>**organizational**behavior

[essentials]

Second Edition

>organizationalbehavior

[essentials]

Second Edition

Steven L. McShane
University of Western Australia

Mary Ann Von Glinow
Florida International University

Boston   Burr Ridge, IL   Dubuque, IA   New York   San Francisco   St. Louis
Bangkok   Bogotá   Caracas   Kuala Lumpur   Lisbon   London   Madrid   Mexico City
Milan   Montreal   New Delhi   Santiago   Seoul   Singapore   Sydney   Taipei   Toronto

McGraw-Hill
Irwin

ORGANIZATIONAL BEHAVIOR: [ESSENTIALS]

Published by McGraw-Hill/Irwin, a business unit of The McGraw-Hill Companies, Inc., 1221 Avenue of the Americas, New York, NY, 10020. Copyright © 2009, 2007 by The McGraw-Hill Companies, Inc. All rights reserved. No part of this publication may be reproduced or distributed in any form or by any means, or stored in a database or retrieval system, without the prior written consent of The McGraw-Hill Companies, Inc., including, but not limited to, in any network or other electronic storage or transmission, or broadcast for distance learning.

Some ancillaries, including electronic and print components, may not be available to customers outside the United States.

This book is printed on acid-free paper.
Printed in China
2 3 4 5 6 7 8 9 0 CTP/CTP 0 9

ISBN   978-0-07-338122-0
MHID   0-07-338122-5

Publisher: *Paul Ducham*
Executive editor: *John Weimeister*
Senior developmental editor: *Christine Scheid*
Marketing manager: *Natalie Zook*
Manager of photo, design & publishing tools: *Mary Conzachi*
Lead production supervisor: *Michael R. McCormick*
Lead designer: *Matthew Baldwin*
Photo research coordinator: *Lori Kramer*
Photo researcher: *Jennifer Blankenship*
Senior media project manager: *Greg Bates*
Senior media project manager: *Susan Lombardi*
Cover and interior design: *George Kokkonas*
Typeface: *10/12 Times Roman*
Compositor: *Aptara, Inc.*
Printer: *CTPS*

Library of Congress Cataloging-in-Publication Data

McShane, Steven Lattimore.
    Organizational behavior : essentials / Steven L. McShane, Mary Ann Von Glinow.—2nd ed.
        p. cm.
    An abridged edition of their comprehensive textbook.
    Includes bibliographical references and index.
    ISBN-13: 978-0-07-338122-0 (alk. paper)
    ISBN-10: 0-07-338122-5 (alk. paper)
    1. Organizational behavior. I. Von Glinow, Mary Ann Young, 1949– II. Title.
HD58.7.M422 2009
658—dc22
                                                                    2008004090

Dedicated with love and devotion to Donna, and to our wonderful daughters, Bryton and Madison

—Steven L. McShane

Dedicated with love to Zack, Emma, and Googun

—Mary Ann Von Glinow

Steven L. McShane   Steven L. McShane is Professor of Management in the UWA Busines School at the University of Western Australia, where he receives high teaching ratings from students in Perth, Singapore, Manila, and other cities in Asia where UWA offers its programs. He is also an Honorary Professor at Universiti Tunku Abdul Rahman (UTAR) in Malaysia and previously taught in the business faculties at Simon Fraser University and Queen's University in Canada. Steve has conducted executive seminars with Nokia, Wesfarmers Group, ALCOA World Alumina Australia, and many other organizations. He is also a popular visiting speaker, having given several dozen talks to faculty and students in a dozen countries over the past three years.

Steve earned his PhD from Michigan State University in organizational behavior, human resource management, and labor relations. He also holds a Master of Industrial Relations from the University of Toronto, and an undergraduate degree from Queen's University in Canada. Steve has served as president of the Administrative Sciences Association of Canada (the Canadian equivalent of the Academy of Management) and director of graduate programs in the business faculty at Simon Fraser University.

Along with co-authoring *Organizational Behavior: [essentials]* 2nd edition, Steve is co-author (with Mary Ann von Glinow) of *Organizational Behavior,* 4th edition (2007), co-author (with Tony Travaglione) of *Organisational Behaviour on the Pacific Rim,* 2nd edition (2007), co-author (with Charles W. L. Hill) of *Principles of Management,* (2008), and the author of *Canadian Organizational Behaviour,* 6th edition (2006). He has also published several dozen articles, book chapters, and conference papers on diverse topics, including values enactment, managerial decision making, organizational learning, socialization of new employees, gender bias in job evaluation, wrongful dismissal, media bias in business magazines, and labor union participation.

Steve enjoys spending his leisure time body-board surfing, canoeing, skiing, and traveling with his wife and two daughters.

Mary Ann Von Glinow   Dr. Von Glinow is a Chair for the Center for International Business Education and Research (CIBER) and is Research Professor of Management and International Business at Florida International University. She also is the 2006 Vice President of the Academy of International Business (AIB) and an editor of JIBS. Previously on the Marshall School faculty of the University of Southern California, she has an MBA and Ph. D in Management Science from The Ohio State University. Dr. Von Glinow was the 1994–1995 President of the Academy of Management, the world's largest association of academicians in management and is a Fellow of the Academy, and the Pan Pacific Business Association. She sits on eleven editorial review boards and numerous international panels. She teaches in executive programs in Latin America, Central America, the Caribbean region, Asia and the U.S.

Dr. Von Glinow has authored over 100 journal atricles and eleven books. Her most recent include *Managing Multinational Teams,* by Elsevier 2005; *Organizational Learning Capability* by Oxford University Press, 1999 (in Chinese and Spanish translation) which won a Gold Book Award from the Ministry of Economic Affairs in Taiwan in 2002. She also has a popular textbook; *Organizational Behavior,* 2007, McGraw-Hill/Irwin and a recently published *OB Essentials* (2007). She heads an international consortium of researchers delving into "Best International Human Resource Management

Practices," and her research in this arena won an award from the American Society for Competitiveness' Board of Trustees. She also received an NSF grant to study globally-distributed work. Dr. Von Glinow is the 2005 Academy of Management recipient of the Distinguished Service Award, one of the Academy's 3 highest honors bestowed.

Mary Ann consults to a number of domestic and multinational enterprises, and serves as a mayoral appointee to the Shanghai Institute of Human Resources in China. Since 1989, she has been a consultant in General Electric's "Workout" and "Change Acceleration Program" including "Coaching to Management." Her clients have included Asia Development Bank, American Express, Diageo, Knight-Ridder, Burger King, Pillsbury, Westinghouse, Southern California Edison, The Aetna, State of Florida, Kaiser Permanente, TWR, Rockwell Int'l, Motorola, N.Y. Life, Amoco, Lucent, and Joe's Stone Crabs, to name a few. She is on the Board of Friends of WLRN, Fielding University, Friends of Bay Oaks, Pan-Pacific Business Association and Animal Alliance in Los Angeles. She is actively involved in several animal welfare organizations and received the 1996 Humanitarian Award of the Year from Miami's Adopt-a-Pet.

[briefcontents]

[contents]

[x]

>part 4

Organizational Processes

[preface]

Students (and instructors!) are busy people. They want an organizational behavior textbook that delivers knowledge efficiently, and yet is readable, interesting, and fulfilling. *Organizational Behavior: [essentials]* 2nd edition aims for that ideal and, according to reviewers and adopters of the premiere edition, we are on the right track.

How do we know what to include and trim out from our popular comprehensive OB textbook? We surveyed dozens of OB instructors about what topics are critical and how they can be most effectively organized. Then, along with our own judgment, we pruned out material within each chapter that didn't satisfy the definition of "essential." We also found a few chapters that, after pruning, could be combined logically with other chapters.

Although this book is less than two-thirds the length of our comprehensive textbook, it doesn't skimp on classroom support. Cases, exercises, and self-assessments are becoming more "essential" than ever in this era of active learning, critical thinking, and outcomes-based teaching, so we include many of these resources.

OB: [essentials] 2nd edition also embraces a "continuous development" approach. We believe that new books should provide new information rather than just repackage content from the comprehensive edition. So, this edition includes new examples as well as plenty of new writing on several OB topics, such as self-concept, organizational effectiveness, conflict management, communication, and organizational culture (ASA theory).

Finally, *OB: [essentials]* 2nd edition includes a judicious number of anecdotes and captioned photos. We believe that these examples help students to remember the content and, quite frankly, make OB theories even more interesting!

Key Features

Organizational Behavior: [essentials] 2nd edition applies four fundamental principles that have made our comprehensive edition one of the best-selling OB books around the world: linking theory with reality, organizational behavior for everyone, contemporary theory foundation, and active learning support.

- *Linking theory with reality.* OB: [essentials] 2nd edition has a strong practical orientation, and this is most evident in the examples that link concepts to real-life incidents in the workplace. For example, you will read about the OB practices that have helped make Pixar Animation Studios a success in the competitive animation feature film business; how an executive at ThedaCare in Wisconsin applied a conflict resolution style that solved an ongoing dispute between nurses and pharmacists; how Whole Foods Markets spreads its successful organizational culture to new stores; and how Johnson & Johnson in India, Europe, the United States, and elsewhere has become one of most admired companies by paying attention to each employee's self-concept and personal values.

- *Organizational behavior for everyone.* OB: [essentials] 2nd edition is written for everyone in organizations. This book is widely adopted in courses for managers, but it also suits students in engineering, pharmacy, accounting, and every other occupation. Fundamentally, we believe that everyone who works in and around organizations needs to understand and make use of organizational behavior knowledge.

- *Contemporary theory foundation.* Scan through the references and you will see that OB: [essentials] 2nd edition is as contemporary conceptually as it is practically. We take contemporary research findings and translate them into understandable ideas with clear connections to workplace events. This contemporary approach includes leading edge knowledge, such as employee self-concept, Schwartz's values model, appreciative inquiry, problems with charismatic leadership, the automaticity and emotionality of perceptions, and emerging views about types of workplace conflict.

- *Active learning support*. Accreditation associ tions are encouraging business schools to include more active learning, critical thinking, and outcomes-based teaching. *OB: [essentials]* 2nd edition supports this trend by offering an assortment of cases, exercises, self-assessments, and video cases to aid the learning process. While some books find it easier to cut corners (and pages) by removing these features, we consider them essential to the learning process.

Supplement Packages

In addition to the content and learning activities provided within *OB: [essentials]* 2nd edition, we are proud to offer students and instructors further resources to improve the learning experience.

For Students   The McGraw-Hill/Irwin Online Learning Center (OLC) is the one-stop hub for additional learning resources. Here are the main features that you will find at the student OLC site:

- *Self-scoring self-assessments*. The three dozen self-assessments summarized in this book are available at the OLC, which allows for rapid self-scoring results, complete with detailed feedback.

- *Additional cases*. Along with the cases provided in this textbook, the OLC offers many others that your instructor might assign for class or assignments.

- *Additional self-assessments*. From the **Build Your Management Skills** collection, these assessments are for those students who want to delve deeper into self-awareness, and for professors who'd like to choose additional exercises, along with a matrix to identify the appropriate topic.

- *Manager's Hot Seat Online* **www. mhhe.com/mhs.** The **Manager's Hot Seat Online** is an interactive Web site in which students watch 15 real managers use their years of experience to solve important management and organizational behavior issues. Students assume the role of the manager as they watch the video and answer multiple-choice questions that pop up during the segment, inviting them to make decisions on the spot. Students learn from the manager's mistakes and successes, and then prepare a report in which they evaluate the manager's approach and defend their reasoning. Ask your local sales representative how you can obtain access to the **Manager's Hot Seat Online** for your course.

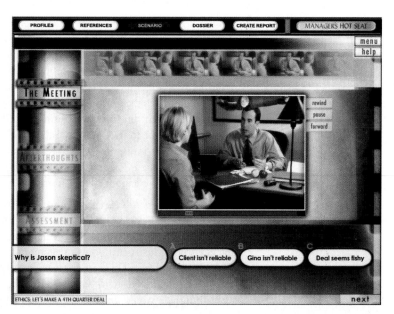

For Instructors   Found on the Instructor Resource CD (ISBN: 0073343447, 13-digit ISBN: 9780073343440):

- *Instructor's Manual.* Includes several resources and aids in every chapter.
- *Test Bank.* Complete with true-false, multiple choice, and essay questions.
- *EZ Test Online*—McGraw-Hill's EZ Test Online is an electronic testing program that allows instructors to create tests from book specific items, accommodates a wide range of question types, and enables instructors to add their own questions. Multiple versions of the test can be created and any test can be exported for use with WebCT, BlackBoard or most other course management systems. EZ Test Online is accessible virtually anywhere via the Web, eliminating the need to install test software. EZ Test Online also generates multiple choice quizzes using iQuiz for iPod. For more information about EZ Test Online, please see the Web site at: www.eztestonline.com.
- *PowerPoint® slides.* A complete set of well-designed slides for each chapter.
- *Video package.* (ISBN: 0073343439, 13-digit ISBN: 9780073343433) A complete set of videos specifically selected by the authors for their interest and relevance.
- *Management in the Movies DVD* (ISBN: 0073317713, 13-digit ISBN: 9780073317717) **Management in the Movies** is available exclusively to adopters of McGraw-Hill textbooks and contains a collection of "Big Screen" Hollywood films that students will recognize. Each movie has been clipped to highlight a specific scene (each is less than two and a half minutes) and linked to specific topics. **Some of the topics include:**

  Groups—*13 Going On 30*
  Ethics—*John Q*
  Diversity—*Inside Man*
  Attitudes, Values, Culture—*Hoosiers*
  Control and Change—*Gung Ho*
  And More!

Along with the DVD, McGraw-Hill provides an instructor manual with suggestions for usage of the clip, clip summaries, and discussion questions to accompany each segment! Ask your McGraw-Hill sales representative how to obtain a copy.

- *Online Learning Center* at **www.mhhe.com/mcshaneEss2e**—If you're looking for a one-stop shopping area for all things OB, look no further than our Web site. Separated into both Instructor and Student areas, each holds a variety of material for instructors to develop and use in their course, and for students to use to review. Instructors will find supplements, additional course materials including downloadable videos and notes, and links to the Group and Video Resource Manual and Manager's Hot Seat Online. Students will find basic material like Chapter quizzes and the Basic PowerPoint outline slides free to use. For a nominal fee, Premium content includes materials like interactive Self-Assessments and Test Your Knowledge quizzes, iPod downloadable content of Narrated PowerPoint slides along with the Chapter quizzes, Quizzes to review the End-of-Chapter videos, a link to the Guide to Online Research, and more.
- *Group and Video Resource Manual: An Instructor's Guide to an Active Classroom* (in print 0073044342 or online at **www.mhhe.com/mobmanual**)—This manual created for instructors contains everything needed to successfully integrate activities into the classroom. Instructor notes to accompany the Self-Assessment exercises, Test Your Knowledge quizzes, Group Exercises, and Manager's Hot Seat videos are located in this one manual along with PowerPoint slides to use in class. Group exercises include everything you would need to use the exercise in class—handouts, figures, etc.

This manual is organized into 25 topics such as ethics, decision-making, change and leadership for easy inclusion in your lecture. The manual includes a matrix that organizes each resource by topic. Students access all of the exercises and self-assessments on their textbook's Web site.

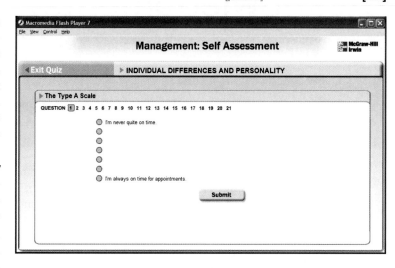

• *"Enhanced" Cartridge for WebCT and Blackboard*—Do you already use **WebCT** or **Blackboard**? Or are you hoping to put more of your course materials **online**? Are you looking for an easy way to assign more materials to your students and manage a gradebook? If so, *Organizational Behavior: [essentials] 2e* comes with McGraw-Hill's new Enhanced Cartridge.

The Enhanced Cartridge is developed to help you get your course up and running with much less time and effort. The content, enhanced with more assignments and more study materials than a standard cartridge, is **pre-populated** into appropriate chapters and content categories. There is no need to cut and paste our content into your course—it's already there! But, you can still choose to hide content we provide and add your own—just as you have before in WebCT and Blackboard. *Organizational Behavior: [essentials] 2e* enhanced cartridge content includes:

• iPod/MP3 content

• Chapter pre- and post-tests

• Gradebook functionality

• Discussion boards

• Additional assignments

• Personalized graphics/banners/icons for your school and much more!

You can choose to package a password card with your text or students can buy access via e-commerce through the book's Web site—for $10. Ask yourMcGraw-Hill sales representative on how to get the enhanced cartridge to accompany *Organizational Behavior: [essentials] 2e* for your course.

[Acknowledgments]

Organizational Behavior: [essentials] 2nd edition symbolizes the power of teamwork. More correctly, it symbolizes the power of a *virtual team* with Mary Ann Von Glinow in Miami, Steve McShane in Perth, Australia, and members of the editorial crew from Chicago and Michigan.

Superb virtual teams require equally superb team members, and we were fortunate to have this in our favor. Sponsoring editor John Weimeister provided reassuring vision and support. Christine Scheid (Senior Developmental Editor) continued to demonstrate superb coordination skills. Mary Conzachi, our lead project manager, is another true professional by handling a tight production schedule with finesse. Matt Baldwin delivered a "cool" design with a textbook cover that captures the innovative and essential themes of this book. We also extend our thanks to Rich Wright for his keen copy editing skills, and to Jennifer Blankenship for successfully tracking down photos from far-flung sources around the world.

Dozens of instructors took time from their busy lives to offer valuable feedback on which topics to include, where topics could be combined, and what other features should be included in this book. We are indebted to all of you for your guidance in *OB: [essentials]* 2nd edition.

Sheryl Alonso,
University of Miami

Kathleen Bates,
California State University—San Marcos

John Bingham,
Brigham Young University

Sandi Deacon Carr,
Boston University

W. Gibb Dyer, Jr.,
Brigham Young University

Deborah E. Gibbons,
Naval Postgraduate School Graduate School of Business and Public Policy

Nell Tabor Hartley,
Robert Morris University

Barbara L. Hassell,
Indiana University/Purdue University

Rusty Juban,
Southeastern Louisiana University

Ricki Ann Kaplan,
East Tennessee State University

John Lipinski,
Robert Morris University

Deborah R. Litvin,
Merrimack College

Janet Logue,
East Tennessee State University

Janice S. Miller,
University of Wisconsin-Milwaukee

Paula Millington,
University of Utah

Donald Otto,
Lindenwood University

Antoinette Phillips,
Southeastern Louisiana University

James D. Powell,
University of North Texas

Edward H. Powley,
Naval Postgraduate School Graduate School of Business and Public Policy

Leslie Sekerka,
Naval Postgraduate School Graduate School of Business and Public Policy

Holly Schroth,
University of California—Berkeley

Karen Tarnoff,
East Tennessee State University

Ed Tomlinson,
John Carroll University

Gina Vega,
Salem State College

Deborah Vidaver-Cohen,
Florida International University

We would also like to extend our sincerest thanks to several instructors whose cases and exercises appear in *OB: [essentials]* 2nd edition:

Alicia Boisnier,
SUNY at Buffalo

Gerard A. Callanan,
West Chester University of Pennsylvania

Sharon Card,
(formerly at) Saskatchewan Institute of Applied Science & Technology

David J. Cherrington,
Brigham Young University

Jeewon Cho,
SUNY at Buffalo

John E. Dittrich,
(formerly at) University of Colorado at Colorado Springs

Mary Gander,
Winona State University

Swee C. Goh,
University of Ottawa

Cheryl Harvey,
Wilfrid Laurier University

Christine Ho,
University of Adelaide

Elizabeth Ho,
Prada Singapore

Glyn Jones,
University of Waikato

Fiona McQuarrie,
University College of the Fraser Valley

Kim Morouney,
Wilfrid Laurier University

David F. Perri,
West Chester University of Pennsylvania

Joseph C. Santora,
Essex County College & TST, Inc.

William Todorovic,
Indiana-Purdue University, Fort Wayne

Edward C. Tomlinson,
John Carroll University

Lisa V. Williams,
SUNY at Buffalo

Robert A. Zawacki,
University of Colorado at Colorado Springs

Along with the reviewers, contributors, and editorial team, Steve McShane would like to extend special thanks to his students in Perth, Manila, and Singapore for sharing their learning experiences and assisting with the development of this book. He is also very grateful to organizational behavior colleagues at the UWA Business School, The University of Western Australia, for their feedback, suggestions, and support. Finally, Steve is forever indebted to his wife Donna McClement and to their wonderful daughters, Bryton and Madison.

Mary Ann would like to thank the many students who have used and hopefully enjoyed this book. I've been stopped on my campus and at occasional meetings by students who wanted to thank me. There are a few who have actually asked for my autograph! (Note, that didn't happen when I was President of the Academy of Management!) Thus it is to the students that I acknowledge many thanks, particularly for making this learning venture fun and exciting. Also, I would like to thank the faculty and staff at Florida International University, who have been very supportive of this effort. By far and away, my coauthor, Steve McShane is the penultimate scholar. He has boundless energy and a mind that doesn't seem to quit, particularly with those late night or early morning e-mails! Steve is also the techno-wizard behind this edition. Finally, I would like to thank my family—John, Rhoda, Lauren, Lindsay, and Christy—as well as some very special people in my life—Janet, Peter, Bill, Karen, Kate, Joanne, Mary, Linda, and Steve. I know I never get a chance to thank them enough, so thank you my friends! I also thank Emma, Zack, Molly, and Googun, my babies! A final note of thanks go to my CIBER family: Tita, Sonia, Juan. Elsa, and KK—you are simply the best! Thank you all, for being there for me.

Steven L. McShane

Mary Ann Von Glinow

>**part I:**

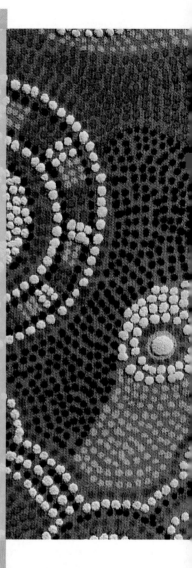

Chapter 1 ....**Introduction to the Field of Organizational Behavior**

Introduction

[chapter 1]

Introduction to the Field of Organizational Behavior

Several organizational behavior practices have helped Pixar Animation Studios to become the world's most successful animation studio.

>learningobjectives

After reading this chapter, you should be able to:

1. Define organizational behavior and organizations, and discuss the importance of this field of inquiry.

2. Diagram an organization from an open systems perspective.

3. Define intellectual capital and describe the organizational learning perspective of organizational effectiveness.

4. Diagnose the extent to which an organization or one of its work units applies high-performance work practices.

5. Explain how the stakeholder perspective emphasizes the importance of values, ethics, and corporate social responsibility.

6. Summarize the five types of individual behavior in organizations.

7. Debate the organizational opportunities and challenges of globalization, workforce diversity, and virtual work.

8. Discuss how employment relationships are changing, and explain why these changes are occurring.

9. Discuss the anchors on which organizational behavior knowledge is based.

One of Robert Iger's first tasks as Walt Disney Co.'s new CEO was to acquire Pixar Animation Studios and put its leaders in charge of Disney's own animation unit, Walt Disney Animation Studios. The studio that brought us Mickey Mouse and the Lion King had become moribund over the past decade, eclipsed by the successes of Pixar and other competitors. Iger didn't spend $7.4 billion just to acquire Pixar's library of award-winning feature films. Disney already had lucrative distribution rights to Pixar's first five films, including any sequels to those films. What Iger wanted from Pixar was far more valuable—the organizational behavior practices that helped Pixar generate a continuous string of blockbuster films, from *Toy Story* to *Ratatouille*.

From its beginnings less than two decades ago, Pixar was built on fundamental organizational behavior principles. Pixar's first principle is that successful companies consist of people with diverse and valued skill sets who effectively coordinate and collaborate with each other. "From the very beginning, we recognized we had to get the best people, technically, from the computer science world, and from the artistic filmmaking animation world, and get them working together," explains John Lasseter, chief creative officer at Pixar (and now Disney). "That, right there, is probably the secret to Pixar."

Pixar's second principle is to strengthen this coordination/collaboration model through long-term employment, rather than short-term project-based contracts that dominate other studios. "The problem with the Hollywood model is that it's generally the day you wrap production that you realize you've finally figured out how to work together," says Randy Nelson, head of Pixar University. "We've made the leap from an idea-centered business to a people-centered business."

Pixar's third principle, which is related to the first two, is teamwork. Pixar's campus in Emeryville, California, was specifically designed to cluster people into teams. At the same time, to encourage cross-fertilization of ideas, the building also creates chance encounters with people from other projects. "You run into people constantly," says Lasseter from a second floor balcony as he waves to a co-worker in the atrium below. "It worked from the minute we arrived. We just blossomed here!"

Compared to most other companies of similar size (Pixar employs around 1,000 employees) and stature, Pixar has an egalitarian no-nonsense culture where people are encouraged to speak honestly about the quality of the work in progress. Quality is a particularly important word around Pixar, representing the company's first priority when making films. This unique culture is supported by the leadership of John Lasseter as well as Edwin Catmull, Pixar's co-founder and president of both Pixar and Disney Animation Studios. "Ed, more than anyone else, provided that leadership to create this very unique Pixar culture," says Pixar CEO Steven Jobs.[1]

//

Coordination, collaboration, communication, creativity, organizational culture, knowledge sharing, leadership, teamwork. These are several critical features behind the success of Pixar Animation Studios and other companies. They are also some of the topics featured in this book. Our main objective is to help you understand behavior in organizations and to work more effectively in organizational settings. We begin in this chapter by introducing you to the field of organizational behavior and why it is important to your career and to organizations. Next, this chapter describes the "ultimate dependent variable" in this field by presenting the four main perspectives of organizational effectiveness. This is followed by an overview of the five types of individual behaviors that are most often studied as dependent variables in organizational behavior. This chapter also introduces three challenges facing organizations—globalization, increasing workforce diversity, and emerging employment relationships—and highlights the anchors that guide organizational behavior knowledge development.

After reading the next section, you should be able to:

1. *Define organizational behavior and organizations, and discuss the importance of this field of inquiry.*

learningobjectives<

>The Field of Organizational Behavior

ORGANIZATIONAL BEHAVIOR (OB): the study of what people think, feel, and do in and around organizations

ORGANIZATIONS: groups of people who work interdependently toward some purpose

Organizational behavior (OB) is the study of what people think, feel, and do in and around organizations. OB researchers systematically study individual, team (including interpersonal), and organizational-level characteristics that influence behavior within work settings. OB emerged as a distinct field around the 1940s, although people have been studying organizations for centuries.[2] **Organizations** are groups of people who work interdependently toward some purpose.[3] Organizations are not buildings or government-registered entities. Rather, they consist of people who interact with each other to achieve a common purpose. Employees have structured patterns of interaction, meaning that they expect each other to complete certain tasks in a coordinated way—in an *organized* way. Organizations also have a collective sense of purpose, whether it's producing animated feature films or building automobiles. "A company is one of humanity's most amazing inventions," says Steven Jobs, CEO of Pixar Animation Studios and Apple, Inc. "It's totally abstract. Sure, you have to build something with bricks and mortar to put the people in, but basically a company is this abstract construct we've invented, and it's incredibly powerful."[4]

Why Study Organizational Behavior?

Organizational behavior instructors face a challenge: One the one hand, students just beginning their careers tend to focus their attention on courses related to specific jobs, such as accounting and marketing.[5] OB doesn't have a specific career path—there is no "vice president of OB"—so instructors have some difficulty conveying the importance of OB to these students. On the other hand, students with several years of work experience place OB courses near the top of their list of important courses. They have directly seen that OB *does make a difference* to their career success. Each one of us has an inherent need to understand and predict the world in which we live.[6] Since much of our time is spent working in or around organizations, OB theories help you to make sense of the workplace. OB theories also give you the opportunity to question and rebuild your personal theories that have developed through observation and experience.

But the main reason why people with work experience value OB is that almost everyone needs to work with other people to get things done, and OB provides the knowledge and tools to work with and through others. Influencing your boss, building a high-performance team, motivating co-workers (or yourself), handling workplace conflicts, and changing employee behavior are just a few of the areas of knowledge and skills offered in organizational behavior. No matter what career path you choose, you'll find that OB concepts play an important role in performing your job and working more effectively within organizations. This practical side of organizational behavior is, according to some experts, a critical feature of the best OB theories.[7]

Organizational Behavior Is for Everyone

Our explanation about why organizational behavior is important for your career success does not assume that you are, or intend to be, a manager. In fact, this book pioneered the notion that OB knowledge is for everyone. Whether you are a geologist, financial analyst, customer service representative, or chief executive officer, you need to understand and apply the many organizational behavior topics that are discussed in this book. Yes, organizations will continue to have managers, but their roles have changed and more importantly, the rest of us are increasingly expected to manage ourselves in the workplace. In the words of one forward-thinking OB writer many years ago: Everyone is a manager.[8]

OB and the Bottom Line

So far, our answer to the question "Why study OB?" has focused on how OB knowledge benefits you as an individual. But organizational behavior knowledge is just as important for the organization's financial health. This was apparent in the opening story about Pixar Animation Studios, which has benefited from several OB concepts and practices. According to one estimate, firms that apply performance-based rewards, employee communication, work–life balance, and other OB practices have three times the level of financial success as companies where these practices are absent. Another study concluded that companies that earn "the best place to work" awards have significantly higher financial and long-term stock market performance. Essentially, these firms leverage the power of OB practices, which translate into more favorable employee attitudes, decisions, and performance. The benefits of OB are well known to Warren Buffett and other financial gurus; they consider the organization's leadership and quality of employees as two of the best predictors of the firm's financial potential.[9]

After reading the next two sections, you should be able to:

2. *Diagram an organization from an open systems perspective.*

3. *Define intellectual capital and describe the organizational learning perspective of organizational effectiveness.*

4. *Diagnose the extent to which an organization or one of its work units applies high-performance work practices.*

5. *Explain how the stakeholder perspective emphasizes the importance of values, ethics, and corporate social responsibility.*

6. *Summarize the five types of individual behavior in organizations.*

learningobjectives<

>Perspectives of Organizational Effectiveness

Almost all organizational behavior theories have the implicit or explicit objective of making organizations more effective.[10] In fact, organizational effectiveness is considered the "ultimate dependent variable" in organizational behavior.[11] The first challenge, however, is to define **organizational effectiveness.** Experts agree that this topic is burdened with too many labels—organizational performance, success, goodness, health, competitiveness, excellence, and so on—with no consensus on the meaning of each label.

Long ago, organizational effectiveness was defined as the extent to which an organization achieved its stated goals.[12] According to this view, Pixar Animation Studios is more effective than Disney's animation unit because Pixar is better at achieving its stated objectives of producing animation features on time, on budget, and on target regarding box office sales. The goal attainment view is no longer accepted, however, because a company can be considered effective simply by establishing easily achievable goals. Also, some goals—such as social responsibility to the community—are so abstract that it would be very difficult to know how well the organization is achieving these goals. A third flaw with the goal attainment definition is that a company might achieve its stated objectives (such as high

ORGANIZATIONAL EFFECTIVENESS: a broad concept represented by several perspectives, including the organization's fit with the external environment, internal subsystems configuration for high-performance, emphasis on organizational learning, and ability to satisfy the needs of key stakeholders

short-term profitability), yet eventually go bankrupt because it didn't invest in product development or production facilities.

How is organizational effectiveness defined today? The answer is that there are several perspectives of effectiveness, so this concept is defined in terms of *all of these perspectives*.[13] Organizations are consider effective when they have a good fit with their external environment; when their internal subsystems are configured for a high-performance workplace; when they are learning organizations; and when they satisfy the needs of key stakeholders. Let's now look at the four perspectives embedded in this definition of organizational effectiveness.

Open Systems Perspective

OPEN SYSTEMS: a perspective that organizations take their sustenance from the environment and, in turn, affect that environment through their output

The **open systems** perspective of organizational effectiveness is one of the earliest and deeply embedded ways of thinking about organizations. In fact, the other major organizational effectiveness perspectives might be considered detailed extensions of the open systems model.[14] As depicted in Exhibit 1.1, the open systems perspective views organizations as complex organisms that "live" within an external environment. The word *open* describes this permeable relationship, whereas *closed systems* can exist without dependence on an external environment.

As open systems, organizations depend on the external environment for resources, including raw materials, employees, financial resources, information, and equipment. Inside the organization are numerous subsystems, such as processes (communication and reward systems), task activities (production, marketing), and social dynamics (informal groups, power relationships). With the aid of technology (such as equipment, work methods, and information), these subsystems transform inputs into various outputs. Some outputs (e.g., products and services) may be valued by the external environment, whereas other outputs (e.g., employee layoffs, pollution) have adverse effects. The organization receives feedback from the external environment regarding the value of its outputs and the availability of future inputs.

[Exhibit 1.1] Open Systems Perspective of Organizations

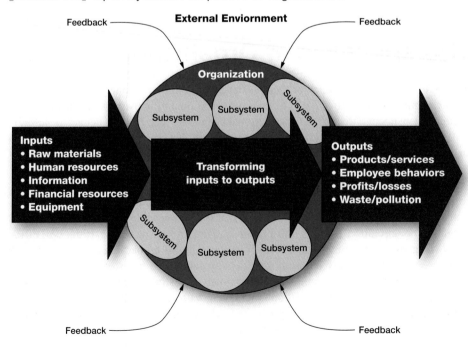

According to the open systems perspective, successful organizations monitor their environments and are able to maintain a close "fit" with those changing conditions.[15] One way they do this is by finding new opportunities to secure essential inputs. For instance, McDonald's Restaurants has developed innovative ways to maintain an adequate supply of people. Years ago, the company was among the first to recruit retirees as employees. Recently, McDonald's UK introduced the Family Contract, an employment arrangement that allows members of the employee's family (spouses, grandparents, and children over the age of 16) to swap shifts without notifying management.[16] Successful organizations also redesign outputs so they remain compatible with needs in the external environment. Food manufacturers have changed their ingredients to satisfy more health-conscious consumers. Grocery stores have added more ethnically diverse foods to reflect increasing ethnic diversity of shoppers.

Internal Subsystems Effectiveness

The open systems perspective considers more than an organization's fit with the external environment. It also considers how well it operates internally, that is, how well the company transforms inputs into outputs. The most common indicator of this internal transformation process is **organizational efficiency** (also called *productivity*), which is the ratio of inputs to outcomes.[17] Companies that produce more goods or services with less labor, materials, and energy are more efficient. However, successful organizations not only have efficient transformation processes; they also have more *adaptive* and *innovative* transformation processes. For example, German engineering conglomerate Siemens AG has an effective transformation process because its subsystems are innovative and responsive, not necessarily the most efficient. "Whether I have additional costs or not doesn't matter as much as the speed to market and the quality of the design," says a Siemens executive. "We're not talking about a pure cost game."[18]

ORGANIZATIONAL EFFICIENCY: the ratio of inputs to outcomes in the organization's transformation process

Organizational Learning Perspective

The open systems perspective has traditionally focused on physical resources that enter the organization and are processed into physical goods (outputs). This was representative of the industrial economy but not the "new economy," where the most valued input is knowledge. Knowledge is the driver of competitive advantage, however, in the **organizational learning** perspective (also called *knowledge management*). Through this lens, organizational effectiveness depends on the organization's capacity to acquire, share, use, and store valuable knowledge.[19]

A growing body of research supports the idea that successful companies are better than others at acquiring, sharing, storing, and using knowledge.[20] Google is a case in point. The company that brought us the ubiquitous Internet search engine acquires knowledge by hiring the best talent, buying entire companies (such as Keyhole, Inc, whose knowledge created Google Earth), and encouraging employees to try out new ideas. In fact, employees are expected to devote a quarter of their time on new ideas of their choosing. Google encourages knowledge sharing in many ways. It has a team-oriented project culture that encourages staff to share information as part of their job. It's campus-like environment (called the Googleplex), increases the chance that employees from different parts of the organization will mingle (and casually share information), whether dining at the company's subsidized gourmet restaurant or playing a game of volleyball in the sports area. Knowledge sharing also occurs through sophisticated information technologies. Along with knowledge acquisition and sharing, Google gives employees more autonomy to apply their newfound knowledge and encourages them to experiment. "Google is truly a learning organization," says Google's chief financial officer George Reyes.[21]

ORGANIZATIONAL LEARNING: a perspective that organizational effectiveness depends on the organization's capacity to acquire, share, use, and store valuable knowledge

Intellectual Capital: The Stock of Organizational Knowledge

INTELLECTUAL
CAPITAL:
company's stock
of knowledge,
including human
capital, structural
capital and
relationship capital

Knowledge acquisition, sharing, and use represents the flow of knowledge. The organizational learning perspective also considers the company's stock of knowledge, called its **intellectual capital.**[22] The most obvious form of intellectual capital is *human capital*—the knowledge that employees carry around in their heads. This is an important part of a company's stock of knowledge, and a huge risk in companies where knowledge is the main competitive advantage. When key people leave, they take with them some of the knowledge that makes the company effective. But even if everyone left the organization, intellectual capital would still remain in the form of *structural capital*. This includes the knowledge captured and retained in an organization's systems and structures, such as documentation of work procedures and physical layout of the production line. Structural capital even includes the organization's finished products because knowledge can be extracted by taking them apart to discover how they work and are constructed (i.e., reverse engineering). Finally, intellectual capital includes *relationship capital*, which is the value derived from an organization's relationships with customers, suppliers, and others who provide added mutual value for the organization.

Organizational Unlearning

The organizational learning perspective states not only that effective organizations learn; they also unlearn routines and patterns of behavior that are no longer appropriate.[23] Unlearning removes knowledge that no longer adds value and, in fact, may undermine the organization's effectiveness. Some forms of unlearning involve replacing dysfunctional policies, procedures, and routines. Other forms of unlearning erase attitudes, beliefs, and assumptions. For instance, employees rethink how they should interact with customers and which is the "best way" to perform a task.

High-Performance Work Practices (HPWP) Perspective

HIGH-
PERFORMANCE
WORK PRACTICES
(HPWP):
a perspective that
effective
organizations
incorporate several
workplace
practices that
leverage the
potential of human
capital

Although the open systems perspective states that successful companies are good at transforming inputs to outputs, it does not offer specific advice about which bundle of subsystems are the most important. Consequently, an entire field of research has blossomed around the objective of identifying internal systems and structures that are associated with successful companies. This research has had various labels over the years, but it is now typically called the study of **high-performance work practices (HPWP).**[24]

The HPWP perspective is based on three propositions:[25]

1. Employees are an important source of competitive advantage. As such, this human capital is (a) valuable—it helps the organization realize opportunities or minimize threats in the external environment, (b) rare—it is not easily available to competitors, (c) difficult to imitate—other firms cannot easily create a similar resource, and (d) nonsubstitutable—competitors cannot rely on technology or other resources as alternatives to human capital.[26]

2. The value of this human capital can be increased through the presence of specific organizational practices. In other words, companies become more effective by investing in employees through the activities these researchers have identified.

3. Most (although not all) HPWP experts state that these organizational practices must be bundled together to maximize their potential. This proposition suggests a synergistic effect, in which these specific activities are mutually reinforcing.

Researchers have investigated numerous organizational practices in various combinations, but a few common activities stand out as high-performance work practices.[27] Two of the

Nucor's Recipe for Success: HPWPs

Many U.S. steel firms either disappeared or reduced their footprint due to globalization over the past 15 years, but not Nucor. The Charlotte, North Carolina-based company grew to become the largest and most profitable steel company in America. What was Nucor's secret to success? A major factor was its high-performance work practices. Nucor employees work in teams and two-thirds of their paycheck depends on team and organizational performance. There is no micromanagement; teams operate most aspects of the work process and each plant is its own profit center. Employees are motivated to run the business efficiently and with high responsiveness. For instance, when an electrical grid failure shut down Nucor's minimill in Arkansas, three Nucor electricians in nearby states immediately went there during their weekend off to help fix the problem.[28]

most widely mentioned high-performance work practices are employee involvement and job autonomy, which typically come together in the form of self-directed teams. As we will learn in several chapters of this book, both activities tend to strengthen employee motivation as well as improve decision making, organizational responsiveness, and commitment to change. Another key variable in the HPWP model is employee competence. Specifically, organizations are more effective when they invest in employee skills and knowledge development, and when they carefully select job applicants with strong skills and performance potential (see Chapter 2). Finally, high-performance organizations link performance and skill development to various forms of financial and nonfinancial rewards valued by employees.

The HPWP perspective is currently popular among scholars and practitioners, but it also has its share of critics. One concern is that many studies try to find out which practices predict organizational performance without theoretically understanding why those practices should have this effect.[29] Theory is essential because it logically explains why a particular practice should *cause* organizations to be more effective. A second concern with the HPWP perspective is that it may satisfy shareholder and customer needs at the expense of employee well-being.[30] Some experts point out that HPWPs increase work stress and that management is reluctant to delegate power or share the financial benefits of productivity improvements. If high-performance work practices improve organizational performance at a cost to employee well-being, then this perspective (along with the open systems and organizational learning perspectives) have not yet painted the entire organizational effectiveness picture. The remaining gaps are mostly filled by the stakeholder perspective of organizational effectiveness.

Stakeholder Perspective

The other three perspectives mainly pay attention to processes and resources, yet they only minimally recognize the importance of relations with **stakeholders.** Stakeholders include individuals, organizations, or other entities who affect, or are affected by, the organization's

STAKEHOLDERS: individuals, organizations, or other entities who affect, or are affected by, the organization's objectives and actions

objectives and actions. They include anyone with a stake in the company, such as employees, shareholders, employees, suppliers, government, communities, consumer and environmental interest groups, and so on. The essence of the stakeholder perspective is that companies must take into account how their actions affect others, which requires them to understand, manage, and satisfy the interests of their stakeholders.[31] The stakeholder perspective personalizes the open systems perspective; it identifies specific people and social entities. It also recognizes that stakeholder relations are dynamic; they can be negotiated and managed, not just taken as a fixed condition.[32]

Consider the troubles that Wal-Mart has faced in recent years.[33] For decades the world's largest retailer was driven to provide customers the lowest possible prices and, through high volume, generate healthy financial returns to stockholders. Yet by emphasizing the needs of customers and stockholders, the company faced increasing hostility from other groups in society. Some interest groups complained that Wal-Mart was destroying America's manufacturing base and promoting unethical business practices (such as child labor) in countries where it purchased goods. Other groups pointed out that Wal-Mart had a poor record of environmental and social responsibility. Still other groups lobbied to keep Wal-Mart out of their communities because the giant retailer typically set up shop in outlying areas (where land is cheap), thereby fading the vibrancy of the community's downtown area. These stakeholder pressure points existed for some time, but Wal-Mart mostly ignored them until they became a serious threat. In fact, Wal-Mart recently created the position "senior director of stakeholder engagement" to ensure that it pays more attention to the fuller set of stakeholders, and to proactively manage those relationships.

Understanding, managing, and satisfying the interests of stakeholders is more challenging than it sounds because stakeholders have conflicting interests and organizations don't have the resources to satisfy every stakeholder to the fullest. Therefore, organizational leaders need to decide how much priority to give each group. One commonly cited factor is to favor stakeholders with the most power.[34] This makes sense when one considers that the most powerful stakeholders hold the greatest threat and opportunity to the company's survival. Yet stakeholder power should not be the only criterion for determining organizational strategy and resource allocation. Ignoring less powerful stakeholders might motivate them to become more powerful. It might also aggravate more powerful stakeholders if ignoring weaker interests violates the norms and standards of society.

Values, Ethics, and Corporate Social Responsibility

VALUES: relatively stable, evaluative beliefs that guide a person's preferences for outcomes or courses of action in a variety of situations

This brings us to one of the key strengths of the stakeholder perspective; it incorporates values, ethics, and corporate social responsibility into the organizational effectiveness equation.[35] To manage the interests of diverse stakeholders, the stakeholder perspective states that leaders ultimately need to rely on their personal and organizational values for guidance. **Values** are relatively stable, evaluative beliefs that guide our preferences for outcomes or courses of action in a variety of situations.[36] Values help us to know what is right or wrong, or good or bad, in the world. As we will learn in more detail in Chapter 2, values are an important part of our self-concept and, as such, motivate our actions. Although values exist within individuals, groups of people might hold the same or similar values, so we tend to ascribe these *shared values* to the team, department, organization, profession, or entire society. Chapter 13 provides details about the importance and dynamics of an organization's shared values.

ETHICS: the study of moral principles or values that determine whether actions are right or wrong and outcomes are good or bad

By incorporating values into organizational effectiveness, the stakeholder perspective also provides the strongest case for ethics and corporate social responsibility. In fact, the stakeholder perspective emerged out of earlier writing on ethics and corporate social responsibility. **Ethics** refers to the study of moral principles or values that determine whether actions are right or wrong and outcomes are good or bad. We rely on our ethical values to determine "the right thing to do." Ethical behavior is driven by the moral principles we use to make decisions. These moral principles represent fundamental values.

CSR Makes Lockheed Martin "Ideal"

When choosing a future employer, college graduates look beyond salary and career opportunities. These factors are important, but recent surveys indicate that the company's ethical standards and corporate social responsibility are also top considerations. These stakeholder considerations have helped Lockheed Martin, the Bethesda, Maryland, aerospace firm, top the list of American-based firms considered "ideal" by undergraduate engineering students. "Students have always been impressed with Lockheed Martin's commitment to diversity and social responsibility," says the CEO of Universum Communications, the company that surveys more than 37,000 students annually. "The company is well known for its charitable contributions and strong values." For example, this photo shows a team of Lockheed Martin employees assisting clean-up of New Orleans following Hurricane Katrina.[37]

Chapter 2 will provide more detail about ethical principles and related influences on moral reasoning.

Corporate social responsibility (CSR) consists of organizational activities intended to benefit society and the environment beyond the firm's immediate financial interests or legal obligations.[38] It is the view that companies have a contract with society, in which they must serve stakeholders beyond stockholders and customers. In some situations, the interests of the firm's stockholders should be secondary to other stakeholders.[39] As part of CSR, many companies have adopted the triple bottom line philosophy. This means that they try to support or earn positive returns in the economic, social, and environmental spheres of sustainability. Firms that adopt the triple bottom line aim to survive and be profitable in the marketplace (economic), but they also intend to maintain or improve conditions for society (social) as well as the physical environment.[40]

The idea that organizations are more effective when they cater to a wide variety of stakeholders has its share of critics. More than 30 years ago, economist Milton Friedman pronounced that "there is one and only one social responsibility of business—to use its resources and engage in activities designed to increase its profits." Although few take this extreme view today, some continue to argue that companies can only benefit other stakeholders if those with financial interests in the company receive first priority. Still, four out of five Americans say that a company's commitment to a social issue is an important factor in deciding whether to work there and whether to buy their products or services. Another poll reported that 97 percent of American and European MBA students would relinquish significant financial benefits to work for an organization with a better reputation for ethics and CSR. Almost 80 percent of Canadians say the company's record of corporate social responsibility has either a moderate or great deal of influence on their decision where to work.[41] In short, leaders may put their organization at risk if they pay attention only to shareholders and ignore the broader corporate social responsibility.[42]

CORPORATE SOCIAL RESPONSIBILITY (CSR): organizational activities intended to benefit society and the environment beyond the firm's immediate financial interests or legal obligations

>Types of Individual Behavior

The four perspectives described over the past few pages—open systems, organizational learning, high-performance work practices, and stakeholders—provide a multidimensional view of what makes companies effective. Within these models, however, are numerous behaviors that employees need to perform that enable companies to interact with their environments; acquire, share, and use knowledge to the best advantage; process inputs to outputs efficiently and responsively; and meet the needs of various stakeholders. While organizational effectiveness is the ultimate dependent variable, these behaviors are the individual-level dependent variables found in most OB research. The five types of employee behavior are task performance, organizational citizenship, counterproductive work behaviors, joining and staying with the organization, and work attendance.

Task Performance

Task performance refers to goal-directed behaviors under the individual's control that support organizational objectives. Task performance behaviors transform raw materials into goods and services or support and maintain the technical activities.[43] For example, foreign exchange traders make decisions and take actions to exchange currencies. Employees in most jobs have more than one performance dimension. Foreign exchange traders must be able to identify profitable trades, work cooperatively with clients and co-workers in a stressful environment, assist in training new staff, and work on special telecommunications equipment without error. Some of these performance dimensions are more important than others, but only by considering all of them can we fully evaluate an employee's contribution to the organization.

Organizational Citizenship

ORGANIZATIONAL CITIZENSHIP BEHAVIORS (OCBs): various forms of cooperation and helpfulness to others that support the organization's social and psychological context

Companies could not effectively compete, transform resources, or serve the needs of their stakeholders if employees performed only their formal job duties. They also need to engage in **organizational citizenship behaviors (OCBs)**—various forms of cooperation and helpfulness to others that support the organization's social and psychological context.[44] In other words, companies require contextual performance (i.e., OCBs) along with task performance.

Organizational citizenship behaviors take many forms. Some are directed toward individuals, such as assisting co-workers with their work problems, adjusting your work schedule to accommodate co-workers, showing genuine courtesy toward co-workers, and sharing your work resources (supplies, technology, staff) with co-workers. Other OCBs represent cooperation and helpfulness toward the organization in general. These include supporting the company's public image, taking discretionary action to help the organization avoid potential problems, offering ideas beyond those required for your own job, attending voluntary functions that support the organization, and keeping up with new developments in the organization.[45]

Counterproductive Work Behaviors

COUNTER-PRODUCTIVE WORK BEHAVIORS, (CWBs): voluntary behaviors that have the potential to directly or indirectly harm the organization

Organizational behavior is interested in all workplace behaviors, including those on the "dark side," collectively known as **counterproductive work behaviors (CWBs).** CWBs are voluntary behaviors that have the potential to directly or indirectly harm the organization. These CWBs can be organized into five categories: abuse of others (e.g., insults and nasty comments), threats (threatening harm), work avoidance (e.g., tardiness), work sabotage (doing work incorrectly), and overt acts (theft). CWBs are not minor concerns. One recent study found that units of a fast-food restaurant chain with higher CWBs had significantly worse performance, whereas organizational citizenship had a relatively minor benefit.[46]

Joining and Staying with the Organization

Task performance, organizational citizenship, and the lack of counterproductive work behaviors are obviously important, but if qualified people don't join and stay with the organization, none of these performance-related behaviors would occur. Attracting and retaining
talented people is particularly important as worries about skills shortages heat up. For instance, a shortage of qualified truck drivers is the main factor restricting growth at Contract
Freighters in Joplin, Missouri. "We have plenty of freight; we have plenty of trucks," says
company president Herb Schmidt, but the "severe shortage" of qualified drivers is making
it impossible to satisfy the growing customer base. Hotels in many parts of the United States
are also struggling to find enough staff to keep up with demand. "We're woefully under-
staffed," says the owner of a St. Petersburg, Florida, resort that employs 265 people and still
has 40 unfilled vacancies. "It's horrible."[47]

Companies survive and thrive not just by hiring people with talent or potential; they also
need to ensure that these employees stay with the company. Companies with high turnover
suffer because of the high cost of replacing people who leave. More important, as was
mentioned earlier in this chapter, much of an organization's intellectual capital is the
knowledge carried around in employees' heads. When people leave, some of this vital
knowledge is lost, often resulting in inefficiencies, poorer customer service, and so forth.
This threat is not trivial: between one-third and one-half of employees say they would
change companies if offered a comparable job.[48]

Why do people quit their jobs? Traditionally, OB experts have identified low job satisfaction as the main cause of turnover. **Job satisfaction** is a person's evaluation of his
or her job and work context (see Chapter 4). Employees become dissatisfied with their
employment relationship, which motivates them to search for and join another organization with better conditions. While job dissatisfaction builds over time and eventually
affects turnover, the most recent opinion is that specific "shock events" trigger the
behavior of searching for another job or submitting our resignation (sometimes without
another job in hand).[49] The boss's unfair decision or a conflict episode with a co-worker
activate strong emotions, which prompt us to seriously consider severing our employment relationship.

> **JOB
> SATISFACTION:**
> person's evaluation
> of his or her job
> and work context

Maintaining Work Attendance

Along with attracting and retaining employees, organizations need everyone to show up for
work at scheduled times. Situational factors—such as a snowstorm or car breakdown—
explain some work absences. Motivation is another factor. Employees who experience job
dissatisfaction or work-related stress are more likely to be absent or late for work because
taking time off is a way to temporarily withdraw from stressful or dissatisfying conditions.
Absenteeism is also higher in organizations with generous sick leave because this benefit
limits the negative financial impact of taking time away from work. Studies have found that
absenteeism is also higher in teams with strong absence norms, meaning that team members tolerate and even expect co-workers to take time off.[50]

learningobjectives<

After reading the next two sections, you should be able to:

7. *Debate the organizational opportunities and challenges of globalization, workforce
   diversity, and virtual work.*

8. *Discuss how employment relationships are changing, and explain why these
   changes are occurring.*

9. *Discuss the anchors on which organizational behavior knowledge is based.*

>Contemporary Challenges for Organizations

An underlying theme of the earlier discussion on organizational effectiveness was that organizations are deeply affected by the external environment. Consequently, they need to anticipate and adjust to environment changes in order to maintain a good fit with their environment. This external environment is continuously changing, but some changes for the past decade and in the decade to come are more profound than others. These changes will require corporate leaders and all other employees to adjust to the new realities. In this section, we highlight three of the major challenges facing organizations: globalization, increasing workforce diversity, and emerging employment relationships.

Globalization

You might not have heard of Fonterra, but chances are that you have purchased or eaten one of its products recently. The New Zealand-based company is the world's largest dairy exporting business and the world's lowest-cost dairy ingredients producer. It operates in 140 countries, employs 20,000 people, and represents 40 percent of the global dairy trade. In many countries, it forms joint partnerships, such as with the Dairy Farmers of America, SanCor in Argentina, and Aria in Europe. Fonterra's current position on the world stage is quite different from a decade ago when three New Zealand dairy companies joined forces. They realized that globalization was shaking up the industry and that they needed to form a global enterprise to survive. The merged company was so globally focused from the outset that it was temporarily called GlobalCo until the name Fonterra was chosen. Fonterra's adjustment to a global operation was not easy. Executives were replaced as the company needed to adopt a different mindset. "A lot of people in the [pre-merger companies] were very New Zealand-centric and culturally did not understand the global challenges of the teams offshore and the different operating companies," acknowledges a Fonterra executive.[51]

GLOBALIZATION: economic, social, and cultural connectivity with people in other parts of the world

Fonterra is a rich example of the globalization of business over the past few decades. **Globalization** refers to economic, social, and cultural connectivity with people in other parts of the world. Fonterra and other organizations globalize when they actively participate in other countries and cultures. Although businesses have traded goods across borders for centuries, the degree of globalization today is unprecedented because information technology and transportation systems allow a much more intense level of connectivity and interdependence around the planet.[52]

Globalization offers numerous benefits to organizations in terms of larger markets, lower costs, and greater access to knowledge and innovation. At the same time, there is considerable debate about whether globalization benefits developing nations, and whether it is primarily responsible for increasing work intensification, as well as reducing job security and work/life balance in developed countries.[53] Globalization is now well entrenched, so the real issue in organizational behavior is how corporate leaders and employees alike can lead and work effectively in this emerging reality[54] OB researchers are turning their attention to this topic. In Project GLOBE, dozens of experts are studying leadership and organizational practices around the world. Another consortium, called the Best Practices Project, is comparing human resources practices in companies across several countries.[55]

Increasing Workforce Diversity

Walk into the offices of Verizon Communications around the United States and you can quickly see that the communications service giant reflects the communities it serves. Minorities make up 30 percent of Verizon's 200,000 workforce and 18 percent of top management positions. Women represent 43 percent of its workforce and 32 percent of top management. Verizon's inclusive culture has won awards from numerous organizations representing Hispanics, African-Americans, gays and lesbians, people with disabilities, and other groups.[56]

Verizon Communications is a model employer and a reflection of the increasing diversity of people living in the United States and in many other countries. The description of Verizon's diversity refers to **surface-level diversity**—the observable demographic or physiological differences in people, such as their race, ethnicity, gender, age, and physical disabilities. Surface-level diversity has changed considerably in the United States over the past few decades. People with nonwhite or Hispanic origin represent one-third of the American population, and this is projected to increase substantially over the next few decades. Within the next 50 years, one in four Americans will be Hispanic, 14 percent will be African-American, and eight percent will be of Asian descent. By 2060, people with European non-Hispanic ethnicity will be a minority.[57]

Diversity also includes differences in the psychological characteristics of employees, including personalities, beliefs, values, and attitudes.[58] We can't directly see this **deep-level diversity,** but it is evident in a person's decisions, statements, and actions. One illustration of deep-level diversity is the different attitudes and expectations held by employees across generational cohorts.[59] *Baby boomers*—people born between 1946 and 1964—seem to expect and desire more job security, and are more intent on improving their economic and social status. In contrast, *Generation-X* employees—those born between 1965 and 1979—expect less job security and are motivated more by workplace flexibility, the opportunity to learn (particularly new technology), and working in an egalitarian and "fun" organization. Meanwhile, some observers suggest that *Generation-Y* employees (those born after 1979) are noticeably self-confident, optimistic, multitasking, and more independent than even Gen-X co-workers. These statements certainly don't apply to everyone in each cohort, but they do reflect the dynamics of deep-level diversity and shifting values and expectations across generations.

> **SURFACE-LEVEL DIVERSITY:** the observable demographic or physiological differences in people, such as their race, ethnicity, gender, age, and physical disabilities

> **DEEP-LEVEL DIVERSITY:** differences in the psychological characteristics of employees, including personalities, beliefs, values, and attitudes

Consequences of Diversity

Diversity presents both opportunities and challenges in organizations.[60] In some circumstances and to some degree, diversity can become a competitive advantage by improving decision making and team performance on complex tasks. Studies suggest that teams with some forms of diversity (particularly occupational diversity) make better decisions on complex problems than do teams whose members have similar backgrounds. One study also found that companies with the highest representation of women on their top management teams experienced significantly better financial performance than firms with the lowest representation of women. Many businesses also report that having a diverse workforce has improved customer service and creativity. For instance, PepsiCo estimates that one-eighth of revenue growth is directly attributable to new products inspired by diversity efforts, such as guacamole-flavored Doritos chips that would appeal to Hispanic customers and a wasabi-flavored snack for Asian-Americans.[61]

Based on this evidence, the popular refrain is that workforce diversity is a sound business proposition. Unfortunately, it's not that simple. In fact, there is growing evidence that most forms of diversity offer both advantages and disadvantages.[62] Teams with diverse employees usually take longer to perform effectively. Diversity brings numerous communication problems as well as "faultlines" in informal group dynamics. Diversity is also a source of conflict, which can lead to lack of information sharing and, in extreme cases, morale problems and higher turnover. But whether or not workforce diversity is a business advantage, companies need to make it a priority because surface-level diversity is a moral and legal imperative. Ethically, companies that offer an inclusive workplace are, in essence, making fair and just decisions regarding employment, promotions, rewards, and so on. Fairness is a well-established influence on employee loyalty and satisfaction. Our main point here, though, is that workforce diversity is the new reality, and that organizations need to adjust to this reality both to survive and to experience its potential benefits for organizational success.

Emerging Employment Relationships

Combine globalization with emerging workforce diversity, and add in new information technology. The resulting concoction has created incredible changes in employment relationships. A few decades ago, most (although not all) employees in the United States, Europe, and similar cultures would finish their workday after eight or nine hours and could separate their personal time from the workday. There were no BlackBerries and no Internet connections to keep staff tethered to work on a 24/7 schedule. Even business travel was more of an exception due to its high cost. Most competitors were located in the same country, so they had similar work practices and labor costs. Today, work hours are longer (although arguably less than 100 years ago), employees experience more work-related stress, and there is growing evidence that family and personal relations are suffering. Little wonder that one of the emerging issues in this new century is for more **work/life balance**—minimizing conflict between work and nonwork demands.[63]

WORK/LIFE BALANCE: the degree to which a person minimizes conflict between work and nonwork demands

Another employment relationship trend is **virtual work,** whereby employees use information technology to perform their jobs away from the traditional physical workplace. The most common form of virtual work, called *telecommuting* or *teleworking,* involves working at home rather than commuting to the office. Virtual work also includes employees connected to the office while on the road or at clients' offices. For instance, nearly 50 percent of employees at Sun Microsystems complete some of their work from home, cafés, drop-in centers, or clients' offices. More than two-thirds of the employees at Agilent Technologies engage in virtual work some or all of the time.[64]

VIRTUAL WORK: work performed away from the traditional physical workplace using information technology

Some research suggests that virtual work, particularly telecommuting, potentially reduces employee stress by offering better work/life balance and dramatically reducing time lost through commuting to the office. AT&T estimates that its telecommuters reduce pollution and are about 10 percent more productive than before they started working from home. Nortel Networks reports that 71 percent of its U.K. staff feels more empowered through virtual work arrangements.[65] Against these potential benefits, virtual workers face a number of real or potential challenges. Family relations may suffer rather than improve if employees lack

Welcome to My Office!

One of Ray Ackley's first decisions each workday is where to put his office. The chief creative officer for Tipping Point Services, a Metro Detroit-based marketing and communications firm, sometimes chooses a popular bakery or café. Other times, he sets up shop in a nearby library (Ackley is shown here at Southfield Public Library). As long as the location has a good Wi-Fi connection and comfortable surroundings, Ackley can get on with his work, which includes communicating with co-workers located elsewhere in Detroit as well as in Delhi, India, and Shanghai, China. Tipping Point Services doesn't even have an official office, although it might eventually establish one. But for now, Ackley and his co-workers prefer the virtual work arrangement. "We made a commitment to be a virtual office because we can," says Ackley. "I can work anywhere, which means I travel less and I can spend more time at home."[66]

sufficient space and resources for a home office. Some virtual workers complain of social isolation and reduced promotion opportunities. Virtual work is clearly better suited to people who are self-motivated, organized, can work effectively with broadband and other technology, and have sufficient fulfillment of social needs elsewhere in their life. They also work better in organizations that evaluate employees by their performance outcomes rather than face time.[67]

>Anchors of Organizational Behavior Knowledge

Globalization, increasing workforce diversity, and emerging employment relationships are just a few of the trends that challenge organizations and make OB knowledge more relevant than ever before. To understand these and other topics, the field of organizational behavior relies on a set of basic beliefs or knowledge structures (see Exhibit 1.2). These conceptual anchors represent the principles on which OB knowledge is developed and refined.

The Multidisciplinary Anchor

Organizational behavior is anchored around the idea that the field should develop from knowledge in other disciplines, not just from its own isolated research base. For instance, psychological research has aided our understanding of individual and interpersonal behavior. Sociologists have contributed to our knowledge of team dynamics, organizational socialization, organizational power, and other aspects of the social system. OB knowledge has also benefited from knowledge in emerging fields such as communications, marketing, and information systems. Some OB experts have recently argued that the field suffers from a "trade deficit"—importing far more knowledge from other disciplines than is exported to other disciplines. While this is a possible concern, organizational behavior has thrived through its diversity of knowledge from other fields of study.[68]

The Systematic Research Anchor

A critical feature of OB knowledge is that it should be based on systematic research, which typically involves forming research questions, systematically collecting data, and testing hypotheses against those data. The result is *evidence-based management,* which involves making decisions and taking actions based on this research evidence. This makes perfect sense, doesn't it? Yet many OB scholars are amazed at how often corporate leaders embrace fads, consulting models, and their own pet beliefs without bothering to find out if they actually work![69]

[**Exhibit 1.2**] Anchors of Organizational Behavior Knowledge

Multidisciplinary anchor	OB should import knowledge from many disciplines
Systematic research anchor	OB should study organizations using systematic research methods
Contingency anchor	OB theory should recognize that the effects of actions often vary with the situation
Multiple levels of analysis anchor	OB knowledge should include three levels of analysis: individual, team, organization

There are many reasons why people have difficulty applying evidence-based management. Leaders and other decision makers are bombarded with so many ideas from newspapers, books, consultant reports, and other sources that it is a challenge to figure out which ones are based on good evidence. Another problem is that good OB research is necessarily generic; it is rarely described in the context of a specific problem in a specific organization. Managers therefore have the difficult task of figuring out which theories are relevant to their unique situation. A third problem is that many consultants and popular book writers are rewarded for marketing their concepts and theories, not for testing to see if they actually work. Indeed, some management concepts have become popular—they are even found in some OB textbooks!—because of heavy marketing, not because of any evidence that they are valid. Finally, as we will learn in Chapter 3, people form perceptions and beliefs quickly and tend to ignore evidence that their beliefs are inaccurate.

The Contingency Anchor

People and their work environments are complex, and the field of organizational behavior recognizes this by stating that a particular action may have different consequences in different situations. In other words, no single solution is best in all circumstances.[70] Of course, it would be so much simpler if we could rely on "one best way" theories, in which a particular concept or practice has the same results in every situation. OB experts do search for simpler theories, but they also remain skeptical about sure-fire recommendations; an exception is somewhere around the corner. Thus, when faced with a particular problem or opportunity, we need to understand and diagnose the situation and select the strategy most appropriate *under those conditions.*[71]

The Multiple Levels of Analysis Anchor

This textbook divides organizational behavior topics into three levels of analysis: individual, team, and organization. The individual level includes the characteristics and behaviors of employees as well as the thought processes that are attributed to them, such as motivation, perceptions, personalities, attitudes, and values. The team level of analysis looks at the way people interact. This includes team dynamics, decisions, power, organizational politics, conflict, and leadership. At the organizational level, we focus on how people structure their working relationships and on how organizations interact with their environments.

Although an OB topic is typically pegged into one level of analysis, it usually relates to multiple levels.[72] For instance, communication is located in this book as a team (interpersonal) process, but we also recognize that it includes individual and organizational processes. Therefore, you should try to think about each OB topic at the individual, team, and organizational levels, not just at one of these levels.

>The Journey Begins

This chapter gives you some background about the field of organizational behavior. But it's only the beginning of our journey. Throughout this book, we will challenge you to learn new ways of thinking about how people work in and around organizations. We begin this process in Chapter 2 by presenting a basic model of individual behavior, then introducing over the next few chapters various stable and mercurial characteristics of individuals that relate to elements of the individual behavior model. Next, this book moves to the team level of analysis. We examine a model of team effectiveness and specific features of high-performance teams. We also look at decision making and creativity, communication, power and influence, conflict, and leadership. Finally, we shift our focus to the organizational level of analysis, where the topics of organizational structure, organizational culture, and organizational change are examined in detail.

>Chapter Summary

Organizational behavior is the study of what people think, feel, and do in and around organizations. Organizations are groups of people who work interdependently toward some purpose. Although OB doesn't have a specific career path, it offers knowledge and skills that are vitally important to anyone who works in organizations. OB knowledge also has a significant effect on the success of organizations. This book takes the view that OB is for everyone, not just managers.

Organizational effectiveness is a multidimensional concept represented by four perspectives: open systems, organizational learning, high-performance work practices, and stakeholders. The open systems perspective says that organizations need to adapt to their external environment and configure their internal subsystems to maximize efficiency and responsiveness. For the most part, the other perspectives of organizational effectiveness are detailed extensions of the open systems model. The organizational learning perspective states that organizational effectiveness depends on the organization's capacity to acquire, share, use, and store valuable knowledge. Intellectual capital is knowledge that resides in an organization, including its human capital, structural capital, and relationship capital. Effective organizations also "unlearn," meaning that they remove knowledge that no longer adds value.

The high-performance work practices (HPWP) perspective states that effective organizations leverage the human capital potential of their employees. Specific HPWPs have been identified, and experts in this field suggest that they need to be bundled together for maximum benefit. The stakeholder perspective states that effective organizations take into account how their actions affect others, which requires them to understand, manage, and satisfy the interests of their stakeholders. This perspective incorporates values, ethics, and corporate social responsibility into the organizational effectiveness equation.

The five main types of workplace behavior are task performance, organizational citizenship, counterproductive work behaviors, joining and staying with the organization, and work attendance. These represent the individual-level dependent variables found in most OB research.

Three environmental shifts that are challenging organizations include globalization, increasing workforce diversity, and emerging employment relationships. Globalization refers to economic, social, and cultural connectivity with people in other parts of the world. Workforce diversity includes both surface-level and deep-level diversity. Two emerging employment relationship changes are demands for work/life balance and virtual work.

Several conceptual anchors represent the principles on which OB knowledge is developed and refined. These anchors include beliefs that OB knowledge should be multidisciplinary and based on systematic research, organizational events usually have contingencies, and organizational behavior can be viewed from three levels of analysis (individual, team, and organization).

>key terms

corporate social responsibility (CSR) 11

counterproductive work behaviors (CWBs) 12

deep-level diversity 15

ethics 10

globalization 14

high-performance work practices (HPWP) 8

intellectual capital 8

job satisfaction 13

open systems 6

organizational behavior (OB) 4

organizational citizenship behaviors (OCBs) 12

organizational effectiveness 5

>critical thinking questions

1. A friend suggests that organizational behavior courses are useful only to people who will enter management careers. Discuss the accuracy of your friend's statement.

2. A number of years ago, employees in a city water distribution department were put into teams and encouraged to find ways to improve efficiency. The teams boldly crossed departmental boundaries and areas of management discretion in search of problems. Employees working in other parts of the city began to complain about these intrusions. Moreover, when some team ideas were implemented, the city managers discovered that a dollar saved in the water distribution unit may have cost the organization two dollars in higher costs elsewhere. Use the open systems perspective to explain what happened here.

3. After hearing a seminar on organizational learning, a mining company executive argues that this perspective ignores the fact that mining companies could not rely on knowledge alone to stay in business. They also need physical capital (such as digging and ore processing equipment) and land (where the minerals are located). In fact, these two may be more important than what employees carry around in their heads. Evaluate the mining executive's comments.

4. A common refrain among executives is "People are our most important asset." Relate this statement to any two of the four perspectives of organizational effectiveness presented in this chapter. Does this statement apply better to some perspectives than to others? Why or why not?

5. Corporate social responsibility is one of the hottest issues in corporate boardrooms these days, partly because it is becoming increasingly important to employees and other stakeholders. In your opinion, why have stakeholders given CSR more attention recently? Does abiding by CSR standards potentially cause companies to have conflicting objectives with some stakeholders in some situations?

6. One of the emerging views of employee turnover is that people often quit their jobs due to "shock events." Describe an experience where a shock event prompted you to act rather than just simmer with dissatisfaction.

7. Look through the list of chapters in this textbook and discuss how globalization could influence each organizational behavior topic.

8. "Organizational theories should follow the contingency approach." Comment on the accuracy of this statement.

>team exercise 1-1

Human Checkers

Purpose   This exercise is designed to help students understand the importance and application of organizational behavior concepts.

Materials   None, but the instructor has more information about the team's task.

Instructions

- *Step 1:* Form teams with six students. If possible, each team should have a private location where team members can plan and practice the required task without being observed or heard by other teams.

- *Step 2:* All teams will receive special instructions in class about the team's assigned task. All teams have the same task and will have the same amount of time to plan and practice the task. At the end of this planning and practice,

each team will be timed while completing the task in class. The team that completes the task in the least time wins.

- *Step 3:* No special materials are required or allowed for this exercise. Although the task is not described here, students should learn the following rules for planning and implementing the task:

   Rule 1: You cannot use any written form of communication or any props to assist in the planning or implementation of this task.

   Rule 2: You may speak to other students in your team at any time during the planning and implementation of this task.

   Rule 3: When performing the task, you must move only in the direction of your assigned destination. In other words, you can only move forward, not backward.

Rule 4: When performing the task, you can move forward to the next space, but only if it is vacant (see Exhibit 1).

Rule 5: When performing the task, you can move forward two spaces, if that space is vacant. In other words, you can move around a student who is one space in front of you to the next space if that space is vacant (see Exhibit 2).

Exhibit 1   **Exhibit 2**

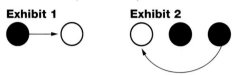

- *Step 4:* When all teams have completed their task, the class will discuss the implications of this exercise for organizational behavior.

Discussion Questions

1. Identify organizational behavior concepts that the team applied to complete this task.

2. What personal theories of people and work teams were applied to complete this task.

3. What organizational behavior problems occurred and what actions were (or should have been) taken to solve them.

>**web** exercise 1-2

Diagnosing Organizational Stakeholders

Purpose   This exercise is designed to help you understand how stakeholders influence organizations as open systems.

Materials   Students need to select a company and, prior to class, retrieve and analyze publicly available information over the past year or two about that company. This may include annual reports, which are usually found on the Web sites of publicly traded companies. Where possible, students should also scan full-text newspaper and magazine databases for articles published over the previous year about the company.

Instructions   The instructor may have students work alone or in groups for this activity. Students will select a company and will investigate the relevance and influence of various stakeholder groups on the organization. Stakeholders will be identified from annual reports, newspaper articles, Web site

statements, and other available sources. Stakeholders should be rank ordered in terms of their perceived importance to the organization.

Students should be prepared to present or discuss their organization's rank ordering of stakeholders, including evidence for this rank ordering.

Discussion Questions

1. What are the main reasons why certain stakeholders are more important than others for this organization?

2. Based on your knowledge of the organization's environmental situation, is this rank order of stakeholders in the organization's best interest, or should specific other stakeholders be given higher priority?

3. What societal groups, if any, are not mentioned as stakeholders by the organization? Does this lack of reference to these unmentioned groups make sense?

>**team** activity/**self-assessment** exercise 1-3

Does It All Make Sense?

Purpose   This exercise is designed to help you understand how organizational behavior knowledge can help you to understand life in organizations.

Instructions   (*Note:* This activity may be done as a self-assessment or as a team activity.) Read each of the statements below and circle whether each statement is true or false, in your opinion. The class will consider the answers to each question and discuss the implications for studying organizational behavior.

Due to the nature of this activity, the instructor will provide information about the most appropriate answer. The scoring key is not found in Appendix B.

1. True False   A happy worker is a productive worker.

2. True False   Decision makers tend to continue supporting a course of action even though information suggests that the decision is ineffective.

3. True False   Organizations are more effective when they prevent conflict among employees.

4. True False   It is better to negotiate alone than as a team.

5. True False   Companies are more effective when they have a strong corporate culture.

6. True False   Employees perform better without stress.

7. True False   Effective organizational change always begins by pinpointing the source of its current problems.

8. True False   Female leaders involve employees in decisions to a greater degree than do male leaders.

9. True False   People who value group harmony and duty to the group (high collectivism) are less likely to value their uniqueness and personal freedom.

10. True False   The best decisions are made without emotion.

11. True False   If employees feel they are paid unfairly, then nothing other than changing their pay will reduce their feelings of injustice.

Find the complete interactive self-assessment at this textbook's Web site at www.mhhe.com/mcshaneEss2e.

>self-assessment exercise 1-4

Telework Disposition Assessment

As companies experiment with telecommuting (also called *teleworking*), they are learning that some employees seem to adapt better than others to this new employment relationship. This self-assessment measures personal characteristics that seem to relate to telecommuting, and therefore provides a rough indication of how well you would adapt to telework.

The instrument asks you to indicate the degree to which you agree or disagree with each of the statements provided. You need to be honest with yourself for a reasonable estimate of your telework disposition. Please keep in mind that this scale only considers your personal characteristics. Other factors, such as organizational, family, and technological systems support, must also be taken into account.

>part II:

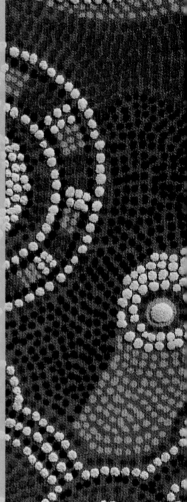

Individual Behavior and Processes

Individual Behavior, Personality, and Values

Johnson & Johnson is one of the world's most respected employers because it recognizes each employee's self-concept and personal values. "We make them feel the company belongs to them," says Narendra Ambwani, the company's managing director in India (shown here).

>learningobjectives

After reading this chapter, you should be able to:

1 Describe the four factors that directly influence voluntary individual behavior and performance.

2 Define personality and discuss what determines an individual's personality characteristics.

3 Summarize the "big five" personality traits in the five-factor model and discuss their influence on organizational behavior.

4 Describe self-concept in terms of self-enhancement, self-verification, and self-evaluation.

5 Explain how social identity theory relates to a person's self-concept.

6 Distinguish personal, shared, espoused, and enacted values, and explain why values congruence is important.

7 Summarize five values commonly studied across cultures.

8 Explain how moral intensity, ethical sensitivity, and the situation influence ethical behavior.

Every Saturday, Vikas Shirodkar takes his daughter to dance lessons and pops into his office at Johnson & Johnson's (J&J) Indian headquarters in Mumbai, which is located next door to the dance class. Doing work at the office saves Shirodkar the trouble of driving home and back again to pick up his daughter after class. After three weeks, Shirodkar received a call from J&J's managing director, Narendra Ambwani, asking if he was overburdened and needed additional staff. Shirodkar was surprised by the question, until Ambwani explained that he noticed the executive's name on the register every Saturday and was concerned about his workload.

The managing director's call was a defining moment for Shirodkar because it reflected J&J's famous credo. Written in 1947, J&J's credo is a value system in which every employee at J&J "must be considered as an individual" and that the company "must respect their dignity and recognize their merit." The credo recognizes employees, customers, communities, and the environment, as well as shareholders. These values and resulting practices have helped J&J become one of the world's top-ranked employers. In India, where job-hopping has become the norm, the average J&J employee has more than 15 years of service. Asked about J&J's success at attracting and retaining talent, India managing director Narendra Ambwani answers: "We make them feel the company belongs to them."

J&J also attracts and retains employees better than most companies by paying attention to each employee's self-concept and personal values. In the United States, for example, J&J's Pharmaceutical Research & Development division discovered that a key ingredient to employee motivation and well-being is for managers to ensure that employees feel valued as contributors to the company's success. This includes giving them a clear sense of direction (i.e., clear role perceptions), involving them in decisions, and expressing trust in their competence. In addition, the European operations of J&J's Global Pharmaceutical Supply Group introduced a new career program that involves employees and takes into account their self-concept. Specifically, the career planning process begins by asking each employee to identify his or her personal values, which are then matched with corresponding job preferences.[1]

///

When asked what makes Johnson & Johnson a successful company, some point to the company's credo, others to its decentralized structure, which encourages entrepreneurial empowerment. But as this opening story reveals, the company's success also comes from treating employees as valued stakeholders, and recognizing that they are ultimately individuals with personal values, personalities, and self-concepts that require dignity, nurturing, and recognition.

This chapter concentrates our attention on the role of the individual in organizations. We begin by presenting the MARS model, which outlines the four drivers of individual behavior and results. Next, we introduce the most stable aspect of individuals—personality—including where our personality comes from, the five main dimensions of personality, and how personality relates to organizational behavior. Our attention then turns to the individual's self-concept, including a person's self-enhancement, self-verification, self-evaluation, and social identity. The latter part of this chapter examines another relatively stable characteristic of individuals: their personal values. We look at type of values, issues of values congruence in organizations, cross-cultural values, and ethical values and practices.

After reading the next section, you should be able to:

1. *Describe the four factors that directly influence voluntary individual behavior and performance.*

learningobjectives<

>MARS Model of Individual Behavior and Performance

For most of the past century, experts in psychology, sociology, and more recently organizational behavior have investigated the direct predictors of individual behavior and performance.[2] One frequently mentioned formula is *performance = ability × motivation,* sometimes known as the "skill and will" model. This formula identifies two characteristics within the person that directly influence behavior and performance. Another popular formula is *performance = person × situation,* where *person* includes individual characteristics, and *situation* represents external influences on the individual's behavior. Role perceptions, the fourth factor that directly predicts behavior and performance, was not identified until the 1960s and continues to be overlooked in many studies on individual behavior.[3]

Exhibit 2.1 illustrates the four factors that directly influence voluntary individual behavior and performance: motivation, ability, role perceptions, and situational factors. These variables are easily remembered by the acronym "MARS."[4] All four factors are important, so behavior and performance would be low when any one of them is low. For example, enthusiastic salespeople (motivation) who understand their job duties (role perceptions) and have sufficient resources (situational factors) will not perform their jobs as well if they lack sufficient knowledge and sales skill (ability). Let's look at each of these four factors in more detail.

Employee Motivation

MOTIVATION: the forces within a person that affect his or her direction, intensity, and persistence of voluntary behavior

Motivation represents the forces within a person that affect his or her direction, intensity, and persistence of voluntary behavior.[5] *Direction* refers to the path along which people engage their effort. This sense of direction of effort reflects the fact that people have choices about where they put their effort. In other words, motivation is goal-directed, not random. People are motivated to arrive at work on time, finish a project a few hours early, or aim for many other targets. The second element of motivation, called *intensity,* is the amount of effort allocated to the goal. For example, two employees might be motivated to finish their project a few hours early (direction), but only one of them puts forth enough

[Exhibit 2.1] MARS Model of Individual Behavior and Results

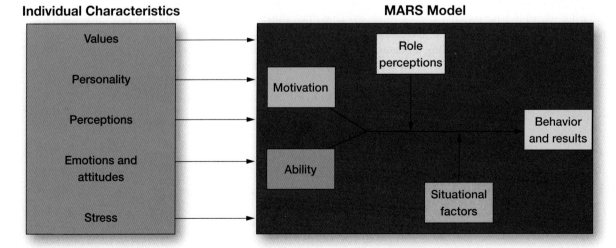

effort (intensity) to achieve this goal. In other words, intensity is all about how much you push yourself to complete the task.

Finally, motivation involves varying levels of *persistence*, that is, continuing the effort for a certain amount of time. Employees sustain their effort until they reach their goal or give up beforehand. To help remember these three elements of motivation, consider the metaphor of driving a car in which the thrust of the engine is your effort. Direction refers to where you steer the car, intensity is how much you put your foot down on the gas pedal, and persistence is for how long you drive toward that destination.

Ability

Employee abilities also make a difference in behavior and task performance. **Ability** includes both the natural aptitudes and learned capabilities required to successfully complete a task. *Aptitudes* are the natural talents that help employees learn specific tasks more quickly and perform them better. For example, some people have a more natural ability than others to manipulate small objects with their fingers (called finger dexterity). There

ABILITY:
the natural aptitudes and learned capabilities required to successfully complete a task

Training the Toyota Way
Poised to become the world's largest automaker, Toyota Motor Company is ramping up its training programs around the world to maintain the company's quality standards. Toyota's training methods make extensive use of visual and cognitive aptitudes that require considerable practice and coaching. For example, trainees learn how to spot defects on metal sheet panels where most of us would see none. They also develop visual gap measuring, such as determining how well the edge of the engine hood lines up with the adjacent part of the front grill. This photo shows Toyota production employee Ray Howley (right) from South Africa learning from master trainer Kazuo Hyodo how to tighten bolts so they are snug without being too tight.[6]

are many physical and mental aptitudes, and our ability to acquire skills is affected by these aptitudes. *Learned capabilities* refer to the skills and knowledge that you have actually acquired. This includes the physical and mental skills you possess as well as the knowledge you acquire and store for later use.

Skills, knowledge, aptitudes, and other personal characteristics that lead to superior performance are bunched together into the concept of **competencies.** The challenge is to match a person's competencies with what each job requires. One strategy is to select applicants whose existing competencies best fit the required tasks. This includes comparing each applicant's competencies with the requirements of the job or work unit. A second approach is to provide training so employees develop required skills and knowledge. Recent evidence suggests that training has a strong influence on organizational performance.[7] The third way to match people with job requirements is to redesign the job so employees are only given tasks within their capabilities.

COMPETENCIES: skills, knowledge, aptitudes, and other personal characteristics that lead to superior performance

Role Perceptions

Employees also require clear role perceptions to perform their job well. Employees have clear role perceptions in three ways. First, they understand the specific tasks assigned to them, meaning that they know the specific duties or consequences for which they are accountable. Second, they understand the priority of their various tasks and performance expectations. For example, employees would know that serving customers should take priority over stocking shelves if the two are required at the same time. This second characteristic of role perceptions also refers to understanding the priority of quality versus quantity in performing the task. The third aspect of role perceptions is understanding the preferred behaviors to accomplish the assigned tasks. This refers to situations where more than one method could be followed to perform the work. Employees with clear role perceptions know which of these methods is preferred by the organization.

Situational Factors

Employee behavior and performance also depends on how well the situation supports their task goals. Situational factors include conditions beyond the employee's immediate control that constrain or facilitate behavior and performance.[8] Some situational characteristics— such as consumer preferences and economic conditions—originate from the external environment and, consequently, are beyond the employee's and organization's control. However, some situational factors—such as time, people, budget, and physical work facilities—are controlled by others in the organization. Corporate leaders need to carefully arrange these conditions so employees can achieve their performance potential.

Motivation, ability, role perceptions, and situational factors affect all voluntary workplace behaviors and their performance outcomes. In the remainder of this chapter, we introduce the most stable characteristics of individuals that impact their motivation, ability, and role perceptions.

>**learning**objectives

After reading the next two sections, you should be able to:

2. *Define personality and discuss what determines an individual's personality characteristics.*

3. *Summarize the "big five" personality traits in the five-factor model and discuss their influence on organizational behavior.*

4. *Describe self-concept in terms of self-enhancement, self-verification, and self-evaluation.*

5. *Explain how social identity theory relates to a person's self-concept.*

>Personality in Organizations

Brigitte Catellier's final hurdle to become vice president of legal affairs at Astral Media Inc wasn't what she anticipated. For seven hours, Catellier sat through eight aptitude, preferences, and personality tests, some of which asked unusual questions such as whether she would prefer to be an astronaut or and acrobat. "I was told very directly there are two candidates and you are both doing the same tests," says Catellier, who was later offered the job at the Montreal, Canada-based media giant. Astral decided a few years ago to include psychological tests in the hiring process, including instruments that measure several personality traits. "This helps us not make mistakes—and we *have* made mistakes from time to time in the past," says Astral's vice president of human resources, referring to people hired whose personality didn't fit the company or job requirements.[9]

Personality is an important individual characteristic, which explains why Astral Media and many other companies are keen to understand the personality traits of job applicants and employees. **Personality** refers to the relatively enduring pattern of thoughts, emotions, and behaviors that characterize a person, along with the psychological processes behind those characteristics.[10] It is, in essence, the bundle of characteristics that make us similar to or different from other people. We estimate an individual's personality in terms of what he or she says and does, and infer the person's internal states—including thoughts and emotions—from these observable behaviors.

> **PERSONALITY:** the relatively enduring pattern of thoughts, emotions, and behaviors that characterize a person, along with the psychological processes behind those characteristics

A basic premise of personality theory is that people have inherent characteristics or traits that can be identified by the consistency or stability of their behavior across time and situations.[11] For example, you probably have some friends who are more talkative than others. You might know some people who like to take chances and others who avoid taking risks. This consistency is an essential requirement for personality theory because it attributes a person's behavior to something within them—their personality—rather than to purely environmental influences.

Of course, people do not act the same way in all situations; they vary their behavior to suit the situation, even if it is at odds with their personality.[12] For example, talkative people remain relatively quiet in a library where "no talking" rules are explicit and strictly enforced. Individuals typically exhibit a wide range of behaviors, yet out of that variety are discernable patterns that we refer to as personality traits. Furthermore, these stable traits predict behavior far into the future. For example, studies report that an individual's personality in childhood predicts various behaviors and outcomes in adulthood, including educational attainment, employment success, marital relationships, illegal activities, and health-risk behaviors.[13]

Personality Determinants: Nature versus Nurture

What determines an individual's personality? Most experts now agree that personality is shaped by both nature and nurture, although the relative importance of each remains an issue. "Nature" refers to our genetic or hereditary origins—the genes that we inherit from our parents. Studies of identical twins, particularly those separated at birth, reveal that heredity has a very large effect on personality; up to 50 percent of variation in behavior and 30 percent of temperament preferences can be attributed to a person's genetic characteristics.[14] In other words, genetic code not only determines our eye color, skin tone, and physical shape; it also has a significant effect on our attitudes, decisions, and behavior.

Some similarities of twins raised apart are surreal. Consider Jim Springer and Jim Lewis, twins who were separated when only four weeks old and didn't meet each other until age 39. In spite of being raised in different families and communities in Ohio, the "Jim twins" held similar jobs, smoked the same type of cigarettes, drove the same make and color of car, spent their vacations on the same Florida beach, had the same woodworking hobby, gave their first sons almost identical names, and had been married twice. Both their first and second wives also had the same first names![15]

Although personality is heavily influenced by heredity, it is also affected to some degree by "nurture"—the person's socialization, life experiences, and other forms of interaction with the environment. Studies have found that the stability of an individual's personality increases up to at least age 30 and possibly to age 50, indicating that some personality development and change occurs when people are young.[16] The main explanation why personality becomes more stable over time is that people form clearer and more rigid self-concepts as they get older. The executive function—the part of the brain that manages goal-directed behavior—tries to keep our behavior consistent with our self-concept.[17] As self-concept becomes clearer and more stable with age, behavior and personality therefore also become more stable. We will discuss self-concept in more detail later in this chapter. The main point here is that personality is not completely determined by heredity; life experiences, particularly early in life, also shape each individual's personality traits.

Personality Traits

One of the most important elements of personality theory is that people possess specific personality traits. Traits are broad concepts that help us to label and understand individual differences. Traits such as sociable, depressed, cautious, and talkative represent clusters of thoughts, feelings, and behaviors that allow us to identify, differentiate, and understand people.[18]

Five-Factor Model of Personality

FIVE-FACTOR MODEL (FFM): The five abstract dimensions representing most personality traits: conscientiousness, emotional stability, openness to experience, agreeableness and extroversion

CONSCIENTIOUS-NESS: a personality dimension describing people who are careful, dependable, and self-disciplined

The English language includes more than 17,000 words that describe an individual's personality. Several decades ago, personality experts scoured *Roget's Thesaurus* and *Webster's Dictionary* to identify these words, then aggregated them into 171 clusters. Further analysis combined these clusters into five abstract personality dimensions. Using more sophisticated techniques, recent investigations identified the same five dimensions—known as the **five-factor model (FFM).**[19] These "Big Five" dimensions, represented by the handy acronym CANOE, are outlined in Exhibit 2.2 and described below:

- *Conscientiousness*—**Conscientiousness** refers to people who are careful, dependable, and self-disciplined. Some scholars argue that this dimension also includes the will to achieve. People with low conscientiousness tend to be careless, less thorough, more disorganized, and irresponsible.
- *Agreeableness*—This includes the traits of being courteous, good-natured, empathic, and caring. Some scholars prefer the label of "friendly compliance" for this dimension, with its opposite being "hostile noncompliance." People with low agreeableness tend to be uncooperative, short-tempered, and irritable.

[**Exhibit 2.2**] Five-Factor Model "Big Five" Personality Dimensions

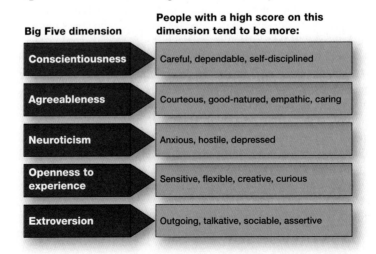

- *Neuroticism*—**Neuroticism** characterizes people with high levels of anxiety, hostility, depression, and self-consciousness. In contrast, people with low neuroticism (high emotional stability) are poised, secure, and calm.

- *Openness to experience*—This dimension is the most complex and has the least agreement among scholars. It generally refers to the extent to which people are sensitive, flexible, creative, and curious. Those who score low on this dimension tend to be more resistant to change, less open to new ideas, and more fixed in their ways.

- *Extroversion*—**Extroversion** characterizes people who are outgoing, talkative, sociable, and assertive. The opposite is introversion, which refers to those who are quiet, shy, and cautious. Introverts do not necessarily lack social skills. Rather, they are more inclined to direct their interests to ideas than to social events. Introverts feel quite comfortable being alone, whereas extroverts do not.

> **NEUROTICISM:** a personality dimension describing people with high levels of anxiety, hostility, depression, and self-consciousness

> **EXTROVERSION:** a personality dimension describing people who are outgoing, talkative, sociable, and assertive

These five personality dimensions are not independent of each other. Conscientiousness, agreeableness, and low neuroticism (high emotional stability) represent a common underlying characteristic broadly described as "getting along"; people with these traits are aware of and more likely to abide by rules and norms of society. The other two dimensions share the common underlying factor called "getting ahead"; people with high scores on extroversion and openness to experience exhibit more behaviors aimed at achieving goals, managing their environment, and advancing themselves in teams.[20]

Personality and Organizational Behavior

Studies report fairly strong associations between personality and a variety of workplace behaviors and outcomes, even when employee ability and other factors are taken into account. Conscientiousness and emotional stability (low neuroticism) stand out as the personality traits that best predict individual performance in almost every job group.[21] Both are motivational components of personality because they energize a willingness to fulfill work obligations within established rules (conscientiousness) and to allocate resources to accomplish those tasks (emotional stability). Various studies have reported that conscientious employees set higher personal goals for themselves, are more motivated, and have higher performance expectations than do employees with low levels of conscientiousness. They also tend to have higher levels of organizational citizenship and work better in organizations that give employees more freedom than in traditional "command and control" workplaces.[22]

The other three personality dimensions predict more specific types of employee behavior and performance. Extroversion is associated with performance in sales and management jobs, where employees must interact with and influence people. Agreeableness is associated with performance in jobs where employees are expected to be cooperative and helpful, such as working in teams, customer relations, and other conflict-handling situations. People high on the openness to experience personality dimension tend to be more creative and adaptable to change. Finally, personality influences employee well-being in various ways. Studies report that personality influences a person's general emotional reactions to their job, how well they cope with stress, and what type of career paths make them happiest.[23]

>Self-Concept: The "I" in Organizational Behavior

To more fully understand individual behavior in organizations, we need to realize that people develop, nurture, and act in ways that maintain and enhance their self-concept. **Self-concept** refers to an individual's self-beliefs and self-evaluations. It is the "Who am I?" and "How do I feel about myself?" that people ask themselves and that guide their decisions and actions. People do not have a single unitary self-concept.[24] Rather,

> **SELF-CONCEPT:** an individual's self-beliefs and self-evaluations

they think of themselves in several ways in various situations. For example, you might think of yourself as a creative employee, a health-conscious vegetarian, and an aggressive skier. A person's self-concept has higher complexity when it consists of many categories.

Along with complexity, self-concept varies in the degree of its consistency. People have high consistency when similar personality traits and values are required across all aspects of self-concept. Low consistency occurs when some aspects of self require personal characteristics that conflict with the characteristics required for other aspects of self. A third structural feature of self-concept is clarity; that is, the degree to which a person's self-conceptions are clearly and confidently described, internally consistent, and stable across time. A clear self-concept necessarily requires a consistent self-concept. Generally, people develop a clearer self-concept as they get older.

These three structural dimensions of self-concept—complexity, consistency, and clarity—influence our adaptability and well-being. People function better when their self-concept has many elements (high complexity) that are compatible with each other (high consistency) and relatively clear. In contrast, people are more rigid and inflexible, and therefore less adaptable, when they view themselves in terms of only a few similar characteristics (low complexity). People also have poorer psychological adjustment when their self-concept is less clear and includes conflicting elements.

Self-Enhancement and Self-Verification

The opening story to this chapter noted that Johnson & Johnson managers discovered a key ingredient to employee motivation and well-being—*ensuring that employees feel valued as contributors to the company's success*. This desire to feel valued is an important aspect of self-concept. We are inherently motivated to promote and protect a self-view of being competent, attractive, lucky, ethical, valued, and so forth.[25] This self-enhancement is observed in many ways. People tend to rate themselves above average, selectively recall positive feedback while forgetting negative feedback, attribute their successes to personal motivation or ability while blaming the situation for their mistakes, and believe that they have a better than average probability of success. We don't see ourselves as above average in all circumstances, but this bias is apparent for conditions that are common rather than rare and that are important to us.[26]

Self-enhancement has both positive and negative consequences in organizational settings. On the positive side, research has found that individuals have better personal adjustment and experience better mental and physical health when they view their self-concept in a positive light. On the negative side, self-enhancement can result in bad decisions. For example, studies report that self-enhancement causes managers to overestimate the probability of success in investment decisions, such as acquiring another company.[27]

Self-Verification

Along with self-enhancement, people are motivated to verify and maintain their existing self-concept.[28] Self-verification stabilizes our self-concept, which, in turn, provides an important anchor to guide our thoughts and actions. Self-verification differs from self-enhancement because people will usually prefer feedback that is consistent with their self-concept even when that feedback is unflattering. Self-verification has several implications for organizational behavior.[29] First, it affects the perceptual process because employees are more likely to remember information that is consistent with their self-concept. Second, the more confident employees are in their self-concept, the less they will accept feedback—positive or negative—that is at odds with their self-concept. Finally, employees are motivated to interact with others who affirm their self-concept, which affects how well they get along with their boss and with co-workers in teams.

Self-Evaluation

Almost everyone strives to have a positive self-concept, but some people have a more positive evaluation of themselves than do others. This self-evaluation is mostly defined in terms of three concepts: self-esteem, self-efficacy, and locus of control.[30]

Self-Esteem

Self-esteem is a fundamental component of self-concept because it represents a global self-evaluation; that is, the extent to which people like, respect, and are satisfied with themselves. People with a high self-esteem are less influenced by others, tend to be persistent in spite of failure, and think more rationally. Self-esteem regarding specific aspects of self (e.g., a good student, a good driver, a good parent) predicts specific thoughts and behaviors, whereas a person's overall self-esteem predicts only large bundles of thoughts and behaviors.[31]

Self-Efficacy

Self-efficacy refers to a person's belief that he or she has the ability, motivation, correct role perceptions, and favorable situation to complete a task successfully.[32] People with high self-efficacy have a can-do attitude. They believe they possess the energy (motivation), resources (situational factors), understanding of the correct course of action (role perceptions), and competencies (ability) to perform the task. In other words, self-efficacy is an individual's perception regarding the MARS model in a specific situation. Although originally defined in terms of specific tasks, self-efficacy is also discussed as a general trait related to self-concept.[33] General self-efficacy is a perception of one's competence to perform across a variety of situations. The higher the person's general self-efficacy, the higher is their overall self-evaluation.

SELF-EFFICACY: a person's belief that he or she has the ability, motivation, correct role perceptions, and favorable situation to complete a task successfully

Locus of Control

A third concept related to a person's evaluation of his or her self-concept is **locus of control,** which is defined as a person's general belief about the amount of control he or she has over personal life events. Individuals who think that events in their life are due mainly to fate/luck or powerful others have an *external locus of control.* Those who feel that they can influence their own destiny have an *internal locus of control.* Locus of control is a generalized belief, so people with an external locus can feel in control in familiar situations (such as performing common tasks). However, their underlying locus of control would be apparent in new situations in which control over events is uncertain.

LOCUS OF CONTROL: a person's general belief about the amount of control he or she has over personal life events

Feeling Valued Adds Value at Fairmont
Yasmeen Youssef's self-confidence was a bit shaky when she and her husband moved from Egypt to Canada a few years ago. "I was worried no one would take a chance on me, would believe in me," she recalls. But any self-doubts slowly disappeared after taking an entry-level job with Fairmont Hotels & Resorts corporate offices in Toronto. "Everything changed when I started working at Fairmont," says Youssef, who is now on Fairmont's human resources team and recently trained new staff in Cairo. "I can't believe the amount of value, care, and respect everyone has extended to me." As North America's largest luxury hotel operator, Fairmont discovered long ago that the secret to employee motivation and well-being is supporting the individual's self-esteem and general self-efficacy. "People want to feel valued and they stay where they feel valued," explain Carolyn Clark, Fairmont's senior vice president of human resources.[34]

People with a higher internal locus of control have a more positive self-evaluation. They also tend to perform better in most employment situations, are more successful in their careers, earn more money, and are better suited for leadership positions. Internals are also more satisfied with their jobs, cope better in stressful situations, and are more motivated by performance-based reward systems.[35]

The Social Self

A person's self-concept can be organized into two fairly distinct categories: personal identity characteristics and social identity characteristics.[36] *Personal identity* consists of characteristics that make us unique and distinct from people in the social groups to which we have a connection. For instance, an unusual achievement that distinguishes you from other people typically becomes a personal identity characteristic. Personal identity refers to something about you as an individual without reference to a larger group. At the same time, human beings are social animals; they have an inherent drive to be associated with others and to be recognized as part of social communities. This drive to belong is reflected in self-concept by the fact that everyone defines themselves to some degree by their association with others.[37]

SOCIAL IDENTITY THEORY: A theory that explains self-concept in terms of the person's unique characteristics (personal identity) and membership in various social groups (social identity)

This social element of self-concept is described in **social identity theory.** According to social identity theory, people define themselves in terms of the groups to which they belong or have an emotional attachment. For instance, someone might have a social identity as an American, a graduate of the University of Massachusetts, and an employee at Oracle Corporation (see Exhibit 2.3). Social identity is a complex combination of many memberships arranged in a hierarchy of importance. One factor determining this importance is how obvious our membership is in the group. We tend to define ourselves by our gender, race, age, and other observable characteristics because other people easily identify our membership in those groups. It is difficult to ignore your gender in a class where most other students are the opposite gender, for example. In that context, gender tends to become a stronger defining feature of your social identity than in social settings where there are many people of the same gender.

Along with our demographic characteristics, group status is typically an important influence on our social identity. We identify with groups that have high status or respect because this aids the self-enhancement of our self-concept. Medical doctors usually define themselves in terms of their profession because of its high status, whereas people in low-status

[Exhibit 2.3] Social Identity Theory Example

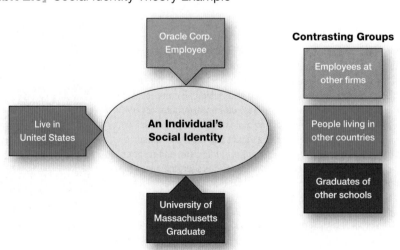

jobs tend to define themselves in terms of nonjob groups. Some people define themselves in terms of where they work because their employer has a favorable reputation in the community. For instance, as the opening vignette to this chapter stated, Johnson & Johnson employees are so proud of and involved in the company that they "feel the company belongs to them." In contrast, people in some other companies never mention where they work because of poor relations with employees and poor reputation in the community.[38]

After reading the next three sections, you should be able to:

6. *Distinguish personal, shared, espoused, and enacted values, and explain why values congruence is important.*

7. *Summarize five values commonly studied across cultures.*

8. *Explain how moral intensity, ethical sensitivity, and the situation influence ethical behavior.*

learningobjectives<

>Values in the Workplace

In addition to personality characteristics and social identities, a person's self-concept consists of their hierarchy of personal values.[39] *Values* are stable, evaluative beliefs that guide our preferences for outcomes or courses of action in a variety of situations. They are perceptions about what is good or bad, right or wrong. Values tell us to what we "ought" to do. They serve as a moral compass that directs our motivation and, potentially, our decisions and actions. Values partly define who we are as individuals and as members of groups with similar values.

People arrange values into a hierarchy of preferences, called a *value system*. Some individuals value new challenges more than they value conformity. Others value generosity more than frugality. Each person's unique value system is developed and reinforced through socialization from parents, religious institutions, friends, personal experiences, and the society in which he or she lives. As such, a person's hierarchy of values is stable and long lasting. For example, one study found that value systems of a sample of adolescents were remarkably similar 20 years later as adults.[40]

Notice that our description of values has focused on individuals, whereas executives often describe values as though they belong to the organization. In reality, values exist only within individuals, which we call *personal values*. However, groups of people might hold the same or similar values, so we tend to ascribe these *shared values* to the team, department, organization, profession, or entire society. The values shared by people throughout an organization (*organizational values*) will receive fuller discussion in Chapter 16 because they are a key part of corporate culture. The values shared across a society (*cultural values*) will receive attention later in this chapter.

Before discussing workplace values in more detail, we need to distinguish between espoused and enacted values.[41] *Espoused values* represent the values that we say we use and, in many cases, think we use. Corporate leaders might say they value environmentalism, creativity, and politeness, whether or not they really do value these things in practice. Values are socially desirable, so people create a positive public image by claiming to believe in values that others expect them to embrace. Also, corporate values are usually considered espoused values because, although leaders might abide by them, we don't know whether lower-level employees share this commitment. *Enacted values,* on the other hand, represent the values we actually rely on to guide our decisions and actions. These values-in-use are apparent by watching people in action. Just as we judge an individual's personality by behavioral tendencies, so too do we judge enacted values by behavioral tendencies.

Types of Values

Values come in many forms, and experts on this topic have devoted considerable attention to organizing them into coherent groups. The model in Exhibit 2.4, developed and tested by social psychologist Shalom Schwartz, has become the most widely studied and generally accepted model today.[42] Schwartz reduced dozens of personal values into these 10 broader domains of values and further organized these domains around two bipolar dimensions.

Along the left side of the horizontal dimension in Schwartz's model is *openness to change,* which represents the extent to which a person is motivated to pursue innovative ways. Openness to change includes the value domains of self-direction (independent thought and action) and stimulation (excitement and challenge). *Conservation,* the opposite end of Schwartz's horizontal dimension, is the extent to which a person is motivated to preserve the status quo. Conservation includes the value clusters of conformity (adherence to social norms and expectations), security (safety and stability), and tradition (moderation and preservation of the status quo).

The vertical dimension in Schwartz's model ranges from self-enhancement to self-transcendence. *Self-enhancement*—how much a person is motivated by self-interest—includes the values of achievement (pursuit of personal success) and power (dominance over others). The opposite of self-enhancement is *self-transcendence,* which refers to the motivation to promote the welfare of others and nature. Self-transcendence includes the values of benevolence (concern for others in one's life) and universalism (concern for the welfare of all people and nature).

Values and Individual Behavior

Personal values guide our decisions and actions to some extent, but this connection isn't always as strong as some would like to believe. Habitual behavior tends to be consistent with our values, but our everyday conscious decisions and actions apply our values much

[**Exhibit 2.4**] Schwartz's Values Circumplex

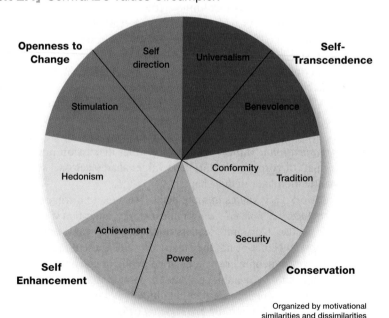

Organized by motivational
similarities and dissimilarities

Sources: S. H. Schwartz, "Universals in the Content and Structure of Values: Theoretical Advances and Empirical Tests in 20 Countries," *Advances in Experimental Social Psychology* 25 (1992), pp. 1–65; S. H. Schwartz and G. Sagie, "Value Consensus and Importance: A Cross-national Study," *Journal of Cross-Cultural Psychology* 31 (July 2000), pp. 465–97.

less consistently. The main reason for the disconnect between personal values and individual behavior is that values are abstract concepts that sound good in theory but are less easily followed in practice.

Three conditions strengthen the linkage between personal values and behavior.[43] First, we are more likely to apply values when we are reminded of them. For example, co-workers tend to treat each other with much more respect and consideration immediately after a senior executive gives a speech on the virtues of benevolence in the workplace. Second, we tend to apply our values only when we can think of specific reasons for doing so. In other words, we need logical reasons for applying a specific value in a specific situation. The third condition that improves the linkage between our values and behavior is the situation. Work environments shape our behavior, at least in the short term, so they necessarily encourage or discourage values-consistent behavior.

Values Congruence

Personal values not only define the person's self-concept; they also affect how comfortable that person is in the organization and working with others. The key concept here is *values congruence,* which refers to the extent that a person's values hierarchy is similar to the values hierarchy of the organization, a co-worker, or other comparison. Organizations benefit from some level of values incongruence because employees with diverse values offer different perspectives, which often leads to better decision making. However, a high level of incongruence has a number of undesirable consequences, including higher stress and turnover as well as lower organizational citizenship, loyalty, and job satisfaction. Values are guideposts, so incongruence also reduces the chance that employees will make decisions compatible with the organization's values.[44]

A second type of values congruence refers to how closely the values apparent in our actions (enacted values) are consistent with what we say we believe in (espoused values). This *espoused-enacted values congruence* is especially important for people in leadership positions because any obvious gap between espoused and enacted values undermines their perceived integrity, a critical feature of effective leaders.

A third type of values congruence refers to the compatibility of an organization's dominant values with the prevailing values of the community or society in which it conducts business.[45] This creates a delicate balancing act, because companies depend on shared values to maintain consistent standards and behaviors, yet need to operate within the values of different cultures around the world. Let's look more closely at how values vary across cultures.

>Values across Cultures

Anyone who has worked long enough in other countries will know that values differ across cultures. Some cultures value group decisions, whereas others think that the leader should take charge. Meetings in Germany usually start on time, whereas they might be half an hour late in Brazil without much concern. We need to be sensitive to the fact that cultural differences exist and, although often subtle, can influence decisions, behavior, and relations among employees.

Individualism and Collectivism

Let's start by looking at the two most commonly mentioned cross-cultural values, individualism and collectivism. **Individualism** is the extent to which we value independence and personal uniqueness. Highly individualist people value personal freedom, self-sufficiency,

INDIVIDUALISM: a cross-cultural value describing the degree to which people in a culture emphasize independence and personal uniqueness

COLLECTIVISM:
a cross-cultural value describing the degree to which people in a culture emphasize duty to groups to which people belong, and to group harmony

control over their own lives, and appreciation of the unique qualities that distinguish them from others. As is shown in Exhibit 2.5, Americans and Italians generally exhibit high individualism, whereas Taiwanese tend to have low individualism. **Collectivism** is the extent to which we value our duty to groups to which we belong and to group harmony. Highly collectivist people define themselves by their group membership and value harmonious relationships within those groups.[46] Americans generally have low collectivism whereas Italians and Taiwanese have relatively high collectivism.

Contrary to popular belief, individualism is not the opposite of collectivism. In fact, an analysis of all previous studies reports that the two concepts are unrelated.[47] Some cultures that highly value duty to one's group do not necessarily give a low priority to personal freedom and self-sufficiency. The distinction between individualism and collectivism makes sense when we realize that people across all cultures define themselves in terms of both their uniqueness (personal identity) and relationship to others (social identity). Some cultures are clearly more of one than the other, but both have a place in a person's values and self-concept.

Other Cross-Cultural Values

POWER DISTANCE:
a cross-cultural value describing the degree to which people in a culture accept unequal distribution of power in a society

UNCERTAINTY AVOIDANCE:
a cross-cultural value describing the degree to which people in a culture tolerate ambiguity (low uncertainty avoidance) or feel threatened by ambiguity and uncertainty (high uncertainty avoidance)

A third frequently mentioned cross-cultural value is **power distance,** which refers to the extent that people accept unequal distribution of power in a society.[48] Those with high power distance accept and value unequal power. They value obedience to authority and are comfortable receiving commands from their superiors without consultation or debate, and prefer to resolve differences through formal procedures rather than directly. In contrast, people with low power distance expect relatively equal power sharing. They view the relationship with their boss as one of interdependence, not dependence; that is, they believe their boss is also dependent on them, so they expect power sharing and consultation before decisions affecting them are made. People in India tend to have high power distance, whereas people in Denmark generally have low power distance.

Uncertainty avoidance is the degree to which people tolerate ambiguity (low uncertainty avoidance) or feel threatened by ambiguity and uncertainty (high uncertainty avoidance). Employees with high uncertainty avoidance value structured situations where rules of conduct and decision making are clearly documented. They usually prefer direct rather than indirect or ambiguous communications. Uncertainty avoidance tends to be high in Italy and Taiwan and very high in Japan. It is generally low in Denmark.

[Exhibit 2.5] Five Cross-Cultural Values in Selected Countries

Country	Individualism	Collectivism	Power distance	Uncertainty Avoidance	Achievement Orientation
United States	High	Low	Medium low	Medium low	Medium high
Denmark	Medium	Medium low	Low	Low	Low
India	Medium high	Medium	High	Medium low	Medium high
Italy	High	High	Medium	High	High
Japan	Medium high	Low	Medium	High	High
Taiwan	Low	High	Medium	High	Medium

Sources: Individualism and collectivism results are from the meta-analysis reported in D. Oyserman, H. M. Coon, and M. Kemmelmeier, "Rethinking Individualism and Collectivism: Evaluation of Theoretical Assumptions and Meta-Analyses," *Psychological Bulletin* 128 (2002), pp. 3–72. The other results are from G. Hofstede, *Culture's Consequences, 2nd ed.* (Thousand Oaks, CA: Sage Publications, 2001).

Achievement-nurturing orientation reflects a competitive versus cooperative view of relations with other people.[49] People with a high achievement orientation value assertiveness, competitiveness, and materialism. They appreciate people who are tough and favor the acquisition of money and material goods. In contrast, people in nurturing-oriented cultures emphasize relationships and the well-being of others. They focus on human interaction and caring rather than competition and personal success. People in Sweden, Norway, and Denmark score very low on achievement orientation (i.e., they have a high nurturing orientation). In contrast, very high achievement orientation scores have been reported in Japan and Hungary, with fairly high scores in the United States and Italy.

Before leaving this topic, we need to point out two concerns about cross-cultural values.[50] One concern is that country scores on power distance, uncertainty avoidance, and achievement-nurturing orientation are based on a survey of IBM employees worldwide more than a quarter century ago. More than 100,000 IBM staff in dozens of countries completed that survey, but these IBM employees might not represent the general population. There is also evidence that values have changed quite a bit in some countries since then. A second concern is the assumption that everyone in a society has similar cultural values. This may be true in a few countries, but multiculturalism—where several microcultures coexist in the same country—is becoming the more common trend. On this point, one study reported significantly different values amongst Javanese, Batik, and Chinese Indonesians. By attributing specific values to an entire society, we are engaging in a form of stereotyping that limits our ability to understand the more complex reality of that society.

> **ACHIEVEMENT NURTURING ORIENTATION:** a cross-cultural value describing the degree to which people in a culture emphasize competitive versus cooperative relations with other people

>Ethical Values and Behavior

When employees are asked to list the most important characteristic they look for in a leader, the top factor isn't intelligence, courage, or even being inspirational. Although these characteristics are important, the most important factor in most surveys is honesty/ethics.[51] *Ethics* refers to the study of moral principles or values that determine whether actions are right or wrong and outcomes are good or bad. People rely on their ethical values to determine "the right thing to do."

Three Ethical Principles

To better understand business ethics, we need to consider three distinct types of ethical principles: utilitarianism, individual rights, and distributive justice.[52] While you might prefer one principle more than the others based on your personal values, all three should be actively considered to put important ethical issues to the test.

- *Utilitarianism*—This principle advises us to seek the greatest good for the greatest number of people. In other words, we should choose the option providing the highest degree of satisfaction to those affected. This is sometimes known as a consequential principle because it focuses on the consequences of our actions, not on how we achieve those consequences. One problem with utilitarianism is that it is almost impossible to evaluate the benefits or costs of many decisions, particularly when many stakeholders have wide-ranging needs and values. Another problem is that most of us are uncomfortable engaging in behaviors that seem, well, unethical, to attain results that are ethical.

- *Individual rights*—This principle reflects the belief that everyone has entitlements that let them act in a certain way. Some of the most widely cited rights are freedom of movement, physical security, freedom of speech, fair trial, and freedom from torture.

The individual rights principle includes more than legal rights; it also includes human rights that everyone is granted as a moral norm of society. One problem with individual rights is that certain individual rights may conflict with others. The shareholders' right to be informed about corporate activities may ultimately conflict with an executive's right to privacy, for example.

- *Distributive justice*—This principle suggests that people who are similar to each other should receive similar benefits and burdens; those who are dissimilar should receive different benefits and burdens in proportion to their dissimilarity. For example, we expect that two employees who contribute equally in their work should receive similar rewards, whereas those who make a lesser contribution should receive less. A variation of the distributive justice principle says that inequalities are acceptable where they benefit the least well off in society. Thus, employees in risky jobs should be paid more if this benefits others who are less well off. One problem with the distributive justice principle is that it is difficult to agree on who is "similar" and what factors are "relevant."

Moral Intensity, Ethical Sensitivity, and Situational Influences

MORAL INTENSITY: the degree to which an issue demands the application of ethical principles

Along with ethical principles, we need to consider the moral intensity of the issue, the individual's ethical sensitivity, and situational factors. **Moral intensity** is the degree to which an issue demands the application of ethical principles. Decisions with high moral intensity are more important, so the decision maker needs to more carefully apply ethical principles to resolve it. Several factors influence the moral intensity of an issue, such as the extent that the issue clearly produces good or bad consequences, others in the society think it is good or evil, the issue quickly affects people, the decision maker feels close to the issue, and how much control the person has over the issue.[53]

ETHICAL SENSITIVITY: a personal characteristic that enables people to recognize the presence and determine the relative importance of an ethical issue

Even if an issue has high moral intensity, some employees might not recognize its ethical importance because they have low **ethical sensitivity.** Ethical sensitivity is a personal characteristic that enables people to recognize the presence and determine the relative importance of an ethical issue.[54] Ethically sensitive people are not necessarily more ethical. Rather, they can more accurately estimate the moral intensity of the issue. The third important factor explaining why good people do bad things is the situation in which the unethical conduct occurs. Employees say they regularly experience pressure from top management that motivates them to lie to customers, breach regulations, or otherwise act unethically.[55] Situational factors do not justify unethical conduct. Rather, we need to recognize these factors so that organizations can reduce their influence in the future.

Supporting Ethical Behavior

Most large and medium-size organizations in the United States and several other countries have developed and communicate ethical codes of conduct. These statements establish the organization's ethical standards and signal to employees that the company takes ethical conduct seriously. However, written ethics codes alone won't prevent wrongdoing in the workplace.[56] To supplement ethics codes, many firms provide ethics training. Some firms, such as food manufacturer H. J. Heinz Co., also rely on an ethics hotline that employees can use to raise ethical issues or concerns about ethical conduct.[57]

These programs seem to have some influence on ethical conduct, but the most powerful foundation is a set of shared values—in other words, a strong organizational culture—that support ethical decisions and behavior. "If you don't have a culture of ethical decision making to begin with, all the controls and compliance regulations you care to deploy won't

Beyond the Ethics Code at Coors

Long before the scandals at Enron, Worldcom, and Tyco, Adolph Coors Co. put together a variety of ethical practices that today makes it one of the best in the United States. A cross-functional team rewrote the Golden, Colorado, brewer's ethics code so it would be clearer and user-friendly. Performance evaluations explicitly consider how well employees model this ethics code. An online training program guides employees through real-world scenarios where they see how the company's ethics principles apply to everyday work situations. The activity is set up as an expedition, where employees progress down a mountain to several "camps," where they must resolve ethics violations. The problems begin with clear violations of the company's ethics code, but later camps have much fuzzier dilemmas requiring more careful thought to underlying values. "The goal of the program is to step beyond rules and guidelines and teach employees how to think, clarify, and analyze situations," says Warren Malmquist, shown here with another Coors ethics leader, Caroline McMichen.[58]

necessarily prevent ethical misconduct," warns Devin Brougham, director of British communications giant Vodafone. Johnson & Johnson, which was described at the beginning of this chapter, has nurtured an ethical culture, supported by its famous credo of respecting key stakeholders. J&J has had ethical shortcomings, but it scores better than most companies due to its deeply entrenched value system. This culture is supported by the ethical conduct and vigilance of corporate leaders. By acting with the highest standards of moral conduct, leaders not only gain support and trust from followers; they serve as role models for the ethical standards that employees are more likely to follow.[59]

>Chapter Summary

Individual behavior is influenced by motivation, ability, role perceptions, and situational factors (MARS). Motivation consists of internal forces that affect the direction, intensity, and persistence of a person's voluntary choice of behavior. Ability includes both the natural aptitudes and learned capabilities required to successfully complete a task. Role perceptions are a person's beliefs about what behaviors are appropriate or necessary in a particular situation. Situational factors are environmental conditions that constrain or facilitate employee behavior and performance.

Personality refers to the relatively enduring pattern of thoughts, emotions, and behaviors that characterize a person, along with the psychological processes behind those characteristics. Most experts now agree that personality is shaped by both nature and nurture. Most personality traits are represented within the five-factor model, which includes conscientiousness, agreeableness, neuroticism, openness to experience, and extroversion. Conscientiousness and emotional stability (low neuroticism) stand out as the personality traits that best predict individual performance in almost every job group. The other three personality dimensions predict more specific types of employee behavior and performance.

Self-concept refers to an individual's self-beliefs and self-evaluations. It has three structural dimensions: complexity, consistency, and clarity. People are inherently motivated to promote and protect their self-concept (called self-enhancement). At the same time, people are motivated to verify and maintain their existing self-concept (called self-verification).

Self-evaluation, an important aspect of self-concept, consists of self-esteem, self-efficacy, and locus of control. Self-esteem is the extent to which people like, respect, and are satisfied with themselves. Self-efficacy refers to a person's belief that he or she has the ability, motivation, correct role perceptions, and favorable situation to complete a task successfully; general self-efficacy is a perception of one's competence to perform across a variety of situations. Locus of control is defined as a person's general belief about the amount of control he or she has over personal life events. Self-concept consists of both personality identity and social identity. Social identity theory explains how people define themselves in terms of the groups to which they belong or have an emotional attachment.

Values are stable, evaluative beliefs that guide our preferences for outcomes or courses of action in a variety of situations. People arrange values into a hierarchy of preferences, called a value system. Espoused values—what we say and think we use as values—are different from enacted values, which are values evident from our actions. Values have been organized into a circle with ten clusters. Values congruence refers to the similarity of value systems between two entities.

Five values that differ across cultures are individualism, collectivism, power distance, uncertainty avoidance, and achievement-nurturing orientation. Three values that guide ethical conduct are utilitarianism, individual rights, and distributive justice. Three factors that influence ethical conduct are the extent that an issue demands ethical principles (moral intensity), the person's ethical sensitivity to the presence and importance of an ethical dilemma, and situational factors that cause people to deviate from their moral values. Companies improve ethical conduct through a code of ethics, ethics training, ethics hot lines, and the conduct of corporate leaders.

>key terms

ability 27	five-factor model (FFM) 30	personality 29
achievement-nurturing orientation 39	individualism 37	power distance 38
collectivism 38	locus of control 33	self-concept 31
competencies 28	moral intensity 40	self-efficacy 33
conscientiousness 30	motivation 26	social identity theory 34
ethical sensitivity 40	neuroticism 31	uncertainty avoidance 38
extroversion 31		

>critical thinking questions

1. An insurance company has high levels of absenteeism among the office staff. The head of office administration argues that employees are misusing the company's sick leave benefits. However, some of the mostly female staff members have explained that family responsibilities interfere with work. Using the MARS model, as well as your knowledge of absenteeism behavior, discuss some of the possible reasons for absenteeism here and how it might be reduced.

2. As the district manager responsible for six stores in a large electronics retail chain, you have had difficulty with the performance of some sales staff. Although they are initially motivated and generally have good

interpersonal skills, many have difficulty with the complex knowledge of the diverse store products, ranging from computers to high-fidelity sound systems. Describe three strategies you might apply to improve the match between the competencies of new sales staff and the job requirements.

3. Research has found compelling evidence that heredity has a strong influence on an individual's personality. What are the implications of this in organizational settings?

4. Suppose that you give all candidates applying for a management trainee position a personality test that measures the five dimensions in the five-factor model. Which personality traits would you consider to be the most important for this type of job? Explain your answer.

5. An important aspect of self-concept is the idea that almost everyone engages in self-enhancement. What problems tend to occur in organizations as a result of this self-enhancement phenomenon? What can organizational leaders do to make use of a person's inherent drive for self-enhancement?

6. This chapter discussed the concept of values congruence in the context of an employee's personal values with the organization's values. But values congruence also relates to the juxtaposition of other pairs of value systems. Explain how values congruence is relevant with respect to organizational versus professional values.

7. People in a particular South American country have high power distance and high collectivism. What does this mean, and what are the implications of this information when you (a senior executive) visit employees working for your company in that country?

8. "All decisions are ethical decisions." Comment on this statement, particularly by referring to the concepts of moral intensity and ethical sensitivity.

>team exercise 2-1

Ethics Dilemma Vignettes

Purpose   This exercise is designed to make you aware of the ethical dilemmas people face in various business situations, as well as the competing principles and values that operate in these situations.

Instructions

The instructor will form teams of four or five students. Team members will read each case below and discuss the extent to which the company's action in each case was ethical. Teams should be prepared to justify their evaluation using ethics principles and perceived moral intensity of each incident.

Case One

An employee at a major food retailer wrote a Weblog (blog) and, in one of his writings, complained that his boss wouldn't let him go home when he felt sick and that his district manager refused to promote him because of his dreadlocks. His blog named the employer, but the employee didn't use his real name. Although all blogs are on the Internet, the employee claims that his was low profile and that it didn't show up when doing a Google search of his name or the company. Still, the employer somehow discovered the blog, figured out the employee's real name, and fired him for "speaking ill-will of the company in a public domain."

Case Two

Computer printer manufacturers usually sell printers at a low margin over cost and generate much more income from subsequent sales of the high-margin ink cartridges required for each printer. One global printer manufacturer now designs its printers so they only work with ink cartridges made in the same region. Ink cartridges purchased in the United States will not work for the same printer model sold in Europe, for example. This "region coding" of ink cartridges does not improve performance. Rather, this action prevents consumers and gray marketers from buying the product at a lower price in another region. The company says this action allows it to maintain stable prices within a region rather than continually changing prices due to currency fluctuations.

Case Three

For the past few years, the design department of a small (40-employee) company has been using a particular software program, but the three employees who use the software have been complaining for more than a year that the software is out of date and is slowing down their performance. The department agreed to switch to a competing software program, costing several thousand dollars. However, the next version won't be released for six months and buying the current version will not allow much discount toward the next version. The company has placed advanced orders for the next version. Meanwhile, one employee was able to get a copy of the current version of the software from a friend in the industry. The company has allowed the three employees to use this current version of the software even though they did not pay for it.

>**self-assessment** exercise 2-2

Identifying Your Dominant Values

Values have taken center stage in organizational behavior. Increasingly, OB experts are realizing that our personal values influence our motivation, decisions, and attitudes. This self-assessment is designed to help you to estimate your personal values and value system. The instrument consists of several words and phrases, and you are asked to indicate whether each word or phrase is highly opposed or highly similar to your personal values, or some point in between these two extremes. As with all self-assessments, you need to be honest with yourself when completing this activity in order to get the most accurate results.

>**self-assessment** exercise 2-3

Individualism-Collectivism Scale

Two of the most important concepts in cross-cultural organizational behavior are individualism and collectivism. This self-assessment measures your levels of individualism and collectivism with one of the most widely adopted measures. This scale consists of several statements, and you are asked to indicate how well each statement describes you. You need to be honest with yourself to receive a reasonable estimate of your level of individualism and collectivism.

>**self-assessment** exercise 2-4

Identifying Your Locus of Control

This self-assessment is designed to help you to estimate the extent to which you have an internal or external locus of control personality. The instrument asks you to indicate the degree to which you agree or disagree with each of the statements provided. As with all self-assessments, you need to be honest with yourself when completing this activity in order to get the most accurate results. The results show your relative position in the internal-external locus continuum and the general meaning of this score.

chapter 3

Perception and Learning in Organizations

Vodafone executive Grahame Maher keeps his perceptions in focus by discarding the executive suite and working close to employees every day.

>learningobjectives

After reading this chapter, you should be able to:

1. Outline the perceptual process.

2. Explain how social identity and stereotyping influence the perceptual process.

3. Describe the attribution process and two attribution errors.

4. Summarize the self-fulfilling prophecy process.

5. Explain how halo, primacy, recency, and false-consensus effects bias our perceptions.

6. Discuss three ways to improve social perception, with specific application to organizational situations.

7. Describe the A-B-C model of behavior modification and the four contingencies of reinforcement.

8. Describe the three features of social learning theory.

9. Diagram and discuss Kolb's experiential learning model.

10. Outline the elements of organizational learning and ways to improve each element.

Don't try looking for Grahame Maher in his office; he doesn't have one. Instead, the Vodafone executive (currently head of the British telecom's Czech Republic operations) uses temporary workspace near employees in various departments. Every few months, he packs up his cell phone, laptop, personal organizer, and a few files, and moves to another department to sharpen his perceptions about the organization. "I haven't had an office for years," says Maher. "[Working among employees] is where I learn most about the business."

Few executives follow Maher's lead by permanently working near frontline staff, but an increasing number improve their understanding of the business by occasionally working in or around frontline jobs. David Neeleman, the founder of New York-based discount airline JetBlue, works in the trenches each month with his baggage handlers and ticket takers. Indianapolis Power & Light (IPL) CEO Ann Murtlow regularly visits line crews in the field, sits in on lineman safety schools, and finds other opportunities to interact with employees throughout the organization. Every new hire at 1-800-GOT-JUNK?, North America's largest rubbish removal company, spends an entire week on a junk removal truck to better understand how the business works. "How can you possibly empathize with someone out in the field unless you've been on the truck yourself?" asks CEO and founder Brian Scudamore.[1]

//

Working in frontline jobs and keeping in close contact with staff and customers is a powerful way for executives and head-office employees to improve their perceptions. **Perception** is the process of receiving information about and making sense of the world around us. It entails deciding which information to notice, how to categorize this information, and how to interpret it within the framework of our existing knowledge. This chapter begins by describing the perceptual process; that is, the dynamics of selecting, organizing, and interpreting external stimuli. Next, we examine the perceptual processes of social identity and stereotyping, attribution, and self-fulfilling prophecy, including biases created within these processes. Four other perceptual biases—halo, primacy, recency, and false consensus—are also briefly introduced. We then identify three potentially effective ways to improve perceptions. The latter part of this chapter looks at three perspectives of learning: behavior modification, social learning theory, and experiential learning, followed by the key elements in organizational learning.

> **PERCEPTION:** the process of receiving information about and making sense of the world around us

>The Perceptual Process

Information from the world around us is filtered through an imperfect perceptual process. Most stimuli that bombard our senses are screened out; the rest are organized and interpreted. The process of attending to some information received by our senses and ignoring other information is called **selective attention.** Selective attention is influenced by characteristics of the person or object being perceived, particularly its size, intensity, motion, repetition, and novelty.[2] For example, a small flashing red light on a nurse station console is immediately noticed because it is bright (intensity), flashing (motion), a rare event (novelty), and has symbolic meaning that a patient's vital signs are failing.

Selective attention is also influenced by the perceiver's characteristics. Emotional markers (worry, happiness, anger) are tagged to incoming stimuli based on a rapid nonconscious evaluation of whether the information supports or undermines our needs and drives. Our expectations also shape the selective attention process. Our assumptions about an employee

> **SELECTIVE ATTENTION:** the process of attending to some information received by our senses and ignoring other information

Detectives Avoid Tunnel Vision with Art Appreciation
Good detective work involves more than forming a good theory about the crime. It also involves *not* forming a theory too early in the investigation. Keith Findley, codirector of the Wisconsin Innocence Project, warns that becoming preoccupied with a single theory causes police to "focus on a suspect, select and filter the evidence that will build a case for conviction, while ignoring or suppressing evidence that points away from guilt." To minimize this selective attention problem, officers in the New York Police Department are attending art classes, where they learn observation skills and develop multiple perspectives. "[The class] reminded me to stop and take in the whole scene and not just have tunnel vision," says NYPD captain David Grossi, who credits the class for helping him to discover evidence outside the area he otherwise would have investigated.[3]

or incident cause us to pay attention to information that supports these assumptions and ignore contrary information. Finally, we nonconsciously screen out information that opposes our self-concept and important beliefs, such as statements and events that undermine political parties that we support.[4]

Perceptual Organization and Interpretation

CATEGORICAL THINKING: organizing people and objects into preconceived categories that are stored in our long-term memory

People make sense of information even before they become aware of it. This sense making partly includes **categorical thinking**—the mostly nonconscious process of organizing people and objects into preconceived categories that are stored in our long-term memory.[5] Categorical thinking relies on a variety of automatic perceptual grouping principles, such as filling in missing pieces of a situation (called *closure*), conceptually grouping people or objects together based on their similarity or proximity to others, or seeing trends that are actually random events.[6]

Making sense also involves interpreting incoming information, and this happens just as quickly as the brain selects and organizes that information. We mentioned that emotional markers are tagged to incoming stimuli, which are essentially quick judgments about whether that information is good or bad for us. For instance, studies have found that people who observe very thin slices of video—as little as three two-second snippets—of an instructor's one-hour lecture give that lecturer similar ratings (optimistic, likeable, anxious, active, etc.) as students who attended the entire class in person.[7] This study, in addition to several others investigating "thin slices" of information, reveal that selective attention as well as perceptual organization and interpretation operate very quickly and to a large extent without our awareness.

Mental Models

MENTAL MODELS: visual or relational images in our mind representing the external world

To achieve our goals with some degree of predictability and sanity, we need road maps of the environments in which we live. These road maps, called **mental models,** are internal representations of the external world.[8] They consist of visual or relational images in our mind, such as what the classroom looks like or conceptually what happens when you submit an assignment late. We rely on mental models to make sense of our environment through perceptual grouping; they fill in the missing pieces, including the causal connection among events. However, mental models also generate expectations that, as we noted earlier, can cause us to overlook important information in the selective attention process.

>Social Identity and Stereotyping

In the previous chapter, we learned that social identity is an important component of a person's self-concept. We define ourselves to a large extent by the groups or collectives to which we belong or identify with. As well as shaping our self-concept, social identity theory explains the dynamics of *social perception*—how we perceive others.[9] This social perception is influenced by three activities in the process of forming and maintaining our social identity: categorization, homogenization, and differentiation.

- *Categorization*. Social identity is a comparative process, and that comparison begins by categorizing people into distinct groups. By viewing someone (including yourself) as a Texan, for example, you remove that person's individuality and, instead, see him or her as a prototypical representative of the group called Texans. This categorization then allows you to distinguish Texans from people who live in, say, California and elsewhere.

- *Homogenization*. To simplify the comparison process, we tend to think that people within each group are very similar to each other. For instance, we think Texans collectively have similar attitudes and characteristics, whereas Californians collectively have their own set of characteristics. Of course, every individual is unique, but we tend to lose sight of this fact when thinking about our social identity and how we compare to people in other social groups.

- *Differentiation*. Social identity fulfills our inherent need to have a distinct and positive self-concept. To achieve this, we do more than categorize people and homogenize them; we also differentiate groups by assigning more favorable characteristics to people in our groups than to people in other groups. This differentiation is often subtle, but it can escalate into a "good guy-bad guy" contrast when groups are in conflict with each other.[10]

Stereotyping in Organizations

Stereotyping is an extension of social identity theory and a product of our natural process of organizing information.[11] Stereotyping has three elements. First, we develop social categories and assign traits that are difficult to observe. For instance, students might form a stereotype that professors are both intelligent and absentminded. Personal experiences shape stereotypes to some extent, but they are mainly provided to us through cultural upbringing and media images (e.g., movie characters). Second, we assign people to one or more social categories based on easily observable information about them, such as their gender, appearance, or physical location. Third, people who seem to belong to the stereotyped group are assigned nonobservable traits associated with the group, such as the example of the intelligent and absentminded professor mentioned above.

> **STEREOTYPING:** the process of assigning traits to people based on their membership in a social category

Stereotyping occurs for three reasons.[12] First, as a form of categorical thinking, it is a natural and mostly nonconscious energy saving process to simplify our understanding of the world. It is easier to remember features of a stereotype than the constellation of characteristics unique to everyone we meet. Second, we have an innate need to understand and anticipate how others will behave. We don't have much information when first meeting someone, so we rely heavily on stereotypes to fill in the missing pieces. People with a stronger need for this cognitive closure have a higher tendency to rely on stereotypes to fill in missing information. Third, we are particularly motivated to rely on negative stereotypes when others threaten our self-concept.[13]

Problems with Stereotyping

Stereotypes are not completely fictional, but neither do they accurately describe every person in that social category. For instance, the widespread "bean counter" stereotype of accountants views people in this profession as "single-mindedly preoccupied with precision and form, methodical and conservative, and a boring joyless character."[14] Although this may be true of some accountants, it is certainly not characteristic of all—or even most—people in this profession.

Another problem with stereotyping is that it lays the foundation for discriminatory behavior. This mostly occurs as *unintentional (systemic) discrimination,* whereby decision makers rely on stereotypes to establish notions of the "ideal" person in specific roles. A person who doesn't fit the ideal tends to receive a less favorable evaluation. In contrast, *intentional discrimination* occurs when people hold unfounded negative emotions and attitudes toward people belonging to a particular stereotyped group. Unintentional discrimination is subtle and often shows up in age discrimination claims, such as the recent case in which Ryanair's recruitment advertising said it was looking for "young dynamic" employees. Recruiters at the Irish discount airline probably didn't intentionally discriminate against older people, but the tribunal concluded that systemic discrimination did occur because none of the job applicants was over 40 years old.[15]

If stereotyping is such a problem, shouldn't we try to avoid this process altogether? Unfortunately, it's not that simple. Most experts agree that categorical thinking (including stereotyping) is an automatic and nonconscious process. Intensive training can minimize stereotype activation to some extent, but for the most part the process is hardwired in our brain cells.[16] Also remember that stereotyping helps us in several valuable (although fallible) ways described earlier: minimizing mental effort, filling in missing information, and supporting our social identity. The good news is that while it is very difficult to prevent the *activation* of stereotypes, we can minimize the *application* of stereotypic information.

>**learning**objectives

After reading the next three sections, you should be able to:

3. Describe the attribution process and two attribution errors.

4. Summarize the self-fulfilling prophecy process.

5. Explain how halo, primacy, recency, and false-consensus effects bias our perceptions.

>Attribution Theory

ATTRIBUTION PROCESS: the perceptual process of deciding whether an observed behavior or event is caused largely by internal or external factors

The **attribution process** involves deciding whether an observed behavior or event is caused mainly by the person (internal factors) or the environment (external factors).[17] Internal factors include the person's ability or motivation, whereas external factors include lack of resources, other people, or just luck. If a co-worker doesn't show up for an important meeting, for instance, we infer either internal attributions (the co-worker is forgetful, lacks motivation, etc.) or external attributions (traffic, a family emergency, or other circumstances prevented the co-worker from attending).

People rely on the three attribution rules shown in Exhibit 3.1 to determine whether someone's behavior mainly has an internal or external attribution. Internal attributions are made when the observed individual behaved this way in the past (high consistency), behaves like this toward other people or in different situations (low distinctiveness), and other people do not behave this way in similar situations (low consensus). On the other hand, an external attribution is made when there is low consistency, high distinctiveness, and high consensus.

To illustrate how these three attribution rules operate, suppose that an employee is making poor-quality products one day on a particular machine. We would probably conclude that

[Exhibit 3.1] Rules of Attribution

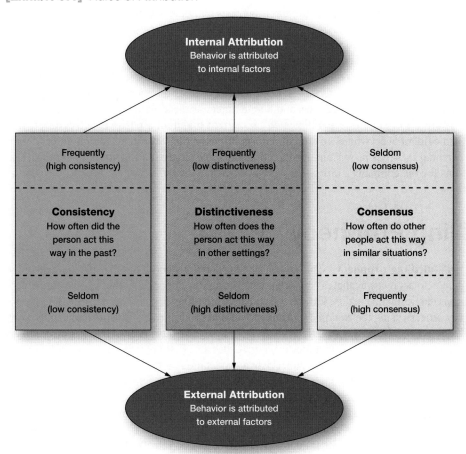

there is something wrong with the machine (an external attribution) if the employee has made good-quality products on this machine in the past (low consistency), the employee makes good-quality products on other machines (high distinctiveness), and other employees have recently had quality problems on this machine (high consensus). We would make an internal attribution, on the other hand, if the employee usually makes poor-quality products on this machine (high consistency), other employees produce good-quality products on this machine (low consensus), and the employee also makes poor-quality products on other machines (low distinctiveness).[18]

Attribution is an essential perceptual process because it forms cause-effect relationships that, in turn, affect how we respond to others' behavior and how we act in the future. How we react to a co-worker's or our own poor performance depends on our internal or external attribution of that performance. Students who make internal attributions about their poor performance are more likely to drop out of their programs, for example.[19]

Attribution Errors

People are far from perfect when making attributions. One bias, called **fundamental attribution error,** refers to our tendency to see the person rather than the situation as the main cause of that person's behavior.[20] If an employee is late for work, observers are more likely to conclude that the person is lazy than to realize that external factors may have caused this behavior. Fundamental attribution error occurs because observers can't easily see the external

FUNDAMENTAL ATTRIBUTION ERROR: the tendency to see the person rather than the situation as the main cause of that person's behavior

factors that constrain the person's behavior. We didn't see the traffic jam that caused the person to be late, for instance. Research suggests that fundamental attribution error is more common in Western cultures than in Asian cultures, where people are taught from an early age to pay attention to the context in interpersonal relations and to see everything connected in a holistic way.[21]

SELF-SERVING BIAS:
the tendency to attribute our favorable outcomes to internal factors and our failures to external factors

Another attribution error, known as **self-serving bias,** is the tendency to attribute our favorable outcomes to internal factors and our failures to external factors. Simply put, we take credit for our successes and blame others or the situation for our mistakes. Self-serving bias is one of several related biases that maintain a positive self-concept. It is also evident everywhere. In annual reports, for example, executives mainly refer to their personal qualities as reasons for the company's successes and to external factors as reasons for the company's failures.[22]

>Self-Fulfilling Prophecy

SELF-FULFILLING PROPHECY:
occurs when our expectations about another person cause that person to act in a way that is consistent with those expectations

Self-fulfilling prophecy occurs when our expectations about another person cause that person to act in a way that is consistent with those expectations. In other words, our perceptions can influence reality. Exhibit 3.2 illustrates the four steps in the self-fulfilling prophecy process using the example of a supervisor and subordinate.[23] The process begins when the supervisor forms expectations about the employee's future behavior and performance. These expectations are sometimes inaccurate, because first impressions are usually formed from limited information. The supervisor's expectations influence his or her treatment of employees. Specifically, high-expectancy employees (those expected to do well) receive more emotional support through nonverbal cues (e.g., more smiling and eye contact), more frequent and valuable feedback and reinforcement, more challenging goals, better training, and more opportunities to demonstrate good performance.

The third step in self-fulfilling prophecy includes two effects of the supervisor's behaviors on the employee. First, through better training and more practice opportunities, a high-expectancy employee learns more skills and knowledge than a low-expectancy employee. Second, the supervisor's displays of confidence increase the employee's self-efficacy,

[Exhibit 3.2] The Self-Fulfilling Prophecy Cycle

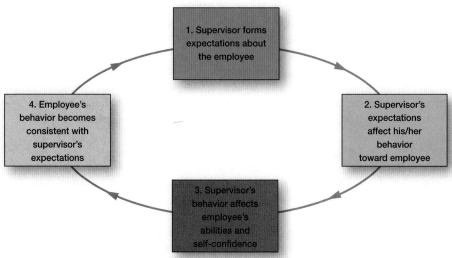

Positive Self-Fulfilling Prophecies Strengthen Cocoplans
After only a dozen years in business, Cocoplans is recognized throughout the Philippines as a top-performing preneeds (superannuation and education) company with excellent customer service. This success is partly due to the way Cocoplans executives perceive their sales staff. "At Cocoplans, we treat sales people as our internal customers, while plan holders are our external customers," explains Cocoplans president Caesar T. Michelena. Michelena believes that by treating employees as customers, Cocoplans managers have positive expectations of those employees, which then results in higher performance results. "It's a self-fulfilling prophecy. If you believe that [employees] will not last, your behavior towards them will show it. . . . You get what you expect."[24]

which results in higher motivation and willingness to set more challenging goals.[25] In the final step, high expectancy employees have higher motivation and better skills, resulting in better performance, while the opposite is true of low-expectancy employees.

There are plenty of examples of self-fulfilling prophecies in work and school settings.[26] Research has found that women score lower on math tests when people around them convey a negative stereotype of women regarding their perceived ability to do math. Women perform better on these tests when they are not exposed to this negative self-fulfilling prophecy. Israeli Defense Force trainees performed better when their instructors received (fictitious) information that they had high potential to succeed in the boot camp program.

Contingencies of Self-fulfilling Prophecy

The self-fulfilling prophecy effect is stronger at the beginning of the relationship, such as when employees are first hired. It is also stronger when several people (rather than just one person) hold the same expectations of the individual. In other words, we might be able to ignore one person's doubts about our potential, but not the collective doubts of several people. The self-fulfilling prophecy effect is also stronger among people with a history of low achievement. High achievers can draw upon their past successes to off-set low expectations, whereas low achievers do not have these past successes to support their self-confidence. Fortunately, the opposite is also true: low achievers respond more favorably than high achievers to positive self-fulfilling prophecy. Low achievers don't receive this positive encouragement very often, so it probably has a strong effect on their motivation to excel.[27]

The main lesson from the self-fulfilling prophecy literature is that leaders need to develop and maintain a positive, yet realistic, expectation toward all employees. This recommendation is consistent with the emerging philosophy of *positive organizational behavior,* which suggests that focusing on the positive rather than negative aspects of life will improve organizational success and individual well-being.

>Other Perceptual Errors

HALO EFFECT: a perceptual error whereby our general impression of a person, usually based on one prominent characteristic, colors our perception of other characteristics of that person

PRIMACY EFFECT: a perceptual error in which we quickly form an opinion of people based on the first information we receive about them

RECENCY EFFECT: a perceptual error in which the most recent information dominates our perception of others

FALSE-CONSENSUS EFFECT: a perceptual error in which we overestimate the extent to which others have beliefs and characteristics similar to our own

Self-fulfilling prophecy, attribution, and stereotyping are among the most common perceptual processes and biases in organizational settings, but there are many others. Four others are briefly described below because they can also bias our perception of the world around us.

Halo effect. Our general impression of a person, usually based on one prominent characteristic, colors our perception of other characteristics of that person.[28] If a supervisor who values punctuality notices that an employee is sometimes late for work, the supervisor might form a negative image of the employee and evaluate that person's other traits and behaviors unfavorably as well. Halo effect is most likely to occur when concrete information about the perceived target is missing or we are not sufficiently motivated to search for it. Instead, we use our general impression of the person to fill in the missing information.

Primacy effect. This is our tendency to quickly form an opinion of people based on the first information we receive about them.[29] This rapid perceptual organization and interpretation occurs because we need to make sense of the world around us. The problem is that first impressions—particularly negative first impressions—are difficult to change. After categorizing someone, we tend to select subsequent information that supports our first impression and screen out information that opposes that impression.

Recency effect. This perceptual bias occurs when the most recent information dominates our perceptions.[30] This effect is most common when making an evaluation involving complex information, particularly among people with limited experience. For instance, auditors must digest large volumes of information in their judgments about financial documents, and the most recent information received prior to the decision tends to get weighted more heavily than information received at the beginning of the audit.

False-consensus effect. Sometimes called the "similar to me" effect, false-consensus effect is a widely observed bias in which we overestimate the extent to which others have beliefs and characteristics similar to our own.[31] Employees who are thinking of quitting their job believe that a large percentage of their co-workers are also thinking about quitting. This bias occurs to some extent because we associate with others who are similar and selectively remember information that is consistent with our own views. We also believe that "everyone does it" to reinforce our self-concept regarding behaviors that do not have a positive image (such as parking illegally).

After reading the next section, you should be able to:

6. *Discuss three ways to improve social perception, with specific application to organizational situations.*

learningobjectives<

>Improving Perceptions

We can't bypass the perceptual process, but we should make every attempt to minimize perceptual biases and distortions. Three potentially effective ways to improve perceptions include awareness of perceptual bias, self-awareness, and meaningful interaction.

Awareness of Perceptual Biases

One of the most obvious and widely practiced ways to reduce perceptual biases is by becoming aware of them. The idea here is that consciously trying to minimize stereotyping, self-serving bias, self-fulfilling prophecy, and other errors can effectively neutralize their effects on the perceptual process. For instance, people who complete the Implicit Association Test (IAT), which detects subtle race, age, and gender bias, are more likely to consciously offset their stereotypic bias.[32] One employee in Alabama who completed the IAT discovered her bias in favor of white people, a group to which she belongs. "My charge is to be color-conscious, not color-blind, and to always explicitly consider how race may affect behaviors and decisions," she said after seeing the results.[33] However, there are limits to how well awareness training reduces perceptual biases. For example, leaders continued to engage in self-fulfilling prophecy effect after receiving training warning them of this effect and encouraging them to practice positive expectations.[34]

Improving Self-Awareness

Knowing yourself—becoming more aware of your values, beliefs, and prejudices—is a powerful way to improve your perceptions.[35] The **Johari Window** is a popular model for understanding how co-workers can increase their mutual understanding.[36] Developed by Joseph Luft and Harry Ingram (hence the name Johari), this model divides information about you into four "windows"—open, blind, hidden, and unknown—based on whether your own values, beliefs, and experiences are known to you and to others (see Exhibit 3.3). The *open area* includes information about you that is known both to you and to others. The *blind area* refers to information that is known to others but not to you. For example, your colleagues might notice that you are self-conscious and awkward when meeting the company chief executive, but you are unaware of this fact. Information known to you but unknown to others is found in the *hidden area*. Finally, the *unknown area* includes your values, beliefs, and experiences that aren't known to you or others.

> **JOHARI WINDOW:** a model of mutual understanding that encourages disclosure and feedback to increase our own open area and reduce the blind, hidden, and unknown areas

The main objective of the Johari Window is to increase the size of the open area so that both you and colleagues are aware of your perceptual limitations. This is partly accomplished by reducing the hidden area through *disclosure*—informing others of your beliefs, feelings, and experiences that may influence the work relationship.[37] The open area also increases through *feedback* from others about your behaviors. This information helps you to reduce your blind area, because co-workers often see things in you that you do not see. Finally, the combination of disclosure and feedback occasionally produces revelations about information in the unknown area.

[Exhibit 3.3] The Johari Window Model of Self-Awareness and
Mutual Understanding

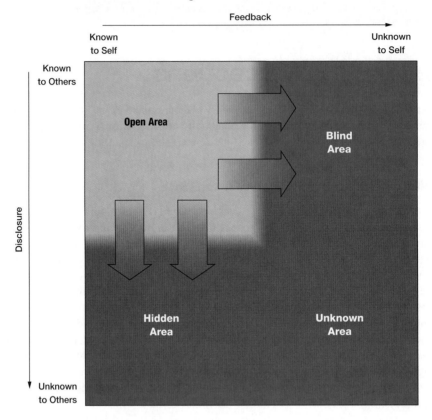

Source: Based on J. Luft, *Group Processes* (Palo Alto, CA: Mayfield, 1984).

Meaningful Interaction

While the Johari Window relies on dialogue, self-awareness and mutual understanding can also improve through *meaningful interaction*.[38] This statement sounds simple enough, but in reality it works only under specific conditions. Participants must have close and frequent interaction working toward a shared goal where they need to rely on each other (i.e., cooperate rather than compete with each other). Everyone should have equal status in that context and should be engaged in a meaningful task. An hour-long social gathering between executives and frontline employees does not satisfy these conditions. On the other hand, having executives work in frontline jobs, which we described at the beginning of this chapter, does seem to represent meaningful interaction. By working in frontline jobs, these executives minimize status differences with other staff, cooperate toward a common goal, and have close and frequent interaction with frontline employees.

Along with reducing reliance on stereotypes, meaningful interaction potentially improves a person's empathy towards others. **Empathy** refers to a person's understanding of and sensitivity to the feelings, thoughts, and situation of others.[39] You have empathy when actively visualizing the other person's situation and feeling that person's emotions in that situation. Empathizing with others improves our sensitivity to external causes of another person's performance and behavior, thereby reducing fundamental attribution error. A supervisor who imagines what it's like to be a single mother, for example, would become more sensitive to the external causes of lateness and other events among these employees.

EMPATHY:
a person's understanding of and sensitivity to the feelings, thoughts, and situation of others

The perceptual process represents the filter through which information passes from the external environment to our brain. As such, it is really the beginning of the learning process, which we discuss next.

After reading the next two sections, you should be able to: **learning**objectives<

7. *Describe the A-B-C model of behavior modification and the four contingencies of reinforcement.*

8. *Describe the three features of social learning theory.*

9. *Diagram and discuss Kolb's experiential learning model.*

10. *Outline the elements of organizational learning and ways to improve each element.*

>Learning in Organizations

Learning is a relatively permanent change in behavior (or behavior tendency) that occurs as a result of a person's interaction with the environment. Learning occurs when the learner behaves differently. For example, we can see that you have "learned" computer skills when you operate the keyboard and windows more quickly than before. Learning occurs when interaction with the environment leads to behavior change. This means that we learn through our senses, such as through study, observation, and experience.

> **LEARNING:** a relatively permanent change in behavior (or behavior tendency) that occurs as a result of a person's interaction with the environment

Some of what we learn is *explicit knowledge,* such as reading information in this book. However, explicit knowledge is really only the tip of the knowledge iceberg. Most of what we know is **tacit knowledge.**[40] Tacit knowledge is not documented; rather, it is acquired through observation and direct experience. For example, airline pilots learn to operate commercial jets more by watching experts and practicing on flight simulators than through lectures. They acquire tacit knowledge by directly experiencing the complex interaction of behavior with the machine's response.

> **TACIT KNOWLEDGE:** knowledge embedded in our actions and ways of thinking, and transmitted only through observation and experience

Three perspectives of learning tacit and explicit knowledge are reinforcement, social learning, and direct experience. Each perspective offers a different angle for understanding the dynamics of learning.

Behavior Modification: Learning Through Reinforcement

One of the oldest perspectives on learning, called **behavior modification** (also known as *operant conditioning* and *reinforcement theory*), takes the rather extreme view that learning is completely dependent on the environment. Behavior modification does not question the notion that thinking is part of the learning process, but it views human thoughts as unimportant intermediate stages between behavior and the environment. The environment teaches us to alter our behaviors so that we maximize positive consequences and minimize adverse consequences.[41]

> **BEHAVIOR MODIFICATION:** a theory that explains learning in terms of the antecedents and consequences of behavior

A-B-Cs of Behavior Modification

The central objective of behavior modification is to change behavior (B) by managing its antecedents (A) and consequences (C). This process is nicely illustrated in the A-B-C model of behavior modification, shown in Exhibit 3.4.[42]

Antecedents are events preceding the behavior, informing employees that certain behaviors will have particular consequences. An antecedent may be a sound from your

[Exhibit 3.4] A-B-Cs of Behavior Modification

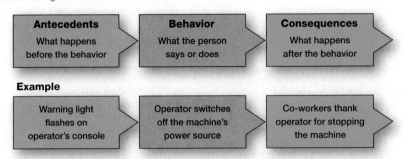

Sources: Adapted from T. K. Connellan, *How to Improve Human Performance* (New York: Harper & Row, 1978), p. 50; F. Luthans and R. Kreitner, *Organizational Behavior Modification and Beyond* (Glenview, IL: Scott, Foresman, 1985), pp. 85–88.

computer signaling that an e-mail has arrived or a request from your supervisor to complete a specific task by tomorrow. These antecedents let employees know that a particular action will produce specific consequences. Notice that antecedents do not cause behaviors. The computer sound doesn't cause us to open our e-mail. Rather, the sound is a cue telling us that certain consequences are likely to occur if we engage in certain behaviors. In behavior modification, *consequences* are events following a particular behavior that influence its future occurrence. Generally speaking, people tend to repeat behaviors that are followed by pleasant consequences and are less likely to repeat behaviors that are followed by unpleasant consequences or no consequences at all.

Contingencies of Reinforcement

Behavior modification identifies four types of consequences, called the *contingencies of reinforcement,* that increase, maintain, or reduce the probability that behavior will be repeated.[43] *Positive reinforcement* occurs when the introduction of a consequence increases or maintains the frequency or future probability of a specific behavior. *Punishment* occurs when a consequence—such as a low exam grade or being ostracized by our co-workers—decreases the frequency or future probability of a behavior.[44]

Negative reinforcement increases or maintains the incidence of behavior by removing or avoiding a consequence. Supervisors apply negative reinforcement when they *stop* criticizing employees whose substandard performance has improved. When the criticism is withheld, employees are more likely to do things that stopped the boss's complaining. Notice that negative reinforcement is not punishment. It actually reinforces behavior by removing punishment. Finally, *extinction* occurs when the target behavior decreases because no consequence follows it. In this respect, extinction is a do-nothing strategy. Generally, behavior that is no longer reinforced tends to disappear; it becomes extinct. Which contingency of reinforcement should we use in the learning process? In most situations, positive reinforcement should follow desired behaviors and extinction (do nothing) should follow undesirable behaviors. This approach is preferred because punishment and negative reinforcement generate negative emotions and attitudes toward the punisher (e.g., supervisor) and organization. However, some form of punishment (dismissal, suspension, demotion, etc.) may be necessary for extreme behaviors, such as deliberately hurting a co-worker or stealing inventory. Indeed, research suggests that, under certain conditions, punishment maintains a sense of equity.[45]

Schedules of Reinforcement

Along with the types of reinforcement, the frequency and timing of those reinforcers also influence employee behaviors.[46] These reinforcement schedules can be continuous or intermittent. The most effective reinforcement schedule for learning new tasks is

Reinforcing the Long (and Healthy) Walk
For many of Horton Group's 350 employees, the best parking spots aren't closest to the building; they are deep in the outfield. The Chicago-based insurance broker reinforces the healthy lifestyle of walking by rewarding staff who take at least 7,000 steps each day—more than twice the normal daily average. The farther they walk, the more points they receive, which can be redeemed for free goods at Amazon.com and other retailers. Participating employees are given a pedometer to measure steps, and have a private Web site that keeps track of their progress.[47]

continuous reinforcement—providing positive reinforcement after every occurrence of the desired behavior. Employees learn desired behaviors quickly and, when the reinforcer is removed, extinction also occurs very quickly.

The best schedule for reinforcing learned behavior is a *variable ratio schedule* in which employee behavior is reinforced after a variable number of times. Salespeople experience variable ratio reinforcement because they make a successful sale (the reinforcer) after a varying number of client calls. They might make four unsuccessful calls before receiving an order on the fifth one, then make 10 more calls before receiving the next order, and so on. The variable ratio schedule makes behavior highly resistant to extinction because it is never expected at a particular time or after a fixed number of accomplishments.

Evaluating Behavior Modification

Everyone practices behavior modification in one form or another. We thank people for a job well done, are silent when displeased, and sometimes try to punish those who go against our wishes. Behavior modification also occurs in various formal programs to reduce absenteeism, improve task performance, encourage safe work behaviors, and promote a healthier lifestyle.[48] One limitation of behavior modification is "reward inflation," in which the reinforcer is eventually considered an entitlement. For this reason, most behavior modification programs must run infrequently and for short durations. A more significant problem, however, is behavior modification's radical view that behavior is learned only through personal interaction with the environment.[49] This view is no longer accepted; instead, learning experts recognize that people also learn by observing others. This learning through observation process is explained by social learning theory.

Social Learning Theory: Learning by Observing

Social learning theory states that much learning occurs by observing others and then modeling the behaviors that lead to favorable outcomes and avoiding behaviors that lead to punishing consequences.[50] This form of learning occurs in three ways: behavior modeling, learning behavior consequences, and self-reinforcement.

- *Behavior modeling.* People learn by observing the behaviors of a role model on the critical task, remembering the important elements of the observed behaviors, and then practicing those behaviors.[51] This is a valuable form of learning because tacit knowledge and skills are mainly acquired from others through observation. As an

SOCIAL LEARNING THEORY: a theory stating that much learning occurs by observing others and then modeling the behaviors that lead to favorable outcomes and avoiding behaviors that lead to punishing consequences

example, it is difficult to document or verbally explain everything about how to bake bread professionally. Student chefs also need to observe the master baker's subtle behaviors.

- *Learning behavior consequences.* People learn the consequences of behavior through logic and observation, not just through direct experience. They logically anticipate consequences after completing a task well or poorly. They also learn behavioral consequences by observing the experiences of other people. You might notice how co-workers mock another employee who dresses formally at work, thereby teaching you to maintain casual attire.[52]

- *Self-reinforcement.* **Self-reinforcement** occurs whenever an employee has control over a reinforcer but doesn't "take" it until completing a self-set goal.[53] For example, you might be thinking about having a snack after you finish reading the rest of this chapter. Raiding the refrigerator is a form of self-induced positive reinforcement for completing this reading assignment. Self-reinforcement takes many forms, such as taking a short walk, watching a movie, or simply congratulating yourself for completing the task.

SELF-REINFORCEMENT: occurs whenever an employee has control over a reinforcer but doesn't "take" it until completing a self-set goal

Learning Through Experience

Along with behavior modification and social learning, employees learn through direct experience. In fact, most tacit knowledge and skills are acquired through experience as well as observation. One of the most enduring models of experiential learning, shown in Exhibit 3.5, views learning as a cyclical four-stage process.[54] *Concrete experience* involves sensory and emotional engagement in some activity. It is followed by *reflective observation,* which involves listening, watching, recording, and elaborating on the experience. The next stage in the learning cycle is *abstract conceptualization.* This is the stage in which we develop concepts and integrate our observations into logically sound theories. The fourth stage, *active experimentation,* occurs when we test our previous experience, reflection, and conceptualization in a particular context. People tend to prefer and operate better in some stages than in others due to their unique competencies and personality. Still, experiential learning requires all four stages in proper balance.

LEARNING ORIENTATION: the extent to which an organization or individual supports knowledge management, particularly opportunities to acquire knowledge through experience and experimentation

One of the most important ingredients for learning through experience is that the organization should possess a strong **learning orientation.**[55] This means that the organization values learning opportunities and, in particular, the generation of new knowledge while employees perform their jobs. If an employee initially fails to perform a task, then the

[**Exhibit 3.5**] Kolb's Experiential Learning Model

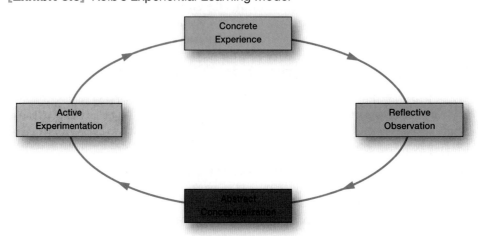

experience might still be a valuable learning opportunity. In other words, organizations achieve a learning orientation culture by rewarding experimentation and recognizing mistakes as a natural part of the learning process. They encourage employees to take reasonable risks to ultimately discover new and better ways of doing things.

>From Individual to Organizational Learning

One of the most popular contemporary perspectives of organizational effectiveness is *organizational learning,* which was defined in Chapter 1 as any structured activity that improves an organization's capacity to acquire, share, and use knowledge in ways that improve its survival and success. Organizational learning is heavily dependent on individual learning, but the capacity to acquire, share, and use knowledge means that companies must establish systems, structures, and organizational values that support the knowledge management process.[56]

- *Knowledge acquisition.* This includes extracting information and ideas from the external environment as well as through insight. One of the fastest and most powerful ways to acquire knowledge is by hiring individuals or acquiring entire companies. Knowledge also enters the organization when employees learn from external sources, such as discovering new resources from suppliers or becoming aware of new trends from clients. A third knowledge acquisition strategy is through experimentation. Companies receive knowledge through insight as a result of research and other creative processes.

- *Knowledge sharing.* This aspect of organizational learning involves distributing knowledge to others across the organization. Although typically associated with computer intranets and digital repositories of knowledge, knowledge sharing also occurs through informal online or face-to-face communication.[57] Most social learning (such as behavioral modeling) and experiential learning are forms of knowledge sharing because the learning is transferred from one employee to another.

- *Knowledge use.* The competitive advantage of knowledge comes from applying it in ways that add value to the organization and its stakeholders. To do this, employees must realize that the knowledge is available and that they have enough freedom to apply it. This requires a culture that supports the learning process.

This chapter has introduced two fundamental activities in human behavior in the workplace: perceptions and learning. These activities involve receiving information from the environment, organizing it, and acting on it as a learning process. Our knowledge about perceptions and learning in the workplace lays the foundation for the next chapter, which looks at workplace emotions and attitudes.

>Chapter Summary

Perception involves selecting, organizing, and interpreting information to make sense of the world around us. Perceptual organization engages categorical thinking—the mostly subconscious process of organizing people and objects into preconceived categories that are stored in our long-term memory. Mental models—internal representations of the external world—also help us to make sense of incoming stimuli.

Social identity theory explains how we perceive people through categorization, homogenization, and differentiation. Stereotyping is a derivative of social identity theory, in which people assign traits to others based on their membership in a social category. Stereotyping economizes mental effort, fills in missing information, and enhances our self-perception and social identity. However, it also lays the foundation for prejudice and systemic discrimination.

The attribution process involves deciding whether an observed behavior or event is caused mainly by the person (internal factors) or the environment (external factors). Attributions are decided by perceptions of the consistency, distinctiveness, and consensus of the behavior. This process helps us to link together the various pieces of our world in cause-effect relationships, but it is also subject to attribution errors, including fundamental attribution error and self-serving bias.

Self-fulfilling prophecy occurs when our expectations about another person cause that person to act in a way that is consistent with those expectations. Essentially, our expectations affect our behavior toward the target person, which then affects the employee's opportunities and attitudes, which then influences his or her behavior. Self-fulfilling prophecies tend to be stronger at the beginning of the relations (such as when employees first join the department), when several people hold the expectations toward the employee, and when the employee has a history of low achievement.

Four other perceptual errors commonly noted in organizations are halo effect, primacy effect, recency effect, and false-consensus effect. We can minimize these and other perceptual problems through awareness of perceptual bias, self-awareness, and meaningful interaction.

Learning is a relatively permanent change in behavior (or behavior tendency) that occurs as a result of a person's interaction with the environment. Much of what we learn is tacit knowledge, which is embedded in our actions without conscious awareness.

The behavior modification perspective of learning states that behavior change occurs by altering its antecedents and consequences. Antecedents are environmental stimuli that provoke (not necessarily cause) behavior. Consequences are events following behavior that influence its future occurrence. Consequences include positive reinforcement, punishment, negative reinforcement, and extinction. The schedules of reinforcement also influence behavior.

Social learning theory states that much learning occurs by observing others and then modeling those behaviors that seem to lead to favorable outcomes and avoiding behaviors that lead to punishing consequences. It also recognizes that we often engage in self-reinforcement. Behavior modeling is effective because it transfers tacit knowledge and enhances the observer's confidence in performing the task.

Many companies now use experiential learning because employees do not acquire tacit knowledge through formal classroom instruction. Kolb's experiential learning model is a cyclical four-stage process that includes concrete experience, reflective observation, abstract conceptualization, and active experimentation.

Organizational learning is any structured activity that improves an organization's capacity to acquire, share, and use knowledge in ways that improve its survival and success. Organizations acquire knowledge through individual learning and experimentation. Knowledge sharing occurs mainly through various forms of communication and training. Knowledge use occurs when employees realize that the knowledge is available and that they have enough freedom to apply it.

>key terms

attribution process 50	false-consensus effect 54	learning 57
behavior modification 57	fundamental attribution error 51	learning orientation 60
categorical thinking 48	halo effect 54	mental models 48
empathy 56	Johari Window 55	perception 47

>critical thinking questions

1. Several years ago, senior executives at energy company CanOil wanted to acquire an exploration company (HBOG) that was owned by another energy company, AmOil. Rather than face a hostile takeover and unfavorable tax implications, CanOil's two top executives met with the CEO of AmOil to discuss a friendly exchange of stock to carry out the transaction. AmOil's chief executive was previously unaware of CanOil's plans and, as the meeting began, the AmOil executive warned that he was there merely to listen. The CanOil executives were confident that AmOil wanted to sell HBOG because energy legislation at the time made HBOG a poor investment for AmOil. AmOil's CEO remained silent for most of the meeting, which CanOil executives interpreted as an implied agreement to proceed to buy AmOil stock on the market. But when CanOil launched the stock purchase a month later, AmOil's CEO was both surprised and outraged. He thought he had given the CanOil executives the cold shoulder, remaining silent to show his disinterest in the deal. The misunderstanding nearly bankrupted CanOil because AmOil reacted by protecting its stock. What perceptual problem(s) likely occurred that led to this misunderstanding?

2. What mental models do you have about attending a college or university lecture? Are these mental models helpful? Could any of these mental models hold you back from achieving the full benefit of the lecture?

3. Do you define yourself in terms of the university or college you attend? Why or why not? What are the implications of your answer for your university or college?

4. During a diversity management session, a manager suggests that stereotypes are a necessary part of working with others. "I have to make assumptions about what's in the other person's head, and stereotypes help me do that," she explains. "It's better to rely on stereotypes than to enter a working relationship with someone from another culture without any idea of what they believe in!" Discuss the merits of and problems with the manager's statement.

5. Describe how a manager or coach could use the process of self-fulfilling prophecy to enhance an individual's performance.

6. Describe a situation in which you used behavior modification to influence someone's behavior. What specifically did you do? What was the result?

7. Why are organizations moving toward the use of experiential approaches to learning? What conditions are required for success?

8. BusNews Corp. is the leading stock market and business news service. Over the past two years, BusNews has experienced increased competition from other news providers. These competitors have brought in the Internet and other emerging computer technologies to link customers with information more quickly. There is little knowledge within BusNews about how to use these computer technologies. Based on the knowledge acquisition processes for knowledge management, explain how BusNews might gain the intellectual capital necessary to become more competitive in this respect.

>class exercise 3-1

The Learning Exercise

Purpose   This exercise is designed to help you understand how the contingencies of reinforcement in behavior modification affect learning.

Materials   Any objects normally available in a classroom will be acceptable for this activity.

Instructions
The instructor will ask for three volunteers, who are then briefed outside the classroom. The instructor will spend a few minutes briefing the remaining students in the class about their duties. Then, one of the three volunteers will enter the room to participate in the exercise. When completed, the second volunteer will enter the room and participates in the exercise. When completed, the third volunteer will enter the class and participates in the exercise.

For students to gain the full benefit of this exercise, no other information will be provided here. However, your instructor will have more details at the beginning of this fun activity.

>**team** exercise 3-2

Who Am I?

Purpose   This exercise is designed to help you understand the elements and implications of social identity theory.

Materials   None.

Instructions

• *Step 1*: Working alone (no discussion with other students), use the form provided here or a piece of paper to write down twelve (12) words or phrases that answer the question "Who am I?" Write your words or phrases describing you as they come to mind; don't worry about their logical order here. Please be sure to fill in all 12 spaces.

Phrases that describe you	Circle S or P
1. I am _____	S P
2. I am _____	S P
3. I am _____	S P
4. I am _____	S P
5. I am _____	S P
6. I am _____	S P
7. I am _____	S P
8. I am _____	S P
9. I am _____	S P
10. I am _____	S P
11. I am _____	S P
12. I am _____	S P

• *Step 2*: Circle the S beside the items that define you in terms of your social identity, such as your demographics and formal or informal membership in a social group or institution (school, company, religious group). Circle the P beside the items that define you in terms of your personal identity; that is, unique personality, values, or experiences that are not connected to any particular social group. Next, underline one or more items that you believe will still be a strong characteristic of you 10 years from now.

• *Step 3*: Form small groups. If you have a team project for this course, your project team would work well for this exercise. Compare your list with the lists that others in your group wrote about themselves. Discuss the following questions in your group and prepare notes for class discussion and possible presentation of these questions:

1. Among members of this team, what was the typical percentage of items representing the person's social versus personal identity? Did some team members have many more or less social identity items compared to other team members? Why do you think these large or small differences in emphasis on social or personal identity occurred?

2. What characteristics did people in your group underline as being the most stable (i.e., remaining the same in 10 years from now)? Were these underlined items mostly social or personal identity features? How similar or different were the underlined items among team members?

3. What do these lists say about the dynamics of your group as a team (whether or not your group for this activity is actually involved in a class project for this course)?

Sources: M. H. Kuhn and T. S. McPartland, "An Empirical Investigation of Self-Attitudes," *American Sociological Review,* 19 (February 1954), pp. 68–76; C. Lay and M. Verkuyten, "Ethnic Identity and Its Relation to Personal Self-Esteem: A Comparison of Canadian-Born and Foreign-Born Chinese Adolescents," *Journal of Social Psychology,* 139 (1999), pp. 288–299; and S. L. Grace and K. L. Cramer, "The Elusive Nature of Self-Measurement: The Self-Construal Scale versus the Twenty Statements Test," *Journal of Social Psychology,* 143 (2003), pp. 649–668.

Find the complete interactive self-assessments at this textbook's Web site at
www.mhhe.com/mcshaneEss2e.

>self-assessment exercise 3-3

Assessing Your Personal Need for Structure

Some people need to "make sense" of things around them more quickly or completely than do other people. This personal need for perceptual structure relates to selective attention as well as perceptual organization and interpretation. This self-assessment is designed to help you to estimate your personal need for perceptual structure. Read each of the statements and decide how much you agree with each according to your attitudes, beliefs, and experiences. It is important for you to realize that there are no right or wrong answers to these questions. This self-assessment is completed alone so that students rate themselves honestly without concerns of social comparison. However, class discussion will focus on the meaning of need for structure in terms of how we engage differently in the perceptual process at work and in other settings.

>self-assessment exercise 3-4

Assessing Your Perspective-Taking (Cognitive Empathy)

Empathy is an important perceptual ability in social relations, but the degree to which people empathize varies considerably. This self-assessment provides an estimate of one form of empathy, known as cognitive empathy or perspective-taking. This means that it measures the level of cognitive awareness of another person's situational and individual circumstances. To complete this scale, indicate the degree to which each of the statements presented does or does not describe you very well. You need to be honest with yourself to reasonably estimate your level of perspective taking. The results show your relative position along the perspective-taking continuum and the general meaning of this score.

>self-assessment exercise 3-5

Assessing Your Emotional Empathy

Empathy is an important perceptual ability in social relations, but the degree to which people empathize varies considerably. This self-assessment provides an estimate of one form of empathy, known as *emotional empathy.* This refers to the extent that you are able to experience the emotions or feelings of the other person. To complete this scale, indicate the degree to which each of the statements presented does or does not describe you very well. You need to be honest with yourself to reasonably estimate your level of emotional empathy. The results show your relative position along the emotional empathy continuum and the general meaning of this score.

chapter 4

Workplace Emotions, Attitudes, and Stress

At CXtec Inc. in Syracuse, New York, job satisfaction and having fun is part of the company's culture.

>learningobjectives

After reading this chapter, you should be able to:

1. Explain how emotions and cognitions (conscious reasoning) influence attitudes and behavior.

2. Identify the conditions that require, and the problems associated with, emotional labor.

3. Describe the four dimensions of emotional intelligence.

4. Summarize the consequences of job dissatisfaction in terms of the exit-voice-loyalty-neglect model.

5. Discuss the effects of job satisfaction on job performance and customer service.

6. Distinguish affective and continuance commitment, and discuss their influences on employee behavior.

7. Describe five strategies to increase organizational (affective) commitment.

8. Define stress and describe the stress experience.

9. Explain why a stressor might produce different stress levels in two people.

10. Identify five ways to manage workplace stress.

After 13 years with the same company, Leslie Tripodi still loves her job. "Honestly, when I wake up, I'm excited to come here," says Tripodi, who works in sales at CXtec Inc., the Syracuse, New York, company that markets computer networking and technology equipment. "I have the best job. I will grow old here. It never occurs to me to leave. I don't know how many people can say that there is high turnover in sales, but not at CXtec."

At CXtec, having fun is more than a bonus; it's built into the company's culture. "Part of our core values is that work is fun," explains Paula Miller, CXtec's director of employee and community relations. Offices at the 350-person company are adorned with colorful clusters of helium-filled balloons, each representing a birthday or performance achievement. Employees enjoy a break room with billiards, foosball, and air hockey, and enjoy occasional minigolf tournaments along the hallways. CXtec has demanding performance goals, but the leadership team tries to balance those demands with personal needs. "If your kid gets sick or your car breaks down or if you just need a day off because you're breaking down, it's no problem," explains CXtec account executive Mi Lee Hill. "[CXtec executives] understand we have a difficult job, and they respect us for that."

These and many other events have made CXtec one of the best medium-sized companies to work for in America, and the top company for creating camaraderie in the workplace. Improving employee well-being through positive emotions also reduces turnover and boosts customer service. "Unlike most employers, I think these people [CXtec's leaders] have figured out that if you keep your people happy, they keep coming back and wanting more," says account representative Amber Clark. "They're happy to work for you."[1]

///

CXtec discovered long ago that emotions and attitudes make a noticeable difference in individual behavior and well-being, as well as in the organization's performance and customer service. Over the past decade, the field of organizational behavior has experienced a sea change in thinking about workplace emotions, so this chapter begins by introducing the concept and explaining why researchers are so eager to discover how emotions influence attitudes and behavior. Next, we consider the dynamics of and the conditions requiring emotional labor. This is followed by the popular topic of emotional intelligence, in which we examine the components of emotional intelligence and ways of improving this ability. The specific work attitudes of job satisfaction and organizational commitment are then discussed, including their association with various employee behaviors and work performance. The final section looks at work-related stress, including the stress experience, four prominent stressors, individual differences in stress, and ways to combat excessive stress.

After reading the next section, you should be able to:

1. *Explain how emotions and cognitions (conscious reasoning) influence attitudes and behavior.*

learningobjectives<

>Emotions in the Workplace

Emotions have a profound effect on almost everything we do in the workplace. This is a strong statement, and one that you would rarely find a decade ago in organizational behavior research or textbooks. Until recently, OB experts assumed that a person's thoughts and actions are governed primarily by conscious reasoning (called *cognitions*). Yet, groundbreaking neuroscience discoveries have revealed that our perceptions, attitudes, decisions,

EMOTIONS:
physiological, behavioral, and psychological episodes experienced toward an object, person, or event that create a state of readiness

and behavior are influenced by both cognition and emotion, and that the latter often has the greater influence.[2]

Emotions are physiological, behavioral, and psychological episodes experienced toward an object, person, or event that create a state of readiness.[3] These "episodes" are very brief events that typically subside or occur in waves lasting from milliseconds to a few minutes. Emotions are directed toward someone or something. For example, we experience joy, fear, anger, and other emotional episodes toward tasks, customers, or a software program we are using. This contrasts with *moods,* which are less intense emotional states that are not directed toward anything in particular.[4] Emotions are experiences. They represent changes in our physiological state (e.g., blood pressure, heart rate), psychological state (e.g., ability to think clearly), and behavior (e.g., facial expression). These emotional reactions are involuntary and often occur without our awareness. Finally, emotions put us in a state of readiness. When we get worried, for example, our heart rate and blood pressure increase to make our body better prepared to engage in fight or flight. Strong emotions also trigger our conscious awareness of a threat or opportunity in the external environment.[5]

There are dozens of emotions, and experts organize them in terms of whether they are positive or negative as well as how much they activate us (demand our attention). Anger is a negative emotion that generates a high level of activation, whereas feeling relaxed is a pleasant emotion that has fairly low activation. Emotions generate a global evaluation (called *core affect*) that something is good or bad, helpful or harmful, to be approached or avoided.[6]

Emotions, Attitudes, and Behavior

ATTITUDES:
the cluster of beliefs, assessed feelings, and behavioral intentions toward a person, object, or event

To understand how emotions influence our thoughts and behavior, we first need to know about attitudes. **Attitudes** represent the cluster of beliefs, assessed feelings, and behavioral intentions toward a person, object, or event (called an *attitude object*).[7] Attitudes are *judgments,* whereas emotions are *experiences.* In other words, attitudes involve conscious logical reasoning, whereas emotions operate as events, often without our awareness. We also experience most emotions briefly, whereas our attitude toward someone or something is more stable over time.

Until recently, attitude experts described attitudes in terms of its three cognitive components illustrated on the left side of Exhibit 4.1: beliefs, feelings, and behavioral intentions. Now, we have good evidence that a parallel emotional process is also at work, shown on the

[Exhibit 4.1] Model of Emotions, Attitudes, and Behavior

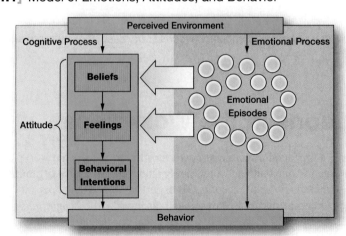

right side of the exhibit.[8] Using attitude toward mergers as an example, let's look more closely at this model, beginning with the traditional cognitive perspective of attitudes.

- *Beliefs.* These are your established perceptions about the attitude object—what you believe to be true. For example, you might believe that mergers reduce job security for employees in the merged firms. Or you might believe that mergers increase the company's competitiveness in this era of globalization. These beliefs are perceived facts that you acquire from past experience and other forms of learning.

- *Feelings.* Feelings represent your positive or negative evaluations of the attitude object. Some people think mergers are good; others think they are bad. Your like or dislike of mergers represents your assessed feelings toward the attitude object. According to the traditional cognitive model of attitudes (left side of the model), feelings are calculated from your beliefs about mergers. If you believe that mergers typically have negative consequences such as layoffs and organizational politics, then you will form negative feelings toward mergers in general or about a specific planned merger in your organization.

- *Behavioral intentions.* Intentions represent your motivation to engage in a particular behavior with respect to the attitude object.[9] Upon hearing that the company will merge with another organization, you might become motivated to quit, or you might intend to complain to management about this decision. Your feelings toward mergers motivates your behavioral intentions, and which actions you choose depends on your past experience, self-concept (values, personality), and social norms of appropriate behavior.

The model in Exhibit 4.1 also illustrates that behavioral intentions directly predict behavior. However, whether your intentions translate into behavior depends on all four elements of the MARS model such as opportunity and ability to act. Attitudes are also more likely to influence behavior when they are strong, meaning that they are anchored by strong emotions.

How Emotions Influence Attitudes and Behavior

Along with the cognitive process, emotions play a central role in forming and changing employee attitudes.[10] As the right side of Exhibit 4.1 illustrates, this process also begins with perceptions. Specifically, the emotional components of our brain quickly and imprecisely tag emotional markers to incoming information based on whether that information supports or threatens our innate drives. These are not calculated feelings; they are automatic and unconscious emotional responses based on very thin slices of sensory information.[11]

Returning to the example of your attitude toward mergers, you might experience excitement, worry, nervousness, or happiness upon learning that your company intends to merge with a competitor. The large dots on the right side of Exhibit 4.1 illustrate the numerous emotional episodes you experience upon hearing the merger announcement, subsequent thinking about the merger, discussion with co-workers about the merger, and so on. These emotions are transmitted to the logical reasoning process, where they swirl around and influence our conscious feelings toward the attitude object.[12] Thus, while consciously evaluating whether the merger is good or bad, your emotions have already formed an opinion, which then sways your conscious evaluation. In fact, we often deliberately "listen in" on our emotions to help us consciously decide whether to support or oppose something.[13] If you experience mainly positive emotions whenever you think about or discuss the merger, then these positive emotional episodes will lean your logical reasoning toward positive feelings regarding the merger.

The dual cognitive-emotional attitude process helps us to understand why CXtec and many other companies want their employees to experience plenty of positive emotional episodes each day. Job satisfaction is shaped by the almost continuous bombardment of emotional experiences people have at work. Those who experience more positive emotions tend to have more favorable attitudes toward their jobs, even when they don't consciously think about these emotional experiences. And when they do think about how they feel about their job, they listen in on the emotions regenerated from past positive or negative events in the workplace.

The influence of both cognitive reasoning and emotions on attitudes is most apparent when they disagree with each other. Everyone occasionally experiences this mental tug-of-war, sensing that something isn't right even though they can't think of any logical reason to be concerned. This conflicting experience indicates that our logical analysis of the situation (left side of Exhibit 4.1) can't identify reasons to support the automatic emotional reaction (right side of Exhibit 4.1).[14] Should we pay attention to our emotional response or our logical analysis? This question is not easy to answer, but some studies indicate that while executives tend to make quick decisions based on their gut feelings (emotional response), the best decisions tend to occur when they spend time logically evaluating the situation.[15] Thus, we should pay attention to both the cognitive and emotional side of the attitude model, and hope they agree with each other most of the time.

One last comment about Exhibit 4.1: Notice the arrow from the emotional episodes to behavior? This indicates that people have direct behavioral reactions to their emotions. Even low-intensity emotions automatically change your facial expressions. High-intensity emotions can have a more powerful effect, which is apparent when an upset employee bangs a fist on the desk or an overjoyed colleague embraces someone nearby. These actions are not carefully thought out. They are automatic emotional responses that serve as coping mechanisms in that situation.[16]

Cognitive Dissonance

COGNITIVE DISSONANCE: occurs when we perceive an inconsistency between our beliefs, feelings, and behavior

Emotions and attitudes usually lead to behavior, but the opposite sometimes occurs through the process of **cognitive dissonance**.[17] Cognitive dissonance occurs when we perceive an inconsistency between our beliefs, feelings, and behavior. When this inconsistency violates our self-concept, it generates emotions that motivate us to change one or more of these elements. Behavior is usually the most difficult element to change, particularly when it is known to everyone, was done voluntarily, and can't be undone. Thus, we usually change our beliefs and feelings to reduce the inconsistency.

>**learning**objectives

After reading the next two sections, you should be able to:

2. Identify the conditions that require, and the problems associated with, emotional labor.

3. Describe the four dimensions of emotional intelligence.

>Managing Emotions at Work

EMOTIONAL LABOR: the effort, planning, and control needed to express organizationally desired emotions during interpersonal transactions

People are expected to manage their emotions in the workplace. They must conceal their frustration when serving an irritating customer, display compassion to an ill patient, and hide their boredom in a long meeting with senior management. These are all forms of **emotional labor**—the effort, planning, and control needed to express organizationally desired emotions during interpersonal transactions.[18] Almost everyone is expected to abide by *display rules* on the job; these are norms requiring us to display specific emotions and to hide other emotions. Emotional labor is higher in jobs requiring a variety of emotions (e.g., anger as well as joy) and more intense emotions (e.g., showing delight rather than smiling weakly), as well as where interaction with clients is frequent and for longer durations. Emotional labor also increases when employees must precisely rather than casually abide by the display rules.[19]

Emotional Display Norms across Cultures

How much we are expected to hide or reveal our true emotions in public depends to some extent on the culture in which we live. Cultural values in some countries—particularly Ethiopia, Korea, Japan, and Austria—expect people to subdue their emotional expression and minimize physical contact with others. Even voice intonation tends to be monotonic. In other countries—notably Kuwait, Egypt, Spain, and Russia—cultural values allow or encourage open display of one's true emotions. People are expected to be transparent in revealing their thoughts and feelings, dramatic in their conversational tones, and animated in their use of nonverbal behaviors to get their message across. These cultural variations in emotional display can be quite noticeable. One survey reported that 83 percent of Japanese believe it is inappropriate to get emotional in a business context, compared with 40 percent of Americans, 34 percent of French, and only 29 percent of Italians. In other words, Italians are more likely to accept or tolerate people who display their true emotions at work, whereas this would be considered rude or embarrassing in Japan.[20]

Emotional Dissonance

Emotional labor can be challenging for most of us because it is difficult to conceal true emotions and to display the emotions required by the job. Joy, sadness, worry and other

Four Seasons Hotels Keeps the Local Temperament
As one of the world's leading operators of luxury hotels, Four Seasons Hotels and Resorts trains employees and audits hotel performance to ensure that guests consistently experience the highest standards of service quality. Yet, Four Seasons also adapts its legendary service to the local culture. "McDonald's is the same all over. We do not want to be that way; we are not a cookie-cutter company," says a Four Seasons executive. One of the most obvious forms of localization is in the way Four Seasons staff are allowed to display emotions that reflect their own culture. "What changes [from one country to the next] is that people do it with their own style, grace, and personality," explains Antoine Corinthios, president of Four Seasons' operations in Europe, Middle East, and Africa. "In some cultures you add the strong local temperament. For example, an Italian concierge has his own style and flair. In Turkey or Egypt you experience different hospitality."[21]

emotions automatically activate a complex set of facial muscles that are difficult to prevent, and equally difficult to fake. Our true emotions tend to reveal themselves as subtle gestures, usually without our awareness. More often than not, observers see when we are faking and sense that we feel a different emotion.[22]

Emotional labor also creates conflict between required and true emotions, called **emotional dissonance.** The larger the gap between the required and true emotions, the more employees tend to experience stress, job burnout, and psychological separation from self.[23] Hiring people with a natural tendency to display the emotions required for the job can minimize this emotional dissonance. For example, The Container Store expects employees to display positive emotions on the job, so its unofficial motto is "Grouchy People Need Not Apply."[24]

> **EMOTIONAL DISSONANCE:** the conflict between required and true emotions

Emotional dissonance is also minimized through *deep acting* rather than *surface acting*.[25] People engage in surface acting when they try to modify their behavior to be consistent with required emotions but continue to hold different internal feelings. For instance, we force a smile while greeting a customer who we consider rude. Deep acting involves changing true emotions to match the required emotions. Rather than feeling irritated by a rude customer, you might view your next interaction with that person as an opportunity to test your sales skills. This change in perspective can potentially generate more positive emotions next time you meet that difficult customer, which produces friendlier displays of emotion. However, deep acting also requires considerable emotional intelligence, which we discuss next.

>Emotional Intelligence

General Motors carefully selected staff for its new GM Holden production facility at Port Melbourne, Australia, but it wasn't long before the project unraveled due to infighting and interpersonal tensions. Consultants called in to analyze the problems offered the following solution: Employees need to improve their emotional intelligence. With this advice, the 30 plant design team members and over 300 other employees completed an emotional intelligence assessment and attended training modules on effective self-expression, understanding others, controlling emotions, and related topics.[26]

> **EMOTIONAL INTELLIGENCE (EI):** the ability to monitor our own and others' feelings and emotions, to discriminate between them and to use this information to guide our thinking and actions

From this experience, executives at General Motors discovered that **emotional intelligence (EI)** can significantly improve individual, team, and organizational effectiveness. EI includes a set of *abilities* to perceive and express emotion, assimilate emotion in thought, understand and reason with emotion, and regulate emotion in oneself and others.[27] One popular model, shown in Exhibit 4.2, organizes EI into four dimensions representing the recognition and regulation of emotions in ourselves and in others.[28] These four dimensions are also found in other models of EI, but experts disagree on the definitive list of abilities representing EI. For example, the authors of the model shown here include a list of "abilities" for each cell, but others warn that the list includes personality traits and personal values (e.g., achievement, optimism) as well as task outcomes (e.g., teamwork, inspirational leadership).[29]

- *Self-awareness.* Self-awareness refers to having a deep understanding of one's own emotions as well as strengths, weaknesses, values, and motives. Self-aware people are better able to eavesdrop in on their emotional responses to specific situations and to use this awareness as conscious information.[30]

- *Self-management.* This represents how well we control or redirect our internal states, impulses, and resources. It includes keeping disruptive impulses in check,

[Exhibit 4.2] Dimensions of Emotional Intelligence

	Self (Personal Competence)	Other (Social Competence)
Recognition of Emotions	Self-Awareness	Social Awareness
Regulation of Emotions	Self-Management	Relationship Management

Sources: D. Goleman, R. Boyatzis, and A. McKee, *Primal Leadership* (Boston: Harvard Business School Press, 2002), Chapter 3; D. Goleman, "An EI-Based Theory of Performance," in C. Cherniss and D. Goleman, (Eds.), *The Emotionally Intelligent Workplace* (San Francisco: Jossey-Bass, 2001), p. 28.

displaying honesty and integrity, being flexible in times of change, maintaining the drive to perform well and seize opportunities, and remaining optimistic even after failure. Self-management involves an inner conversation that guides our behavior.

- *Social awareness.* Social awareness is mainly about *empathy*—having understanding and sensitivity to the feelings, thoughts, and situation of others (see Chapter 3). This includes understanding another person's situation, experiencing the other person's emotions, and knowing that person's needs even though unstated. Social awareness extends beyond empathy to include being organizationally aware, such as sensing office politics and understanding social networks.

- *Relationship management.* This dimension of EI refers to managing other people's emotions. It is linked to a wide variety of practices, such as inspiring others, influencing people's beliefs and feelings, developing others' capabilities, managing change, resolving conflict, cultivating relationships, and supporting teamwork and collaboration.

These four dimensions of emotional intelligence form a hierarchy.[31] Self-awareness is the lowest level of EI because it does not require the other dimensions; instead, it is a prerequisite for the other three dimensions. Self-management and social awareness are necessarily above self-awareness in the EI hierarchy. You can't manage your own emotions (self-management) if you aren't good at knowing your own emotions (self-awareness). Relationship management is the highest level of EI because it requires all three other dimensions. In other words, we require a high degree of emotional intelligence to master relationship management because this set of competencies requires sufficiently high levels of self-awareness, self-management, and social awareness.

Most jobs involve social interaction with co-workers or external stakeholders, so employees need emotional intelligence to work effectively. Research indicates that people with high EI are better at interpersonal relations, perform better in jobs requiring emotional labor, are superior leaders, make better decisions involving social exchanges, and are more successful in many aspects of job interviews. Teams whose members have high emotional intelligence initially perform better than teams with low EI.[32] However, emotional intelligence does not improve some forms of performance, such as tasks that require minimal social interaction.[33]

Improving Emotional Intelligence

Emotional intelligence is associated with some personality traits, as well as with the emotional intelligence of one's parents.[34] However, GM Holden and other companies put employees through EI training programs because EI can also be learned in adulthood to some extent.[35] Personal coaching, plenty of practice, and frequent feedback are particularly effective at developing EI. EI also increases with age; it is part of the process called maturity. Overall, emotional intelligence offers considerable potential, but we also have a lot to learn about its measurement and effects on people in the workplace.

This chapter has laid out the model of emotions and attitudes, and introduced emotional intelligence as the means by which we manage emotions in the workplace. The next two sections of this chapter introduce the concepts of job satisfaction and organizational commitment. These two attitudes are so important in our understanding of workplace behavior that some experts suggest that together they should be called "overall job attitude."[36]

>**learning**objectives

After reading the next two sections, you should be able to:

4. Summarize the consequences of job dissatisfaction in terms of the exit-voice-loyalty-neglect model.

5. Discuss the effects of job satisfaction on job performance and customer service.

6. Distinguish affective and continuance commitment, and discuss their influences on employee behavior.

7. Describe five strategies to increase organizational (affective) commitment.

>Job Satisfaction

Job satisfaction, a person's evaluation of his or her job and work context, is probably the most studied attitude in organizational behavior.[37] It is an *appraisal* of the perceived job characteristics, work environment, and emotional experiences at work. Satisfied employees have a favorable evaluation of their job, based on their observations and emotional experiences. Job satisfaction is best viewed as a collection of attitudes about different aspects of the job and work context. You might like your co-workers but be less satisfied with workload, for instance.

How satisfied are employees at work? Exhibit 4.3 reveals that more than 85 percent of Americans are moderately or very satisfied with their jobs, a level that has been consistent for most years over the past three decades.[38] Global surveys estimate that Americans also have high levels of job satisfaction compared with people in most other countries.[39] Can we conclude from these results that Americans are happy at work? Possibly, but not as much as these statistics suggest. The problem is that surveys often use a single direct question, such as "How satisfied are you with your job?" Many dissatisfied employees are reluctant to reveal their feelings in a direct question because this is tantamount to admitting that they made a poor job choice and are not enjoying life. In fact, these surveys also report that employees rate almost all aspects of their job lower than their overall score.[40]

EXIT-VOICE-LOYALTY-NEGLECT (EVLN) MODEL: the four ways, as indicated in the name, that employees respond to job dissatisfaction

Job Satisfaction and Work Behavior

Job satisfaction affects many types of individual behavior. A useful template to organize and understand the consequences of job dissatisfaction is the **exit-voice-loyalty-neglect**

[**Exhibit 4.3**] Job Satisfaction Stability in America: 1972–2006

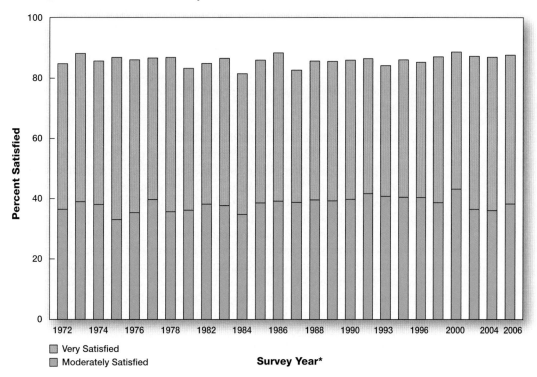

*Surveys were not conducted in all years.
Question Wording: "On the whole how satisfied are you with the work you do—would you say you are very satisfied, moderately satisfied, a little dissatisfied, or very dissatisfied?"
Source: T. W. Smith, *Job Satisfaction in America: Trends and Socio-Demographic Correlates*, (Chicago: National Opinion Research Center/University of Chicago, August 2007).

(EVLN) model. As the name suggests, the EVLN model identifies four ways that employees respond to dissatisfaction:[41]

- *Exit.* Exit refers to leaving the organization, transferring to another work unit, or at least trying to exit the dissatisfying situation. Exit usually follows specific "shock events," such as when your boss treats you unfairly.[42] These shock events generate strong emotions that energize employees to think about and search for alternative employment.

- *Voice.* Voice refers to any attempt to change, rather than escape from, the dissatisfying situation. Voice can be a constructive response, such as recommending ways for management to improve the situation, or it can be more confrontational, such as by filing formal grievances.[43] In the extreme, some employees might engage in counterproductive behaviors to get attention and force changes in the organization.

- *Loyalty.* Loyalty has been described in different ways, but the most widely held view is that "loyalists" are employees who respond to dissatisfaction by patiently waiting— some say they "suffer in silence"—for the problem to work itself out or get resolved by others.[44]

- *Neglect.* Neglect includes reducing work effort, paying less attention to quality, and increasing absenteeism and lateness. It is generally considered a passive activity that has negative consequences for the organization.

Which of the four EVLN alternatives do employees use? It depends on the person and situation.[45] One determining factor is the person's self-concept. Some people avoid the self-image as a complainer, whereas others view themselves very much as taking action when they dislike a work situation. This self-concept relates to personal and cultural values as well as personality. For example, people with a high-conscientiousness personality are less likely to engage in neglect and more likely to engage in voice. Past experience also influences which EVLN action is applied. Employees who were unsuccessful with voice in the past are more likely to engage in exit or neglect when experiencing job dissatisfaction in the future. Finally, the response to dissatisfaction depends on the situation. Employees are less likely to use the exit option when there are few alternative job prospects, for example.

Job Satisfaction and Performance

For almost a century, OB researchers have challenged the popular belief that "a happy worker is a productive worker." For most of that time, they concluded that job satisfaction has a minimal effect on job performance. Now, the evidence suggests that the popular saying may be correct after all; there is a *moderate* relationship between job satisfaction and job performance. In other words, happy workers really are more productive workers *to some extent.*[46] Even with a moderate association between job satisfaction and performance, there are a few underlying reasons why the relationship isn't even stronger. One argument is that general attitudes (such as job satisfaction) don't predict specific behaviors very well. As we learned with the EVLN model, job dissatisfaction can lead to a variety of outcomes rather than lower job performance (neglect). Some employees continue to work productively while they complain (voice), look for another job (exit), or patiently wait for the problem to be fixed (loyalty).

A second explanation is that job performance leads to job satisfaction (rather than vice versa), but only when performance is linked to valued rewards. Higher performers receive more rewards and, consequently, are more satisfied than low-performing employees who receive fewer rewards. The connection between job satisfaction and performance isn't stronger because many organizations do not reward good performance. The third explanation is that job satisfaction influences employee motivation, but doesn't affect performance in jobs where employees have little control over their job output (such as assembly line work).

Job Satisfaction and Customer Satisfaction

Another popular belief is that happy customers are the result of happy employees. "It just seems common sense to me that if you start with a happy, well-motivated workforce, you're much more likely to have happy customers," suggests Virgin Group founder Sir Richard Branson.[47] Fortunately, research generally agrees that job satisfaction has a positive effect on customer service.[48] There are two main reasons for this relationship. First, employees are usually in a more positive mood when they feel satisfied with their job and working conditions. Employees in a good mood display friendliness and positive emotions more naturally and frequently, which create positive emotions for customers. Second, satisfied employees are less likely to quit their jobs, so they have better knowledge and skills to serve clients. Lower turnover also gives customers the same employees to serve them, so there is more consistent service. There is some evidence that customers build their loyalty to specific employees, not to the organization, so keeping employee turnover low tends to build customer loyalty.[49]

Before leaving the topic of job satisfaction, we should mention that job satisfaction does more than improve work behaviors and customer satisfaction. Job satisfaction is also an ethical issue that influences the organization's reputation in the community. People spend a large portion of their time working in organizations, and many societies now expect companies to provide work environments that are safe and enjoyable. Indeed, employees in several countries closely monitor ratings of the best companies to work for, an indication that employee satisfaction is a virtue worth considerable goodwill to employers. This virtue is

Happy Employees Equal Happy Customers
Wegmans Food Markets has an unusual motto: Employees first, customers second. The grocery chain definitely puts its 33,000 employees in New York and four nearby states on top of its stakeholder list. They enjoy above average pay, health benefits, and other perks, resulting in labor costs of about 16 percent of sales compared to 12 percent at most supermarkets. Perhaps more important is that employees feel welcome and valued. "It's more of you're not part of a company, you're part of a family," says Katie Southard, who works in customer service at a Wegmans' store in Rochester, New York. "You're treated as an individual, not just one of the 350 persons in the store." Why don't customers come first? Wegmans' rationale is that you can't have happy customers if employees don't have high morale. Their theory seems to work: Wegmans enjoys one of the highest levels of customer loyalty and lowest levels of employee turnover in the industry.[50]

apparent when an organization has low job satisfaction. The company tries to hide this fact and, when morale problems become public, corporate leaders are usually quick to improve the situation.

>Organizational Commitment

Along with job satisfaction, organizational commitment is a central and arguably critical attitude is successful companies. **Organizational (affective) commitment** refers to the employee's emotional attachment to, identification with, and involvement in a particular organization.[51] This definition refers specifically to *affective commitment* because it is an emotional attachment—our feelings of loyalty—to the organization.

Organizational (affective) commitment is different from **continuance commitment.** While organizational commitment is an emotional bond to the organization, continuance commitment is a calculative attachment.[52] Employees have high continuance commitment when they do not particularly identify with the organization where they work but feel bound to remain there because it would be too costly to quit. In other words, they choose to stay because the calculated (typically financial) value of staying is higher than the value of working somewhere else. You can tell someone has high calculative commitment when they say: "I hate this place but can't afford to quit!" This reluctance to quit may be due to the risk of losing a large bonus by leaving early or because they are well established in the community where they work.[53]

Consequences of Organizational Commitment

Organizational commitment can be a significant competitive advantage.[54] Loyal employees are less likely to quit their jobs and be absent from work. They also have higher work motivation and organizational citizenship, as well as somewhat higher job performance. Organizational commitment also improves customer satisfaction because long-tenure employees have better knowledge of work practices, and clients like to do business with the same employees. One warning is that employees with very high loyalty tend to have high conformity, which results in lower creativity. There are also cases of dedicated employees who violated laws to defend the organization. However, most companies suffer from too little rather than too much employee loyalty.

ORGANIZATIONAL (AFFECTIVE) COMMITMENT: the employee's emotional attachment to, identification with, and involvement in a particular organization

CONTINUANCE COMMITMENT: an employee's calculative attachment to the organization, whereby an employee is motivated to stay only because leaving would be costly

While affective commitment is beneficial, research suggests that continuance commitment can be dysfunctional. In fact, employees with high levels of continuance commitment tend to have *lower* performance ratings and are *less* likely to engage in organizational citizenship behaviors. Furthermore, unionized employees with high continuance commitment are more likely to use formal grievances, whereas employees with high affective commitment engage in more constructive problem solving when employee–employer relations sour.[55] Although some level of financial connection may be necessary, employers should not confuse continuance commitment with employee loyalty. Employers still need to win employees' hearts (affective commitment) beyond tying them financially to the organization (continuance commitment).

Building Organizational Commitment

There are almost as many ways to build organizational loyalty as topics in this textbook, but the following list is most prominent in the literature.

- *Justice and support.* Affective commitment is higher in organizations that fulfill their obligations to employees and abide by humanitarian values, such as fairness, courtesy, forgiveness, and moral integrity. These values relate to the concept of organizational justice that we discuss in the next chapter. Similarly, organizations that support employee well-being tend to cultivate higher levels of loyalty in return.[56]

- *Shared values.* The definition of affective commitment refers to a person's identification with the organization, and that identification is highest when employees believe their values are congruent with the organization's dominant values. Also, employees experience more comfort and predictability when they agree with the values underlying corporate decisions. This comfort increases their motivation to stay with the organization.[57]

TRUST: positive expectations one person has toward another person in situations involving risk

- *Trust.* **Trust** refers to positive expectations one person has toward another person in situations involving risk.[58] Trust means putting faith in the other person or group. It is also a reciprocal activity: To receive trust, you must demonstrate trust. Employees identify with and feel obliged to work for an organization only when they trust its leaders. This explains why layoffs are one of the greatest blows to employee loyalty—by reducing job security, companies reduce the trust employees have in their employer and the employment relationship.[59]

- *Organizational comprehension.* Affective commitment is a person's identification with the company, so it makes sense that this attitude is strengthened when employees understand the company, including its past, present, and future. Thus, loyalty tends to increase with open and rapid communication to and from corporate leaders, as well as with opportunities to interact with co-workers across the organization.[60]

- *Employee involvement.* Employee involvement increases affective commitment by strengthening the employee's social identity with the organization. Employees feel that they are part of the organization when they take part in decisions that guide the organization's future. Employee involvement also builds loyalty because giving this power is a demonstration of the company's trust in its employees.

Organizational commitment and job satisfaction represent two of the most often studied and discussed attitudes in the workplace. Each is linked to emotional episodes and cognitive judgments about the workplace and relationship with the company. Emotions also play an important role in another concept that is on everyone's mind these days: stress. The final section of this chapter provides a brief overview of stress and how it can be managed.

After reading the next section, you should be able to:

learningobjectives<

8. *Define stress and describe the stress experience.*
9. *Explain why a stressor might produce different stress levels in two people.*
10. *Identify five ways to manage workplace stress.*

>Work-Related Stress and Its Management

Josh Holmes has fond memories of working at Electronic Arts (EA), but admits that the long hours at the electronic games company were stressful. "From the minute I joined [EA], I put every waking hour of my day into my work. . . . It definitely took its toll," says Holmes. After 10 years at EA, Holmes was burned out, so he quit. "We had done a lot of really long, grueling hours. I know I was thinking that there's got to be a way to do things a little differently." So, in their quest for a less-stressful electronic games company, Holmes and three other senior EA staff formed Propaganda Games (now a creative center within Disney's video game division), with the unique values of creativity, risk-taking, and work/life balance. "We want you to come into the studio, do great work, then get out and live your life," says Propaganda's Web site. "We foster a startup attitude without the startup stress."[61]

Stress is an adaptive response to a situation that is perceived as challenging or threatening to the person's well-being.[62] The stress response is a complex emotion that produces physiological changes to prepare us for "fight or flight"—to defend the threat or flee from it. Specifically, our heart rate increases, muscles tighten, breathing speeds up, and perspiration increases. Our body also moves more blood to the brain, releases adrenaline and other hormones, fuels the system by releasing more glucose and fatty acids, activates systems that sharpen our senses, and conserves resources by shutting down our immune system.

STRESS: an adaptive response to a situation that is perceived as challenging or threatening to the person's well-being

We often hear about stress as a negative experience. This is known as *distress*—the degree of physiological, psychological, and behavioral deviation from healthy functioning. However, some level of stress—called *eustress*—is also a necessary part of life because it activates and motivates people to achieve goals, change their environments, and succeed in life's challenge.[63] Our focus will be on the causes and management of distress, because it has become a chronic problem in many societies.

General Adaptation Syndrome

The stress experience, called the **general adaptation syndrome,** is an automatic defense system to help us cope with environmental demands. It occurs through the three stages shown in Exhibit 4.4.[64] The *alarm reaction* stage occurs when a threat or challenge activates the physiological stress responses that were noted earlier. The individual's energy level and coping effectiveness decrease in response to the initial shock. The second stage, *resistance,* activates various biochemical, psychological, and behavioral mechanisms that give us more energy and engage coping mechanisms to overcome or remove the source of stress. To focus energy on the source of the stress, the body reduces resources to the immune system during this stage.

GENERAL ADAPTATION SYNDROME: a model of the stress experience, consisting of three stages: alarm reaction, resistance and exhaustion

People have a limited resistance capacity and, if the source of stress persists, they will eventually move into the third stage, *exhaustion.* Most of us are able to remove the source of stress or remove ourselves from that source before becoming too exhausted. However, people who frequently reach exhaustion have increased risk of long-term physiological and psychological damage.[65]

[Exhibit 4.4] General Adaptation Syndrome

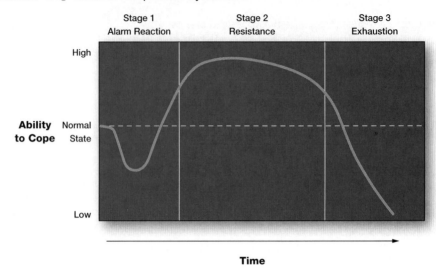

Source: Adapted from H. Selye, *The Stress of Life* (New York: McGraw-Hill, 1956).

Consequences of Distress

Stress takes its toll on the human body.[66] Many people experience tension headaches, muscle pain, and related problems mainly due to muscle contractions from the stress response. Studies have found that high stress levels also contribute to cardiovascular disease, including heart attacks and strokes. They also produce various psychological consequences, such as job dissatisfaction, moodiness, depression, and lower organizational commitment. Furthermore, various behavioral outcomes have been linked to high or persistent stress, including lower job performance, poor decision making, and increased workplace accidents and aggressive behavior. Most people react to stress through fight or flight, so increased absenteeism is another outcome because it is a form of flight.[67]

Stressors: The Causes of Stress

STRESSORS:
any environmental
conditions that
place a physical or
emotional demand
on the person

The general adaptation syndrome describes the stress experience, but to manage work-related stress, we must understand its causes, known as stressors. **Stressors** include any environmental conditions that place a physical or emotional demand on the person.[68] There are numerous stressors in the workplace and in life generally. In this section, we'll highlight three of the most common stressors: harassment and incivility, workload, and lack of task control.

Harassment and Incivility

**PSYCHOLOGICAL
HARASSMENT:**
repeated and
hostile or unwanted
conduct, verbal
comments, actions
or gestures that
affect an
employee's dignity
or psychological or
physical integrity
and that result in a
harmful work
environment for the
employee

One of the fastest growing sources of workplace stress is **psychological harassment.** Psychological harassment includes repeated and hostile or unwanted conduct, verbal comments, actions or gestures that affect an employee's dignity or psychological or physical integrity and that result in a harmful work environment for the employee. This definition covers a broad landscape of behaviors, from threats and bullying to subtle yet persistent forms of incivility.[69] More than 70 percent of Americans think people are less civil today than 20 years ago; 10 percent say they witness incivility daily in their workplaces and are targets of that abuse at least once each week.[70] Psychological harassment also permeates throughout workplaces in other countries. For example, two studies reported that more than half of UK human resource managers and Australian lawyers say they have been bullied or intimidated.[71]

Sexual harassment is a type of harassment in which a person's employment or job performance is conditional on unwanted sexual relations (called *quid pro quo*), and/or the person experiences sexual conduct from others (such as posting pornographic material) that unreasonably interferes with work performance or creates an intimidating, hostile, or offensive working environment (called *hostile work environment*). The number of charges alleging sexual harassment in the United States has declined steadily from 16,000 in 2000 to less than 13,000 today. The Equal Employment Opportunity Commission attributes the improvement to better supervisor training and concerted management action to address harassment issues before they reach litigation.

> **SEXUAL HARASSMENT:** unwelcome conduct of a sexual nature that detrimentally affects the work environment or leads to adverse job-related consequences for its victims

Work Overload

A half-century ago, social scientists predicted that technology would allow employees to enjoy a 15-hour workweek at full pay by 2030.[72] So far, it hasn't turned out that way. Americans experience considerable *work overload*—working more hours and more intensely during those hours than they can reasonably cope. Surveys by the Families and Work Institute report that 44 percent of Americans say they are overworked, up from 28 percent who felt this way three years earlier. This work overload is also the main cause of work-family conflicts, because overworked employees have insufficient time to satisfy their nonwork roles of being a parent, spouse, and so forth.[73]

Some writers suggest that the rising workload is caused by globalization and its demands for more work efficiency. A second cause, according to a recent study, is that many people are caught up in consumerism; they want to buy more goods and services, which requires more income through longer work hours. A third reason, called the *ideal worker norm,* is that professionals expect themselves and others to work longer work hours. For many, toiling away far beyond the normal workweek is a badge of honor, a symbol of their superhuman capacity to perform above others.[74] This badge of honor is particularly pronounced in several (but not all) Asian countries, to the point where "death from overwork" is now part of the common language (*karoshi* in Japanese and *guolaosi* in Chinese).

Asian Professionals are Dying to Get Ahead

Throughout Asia, professionals are working long work hours as a badge of honor. For some, it's a short-lived honor. According to the Japanese government, employees who work more than 80 hours of overtime per month have a significantly higher risk of *karoshi*—death from overwork. Currently, more than 20 percent of male Japanese employees exceed that level of overtime. Governments in South Korea—which has among the world's highest average work hours—and Taiwan are also paying closer attention to workplace casualties linked to long work hours. In China, the media are now using the term *guolaosi* (overwork death) to describe this disturbing trend. In one recent incident, two young faculty members at China's top engineering school died suddenly, apparently from exhaustion and overwork. The Chinese media, itself, seems to suffer from *guolaosi*. A study of journalists in China's major news outlets revealed that the average age at the time of death was 46 years. Long hours and corresponding poor lifestyle were identified as factors in the shorter life expectancy.[75]

Low Task Control

As a private driver for an executive in Jakarta, Eddy knows that traffic jams are a way of life in Indonesia's largest city. "Jakarta is traffic congestion," he complains. "All of the streets in the city are crowded with vehicles. It is impossible to avoid this distressing fact every day." Eddy's boss complains when traffic jams make him late for appointments, which makes matters even more stressful.[76] Eddy and many other people experience stress due to a lack of task control. Along with driving through congested traffic, low task control occurs where the work is paced by a machine, the job involves monitoring equipment, or the work schedule is controlled by someone else. Computers, cell phones, and other technology also increase stress by limiting a person's control of time and privacy.[77]

The degree to which low task control is a stressor increases with the burden of responsibility the employee must carry. Assembly line workers have low task control, but their stress can also be fairly low if their level of responsibility is also low. In contrast, sports coaches are under immense pressure to win games (high responsibility), yet have little control over what happens on the playing field (low task control). Similarly, Eddy (the Jakarta driver) is under pressure to get his employer to a particular destination on time (high responsibility), yet he has little control over traffic congestion (low task control).

Individual Differences in Stress

People have different stress experiences when exposed to the same stressor due to unique personal characteristics. One reason is that they have different threshold levels of resistance to the stressor. Those who exercise and have healthy lifestyles have a larger store of energy to cope with high stress levels. A second reason for different stress responses is that people use different coping strategies, some of which are more effective than others. Research suggests that employees who try to ignore or deny the existence of a stressor suffer more in the long run than those who try to find ways to weaken the stressor and seek social support.[78]

RESILIENCE: the capability of individuals to cope successfully in the face of significant change, adversity, or risk

A third reason why some people experience less stress than others is that they have higher resilience.[79] **Resilience** is the capability of individuals to cope successfully in the face of significant change, adversity, or risk. Those with high resilience are able to withstand adversity as well as recover more quickly from it. Resilient people possess personality traits (such as high extroversion and low neuroticism) that generate more optimism, confidence, and positive emotions. Resilience also involves specific competencies and behaviors to respond and adapt more effectively to stressors. Research indicates that resilient people have higher emotional intelligence and good problem-solving skills. They also apply productive coping strategies, such as analyzing the sources of stress and finding ways to neutralize these problems.[80]

WORKAHOLIC: a person who is highly involved in work, feels compelled to work and has a low enjoyment of work

While resilience helps people to withstand stress, another personal characteristic—workaholism—attracts more stressors and weakens the capacity to cope with them. The classic **workaholic** (also called *work addict*) is highly involved in work, feels compelled or driven to work because of inner pressures, and has a low enjoyment of work. Workaholics are compulsive and preoccupied with work, often to the exclusion and detriment of personal health, intimate relationships, and family.[81] Classic workaholics are more prone to job stress and have significantly higher scores on scales of depression, anxiety, and anger.[82]

Managing Work-Related Stress

Some degree of stress is good (eustress), but for the most part employees and employers need to figure out how to minimize distress. Most stress management strategies can be organized into five categories: remove the stressor, withdraw from the stressor, change stress perceptions, control stress consequences, and receive social support.

- *Remove the stressor*. While other stress management strategies try to keep employees "stress-fit," the best solution is to get rid of (or minimize) the conditions that cause high stress. This would include assigning employees to jobs that match their skills and preferences, reducing excessive workplace noise, having a complaint system and corrective action against harassment, and giving employees more control over the work process. Work/life balance initiatives also fall into this category, such as offering flexible work schedules, job sharing, telecommuting, personal leave, and child care support.[83]

- *Withdraw from the stressor*. Employees withdraw from stressors by taking work breaks, days off, vacations, and sabbaticals. In fact, research indicates that leisure time significantly improves the employees' ability to cope with work-related stress.[84]

- *Change stress perceptions*. Earlier, we learned that employees experience different stress levels because they have different levels of resilience, including self-confidence and optimism. Consequently, corporate leaders need to look at ways for employees to strengthen their confidence and self-esteem so that job challenges are not perceived as threatening. A study of newly hired accountants reported that personal goal setting and self-reinforcement can also reduce the stress that people experience when they enter new work settings. Humor can also improve optimism and create positive emotions by taking some psychological weight off the situation.[85]

- *Control stress consequences*. Companies can reduce the adverse consequences of high stress by ensuring that employees maintain healthy lifestyles.[86] Some companies provide on-site exercise facilities or subsidize the cost of offsite fitness centers. A few firms, such as AstraZeneca, encourage employees to practice relaxation and meditation techniques during the workday. Others offer more comprehensive wellness programs that educate and support employees in better nutrition and fitness, regular sleep, and other good health habits.

- *Receive social support*. Social support occurs when co-workers, supervisors, family members, friends, and others, provide emotional and/or informational support to buffer the stress experience. Potentially, it improves the person's resilience (particularly their optimism and self-confidence) because support makes people feel valued and worthy. Social support also provides information to help employees interpret, comprehend, and possibly remove the stressor. For instance, social support might reduce a new employee's stress because co-workers describe ways to handle difficult customers. Seeking social support is called a "tend and befriend" response to stress, and research suggests that women often follow this route rather than the fight-or-flight response mentioned earlier.[87]

Employee emotions, attitudes, and stress influence employee behavior mainly through motivation. Recall, for instance, that behavioral intentions are judgments or expectations about the motivation to engage in a particular behavior. The next chapter introduces the prominent theories of employee motivation as well as applied practices that increase and support motivation.

>Chapter Summary

Emotions are physiological, behavioral, and psychological episodes experienced toward an object, person, or event that create a state of readiness. Emotions differ from attitudes, which represent the cluster of beliefs, feelings, and behavioral intentions toward a person, object, or event. Beliefs are a person's established perceptions about the attitude object.

Feelings are positive or negative evaluations of the attitude object. Behavioral intentions represent a motivation to engage in a particular behavior with respect to the target.

Attitudes have traditionally been described as a purely rational process in which beliefs predict feelings, which predict behavioral intentions, which predict behavior. We now know that emotions have an equal or greater influence. This dual process is apparent when we internally experience a conflict between what logically seems good or bad and what we emotionally feel is good or bad in a situation. Emotions also affect behavior directly. Behavior sometimes influences our subsequent attitudes through cognitive dissonance.

Emotional labor refers to the effort, planning, and control needed to express organizationally desired emotions during interpersonal transactions. This is more common in jobs requiring a variety of emotions and more intense emotions, as well as where interaction with clients is frequent and for longer durations. Cultures also differ in the norms of displaying or concealing a person's true emotions. Emotional dissonance occurs when required and true emotions are incompatible with each other. Deep acting can minimize this dissonance, as can the practice of hiring people with a natural tendency to display desired emotions.

Emotional intelligence is the ability to perceive and express emotion, assimilate emotion in thought, understand and reason with emotion, and regulate emotion in oneself and others. This concept includes four components arranged in a hierarchy: self-awareness, self-management, social awareness, and relationship management. Emotional intelligence can be learned to some extent, particularly through personal coaching.

Job satisfaction represents a person's evaluation of his or her job and work context. The exit-voice-loyalty-neglect model outlines four possible consequences of job dissatisfaction. Job satisfaction has a moderate relationship with job performance and with customer satisfaction. Affective organizational commitment (loyalty) refers to the employee's emotional attachment to, identification with, and involvement in a particular organization. This contrasts with continuance commitment, which is a calculative bond with the organization. Companies build loyalty through justice and support, shared values, trust, organizational comprehension, and employee involvement.

Stress is an adaptive response to a situation that is perceived as challenging or threatening to the person's well-being. The stress experience, called the general adaptation syndrome, involves moving through three stages: alarm, resistance, and exhaustion. Stressors are the causes of stress and include any environmental conditions that place a physical or emotional demand on the person. Three stressors that have received considerable attention are harassment (including incivility), work overload, and low task control.

Two people exposed to the same stressor may experience different stress levels. Many interventions are available to manage work-related stress, including removing the stressor, withdrawing from the stressor, changing stress perceptions, controlling stress consequences, and receiving social support

>key terms

attitudes 68	emotions 68	resilience 82
cognitive dissonance 70	exit-voice-loyalty-neglect (EVLN) model 74	sexual harassment 81
continuance commitment 77	general adaptation syndrome 79	stress 79
emotional dissonance 72		stressors 80
emotional intelligence (EI) 72	organizational (affective) commitment 77	trust 78
emotional labor 70	psychological harassment 80	workaholic 82

>critical thinking questions

1. A recent study reported that college instructors are frequently required to engage in emotional labor. Identify the situations in which emotional labor is required for this job. In your opinion, is emotional labor more troublesome for college instructors or for telephone operators working at a 911 emergency service?

2. "Emotional intelligence is more important than cognitive intelligence in influencing an individual's success." Do you agree or disagree with this statement? Support your perspective.

3. Describe a time when you effectively managed someone's emotions. What happened? What was the result?

4. "Happy employees create happy customers." Explain why this statement might be true, and identify conditions in which it might not be true.

5. What factors influence an employee's organizational loyalty?

6. Is being a full-time college or university student a stressful role? Why or why not? Contrast your response with other students' perspectives.

7. Two recent college graduates join the same major newspaper as journalists. Both work long hours and have tight deadlines to complete their stories. They are under constant pressure to scout out new leads and be the first to report new controversies. One journalist is increasingly fatigued and despondent and has taken several days of sick leave. The other is getting the work done and seems to enjoy the challenges. Use your knowledge of stress to explain why these two journalists are reacting differently to their jobs.

8. A senior official of a labor union stated: "All stress management does is help people cope with poor management. [Employers] should really be into stress reduction." Discuss the accuracy of this statement.

>class exercise 4-1

Stem-and-Probe Interview Activity

Purpose   To help students experience the effects of emotional experiences on behavior.

Materials   None

Instructions
This simple, yet powerful, exercise consists of students conducting and receiving a detailed stem-and-probe interview with other students in the class. Each student will have an opportunity to interview and be interviewed. However, to increase the variation and novelty of this experience, the student conducting the first interview should *not* be interviewed by the student who was just interviewed. Instead, the instructor should either forms groups of four students (two pairs) at the beginning of this exercise, or have two pairs of students swap after the first round. Each of the two sets of interviews should take 10 to 15 minutes and use a stem-and-probe interview method. The stem-and-probe method, as well as the topic of the interview, are described next.

Stem-and-probe interviewing.   This interview method attempts to receive more detail from the interviewee than typically occurs in semi-structured or structured interviews. The main interview question, called the *stem* is followed by a series of probing questions that encourages the interviewee to provide more details relating to a particular incident or situation. The stem question for this exercise is provided below. There are several probes

that the interviewee can use to elicit more detail, and the best probe depends on the circumstances, such as what information has already been provided. Some common probe questions include "Tell me more about that"; "What did you do next?"; "Could you explain that further, please?"; "What else can you remember about that event?" Notice that each of these probes is open-ended, not closed-ended questions such as "Is there anything else you want to tell me" in which a simple yes or no answer is possible. Stem-and-probe interviewing also improves when the interviewer engages in active listening and isn't afraid of silence—giving the interviewee time to think and motivating them to fill in the silence with new information.

Interview Topic.   In both sets of interviews, the stem question is:

> Describe two or three things you did this past week that made someone else feel better.

Through this interview process, the interviewer's task is to receive as much information as possible (that the interviewee is willing to divulge) about the details of these two or three things that the interviewee did over the past week.

Following the two sets of interviews (where each student has interviewed and been interviewed once), the class will discuss the emotional and attitudinal dynamics of this activity.

>**team** exercise 4-2

Stage Fright!

Purpose   This exercise is designed to help you to diagnose a common stressful situation and determine how stress management practices apply to this situation.

Background   Stage fright—including the fear of public speaking—is one of the most stressful experiences many people have in everyday life. According to some estimates, nearly three-quarters of us frequently get stage fright, even when speaking or acting in front of a small audience. Stage fright is an excellent topic for this team activity on stress management because the psychological and physiological symptoms of stage fright are really symptoms of stress. In other words, stage fright is the stress experience in a specific context involving a public audience. Based on the personal experiences of team members, your team is asked to identify the symptoms of stage fright and to determine specific stress management activities that effectively combat stage fright.

Instructions

- *Step 1:* Students are organized into teams, typically 4 to 6 students per team. Ideally, each team should have one or more people who acknowledge that they have experienced stage fright.

- *Step 2:* Each team's first task is to identify the symptoms of stage fright. The best way to organize these symptoms is to look at the three categories of stress outcomes described in the textbook: physiological, psychological, and behavioral. The specific stage fright symptoms may be different from the stress outcomes described in the textbook, but the three broad categories are relevant. Teams should be prepared to identify several symptoms and to present one or two specific examples of stage fright symptoms based on personal experiences of team members. (Please remember that individual students are not required to describe their experiences to the entire class.)

- *Step 3:* Each team's second task is to identify specific strategies people could or have applied to minimize stage fright. The five categories of stress management presented in the textbook will likely provide a useful template in which to organize the specific stage fright management activities. Each team should document several strategies to minimize stage fright and be able to present one or two specific examples to illustrate some of these strategies.

- *Step 4:* The class will congregate to hear each team's analysis of symptoms and solutions to stage fright. This information will then be compared to the stress experience and stress management practices, respectively.

Find the complete interactive self-assessments at this textbook's Web site at
www.mhhe.com/mcshaneEss2e.

>**self-assessment** exercise 4-3

School Commitment Scale

This self-assessment is designed to help you understand the concept of organizational commitment and to assess your commitment to the college or university you are currently attending. The concept of commitment is as relevant to students enrolled in college or university courses as it is to employees working in various organizations. This self-assessment adapts a popular organizational commitment instrument so it refers to your commitment as a student to the school where you are attending this program. Select the response for each statement that best fits your personal belief. This self-assessment is completed alone so that students rate themselves honestly without concerns of social comparison. However, class discussion will focus on the meaning of the different types of organizational commitment and how well this scale applies to the commitment of students toward the college they are attending.

>self-assessment exercise 4-4

Dispositional Mood Scale

This self-assessment is designed to help you understand mood states or personality traits of emotions and to assess your own mood or emotions-based personality. This self-assessment consists of several words representing various emotions that you might have experienced. For each word presented, indicate the extent to which you have felt this way generally across all situations *over the past six months*. You need to be honest with yourself to receive a reasonable estimate of your mood state or personality trait on these scales. The results provide an estimate of your level on two emotional personality scales. This instrument is widely used in research, but it is only an estimate. You should not assume that the results are accurate without a more complete assessment by a trained professional.

>self-assessment exercise 4-5

Work Addiction Risk Test

This self-assessment is designed to help you to identify the extent to which you are a workaholic. This instrument presents several statements, and asks you to indicate the extent to which each statement is true of your work habits. You need to be honest with yourself for a reasonable estimate of your level of workaholism.

>self-assessment exercise 4-6

Connor-Davidson Resilience Scale

This self-assessment is designed to help you to estimate your personal level of resilience. Please indicate the extent that each statement in this instrument is true for you *over the past month*. It is important for you to realize that there are no right or wrong answers to these questions. This self-assessment is completed alone so that you can complete this instrument honestly without concerns of social comparison. However, class discussion will focus on the meaning of resilience and how it relates to workplace stress.

>**self-assessment** exercise 4-7

Perceived Stress Scale

This self-assessment is designed to help you to estimate your perceived general level of stress. The items in this scale ask you about your feelings and thoughts during the last month. In each case, please indicate how often you felt or thought a certain way. You need to be honest with yourself for a reasonable estimate of your general level of stress.

>**self-assessment** exercise 4-8

Stress Coping Preference Scale

This self-assessment is designed to help you to identify the type of coping strategy you prefer to use in stressful situations. This scale lists a variety of things you might do when faced with a stressful situation. You are asked how often you tend to react in these ways. You need to be honest with yourself for a reasonable estimate of your preferred coping strategy.

[chapter 5]

Employee Motivation:
Foundations and Practices

Panafric Hotel in Nairobi, Kenya, motivates its employees through plenty of praise and recognition.

>**learning**objectives

After reading this chapter, you should be able to:

1. Diagram and discuss the relationship between human drives, needs, and behavior.

2. Summarize Maslow's needs hierarchy and discuss Maslow's contribution to the field of motivation.

3. Summarize McClelland's learned needs theory, including the three needs he studied.

4. Describe four-drive theory and discuss its implications for motivating employees.

5. Diagram the expectancy theory model and discuss its practical implications for motivating employees.

6. Describe the characteristics of effective goal setting and feedback.

7. Summarize equity theory and describe how to improve procedural justice.

8. Diagram the job characteristics model of job design and use its elements to explain how to improve motivation through job enrichment.

9. Define empowerment and identify strategies to support empowerment.

David Gachuru lives by a motto that motivates employees more than money: "If an employee's work calls for a thumbs-up, I will appreciate him or her as many times as possible." Translating this advice into practice is a daily event for the general manager of Panafric Hotel in Nairobi, Kenya. In addition to thanking staff personally and through e-mails, Gachuru holds bi-monthly meetings where top performing employees are congratulated and receive paid holidays with their family. Employee achievements are also celebrated in the hotel's newsletter, which is distributed to guests as well as employees. Panafric Hotel and other firms are returning to good old-fashioned praise and recognition to motivate staff. Share options can evaporate and incentive plans might backfire, whereas a few words of appreciation almost always create a warm glow of satisfaction and a renewed energy.

Along with recognition from managers, approximately one-third of large American firms rely on peer recognition as one of the ways to motivate employees. Among them is Yum Brands Inc., the parent company of KFC, Taco Bell, and Pizza Hut. Yum's restaurants around the world use a recognition program in which employees reward colleagues with "Champs" cards, an acronym for KFC's values (cleanliness, hospitality, etc.). The Ritz Carlton Hotel in Kuala Lumpur, Malaysia, which is rated as one of the best places to work in Asia, applies a similar peer recognition process using First Class Cards. Nancy Teoh, Ritz Carlton Kuala Lumpur's human resources manager, explains that "congratulatory messages or words of appreciation are written down by any member of the team to another and even as far as from the hotel and corporate senior leaders." Teoh adds: "This serves as a motivational aspect of the work environment."[1]

From Panafric Hotel in Africa to KFC restaurants around the world, corporate leaders are trying to find ways to create a more motivated and engaged workforce. Recall from Chapter 2 that **motivation** refers to the forces within a person that affect the direction, intensity, and persistence of voluntary behavior.[2] Motivated employees are willing to exert a particular level of effort (intensity), for a certain amount of time (persistence), toward a particular goal (direction). Motivation is one of the four essential drivers of individual behavior and performance, and consequently is important to an organization's success. However, most employers—92 percent of them, according to one major survey—say that motivating employees is as difficult or has become more difficult in recent years. The challenge of motivating staff is particularly true for younger people in the workforce. According to one report, more than 40 percent of employees aged 25 to 34 sometimes or frequently feel de-motivated compared to 30 percent of employees in the 35 to 44 age bracket and just 18 percent of those 45 to 54 years of age.[3]

MOTIVATION: the forces within a person that affect the direction, intensity, and persistence of voluntary behavior

We begin this chapter by introducing concepts and theories related to human drives and needs, including Maslow's well-known needs hierarchy theory, McClelland's learned needs theory, and four-drive theory. Next, we turn our attention to a rational decision model of employee motivation, called expectancy theory. This is followed by an overview of the key elements of goal setting and feedback as well as equity theory and procedural justice. The latter part of this chapter describes two applied performance practices: job design and empowerment, including specific job design strategies to motivate employees as well as conditions that support empowerment.

After reading this section, you should be able to:

1. *Diagram and discuss the relationship between human drives, needs, and behavior.*
2. *Summarize Maslow's needs hierarchy and discuss Maslow's contribution to the field of motivation.*
3. *Summarize McClelland's learned needs theory, including the three needs he studied.*
4. *Describe four-drive theory and discuss its implications for motivating employees.*

learningobjectives<

>Needs, Drives, and Employee Motivation

One of the first barriers to understanding employee motivation is the confusing and contradictory array of words describing the internal source of individual effort. Innate drives, learned needs, motivations, instincts, secondary drives, primary needs, and other phrases have been used in almost chaotic fashion, often within the same article.[4] We offer the following working definitions, but you should be aware that these terms may be used differently by some other writers.

DRIVES: neural states that energize individuals to correct deficiencies or maintain an internal equilibrium

Drives are neural states that energize individuals to correct deficiencies or maintain an internal equilibrium.[5] This means that drives (also called *primary needs*, *fundamental needs,* or *innate motives*) are hardwired in the brain. They serve as the "prime movers" of behavior by activating emotions, which put us in a state of readiness to act. Although typically overlooked in organizational behavior, emotions play a central role in motivation.[6] In fact, both words (emotion and motivation) come from the same Latin word, *movere,* which means "to move." Drive theories popular a half-century ago ultimately failed because they limited drives to physiological essentials, such as hunger and thirst. Now, experts conclude that people also have nonphysiological drives, such as the drive for social interaction, to understand the immediate environment, as well as to defend oneself against physiological and psychological harm.[7] In short, to the best of our current knowledge, drives and emotions represent the primary sources of employee motivation.

NEEDS: goal-directed forces that people experience

We define **needs** as goal-directed forces that people experience. Needs are drive-generated emotions that people have consciously or nonconsciously directed toward particular goals to correct deficiencies or imbalances. As Exhibit 5.1 illustrates, most needs are shaped by the individual's self-concept (including personality and values), social norms, and past experience.[8] These personal characteristics can amplify or suppress some needs, which explains why people have different need levels in the same situation. People who define themselves as very sociable would have a strong need for social interaction if alone for a while, whereas other people would experience a less intense need to socialize. Self-concept, social norms, and past experience also regulate a person's motivated goals and behavior. For example, you might have noticed how strangers in some cultures will walk up to you and ask what you are doing, whereas the curiosity that motivated this forward behavior is suppressed in other cultures. Similarly, in one organization you might be expected to openly disagree with a co-worker about a problem, whereas you would suppress this desire to complain in another company where disagreement is discouraged.

We have presented this detail about needs and drives for a few reasons.[9] First, the field of organizational behavior has been woefully slow to acknowledge the central role of emotions in employee motivation, which will be apparent when reviewing most motivation theories in this chapter. Second, as mentioned, motivation theories use the terms needs,

[Exhibit 5.1] Drives, Needs, and Behavior

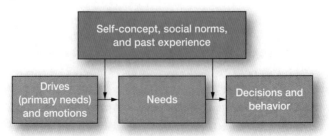

drives, and motivations so loosely that they make it difficult to compare theories, so it is important to settle this confusion at the outset. Third, Exhibit 5.1 provides a useful template to understand various motivation theories. The remainder of this section describes theories that try to explain the dynamics of drives and needs. Later theories in this chapter explain how experiences—such as expectancies, feedback, and work experiences—influence the motivation process.

Maslow's Needs Hierarchy Theory

By far, the most widely known theory of human motivation is **Maslow's needs hierarchy theory.** Developed by psychologist Abraham Maslow in the 1940s, the model condenses and integrates the long list of needs that had been studied previously into a hierarchy of five basic categories (from lowest to highest):[10]

MASLOW'S NEEDS HIERARCHY THEORY: a motivation theory of needs arranged in a hierarchy, whereby people are motivated to fulfill a higher need as a lower one becomes gratified

Physiological. The need for food, air, water, shelter, and so on.

Safety. The need for a secure and stable environment and the absence of pain, threat, or illness.

Belongingness/love. The need for love, affection, and interaction with other people.

Esteem. The need for self-esteem through personal achievement as well as social esteem through recognition and respect from others.

Self-actualization. The need for self-fulfillment, realization of one's potential.

In addition to these five categories, Maslow identified the desire to know and for aesthetic beauty as two drives that do not fit within the hierarchy.

Maslow's list represents drives (primary needs) because they are described as innate and universal. According to Maslow, we are motivated simultaneously by several needs, but the strongest source is the lowest unsatisfied need at the time. As the person satisfies a lower level need, the next higher need in the hierarchy becomes the primary motivator and remains so even if never satisfied. Physiological needs are initially the most important and people are motivated to satisfy them first. As they become gratified, the desire for safety emerges as the strongest motivator. As safety needs are satisfied, belongingness needs become most important, and so forth. The exception to this need fulfillment process is self-actualization; as people experience self-actualization, they desire more rather than less of this need. Thus, while the bottom four groups are *deficiency needs* because they become activated when unfulfilled, self-actualization is known as a *growth need* because it continues to develop even when fulfilled.

Limitations and Contributions of Maslow's Theory

In spite of its popularity, Maslow's needs hierarchy theory has been dismissed by most motivation experts.[11] Maslow developed the theory based only on his professional observations and was later surprised that it was so widely accepted before anyone tested it! Empirical studies have concluded that the five needs are not separate from each other, and that people do not consistently progress through the hierarchy. For example, some people strive more for self-esteem before their belongingness needs have been satisfied. The theory also assumes that needs priorities shift over months or years, whereas needs priorities likely rise and fall more frequently with the situation.

Although needs hierarchy theory has failed the reality test, Maslow deserves much credit for dramatically changing the study of human motivation. He brought a more holistic perspective by introducing the notion that needs are related to each other and, consequently, should be studied together. Previously, motivation experts had splintered needs and drives

POSITIVE ORGANIZATIONAL BEHAVIOR: a perspective of organizational behavior that focuses on building positive qualities and traits within individuals or institutions as opposed to focusing on what is wrong with them

into dozens of categories, each studied in isolation using nontypical subjects (usually animals or people with severe psychological dysfunctions).[12] Second, Maslow argued that higher order needs are influenced by social dynamics and culture, not just instincts. Previously, motivation experts were preoccupied with instinctive behavior. Finally, Maslow encouraged motivation experts to pay attention to strengths rather than deficiencies. He championed the notion that people are naturally motivated to reach their potential, and that organizations and societies need to be structured to help people continue and develop this motivation.[13] As such, Maslow is recognized as one of the founders of **positive organizational behavior** (a variation of *positive psychology*), which focuses on building positive qualities and traits within individuals or institutions as opposed to focusing on what is wrong with them.[14]

What's Wrong with Needs Hierarchy Models?

ERG THEORY: a needs hierarchy theory consisting of three fundamental needs—existence, relatedness, and growth

Maslow's theory is not the only attempt to map employee needs onto a single hierarchy. Another hierarchy model, called **ERG theory,** reorganizes Maslow's five groups into three—existence, relatedness, and growth.[15] Unlike Maslow's theory, which only explained how people progress up the hierarchy, ERG theory also describes how people regress down the hierarchy when they fail to fulfill higher needs. ERG theory seems to explain human motivation somewhat better than Maslow's needs hierarchy, but that's mainly because it is easier to cluster human needs around ERG's three categories than Maslow's five categories. Otherwise, the research indicates that ERG theory only marginally improves our understanding of human needs.[16]

Why have Maslow's needs hierarchy, ERG theory, and other needs hierarchies largely failed to explain the dynamics of employee needs? The most glaring explanation is that people don't fit into a single universal needs hierarchy. Some people place social status at the top of their personal hierarchy; others consider personal development and growth an ongoing priority over social relations or status. There is increasing evidence that needs hierarchies are unique, not universal, because needs are strongly influenced by each individual's self-concept, including personal values and social identity. If your most important values lean toward stimulation and self-direction, you probably pay more attention to self-actualization needs. If power and achievement are at the top of your value system, then status needs will likely be at the top of your needs hierarchy. This connection between values and needs suggests that a needs hierarchy is unique to each person and can change over time, just as values change over a lifetime.[17]

Learned Needs Theory

Earlier in this chapter we said that drives (primary needs) are innate whereas needs are shaped, amplified, or suppressed through self-concept, social norms, and past experience. Maslow noted that individual characteristics influence the strength of "social needs." However, psychologist David McClelland further pushed this idea that need strength can be altered through social influences.

McClelland examined three of these "learned" needs.[18] People with a strong *need for achievement (nAch)* value competition against a standard of excellence; they want to accomplish reasonably challenging goals through their own effort. *Need for affiliation (nAff)* refers to a desire to seek approval from others, conform to their wishes and expectations, and avoid conflict and confrontation. People with a high *need for power (nPow)* want to exercise control over others and are concerned about maintaining their leadership position. Those who enjoy their power to advance personal interests have *personalized power*. Others mainly have a high need for *socialized power* because they desire power as a means to help others. Effective leaders have a high need for socialized rather than personalized power.

McClelland's research supported his theory that needs can be learned (more accurately, strengthened or weakened). In particular, he developed achievement motivation training programs in which trainees wrote achievement-oriented stories, practiced achievement-oriented behaviors in business games, and completed a detailed achievement plan for the next two years.[19] These programs apparently strengthened the need for achievement in most participants.

Four-Drive Theory

One of the central messages of this chapter is that emotions play a central role in employee motivation. This view is supported by a groundswell of research in neuroscience, but is almost completely absent from contemporary motivation theories in organizational behavior. Also, social scientists in several fields (psychology, anthropology, etc.) increasingly agree that human beings have several hardwired drives, including social interaction, learning, and dominance. One of the few theories to apply this emerging knowledge is **four-drive theory**.[20] Developed by Harvard Business School professors Paul Lawrence and Nitin Nohria, four-drive theory states that everyone has the drive to acquire, bond, learn, and defend:

> **FOUR-DRIVE THEORY:** a motivation theory based on the innate drives to acquire, bond, learn, and defend that incorporates both emotions and rationality

- *Drive to acquire.* This is the drive to seek, take, control, and retain objects and personal experiences. The drive to acquire extends beyond basic food and water; it includes enhancing one's self-concept through relative status and recognition in society.[21] Thus, it is the foundation of competition and the basis of our need for esteem.

- *Drive to bond.* This is the drive to form social relationships and develop mutual caring commitments with others. It also explains why people form social identities by aligning their self-image with various social groups (see Chapter 2). It may also explain why people who lack social contact are more prone to serious health problems.[22] The drive to bond motivates people to cooperate and, consequently, is a fundamental ingredient in the success of organizations and the development of societies.

- *Drive to learn.* This is the drive to satisfy our curiosity, to know and understand ourselves and the environment around us.[23] When observing something that is inconsistent with or beyond our current knowledge, we experience a tension that motivates us to close that information gap.

- *Drive to defend.* This is the drive to protect ourselves physically and socially. Probably the first drive to develop, it creates a "fight-or-flight" response in the face of personal danger. The drive to defend goes beyond protecting our physical self. It includes defending our relationships, our acquisitions, and our belief systems.

These four drives are innate and universal, meaning that they are hardwired in our brains through evolution and are found in all human beings. They are also independent of each other. There is no hierarchy of drives, so one drive is neither dependent on nor inherently inferior or superior to another drive. Four-drive theory also states that these four drives are a complete set—there are no other fundamental drives excluded from the model. Another key feature is that three of the four drives are "proactive"—we regularly try to fulfill them. Only the drive to defend is reactive. Thus, any notion of fulfilling drives is temporary, at best.

How Drives Influence Employee Motivation

In addition to identifying a list of core drives, four-drive theory draws from current neuroscience knowledge to explain how drives translate into goal-directed effort. To begin with, recall from previous chapters that every meaningful bit of information we receive is quickly and nonconsciously tagged with emotional markers that subsequently shape our logical analysis of the situation.[24] According to four-drive theory, these four drives determine which emotions are tagged to incoming stimuli. Suppose your department has just received

[Exhibit 5.2] Four-Drive Theory of Motivation

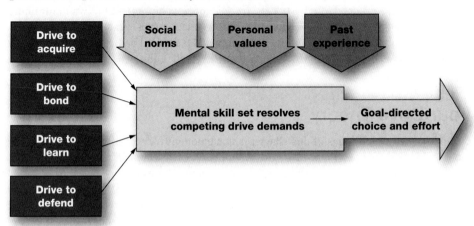

Source: Based on information in P. R. Lawrence and N. Nohria. *Driven: How Human Nature Shapes Our Choices.* (San Francisco: Jossey-Bass, 2002).

a new computer program that you are curious to try out (triggered by your drive to learn). However, your boss says that you are not experienced enough to use the new system yet, which makes you somewhat angry (triggered by your drive to defend against the "inexperience" insult). Both the curiosity about the software program and your anger from the boss's beliefs about your experience demand your attention and energize you to act.

Four-drive theory states that competing drives (i.e. conflicting emotions) demand our attention, which causes us to choose a course of action based on our social norms, past experience, and personal values (see Exhibit 5.2). In other words, our conscious analysis of competing demands from the four drives generates needs that energize us to act in ways acceptable to society and our own moral compass.[25]

Evaluating Four-Drive Theory

Although four-drive theory was introduced very recently, it is based on a deep foundation of research that dates back more than three decades. The drives have been identified from psychological and anthropological studies. The translation of drives into goal-directed behavior originates from considerable research on emotions and neural processes. The theory avoids the assumption that everyone has the same needs hierarchy, and explains why needs vary from one person to the next. Notice, too, that four-drive theory is both holistic (it integrates several drives) and humanistic (it acknowledges the role of human thought and social influences rather than just instinct). Maslow had identified these two principles as important features of a motivation theory. Four-drive theory also provides a much clearer understanding about the role of emotional intelligence in employee motivation and behavior. Employees with high emotional intelligence are more sensitive to competing demands from the four drives, are better able to avoid impulsive behavior from those drives, and can judge the best way to act to fulfill those drive demands in a social context.

Even with its well-researched foundations, four-drive theory is far from complete. First, most experts would question one or more of the drives identified in the theory, typically pointing to one or two others that should be included. Second, social norms, personal values, and past experience probably don't represent the full set of individual characteristics that translate emotions into goal-directed effort. For example, other elements of self-concept beyond personal values, such as personality and social identity, likely play a significant role.

Sony Suffers from Lack of Four-Drive Balance
According to four-drive theory, companies that help employees fulfill one drive much more than the others will face long-term problems. This seems to explain the current challenges facing Sony. The Japanese company, which led the electronics world a decade ago with its Walkman and Playstation innovations, is now struggling to keep up with competitors. One reason for the current difficulties is that Sony executives allowed a hypercompetitive culture to develop where engineers were encouraged to outdo each other rather than work together. This competitive culture fed employees' drive to acquire, but the lack of balance with the drive to bond led to infighting and information hoarding. For instance, competitive rivalries within Sony delayed the company's launch of a digital music player and online music service to compete against Apple's iPod and iTunes music Web site.[26]

Practical Implications of Four-Drive Theory

The main recommendation from four-drive theory is to ensure that individual jobs and workplaces provide a balanced opportunity to fulfill the drive to acquire, bond, learn, and defend.[27] There are really two key recommendations here. The first one is that everyone continuously seeks fulfillment of their innate drives. Thus, the best workplaces for motivation and morale provide sufficient rewards, learning opportunities, social interaction, and so forth for all employees. The second recommendation is that these four drives must be kept in "balance"; that is, organizations should avoid too much or too little opportunity to fulfill each drive. The reason for this advice is that the four drives counterbalance each other. An organization that energizes the drive to acquire without the drive to bond may eventually suffer from organizational politics and dysfunctional conflict. Change and novelty in the workplace will aid the drive to learn, but too much of it will trigger the drive to defend to such an extent that employees become territorial and resistant to change. Thus, the workplace should offer enough opportunity to keep all four drives in balance.

After reading the next three sections, you should be able to: **learning**objectives<

5. *Diagram the expectancy theory model and discuss its practical implications for motivating employees.*

6. *Describe the characteristics of effective goal setting and feedback.*

7. *Summarize equity theory and describe how to improve procedural justice.*

>Expectancy Theory of Motivation

EXPECTANCY THEORY:
a motivation theory based on the idea that work effort is directed towards behaviors that people believe will lead to desired outcomes

The theories described so far mainly explain the internal origins of employee motivation. But how do these drives and needs translate into specific effort and behavior? One of the best theories to answer this question is expectancy theory of motivation. **Expectancy theory** is based on the idea that work effort is directed toward behaviors that people believe will lead to desired outcomes.[28] As illustrated in Exhibit 5.3, an individual's effort level depends on three factors: effort-to-performance (E-to-P) expectancy, performance-to-outcome (P-to-O) expectancy, and outcome valences (V). Employee motivation is influenced by all three components of the expectancy theory model. If any component weakens, motivation weakens.

- *E-to-P expectancy.* This refers to the individual's perception that his or her effort will result in a particular level of performance. In some situations, employees may believe that they can unquestionably accomplish the task (a probability of 1.0). In other situations, they expect that even their highest level of effort will not result in the desired performance level (a probability of 0.0). In most cases, the E-to-P expectancy falls somewhere between these two extremes.

- *P-to-O expectancy.* This is the perceived probability that a specific behavior or performance level will lead to particular outcomes. In extreme cases, employees may believe that accomplishing a particular task (performance) will definitely result in a particular outcome (a probability of 1.0), or they may believe that this outcome will have no effect on successful performance (a probability of 0.0). More often, the P-to-O expectancy falls somewhere between these two extremes.

- *Outcome valences.* A valence is the anticipated satisfaction or dissatisfaction that an individual feels toward an outcome. It ranges from negative to positive. (The actual range doesn't matter; it may be from -1 to $+1$, or from -100 to $+100$.) An outcome valence represents a person's anticipated satisfaction with the outcome.[29] Outcomes have a positive valence when they are consistent with our values and satisfy our needs; they have a negative valence when they oppose our values and inhibit need fulfillment.

[**Exhibit 5.3**] Expectancy Theory of Motivation

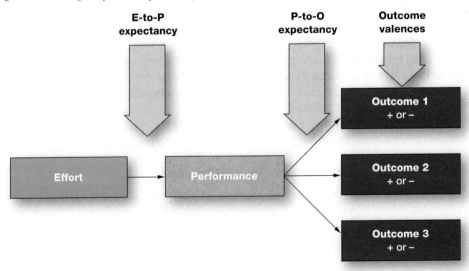

Expectancy Theory in Practice

One of the appealing characteristics of expectancy theory is that it provides clear guidelines for increasing employee motivation.[30] Here are some of the main recommendations for each of the theory's three components:

Increasing E-to-P Expectancies

E-to-P expectancies can increase by assuring employees that they have the necessary competencies, clear role perceptions, and necessary resources to reach the desired levels of performance. Matching employees to jobs based on their abilities and clearly communicating the tasks required for the job is an important part of this process. Similarly, E-to-P expectancies are learned, so behavioral modeling and supportive feedback (positive reinforcement) typically strengthen employee self-confidence.

Increasing P-to-O Expectancies

The most obvious ways to improve P-to-O expectancies are to measure employee performance accurately and distribute more valued rewards to those with higher job performance. P-to-O expectancies are perceptions, so employees need to know how higher performance will result in higher rewards. This occurs by explaining how specific rewards are connected to specific past performance, and by using examples, anecdotes, and public ceremonies to illustrate when behavior has been rewarded.

Increasing Outcome Valences

Everyone has unique values and experiences, which translates into different needs at different times. Consequently, individualizing rather than standardizing rewards and other performance outcomes is an important ingredient in employee motivation. At the same time, leaders need to watch out for countervalent outcomes—consequences with negative valences that reduce rather than enhance employee motivation. For example, peer pressure may cause some employees to perform their jobs at the minimum standard even though formal rewards and the job itself would otherwise motivate them to perform at higher levels.

Overall, expectancy theory is a useful model that explains how people rationally figure out the best direction, intensity, and persistence of effort. It has been tested in a variety of situations and predicts employee motivation in different cultures.[31] However, critics have a number of concerns with how the theory has been tested. Another concern is that expectancy theory ignores the central role of emotion in employee effort and behavior. The valence element of expectancy theory captures some of this emotional process, but only peripherally.[32]

>Goal Setting and Feedback

Goal setting is the process of motivating employees and clarifying their role perceptions by establishing performance objectives. It potentially improves employee performance in two ways: (1) by stretching the intensity and persistence of effort and (2) by giving employees clearer role perceptions so that their effort is channeled toward behaviors that will improve work performance. Goal setting is more complex than simply telling someone to "do your best." Instead, it requires six conditions to maximize task effort and performance: specific goals, relevant goals, challenging goals, goal commitment, participation in goal formation (sometimes), and goal feedback.[33]

GOAL SETTING: the process of motivating employees and clarifying their role perceptions by establishing performance objectives

- *Specific goals.* Employees put more effort into a task when they work toward specific goals rather than "do your best" targets. Specific goals have measurable levels of change over a specific and relatively short time frame, such as "reduce scrap rate by 7 percent over the next six months."

- *Relevant goals.* Goals must also be relevant to the individual's job and within his or her control. For example, a goal to reduce waste materials would have little value if employees don't have much control over waste in the production process.

- *Challenging goals.* Challenging goals (rather than easy ones) cause people to raise the intensity and persistence of their work effort and to think through information more actively. They also fulfill a person's achievement or growth needs when the goal is achieved.

- *Goal commitment.* Ideally goals should be challenging without being so difficult that employees lose their motivation to achieve them.[34] This is the same as the E-to-P expectancy that we learned about in the section on expectancy theory. The lower the E-to-P expectancy that the goal can be accomplished, the less committed (motivated) the employee is to the goal.

- *Goal participation* (sometimes). Goal setting is usually (but not always) more effective when employees participate in setting goals.[35] Participation potentially increases goal commitment compared to goals set alone by the supervisor. Participation may also improve goal quality, because employees have valuable information and knowledge that may not be known to those who initially formed the goal.

- *Goal feedback.* Feedback is another necessary condition for effective goal setting.[36] Feedback is any information that lets us know whether we have achieved the goal or are properly directing our effort toward it. Feedback redirects our effort, but it potentially also fulfills our growth needs. Feedback is so central to goal setting that we will look more closely at it next.

Characteristics of Effective Feedback

Whirlpool Corp. employees complained they weren't getting enough feedback from their bosses, so the appliance manufacturer asked managers to meet with their immediate subordinates quarterly rather than the previous schedule of every six months. Jeffrey Davidoff, head of marketing for Whirlpool's North American consumer brands, has taken the feedback frequency even further; he meets with his eight direct reports for up to 45 minutes every two weeks. "I'm noticing much better results," Mr. Davidoff says.[37]

As Whirlpool managers are learning, feedback is a potentially important practice in employee motivation and performance. In addition to clarifying role perceptions and improving employee skills and knowledge, feedback motivates when it is constructive and when employees have a strong self-efficacy.[38] As with goal setting, feedback should be *specific* and *relevant*. It should also be *timely* —available as soon as possible after the behavior or results so employees see a clear association between their actions and the consequences. Feedback should also be *sufficiently frequent*. New employees require more frequent feedback to aid their learning. Some jobs (e.g., executives) necessarily have less frequent feedback because the consequences of their actions take longer than in, say, a cashier's job. Finally, feedback should be *credible,* such as from people with no vested interest or from reliable monitoring devices.

Goal setting represents one of the "tried and true" theories in organizational behavior, so much so that a recent survey of professors identified it as one of the top OB theories in terms of validity and usefulness.[39] In partnership with goal setting, feedback also has an excellent reputation for improving employee motivation and performance. At the same time, putting goal setting into practice is far from perfect.[40] One

Executive Feedback Drives Through the Dashboard

Corporate intranets now allow many executives to receive feedback instantaneously on their computer, usually in the form of graphic output on an executive dashboard. Verizon CIO Shaygan Kheradpir (shown here) appreciates the instant feedback provided by his dashboard, which is a huge plasma screen on the wall of his office. Called the "Wall of Shaygan," the screen displays the status of more than 100 network systems around the country in green, yellow, or red lights. Another part of the screen also shows sales, voice portal volumes, call center results, and other business metrics.[41]

concern is that goal setting tends to focus employees on a narrow subset of measurable performance indicators while ignoring aspects of job performance that are difficult to measure. The saying, "What gets measured, gets done" applies here. A second problem is that when tied to financial rewards, many employees are motivated to make their goals easy (while making the boss think they are difficult) so they have a higher probability of the bonus or pay increase. As a former chief executive at Ford once quipped: "At Ford, we hire very smart people. They quickly learn how to make relatively easy goals look difficult!"[42] A third problem is that setting performance goals is effective in established jobs, but seems to interfere with the learning process in new, complex jobs. Thus, we need to be careful not to apply goal setting where an intense learning process is occurring.

>Organizational Justice

Most corporate leaders know that treating employees fairly is both morally correct and good for employee motivation, loyalty, and well-being. Yet, feelings of injustice are regular occurrences in the workplace. To minimize these incidents, we need to first understand that there are two forms of organizational justice: distributive justice and procedural justice.[43] **Distributive justice** refers to perceived fairness in the outcomes we receive relative to our contributions and the outcomes and contributions of others. **Procedural justice,** on the other hand, refers to perceived fairness of the procedures used to allocate resources as well as treatment of others throughout that exchange process.

Equity Theory

What is considered "fair" varies with each person and situation, but one theory that helps to understand this concept is **equity theory.**[44] According to this theory, feelings of equity or inequity occur when employees compare their own outcome/input ratio to the outcome/input ratio of some other person. The outcome/input ratio is the value of the outcomes you receive divided by the value of inputs you provide in the exchange relationship. Inputs include such things as skill, effort, reputation, performance, experience, and hours worked. Outcomes are what employees receive from the organization in exchange for the inputs, such as pay, promotions, recognition, preferential treatment, or preferred jobs in the future.

DISTRIBUTIVE JUSTICE: perceived fairness in the outcomes we receive relative to our contributions and the outcomes and contributions of others

PROCEDURAL JUSTICE: perceived fairness of the procedures used to allocate resources as well as treatment of others throughout that exchange process

EQUITY THEORY: a theory that explains how people develop perceptions of fairness in the distribution and exchange of resources

Equity theory states that we compare our outcome/input ratio with a *comparison other*.[45] The comparison other may be another person or group of people in the same job, another job, or another organization. Some research suggests that employees frequently collect information on several referents to form a "generalized" comparison other.[46] For the most part, however, the comparison other varies from one person to the next and is not easily identifiable.

People develop feelings of equity or inequity by comparing their own outcome/input ratio with the comparison other's ratio. In the equity condition, people believe that their outcome/input ratio is similar to the ratio of the comparison other. People experience underreward inequity when they believe their ratio is lower than the comparison other's ratio. Overreward inequity occurs when people believe their ratio of outcomes/inputs is higher than the comparison other's ratio. However, overreward inequity isn't as common as underreward inequity because people change their perceptions to justify the higher outcomes.

Inequity and Employee Motivation

How does the equity evaluation relate to employee motivation? The answer is that feelings of inequity generate negative emotions and, as we have pointed out throughout this chapter, emotions are the engines of motivation. In the case of inequity, people are motivated to reduce the emotional tension. Here are the main ways that people correct inequity feelings when they are underrewarded compared to a co-worker (comparison other):[47]

- *Reduce our inputs*. Perform at a lower level, give fewer helpful suggestions, engage in less organizational citizenship behavior.

- *Increase our outcomes*. Ask for a pay increase, make unauthorized use of company resources.

- *Increase the comparison other's inputs*. Subtly ask the better off co-worker to do a larger share of the work to justify his/her higher pay or other outcomes.

- *Reduce comparison other's outcomes*. Ask the boss to stop giving favorable treatment to the co-worker.

- *Change our perceptions*. Believe the co-worker really is doing more (e.g., working longer hours), or that the higher outcomes (e.g., better office) he/she receives really aren't so much better than what you get.

- *Change the comparison other*. Compare yourself to someone else closer to your situation (job duties, pay scale).

- *Leave the field*. Avoid thinking about the inequity by keeping away from the office where the co-worker is located, taking more sick leave, moving to another department, or quitting the job.

Although the categories remain the same, people who feel overreward inequity would, of course, act differently. For example, overrewarded employees don't usually reduce the inequity tension by working harder. Instead, they might encourage the co-worker to work at a more leisurely pace or, equally likely, change their perceptions to justify why they are given more favorable outcomes.

Evaluating Equity Theory

Equity theory is widely studied and quite successful at predicting various situations involving feelings of workplace injustice.[48] However, equity theory isn't so easy to put into practice because it doesn't identify the "comparison other" and doesn't indicate which inputs or outcomes are most valuable to each employee. The best solution here is for leaders to know their employees well enough to minimize the risk of inequity feelings. Open communication is also the key, so employees can let decision makers know when they feel their decisions are unfair. A second problem is that equity theory accounts for only some of our feelings of fairness or justice in the workplace. Experts now say that procedural justice is at least as important as distributive justice.

Procedural Justice

Recall that procedural justice refers to perceived fairness of the resource allocation procedures and treatment of others throughout that process. How do companies improve procedural fairness?[49] A good place to start is by giving employees "voice" in the process; encourage them to present their facts and perspectives on the issue. It is also important that the decision maker is unbiased, relies on complete and accurate information, applies existing policies consistently, and has listened to all sides of the dispute. If employees still feel unfairness in the allocation of resources, these feelings tend to weaken if the company has a way of appealing the decision to a higher authority. Finally, people usually feel better when they are treated with respect and are given a full explanation of the decision. If employees believe a decision is unfair, refusing to explain how the decision was made could fuel those feelings of inequity.

After reading the next two sections, you should be able to:

learningobjectives<

8. *Diagram the job characteristics model of job design and use its elements to explain how to improve motivation through job enrichment.*

9. *Define empowerment and identify strategies to support empowerment.*

>Job Design

How do you build a better job? That question has challenged organizational behavior experts as well as psychologists, engineers, and economists for a few centuries. Some jobs have very few tasks and usually require very little skill. Other jobs are immensely complex and require years of learning to master them. From one extreme to the other, jobs have different effects on work efficiency and employee motivation. The challenge, at least from the organization's perspective, is to find the right combination so work is performed efficiently but employees are motivated and engaged.[50] This challenge requires careful **job design**—the process of assigning tasks to a job, including the interdependency of those tasks with other jobs. To understand how jobs affect motivation and performance, let's begin by describing early job design efforts aimed at increasing work efficiency through job specialization.

> **JOB DESIGN:** the process of assigning tasks to a job, including the interdependency of those tasks with other jobs

Job Design and Work Efficiency

Throughout the first half of the 20th century, industry experts and academics spent a lot of time figuring out how to increase employee performance by dividing work into narrower tasks. This **job specialization** is a widespread practice even today. For example, Chrysler's assembly line employees current have an average job cycle of about 64.5 seconds, which means that they repeat the same set of tasks about 58 times each hour and about 230 times before they take a meal break.[51] Some call centers also rely on job specialization; employees repeat the same structured dialogue and are assigned to a limited number of customer issues.[52]

> **JOB SPECIALIZATION:** the result of division of labor in which each job includes a subset of the tasks required to complete the product or service

Why would companies divide work into such tiny bits? The simple answer is that job specialization improves work efficiency. Job specialization potentially increases work efficiency because employees have fewer tasks to juggle and therefore spend less time changing activities. They also require fewer physical and mental skills to accomplish the assigned work, so less time and resources are needed for training. A third reason is that employees practice their tasks more frequently with shorter work cycles, so jobs are mastered quickly. A fourth reason why work efficiency increases is that employees with specific aptitudes or skills can be matched more precisely to the jobs for which they are best suited.[53]

One of the strongest advocates of job specialization was Frederick Winslow Taylor, an American industrial engineer who introduced the principles of **scientific management** in the early 1900s.[54] According to Taylor, the most effective companies have detailed procedures and work practices developed by engineers, enforced by supervisors, and executed by employees. Taylor and other industrial engineers demonstrated that scientific management significantly improves work efficiency. No doubt, some of the increased productivity can be credited to the training, goal setting, and work incentives, but job specialization quickly became popular in its own right.

SCIENTIFIC MANAGEMENT: systematically partitioning work into its smallest elements and standardizing tasks to achieve maximum efficiency

Problems with Job Specialization

Frederick Taylor and his contemporaries focused on how job specialization reduces labor "waste" by improving the mechanical efficiency of work (i.e. matching skills, faster learning, less switch-over time). Yet, they didn't seem to notice how this extreme job specialization made jobs tedious, trivial, and socially isolating. Employee turnover and absenteeism tends to be higher in specialized jobs with very short time cycles. Job specialization often reduces work quality because employees see only a small part of the process.[55]

Job Design and Work Motivation

JOB CHARACTERISTICS MODEL: a job design model that relates the motivational properties of jobs to specific personal and organizational consequences of those properties

Industrial engineers may have overlooked the motivational effect of job characteristics, but it is now the central focus of many job design changes. This motivational perspective is nicely laid out in the **job characteristics model,** shown in Exhibit 5.4.[56] All jobs can be examined in terms of five core dimensions and, under the right conditions, employees are more motivated and satisfied when jobs have higher levels of these characteristics.

SKILL VARIETY: the extent to which employees must use different skills and talents to perform tasks within their job

- *Skill variety.* **Skill variety** refers to the use of different skills and talents to complete a variety of work activities. For example, sales clerks who normally only serve customers might be assigned the additional duties of stocking inventory and changing storefront displays.
- *Task identity.* **Task identity** is the degree to which a job requires completion of a whole or identifiable piece of work, such as assembling an entire broadband modem rather than just soldering in the circuitry.
- *Task significance.* **Task significance** is the degree to which the job affects the organization and/or larger society.
- *Autonomy.* Jobs with high levels of autonomy provide freedom, independence, and discretion in scheduling the work and determining the procedures to be used to complete the work. In autonomous jobs, employees make their own decisions rather than relying on detailed instructions from supervisors or procedure manuals.
- *Job feedback.* Job feedback is the degree to which employees can tell how well they are doing based on direct sensory information from the job itself. Airline pilots can tell how well they land their aircraft and road crews can see how well they have prepared the road bed and laid the asphalt.

TASK IDENTITY: the degree to which a job requires completion of a whole or an identifiable piece of work

TASK SIGNIFICANCE: the degree to which the job has a substantial impact on the organization and/or larger society

These five core job characteristics affect employee motivation and satisfaction through three critical psychological states. Skill variety, task identity, and task significance directly influence the job's *experienced meaningfulness*—the belief that one's work is worthwhile

[Exhibit 5.4] The Job Characteristics Model

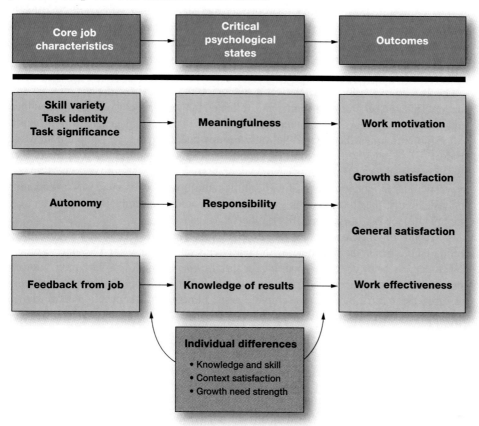

Source: J. R. Hackman and G. Oldham, *Work Redesign* (Pearson Education, Inc., Upper Saddle River, NJ., © 1980), p. 90. Electronically reproduced with permission.

or important. Autonomy directly contributes to *experienced responsibility*—where employees feel personally accountable for the outcomes of their efforts. Job feedback affects the third critical psychological state, *knowledge of results.*

Individual Differences

Job design doesn't increase work motivation for everyone in every situation. Employees must have the required skills and knowledge to master the more challenging work. Otherwise, job design tends to increase stress and reduce job performance. The original model also suggests that creating motivating jobs will not motivate employees who are dissatisfied with their work context (e.g., working conditions, job security) or who have a low-growth need strength. However, research findings have been mixed, suggesting that employees might be motivated by job design no matter how they feel about their job context or how high or low they score on growth needs.[57]

Job Enrichment

The job characteristics model is a good template for figuring out how to motivate employees through job redesign. However, OB experts now believe that some of these five dimensions have a stronger effect than others on employee motivation. For instance, simply adding more tasks to a job (i.e., increasing skill variety alone) doesn't motivate employees much. Instead, the evidence points to autonomy as the core dimension to consider when trying to enrich the motivational potential of jobs.[58]

JOB ENRICHMENT: occurs when employees are given more responsibility for scheduling, coordinating and planning their own work

Autonomy is at the heart of **job enrichment,** which occurs when employees are given more responsibility for scheduling, coordinating, and planning their own work.[59] Generally, people in enriched jobs experience higher job satisfaction and work motivation, along with lower absenteeism and turnover. Product and service quality tend to improve because job enrichment increases the jobholder's felt responsibility and sense of ownership over the product or service.[60]

One way to increase job enrichment is by combining highly interdependent tasks into one job. This *natural grouping* approach is reflected in the video journalist job. Video journalist combines the tasks of a camera operator, sound engineer, and narrator. It is an example of job enrichment because it naturally groups tasks together to complete an entire product (i.e., a news clip). By forming natural work units, jobholders have stronger feelings of responsibility for an identifiable body of work. They feel a sense of ownership and, therefore, tend to increase job quality. Forming natural work units increases task identity and task significance because employees perform a complete product or service and can more readily see how their work affects others.

A second job enrichment strategy, called *establishing client relationships,* involves putting employees in direct contact with their clients rather than using the supervisor as a go-between. By being directly responsible for specific clients, employees have more information and can make decisions affecting those clients.[61] Establishing client relationships also increases task significance because employees see a line-of-sight connection between their work and consequences for customers.

>Empowerment Practices

A large American hotel had a policy that if a guest questioned his/her bill, front-desk staff were supposed to defend the bill no matter what. If the guest asked to speak with the manager, the manager would override the charge. The hotel manager thought this "good cop, bad cop" approach was useful, but Rick Garlick, a consultant hired by the hotel, suggested that they immediately change the policy. Instead, front-desk staff should have the autonomy to decide alone whether the complaint was justified. The result? Within a few months, the hotel's guest satisfaction scores soared from near the bottom to near the top among hotels in the company's chain. "Empowering employees was one of a number of key improvements in manager-staff relations that ultimately resulted in much higher guest satisfaction," says Garlick.[62]

EMPOWERMENT: a psychological concept in which people experience more self-determination, meaning, competence and impact regarding their role in the organization

Empowerment is a term that has been loosely tossed around in corporate circles and has been the subject of considerable debate among academics.[63] However, the most widely accepted definition is that empowerment is represented by four dimensions: self-determination, meaning, competence, and impact of the individual's role in the organization.[64]

- *Self-determination.* Empowered employees feel that they have freedom, independence, and discretion over their work activities.

- *Meaning.* Employees who feel empowered care about their work and believe that what they do is important.

- *Competence.* Empowered people are confident about their ability to perform the work well and have a capacity to grow with new challenges.

- *Impact.* Empowered employees view themselves as active participants in the organization; that is, their decisions and actions have an influence on the company's success.

Supporting Empowerment

Chances are that you have heard corporate leaders say they are "empowering" the workforce. What these executives really mean is that they are changing the work environment to support empowerment.[65] Numerous individual, job design, and organizational or work context factors support empowerment. At the individual level, employees must possess the necessary competencies to be able to perform the work as well as handle the additional decision-making requirements.[66]

Job characteristics strongly influence the dynamics of empowerment.[67] To generate beliefs about self-determination, employees must work in jobs with a high degree of autonomy with minimal bureaucratic control. To maintain a sense of meaningfulness, jobs must have high levels of task identity and task significance. And to maintain a sense of self-confidence, jobs must provide sufficient feedback.

Several organizational and work context factors also influence empowerment. Employees experience more empowerment in organizations where information and other resources are easily accessible. Empowerment also requires a *learning orientation* culture, where employee learning is encouraged and reasonable mistakes are viewed as a natural part of the learning process. Furthermore, empowerment requires corporate leaders who trust employees and are willing to take the risks that empowerment creates.[68]

With the right individuals, job characteristics, and organizational environment, empowerment can have a noticeable effect on motivation and performance. For instance, a study of bank employees concluded that empowerment improved customer service and tended to reduce conflict between employees and their supervisors. Other research links empowerment with higher trust in management, which ultimately influences job satisfaction, belief and acceptance of organizational goals and values, and organizational commitment. Empowerment also tends to increase personal initiative because employees identify with and assume more psychological ownership of their work.[69]

Kambuku Empowerment

A few years ago, Pretoria Portland Cement (PPC) was a top-down, autocratic organization where managers gave "oodles of supervision and checking that people do the right things," recalls PPC chief executive John Gomersall. Now, under an initiative called *Kambuku* (named after one of Africa's largest tusked elephants), PPC has "passed the ownership to the people." Departments and teams are given much more autonomy. Company leaders seek out employee ideas, offer continuous training, and reward teams and individuals for their performance. The result has been a dramatic increase in employee morale and empowerment. Chief operating officer Orrie Fenn explains the transformation: "Empowered employees ensure a committed workforce, which eventually translates into sustainable business performance."[70]

>Chapter Summary

Motivation refers to the forces within a person that affect his or her direction, intensity, and persistence of voluntary behavior in the workplace. Drives (also called primary needs) are neural states that energize individuals to correct deficiencies or maintain an internal equilibrium. They are the "prime movers" of behavior by activating emotions, which put us in a state of readiness to act. Needs—goal-directed forces that people experience—are shaped by the individual's self-concept (including personality and values), social norms, and past experience.

Maslow's needs hierarchy groups needs into a hierarchy of five levels and states that the lowest needs are initially most important, but higher needs become more important as the lower ones are satisfied. Although very popular, the theory lacks research support, as does ERG theory, which attempted to overcome some of the limitations in Maslow's needs hierarchy. Both models assume that everyone has the same hierarchy, whereas the emerging evidence suggests that needs hierarchies vary from one person to the next based on their personal values.

McClelland's learned needs theory argues that needs can be strengthened through learning. The three needs studied in this respect have been need for achievement, need for power, and need for affiliation. Four-drive theory states that everyone has four innate drives—the drive to acquire, bond, learn, and defend. These drives activate emotions that we regulate through a skill set that considers social norms, past experience, and personal values. The main recommendation from four-drive theory is to ensure that individual jobs and workplaces provide a balanced opportunity to fulfill the four drives.

Expectancy theory states that work effort is determined by the perception that effort will result in a particular level of performance (E-to-P expectancy), the perception that a specific behavior or performance level will lead to specific outcomes (P-to-O expectancy), and the valences that the person feels for those outcomes. The E-to-P expectancy increases by improving the employee's ability and confidence to perform the job. The P-to-O expectancy increases by measuring performance accurately, distributing higher rewards to better performers, and showing employees that rewards are performance-based. Outcome valences increase by finding out what employees want and using these resources as rewards.

Goal setting is the process of motivating employees and clarifying their role perceptions by establishing performance objectives. Goals are more effective when they are specific, relevant, and challenging; have employee commitment; and are accompanied by meaningful feedback. Participative goal setting is important in some situations. Effective feedback is specific, relevant, timely, credible, and sufficiently frequent.

Organizational justice consists of distributive justice (perceived fairness in the outcomes we receive relative to our contributions and the outcomes and contributions of others) and procedural justice (fairness of the procedures used to decide the distribution of resources). Equity theory has four elements: outcome/input ratio, comparison other, equity evaluation, and consequences of inequity. The theory also explains what people are motivated to do when they feel inequitably treated. Along with equity of the distribution of resources, companies need to consider fairness in the process of making resource allocation decisions.

Job design refers to the process of assigning tasks to a job, including the interdependency of those tasks with other jobs. Job specialization subdivides work into separate jobs for different people. This increases work efficiency but may also have adverse effects on job performance. The job characteristics model is a template for job redesign that specifies core job dimensions, psychological states, and individual differences. Two ways to enrich jobs are clustering tasks into natural groups and establishing client relationships.

Empowerment is a psychological concept represented by four dimensions: self-determination, meaning, competence, and impact regarding the individual's role in the organization. Job design is a major influence on empowerment, particularly autonomy, task identity, task significance, and job feedback. Empowerment is also supported at the organizational level through a learning orientation culture, sufficient information and resources, and corporate leaders who trust employees.

>**key** terms

distributive justice 101	goal setting 99	needs 92
drives 92	job characteristics model 104	positive organizational behavior 94
empowerment 106	job design 103	procedural justice 101
equity theory 101	job enrichment 106	scientific management 104
ERG theory 94	job specialization 103	skill variety 104
expectancy theory 98	Maslow's needs hierarchy theory 93	task identity 104
four-drive theory 95	motivation 91	task significance 104

>**critical thinking** questions

1. Four-drive theory is conceptually different from the Maslow's needs hierarchy theory (as well as ERG theory) in several ways. Describe these differences. At the same time, needs are based on drives, so the four drives should parallel the seven needs that Maslow identified (five in the hierarchy and two additional needs). Map Maslow's needs onto the four drives in four-drive theory.

2. Use all three components of expectancy theory to explain why some employees are motivated to show up for work during a severe storm whereas others make no effort to leave their home.

3. Two friends who have just completed an organizational behavior course at another college inform you that employees must fulfill their need for self-esteem and social esteem before they can reach their full potential through self-actualization. What theory are these friends referring to? How does this statement differ from what you learned about that theory in this textbook?

4. Using your knowledge of the characteristics of effective goals, establish two meaningful goals related to your performance in this class.

5. Several service representatives are upset that the newly hired representative with no previous experience will be paid $3,000 a year above the usual starting salary in the pay range. The department manager explained that the new hire would not accept the entry-level rate, so the company raised the offer by $3,000. All five reps currently earn salaries near the top of the scale ($15,000 higher than the new recruit), although they all started at the minimum starting salary a few years earlier. Use equity theory to explain why the five service representatives feel inequity in this situation.

6. Organizational injustice can occur in the classroom as well as in the workplace. Identify classroom situations in which you experienced feelings of injustice. What can instructors do to maintain an environment that fosters both distributive and procedural justice?

7. Most of us have watched pizzas being made while waiting in a pizzeria. What level of job specialization do you usually notice in these operations? Why does this high or low level of specialization exist? If some pizzerias have different levels of specialization than others, identify the contingencies that might explain these differences.

8. Can a manager or supervisor "empower" an employee? Discuss fully.

>team exercise 5-1

Needs Priority Exercise

Purpose   This class exercise is designed to help you understand the characteristics and contingencies of employee needs in the workplace.

Instructions

• *Step 1:* The table below lists in alphabetical order 14 characteristics of the job or work environment. Working alone, use the far left column to rank order these characteristics in terms of how important they are to you personally. Write in "1" beside the most important characteristic,

"2" for the second most important, and so on through to "14" for the least important characteristic on this list.

• *Step 2:* In the second column, rank order these characteristics in the order that you think Human Resource managers believe are important for their employees.

• *Step 3:* Your instructor will provide results of a recent large-scale survey of employees. When these results are presented, identify the reasons for any noticeable differences. Relate these differences to your understanding of the emerging view of employee needs and drives in work settings.

Importance to You	What HR Managers Believe Are Important to Employees	
_____	_____	Autonomy and independence
_____	_____	Benefits (health care, dental, etc.)
_____	_____	Career development opportunities
_____	_____	Communication between employees and senior mgmt
_____	_____	Compensation/pay
_____	_____	Feeling safe in the work environment
_____	_____	Flexibility to balance work/life issues
_____	_____	Job security
_____	_____	Job specific training
_____	_____	Management recognition of employee job performance
_____	_____	Opportunities to use skills/abilities
_____	_____	Organization's commitment to professional development
_____	_____	Relationship with immediate supervisor
_____	_____	The work itself

>team exercise 5-2

A Question of Feedback

Purpose   This exercise is designed to help you understand the importance of feedback, including problems that occur with imperfect communication in the feedback process.

Materials   The instructor will distribute a few pages of exhibits to one person on each team. The other students will require a pencil with eraser and blank paper. Movable chairs and tables in a large area are helpful.

Instructions

• *Step 1:* The class is divided into pairs of students. Each pair is ideally located in a private area, away from other students and where one person can write. One student is given the pages of exhibits from the instructor. The other student in each pair is not allowed to see these exhibits.

• *Step 2:* The student holding the materials will describe each of the exhibits and the other student's task is to accurately replicate each exhibit. The pair of students can compare the replication with the original at the end of each drawing. They may also switch roles for each exhibit, if they wish. If roles are switched, the instructor must distribute exhibits separately to each student so that they are not seen by the other person. Each exhibit has a different set of limitations, as described below:

- *Exhibit 1:* The student describing the exhibit cannot look at the other student or his/her diagram. The student drawing the exhibit cannot speak or otherwise communicate with the person describing the exhibit.

- *Exhibit 2:* The student describing the exhibit may look at the other student's diagram. However, he/she may only say "Yes" or "No" when the student drawing

the diagram asks a specific question. In other words, the person presenting the information can only use these words for feedback and only when asked a question by the writer.

- *Exhibit 3:* (optional—if time permits) The student describing the exhibit may look at the other student's diagram and may provide any feedback at any time to the person replicating the exhibit.

- *Step 3:* The class will gather to debrief this exercise. This may include discussion on the importance of feedback, and the characteristics of effective feedback for individual motivation and learning.

Source: © 2001 Steven L. McShane

Find the complete interactive self-assessments at this textbook's Web site at
www.mhhe.com/mcshaneEss2e.

>self-assessment exercise 5-3

Measuring Your Equity Sensitivity

Equity theory states that feelings of equity are determined by the perceived outcome/input ratio between yourself and another person or source (the comparison other). However, people have different degrees of equity sensitivity; that is, their reaction to various outcome/input ratios. This self-assessment estimates your level of equity

sensitivity. Read each of the statements and indicate the response that best reflects your opinion of that statement. This exercise is completed alone so students assess themselves honestly without concerns of social comparison. However, class discussion will focus on equity theory and the effect of equity sensitivity on perceptions of fairness in the workplace.

>self-assessment exercise 5-4

Measuring Your Growth Need Strength

Abraham Maslow's needs hierarchy theory distinguished between deficiency needs and growth needs. Deficiency needs become activated when unfulfilled, such as the need for food or belongingness. Growth needs, on the other hand, continue to develop even when temporary fulfilled. Maslow identified self-actualization as the only category of growth needs. Research has found that Maslow's needs hierarchy theory overall doesn't fit reality, but specific

elements such as the concept of growth needs have not been rejected. This self-assessment is designed to estimate your level of growth need strength. This instrument asks you to consider what it is about a job that is most important to you. Please indicate which of the two jobs you personally would prefer if you had to make a choice between them. In answering each question, assume that everything else about the jobs is the same. Pay attention only to the characteristics actually listed.

>self-assessment exercise 5-5

Student Empowerment Scale

Empowerment is a concept that applies to people in a variety of situations. This instrument is specifically adapted to your position as a student at this college or university. Indicate the extent to which you agree or disagree with each statement in this instrument, then request the results, which provide an overall score as well as scores on each of the four dimensions of empowerment. Complete each item honestly to get the best estimate of your level of empowerment.

>self-assessment exercise 5-6

What is Your Attitude toward Money?

Money is an important part of the employment relationship and, as we read in this chapter, is often mentioned in the context of various motivation theories such as needs/drives, expectancy theory, goal setting, and equity theory. However, people have rather diverse reactions to money, so the effect of financial rewards on motivation can get complicated. This self-assessment is designed to help you to understand the types of attitudes toward money and to assess your attitude toward money. Read each of the statements in this scale and indicate the response that you believe best reflects your position regarding the statement. This exercise is completed alone so students assess themselves honestly without concerns of social comparison. However, class discussion will focus on what money means to people, including the dimensions measured here.

chapter 8

Decision Making and Creativity

Radical Entertainment founder Ian Wilkinson (third from right) meets with employees every week to reinforce the Vancouver-based games developer's emphasis on creative decision making and employee involvement.

>learningobjectives

After reading this chapter, you should be able to:

1. Describe the six stages in the rational choice decision process.

2. Explain why people have difficulty identifying problems and opportunities, and identify ways to minimize these limitations.

3. Contrast the rational choice assumptions about evaluating alternatives with observations from organizational behavior.

4. Describe three ways in which emotions influence the selection of alternatives.

5. Outline how intuition operates.

6. Describe four causes of escalation of commitment.

7. Describe four benefits of employee involvement in decision making.

8. Identify four contingencies that affect the optimal level of employee involvement.

9. Outline the four steps in the creative process.

10. Describe the characteristics of employees who tend to be more creative, as well as workplace conditions and activities that support creativity.

What does a swarm of robot bees sound like? Cory Hawthorne tried to figure that out by listening to dozens of sounds and loops. Suddenly, eureka! The sound effects specialist at Radical Entertainment found the right combination when he mixed his humming through a kazoo with the noise of operating an electric beard trimmer across the surface of his bathtub. The robot bees now had a menacing audio effect in the electronic game that Hawthorne was working on, "The Simpsons: Hit and Run."

Radical depends on Cory Hawthorne and its other 230 employees to have plenty of "eureka!" moments in order to succeed in the competitive video game marketplace. "People are hugely empowered to be creative, to go beyond the call of duty to come up with great ideas and to actually implement them," says Danielle Michael, vice-president of business development of the Vancouver, Canada, company (now a division of Los Angeles-based Vivendi Universal Games). To help guide employee decision making, posters hung throughout Radical's headquarters state the company's succinct values, including "Take risks, always learn." Wilkinson takes these values seriously. He lunches with a half-dozen employees each week (as shown in this photo; Wilkinson is third from the right), encouraging them to apply the company's values in their everyday decisions.[1]

Employees at Radical Entertainment are in the creativity business, but every organization depends on creativity to some extent in almost all decisions. **Decision making** is a conscious process of making choices among alternatives with the intention of moving toward some desired state of affairs.[2] This chapter begins by outlining the rational choice paradigm of decision making. Then, we examine this perspective more critically by recognizing how people identify problems and opportunities, choose among alternatives, and evaluate the success of their decisions differently from the rational model. Bounded rationality, escalation of commitment, and intuition are three prominent topics in this section. Next, we explore the role of employee involvement in decision making, including the benefits of involvement and the factors that determine the optimal level of involvement. The final section of this chapter examines the factors that support creativity in decision making, including characteristics of creative people, work environments that support creativity, and creativity activities.

> **DECISION MAKING:** a conscious process of making choices among alternatives with the intention of moving toward some desired state of affairs

After reading the next two sections, you should be able to:

1. *Describe the six stages in the rational choice decision process.*

2. *Explain why people have difficulty identifying problems and opportunities, and identify ways to minimize these limitations.*

learningobjectives<

>Rational Choice Paradigm of Decision Making

> **RATIONAL CHOICE PARADIGM:** a deeply held perspective of decision making that people should—and typically do—make decisions based on pure logic and rationality

For most of written history, philosophers, economists, and other scholars in Western societies have stated or assumed that people should—and typically do—make decisions based on pure logic or rationality. This **rational choice paradigm** began 2,500 years ago when Plato and his contemporaries in ancient Greece raised logical debate and reasoning to a fine art. About 500 years ago, several European philosophers emphasized that the ability to make logical decisions is one of the most important accomplishments of

[Exhibit 6.1] Rational Choice Decision-Making Process

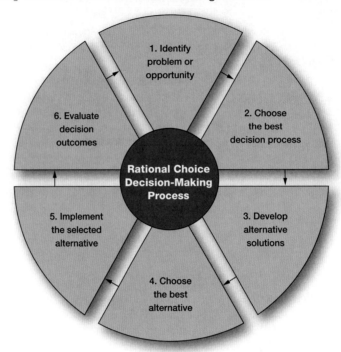

human beings. By the 1900s, social scientists and mathematicians had developed elegant rational choice models and formulae that are now embedded in operations research and other decision sciences.[3]

Exhibit 6.1 illustrates the rational choice process.[4] The first step is to identify the problem or recognize an opportunity. A problem is a deviation between the current and the desired situation—the gap between "what is" and "what ought to be." This deviation is a symptom of more fundamental root causes that need to be corrected.[5] An opportunity is a deviation between current expectations and a potentially better situation that was not previously expected. In other words, decision makers realize that some decisions may produce results beyond current goals or expectations.

The second step involves deciding how to process the decision.[6] For example, we need to consider whether we are facing a routine issue (called a *programmed decision*) that requires following standard operating procedure developed from past experience, or a novel situation (called a *nonprogrammed decision*) that requires working through all steps in the decision model. The third step in the decision model is to develop a list of possible solutions. This usually begins by searching for ready-made solutions, such as practices that have worked well on similar problems. If an acceptable solution cannot be found, then decision makers need to design a custom-made solution or modify an existing one.

The fourth step is to choose from among the alternatives. The rational choice paradigm assumes that people naturally select the alternative with the highest *subjective expected utility,* meaning that they choose the option with the most favorable outcomes or "highest payoff."[7] The rational choice paradigm assumes that decision makers can figure out which alternative has the highest value by identifying all the outcomes for every alternative and the probability that they will occur. The fifth step is to implement the selected alternative.

This is followed by the sixth step, evaluating whether the gap has narrowed between "what is" and "what ought to be."

Problems with the Rational Choice Paradigm

The rational choice paradigm seems so logical, yet it rarely exists in practice. One reason is that the model assumes people are efficient and logical information processing machines. But as the next few pages will reveal, people have difficulty recognizing problems; they cannot (or will not) simultaneously process the huge volume of information needed to identify the best solution; and they have difficulty recognizing when their choices have failed. The second reason why the rational model doesn't fit reality is that it focuses on logical thinking and completely ignores the fact that emotions also influence—perhaps even dominate—the decision-making process. As we shall discover, emotions both support and interfere with our quest to make better decisions.[8] With these points in mind, let's look again at each step of decision making, but with more detail about what really happens.

>Identifying Problems and Opportunities

When Albert Einstein was asked how he would save the world in one hour, he replied that the first 55 minutes should be spent defining the problem and the last 5 minutes solving it.[9] Einstein's point is that problem identification is not just the first step in decision making; it is arguably the most important step. But problems and opportunities are not so-labeled when they cross our desk. Instead, we need to examine information to determine whether something is wrong or that an opportunity is available.

To some extent, this discovery process occurs through conscious evaluation of the facts and persuasive arguments by other people. But problem recognition generally occurs during the mostly nonconscious processes of perceptual selective attention and attitude formation (described in Chapters 3 and 4, respectively).[10] Specifically, we evaluate information as soon as we perceive it by attaching emotional markers (worry, caution, elation, etc.) to that information. These rapid emotional responses, together with logical analysis and the emotions triggered by that analysis, determine whether you perceive something as a problem, opportunity, or irrelevant.

Problems with Problem Identification

The problem identification stage is, itself, filled with problems. Here are five of the most widely recognized concerns:[11]

1. *Stakeholder framing.* Employees, clients, and other stakeholders with vested interests try to "frame" the situation by persuading decision makers that the available information points to a problem, an opportunity, or does not have any importance at all. This framing of facts tends to short-circuit the decision maker's full assessment of the situation.

2. *Perceptual defense.* People sometimes block out or actively reject bad news as a coping mechanism. This perceptual defense is more common when people have limited control over the situation.[12] For example, an investigation of the space shuttle Columbia disaster revealed that NASA managers rejected suggestions and evidence that the shuttle and its seven crew members were in trouble.

3. *Mental models.* Mental models—cognitive templates or images of the external world—provide stability and predictability in our lives, but they also produce assumptions and

expectations that prevent us from seeing unique problems or opportunities. If an idea doesn't fit the existing mental model of how things should work, then the idea is dismissed as unworkable.

4. *Decisive leadership*. Studies report that people view leaders as more effective when they are decisive decision makers. Consequently, eager to look like an effective leader, many decision makers quickly zero in on a problem and its solution. Unfortunately, this decisiveness limits careful analysis of facts and logic which, according to research, tends to produce inferior decisions.[13]

5. *Solution-focused problems*. Decision makers often find a solution almost as soon as the problem is identified.[14] Indeed, problems are sometimes defined in terms of pet solutions, such as "The problem is that we need more control over our suppliers." This solution-focused problem definition occurs because it provides comforting closure to the otherwise ambiguous and uncertain nature of problems. Some decision makers take this solution focus a step further by seeing all problems in terms of strategies that have worked well for them in the past, even though they were applied under different circumstances. Again, the familiarity of past solutions makes the current problem less ambiguous or uncertain.

No Problem, Houston?

In February 2003, the NASA space shuttle Columbia disintegrated during re-entry over Texas and other western states, killing all seven crewmembers. The disintegration was technically caused by a hole in the left wing created by a large piece of foam debris during lift-off. However, a special accident investigation board concluded that NASA's middle management continually resisted attempts to recognize that the Columbia was in trouble, and therefore made no attempt to prevent loss of life. For example, photos from military satellites would have determined whether the foam caused serious wing damage. But when a team of engineers requested these photos, NASA management shot back an e-mail just 26 minutes later rejecting the request without explanation. Managers also questioned tests suggesting that a chunk of foam debris could cause wing damage, yet were quick to accept a faulty test showing that the foam could not damage the wing. In addition, the accident board reported that NASA managers criticized those who believed that a problem existed. One engineer was called "alarmist"; NASA's lead flight director said that the "rationale was lousy" in a report submitted by an engineering team concerned about the wing damage. In one meeting, Columbia's lead flight director candidly admitted: "I don't think there is much we can do, so you know it's not really a factor during the flight because there isn't much we can do about it."[15]

Identifying Problems and Opportunities More Effectively

Recognizing problems and opportunities will always be a challenge, but the process can be improved through awareness of these perceptual and diagnostic limitations. By recognizing the limitations of their mental models, for instance, decision makers might see opportunities or problems that mental models would cause them to overlook. A second strategy is to discover blind spots in problem identification by hearing how others perceive certain information and diagnose problems. Opportunities also become apparent when outsiders explore this information from their different mental models. Third, leaders require considerable willpower to resist appearing decisive when a more thoughtful examination of the situation should occur. Finally, successful decision makers experience "divine discontent," in which they are never satisfied with the status quo.[16]

After reading the next two sections, you should be able to: **learning**objectives<

3. *Contrast the rational choice assumptions about evaluating alternatives with observations from organizational behavior.*

4. *Describe three ways in which emotions influence the selection of alternatives.*

5. *Outline how intuition operates.*

6. *Describe four causes of escalation of commitment.*

>Evaluating and Choosing Alternatives

According to the rational choice paradigm, decision makers are able to evaluate and choose alternatives because they have well-articulated and agreed upon organizational goals, that they efficiently and simultaneously process facts about all alternatives and the consequences of those alternatives, and that they choose the alternative with the highest payoff. Nobel Prize–winning organizational scholar Herbert Simon questioned these assumptions half a century ago. He argued that people engage in **bounded rationality** because they process limited and imperfect information and rarely select the best choice.[17] Exhibit 6.2 contrasts rational choice assumptions with observations from Simon and other OB researchers about how people actually evaluate and choose alternatives.

BOUNDED RATIONALITY: processing limited and imperfect information and satisficing rather than maximizing when choosing between alternatives

The rational choice paradigm assumes that organizational goals are clear and agreed-upon, because this is essential to identify "what ought to be" and, therefore, provides a standard against which each alternative is evaluated. In reality, organizational goals are often ambiguous or in conflict with each other, so it isn't easy to figure out the best alternative.

The rational choice paradigm also makes several assumptions about the human capacity to process information. It assumes that decision makers can process information about all alternatives and their consequences, whereas this is not possible in reality. Instead, people evaluate only a few alternatives and only some of the main outcomes of those alternatives.[18] Also, decision makers typically look at alternatives sequentially rather than all at the same time. As a new alternative comes along, it is compared against an **implicit favorite**—a preferred alternative that the decision maker uses repeatedly as a comparison.[19] Unfortunately, people tend to distort information and temporarily change the importance of decision criteria so their implicit favorite comes out ahead even when the alternative is superior.[20]

IMPLICIT FAVORITE: a preferred alternative that the decision maker uses repeatedly as a comparison

Finally, the rational choice paradigm assumes that decision makers choose the alternative with the highest subjective expected utility. But OB research reports that people select the

[Exhibit 6.2] Rational Choice Assumptions versus Organizational Behavior Findings about Choosing Alternatives

Rational choice paradigm assumptions	Observations from organizational behavior
Goals are clear, compatible, and agreed upon.	Goals are ambiguous, in conflict, and lack full support.
Decision makers can calculate all alternatives and their outcomes.	Decision makers have limited information processing abilities.
Decision makers evaluate all alternatives simultaneously.	Decision makers evaluate alternatives sequentially.
Decision makers use absolute standards to evaluate alternatives.	Decision makers evaluate alternatives against an implicit favorite.
Decision makers use factual information to choose alternatives.	Decision makers process perceptually distorted information.
Decision makers choose the alternative with the highest payoff.	Decision makers choose the alternative that is good enough (satisficing).

SATISFICING: selecting a solution that is satisfactory or "good enough," rather than optimal or "the best"

alternative that is acceptable or "good enough." In other words, they engage in **satisficing** rather than maximizing. Satisficing occurs because it isn't possible to identify every alternative, and information about available alternatives is imperfect or ambiguous. Satisficing also occurs because, as mentioned already, decision makers tend to evaluate alternatives sequentially, not all at the same time. They evaluate each alternative against the implicit favorite and eventually select an option that scores above a subjective minimum point considered to be good enough to satisfy their needs or preferences.[21]

Evaluating Opportunities

Opportunities are just as important as problems, but what happens when an opportunity is "discovered" is quite different from the process of problem solving. According to a recent study of decision failures, decision makers do not evaluate several alternatives when they find an opportunity; after all, the opportunity *is* the solution, so why look for others! An opportunity is usually experienced as an exciting and rare revelation, so decision makers tend to have an emotional attachment to the opportunity. Unfortunately, this emotional preference motivates decision makers to apply the opportunity and short-circuit any detailed evaluation of it.[22]

Emotions and Making Choices

Herbert Simon and others demonstrated that people evaluate alternatives imperfectly, but they neglected to mention another glaring weakness with the rational choice paradigm—it completely ignores the role of emotions in human decision making. Emotions affect the evaluation of alternatives in three ways. First, the emotional marker process described earlier in this chapter as well as in previous chapters determines our preferences for each alternative. Our brain attaches specific emotions to information about each alternative, and our preferred alternative is strongly influenced by those initial emotional markers. Logical analysis also influences which alternative we choose, but even this logical information receives emotional tags, which then sway our preferences.

Second, moods and specific emotions influence the *process* of evaluating alternatives. For instance, we pay more attention to details when in a negative mood, possibly because a negative mood signals that there is something wrong that requires attention. When in a positive mood, on the other hand, we pay less attention to details and rely on a more programmed decision routine. When angry, decision makers are more likely to speed up the choice process and tend to be more optimistic about the success of risky alternatives.[23]

The third effect of emotions on the evaluation of alternatives is through a process called "emotions as information." Marketing research has found that we listen in on our emotions to provide guidance when making choices.[24] This temporary sensitivity to our emotional state influences our preference for each alternative. Influenced by their personality traits, some people pay more attention to these gut feelings.[25] But all of us use our emotions as information to some degree. This phenomenon ties directly into our next topic, intuition.

Intuition and Making Choices

Intuition is the ability to know when a problem or opportunity exists and to select the best course of action without conscious reasoning.[26] Intuition is both an emotional experience and a rapid unconscious analytic process. As was mentioned in the previous section, the gut feelings we experience are emotional signals that have enough intensity to make us consciously aware of them. These signals warn us of impending danger, or motivate us to take advantage of an opportunity. Some intuition also directs us to preferred choices relative to other alternatives in that situation.

INTUITION: the ability to know when a problem or opportunity exists and to select the best course of action without conscious reasoning

All gut feelings are emotional signals, but not all emotional signals are intuition. False intuition occurs when we have emotional reactions without relevant experience, whereas real intuition involves rapidly comparing what we see or otherwise sense with mental patterns or templates implicitly learned over time.[27] We rapidly match these templates with the current situation, and this pattern-matching process generates emotions that motivate us to act. These images are mental models because they usually include anticipated cause-effect relationships, allowing us to anticipate future events from current observations. Studies have also found that chess masters receive emotional signals when they sense an opportunity through quick observation of a chessboard. They can't immediately explain why they see a favorable move on the chessboard—they just feel it.

Making Choices More Effectively

It is very difficult to get around the human limitations of making choices, but a few strategies may help. Decisions tend to have a higher failure rate when leaders are decisive rather than contemplative. By systematically evaluating alternatives, decision makers minimize the implicit favorite and satisficing problems that occur when relying on general subjective judgments. Intuition still figures into this analysis, but so does careful consideration of relevant information.[28]

Another issue is how to minimize the adverse effects of emotions on the decision process. The first recommendation here is that we need to be constantly aware that decisions are influenced by both rational and emotional processes. With this awareness, some decision makers deliberately revisit important issues so they look at the information in different moods and have allowed their initial emotions to subside. Others practice **scenario planning,** in which they anticipate emergencies long before they occur, so that

SCENARIO PLANNING: a systematic process of thinking about alternative futures and what the organization should do to anticipate and react to those environments

alternative courses of action are evaluated without the pressure and emotions that occur during real emergencies.[29]

>Implementing Decisions

Implementing decisions is often skipped over in most writing about the decision-making process. Yet leading business writers advise that translating decisions into action is one of the most important and challenging tasks of leaders.[30] A recent survey of 3,600 bosses identified the "drive for results" as one of the five most important competencies of effective managers. This evidence is backed up by Larry Bossidy's experience leading thousands of managers. "When assessing candidates, the first thing I looked for was energy and enthusiasm for execution," says the former CEO of Honeywell and Allied Signal. The art and science of implementing decisions will be covered more fully in later chapters, particularly those on leadership and organizational change.

>Evaluating Decision Outcomes

ESCALATION OF COMMITMENT: the tendency to repeat an apparently bad decision or allocate more resources to a failing course of action

Contrary to the rational choice paradigm, decision makers aren't so logical when evaluating the effectiveness of their decisions. The most widely studied evidence of this is called **escalation of commitment**—the tendency to repeat an apparently bad decision or allocate more resources to a failing course of action.[31] There are plenty of escalation examples, including Scotland's new parliament building, a subway extension project in Tokyo, an automated baggage handling system at Denver International Airport, and the Irish government's recent cost blowout for its health department's computer system.

Why are people led deeper and deeper into failing projects? There are several reasons, including self-justification, prospect theory effect, perceptual blinders, and closing costs.

- *Self-justification*. Individuals are motivated to maintain their course of action when they have a high need to justify their decision. This self-justification is particularly evident when decision makers are personally identified with the project and have staked their reputations to some extent on the project's success.[32] The cost of the Irish health department's computer system likely escalated for this reason. Senior health administrators continued to support the project long after the finance department and others were convinced otherwise.

PROSPECT THEORY: an effect in which losing a particular amount is more disliked than gaining the same amount

- *Prospect theory effect*. Researchers have discovered that we dislike losing a particular amount more than we like gaining the same amount. We also take fewer risks to receive gains and take more risks to avoid losses. This effect, called **prospect theory,** is a second explanation for escalation of commitment. Stopping a project is a certain loss, which is more painful to most people than the uncertainty of success associated with continuing to fund the project. Given the choice, decision makers choose the less painful option.[33] The prospect theory effect may have escalated the Irish health department's computer project because leaders remained optimistic that the problems could be fixed in spite of the odds.

- *Perceptual blinders*. Escalation of commitment sometimes occurs because decision makers do not see the problems soon enough. They unconsciously screen out or explain away negative information to protect self-esteem. Serious problems initially look like random errors along the trend line to success. Even when they see that

Irish Health under re-PPARS

In the mid-1990s, executives at five health boards across Ireland decided to develop a common payroll system, called PPARS (payroll, payment, and related systems). Using well-established SAP software, the project would be done in three years at a total estimated cost of US $12 million. Health department officials were enthusiastic about PPARS' many benefits, but four years later the system was still far from completion even though costs had more than doubled to $25 million. Asked in 2002 to evaluate the project, Hay Associates concluded that PPARS was worth continuing, even if only to recoup the funds spent so far. The catch, however, was that the government needed to fork over another US $120 million, which it agreed to do. By 2005, Ireland's finance department was sounding alarm bells that PPARS' costs had spiraled out of control and the operational parts of the system were error-prone. The most embarrassing example was a health department employee who received a $1.5 million paycheck one week. The Irish government halted rollout of PPARS, yet senior health officials remained confident in its success, ordering staff as late as May 2007 to "realize the benefits" of the system. PPARS was officially axed in July 2007. The estimated cost of the failed project: somewhere between US $250–350 million.[34]

something is wrong, the information is sufficiently ambiguous that it can be misinterpreted or justified.

• *Closing costs.* Even when a project's success is in doubt, decision makers will persist because the costs of ending the project are high or unknown. Terminating a major project may involve large financial penalties, a bad public image, or personal political costs.

These four conditions make escalation of commitment look irrational. Usually it is, but there are exceptions. Recent studies suggest that throwing more money into a failing project is sometimes a logical attempt to further understand an ambiguous situation. This strategy is essentially a variation of testing unknown waters. By adding more resources, the decision maker gains new information about the effectiveness of these funds, which provides more feedback about the project's future success. This strategy is particularly common where the project has high closing costs.[35]

Evaluating Decision Outcomes More Effectively

One of the most effective ways to minimize escalation of commitment is to separate decision choosers from decision evaluators. This minimizes the self-justification effect because the person responsible for evaluating the decision is not connected to the original decision. A second strategy is to publicly establish a preset level at which the decision is abandoned or reevaluated. However, conditions are often so complex that it is difficult to identify an appropriate point to abandon a project.[36] Finally, projects might have less risk of escalation if several people are involved. Co-workers continuously monitor each other and might notice problems sooner than someone working alone on the project. Employee involvement offers these and other benefits to the decision-making process, as we learn next.

>**learning**objectives

After reading the next two sections, you should be able to:

7. *Describe four benefits of employee involvement in decision making.*

8. *Identify four contingencies that affect the optimal level of employee involvement.*

9. *Outline the four steps in the creative process.*

10. *Describe the characteristics of employees who tend to be more creative, as well as workplace conditions and activities that support creativity.*

>Employee Involvement in Decision Making

EMPLOYEE INVOLVEMENT: the degree to which employees influence how their work is organized and carried out

In this world of rapid change and increasing complexity, leaders rarely have enough information to make the best decision alone. Whether this information is about reducing costs or improving the customer experience, employee involvement can potentially solve problems or realize opportunities more effectively. **Employee involvement** (also called *participative management*) refers to the degree to which employees influence how their work is organized and carried out.[37] Every organization has some form and various levels of employee involvement. At the lowest level, participation involves asking employees for information. They do not make recommendations and might not even know what the problem is about. At a moderate level of involvement, employees are told about the problem and provide recommendations to the decision maker. At the highest level of involvement, the entire decision-making process is handed over to employees. They identify the problem, choose the best alternative, and implement their choice.

Benefits of Employee Involvement

Involving employees in decision making offers a number of potential advantages.[38] It improves problem identification because employees are usually the first to know when something goes wrong with production, customer service, or many other subsystems within the organization. In a well-managed meeting, employee involvement also creates synergy that can generate more and better solutions than when these people work alone. A third advantage of employee involvement is that people collectively tend to be better than individuals at picking the best alternative when they have diverse perspectives and a broad representation of values.[39] Along with improving decision quality, employee involvement tends to strengthen employee commitment to the decision. Rather than viewing themselves as agents of someone else's decision, staff members feel personally responsible for its success.

High Involvement Keeps Thai Carbon Black in the Black

Thai Carbon Black, which makes the black coloring agent in tires, inks, and many other products, views all of its employees as problem solvers. "The 'can do' attitude of every employee is important," says Subburaman Srinivasan, president of the Thai-Indian joint venture. Each year, the staff submits over 600 productivity improvement suggestions, placing their ideas in one of the little red boxes located around the site. Participatory management meetings are held every month, where employees are encouraged to come up with new ideas on ways to improve day-to-day operations. For instance, the company cut its transport costs by more than 10 percent after employees developed a special shipping bag allowing packers to stuff more product into the same volume. Thanks in part to this emphasis on employee involvement, Thai Carbon Black is one of the few companies outside Japan to receive the Deming Prize for total quality management. It has also received the Thailand Quality Class award, *Forbes* magazine's recognition as one of the best managed companies, and Hewitt Associates' ranking as one of the best employers in Asia and Thailand.[40]

Contingencies of Employee Involvement

As with most OB topics, the optimal level of employee involvement depends on the situation. The four main contingencies are decision structure, source of decision knowledge, decision commitment, and risk of conflict in the decision process.

- *Decision structure.* Employee involvement is unnecessary when the problem is routine; that is, it has been identified in the past and standard procedures developed with a ready-made solution. Instead, the benefits of employee involvement increase with the novelty and complexity of the problem or opportunity.

- *Source of decision knowledge.* Subordinates should be involved in some level of decision making when the leader lacks sufficient knowledge and subordinates have additional information to improve decision quality. In many cases, employees are closer to customers and production activities, so they often know where the company can save money, improve product or service quality, and realize opportunities.[41]

- *Decision commitment.* Participation tends to improve employee commitment to the decision. If employees are unlikely to accept a decision made without their involvement, then some level of participation is usually necessary.

- *Risk of conflict.* Two types of conflict undermine the benefits of employee involvement. First, if employee goals and norms conflict with the organization's goals, then only a low level of employee involvement is advisable. Second, the degree of involvement depends on whether employees will reach agreement on the preferred solution. If conflict is likely, then high involvement (i.e., where employees make the decision alone) would be difficult to achieve.

Employee involvement is an important component of the decision-making process. To make the best decisions, we need to involve people who have the most valuable information and who will increase commitment to implement the decision. Another important component of decision making is creativity, which we discuss next.

>Creativity

CREATIVITY:
the development of original ideas that make a socially recognized contribution

The opening story to this chapter describes how Radical Entertainment depends on creativity (as well as employee involvement) to make effective decisions. **Creativity** is the development of original ideas that make a socially recognized contribution.[42] Although there are unique conditions for creativity that we discuss over the next few pages, it is really part of the decision-making process described earlier in the chapter. We rely on creativity to find problems, identify alternatives, and implement solutions.

One of the earliest and most influential models of creativity is shown in Exhibit 6.3.[43] The first stage is preparation, which involves developing a clear understanding of what you are trying to achieve through a novel solution, then actively studying information seemingly related to the topic. The second stage, called incubation, is the stage of reflective thought. We put the problem aside, but our mind is still working on it in the background.[44] The important condition here is to maintain a low-level awareness by frequently revisiting the problem. Incubation does not mean that you forget about the problem or issue. Incubation

DIVERGENT THINKING:
reframing the problem in a unique way and generating different approaches to the issue

assists **divergent thinking**—reframing the problem in a unique way and generating different approaches to the issue. This contrasts with convergent thinking—calculating the conventionally accepted "right answer" to a logical problem. Divergent thinking breaks us away from existing mental models so we can apply concepts or processes from completely different areas of life.

Insight, the third stage of creativity, refers to the experience of suddenly becoming aware of a unique idea.[45] Insight is often visually depicted as a light bulb, but a better image would be a brief flash of light or a flickering candle because these bits of inspiration are fleeting and can be quickly lost if not documented. Insights are merely rough ideas. Their usefulness still requires verification through conscious evaluation and experimentation. Thus, although verification is labeled the final stage of creativity, it is really the beginning of a long process of experimentation and further creativity.

[Exhibit 6.3] The Creative Process Model

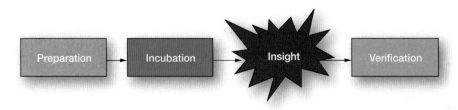

Creative People and Work Environments

Everyone is creative, but some people seem to be more creative than others. One of the main features of creative people is above-average intelligence to synthesize information, analyze ideas, and apply their ideas.[46] Second, people with higher creativity are more persistent. New ideas require lots of trial and error, particularly in the face of doubters. Persistence drives creative people to continue developing and testing after others have given up. This persistence is based on a high need for achievement and a moderate or high degree of self-confidence.[47]

A third feature of creative people is that they possess sufficient knowledge and experience about the subject matter.[48] At the same time, too much knowledge about the topic can undermine creativity because people develop deeply held mental models that lead to "mindless behavior," whereby they stop questioning their assumptions.[49] The fourth characteristic of creative people is that they have an inventive thinking style. Creative types are divergent thinkers and risk takers. They are not bothered about making mistakes or working with ambiguous information. They take a broad view of problems, don't like to abide by rules or status, and are unconcerned about social approval of their actions.[50]

Organizational Conditions Supporting Creativity

Hiring creative people is only part of the creativity equation. Corporate leaders also need to maintain a work environment that supports the creative process for everyone.[51] There is no single ideal environment in which creativity flourishes.[52] However, several conditions seem to support creative thinking. One of the most important conditions is that the organization has a *learning orientation;* that is, leaders recognize that employees make reasonable mistakes as part of the creative process. Motivation from the job itself is another important condition for creativity.[53] Employees tend to be more creative when they believe their work has a substantial impact on the organization and/or larger society (i.e., task significance) and when they have the freedom to pursue novel ideas without bureaucratic delays (i.e., autonomy). Creativity is about changing things, and change is possible only when employees have the authority to experiment.

Other conditions known to improve creativity are open communication, sufficient resources, a reasonable level of job security, and leader support. Time pressure tends to have a U-shaped effect on creativity; extreme time pressures are well-known creativity inhibitors, but lack of pressure can also undermine creativity.[54]

Activities That Encourage Creativity

Along with hiring creative people and giving them a supportive work environment, organizations have introduced numerous activities that attempt to crank up the creative potential. One set of activities encourages employees to redefine the problem. This occurs when we revisit old projects that have been set aside. After a few months of neglect, these projects might be seen in new ways.[55] Another strategy involves asking people unfamiliar with the issue (preferably with different expertise) to explore the problem with you. By verbalizing the problem, listening to questions, and hearing what others think, you are more likely to form new perspectives on the issue.[56]

A second set of creativity activities try to assist free thinking so that people break out of their rigid mental models. These activities range from art classes to improvisational storytelling and acting. For example, British media giant OMD sends employees to two-day retreats in the countryside where they play grapefruit croquet, chant like medieval monks, and pretend to be dog collars. "Being creative is a bit like an emotion—we need to be stimulated," explains Harriet Frost, one of OMD's specialists in building creativity. "The same is true for our imagination and its ability to come up with new ideas. You can't just sit in a room and devise hundreds of ideas."[57]

A third creativity-building strategy, called *cross-pollination,* occurs when people from different areas of the organization exchange ideas.[58] Radical Entertainment, introduced at the beginning of this chapter, uses cross-pollination through its monthly "game fair" day, in which teams show off their products and make presentations to other teams in the organization. IDEO, the California-based product design company, has a similar effect by mixing together employees from different past projects so they share new knowledge with each other.

Cross-pollination highlights the fact that most creative ideas are generated through teams and informal social interaction. This probably explains why Jonathon Ive, the award-winning designer of Apple Computer products, always refers to his team's creativity rather than his own. "The only time you'll hear [Jonathan Ive] use the word 'I' is when he's naming some of the products he helped make famous: iMac, iBook, iPod," says one writer.[59] The next chapter examines the foundations of team effectiveness and identifies ways to improve decision making and creativity in team settings.

>Chapter Summary

Decision making is a conscious process of making choices among one or more alternatives with the intention of moving toward some desired state of affairs. The rational choice paradigm of decision making includes identifying problems and opportunities, choosing the best decision style, developing alternative solutions, choosing the best solution, implementing the selected alternative, and evaluating decision outcomes.

The ability to effectively identify problems and opportunities is biased or undermined by stakeholder framing, perceptual defense, mental models, decisiveness, and solution-focused thinking. We can minimize these challenges by being aware of these problems, discussing the situation with other people, minimizing decisiveness, and maintaining divine discontent with the status quo.

Evaluating and choosing alternatives is often challenging because organizational goals are ambiguous or in conflict, human information processing is incomplete and subjective, and people tend to satisfice rather than maximize. Decision makers also short-circuit the evaluation process when faced with an opportunity rather than a problem. Emotions shape our preferences for alternatives and the process we follow to evaluate alternatives. We also listen in to our emotions for guidance when making decisions. This latter activity relates to intuition—the ability to know when a problem or opportunity exists and to select the best course of action without conscious reasoning. Intuition is both an emotional experience and a rapid unconscious analytic process that involves both pattern matching and action scripts.

People generally make better choices by systematically evaluating alternatives. Scenario planning can help to make future decisions without the pressure and emotions that occur during real emergencies.

Escalation of commitment makes it difficult to accurately evaluate decision outcomes. Escalation is mainly caused by self-justification, the prospect theory effect, perceptual blinders, and closing costs. These problems are minimized by separating decision choosers from decision evaluators, establishing a preset level at which the decision is abandoned or reevaluated, relying on more systematic and clear feedback about the project's success, and involving several people in decision making.

Employee involvement refers to the degree that employees influence how their work is organized and carried out. The level of involvement may range from an employee providing specific information to management without knowing the problem or issue, to complete involvement in all phases of the decision process. Employee involvement may lead to higher decision quality and commitment, but several contingencies need to be considered, including the decision structure, source of decision knowledge, decision commitment, and risk of conflict.

Creativity is the development of original ideas that make a socially recognized contribution. The four creativity stages are preparation, incubation, insight, and verification. Incubation assists divergent thinking, which involves reframing the problem in a unique way and generating different approaches to the issue. Four of the main features of creative people are intelligence, subject-matter knowledge and experience, persistence, and inventive thinking style. Creativity is also strengthened for everyone when the work environment supports a learning orientation, the job is highly motivating (i.e., high job enrichment), the organization provides a reasonable level of job security, and project leaders provide appropriate goals, time pressure, and resources. Three types of activities that encourage creativity are redefining the problem, free-thinking activities, and cross-pollination.

>key terms

bounded rationality 119	employee involvement 124	prospect theory 122
creativity 126	escalation of commitment 122	rational choice paradigm 115
decision making 115	implicit favorite 119	satisficing 120
divergent thinking 126	intuition 121	scenario planning 121

>critical thinking questions

1. A management consultant is hired by a manufacturing firm to determine the best site for its next production facility. The consultant has had several meetings with the company's senior executives regarding the factors to consider when making the recommendation. Discuss the decision-making problems that might prevent the consultant from choosing the best site location.

2. You have been asked to personally recommend a new travel agency to handle all airfare, accommodation, and related travel needs for your organization of 500 staff. One of your colleagues, who is responsible for the company's economic planning, suggests that the best travel agent could be selected mathematically by inputting the relevant factors for each agency and the weight (importance) of each factor. What decision-making approach is your colleague recommending? Is this recommendation a good idea in this situation? Why or why not?

3. Intuition is both an emotional experience and an unconscious analytic process. One problem, however, is that not all emotions signaling that there is a problem or opportunity represent intuition. Explain how we would know if our "gut feelings" are intuition or not, and if not intuition, suggest what might be causing them.

4. A developer received financial backing for a new business financial center along a derelict section of the waterfront, a few miles from the current downtown area of a large European city. The idea was to build several high-rise structures, attract large tenants to those sites, and have the city extend transportation systems out to the new center. Over the next decade, the developer believed that others would build in the area, thereby attracting the regional or national offices of many financial institutions. Interest from potential tenants was much lower than initially predicted and the city did not build transportation systems as quickly as expected. Still, the builder proceeded with the original plans. Only after financial support was curtailed did the developer reconsider the project. Using your knowledge of escalation of commitment, discuss three possible reasons why the developer was motivated to continue with the project.

5. Ancient Book Company has a problem with new book projects. Even when others are aware that a book is far behind schedule and may engender little public interest, sponsoring editors are reluctant to terminate contracts with authors whom they have signed. The result is that editors invest more time with these projects than on more fruitful projects. As a form of escalation of commitment, describe two methods that Ancient Book Company can use to minimize this problem.

6. Employee involvement applies just as well to the classroom as to the office or factory floor. Explain how student involvement in classroom decisions typically made by the instructor alone might improve decision quality. What potential problems may occur in this process?

7. Think of a time when you experienced the creative process. Maybe you woke up with a brilliant (but usually sketchy and incomplete) idea, or you solved a baffling problem while doing something else. Describe this incident to your class and explain how the experience followed the creative process.

8. Two characteristics of creative people are that they have relevant experience and are persistent in their quest. Does this mean that people with the most experience and the highest need for achievement are the most creative? Explain your answer.

>team exercise 6-1

Employee Involvement Incidents

Incident 1: The Sugar Substitute Research Decision

You are the head of research and development (R&D) for a major beer company. While working on a new beer product, one of the scientists in your unit seems to have tentatively identified a new chemical compound that has few calories but tastes closer to sugar than current sugar substitutes. The company has no foreseeable need for this product, but it could be patented and licensed to manufacturers in the food industry.

The sugar substitute discovery is in its preliminary stages and would require considerable time and resources before it would be commercially viable. This means that it would necessarily take some resources away from other projects in the lab. The sugar substitute project is beyond your technical expertise, but some of the R&D lab researchers are familiar with that field of chemistry. As with most forms of research, it is difficult to determine the amount of research required to further identify and perfect the sugar substitute. You do not know how much demand is expected for this product. Your department has a decision process for funding projects that are behind schedule. However, there are no rules or precedents about funding projects that would be licensed but not used by the organization.

The company's R&D budget is limited and other scientists in your work group have recently complained that they require more resources and financial support to get their projects completed. Some of these other R&D projects hold promise for future beer sales. You believe that most researchers in the R&D unit are committed to ensuring company's interests are achieved.

Incident 2: Coast Guard Cutter Decision Problem

You are the captain of a 200-foot Coast Guard cutter, with a crew of 16, including officers. Your mission is general at-sea search and rescue. At 2:00 A.M. this morning, while en route to your home port after a routine 28-day patrol, you received word from the nearest Coast Guard station that a small plane had crashed 60 miles offshore. You obtained all the available information concerning the location of the crash, informed your crew of the mission, and set a new course at maximum speed for the scene to commence a search for survivors and wreckage.

You have now been searching for 20 hours. Your search operation has been increasingly impaired by rough seas, and there is evidence of a severe storm building. The atmospherics associated with the deteriorating weather have made communications with the Coast Guard station impossible. A decision must be made shortly about whether to abandon the search and place your vessel on a course that would ride out the storm (thereby protecting the vessel and your crew, but relegating any possible survivors to almost certain death from exposure) or to continue a potentially futile search and the risks it would entail.

Before losing communications, you received an update weather advisory concerning the severity and duration of the storm. Although your crew members are extremely conscientious about their responsibility, you believe that they would be divided on the decision of leaving or staying.

Discussion Questions (for both incidents)

1. To what extent should your subordinates be involved in this decision? Select one of the following levels of involvement:

- *No involvement*: You make the decision alone without any participation from subordinates.

- *Low involvement*: You ask one or more subordinates for information relating to the problem, but you don't ask for their recommendations and might not mention the problem to them.

- *Medium involvement*: You describe the problem to one or more subordinates (alone or in a meeting) and ask for any relevant information as well as their recommendations on the issue. However, you make the final decision, which might or might not reflect their advice.

- *High involvement*: You describe the problem to subordinates. They discuss the matter, identify a solution without your involvement (unless they invite your ideas), and implement that solution. You have agreed to support their decision.

2. What factors led you to choose this level of employee involvement rather than the others?

3. What problems might occur if less or more involvement occurred in this incident (where possible)?

Sources: The Sugar Substitute Research Decision is written by Steven L. McShane, © 2002. The Coast Guard cutter case is adapted from V. H. Vroom and A. G. Jago, *The New Leadership: Managing Participation in Organizations* (Englewood Cliffs, NJ: Prentice Hall, 1988). © 1987 V. H. Vroom and A. G. Jago. Used with permission of the authors.

>team exercise 6-2

Where in the World Are We?

Purpose   This exercise is designed to help you understand the potential advantages of involving others in decisions rather than making decisions alone.

Materials   Students require an unmarked copy of the map of the United States with grid marks (Exhibit 2). Students are not allowed to look at any other maps or use any other materials. The instructor will provide a list of communities located somewhere on Exhibit 2. The instructor will also provide copies of the answer sheet after students have individually and in teams estimated the locations of communities.

Instructions

- *Step 1*: Write down in Exhibit 1 the list of communities identified by your instructor. Then, working alone, estimate the location in Exhibit 2 of these communities, all of which are in the United States. For example, mark a small "1" in Exhibit 2 on the spot where you believe the first community is located. Mark a small "2" where you think the second community is located, and so on. Please be sure to number each location clearly and with numbers small enough to fit within one grid space.

- *Step 2*: The instructor will organize students into approximately equal-sized teams (typically five or six people per team). Working with your team members, reach a consensus on the location of each community listed in Exhibit 1. The instructor might provide teams with a separate copy of this map, or each member can identify the team's numbers using a different colored pen on their individual maps. The team's decision for each location should occur by consensus, not voting or averaging.

- *Step 3:* The instructor will provide or display an answer sheet, showing the correct locations of the communities. Using this answer sheet, students will count the minimum number of grid squares between the location they individually marked and the true location of each community. Write the number of grid squares in the second column of Exhibit 1, then add up the total. Next, count the minimum number of grid squares between the location the team marked and the true location of each community. Write the number of grid squares in the third column of Exhibit 1, then add up the total.

- *Step 4*: The instructor will ask for information about the totals and the class will discuss the implication of these results for employee involvement and decision making.

[Exhibit 1] List of Selected Communities in the United States of America

Number	Community	Individual Distance in Grid Units from the True Location	Team Distance in Grid Units from the True Location
1.	_____	_____	_____
2.	_____	_____	_____
3.	_____	_____	_____
4.	_____	_____	_____
5.	_____	_____	_____
6.	_____	_____	_____
7.	_____	_____	_____
8.	_____	_____	_____
		Total: _____	Total: _____

Source: © 2002 Steven L. McShane

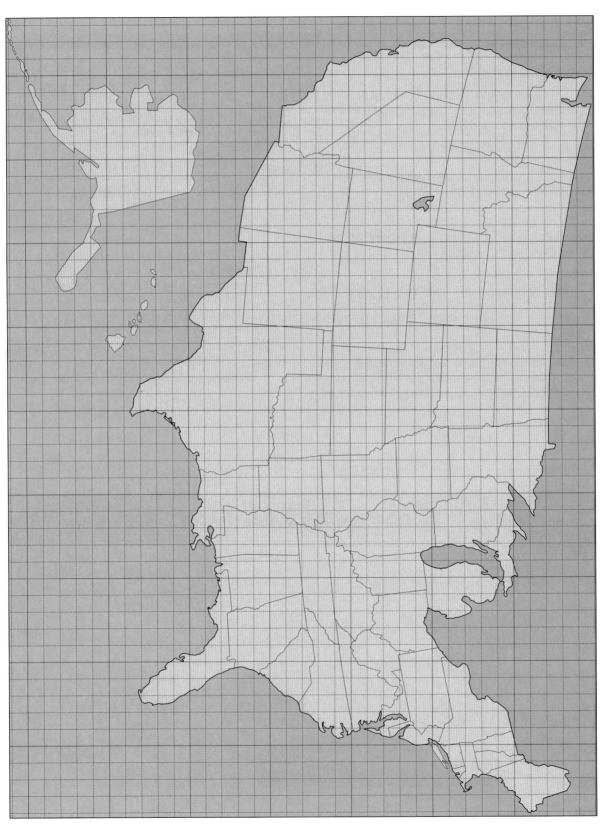

[Exhibit 2] Map Showing the United States of America

>**class** exercise 6-3

Creativity Brainbusters

Purpose　This exercise is designed to help students understand the dynamics of creativity and team problem solving.

Instructions

This exercise may be completed alone or in teams of three or four people. If teams are formed, students who already know the solutions to one or more of these problems should identify themselves and serve as silent observers. When finished (or, more likely, time is up), the instructor will review the solutions and discuss the implications of this exercise. In particular, be prepared to discuss what you needed to solve these puzzles and what may have prevented you from solving them more quickly (or at all).

1. Double Circle Problem

Draw two circles, one inside the other, with a single line and with neither circle touching the other (as shown below). In other words, you must draw both of these circles without lifting your pen (or other writing instrument).

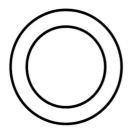

2. Nine Dot Problem

Below are nine dots. Without lifting your pencil, draw no more than four straight lines that pass through all nine dots.

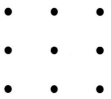

3. Nine Dot Problem Revisited

Referring to the nine dot exhibit above, describe how, without lifting your pencil, you could pass a pencil line through all dots with three (3) or fewer straight lines.

4. Word Search

In the following line of letters, cross out five letters so that the remaining letters, without altering their sequence, spell a familiar English word.

C F R I V E E L A T E T I T E V R S E

5. Burning Ropes

You have two pieces of rope of unequal lengths and a box of matches. In spite of their different lengths, each piece of rope takes one hour to burn; however, parts of each rope burn at unequal speeds. For example, the first half of one piece might burn in ten minutes. Use these materials to accurately determine when 45 minutes has elapsed.

**Find the complete interactive self-assessments at this textbook's Web site at
www.mhhe.com/mcshaneEss2e.**

>**self-assessment** exercise 6-4

Measuring Your Creative Personality

This self-assessment is designed to help you to measure the extent to which you have a creative personality. Our creative potential depends on our personality, values, and competencies. This self-assessment estimates your level of creative potential as a personality characteristic. It consists of an adjective checklist with 30 words that may or may not describe you. You are asked to indicate which words you think accurately describe you. Please DO NOT select the boxes for words that do not describe you. This exercise is completed alone so students assess themselves without concerns of social comparison. However, class discussion will focus on how this scale might be applied in organizations, and the limitations of measuring creativity in work settings.

>self-assessment exercise 6-5

Testing Your Creative Bench Strength

This self-assessment takes the form of a self-scoring quiz. It consists of 12 questions that require divergent thinking to identify the correct answers. For each question, type in your answer in the space provided. When finished, look at the correct answer for each question, along with the explanation for that answer

>self-assessment exercise 6-6

Decision-Making Style Inventory

People have different styles of decision making that are reflected in how they identify problems or opportunities and make choices. This self-assessment estimates your decision-making style through a series of statements describing how individuals go about making important decisions. Please indicate whether you agree or disagree with each statement.

Answer each item as truthfully as possible so that you get an accurate estimate of your decision-making style. This exercise is completed alone so students assess themselves honestly without concerns of social comparison. However, class discussion will focus on the decision-making style that people prefer in organizational settings.

[part 2. case 1] Fran Hayden Joins Dairy Engineering

By Glyn Jones, University of Waikato, New Zealand

Dairy Engineering (NZ) Ltd has its headquarters in Hamilton, New Zealand, with manufacturing plants in South Auckland and Christchurch. The company manufactures equipment for the dairy industry. In its early years it focused on the domestic market but in the last five years has expanded into the export market. The company employs 450 people, which makes it a large company by New Zealand standards.

The case focuses on events in the accounting department at the head office, which is organized into two sections: cost accounting and management information services (MIS). The accounting department is structured as is shown in Exhibit 1.

Fran, the New Graduate

Fran Hayden is in the final year of her Bachelor of Management Studies (BMS) degree at the University of Waikato where she has proved to be a high achiever. Fran was interested in a position with Dairy Engineering because of the opportunity to gain practical experience, the higher starting salary offered in the industry, and that her boyfriend lived in that community.

Fran sent her curriculum vitae to the company and two weeks later was invited to an interview with the chief accountant. She was surprised at the end of the interview to be offered the position of assistant cost accountant. Fran said she would like to think it over. Two weeks later when she had still not replied she received a telephone call from Rob asking if she was going to take the position. Still not totally convinced, Fran decided nonetheless to accept the offer.

The First Day at Work

Like many of her peers, Fran was glad to be leaving the university after four years of study. She was looking forward to having money to spend as well as reducing her student debt. In order to look the part she had gone further into debt to buy new "corporate clothing."

On reporting to the accounting department she got her first shock in the real world. No one was expecting her! Even worse, she found that there was no vacancy for her in cost accounting. Instead, she had been assigned to MIS.

Fran was taken to MIS by one of her new colleagues, Mike, who introduced her to her colleagues, Tom and Adrian. They seemed to be a friendly bunch as apparently was her boss, Peter Bruton, who explained that her main duties were to assist with compiling information for the monthly management report known as *Big Brother*.

After two weeks the time came for compiling *Big Brother*. Fran found that her part was almost entirely clerical and consisted of photocopying, collating, binding, punching, and stamping the pages of the report. She then had to hand-deliver copies of the report to the senior manager at headquarters.

After *Big Brother* was completed, Fran found again she had little to do. She began to wonder why MIS needed four people.

The Big Opportunity

One afternoon, out of the blue, the chief accountant called Fran to his office to tell her about an upcoming

[**Exhibit 1**] Description of Employees in the Case

Name	Position	Description
Rob Poor	Chief Accountant	Rob is the accounting department manager. He is 40 years old, a qualified accountant with a chartered accounting (ACA) qualification. He has been with the company for six years. He is an unassuming person regarded as a bit "soft" by his staff.
Vernon Moore	Chief Cost Accountant	Vernon is 30 years old, also a graduate with an ACA qualification. He joined the company 18 months ago. He is considered an easy-going type and is well liked by his staff.
Peter Bruton	Management Accountant	Peter is 37 years old with a science degree in dairy technology. He is also studying part-time for a management degree through Massey University. He is regarded as "moody" and not well liked by his staff.

management workshop to be held in Auckland on performance measurement. Rob talked about the importance of staff development and that he would like to see one of his younger staff attending the workshop. He then asked Fran if she would be interested? She jumped at the opportunity. Unfortunately her boss was away on two weeks leave at the time but Rob said he would talk with Peter.

Fran enjoyed the workshop, particularly rubbing shoulders with experienced managers, staying at an Auckland hotel, and generally acting the management part. Even before returning to Hamilton, she wrote a detailed report on the workshop for the chief accountant.

On her return to Hamilton, however, she found all was far from well. On Sunday evening, Fran was telephoned by her colleague Mike with some disturbing news. When Peter returned to work to find that Fran was in Auckland, he was furious, complaining that he had not been consulted and that his authority was being undermined.

> PETER: Fran is no longer employed in his section.

Fran returned to work full of trepidation only to find that the expected encounter with her boss did not take place because he was in Christchurch. She handed two copies of her report on the workshop to the chief accountant's secretary before taking the opportunity of her boss's absence to seek the advice of her colleagues:

> FRAN: I am really worried. What do you think I should do?
>
> ADRIAN: Stop worrying about it. He's just letting off steam. I have seen this all before. He'll get over it.
>
> FRAN: Come on; get serious. He is my boss! He can make things very difficult for me.
>
> MIKE: I think you should talk with Rob. After all, he's the one who suggested you go. It's not like it was your idea. He has to stick up for you.

The next day Fran managed to get an appointment with the chief accountant. She started by saying that she found the workshop very useful. She then brought up her fears about Peter's displeasure with her attendance at the workshop, to which the chief accountant responded:

> ROB: Well yes, he was a bit upset but don't worry, I will sort it out. The report was really good. By the way, I think you should treat it as

confidential. Don't show it to anyone or discuss it with anyone. Is that ok? Don't worry about this. I assure you that I will sort it out.

Fran left the meeting feeling reassured but also a bit puzzled, wondering how Rob could have read her report in such a short time.

On Thursday Peter returned to work and just before lunch called Fran into his office where he proceeded to attack her verbally, saying that she had connived behind his back to attend the workshop and that she had never asked for his permission. He said that he realized she was an intelligent girl but that she was sneaky. He went on:

> PETER: You had better know which side your bread is buttered on—that for better or worse, you are in my section. No other section would want you.

He then called Mike in and told him:

> PETER: I don't want Fran wasting any more time—she is not to make any private calls from work.

Later, in confidence, he also told Janet, one of the administration clerks:

> PETER: Don't go talking with Fran—she has far too much work to catch up on.

Naturally Janet did tell Fran!

The following week, Vernon happened to pass Fran in the corridor and stopped to talk with her. Fran had met Vernon only briefly during her first week in the company and was surprised when he asked her why she looked so miserable? She explained and he said that they had better talk with the chief accountant, and taking Fran with him, went to Rob's office. Vernon said that they needed a word, and Fran listened as Vernon outlined the situation to Rob. Fran made it clear that if Peter continued to treat her this way, she would have to ask for a transfer. She also said that there was certainly not enough work in MIS to keep her occupied for more than a day or so each week.

The chief accountant listened and then asked her to give him a written report of what had happened since she had joined the company, including the latest incident with her boss. This, he said, would be brought up at the next senior management meeting. On the weekend Fran wrote the report, which included a request for a transfer out of MIS on the basis of the lack of work and her boss's attitude toward her. On Monday morning she handed her report to the chief accountant's secretary.

Fran expected a reply but, by early afternoon, had heard nothing. At the end of the day, however, Peter called all his staff into his office. He was obviously in a good mood and told them that he had put his plan for revising *Big Brother* to the management meeting and had received an enthusiastic response. As he spoke, Fran noticed the color draining out of Mike's face. On the way out, he told her that what Peter was describing was *his* revision plans, not Peter's own plans. Mike resolved never to give his boss another one of his ideas telling Fran:

MIKE: He just uses other people's brains—but that's the last time he uses mine.

Fran drove home from work feeling despondent. She wished she had never joined the company. Her job was boring, almost entirely clerical, and certainly did not require a degree. She was also taking the stresses home, resulting in quarrels with her boyfriend and roommates.

Fran concluded that she had only two alternatives: a transfer or resignation. But to leave her job after less than five months would hardly impress any future employer. In desperation, she went to talk with Vernon who she thought would be sympathetic but received more unwelcome news: He told her about the outcome of the senior management meeting. Contrary to Fran's expectation, the chief accountant had not confronted Peter. In fact, it appeared he had been eclipsed by Peter's presentation for the revision of *Big Brother* and the chief accountant had not attempted to raise the issue.

Vernon was frank—she must either transfer or resign. Then, to Fran's surprise, he suggested she apply for a position in his section that would become vacant in three weeks. One of his assistant accountants was leaving to go overseas on short notice and he did not have a replacement. Vernon cautioned however that Fran's only chance was to apply directly to the chief accountant—that would force the issue. With a formal, written application before him, the chief accountant would have to make a decision. Just as certainly, Peter would resist the request. Later Fran drafted a letter to Rob requesting that she be transferred from MIS to the upcoming position in cost accounting.

The Confrontation

The next morning, Fran took her request to the chief accountant, but after reading it he said:

ROB: You really needn't have done this, you know—I intended dealing with the situation.

Fran left Rob's office wondering what to believe. From her desk she watched as Peter made his way across to the chief accountant's office. The meeting was brief. Five minutes later, he left Rob's office and as he passed by, he said, in a loud voice:

PETER: Fran, you are finished at this company.

Fran saw her colleagues duck their heads down and pretend to be working. No one envied her position. She wondered how, in such a short time, she has ended up in such a situation.

[part 2. case 2] From Lippert-Johanson Incorporated to Fenway Waste Management

By Lisa V. Williams, Jeewon Cho, and Alicia Boisnier, SUNY at Buffalo

Part One

Catherine O'Neill was very excited to be graduating from Flagship University at the end of the semester. She had always been interested in accounting, following from her father's lifelong occupation, and she very much enjoyed the challenging major. She was involved in many highly regarded student clubs in the business school and worked diligently to earn good grades. Now her commitment to the profession would pay off, she hoped, as she turned her attention to her job search. In late fall, she had on-campus interviews with several firms, but her interview with the prestigious Lippert-Johanson Incorporated (LJI) stood out in her mind as the most attractive opportunity. That's why Catherine was thrilled to learn she made it to the next level of interviews, to be held at the firm's main office later that month.

When Catherine entered the elegant lobby of LJI's New York City offices, she was immediately impressed by all there was to take in. Catherine had always been one to pay attention to detail, and her acute observations of her environment had always been an asset. She was able to see how social and environmental cues told her what was expected of her, and she always set out to meet and exceed those expectations. On a tour of the office, she had already begun to size up her prospective workplace. She appreciated the quiet, focused work atmosphere. She liked how everyone was dressed: most wore suits and their conservative apparel supported the professional attitudes that seemed to be omnipresent. People spoke to her in a formal, but friendly manner, and seemed enthusiastic. Some of them even took the time to greet her as she was guided to the conference room for her individual interviews. "I like the way this place feels and I would love to come to work here every day," Catherine thought. "I hope I do well in my interview!"

Before she knew it, Catherine was sitting in a well-appointed office with one of the eight managers in the firm. Sandra Jacobs was the picture of a professional woman, and Catherine naturally took her cue from her about how to conduct herself in the interview. It seemed to go very quickly, although the interview lasted an hour. As soon as Catherine left the office, she could not wait to phone her father about the interview. "I loved it there and I just know I'm a good fit!" she told her proud father. "Like them, I believe it is important to have the highest ethical standards and quality of work. Ms. Jacobs really emphasized the mission of the firm, as well as its policies. She did say that all the candidates have an excellent skill set and are well qualified for the job, so mostly, they are going to base their hiring decision on how well they think each of us will fit into the firm. Reputation is everything to an accounting firm. I learned that from you, Dad!"

After six weeks of apprehensive waiting, Catherine's efforts were rewarded when LJI and another firm contacted her with job offers. Catherine knew she would accept the offer from LJI. She saw the firm as very ethical, with the highest standards for work quality, and an excellent reputation. Catherine was grateful to have been selected from such a competitive hiring process. "There couldn't be a better choice for me! I'm so proud to become a member of this company!"

Catherine's first few days at LJI were a whirlwind of a newcomer's experiences. She had meetings with her supervisor to discuss the firm's mission statement, her role in the firm, and what was expected of her. She was also told to spend some time looking at the employee handbook that covers many important policies of the firm, such as dress code, sick time, grievances, the chain of command and job descriptions, and professional ethics. Everyone relied on the handbook to provide clear guidance about what is expected of each employee. Also, Catherine was informed that she would soon begin participating in continuing professional education, which would allow her to update her skills and knowledge in her field. "This is great," thought Catherine, "I'm so glad to know the firm doesn't just talk about its high standards, it actually follows through with action."

What Catherine enjoyed most about her new job were her warm and welcoming colleagues who invited her to their group lunches beginning her first day. They talked about work and home; they seemed close, both professionally and personally. She could see that everyone had a similar attitude about work: they cared about their work and the firm, they took responsibility for their own tasks, but they also helped one another out. Catherine also got involved in LJI activities outside of work, like their baseball and soccer teams, happy hours, picnics and parties, and enjoyed the chance to mingle with her co-workers. In what seemed like no time at all, Catherine started to really see herself as a fully integrated member of LJI.

Before tax season started, Catherine attended some meetings of the AICPA and other professional accounting societies. There, she met many accountants from other firms who all seemed very impressed when she told them where she worked. Catherine's pride and appreciation for being a member of LJI grew as she realized how highly regarded the firm is among others in the accounting industry.

Part Two

Over the past seven years, Catherine's career in New York has flourished. Her reputation as one of the top tax accountants in her company is well established, and is recognized by colleagues outside the firm as well. However, Catherine entered a new chapter of her life when she married Ted Lewis, an oncology intern, who could not turn down an offer of residency at a top cancer center in upstate New York. Wanting to support Ted's once-in-a-lifetime career opportunity, Catherine decided it was time to follow the path of many of her colleagues and leave public accounting for a position that would be more conducive to starting a family. Still, her heart was in the profession, so she took an available position as a controller of a small recycling company located a few miles from Catherine and Ted's new upstate New York home. She knew that with this position she could both have children and maintain her career.

Fenway Waste Management is small—about 35 employees. There are about 25 people who work in the warehouse, three administrative assistants, two supervisors, and five people in management. Catherine is finding she has to adjust to her new position and surroundings. Often, she has found herself doing work that formally belonged to someone else; because it is a small company, managers seem to wear many hats. This was quite different from what she had experienced at LJI. In addition, the warehousemen often have to work with greasy materials, and sometimes track the grease into the offices. Catherine half-laughed and half-worried when she saw a piece of paper pinned to the wall that said, "Clean Up After Yourself!" She supposed that the nature of the business was why the offices are functional, but furnished with old pieces. She couldn't imagine having a business meeting there! Also, for most of the employees, the casual dress matches the causal attitudes. But, Catherine continued to wear a dressed-down version of her formal LJI attire, even though her new co-workers considered her overdressed.

With all the changes Catherine has experienced, she has maintained one familiar piece of her past. Although it is not required for her new position, Catherine still attends AICPA meetings and makes a point to continue updating her knowledge of current tax laws. At this year's conference, she told a former colleague, "Being here, I feel so much more like myself—I am so much more connected to these people and this environment than to those at my new job. It's too bad I don't feel this way at Fenway. I guess I'm just more comfortable with professionals who are similar to me."

[part 2. case 3] Keeping Suzanne Chalmers

By Steven L McShane, The University of Western Australia*

Thomas Chan hung up the telephone and sighed. The vice president of software engineering at Advanced Photonics Inc. (API) had just spoken to Suzanne Chalmers, who called to arrange a meeting with Chan later that day. She didn't say what the meeting was about, but Chan almost instinctively knew that Suzanne was going to quit after working at API for the past four years. Chalmers is a software engineer in Internet Protocol (IP), the software that directs fiber-optic light through API's routers. It is very specialized work, and Suzanne is one of API's top talents in that area.

Thomas Chan had been through this before. A valued employee would arrange a private meeting. The meeting would begin with a few pleasantries, then the employee announces that he or she wants to quit. Some employees say they are leaving because of the long hours and stressful deadlines. They say they need to decompress, get to know the kids again, or whatever. But that's not usually the real reason. Almost every organization in this industry is scrambling to keep up with technological advances and the competition. Employees would just leave one stressful job for another one.

Also, many of the people who leave API join a start-up company a few months later. These start-up firms can be pressure cookers where everyone works 16 hours each day and has to perform a variety of tasks. For example, engineers in these small firms might have to meet customers or work on venture capital proposals rather than focus on specialized tasks related to their knowledge. API now has over 6,000 employees, so it is easier to assign people to work that matches their technical competencies.

No, the problem isn't the stress or long hours, Chan thought. The problem is money—too much money. Most of the people who leave are millionaires. Suzanne Chalmers is one of them. Thanks to generous share options that have skyrocketed on the stock markets, many employees at API have more money than they can use. Most are under 40 years old, so it's too early for them to retire. But their financial independence gives them less reason to remain with API.

The Meeting

The meeting with Suzanne Chalmers took place a few hours after the telephone call. It began like the others, with the initial pleasantries and brief discussion about progress on the latest fiber-optic router project. Then, Suzanne made her well-rehearsed statement: "Thomas, I've really enjoyed working here, but I'm going to leave Advanced Photonics." Suzanne took a breath, then looked at Chan. When he didn't reply after a few seconds, she continued: "I need to take time off. You know, get away to recharge my batteries. The project's nearly done and the team can complete it without me. Well, anyway, I'm thinking of leaving."

Chan spoke in a calm voice. He suggested that Suzanne should take an unpaid leave for two or maybe three months, complete with paid benefits, then return refreshed. Suzanne politely rejected that offer, saying that she needs to get away from work for a while. Thomas then asked Suzanne whether she was unhappy with her work environment—whether she was getting the latest computer technology to do her work and whether there were problems with co-workers. The workplace was fine, Susanne replied. The job was getting a bit routine, but she had a comfortable workplace with excellent co-workers.

Chan then apologized for the cramped workspace, due mainly to the rapid increase in the number of people hired over the past year. He suggested that if Suzanne took a couple of months off, API would give her special treatment with a larger work space with a better view of the park behind the campus-like building when she returned. She politely thanked Chan for that offer, but it wasn't what she needed. Besides, it wouldn't be fair to have a large work space when other team members work in smaller quarters.

Chan was running out of tactics, so he tried his last hope: money. He asked whether Suzanne had higher offers. Suzanne replied that she regularly received calls from other companies, and some of them offered more money. Most were start-up firms that offered a lower salary but higher potential gains in share options. Chan knew from market surveys that Suzanne was already paid well in the industry. He also knew that API couldn't compete on share option potential. Employees working in start-up firms sometimes saw their shares increase by five or ten times their initial value, whereas shares at API and other large firms increased more slowly. However, Chan promised Suzanne that he would recommend that she receive a significant raise—maybe 25 percent more—and more share options. Chan added that Chalmers was one of API's most valuable employees and that the company would suffer if she left the firm.

The meeting ended with Chalmers promising to consider Chan's offer of higher pay and share options. Two days later, Chan received her resignation in writing. Five months later, Chan learned that after a few months traveling with her husband, Chalmers joined a start-up software firm in the area.

[part 2. case 4] Perfect Pizzeria

By J. E. Dittrich and R. A. Zawacki*

Perfect Pizzeria in Southville, deep in southern Illinois, is the chain's second-largest franchise. The headquarters is located in Phoenix, Arizona. Although the business is prospering, it has employee and managerial problems.

Each operation has one manager, an assistant manager, and from two to five night managers. The managers of each pizzeria work under an area supervisor. There are no systematic criteria for being a manager or becoming a manager trainee. The franchise has no formalized training period for the manager. No college education is required. The managers for whom the case observer worked during a four-year period were relatively young (ages 24 to 27), and only one had completed college. They came from the ranks of night managers, assistant managers, or both. The night managers were chosen for their ability to perform the duties of the regular employees. The assistant managers worked a two-hour shift during the luncheon period five days a week to gain knowledge about bookkeeping and management. Those becoming managers remained at that level unless they expressed interest in investing in the business.

The employees were mostly college students, with a few high school students performing the less challenging jobs. Because Perfect Pizzeria was located in an area with few job opportunities, it was relatively easy for it to fill its employee quotas. All the employees, with the exception of the manager, were employed part-time. Consequently, they earned only the minimum wage.

The Perfect Pizzeria system is devised so that food and beverage costs and profits are set up according to a percentage. If the percentage of food unsold or damaged in any way is very low, the manager gets a bonus. If the percentage is high, the manager does not receive a bonus; rather, he or she receives only his or her normal salary.

There are many ways in which the percentage can fluctuate. Because the manager cannot be in the store 24 hours a day, some employees make up for their paychecks by helping themselves to the food. When a friend comes in to order a pizza, extra ingredients are

*John E. Dittrich and Robert A. Zawacki, *People and Organizations* (Plano, TX: Business Publications, 1981), pp. 126–28. Used by permission of McGraw-Hill/Irwin.

put on the friend's pizza. Occasional nibbles by 18 to 20 employees throughout the day at the meal table also raise the percentage figure. An occasional bucket of sauce may be spilled or a pizza accidentally burned. Sometimes the wrong size of pizza may be made.

In the event of an employee mistake or a burned pizza by the oven person, the expense is supposed to come from the individual. Because of peer pressure, the night manager seldom writes up a bill for the erring employee. Instead, the establishment takes the loss and the error goes unnoticed until the end of the month when the inventory is taken. That's when the manager finds out that the percentage is high and that there will be no bonus.

In the present instance, the manager took retaliatory measures. Previously, each employee was entitled to a free pizza, salad, and all the soft drinks he or she could drink for every 6 hours of work. The manager raised this figure from 6 to 12 hours of work. However, the employees had received these 6-hour benefits for a long time. Therefore, they simply took advantage of the situation whenever the manager or the assistant was not in the building. Although the night managers theoretically had complete control of the operation in the evenings, they did not command the respect that the manager or assistant manager did. That was because night managers received the same pay as the regular employees, could not reprimand other employees, and were basically the same age or sometimes even younger than the other employees.

Thus, apathy grew within the pizzeria. There seemed to be a further separation between the manager and his workers, who started out to be a closely knit group. The manager made no attempt to alleviate the problem, because he felt it would iron itself out. Either the employees who were dissatisfied would quit or they would be content to put up with the new regulations. As it turned out, there was a rash of employee dismissals. The manager had no problem in filling the vacancies with new workers, but the loss of key personnel was costly to the business.

With the large turnover, the manager found he had to spend more time in the building, supervising and sometimes taking the place of inexperienced workers. This was in direct violation of the franchise regulation, which stated that a manager would act as a supervisor and at no time take part in the actual food preparation.

Employees were not placed under strict supervision with the manager working alongside them. The operation no longer worked smoothly because of differences between the remaining experienced workers and the manager concerning the way in which a particular function should be performed.

Within a two-month period, the manager was again free to go back to his office and leave his subordinates in charge of the entire operation. During this two-month period, in spite of the differences between experienced workers and the manager, the unsold/damaged food percentage had returned to the previous low level and the manager received a bonus each month. The manager felt that his problems had been resolved and that conditions would remain the same, since the new personnel had been properly trained.

It didn't take long for the new employees to become influenced by the other employees. Immediately after the manager had returned to his supervisory role, the unsold/damaged food percentage began to rise. This time the manager took a bolder step. He cut out *any* benefits that the employees had—no free pizzas, salads, or drinks. With the job market at an even lower ebb than usual, most employees were forced to stay. The appointment of a new area supervisor made it impossible for the manager to work behind the counter, because the supervisor was centrally located in Southville.

The manager tried still another approach to alleviate the rising unsold/damaged food percentage problem and maintain his bonus. He placed a notice on the bulletin board, stating that if the percentage remained at a high level, a lie detector test would be given to all employees. All those found guilty of taking or purposefully wasting food or drinks would be immediately terminated. This did not have the desired effect on the employees, because they knew if they were all subjected to the test, all would be found guilty and the manager would have to dismiss all of them. This would leave him in a worse situation than ever.

Even before the following month's unsold/damaged food percentage was calculated, the manager knew it would be high. He had evidently received information from one of the night managers about the employees' feelings toward the notice. What he did not expect was that the percentage would reach an all-time high. That is the state of affairs at the present time.

>part III:

Team Processes

chapter 7

Team Dynamics

Whole Foods relies on teams to more effectively serve customers and fulfill employee needs.

>learningobjectives

After reading this chapter, you should be able to:

1. Define teams and discuss their benefits and limitations.
2. Explain why people are motivated to join informal groups.
3. Diagram the team effectiveness model.
4. Discuss how task characteristics, team size, and team composition influence team effectiveness.
5. Summarize the team development process.
6. Discuss how team norms develop, and how they may be altered.
7. List six factors that influence team cohesion.
8. Discuss the characteristics and factors required for success of self-directed teams and virtual teams.
9. Identify four constraints on team decision making.
10. Discuss the advantages and disadvantages of four structures that potentially improve team decision making.

When John Mackey co-founded Whole Foods Market in 1980, he adopted one of the central recommendations from the then-popular Japanese management books: successful companies rely on teams more than individuals. Even today with almost 200 stores employing 40,000 people in the United States, Canada, and the United Kingdom, Whole Foods remains true to its team-based structure. Every Whole Foods store is divided into about 10 teams, such as the prepared-foods team, the cashier/front-end team, and the seafood team. Teams are "self-directed" because team members make the decisions about their work unit with minimal interference from management. Each team is responsible for managing inventory, labor productivity, and gross margins. Team members make many of the product-placement decisions, a sharp contrast to the centralized purchasing decisions in most grocery chains.

Whole Foods teams also decide on whether new hires get to remain as permanent team members. After a recruit is temporarily employed for 30 to 45 days, team members vote on whether the individual should become a permanent member; at least two-thirds must vote in favor for the recruit to join the team permanently. Team members take these hiring decisions seriously because their monthly bonuses are based on team performance. Every four weeks, the company calculates each team's performance against goals and cost efficiencies. When the team finds ways to work more effectively, the unused budget is divided among them. This team bonus can add up to hundreds of extra dollars in each paycheck.[1]

///

Several factors explain why Whole Foods Market has become a retail success story and one of the best places to work in America, but the company's focus on teams is clearly one of those factors. This focus on teamwork extends to most industries. At General Electric's (GE) Aircraft Engines division in Durham, North Carolina, employees are organized into more than a dozen 16-member teams who receive feedback and rewards based partially on team performance. Ford Motor Company's legal department was recently identified as one of the best legal departments in the country, partly because almost everything the department does is achieved through project teams. C&S Wholesale Grocers, the second-largest grocery wholesaler in the United States, created self-directed teams throughout its warehouse operation, resulting in significantly higher productivity and lower absenteeism.[2]

This chapter begins by defining teams and examining the reasons why organizations rely on teams and why people join informal groups in organizational settings. Several types of teams are described, including the increasing prevalence of self-directed teams and virtual teams. A large segment of this chapter examines a model of team effectiveness, which includes team and organizational environment, team design, and the team processes of development, norms, cohesion, and trust. The final section of this chapter looks at the challenges and strategies for making better decisions in teams.

After reading the next two sections, you should be able to:

1. *Define teams and discuss their benefits and limitations.*
2. *Explain why people are motivated to join informal groups.*

learningobjectives<

>Teams and Informal Groups

Teams are groups of two or more people who interact and influence each other, are mutually accountable for achieving common goals associated with organizational objectives, and perceive themselves as a social entity within an organization.[3] This definition has a few important components worth repeating. First, all teams exist to fulfill some purpose,

TEAMS:
groups of two or more people who interact and influence each other, are mutually accountable for achieving common goals associated with organizational objectives, and perceive themselves as a social entity within an organization

[Exhibit 7.1] Types of Teams in Organizations

Team Type	Description
Departmental teams	Employees have similar or complementary skills located in the same unit of a functional structure; usually minimal task interdependence because each person works with employees in other departments.
Production/service/ leadership teams	Typically multiskilled (employees have diverse competencies), team members collectively produce a common product/service or make ongoing decisions; production/service teams typically have an assembly line type of interdependence, whereas leadership teams tend to have tight interactive (reciprocal) interdependence.
Self-directed teams	Similar to production/service teams except (1) they are organized around work processes that complete an entire piece of work requiring several interdependent tasks, and (2) they have substantial autonomy over the execution of those tasks (i.e., they usually control inputs, flow, and outputs with little or no supervision).
Advisory teams	Teams that provide recommendations to decision makers; includes committees, advisory councils, work councils, and review panels; may be temporary, but often permanent, some with frequent rotation of members.
Task force (project) teams	Usually multiskilled, temporary teams whose assignment is to solve a problem, realize an opportunity, or design a product or service.
Skunkworks	Multiskilled teams that are usually located away from the organization and relatively free of its hierarchy; often initiated by an entrepreneurial team leader who borrows people and resources (*bootlegging*) to design a product or develop a service.
Virtual teams	Formal teams whose members operate across space, time, and organizational boundaries and are linked through information technologies to achieve organizational tasks; may be a temporary task force or permanent service team.
Communities of practice	May be informal groups, but increasingly formal teams bound together by shared expertise and passion for a particular activity or interest; main purpose is to share information; often rely on information technologies as main source of interaction (i.e., a specific form of virtual team).

such as assembling a product, providing a service, designing a new manufacturing facility, or making an important decision. Second, team members are held together by their interdependence and need for collaboration to achieve common goals. All teams require some form of communication so members can coordinate and share common objectives. Third, team members influence each other, although some members are more influential than others regarding the team's goals and activities. Finally, a team exists when its members perceive themselves to be a team.

Exhibit 7.1 briefly describes various types of teams in organizations. Some teams are permanent, while others are temporary; some are responsible for making products or providing services, while others exist to make decisions or share knowledge. Each type of team has been created deliberately to serve an organizational purpose. Some teams, such as skunkworks teams, are not initially sanctioned by management, yet are called "teams" because members clearly work toward an organization objective.

Informal Groups

Although most of our attention in this chapter is on formal teams, employees also belong to informal groups. All teams are groups, but many groups do not satisfy our definition of teams. Groups include people assembled together whether or not they have any interdependence or organizationally focused objective. The friends you meet for lunch are an *informal group,* but wouldn't be called a team because they have little or no interdependence (each person could just as easily eat lunch alone) and no organizationally-mandated purpose (which is why they are "informal"). Instead, they exist primarily for the benefit of their members. Although the terms are used interchangeably, "teams" has largely replaced "groups" in the language of business when referring to employees who work together to complete tasks.[4]

People join informal groups for several reasons, each of which also applies to a person's motivation to be members of formal teams. One reason is that human beings are social animals. Our drive to bond is hardwired through evolutionary development, which creates a need to belong to informal groups.[5] This is evident by the fact that people invest considerable time and effort forming and maintaining social relationships without any special circumstances or ulterior motives. A second explanation is provided by social identity theory, which states that individuals define themselves by their group affiliations. Thus, we join groups—particularly those viewed favorably by others and that are similar to our existing values—because they shape and reinforce our self-image.[6]

A third reason why people form informal groups and are motivated to be on formal teams is that they accomplish tasks that cannot be achieved by individuals working alone. For example, employees will sometimes create a group to oppose organizational changes because the group collectively has more power than individuals complaining alone. A fourth explanation for informal groups is that in stressful situations we are comforted by the mere presence of other people and are therefore motivated to be near them. When in danger, people congregate near each other even though it serves no apparent purpose. Similarly, employees tend to mingle more often when hearing rumors that the company might be sold.[7]

>Advantages and Disadvantages of Teams

Why do Whole Foods, GE, Ford, C&S Wholesale Grocers, and many other organizations rely so heavily on teams rather than individuals? The answer to this question has a long history, dating back to research on British coal mining in the 1940s and the Japanese economic miracle of the 1970s.[8] These early studies and a huge number of investigations since then have revealed that *under the right conditions,* teams make better decisions, develop better products and services, and create a more engaged workforce compared with employees working alone.[9] Similarly, team members can quickly share information and coordinate tasks, whereas these processes are slower and prone to more errors in traditional departments led by supervisors. Teams typically provide superior customer service because they provide more breadth of knowledge and expertise to customers than individual "stars" can offer.

In many situations, people are potentially more motivated when working in teams than alone.[10] One reason for this motivation is that, as we mentioned a few paragraphs ago, employees have a drive to bond and are motivated to fulfill the goals of groups to which they belong. This motivation is particularly strong when the team is part of the employee's social identity. Second, people are more motivated in teams because they are accountable to fellow team members, who monitor performance more closely than a traditional supervisor. This is particularly true where the team's performance depends on the worst performer, such as on an assembly line where how fast the product is assembled depends on the speed of the slowest employee. Third, under some circumstances, performance improves when employees work near others because co-workers become benchmarks of comparison. Employees are also motivated to work harder because of apprehension that their performance will be compared to others' performance.

The Trouble with Teams

In spite of the many benefits of teams, they are not always as effective as individuals working alone.[11] Teams are usually better suited to work that is sufficiently complex, such as designing a building or auditing a company's financial records. Under these circumstances, the necessary knowledge and skills are not typically found within one person, the work is performed more efficiently by dividing its tasks into more specialized roles, and people in those specialized roles require frequent coordination with each other. In contrast, work is typically performed more effectively by individuals alone when they have all the necessary knowledge and skills and the work cannot be divided into specialized tasks or is not complex enough to benefit from specialization. Even where the work can and should be specialized, a team structure might not be necessary if the tasks performed by several people require minimal coordination.

PROCESS LOSSES: resources (including time and energy) expended toward team development and maintenance rather than the task

The main problem with teams is that they have additional costs called **process losses**—resources (including time and energy) expended toward team development and maintenance rather than the task.[12] It is much easier for someone to coordinate his or her own actions than with other people. As we will learn in this chapter, to perform well, team members need to agree and develop mutual understanding of their goals, the strategy to accomplish those goals, their specific roles, and informal rules of conduct.[13] These team requirements divert time and energy away from performing the work. The process loss problem is particularly apparent when adding new people to the team. Team performance suffers when a team adds members, because those employees need to learn how the team operates and how to coordinate efficiently with other team members. The software industry even has a name for this. **Brooks's law** (also called the "mythical man-month") says that adding more people to a late software project only makes it later!

BROOKS'S LAW: also called the "mythical man-month", this principle says that adding more people to a late software project only makes it later

Social Loafing

SOCIAL LOAFING: occurs when people exert less effort (and usually perform at a lower level) when working in teams than when working alone

Perhaps the best-known limitation of teams is the risk of productivity loss due to **social loafing.** Social loafing occurs when people exert less effort (and usually perform at a lower level) when working in teams than when working alone.[14] It is most likely to occur in large teams where individual output is difficult to identify. This particularly includes situations in which team members work alone toward a common output pool. Under these conditions, employees aren't as worried that their performance will be noticed. Therefore, one way to minimize social loafing is to make each team member's contribution more noticeable, such as by reducing the size of the team or measuring each team member's performance. Social loafing is also less likely to occur when the task is interesting, because individuals have a higher intrinsic motivation to perform their duties. It is less common when the group's objective is important, possibly because individuals experience more pressure from other team members to perform well. Finally, social loafing occurs less frequently among members who value team membership and believe in working toward the team's objectives.[15]

>**learning**objectives

After reading the next two sections, you should be able to:

3. *Diagram the team effectiveness model.*

4. *Discuss how task characteristics, team size, and team composition influence team effectiveness.*

>A Model of Team Effectiveness

Why are some teams effective while others fail? This question has challenged organizational researchers for some time and, as you might expect, numerous models of team effectiveness have been proposed over the years.[16] Exhibit 7.2 presents the model of team effectiveness that pulls together the main concepts on team effectiveness and will be examined closely over the next several pages. Although this model shows how the concepts

[Exhibit 7.2] Team Effectiveness Model

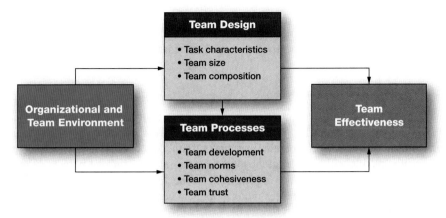

relate to each other, it is best viewed as a template of several theories. For example, the team effectiveness model refers to team composition and team cohesion, both of which have specific theories and models to explain how those concepts operate.

Team effectiveness has three components.[17] First, effective teams have high performance; that is, they achieve their objectives. Second, team effectiveness relates to the satisfaction and well-being of its members. People join and remain members of teams to fulfill their personal needs, so effectiveness is partly measured by this need fulfillment. Third, team effectiveness relates to the team's ability to survive. It must be able to maintain the commitment of its members, particularly during the turbulence of the team's development. Without this commitment, people leave and the team will fall apart. This element of team effectiveness also includes the ability to secure sufficient resources and find a benevolent environment in which to operate.

>Organizational and Team Environment

The organizational and team environment represents all of the factors beyond the team's boundaries that influence its effectiveness. Team members tend to work together more effectively when they are at least partly rewarded for team performance.[18] For instance, part of an employee's paycheck at Whole Foods Market is determined by the team's productivity. Communication systems can influence team effectiveness, particularly in virtual teams, which are highly dependent on information technologies to coordinate work. Another environmental factor is the organizational structure; teams flourish when organized around work processes because it increases interaction among team members. High-performance teams also depend on organizational leaders who provide support and strategic direction while team members focus on operational efficiency and flexibility.[19]

Along with these conditions, the physical layout of the team's workspace can make a difference. Pixar Animation Studios and Fifth Third Securities are two companies that have specifically designed the work area to improve communication among team members. Medrad, Inc., the Indianola, Pennsylvania, medical device manufacturer, found that one of the best ways to support teams was by replacing the straight-line assembly line with a clustered production arrangement in which members of each team work more closely in U-shaped work cells. A successful trial confirmed that the U-shaped cell physical arrangement improved team performance by improving the ability of team members to observe and assist each other.[20]

>Team Design Elements

Along with setting up a team-friendly environment, managers need to carefully design the team itself, including task characteristics, team size, team composition, and team roles.

Task Characteristics

What type of work is best for teams? As we noted earlier, teams operate better than individuals working alone on work that is sufficiently complex, such as launching the business in a new market, developing a computer operating system, or constructing a bridge. Complex work requires skills and knowledge beyond the competencies of one person. Teams are particularly well-suited when this complex work can be divided into more specialized roles, and people in those specialized roles require frequent coordination with each other. Some evidence also suggests that teams work best with well-structured tasks because it is easier to coordinate work among several people.[21] The challenge, however, is to find tasks with the uncommon combination of being both well structured and complex.

TASK INTER-DEPENDENCE: the extent that team members must share materials, information, or expertise in order to perform their jobs

One task characteristic that is particularly important for teams is **task interdependence**—the extent that team members must share materials, information, or expertise in order to perform their jobs.[22] Task interdependence represents the collective degree of mutual dependence team members have on each other for resources. *Pooled interdependence* produces minimal interdependence, such as when team members share machinery, support staff, or some other resource from a common source. Interdependence is higher under *sequential interdependence,* in which the output of one person is the direct input for another person or unit (similar to relations among employees on an assembly line). *Reciprocal interdependence,* in which work output is exchanged back and forth among individuals, produces the highest degree of interdependence. Employees with reciprocal interdependence should almost always be organized into teams to facilitate coordination in their interwoven relationship. The general rule is that the higher the level of task interdependence, the greater the need for teams rather than individuals working alone. However, this rule applies when team members have the same task goals, such as serving the same clients or collectively assembling the same product. When team members have different goals, teamwork might create more conflict than individuals who are supervised.

Team Size

The most effective teams have the right number of team members. One popular (but untested) rule is that the optimal team size is somewhere between five to seven people. In reality, the optimal team size depends on a few things. Teams with a dozen or more people are typically less effective because they consume more time and effort coordinating their roles and resolving differences (i.e., higher process losses). A somewhat extreme example is Whole Foods' 140-person cashier team in New York City's Columbus Circle. A team this large is too difficult to coordinate, and team members lack cohesion, so Whole Foods divides the group into smaller teams with a dozen employees on each team. All cashiers meet as one massive group every month to discuss production issues, but the smaller teams work more effectively on a day-to-day basis.[23]

Although companies usually need to break up large teams, they also run into trouble when teams are too small to accomplish the team's objectives. So, teams should be large enough to provide the necessary competencies and perspectives to perform the work, yet small enough to maintain efficient coordination and meaningful involvement of each member.

Team Composition

Choosing a new team member is too important a decision at Whole Foods Market to be left to management. Instead, as this chapter's opening vignette noted, new hires are approved for permanent employment by their teammates. To work effectively in a team, employees must have more than technical skills and self-leadership to perform their own work; they must also be able and willing to support team dynamics. The most frequently mentioned characteristics or behaviors of effective team members are cooperation, coordination, communication, psychological support, and conflict resolution. The first three mainly (but not entirely) are task-related, while the last two mostly assist team maintenance:[24]

- *Cooperation.* Effective team members are willing and able to work together rather than alone. This includes sharing resources and being sufficiently adaptive or flexible to accommodate the needs and preferences of other team members, such as rescheduling use of machinery so another team member with a tighter deadline can use it.

- *Coordination.* Effective team members actively manage the team's work so it is performed efficiently and harmoniously. For example, effective team members keep the team on track and help to integrate the work performed by different members. This typically requires effective team members to know the work of other team members, not just their own.

- *Communication.* Effective team members transmit information freely (rather than hoarding), efficiently (using the best channel and language), and respectfully (minimizing arousal of negative emotions). They also listen actively to co-workers.

- *Psychological support.* Effective team members help co-workers to maintain a positive and healthy psychological state. They show empathy, provide psychological comfort, and build co-worker feelings of confidence and self-worth.

- *Conflict resolution.* Conflict is inevitable in social settings, so effective team members have the skills and motivation to resolve dysfunctional disagreements among team members. This requires effective use of various conflict handling styles as well as diagnostic skills to identify and resolve the structural sources of conflict.

These characteristics of effective team members are associated with conscientiousness and extroversion personality traits, as well as with emotional intelligence. Furthermore, the old saying "one bad apple spoils the barrel" may apply to teams because one team member who is low on these teamwork competencies may undermine the dynamics of the entire team.[25]

Another important dimension of team composition is diversity.[26] Teams whose members have diverse knowledge, skills, and perspectives are generally more effective in situations involving complex problems requiring innovative solutions. One reason is that people from different backgrounds see a problem or opportunity from different perspectives. A second reason is that they usually have a broader knowledge base. A third reason favoring teams with diverse members is that they provide better representation of the team's constituents, such as other departments or clients from similarly diverse backgrounds. However, diverse employees take longer to become a high-performing team. They are also more susceptible to "faultlines"—hypothetical dividing lines that may split a team into subgroups along gender, ethnic, professional, or other dimensions. Faultlines increase the risk of dysfunctional conflict and other behaviors that undermine team effectiveness.

Identifying Effective Team Players in Gourami
Shell discovered long ago that it isn't easy to measure team competencies in a job interview. Instead, the global energy company launched the Shell Gourami Business Challenge, a five-day event in which four dozen engineering and business university students are split into several teams (exploration, refining, finance, marketing, etc.) and must develop and present a five-year business strategy for Shell in the fictitious nation of Gourami. Introduced in Europe a decade ago, and more recently in North America and Asia, participants first attended a cultural sensitivity briefing, but the effects of team diversity are still apparent throughout the exercise. One Filipino student in the Asian Gourami Challenge felt initial tension because the Australian team members were "more straightforward and tell you right away if you're doing something right or wrong." Another Asian participant said the Gourami game made him realize how diversity affects the team's development and performance. "I learnt how cultural aspects can affect the way a team works together, and how to handle working with an international group."[27]

>**learning**objectives

After reading the next two sections, you should be able to:

5. *Summarize the team development process.*
6. *Discuss how team norms develop, and how they may be altered.*
7. *List six factors that influence team cohesion.*

>Team Processes

The third set of elements in the team effectiveness model, collectively known as team processes, includes team development, norms, cohesion, and trust. These represent evolving dynamics that the team shapes and reshapes over time.

Team Development

A few years ago, the National Transportation Safety Board (NTSB) studied the circumstances under which airplane cockpit crews were most likely to have accidents and related problems. What they discovered was startling: 73 percent of all incidents took place on the crew's first day, and 44 percent occurred on the crew's very first flight together. This isn't an isolated example. NASA studied fatigue of pilots after returning from multiple-day trips. Fatigued pilots made more errors in the NASA flight simulator, as one would expect. But the NASA researchers didn't expect the discovery that fatigued crews who had worked together made fewer errors than did rested crews who had not yet flown together.[28]

The NTSB and NASA studies reveal that team members must resolve several issues and pass through several stages of development before emerging as an effective work unit. They need to get to know and trust each other, understand and agree upon their respective roles, discover appropriate and inappropriate behaviors, and learn how to coordinate with each other. The longer that team members work together, the better they develop common

[Exhibit 7.3] Stages of Team Development

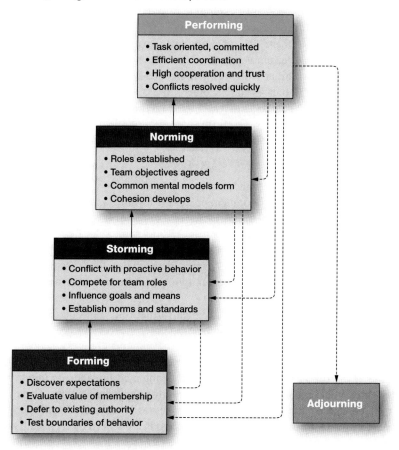

or complementary mental models, mutual understanding, and effective performance routines to complete the work.

A popular model that captures many team development activities is shown in Exhibit 7.3.[29] The model shows teams moving systematically from one stage to the next, while the dashed lines illustrate that teams might fall back to an earlier stage of development as new members join or other conditions disrupt the team's maturity. *Forming,* the first stage of team development is a period of testing and orientation in which members learn about each other and evaluate the benefits and costs of continued membership. People tend to be polite, will defer to authority, and try to find out what is expected of them and how they will fit into the team. The *storming* stage is marked by interpersonal conflict as members become more proactive and compete for various team roles. Members try to establish norms of appropriate behavior and performance standards.

During the *norming* stage, the team develops its first real sense of cohesion as roles are established and a consensus forms around group objectives and a common or complementary team-based mental model. By the *performing* stage, team members have learned to efficiently coordinate and resolve conflicts. In high-performance teams, members are highly cooperative, have a high level of trust in each other, are committed to group objectives, and identify with the team. Finally, the *adjourning* stage occurs when the team is about to disband. Team members shift their attention away from task orientation to a relationship focus.

The five-stage model is consistent with what students experience on team projects, but it is far from a perfect representation of the team development process.[30] For instance, it does not show that some teams remain in a particular stage longer than others. It also blurs two distinct processes during team development: membership and competence.[31] The membership development process occurs as employees make the transition from viewing the team as something "out there" to something that is part of themselves. In other words, team development occurs when employees shift their view of the team from "them" to "us." This relates to becoming familiar with the team, making it part of their social identity, and shaping the team to better fit their ideal. The other process—developing team competence—includes several changes related to team learning. Team members develop habitual routines that increase work efficiency. They also form shared or complementary mental models regarding team resources, goals and tasks, social interaction, and characteristics of other team members.[32]

Team Roles

ROLE:
a set of behaviors that people are expected to perform because they hold certain positions in a team and organization

An important part of the team development process is forming and reinforcing team roles. A **role** is a set of behaviors that people are expected to perform because they hold certain positions in a team and organization.[33] In a team setting, some roles help the team achieve its goals; other roles maintain relationships within the team. Some team roles are formally assigned to specific people. For example, team leaders are usually expected to initiate discussion, ensure that everyone has an opportunity to present their views, and help the team reach agreement on the issues discussed.

Although team members are usually assigned formal roles (and therefore are part of team design), we have introduced the topic here because roles are merely assigned to team members. Instead, throughout the continuous team development process, people vary their formal roles to suit their personality and values as well as the wishes of other team members. Furthermore, many roles exist informally, such as being a cheerleader, an initiator of new ideas, or an advisor that encourages the group to soberly rethink their actions. These informal roles are shared by the entire team, but many are eventually associated with specific team members. Again, this informal role assignment process is influenced by each team member's personal preferences (personality and values) as well as through negotiated dynamics with other team members.[34]

Team Norms

NORMS:
the informal rules and shared expectations that groups establish to regulate the behavior of their members

Norms are the informal rules and shared expectations that groups establish to regulate the behavior of their members. Norms apply only to behavior, not to private thoughts or feelings. Furthermore, norms exist only for behaviors that are important to the team.[35] Norms are enforced in various ways. Co-workers grimace if we are late for a meeting or make sarcastic comments if we don't have our part of the project completed on time. Norms are also directly reinforced through praise from high-status members, more access to valued resources, or other rewards available to the team. But team members often conform to prevailing norms without direct reinforcement or punishment because they identify with the group and want to align their behavior with the team's values. The more closely the person's social identity is connected to the group, the more the individual is motivated to avoid negative sanctions from that group.[36]

How Team Norms Develop

Norms develop as soon as teams form because people need to anticipate or predict how others will act. Even subtle events during the team's formation, such as how team members initially greet each other and where they sit in the first meetings, can initiate norms that are later difficult to change. Norms also form as team members discover behaviors that help them function more effectively (such as the need to respond quickly to e-mail). In particular, a critical event in the team's history can trigger formation of a norm or sharpen a previously vague one. A third influence on team norms is the past experiences and values that members bring to the team. If members of a new team value work/life balance, then norms are likely to develop that discourage long hours and work overload.[37]

Preventing and Changing Dysfunctional Team Norms

Team norms often become deeply anchored, so the best way to avoid norms that undermine organizational success or employee well-being is to establish desirable norms when the team is first formed. One way to do this is to clearly state desirable norms as soon as the team is created. Another approach is to select people with appropriate values. If organizational leaders want their teams to have strong safety norms, then they should hire people who already value safety and clearly identify the importance of safety when the team is formed.

The suggestions so far refer to new teams, but how can organizational leaders maintain desirable norms in older teams? First, as one recent study affirmed, leaders often have the capacity to alter existing norms.[38] By speaking up or actively coaching the team, they can often subdue dysfunctional norms while developing useful norms. Team-based reward systems can also weaken counterproductive norms; however, studies report that employees might continue to abide by team norms (such as limiting output) even though their compliant behavior reduces their paycheck. Finally, if dysfunctional norms are deeply ingrained and the previous solutions don't work, it may be necessary to disband the group and replace it with people having more favorable norms.

Team Cohesion

Team cohesion refers to the degree of attraction people feel toward the team and their motivation to remain members. It is a characteristic of the team, including the extent to which its members are attracted to the team, are committed to the team's goals or tasks, and feel a collective sense of team pride.[39] Thus, team cohesion is an emotional experience, not just a calculation of whether to stay or leave the team. It exists when team members make the team part of their social identity.

> **TEAM COHESION:** the degree of attraction people feel toward the team and their motivation to remain members

Influences on Team Cohesion

Several factors influence team cohesion: member similarity, team size, member interaction, difficult entry, team success, and external competition or challenges. For the most part, these factors reflect the individual's social identity with the group and beliefs about how team membership will fulfill personal needs.

- *Member similarity.* For more than 2,000 years, philosophers and researchers have observed that people with similar backgrounds and values are more comfortable and attractive to each other. In team settings, this similarity-attraction effect means that teams have higher cohesion—or become cohesive more quickly—when members are similar to each other. The adverse effect of team diversity on cohesion depends on the type of diversity, however. For example, teams consisting of people from different job groups seem to gel together just as well as teams of people from the same job.[40]

- *Team size.* Smaller teams tend to have more cohesion than larger teams because it is easier for a few people to agree on goals and coordinate work activities. However, small teams have less cohesion when they lack enough members to perform the required tasks.

- *Member interaction.* Teams tend to have more cohesion when team members interact with each other fairly regularly. This occurs when team members perform highly interdependent tasks and work in the same physical area.

- *Somewhat difficult entry.* Teams tend to have more cohesion when entry to the team is restricted. The more elite the team, the more prestige it confers on its members, and the more they tend to value their membership in the unit. At the same time, research suggests that severe initiations can weaken team cohesion because of the adverse effects of humiliation, even for those who successfully endure the initiation.[41]

• *Team success.* Cohesion is both emotional and instrumental, with the latter referring to the notion that people feel more cohesion to teams that fulfill their needs and goals. Consequently, cohesion increases with the team's level of success.[42] Furthermore, individuals are more likely to attach their social identity to successful teams than to those with a string of failures.

• *External competition and challenges.* Team cohesion tends to increase when members face external competition or a valued objective that is challenging. This might include a threat from an external competitor or friendly competition from other teams. Employees value their membership on the team because of its ability to overcome the threat or competition, and as a form of social support. However, cohesion can dissipate when external threats are severe because these threats are stressful and cause teams to make less effective decisions.[43]

Consequences of Team Cohesion

Every team must have some minimal level of cohesion to maintain its existence. People who belong to high-cohesion teams are motivated to maintain their membership and to help the team perform effectively. Compared to low-cohesion teams, high-cohesion team members spend more time together, share information more frequently, and are more satisfied with each other. They provide each other with better social support in stressful situations.[44]

Members of high-cohesion teams are generally more sensitive to each other's needs and develop better interpersonal relationships, thereby reducing dysfunctional conflict. When conflict does arise, members tend to resolve these differences swiftly and effectively. With better cooperation and more conformity to norms, high-cohesion teams usually perform better than low-cohesion teams.[45] However, this only holds true when team norms are compatible with organizational values and objectives. Cohesion motivates employees to perform at a level more consistent with team norms, so when those norms conflict with the organization's success (such as when norms support high absenteeism or acting unethically), high cohesion will reduce team performance.[46]

Team Trust

TRUST:
a psychological state comprising the intention to accept vulnerability based on positive expectations of the intent or behavior of another person

Any relationship—including the relationship among team members—depends on a certain degree of trust.[47] **Trust** is a psychological state comprising the intention to accept vulnerability based on positive expectations of the intent or behavior of another person. A high level of trust occurs when others affect you in situations where you are at risk, but you believe they will not harm you. Trust includes both your beliefs and conscious feelings about the relationship with other team members. In other words, a person both logically evaluates the situation as trustworthy and feels that it is trustworthy.[48] Trust can also be understood in terms of the foundation of that trust. From this perspective, people trust others based on three foundations: calculus, knowledge, and identification (see Exhibit 7.4).

Calculus-based trust represents a logical calculation that other team members will act appropriately because they face sanctions if their actions violate reasonable expectations.[49] It offers the lowest potential trust and is easily broken by a violation of expectations. Generally, calculus-based trust alone cannot sustain a team's relationship, because it relies on deterrence. *Knowledge-based trust* is based on the predictability of another team member's behavior. Even if we don't agree with a particular team member's actions, his or her consistency generates some level of trust. Knowledge-based trust also relates to confidence in the other person's

[Exhibit 7.4] Three Foundations of Trust in Teams

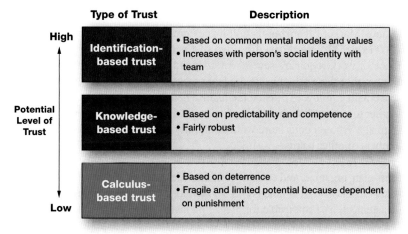

ability or competence, such as when you trust a physician.[50] Knowledge-based trust offers a higher potential level of trust and is more stable because it develops over time.

Identification-based trust is based on mutual understanding and an emotional bond among team members. It occurs when team members think like, feel like, and act like each other. High-performance teams exhibit this level of trust because they share the same values and mental models. Identification-based trust is potentially the strongest and most robust of all three types of trust. The individual's self-image is based partly on membership in the team and he/she believes their values highly overlap, so any transgressions by other team members are quickly forgiven. People are more reluctant to acknowledge a violation of this high-level trust because it strikes at the heart of their self-image.

Dynamics of Team Trust

Employees typically join a team with a moderate or high level—not a low level—of trust in their new co-workers. The main explanation for the initially high trust (called *swift trust*) in organizational settings is that people usually believe their teammates are reasonably competent (knowledge-based trust) and they tend to develop some degree of social identify with the team (identification-based trust). Even when working with strangers, most of us display some level of trust, if only because it supports our self-concept of being a nice person.[51] However, trust is fragile in new relationships because it is based on assumptions rather than well-established experience. Consequently, recent studies report that trust tends to decrease rather than increase over time. This is unfortunate because employees become less forgiving and less cooperative toward others as their level of trust decreases, which undermines team and organizational effectiveness.[52]

The team effectiveness model is a useful template for understanding how teams work—and don't work—in organizations. With this knowledge in hand, let's briefly investigate two types of teams that have received considerable attention amongst OB experts and practitioners: self-directed teams and virtual teams.

After reading the next two sections, you should be able to: **learning**objectives<

8. *Discuss the characteristics and factors required for success of self-directed teams and virtual teams.*

9. *Identify four constraints on team decision making.*

10. *Discuss the advantages and disadvantages of four structures that potentially improve team decision making.*

>Self-Directed Teams

Whole Foods Market organizes its employees not just into teams, but into **self-directed teams (SDTs).** SDTs are defined by two distinctive features.[53] First, they complete an entire piece of work requiring several interdependent tasks. This high interdependence is important because the work clusters the team members together and minimizes their interdependence with employees outside the team. The result is a close-knit group that depends on each other to accomplish their individual tasks. For example, employees in the prepared-foods team at a Whole Foods store would naturally work more closely with each other than with members of other teams.

Second, SDTs have substantial autonomy over the execution of their tasks. In particular, these teams plan, organize, and control work activities with little or no direct involvement of a higher-status supervisor. At Whole Foods Market, for example, every store team "gets a profit-and-loss statement, it's responsible for managing inventory, labor productivity, gross margins; and its members are responsible for many of the product-placement decisions," says Whole foods co-founder and CEO John Mackey.[54] And when Chrysler introduced SDTs in its Belvidere, Wisconsin, plant, supervisors learned to give teams more control over their work process. Belvidere plant manager Kurt Kavajecz recalls one such example: "This traditional first-line supervisor, who is used to putting out fires and reacting to crises, came into the new area and was amazed because the team members and the team leaders were running the area."[55]

Almost all of the top-rated manufacturing firms in the United States rely on self-directed teams.[56] The popularity of SDTs is consistent with research indicating that self-directed teams potentially increase both productivity and job satisfaction. For instance, one study found that car dealership service shops that organize employees into SDTs were significantly more profitable than shops where employees work without a team structure. Another study reported that both short- and long-term measures of customer satisfaction increased after street cleaners in a German city were organized into SDTs.[57]

Chrysler's Lean Self-Directed Teams

Chrysler president Tom LaSorda believes that one of the key success factors for the automaker's future is "smart manufacturing," which includes introducing lean manufacturing in plants operated by self-directed teams (SDTs). SDTs were introduced a decade ago at Chrysler's operations in Mexico. The plant in Saltillo, Mexico, (where LaSorda is shown here greeting employees) organizes employees into teams of a dozen people responsible for a specific set of integrated tasks, including maintenance, quality control, safety, and productivity in that work area. Now, Chrysler is introducing SDTs in its U.S. plants. To assist the culture change, team leaders completed 40 hours of training to understand their new role, and the physical workspace was rearranged to create a more intimate team environment.[58]

Success Factors for Self-Directed Teams

Self-directed teams probably would add value in most organizations, but several conditions must be in place to realize their benefits.[59] In addition to managing the team dynamics issues described earlier in this chapter, SDTs operate best when they are responsible for an entire work process, such as making an entire product or providing a service. This organization around a work process keeps each team sufficiently independent from other teams, yet demands a relatively high degree of interdependence among employees within the team.[60] SDTs should also have sufficient autonomy to organize and coordinate their work. This autonomy allows them to respond more quickly and effectively to client and stakeholder demands. It also motivates team members through feelings of empowerment. Finally, SDTs are more successful when the technology supports coordinating and communication among team members and increases job enrichment.[61] Too often, management calls a group of employees a "team," yet the work layout, assembly line structure, and other technologies isolate employees from each other.

>Virtual Teams

PricewaterhouseCoopers (PwC) employs 190 training professionals in 70 offices across the United States. These professionals, along with many more consultants and academics who provide employee development services, routinely form virtual teams for new projects. "Virtual teaming is the norm for us," says Peter Nicolas, a PwC learning solutions manager in Florham Park, New Jersey.[62] PricewaterhouseCoopers makes better use of its human capital by creating **virtual teams.** Virtual teams are teams whose members operate across space, time, and organizational boundaries and are linked through information technologies to achieve organizational tasks.[63] Virtual teams differ from traditional teams in two ways: (1) they are not usually co-located (work in the same physical area), and (2) due to their lack of co-location, members of virtual teams depend primarily on information technologies rather than face-to-face interaction to communicate and coordinate their work effort.

> **VIRTUAL TEAMS:** teams whose members operate across space, time, and organizational boundaries and are linked through information technologies to achieve organizational tasks

According to one estimate, more than 60 percent of employees in professions are members of a virtual team at some point during the year. In global companies such as IBM, almost everyone in knowledge work is part of a virtual team. One reason why virtual teams have become so widespread is that information technologies have made it easier than ever before to communicate and coordinate with people at a distance.[64] The shift from production-based to knowledge-based work is a second reason why virtual teamwork is feasible. It isn't yet possible to make a product when team members are located apart, but most of us now make decisions and ideas.

Information technologies and knowledge-based work make virtual teams *possible,* but organizational learning and globalization are two reasons why they are increasingly *necessary*. Virtual teams represent a natural part of the organizational learning process because they encourage employees to share and use knowledge where geography limits more direct forms of collaboration. Globalization makes virtual teams increasingly necessary because employees are spread around the planet rather than around one city. Thus, global businesses depend on virtual teamwork to leverage their human capital.

Success Factors for Virtual Teams

Virtual teams have all of the challenges of traditional teams along with the complications of distance and time. Fortunately, OB researchers have been keenly interested in virtual teams, and their studies are now yielding ways to improve virtual team effectiveness.[65]

First, along with the list of team competencies described earlier in this chapter, members of successful virtual teams require the ability to communicate easily through technology, strong self-leadership skills to motivate and guide their behavior without peers or bosses nearby, and higher emotional intelligence so they can decipher the feelings of teammates from e-mail and other limited communication media. Second, studies have found that leaders typically impose technology on virtual teams rather than allow them to adopt technology that suits their needs at a particular time. The best situation occurs where virtual teams have a toolkit of communication vehicles (e-mail, virtual white boards, video conferencing, etc.), which gain and lose importance over different parts of the project.

The final recommendation is that virtual team members should meet face-to-face fairly early in the team development process. This idea may seem contradictory to the entire notion of virtual teams, but so far, no technology has replaced face-to-face interaction for high-level bonding and mutual understanding. For instance, when IBM formed a virtual team to build an electronic customer-access system for Shell, employees from both firms began with an "all hands" face-to-face gathering to assist the team development process. The two firms also made a rule that the dispersed team members should have face-to-face contact at least once every six weeks throughout the project. Without this, "after about five or six weeks we found some of that communication would start to break down," says Sharon Hartung, the IBM co-manager for the project.[66]

>Team Decision Making

Self-directed work teams, virtual teams, and practically all other groups are expected to make decisions. Under certain conditions, teams are more effective than individuals at identifying problems, choosing alternatives, and evaluating their decisions. To leverage these benefits, however, we first need to understand the constraints on effective team decision making. Then, we look at specific team structures that try to overcome these constraints.

Constraints on Team Decision Making

Anyone who has spent enough time in the workplace can reel off several ways in which teams stumble in decision making. The four most common problems are time constraints, evaluation apprehension, pressure to conform, and groupthink.

Time Constraints

There's a saying that "committees keep minutes and waste hours." This reflects the fact that teams take longer than individuals to make decisions.[67] Unlike individuals, teams require extra time to organize, coordinate, and maintain relationships. The larger the group, the more time is required to make a decision. Team members need time to learn about each other and build rapport. They need to manage an imperfect communication process so that there is sufficient understanding of each other's ideas. They also need to coordinate roles and rules of order within the decision process.

Another time-related constraint found in most team structures is that only one person can speak at a time.[68] This problem, known as **production blocking,** undermines idea generation in several ways. First, team members need to listen in on the conversation to find an opportune time to speak up, and this monitoring makes it difficult for them to concentrate on their own ideas. Second, ideas are fleeting, so the longer they wait to speak up, the more likely these flickering ideas will die out. Third, team members might remember their fleeting thoughts by concentrating on them, but this causes them to pay less attention to the

PRODUCTION BLOCKING: a time constraint in team decision making due to the procedural requirement that only one person may speak at a time

conversation. By ignoring what others are saying, team members miss other potentially good ideas as well as the opportunity to convey their ideas to others in the group.

Evaluation Apprehension

Individuals are reluctant to mention ideas that seem silly because they believe (often correctly) that other team members are silently evaluating them.[69] This **evaluation apprehension** is based on the individual's desire to create a favorable self-presentation and a need to protect self-esteem. It is most common in meetings attended by people with different levels of status or expertise, or when members formally evaluate each other's performance throughout the year (as in 360-degree feedback). Creative ideas often sound bizarre or illogical when first presented, so evaluation apprehension tends to discourage employees from mentioning them in front of co-workers.

EVALUATION APPREHENSION: occurs when individuals are reluctant to mention ideas that seem silly because they believe (often correctly) that other team members are silently evaluating them

Pressure to Conform

Team cohesion leads employees to conform to the team's norms. This control keeps the group organized around common goals, but it may also cause team members to suppress their dissenting opinions, particularly when a strong team norm is related to the issue. When someone does state a point of view that violates the majority opinion, other members might punish the violator or try to persuade him or her that the opinion is incorrect. Conformity can also be subtle. To some extent, we depend on the opinions that others hold to validate our own views. If co-workers don't agree with us, then we begin to question our own opinions even without overt peer pressure.

Groupthink

Groupthink is the tendency of highly cohesive groups to value consensus at the price of decision quality.[70] Groupthink goes beyond the problem of conformity by focusing on how decisions go awry when team members try to maintain harmony. This desire for harmony exists as a group norm and is most apparent when team members have a strong social identity with the group. Along with a desire for harmony, groupthink supposedly occurs when the team is isolated from outsiders, the team leader is opinionated (rather than impartial), the team is under stress due to an external threat, the team has experienced recent failures or other decision-making problems, and the team lacks clear guidance from corporate policies or procedures.

GROUPTHINK: the tendency of highly cohesive groups to value consensus at the price of decision quality

Although the word "groupthink" is now part of everyday language, the concept is quickly losing favor among OB experts. The symptoms of groupthink don't cluster together as the concept assumes, and some of these characteristics actually tend to improve rather than undermine decision making in some situations.[71] However, at least one element of groupthink—overconfidence—does create problems in team decision making. Studies consistently report that highly confident teams have a false sense of invulnerability, which makes them less attentive in decision making than are moderately confident teams.[72]

Team Structures to Improve Decision Making

There is plenty of research revealing problems with team decision making, but several solutions also emerge from these bad-news studies. Team members need to be confident in their decision making, but not so confident that they collectively feel invulnerable. This calls for team norms that encourage critical thinking as well as team membership with sufficient diversity. Checks and balances need to be in place to prevent one or two people from dominating the discussion. The team should also be large enough to possess the collective knowledge to resolve the problem, yet small enough that the team doesn't consume too much time or restrict individual input.

NASA's Constructive Conflict Room

The ill-fated flight of the space shuttle Columbia was a wake-up call for how NASA's mission management team makes decisions. The Columbia accident investigation team concluded that concerns raised by engineers were either deflected or watered down because the mission management team appeared to be "immersed in a culture of invincibility" and hierarchical authority discouraged constructive debate. If top decision makers had more fully considered the extent of damage during takeoff, they might have been able to save

Columbia's seven crew members. To foster more open communications and constructive debate, the mission management team's assigned-seating rectangular table has been replaced by a C-shaped arrangement where people sit wherever they want (shown in photo). None of the 24 members stands out above the others in the new set-up. Around the walls of the room are pearls of wisdom reminding everyone of the pitfalls of team decision making. "People in groups tend to agree on courses of action which, as individuals, they know are stupid," warns one poster.[73]

Team structures also help to minimize the problems described over the previous few pages. Four structures potentially improve team decision making in team settings: constructive conflict, brainstorming, electronic brainstorming, and nominal group technique.

Constructive Conflict

A popular way to improve team decision making at Corning Inc. is to assign promising ideas to two-person teams, who spend up to four months analyzing the feasibility of their assigned idea. The unique feature about this process is that the team is deliberately designed so that one person is from marketing, while the other has technical expertise. This oil-and-water combination sometimes ruffles feathers, but it seems to generate better ideas and evaluations. "We find great constructive conflict this way," says Deborah Mills, who leads Corning's early-stage marketing team.[74]

CONSTRUCTIVE CONFLICT: (also known as task or cognitive conflict) occurs when people focus their discussion on the issue while maintaining respectfulness for people having other points of view

Constructive conflict (also known as *task or cognitive conflict*) occurs when people focus their discussion on the issue while maintaining respectfulness for people having other points of view. This conflict is called "constructive" because different viewpoints are encouraged so that ideas and recommendations can be clarified, redesigned, and tested for logical soundness. The main advantage of this debate is that it presents different points of view, which encourages everyone to reexamine their assumptions and logic. The main challenge with constructive conflict is that healthy debate too often slides into personal attacks, which may explain why the evidence of constructive conflict on team decision making is inconsistent.[75] We will explore this issue further in Chapter 10, along with specific strategies to minimize the emotional effects of conflict while maintaining constructive debate.

Brainstorming

Brainstorming tries to leverage the creative potential of teams by establishing four simple rules: (1) speak freely—describe even the craziest ideas; (2) don't criticize others or their ideas; (3) provide as many ideas as possible—the quality of ideas increases with the quantity of ideas; and (4) build on the ideas that others have presented. These rules are supposed to encourage divergent thinking while minimizing evaluation apprehension and other team dynamics problems. Lab studies using university students concluded many years ago that brainstorming isn't so effective, largely because production blocking and evaluation apprehension still interfere with team dynamics.[76]

However, brainstorming may be more beneficial than the earlier studies indicated.[77] The earlier lab studies measured the number of ideas generated, whereas recent investigations within companies that use brainstorming indicate that this team structure results in more *creative* ideas, which is the main reason why companies use brainstorming. Also, evaluation apprehension is less of a problem in high-performing teams that embrace a learning orientation culture than for students brainstorming in lab experiments. Another overlooked advantage of brainstorming is that participants interact and participate directly, thereby increasing decision acceptance and team cohesion. Finally, brainstorming sessions often spread enthusiasm, which tends to generate more creativity. Overall, while brainstorming might not always be the best team structure, it seems to be more valuable than some of the earlier research studies indicated.

> **BRAINSTORMING:**
> a freewheeling, face-to-face meeting where team members aren't allowed to criticize, but are encouraged to speak freely, generate as many ideas as possible, and build on the ideas of others

Electronic Brainstorming

Electronic brainstorming is a recent form of brainstorming that relies on networked computers to submit and share creative ideas. After receiving the question or issue, participants enter their ideas using special computer software. The ideas are distributed anonymously to other participants, who are encouraged to piggyback on those ideas. Team members eventually vote electronically on the ideas presented. Face-to-face discussion usually follows. Electronic brainstorming can be quite effective at generating creative ideas with minimal production blocking, evaluation apprehension, or conformity problems.[78] Despite these numerous advantages, electronic brainstorming seems to be too structured and technology-bound for some executives. Some leaders may also feel threatened by the honesty of statements generated through this process and by their limited ability to control the discussion.

> **ELECTRONIC BRAINSTORMING:**
> a recent form of brainstorming that relies on networked computers to submit and share creative ideas

Nominal Group Technique

Nominal group technique is a variation of traditional brainstorming that tries to combine the benefits of team decision making without the problems mentioned earlier.[79] The method is called nominal because participants form a group in name only during two of its three stages. After the problem is described, team members silently and independently write down as many solutions as they can. In the second stage, participants describe their solutions to the other team members, usually in a round-robin format. As with brainstorming, there is no criticism or debate, although members are encouraged to ask for clarification of the ideas presented. In the third stage, participants silently and independently rank order or vote on each proposed solution. Nominal group technique tends to generate a higher number and better-quality ideas compared with traditional interacting and possibly brainstorming groups.[80] Due to its high degree of structure, nominal group technique usually maintains a high task orientation and relatively low potential for conflict within the team. However, production blocking and evaluation apprehension still occur to some extent.

> **NOMINAL GROUP TECHNIQUE:**
> a variation of traditional brainstorming that tries to combine the benefits of team decision making without the problems mentioned earlier

>Chapter Summary

Teams are groups of two or more people who interact and influence each other, are mutually accountable for achieving common goals associated with organizational objectives, and perceive themselves as a social entity within an organization. All teams are groups, because they consist of people with a unifying relationship; not all groups are teams, because some groups do not have purposive interaction.

People join informal groups (and are motivated to be on formal teams) for four reasons: (1) people have an innate drive to bond, (2) group membership is an inherent ingredient in a person's self-image, (3) some personal goals are accomplished better in groups, and (4) individuals are comforted in stressful situations by the mere presence of other people. Teams have become popular because they tend to make better decisions, support the knowledge management process, and provide superior customer service. People also tend to be more motivated working in teams. However, teams are not always as effective as individuals working alone. Process losses and social loafing are two particular concerns that drag down team performance.

Team effectiveness includes the team's ability to achieve its objectives, fulfill the needs of its members, and maintain its survival. The model of team effectiveness considers the team and organizational environment, team design, and team processes. Three team design elements are task characteristics, team size, and team composition. Teams tend to be better suited for complex work and where tasks among employees have high interdependence. Teams should be large enough to perform the work, yet small enough for efficient coordination and meaningful involvement. Effective teams are composed of people with the competencies and motivation to perform tasks in a team environment. Team member diversity has advantages and disadvantages for team performance.

Teams develop through the stages of forming, storming, norming, performing, and eventually adjourning. Within these stages are two distinct team development processes: membership and team competence. Teams develop norms to regulate and guide member behavior. These norms may be influenced by initial experiences, critical events, and the values and experiences that team members bring to the group. Team cohesion—the degree of attraction people feel toward the team and their motivation to remain members—increases with member similarity, smaller team size, higher degree of interaction, somewhat difficult entry, team success, and external challenges. Cohesion increases team performance when the team's norms are congruent with organizational goals. Trust is a psychological state comprising the intention to accept vulnerability based on positive expectations of the intent or behavior of another person. People trust others based on three foundations: calculus, knowledge, and identification.

Self-directed teams (SDTs) complete an entire piece of work requiring several interdependent tasks, and they have substantial autonomy over the execution of their tasks. SDTs potentially increase both productivity and job satisfaction, but these benefits occur only when the team is responsible for an entire work process, has sufficient autonomy to organize and coordinate their work, and when the technology supports coordinating and communication among team members and increases job enrichment.

Members of virtual teams operate across space, time, and organizational boundaries and are linked through information technologies to achieve organizational tasks. Virtual teams are more effective when their members have certain competencies (communicating through technology, self-leadership, and higher emotional intelligence), where the team has the freedom to choose the preferred communication channels, and where virtual team members meet face-to-face fairly early in the team development process.

Team decisions are impeded by time constraints, evaluation apprehension, conformity to peer pressure, and groupthink (specifically overconfidence). Four structures potentially improve decision making in team settings: constructive conflict, brainstorming, electronic brainstorming, and nominal group technique.

>key terms

brainstorming 163	nominal group technique 163	social loafing 148
Brooks's law 148	norms 154	task interdependence 150
constructive conflict 162	process losses 148	team cohesion 155
electronic brainstorming 163	production blocking 160	teams 145
evaluation apprehension 161	role 154	trust 156
groupthink 161	self-directed teams (SDTs) 158	virtual teams 159

>critical thinking questions

1. Informal groups exist in almost every form of social organization. What types of informal groups exist in your classroom? Why are students motivated to belong to these informal groups?

2. The late management guru Peter Drucker said: "The now-fashionable team in which everybody works with everybody on everything from the beginning rapidly is becoming a disappointment." Discuss three problems associated with teams.

3. You have been put in charge of a cross-functional task force that will develop enhanced Internet banking services for retail customers. The team includes representatives from marketing, information services, customer service, and accounting, all of whom will move to the same location at headquarters for three months. Describe the behaviors you might observe during each stage of the team's development.

4. You have just been transferred from the Kansas office to the Denver office of your company, a national sales organization of electrical products for developers and contractors. In Kansas, team members regularly called customers after a sale to ask whether the products arrived on time and whether they are satisfied. But when you moved to the Denver office, no one seemed to make these follow-up calls. A recently hired co-worker explained that other co-workers discouraged her from making those calls. Later, another co-worker suggested that your follow-up calls were making everyone else look lazy. Give three possible reasons why the norms in Denver might be different from those in the Kansas office, even though the customers, products, sales commissions, and other characteristics of the workplace are almost identical.

5. You have been assigned to a class project with five other students, none of whom you have met before. To what extent would team cohesion improve your team's performance on this project? What actions would you recommend to build team cohesion among student team members in this situation?

6. Suppose that you were put in charge of a virtual team where each member is located in different cities around the country or region. What tactics could you use to build and maintain team trust, as well as minimize the decline in trust that often occurs in teams?

7. You are responsible for convening a major event in which senior officials from several state governments will try to come to agreement on environmental issues. It is well known that some officials posture so they appear superior, whereas others are highly motivated to solve the environmental problems that cross adjacent states. What team decision-making problems are likely to be apparent in this government forum, and what actions can you take to minimize these problems?

8. Carmel Technologies wants to use brainstorming with its employees and customers to identify new uses for its technology. Advise Carmel's president about the potential benefits of brainstorming, as well as its potential limitations.

>team exercise 7-1

Team Tower Power

Purpose   This exercise is designed to help you understand team roles, team development, and other issues in the development and maintenance of effective teams.

Materials   The instructor will provide enough Duplo/ Megblok pieces or similar materials for each team to complete the assigned task. All teams should have an identical (or very similar) amount and type of pieces. The instructor will need a measuring tape and stopwatch. Students may use writing materials during the design stage (Step 2 below). The instructor will distribute a Team Objectives Sheet and Tower Specifications Effectiveness Sheet to all teams.

Instructions

- *Step 1*: The instructor will divide the class into teams. Depending on class size and space available, teams may have between four to seven members, but all should be approximately equal size.

- *Step 2*: Each team is given 20 minutes to design a tower that uses only the materials provided, is free-standing, and provides an optimal return on investment. Team members may wish to draw their tower on paper or flip chart to assist the tower's design. Teams are free to practice building their tower during this stage. Preferably, teams are assigned to their own rooms so the design can be created privately. During this stage, each team will complete the Team Objectives Sheet distributed by the instructor. This sheet requires the Tower Specifications Effectiveness Sheet, also distributed by the instructor.

- *Step 3:* Each team will show the instructor that it has completed its Team Objectives Sheet. Then, with all teams in the same room, the instructor will announce the start of the construction phase. The time elapsed for construction will be closely monitored and the instructor will occasionally call out time elapsed (particularly if there is no clock in the room).

- *Step 4:* Each team will advise the instructor as soon as it has completed its tower. The team will write down the time elapsed that the instructor has determined. It may be asked to assist the instructor by counting the number of blocks used and height of the tower. This information is also written on the Team Objectives Sheet. Then, the team calculates its profit.

- *Step 5:* After presenting the results, the class will discuss the team dynamics elements that contribute to team effectiveness. Team members will discuss their strategy, division of labor (team roles), expertise within the team, and other elements of team dynamics.

Source: Several published and online sources describe variations of this exercise, but there is no known origin to this activity.

Find the complete interactive self-assessments at this textbook's Web site at
www.mhhe.com/mcshaneEss2e.

>self-assessment exercise 7-2

Team Roles Preferences Scale

Teams depend on their members to fulfill several roles related to the task and maintenance of the team. This self-assessment is designed to help you to identify your preferred roles in meetings and similar team activities. Read each of the statements in this instrument and indicate the response that you believe best reflects your position regarding each statement. This exercise is completed alone so students assess themselves honestly without concerns of social comparison. However, class discussion will focus on the roles that people assume in team settings. This scale only assesses a few team roles.

>self-assessment exercise 7-3

The Team Player Inventory

How much do you like working in teams? Some of us avoid teams wherever possible; others tolerate team work; still others thrive in team environments. This exercise is designed to help you estimate the extent to which you are positively predisposed to work in teams. Read each statement in this scale and indicate the extent to which you agree or disagree with that statement. This exercise is completed alone so students assess themselves honestly without concerns of social comparison. However, class discussion will focus on the characteristics of individuals who are more or less compatible with working in teams.

>self-assessment exercise 7-3

Propensity to Trust Scale

Trust is a psychological state comprising the intention to accept vulnerability based on positive expectations of the intent or behavior of another person. While trust varies from one situation to the next, some people have a higher or lower propensity to trust. In other words, some people are highly trusting of others, even when first meeting them, whereas others have difficulty trusting anyone, even over a long time. This self-assessment provides an estimate of your propensity to trust. Indicate your preferred response to each statement, being honest with yourself for each item. This self-assessment is completed alone, although class discussion will focus on the meaning of propensity to trust, why it varies from one person to the next, and how it affects teamwork.

[chapter 8]

Communicating in Teams and Organizations

Standing in front of Beijing's Forbidden City, IBM chief executive Sam Palmisano communicates through his Second Life avatar to several thousand employees worldwide.

>learningobjectives

After reading this chapter, you should be able to:

1. Explain why communication is important in organizations.

2. Diagram the communication process and identify four ways to improve this process.

3. Discuss problems with communicating through electronic mail.

4. Identify two ways in which nonverbal communication differs from verbal communication.

5. Appraise the appropriateness of a communication medium for a particular situation based on social influence and media richness factors.

6. Identify four common communication barriers.

7. Discuss the degree to which men and women communicate differently.

8. Outline the key strategies for getting your message across and engaging in active listening.

9. Summarize three communication strategies in organizational hierarchies.

10. Debate the benefits and limitations of the organizational grapevine.

Imagine IBM chief executive Samuel Palmisano speaking to a throng of 7,000 employees with Beijing's famous Forbidden City towering behind him. Does this scenario sound a bit too fantastic to be real? Well, Palmisano *was* recently in Beijing speaking face-to-face to about 2,000 staff in an auditorium, but he also communicated part of his talk to another 5,000 IBMers through his avatar (graphic character representing a person) in front of a virtual version of the Forbidden City on the Second Life Web site.

Second Life, an online world where individuals can cruise around various islands, is becoming one of IBM's venues for sharing information. Along with Palmisano's virtual town hall meeting, IBMers have held hundreds of virtual meetings at a large boardroom that IBM created at its Second Life premises.

Audio and video communication is possible, but most gatherings use written text messages to the entire group or privately to others attending. Unlike instant messaging text chats, however, the avatars in IBM's Second Life meetings add a personal touch that improves the communication experience.

"Second Life allows you to strike up a natural conversation that you can't do on a two-dimensional Web site," says Michael Rowe, head of IBM's digital convergence team. The avatars add a nonverbal communication element that enriches the interaction. "There's a sense that you're actually at the meeting," explains Chuck Hamilton, director of IBM's center for advanced learning. "If I stop moving my mouse, eventually my avatar will slump forward, and the other people in the room will say, 'Hey, Chuck, are you still there?'"[1]

Information technologies have transformed how we communicate in organizations, yet we may still be at the beginning of this revolution. Wire cablegrams and telephones introduced a century ago are giving way to e-mail, instant messaging, weblogs, podcasting, and virtual reality social networking. Each of these inventions creates fascinating changes in how people communicate with each other in the workplace, as well as new opportunities to improve organizational effectiveness and employee well-being.

Communication refers to the process by which information is transmitted and *understood* between two or more people. We emphasize the word "understood" because transmitting the sender's intended meaning is the essence of good communication. This chapter begins by discussing the importance of effective communication and outlining a model of the communication process. Next, we identify types of communication channels, including computer-mediated communication, followed by factors to consider when choosing a communication medium. This chapter then identifies barriers to effective communication. This is followed by an overview of ways to communicate in organizational hierarchies and the pervasive organizational grapevine.

> **COMMUNICATION:** the process by which information is transmitted and *understood* between two or more people

After reading the next two sections, you should be able to:

learningobjectives<

1. Explain why communication is important in organizations.
2. Diagram the communication process and identify four ways to improve this process.

>The Importance of Communication

Effective communication is vital to all organizations, so much so that no company could exist without it. The reason? In Chapter 1 we defined organizations as groups of people who work interdependently toward some purpose. People can only work interdependently through communication. Communication is the vehicle through which people clarify their expectations and coordinate work, which allows them to achieve organizational objectives more efficiently and effectively. Chester Barnard, a telecommunications CEO and a respected pioneer in organizational behavior theory, stated this point back in 1938: "An organization is born when there are individuals who are able to communicate."[2]

Along with coordinating work, communication is an important instrument for organizational learning and decision making. Organizations operate as open systems in their environment; their survival and success depend on acquiring information from the external environment (as well as through experimentation), and sharing that information with people who can best use it to perform their jobs. These processes of acquiring and sharing information depend on various forms of communication. Effective communication minimizes "silos of knowledge," a situation in which knowledge is cloistered rather than distributed to those who require the information to make better decisions and perform their jobs more effectively.[3]

Communication also aids employee well-being.[4] Employees cope better when co-workers communicate information that helps to manage the situation, such as describing proper work procedures or how to remain on good terms with the boss. However, the communication process itself is critical to personal well-being because it fulfills the drive to bond and validates the individual's worth and identity. Social interaction is so important that people who experience social isolation are much more susceptible to colds, cardiovascular disease, and other physical and mental illnesses.[5] Communicating with others is partially the means through which individuals define themselves; that is, maintain their social identity. This occurs even in the virtual world of Second Life. "In Second Life we gather and mingle before the meeting, and when it finishes, some people stop and talk again," explains Ian Hughes, an IBM employee who attends these virtual meetings as a pudgy avatar with spiky green hair. "We start to form social networks and the kinds of bonds you make in real life."[6]

>A Model of Communication

The communication model presented in Exhibit 8.1 provides a useful "conduit" metaphor for thinking about the communication process.[7] According to this model, communication flows through channels between the sender and receiver. The sender forms a message and encodes it into words, gestures, voice intonations, and other symbols or signs. Next, the

[Exhibit 8.1] The Communication Process Model

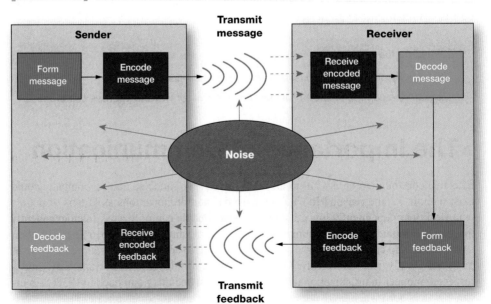

encoded message is transmitted to the intended receiver through one or more communication channels (media). The receiver senses the incoming message and decodes it into something meaningful. Ideally, the decoded meaning is what the sender had intended.

In most situations, the sender looks for evidence that the other person received and understood the transmitted message. This feedback may be a formal acknowledgment, such as "Yes, I know what you mean," or indirect evidence from the receiver's subsequent actions. Notice that feedback repeats the communication process. Intended feedback is encoded, transmitted, received, and decoded from the receiver to the sender of the original message. This model recognizes that communication is not a free-flowing conduit. Rather, the transmission of meaning from one person to another is hampered by noise—the psychological, social, and structural barriers that distort and obscure the sender's intended message. If any part of the communication process is distorted or broken, the sender and receiver will not have a common understanding of the message.

Improving Communication through Encoding and Decoding

The communication model suggests that communication effectiveness depends on the ability of sender and receiver to efficiently and accurately encode and decode information. Experts have identified four ways to improve this process.[8] One way is to ensure that both parties have similar "codebooks"—dictionaries of symbols, language, gestures, idioms, and other tools used to convey information. In addition to improving encoding and decoding accuracy, having similar codebooks improves communication efficiency because there is less need for redundancy (such as saying the same thing in different ways) and confirmation feedback.

Second, the encoding-decoding process improves when both parties have similar mental models about the context of the information. Mental models are internal representations of the external world that allow us to visualize elements of a setting and relationships among those elements (see Chapter 3). When sender and receiver have common mental models, they share a common understanding of the context relating to the information, so less communication is necessary. For instance, two NASA astronauts familiar with the space shuttle would be able to communicate information about a specific piece of equipment in the shuttle much more quickly and accurately than if an astronaut tried to communicate the same information to someone who was unfamiliar with the intricacies of the space shuttle.

A third factor is familiarity with the message topic. As people become more familiar with the subject matter, they develop more efficient or colorful scripts to describe the subject. This is similar to the effect of job training or sports practice. The more experience and practice gained at communicating a subject, the more one learns how to effectively transmit that information to others. Finally, the encoding-decoding process tends to improve with the sender and receiver's proficiency with the communication channel. If you learn that a co-worker doesn't work well with e-mail, you might try to improve communication effectiveness by telephoning that person more often instead of sending e-mails.[9]

After reading the next two sections, you should be able to: **learning**objectives<

3. *Discuss problems with communicating through electronic mail.*
4. *Identify two ways in which nonverbal communication differs from verbal communication.*
5. *Appraise the appropriateness of a communication medium for a particular situation based on social influence and media richness factors.*

>Communication Channels

A critical part of the communication model is the channel or medium through which information is transmitted. There are two main types of channels: verbal and nonverbal. Verbal communication includes any oral or written means of transmitting meaning through words. Nonverbal communication, which we discuss later, is any part of communication that does not use words.

Verbal Communication

Different forms of verbal communication should be used in different situations. Face-to-face interaction is usually better than written methods for transmitting emotions and persuading the receiver. This is because nonverbal cues accompany oral communications, such as voice intonations and use of silence. Furthermore, face-to-face interaction provides the sender with immediate feedback from the receiver and the opportunity to adjust the emotional tone of the message accordingly. Written communication is more appropriate for recording and presenting technical details. This is because ideas are easier to follow when written down than when communicated orally. Traditionally, written communication has taken longer to prepare and transmit, but electronic mail, weblogs, and other computer-mediated communication channels have significantly improved written communication efficiency.

Computer-mediated Communication

Two decades ago, computer-mediated communication was a novel development in communication theory and practice. Today, it seems that many of us rely more on this medium than the old-fashioned options. By far, the most widely used of these is electronic mail (e-mail), which has revolutionized the way we communicate in organizational settings. E-mail has become the medium of choice in most workplaces because messages are quickly written, edited, and transmitted. Information can be appended and conveyed to many people with a simple click of a mouse. E-mail is asynchronous (messages are sent and received at different times), so there is no need to coordinate a communication session. E-mail software has also become an efficient filing cabinet.[10] Employees increasingly rely on e-mail to filter, store, sort, and search messages and attachments far more quickly than is possible with paper-based memos.

E-mail tends to be the preferred medium for coordinating work (e.g., confirming deadlines with a co-worker's schedule) and for sending well-defined information for decision making. It often increases the volume of communication and significantly alters the flow of that information within groups and throughout the organization.[11] Specifically, it reduces some face-to-face and telephone communication but increases communication with people further up the hierarchy. Some social and organizational status differences still exist with e-mail,[12] but they are somewhat less apparent than in face-to-face communication. By hiding age, race, and other features, e-mail reduces stereotype biases. However, it also tends to increase reliance on stereotypes when we are already aware of the other person's personal characteristics.[13]

Problems with E-Mail

In spite of the wonders of e-mail, anyone who has used this communication medium knows that it has its limitations. Here are the top four complaints:

1. *Poor medium for communicating emotions.* People rely on facial expressions and other nonverbal cues to interpret the emotional meaning of words, and e-mail lacks

this parallel communication channel. Senders try to clarify the emotional tone of their messages by using expressive language ("Wonderful to hear from you!"), highlighting phrases in boldface or quotation marks, and inserting graphic faces (called emoticons or "smileys") representing the desired emotion. These actions help, but do not replace the full complexity of real facial expressions, voice intonation, and hand movements.[14]

2. *Reduces politeness and respect.* E-mail messages are often less diplomatic than written letters because individuals can post e-mail messages before their emotions subside. Also, e-mail has low social presence (which makes it more impersonal), so people are more likely to write things that they would never say in face-to-face conversation. Fortunately, research has found that e-mail diplomacy increases as teams move to later stages of development and when explicit norms and rules of communication are established.[15]

3. *Poor medium for ambiguous, complex, and novel situations.* E-mail requires a moderate level of mutual understanding between the sender and receiver. Coordinating through e-mail in ambiguous, complex, and novel situations, on the other hand, requires communication channels that quickly send a larger volume of information and offer equally rapid feedback. In other words, when the issue gets messy, stop e-mailing and start talking, preferably face-to-face.

4. *Contributes to information overload.* E-mail contributes to information overload, which we'll discuss in more detail later in this chapter.[16] An estimated 22.3 trillion e-mails are now transmitted annually, up from just 1.1 trillion in 1998. According to one survey, professionals spend an average of two hours per day processing e-mail. The e-mail glut occurs because they can be easily created and copied to many people without much effort. The number of e-mail messages will probably decrease as people become more familiar with it, but to date e-mail volume continues to rise.

Social Network Communication

The opening story to this chapter described how IBM is experimenting with innovative forms of computer-mediated communication. In fact, while e-mail likely remains the most popular medium, IBMers have flocked to computer-mediated technologies that support *social networking.*[17] These technologies cluster people around themes or events (such as synchronous conversation), resulting in closer interaction in the communication experience. Indeed, some social networking technologies—online forums and instant messaging are two examples—gain value and potential when more people are clustered and linked to the technology.[18]

Flaming E-mails
Executives at Admiral Insurance are concerned that the electronic communication medium is making staff at the Welsh company less polite to each other and to customers. "It is much easier to have a row by e-mail than it is face-to-face, and people are often ruder as a result," says Admiral spokesperson Justin Beddows. "Orders can be issued out and people can be quite abrupt because they feel protected by the distance the e-mail provides. But once an abusive e-mail is sent out, there is no getting it back and it can cause a rift that cannot be resolved easily." Along with reminding employees of e-mail's limitations as a communication medium, Admiral executives occasionally try to wean staff from e-mail dependence. "We hold 'no e-mail days' to encourage people to get off their backsides and visit people face-to-face," says Beddows.[19]

A virtual visit to Second Life is social networking because people interact in real time around an event, such as a participating in conversation or attending a presentation. Instant messaging (IM) is another form of social networking because organizations create IM communities that cluster employees around specific themes, typically fields of expertise. Employees belong to several IM communities, each with its own directory of members. **Wikis**—collaborative web spaces in which anyone in a group can write, edit, or remove material from the Web site—are becoming one of the most promising forms of social network communication. IBM introduced wikis just a couple of years ago, but already has 20,000 of them, involving 100,000 employees. Wikis are discussed in more detail later in this chapter.

Nonverbal Communication

Nonverbal communication includes facial gestures, voice intonation, physical distance, and even silence. This communication channel is necessary where noise or physical distance prevents effective verbal exchanges and the need for immediate feedback precludes written communication. But even in quiet face-to-face meetings, most information is communicated nonverbally. Rather like a parallel conversation, nonverbal cues signal subtle information to both parties, such as reinforcing their interest in the verbal conversation or demonstrating their relative status in the relationship.[20]

Nonverbal communication differs from verbal communication in a couple of ways. First, it is less rule-bound than verbal communication. We receive a lot of formal training on how to understand spoken words, but very little on understanding the nonverbal signals that accompany those words. Consequently, nonverbal cues are generally more ambiguous and susceptible to misinterpretation. At the same time, many facial expressions (such as smiling) are hardwired and universal, thereby providing the only reliable means of communicating across cultures.

The other difference between verbal and nonverbal communication is that the former is typically conscious, whereas most nonverbal communication is automatic and unconscious. We normally plan the words we say or write, but we rarely plan every blink, smile, or other gesture during a conversation. Indeed, as we just mentioned, many of these facial expressions communicate the same meaning across cultures because they are hardwired nonconscious responses to human emotions.[21] For example, pleasant emotions cause the brain center to widen the mouth, whereas negative emotions produce constricted facial expressions (squinting eyes, pursed lips, etc.).

>Choosing the Best Communication Medium

Which communication channel is most appropriate in a particular situation? One set of factors fall under the category called social influence.[22] Probably the most important social influence factor is organization and team norms regarding the use of specific communication channels. Norms partly explain why telephone conversations are more common among staff in some firms, whereas e-mail or instant messaging is the medium of choice in other organizations. Some companies expect employees to meet face-to-face, whereas meetings and similar conversations are rare events elsewhere. Norms also shape the use of communication media for people in specific positions. For instance, front-line employees are more likely to write an e-mail and less likely to telephone or personally visit the company's CEO.

A second social influence factor is individual preferences for specific communication channels.[23] You may have discovered that a co-worker prefers e-mail rather than voice mail, or wants to meet in person more than you think is necessary. These preferences are due to personality traits as well as previous experience and reinforcement with particular channels. A third social influence on communication channel choice is the symbolic meaning of a channel. Communication channels are viewed as more personal or impersonal, professional versus casual, cool versus out of touch, and so on. For example, stories about employees getting laid off or fired through e-mails or text messages make front-page headlines because the communication medium is considered inappropriate (too impersonal) for transmission of that particular information.[24]

Media Richness

Along with social influences, people select communication media based on their **media richness.** Media richness refers to the medium's data-carrying capacity—the volume and variety of information that can be transmitted during a specific time.[25] Exhibit 8.2 illustrates various communication channels arranged in a hierarchy of richness, with face-to-face interaction at the top and lean data-only reports at the bottom. A communication channel has high richness when it is able to convey multiple cues (such as both verbal and nonverbal information), allows timely feedback from receiver to sender, allows the sender to customize the message to the receiver, and makes use of complex symbols (such as words and phrases with multiple meanings). Face-to-face communication is at the top of

> **MEDIA RICHNESS:** the medium's data-carrying capacity, that is, the volume and variety of information that can be transmitted during a specific time

[Exhibit 8.2] Media Richness Hierarchy

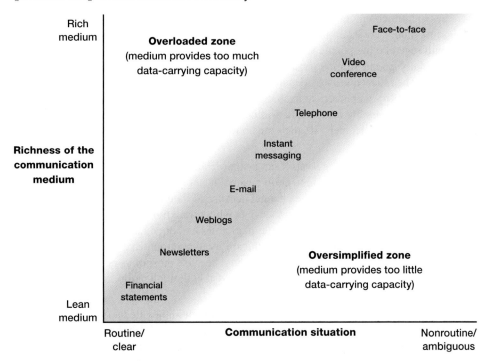

Source: Based on R. Lengel and R. Daft, "The Selection of Communication Media as an Executive Skill," *Academy of Management Executive* 2, no. 3 (August, 1988), p. 226; R. L. Daft and R. H. Lengel, "Information Richness: A New Approach to Managerial Behavior and Organization Design," *Research in Organizational Behavior,* 1984, p. 199.

media richness because it allows us to communicate both verbally and nonverbally at the same time, to receive feedback almost immediately from the receiver, to quickly adjust our message and style, and to use complex language such as metaphors and idioms (e.g., "spilling the beans").

According to media richness theory, rich media are better than lean media when the communication situation is nonroutine and ambiguous. In nonroutine situations (such as an unexpected and unusual emergency), the sender and receiver have little common experience, so they need to transmit a large volume of information with immediate feedback. Lean media work well in routine situations because the sender and receiver have common expectations through shared mental models. Ambiguous situations also require rich media because the parties must share large amounts of information with immediate feedback to resolve multiple and conflicting interpretations of their observations and experiences.[26] Choosing the wrong medium reduces communication effectiveness. When the situation is routine or clear, using a rich medium—such as holding a special meeting—would seem like a waste of time. On the other hand, if a unique and ambiguous issue is handled through e-mail or another lean medium, then issues take longer to resolve and misunderstandings are more likely to occur.

Evaluating Media Richness Theory

Although research generally supports the relevance of media richness for traditional channels (face-to-face, written memos, etc.), the evidence is mixed when computer-mediated communication channels are studied. Three factors seem to override or blur the medium's richness:

1. *The ability to multicommunicate.* Unlike most traditional communication channels, particularly those with high media richness, emerging technologies allow employees to multicommunicate—engage in two or more communication events at the same time.[27] For example, you might be paying attention to discussion at a meeting with several other people while simultaneously instant messaging with a client. Similarly, people routinely scan Web pages while carrying on telephone conversations. The reduced sensory demand for most forms of computer-mediated communication allow employees to exchange information through multiple channels at the same time, possibly resulting in as much information processing as occurs through one traditional channel with high media richness (e.g., a face-to-face one-on-one conversation).

2. *More varied proficiency levels.* Some experts point out that the richness of a computer-mediated communication channel is not fixed; some people can "push" more information through the channel because of their higher proficiency. Experienced Blackberry users, for instance, can whip through messages in a flash, whereas new users struggle to type e-mail notes and organize incoming messages. In contrast, there is less variation in the ability to communicate through traditional channels (e.g., casual conversation, memos) because most of us develop good levels of proficiency throughout life and possibly through hardwired evolutionary development.[28]

3. *Social distractions of rich channels.* Channels with higher media richness tend to have higher social interaction. But the social dynamics of rich media tend to distract people from efficiently processing the message content.[29] Instead, the sender and receiver focus on their relative status, and engage in activities that maintain their self-worth and status. This social distraction reduces efficiency at transmitting and receiving information, which sometimes makes rich media less effective than leaner media that have less social interaction.

After reading the next two sections, you should be able to:

6. *Identify four common communication barriers.*

7. *Discuss the degree to which men and women communicate differently.*

learningobjectives<

>Communication Barriers (Noise)

In spite of the best intentions of sender and receiver to communicate, several barriers (called "noise" earlier in Exhibit 8.1) inhibit the effective exchange of information. One barrier is the imperfect perceptual process of both sender and receiver. As receivers, we don't listen as well as senders assume, and our needs and expectations influence what signals get noticed and ignored. We aren't any better as senders, either. Some studies suggest that we have difficulty stepping out of our own perspectives and stepping into the perspectives of others, so we overestimate how well other people understand the message we are communicating.[30]

Even if the perceptual process is well tuned, messages sometimes get filtered on their way up or down the corporate hierarchy. Filtering may involve deleting or delaying negative information or using less harsh words so the message sounds more favorable.[31] Filtering is most common where the organization rewards employees who communicate mainly positive information and among employees with strong career mobility aspirations.

Language issues can be huge sources of communication noise because sender and receiver might not have the same "codebook." They might not speak the same language, or might have different meanings for particular words and phrases. For example, a French executive might call an event a "catastrophe" as a casual exaggeration, whereas someone in Germany usually interprets this word literally as an earthshaking event.[32] Jargon, which includes specialized words and phrases for specific occupations or groups, is designed to improve communication efficiency. However, it has the opposite effect when senders use jargon on people who do not possess the jargon codebook.

Even when both people use the same language and codebook, they might interpret words and phrases differently. The question "Can you close the door?" might be (a) telling you to shut the door, or it might be asking (b) whether you are physically able to shut the door, (c) whether the door is designed such that it can be shut, or (d) whether shutting the door is permitted.[33] The ambiguity of language isn't always dysfunctional noise.[34] Corporate leaders sometimes rely on metaphors and other vague language to describe ill-defined or complex ideas. Ambiguity is also used to avoid conveying or creating undesirable emotions.

Information Overload

Start with a daily avalanche of e-mail, then add in voice mail, cell phone text messages, PDF file downloads, Web pages, hard copy documents, instant messages, blogs, wikis, and other sources of incoming information. Together, you have created a perfect recipe for **information overload.**[35] Information overload occurs when the volume of information received exceeds the person's capacity to get through it. Employees have a certain *information processing capacity*—the amount of information that they are able to process in a fixed unit of time. At the same time, jobs have a varying *information load*—the amount of information to be processed per unit of time.[36]

Information overload creates noise in the communication system because information gets overlooked or misinterpreted when people can't process it fast enough. It has also become a common cause of workplace stress. These problems can be minimized by

INFORMATION OVERLOAD: occurs when the volume of information received exceeds the person's capacity to get through it

increasing our information processing capacity, reducing the job's information load, or through a combination of both. Information processing capacity increases when we learn to read faster, scan through documents more efficiently, and remove distractions that slow information processing speed. Time management also increases information processing capacity. When information overload is temporary, information processing capacity can increase by working longer hours. Information load can be reduced by buffering, omitting, and summarizing. Buffering involves having incoming communication filtered, usually by an assistant. Omitting occurs when we decide to overlook messages, such as using software rules to redirect e-mails from distribution lists to folders that we never look at. An example of summarizing would be where we read executive summaries rather than the full report.

>Cross-Cultural and Gender Communication

As globalization and cultural diversity increase, you can be sure that cross-cultural communication problems will also increase.[37] Language is the most obvious cross-cultural communications challenge. Words are easily misunderstood in verbal communication, either because the receiver has a limited vocabulary or the sender's accent distorts the usual sound of some words. Voice intonation is another cross-cultural communication barrier, because how loudly, deeply, and quickly we speak sends secondary messages that have different meaning in different cultures.

Communication includes silence, but its use and meaning varies from one culture to another.[38] A recent study estimated that silence and pauses represented 30 percent of conversation time between Japanese doctors and patients, compared to only 8 percent of the time between American doctors and patients. In Japan, silence symbolizes respect and indicates that the listener is thoughtfully contemplating what has just been said.[39] Similarly, Japanese people usually stop talking when they are interrupted, whereas talking over the other person's speech is more common in Brazil and some other countries. Indeed, Brazilians are more likely to view interruptions as evidence that the other person is involved in the conversation!

Thumbs-up for Cross-Cultural (Mis)communication
Patricia Oliveira made several cultural adjustments when she moved from Brazil to Australia. One of the more humorous incidents occurred in the Melbourne office where she works. A co-worker would stick his thumbs up when asked about something, signaling that everything was OK. But the gesture had a totally different meaning to Oliveira and other people from Brazil. "He asked me why I was laughing and I had to explain that in Brazil, that sign means something not very nice," recalls Oliveira. "After that, everyone started doing it to the boss. It was really funny."[40]

Nonverbal Differences

Nonverbal communication represents another potential area for misunderstanding across cultures. Many nonconscious or involuntary nonverbal cues (such as smiling) have the same meaning around the world, but deliberate gestures often have different interpretations. For example, most of us shake our head from side to side to say "No," but a variation of head shaking means "I understand" to many people in India. Filipinos raise their eyebrows to give an affirmative answer, yet Arabs interpret this expression (along with clicking one's tongue) as a negative response. Most Americans are taught to maintain eye contact with the speaker to show interest and respect, whereas people in some other cultures learn at an early age to show respect by looking down when an older or more senior person is talking to them.[41]

Gender Differences in Communication

Men and women have similar communication practices, but there are subtle distinctions that can occasionally lead to misunderstanding and conflict. One distinction is that men are more likely than women to view conversations as negotiations of relative status and power. They assert their power by directly giving advice to others (e.g., "You should do the following") and using combative language. There is also evidence that men dominate the talk time in conversations with women, as well as interrupt more and adjust their speaking style less than do women.[42]

Men engage in more "report talk," in which the primary function of the conversation is impersonal and efficient information exchange. Women also do report talk, particularly when conversing with men, but conversations among women have a higher incidence of relationship building through "rapport talk." Women make more use of indirect requests ("Do you think we should . . ."), apologize more often, and seek advice from others more quickly than do men. Finally, research fairly consistently indicates that women are more sensitive than men to nonverbal cues in face-to-face meetings.[43] Together, these conditions can create communication conflicts. Women who describe problems get frustrated that men offer advice rather than rapport, whereas men become frustrated because they can't understand why women don't appreciate their advice.

After reading the next two sections, you should be able to:

learningobjectives<

8. Outline the key strategies for getting your message across and engaging in active listening.
9. Summarize three communication strategies in organizational hierarchies.
10. Debate the benefits and limitations of the organizational grapevine.

>Improving Interpersonal Communication

Effective interpersonal communication depends on the sender's ability to get the message across and the receiver's performance as an active listener. In this section, we outline these two essential features of effective interpersonal communication.

Getting Your Message Across

This chapter began with the statement that effective communication occurs when the other person receives and understands the message. To accomplish this difficult task, the sender must learn to empathize with the receiver, repeat the message, choose an appropriate time for the conversation, and be descriptive rather than evaluative.

- *Empathize.* Recall from the earlier chapters that empathy is a person's ability to understand and be sensitive to the feelings, thoughts, and situation of others. In conversations, this involves putting yourself in the receiver's shoes when encoding the message. For instance, be sensitive to words that may be ambiguous or trigger the wrong emotional response.
- *Repeat the message.* Rephrase the key points a couple of times. The saying "Tell them what you're going to tell them; tell them; then tell them what you've told them" reflects this need for redundancy.

- *Use timing effectively*. Your message competes with other messages and noise, so find a time when the receiver is less likely to be distracted by these other matters.

- *Be descriptive*. Focus on the problem, not the person, if you have negative information to convey. People stop listening when the information attacks their self-esteem. Also, suggest things the listener can do to improve, rather than point to him or her as a problem.

Active Listening

"Nature gave people two ears but only one tongue, which is a gentle hint that they should listen more than they talk." To follow this advice, we need to recognize that listening is a process of actively sensing the sender's signals, evaluating them accurately, and responding appropriately. These three components of listening—sensing, evaluating, and responding— reflect the listener's side of the communication model described at the beginning of this chapter. Listeners receive the sender's signals, decode them as intended, and provide appropriate and timely feedback to the sender (see Exhibit 8.3). Active listeners constantly cycle through sensing, evaluating, and responding during the conversation and engage in various activities to improve these processes.[44]

Sensing

Sensing is the process of receiving signals from the sender and paying attention to them. Active listeners improve sensing in three ways. First, they postpone evaluation by not forming an opinion until the speaker has finished. Second, they avoid interrupting the speaker's conversation. Third, they remain motivated to listen to the speaker.

Evaluating

This component of listening includes understanding the message meaning, evaluating the message, and remembering the message. To improve their evaluation of the conversation, active listeners empathize with the speaker—they try to understand and be sensitive to the speaker's feelings, thoughts, and situation. Evaluation also improves by organizing the speaker's ideas during the communication episode.

[Exhibit 8.3] Active Listening Process and Strategies

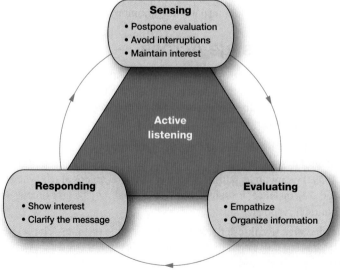

Responding

Responding, the third component of listening, is feedback to the sender, which motivates and directs the speaker's communication. Active listeners accomplish this by maintaining sufficient eye contact and sending back channel signals (e.g., "I see"), both of which show interest. They also respond by clarifying the message—rephrasing the speaker's ideas at appropriate breaks ("So you're saying that . . . ?").

>Improving Communication throughout the Hierarchy

So far, we have focused on "micro-level" issues in the communication process, namely, the dynamics of sending and receiving information between two people or a small cluster of people. But in this era where knowledge is competitive advantage, corporate leaders also need to maintain an open flow of communication up, down, and across the organization. In this section, we discuss three communication strategies: workspace design, blogs/wikis/e-zines, and direct communication with top management.

Workspace Design

The ability and motivation to communicate is partially influenced by the physical space in which employees work.[45] The location and design of hallways, offices, cubicles, and communal areas (cafeterias, elevators) all shape whom we speak to as well as the frequency of that communication. Pixar Animation Studios has leveraged the power of workspaces by constructing a campus in Emeryville, California, that clusters teams and encourages more casual communication among team members. At the same time, the campus encourages happenstance interactions with people on other teams. Pixar executives call this the "bathroom effect," because team members must leave their isolated pods to fetch their mail, have lunch, or visit the restroom.[46]

Kowloon Shangri-La's "State of the Hotel" Meetings
Communicating with employees can be a challenge when the organization is a large hotel that operates around the clock. But these conditions haven't prevented senior management at Kowloon Shangri-La from holding "state of the hotel" meetings with all 700 staff twice each year. Two sessions are held—one in the morning, the other in the afternoon—so all employees at the Hong Kong hotel can attend without leaving the hotel short staffed. General manager Mark Heywood conducts no-holds-barred sessions in which employees are updated on the hotel's financial performance, upcoming events, and renovations. "It's a chance to communicate about the good, the bad, and the ugly," says Heywood. "We don't just share good news and positive things." He also outlines his vision for the hotel and reinforces its "one team—one way" culture.[47]

One of the most popular workspace strategies is to replace traditional offices with open space arrangements, where all employees (including management) work in the same open area. One recent convert to open space is Continuum, the Boston-based design and innovation firm. "We do not have doors," explains a Continuum executive. "It's structured that way to stimulate conversation and to allow people to work collaboratively. Anyone from the chief operating officer to our interns shares space and sits next to each other. You can stop in and have a conversation with anyone, anytime you want."[48] People do communicate more with fewer walls, but research also suggests that open office design potentially increases employee stress due to the loss of privacy and personal space.[49] The challenge is to balance privacy with opportunities for social interaction.

Wikis, Blogs, and E-Zines

For decades, employees have received official company news through hard copy newsletters and magazines. Many firms still use these communication devices, but most have supplemented or replaced them completely with Web-based or PDF-only format newsletters, called *e-zines*. E-zines can prepare and distribute company news quickly, but employees are increasingly skeptical of information that has been screened and packaged by management. So, some adventurous firms are encouraging employees to write any news they see fit on their own weblogs (blogs). IBM is a pioneer in this area through BlogCentral, an inward-facing (i.e., for IBM employees' eyes only) blog-hosting service where several thousand employees blog about their own news of the week. A search engine helps staff find important information on any of the several thousand blogs.

Earlier in this chapter we introduced wikis as collaborative web spaces in which anyone in a group can write, edit, or remove material from the Web site. Wikipedia, the popular online encyclopedia, is a massive public example of a wiki. Wikis hold considerable promise for organizational communication because they are democratic, collaborative social networking spaces that rapidly document new knowledge. IBM introduced wiki technology a few years ago in the form of WikiCentral, which is now used by more than one-third of its employees. One of IBM's many wiki projects involved accumulating ideas and issues from several employees about a new patent policy within IBM. "Wikis are good for project management, for to-do's, status reports, creating an issues log—you're always up to date," explains Brad Kasell, an IBM manager for emerging technologies. "There's no collating reports from everyone at the end of the week for an update." The accuracy of wikis depends on the quality of participants, but Kasell says that errors are quickly identified by IBM's online community.[50]

Direct Communication with Top Management

MANAGEMENT BY WALKING AROUND (MBWA): a communication practice in which executives get out of their offices and learn from others in the organization through face-to-face dialogue

"The best fertilizer in any field is that of the farmer's footsteps!" This old Chinese saying means that farms are most successful when the farmers spend time in the fields directly observing the crop's development. In an organizational context, this means that to fully understand the issues, senior executives need to get out of the executive suite and meet directly with employees at all levels and on their turf. Nearly 40 years ago, people at Hewlett-Packard coined a phrase for this communication strategy: **management by walking around (MBWA).**[51]

Along with MBWA, executives are getting more direct communication with employees through "town hall meetings," where large groups of employees hear about a merger or other special news directly from the key decision makers. Some executives also conduct employee roundtable forums to hear opinions from a small representation of staff about various issues. All of these direct communication strategies potentially minimize filtering because executives listen directly to employees. They also help executives acquire a deeper meaning and quicker understanding of internal organizational problems. A third benefit of direct communication is that employees might have more empathy for decisions made further up the corporate hierarchy.

>Communicating through the Grapevine

No matter how much corporate leaders try to communicate through e-zines, blogs, wikis, MBWA, and other means, employees will still rely on the oldest communication channel: the corporate **grapevine.** The grapevine is an unstructured and informal network founded on social relationships rather than organizational charts or job descriptions. What do employees think about the grapevine? Surveys of employees in two U.S. firms— one in Florida, the other in California—provide the answer. Both surveys found that almost all employees use the grapevine, but very few of them prefer this source of information. The Californian survey also reported that only one-third of employees believe grapevine information is credible. In other words, employees turn to the grapevine when they have few other options.[52]

> **GRAPEVINE:** an unstructured and informal network founded on social relationships rather than organizational charts or job descriptions

Grapevine Characteristics

Research conducted several decades ago reported that the grapevine transmits information very rapidly in all directions throughout the organization. The typical pattern is a cluster chain, whereby a few people actively transmit rumors to many others. The grapevine works through informal social networks, so it is more active where employees have similar backgrounds and are able to communicate easily. Many rumors seem to have at least a kernel of truth, possibly because they are transmitted through media-rich communication channels (e.g., face-to-face) and employees are motivated to communicate effectively. Nevertheless, the grapevine distorts information by deleting fine details and exaggerating key points of the story.[53]

Some of these characteristics might still be true, but other features of the grapevine would have changed due to the dramatic effects of information technologies in the workplace. E-mail, instant messages, and even blogs have replaced the traditional watercooler as sources of gossip. Social networks have expanded as employees communicate with each other around the globe, not just around the next cubicle. Public blogs and Web forums have extended gossip to anyone, not just employees connected to social networks.

Grapevine Benefits and Limitations

Should the grapevine be encouraged, tolerated, or quashed? The difficulty in answering this question is that the grapevine has both benefits and limitations.[54] One benefit, as was mentioned earlier, is that employees rely on the grapevine when information is not available through formal channels. It is also the main conduit through which organizational stories and other symbols of the organization's culture are communicated. A third benefit of the grapevine is that this social interaction relieves anxiety. This explains why rumor mills are most active during times of uncertainty.[55] Finally, the grapevine is associated with the drive to bond. Being a recipient of gossip is a sign of inclusion, according to evolutionary psychologists. Trying to quash the grapevine is, in some respects, an attempt to undermine the natural human drive for social interaction.[56]

While the grapevine offers these benefits, it is not a preferred communication medium. Grapevine information is sometimes so distorted that it escalates rather than reduces employee anxiety. Furthermore, employees develop more negative attitudes toward the organization when management is slower than the grapevine in communicating information. What should corporate leaders do with the grapevine? The best advice seems to be to listen to the grapevine as a signal of employee anxiety, then correct the cause of this anxiety. Some companies also listen to the grapevine and step in to correct blatant errors and fabrications. Most important, corporate leaders need to view the grapevine as a competitor, and eventually win the challenge to inform employees before they receive the news through the grapevine.

>Chapter Summary

Communication refers to the process by which information is transmitted and *understood* between two or more people. Communication supports work coordination, organizational learning, decision making, and employee well-being. The communication process involves forming, encoding, and transmitting the intended message to a receiver, who then decodes the message and provides feedback to the sender. Effective communication occurs when the sender's thoughts are transmitted to and understood by the intended receiver. Four ways to improve this process is for both sender and receiver to have common codebooks of symbols, to share common mental models, to be familiar with the message topic, and to be proficient with the communication channel.

The two main types of communication channels are verbal and nonverbal. Various forms of computer-mediated communication are widely used in organizations, with e-mail the most popular. Although efficient and a useful filing cabinet, e-mail is relatively poor at communicating emotions; it tends to reduce politeness and respect; it is an inefficient medium for communicating in ambiguous, complex, and novel situations; and it contributes to information overload. Social network communication, such as instant messaging, wikis, and virtual reality platforms are also gaining popularity as forms of communication. Nonverbal communication includes facial gestures, voice intonation, physical distance, and even silence. Unlike verbal communication, nonverbal communication is less rule-bound and is mostly automatic and unconscious.

The most appropriate communication medium partly depends on social influence factors, including organization and team norms, individual preferences for specific communication channels, and the symbolic meaning of a channel. A communication medium should also be chosen for its data-carrying capacity (media richness). Nonroutine and ambiguous situations require rich media. However, we also need to recognize that lean media allow people to multicommunicate, that the capacity of computer-mediated communication is varied due to the proficiency of individual users, and that social distractions can reduce the efficient processing of information in high media-richness channels.

Several barriers create noise in the communication process. People misinterpret messages because of perceptual biases. Some information is filtered out as it gets passed up the hierarchy. Jargon and ambiguous language are barriers when the sender and receiver have different interpretations of the words and symbols used. People also screen out or misinterpret messages due to information overload. These problems are often amplified in cross-cultural settings because of language barriers and differences in meaning of nonverbal cues. There are also some communication differences between men and women, such as the tendency for men to exert status and engage in report talk in conversations, whereas women use more rapport talk and are more sensitive than are men to nonverbal cues.

To get a message across, the sender must learn to empathize with the receiver, repeat the message, choose an appropriate time for the conversation, and be descriptive rather than evaluative. Listening includes sensing, evaluating, and responding. Active listeners support these processes by postponing evaluation, avoiding interruptions, maintaining interest, empathizing, organizing information, showing interest, and clarifying the message.

Some companies try to encourage communication through workspace design, as well as through wikis, blogs, and e-zines, Some executives also meet directly with employees, either through management by walking around (MBWA) or other arrangements, to facilitate communication across the organization.

In any organization, employees rely on the grapevine, particularly during times of uncertainty. The grapevine is an unstructured and informal network founded on social relationships rather than organizational charts or job descriptions. Although early research identified several unique features of the grapevine, some of these features may be changing as the Internet plays an increasing role in grapevine communication.

>key terms

communication 169

grapevine 183

information overload 177

management by walking around (MBWA) 182

media richness 175

wikis 174

>critical thinking questions

1. You have been hired as a consultant to improve communication between engineering and marketing staff in a large high-technology company. Use the communication model and the four ways to improve that process to devise strategies to improve communication effectiveness among employees between these two work units.

2. A company in a country that is just entering the information age intends to introduce electronic mail for office staff at its three buildings located throughout the city. Describe two benefits as well as two potential problems that employees will likely experience with this medium.

3. Instant messaging has become increasingly popular in organizations over the past few years. What are the advantages and disadvantages of this communication medium?

4. Senior management at a consumer goods company wants you to investigate the feasibility of using a virtual reality platform (such as Second Life) for monthly online meetings involving its three-dozen sales managers located in several cities and countries. Use the social influence and media richness factors described in this chapter to identify information you need to consider when conducting this evaluation.

5. Under what conditions, if any, do you think it is appropriate to use e-mail to notify an employee that he or she has been laid off or fired? Why is e-mail usually considered an inappropriate channel to convey this information?

6. Explain why men and women are sometimes frustrated with each other's communication behaviors.

7. In your opinion, has the introduction of e-mail and other information technologies increased or decreased the amount of information flowing through the corporate grapevine? Explain your answer.

8. Wikis are collaborative Web sites where anyone in the group can post, edit, or delete any information. Where might this communication technology be most useful in organizations?

>team exercise 8-1

Active Listening Exercise

By Mary Gander, Winona State University

Purpose   This exercise is designed to help you understand the dynamics of active listening in conversations and to develop active listening skills.

Instructions

For each of the four vignettes presented below, student teams (or students working individually) will compose three statements that demonstrate active listening. Specifically, one statement will indicate that you show empathy for the situation; the second asks for clarification and detail in a nonjudgmental way; and the third statement will provide nonevaluative feedback to the speaker. Here are details about each of these three types of responses:

- **Showing empathy—Acknowledge feelings.** Sometimes it sounds like the speaker wants you to agree with him/her but, in reality, they mainly want you to understand how they feel. "Acknowledging feelings" involves taking in their statements, but looking at the "whole message"— including body language, tone of voice, and level of arousal—and trying to determine what emotion they are conveying. Then you let them know that you realize they are feeling that emotion by just acknowledging it in a sentence.

- **Asking for clarification and detail while withholding your judgment and own opinions.** This conveys that you are making a good effort to understand and not just trying to push your opinions onto them. To formulate a relevant question in asking for more clarification, you will have to listen carefully to what they say. Frame your question as someone trying to understand in more detail, often asking for a specific example is useful. This also helps the speaker evaluate their own opinions and perspective.

- **Providing nonevaluative feedback—feeding back the message you heard.** This will allow the speaker to determine if he/she really got the message across to you and help prevent troublesome miscommunication. It will also help the speaker become more aware of how he/she is coming across to another person (self-evaluation). Just think about what the speaker is conveying and paraphrase it in your own words, and say it back to the speaker (without judging the correctness or merit of what they said), asking him/her if that is what they meant.

After teams (or individual students) have prepared the three statements for each vignette, the instructor will ask them to present their statements and explain how these statements satisfy the active listening criteria.

First Vignette   A colleague stops by your desk and says, "I am tired of the lack of leadership around here. The boss is so wishy-washy, he can't get tough with some of the slackers around here. They just keep milking the company, living off the rest of us. Why doesn't management do something about these guys? And *you* are always so supportive of the boss; he's not as good as you make him out to be."

Develop three statements that respond to the speaker in this vignette by (a) showing empathy, (b) seeking clarification, and (c) providing nonevaluative feedback.

Second Vignette   Your co-worker stops by your cubicle. Her voice and body language show stress, frustration, and even some fear. You know she has been working hard and has a strong need to get her work done on time and done well. You are trying to concentrate on some work and have had a number of interruptions already. She just abruptly interrupts you and says, "This project is turning out to be a mess, why can't the other three people on my team quit fighting each other?"

Develop three statements that respond to the speaker in this vignette by (a) showing empathy, (b) seeking clarification, and (c) providing nonevaluative feedback.

Third Vignette   One of your subordinates is working on an important project. He is an engineer who has good technical skills and knowledge and was selected for the project team because of that. He stops by your office and appears to be quite agitated, his voice is loud and strained, and his face has a look of bewilderment. He says, "I'm supposed to be working with four other people from four other departments on this new project, but they never listen to my ideas and seem to hardly know I'm at the meeting!"

Develop three statements that respond to the speaker in this vignette by (a) showing empathy, (b) seeking clarification, and (c) providing nonevaluative feedback.

Fourth Vignette   Your subordinate comes into your office in a state of agitation, and asks if she can talk to you. She is polite and sits down. She seems calm and does not have an angry look on her face. However, she says, "It seems like you consistently make up lousy schedules, you are unfair and unrealistic in the kinds of assignments you give certain people, me included. Everyone else is so intimidated they don't complain but I think you need to know that this isn't right and it's got to change."

Develop three statements that respond to the speaker in this vignette by (a) showing empathy, (b) seeking clarification, and (c) providing nonevaluative feedback.

Source: Reprinted with permission of Mary Gander, Winona State University.

>team exercise 8-2

Cross-Cultural Communication Game

Purpose   This exercise is designed to develop and test your knowledge of cross-cultural differences in communication and etiquette.

Materials   The instructor will provide one set of question/answer cards to each pair of teams.

Instructions

- *Step 1*: The class is divided into an even number of teams. Ideally, each team would have three students. (Two- or four-student teams are possible if matched with an equal-sized team.) Each team is then paired with another team and the paired teams (team "A" and team "B") are assigned a private space away from other matched teams.

- *Step 2*: The instructor will hand each pair of teams a stack of cards with the multiple-choice questions face down. These cards have questions and answers about cross-cultural differences in communication and etiquette. No books or other aids are allowed.

- *Step 3*: The exercise begins with a member of team A picking up one card from the top of the pile and asking the question on that card to both people on team B. The information given to team B includes the question and all alternatives listed on the card. Team B has 30 seconds after the question and alternatives have been read to give an answer. Team B earns one point if the correct answer is given. If team B's answer is incorrect, however, team A earns that point. Correct answers to each question are indicated on the card and, of course, should not be revealed until the question is correctly answered or time is up. Whether or not team B answers correctly, it picks up the next card on the pile and asks it to members of team A. In other words, cards are read alternatively to each team. This procedure is repeated until all of the cards have been read or time has elapsed. The team receiving the most points wins.

Important note: The textbook provides very little information pertaining to the questions in this exercise. Rather, you must rely on past learning, logic, and luck to win.

Source: © 2001 Steven L. McShane.

Find the complete interactive self-assessments at this textbook's Web site at www.mhhe.com/mcshaneEss2e.

>self-assessment exercise 8-3

Active Listening Skills Inventory

This self-assessment is designed to help you estimate your strengths and weaknesses on various dimensions of active listening. Think back to face-to-face conversations you have had with a co-worker or client in the office, hallway, factory floor, or other setting. Indicate the extent that each item in this instrument describes your behavior during those conversations. Answer each item as truthfully as possible so that you get an accurate estimate of where your active listening skills need improvement. This exercise is completed alone so students assess themselves honestly without concerns of social comparison. However, class discussion will focus on the important elements of active listening.

chapter 9

Power and Influence in the Workplace

National Australia Bank rogue trader Luke Duffy (shown here after sentencing) and his colleagues created losses of $350 million, thanks in part to Duffy's power and influence tactics.

>**learning**objectives

After reading this chapter, you should be able to:

1. Define power and countervailing power.
2. Describe the five bases of power in organizations.
3. Explain how information relates to power in organizations.
4. Discuss the four contingencies of power.
5. Summarize the effects of power on the powerholder's own performance and well-being.
6. Summarize the eight types of influence tactics.
7. Discuss three contingencies to consider when deciding which influence tactic to use.
8. Distinguish influence from organizational politics.
9. Describe the organizational conditions and personal characteristics that support organizational politics.
10. Identify ways to minimize organizational politics.

For three long days, junior trader Dennis Gentilin received the cold shoulder from his boss, Luke Duffy. As head of National Australia Bank's (NAB) foreign currency options desk in Melbourne, Duffy was angry that Gentilin notified Duffy's boss that Duffy was carrying forward trading losses (called *smoothing*), which was recently prohibited. On the fourth day, Duffy launched into a tirade: "I felt like . . . killing someone the other day," Duffy apparently said pointedly to Gentilin. "If you want to stay in the team, I demand loyalty and don't want you going to Dillon [Duffy's boss] about what's happening in the team."

Gentilin later told authorities that, due to their expertise, Duffy and other senior traders were "untouchables" who were given free rein at NAB. "They just created this power base where they were laws unto themselves," claims Gentilin. Duffy also mocked and intimidated employees into submission. He referred to one of NAB's traders in London as "the London stench boy" because the London trader "was always making a stink about things." Duffy warned a junior trader, Vanessa McCallum, not to cross him, saying that another employee who had done so was now making bread for a living. When testifying against Duffy in court, McCallum recalled: "My greatest fear was, if nothing is wrong, I'm going to have to leave the desk because you had to be loyal to Luke."

But something did go very wrong. When Duffy's team bet against a rising Australian dollar, they began an escalating series of cover-ups, including creation of fictitious trades to offset the losses. The unrestrained power and influence of Duffy and other senior traders in Melbourne and London kept everyone in line, resulting in more than 800 breaches of the bank's trading limits. Gentilin and McCallum eventually notified senior management, but by then the damage had been done. Within a year, the rogue team had amassed US$300 million in losses. Duffy and three other traders were jailed for securities violations. The chief executive and chairman of National Australia Bank lost their jobs.[1]

//

The National Australia Bank saga illustrates how power and influence can have profound consequences for employee behavior and the organization's success. Although this story has an unhappy ending, power and influence can equally influence ethical conduct and improve corporate performance. The reality is that no one escapes from organizational power and influence. Power and influence exist in every business and, according to some writers, in every decision and action.

This chapter unfolds as follows: First, we define power and present a basic model depicting the dynamics of power in organizational settings. The chapter then discusses the five bases of power, as well as information as a power base. Next, we look at the contingencies necessary to translate those sources into meaningful power. The latter part of this chapter examines the various types of influence in organizational settings as well as the contingencies of effective influence strategies. The final section of this chapter looks at situations in which influence becomes organizational politics, as well as ways of minimizing dysfunctional politics.

After reading the next three sections, you should be able to:

learningobjects <

1. *Define power and countervailing power.*
2. *Describe the five bases of power in organizations.*
3. *Explain how information relates to power in organizations.*
4. *Discuss the four contingencies of power.*
5. *Summarize the effects of power on the powerholder's own performance and well-being.*

>The Meaning of Power

POWER:
the capacity of a person, team, or organization to influence others

Power is the capacity of a person, team, or organization to influence others.[2] Power is not the act of changing someone's attitudes or behavior; it is only the potential to do so. People frequently have power they do not use; they might not even know they have power. Also, power is not a personal feeling of power. You might feel powerful or think you have power over someone else, but this is not power unless you actually have the capacity to influence that person. The most basic prerequisite of power is that one person or group believes it is dependent on another person or group for a resource of value.[3] This relationship, shown in Exhibit 9.1, occurs where person A has power over person B by controlling something that person B wants. You might have power over others by controlling a desired job assignment, useful information, important resources, or even the privilege of being associated with you! However, power requires the *perception* of dependence, so people might gain power by convincing others that they have something of value, whether or not they actually control that resource. Thus, power exists when others believe that you control resources they want.

COUNTERVAILING POWER:
the capacity of a person, team or organization to keep a more powerful person or group in the exchange relationship

Although dependence is a key element of power relationships, it is really more accurate to say that the parties are *interdependent*.[4] In Exhibit 9.1, person A dominates in the power relationship, but person B also has some **countervailing power**—enough power to keep person A in the exchange relationship and ensure that they use their dominant power judiciously. For example, executives have power over subordinates by controlling their job security and promotional opportunities. At the same time, employees have countervailing power by possessing skills and knowledge to keep production humming and customers happy, something that executives can't accomplish alone. Finally, the power relationship depends on some minimum level of trust. Trust indicates a level of expectation that the more powerful party will deliver the resource. For example, you trust your employer to give you a paycheck at the end of each pay period. Even those in extremely dependent situations will usually walk away from the relationship if they lack a minimum level of trust in the more powerful party.

>Sources of Power in Organizations

Power derives from several sources and a few contingencies that determine the potential of those power sources.[5] Three sources of power—legitimate, reward, and coercive—originate mostly from the powerholder's formal position or informal role. In other words, the person is granted these power bases formally by the organization or informally by co-workers. Two

[Exhibit 9.1] Dependence in the Power Relationship

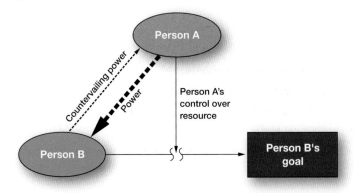

other sources of power—expert and referent—originate from the powerholder's own characteristics; that is, they bring these power bases to the organization. Sources of power are resources that help the dependent person directly or indirectly achieve his or her goals. For example, your expertise is a source of power when others need that expertise to accomplish their objectives.

Legitimate Power

Legitimate power is an agreement among organizational members that people in certain roles can request specific behaviors of others. This perceived right originates from formal job descriptions as well as informal rules of conduct. This legitimate power extends to employees, not just managers. For example, an organization might give employees the right to request customer files if this information is required for their job. Legitimate power depends on more than job descriptions. It also depends on mutual agreement from those expected to abide by this authority. Your boss's power to make you work overtime partly depends on your agreement to this authority. Thus, legitimate power operates within a "zone of indifference"—the range within which people are willing to accept someone else's authority.[6]

> **LEGITIMATE POWER:** an agreement among organizational members that people in certain roles can request specific behaviors of others

The size of this zone of indifference (and, consequently, the magnitude of legitimate power) increases with the extent that the powerholder is trusted and makes fair decisions. Some people are also more obedient than others to authority, particularly those who value conformity and tradition. People in high power distance cultures (i.e., those who accept an unequal distribution of power) also tend to have higher obedience to authority compared with people in low power distance cultures. The organization's culture represents a third factor. A 3M scientist might continue to work on a project after being told by superiors to stop working on it because the 3M culture supports an entrepreneurial spirit, which includes ignoring your boss's authority from time to time.[7]

Reward Power

Reward power is derived form the person's ability to control the allocation of rewards valued by others and to remove negative sanctions (i.e., negative reinforcement). Managers have formal authority that gives them power over the distribution of organizational rewards such as pay, promotions, time off, vacation schedules, and work assignments. Employees also have reward power over their bosses through the use of 360-degree feedback systems. Employee feedback affects supervisors' promotions and other rewards, so they tend to behave differently toward employees after 360-degree feedback is introduced.

Coercive Power

Coercive power is the ability to apply punishment. In the opening story to this chapter, Luke Duffy demonstrated his coercive power by reprimanding and threatening employees into submission. Employees also have coercive power, ranging from sarcasm to ostracism, to ensure that co-workers conform to team norms. Many firms also rely on the coercive power of team members to control co-worker behavior. For instance, when asked how AirAsia maintained attendance and productivity after the Kuala Lumpur-based discount airline removed the time clocks, chief executive Tony Fernandes replied: "Simple. Peer pressure sees to that. The fellow employees, who are putting their shoulders to the wheel, will see to that."[8]

Expert Power

For the most part, legitimate, reward, and coercive power originate from the position.[9] In contrast, expert power originates from within the person. It is an individual's or work unit's capacity to influence others by possessing knowledge or skills that they value. Luke Duffy and other "untouchables" mentioned in the opening story had expert power over senior executives at National Australia Bank, apparently to the point that they performed much of their work with minimal checks and balances. Employees are also gaining expert power as our society moves from an industrial to a knowledge-based economy.[10] The reason is that employee knowledge becomes the means of production and is ultimately outside the control of those who own the company. And without this control over production, owners are more dependent on employees to achieve their corporate objectives.

REFERENT POWER: the capacity to influence others based on an identification with and respect for the power-holder

Referent Power

People have **referent power** when others identify with them, like them, or otherwise respect them. Like expert power, referent power comes from within the person. It is largely a function of the person's interpersonal skills and usually develops slowly. Referent power is usually associated with charismatic leadership. Experts have difficulty agreeing on the meaning of *charisma,* but it is most often described as a form of interpersonal attraction whereby followers ascribe almost magical powers of attraction to the charismatic individual.[11] Some experts describe charisma as a special "gift" or trait within the charismatic person, while others say it is mainly in the eyes of the beholder. However, all agree that charisma produces a high degree of trust, respect, and devotion toward the charismatic individual.

Trendspotters Have Information Power

People who can forecast the future are worth their weight in gold. The reason is this: Information about the future helps companies to cope with environmental uncertainties. Corporate leaders can ramp up production to cash in on growing demand, and can take corrective action to minimize damage from falling demand. "It's good to have advance-warning radar about what's happening among consumers," says London-based trendspotter Zoe Lazarus. Lazarus and Richard Welch in New York (both shown here) jointly lead a trend analysis unit for Lowe Worldwide, one of several ad agencies that have recently introduced trend analysis teams that peer into the future. Along with scanning offbeat magazines (*Sleazenation, Relax*), Lazarus and Welch anticipate social changes by listening to more than 500 bartenders, photographers, disc jockeys, architects, journalists, designers, and other "influencers" in 52 cities across several countries. "[We're] looking for leading-edge trends that will eventually filter into the mainstream in one to two years' time, changing patterns in leisure behavior, holiday destinations, music choices, as well as fashion trends," Lazarus explains.[14]

Information and Power

Information is power.[12] In one form, people gain information power when they control (through legitimate power) the flow of information to others. Employees are ultimately dependent on these information gatekeepers to release the information required to perform their jobs. Also, by deciding what information is distributed to whom, those who control information flow also control perceptions of the situation by releasing information favoring one perspective more than another.[13]

The other form of information power relates to expert power. Specifically, employees have more power if they seem to be able to cope with organizational uncertainties. Organizations are more effective when they can cope with uncertainties in the external environment. Therefore, individuals and work units gain power by offering one or more of the following ways to cope with uncertainty, with the first being the most powerful:[15]

- *Prevention*. The most effective strategy is to prevent environmental changes from occurring. For example, financial experts acquire power by preventing the organization from experiencing a cash shortage or defaulting on loans.

- *Forecasting*. The next best strategy is to predict environmental changes or variations. In this respect, marketing specialists gain power by predicting changes in consumer preferences.

- *Absorption*. People and work units also gain power by absorbing or neutralizing the impact of environmental shifts as they occur. An example is the ability of maintenance crews to come to the rescue when machines break down and the production process stops.

>Contingencies of Power

Let's say that you have expert power by virtue of your ability to forecast and possibly even prevent dramatic changes in the organization's environment. Does this expertise mean that you are influential? Not necessarily, because the sources of power operate at full capacity only under certain conditions. Four important contingencies of power are substitutability, centrality, discretion, and visibility.[16]

Substitutability

Substitutability refers to the availability of alternatives. Power is strongest when someone has a monopoly over a valued resource. Conversely, power decreases as the number of alternative sources of the critical resource increases. If you—and no one else—have expertise across the organization on an important issue, you would be more powerful than if several people in your company possess this valued knowledge. Substitutability refers not only to other sources that offer the resource, but also to substitutions of the resource itself. For instance, labor unions are weakened when companies introduce technologies that replace the need for their union members. Technology is a substitute for employees and, consequently, reduces union power.

SUBSTITUTABILITY: a contingency of power referring to the availability of alternatives

Nonsubstitutability is strengthened by controlling access to the resource. Professions and labor unions gain power by controlling knowledge, tasks, or labor to perform important activities. For instance, the medical profession is powerful because it controls who can perform specific medical procedures. Labor unions that dominate an industry effectively control access to labor needed to perform key jobs. Employees become nonsubstitutable when they possess knowledge (such as operating equipment or serving clients) that is not documented or readily available to others. Nonsubstitutability also occurs when people differentiate their resource from the alternatives. Some people claim that consultants use this tactic. They take skills and knowledge that many consulting firms can provide and wrap them into a package (with the latest buzz words, of course) so that it looks like a service that no one else can offer.

Centrality

Centrality refers to the degree and nature of interdependence between the powerholder and others.[17] Think about your own centrality for a moment: If you decided not to show up for work or school tomorrow, how many people would be affected, and how much time

CENTRALITY: a contingency of power referring to the degree and nature of interdependence between the powerholder and others

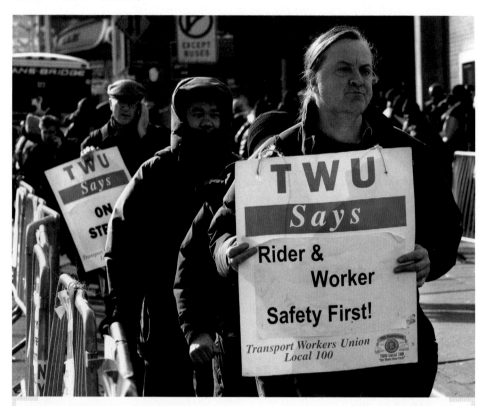

The Centrality of New York Transit

New York City's seven million commuters were on the receiving end of "centrality" of power a few years ago when transit workers illegally walked off the job for three days. The strike's effect on commuters and businesses was immediate and widespread, amplified by the strike's occurrence during the peak Christmas-shopping season. Even with the city center restricted to car pools, the roads quickly became clogged with cars. Some businesses estimated that half of their employees did not arrive to work or were very late. Several public schools started two hours later than usual. According to New York City's mayor, the three-day stoppage cost the city and its businesses more than $1 billion. "[The Metropolitan Transit Authority] told us we got no power, but we got power," said one striking transit worker. "We got the power to stop the city." The strike ended after three days because courts imposed heavy fines on the transit union and promised jail terms for its leaders.[18]

would pass before they are affected? If you have high centrality, most people in the organization would be adversely affected by your absence, and they would be affected quickly. For example, airline pilots have high centrality because the airline could not operate planes without them. If pilots refused to work, the airline's critical business operations would be shut down immediately.

Discretion

The freedom to exercise judgment—to make decisions without referring to a specific rule or receiving permission from someone else—is another important contingency of power in organizations. Consider the plight of first-line supervisors. It may seem that they have legitimate, reward, and coercive power over employees, but this power is often curtailed by specific rules. The lack of discretion makes supervisors less powerful than their positions would indicate. "Middle managers are very much 'piggy-in-the-middle,'" complains a middle manager at Britain's National Health System. "They have little power, only what senior managers are allowed to give them."[19] More generally, research indicates that managerial discretion varies considerably across industries, and that managers with an internal locus of control are viewed as more powerful because they don't act like they lack discretion in their job.[20]

Visibility

People who control valued resources or knowledge will yield power only when others are aware of these power bases, in other words, when it is visible. One way to increase visibility is to take people-oriented jobs and work on projects that require frequent interaction with senior executives. "You can take visibility in steps," advises an executive at a U.S. pharmaceutical firm. "You can start by making yourself visible in a small group, such as a staff meeting. Then when you're comfortable with that, seek out larger arenas."[21]

Another way to gain visibility is by working in a location where people see you more often, such as an office closest to the elevator or office coffee room. People often use public symbols as subtle (and not-so-subtle) cues to make their power sources known to others. Many professionals display their educational diplomas and awards on office walls to remind visitors of their expertise. Medical professionals wear white coats with a stethoscope around their neck to symbolize their legitimate and expert power in hospital settings. Other people play the game of "face time"—spending more time at work and showing that they are working productively. **Mentoring**—a relationship in which a more senior member of the organization provides coaching and other career development support to a junior member—also increases power through visibility. Specifically, mentors help to expose the junior employee's talents, such as by giving the junior person access to visible tasks and more interaction opportunities with key decision makers in the organization.[22]

> **MENTORING:** a relationship in which a more senior member of the organization provides coaching and other career development support to a junior member—also increases power through visibility

Social Networking and Power

"It's not what you know, but who you know that counts!" This often-heard statement reflects the fact that employees get ahead not just by developing their competencies, but by *networking*—cultivating social relationships with others to accomplish one's goals. Networking increases a person's power in three ways. First, networks represent a critical component of **social capital**—the knowledge and other resources available to people or social units (teams, organizations) due to a durable network that connects them to others. Networks consist of people who trust each other, which increases the flow of knowledge among those within the network. The more you network, the more likely you will receive valuable information that increases your expert power in the organization.[23]

> **SOCIAL CAPITAL:** the knowledge and other resources available to people or social units (teams, organizations) due to a durable network that connects them to others

Second, people tend to identify more with partners within their own networks, which increases referent power among people within each network. This network-based referent power may lead to more favorable decisions by others in the network. Finally, effective networkers are better known by others in the organization, so their talents are more readily recognized. This power increases when networkers place themselves in strategic positions in the network, thereby gaining centrality.[24] For example, these people might be regarded as the main person who distributes information in the network or who keeps the network connected through informal gatherings.

Consequences of Power

How does power affect the powerholder? We partly answered this question earlier in this book when describing *empowerment*—an individual's feelings of self-determination, meaning, competence, and impact in the organization. Employees are more likely to feel empowered when they work in enriched jobs and in companies with a strong learning orientation. Empowered employees are more motivated, have higher job satisfaction and organizational commitment, and usually perform their jobs better. In addition, research suggests that as people become more powerful, they are more goal-directed and tend to act on their environment rather than hide from it.

At the same time, increasing power over others can potentially undermine an individual's effectiveness and interpersonal relations. Some studies have found that people who have (or believe they have) more power over others are more likely to cling to stereotypes, have more difficulty empathizing, and generally have less-accurate perceptions compared with people with less power. They also engage in more automatic rather than mindful thinking, possibly because powerful people are less concerned about the consequences of their actions.[25]

>**learning**objectives

After reading the following section, you should be able to:

6. *Summarize the eight types of influence tactics.*

7. *Discuss three contingencies to consider when deciding which influence tactic to use.*

>Influencing Others

INFLUENCE:
any behavior that
attempts to
alter someone's
attitudes or
behavior

Up to this point, we have focused on the sources and contingencies of power. But power is only the capacity to influence others. It represents the potential to change someone's attitudes and behavior. **Influence,** on the other hand, refers to any behavior that attempts to alter someone's attitudes or behavior.[26] Influence is power in motion. It applies one or more power bases to get people to alter their beliefs, feelings, and activities. Consequently, our interest in the remainder of this chapter is on how people use power to influence others.

Influence tactics are woven throughout the social fabric of all organizations. This is because influence is an essential process through which people coordinate their effort and act in concert to achieve organizational objectives. Indeed, influence is central to the definition of leadership. Influence operates down, across, and up the corporate hierarchy. Executives ensure that subordinates complete required tasks. Employees influence co-workers to help them with their job assignments. Subordinates engage in upward influence tactics so corporate leaders make decisions compatible with subordinates' needs and expectations.

Types of Influence Tactics

Organizational behavior researchers have devoted considerable attention to the various types of influence tactics found in organizational settings. They do not agree on a definitive list, but the most commonly mentioned influence tactics are identified in Exhibit 9.2 and described over the next few pages.[27] The first five are known as

[Exhibit 9.2] Types of Influence Tactics in Organizations

Influence Tactic	Description
Hard influence tactics	
Silent authority	Influencing behavior through legitimate power without explicitly referring to that power base.
Assertiveness	Actively applying legitimate and coercive power by applying pressure or threats.
Information control	Explicitly manipulating someone else's access to information for the purpose of changing their attitudes and/or behavior.
Coalition formation	Forming a group that attempts to influence others by pooling the resources and power of its members.
Upward appeal	Gaining support from one or more people with higher authority or expertise.
Soft influence tactics	
Ingratiation/impression management	Attempting to increase liking by, or perceived similarity to, some targeted person.
Persuasion	Using logical arguments, factual evidence, and emotional appeals to convince people of the value of a request.
Exchange	Promising benefits or resources in exchange for the target person's compliance.

"hard" influence tactics because they force behavior change through position power (legitimate, reward, and coercion). The latter three—ingratiation and impression management, persuasion, and exchange—are called "soft" influence tactics because they rely more on personal sources of power (referent, expert) and appeal to the target person's attitudes and needs.

Silent Authority

The silent application of authority occurs where someone complies with a request because of the requester's legitimate power as well as the target person's role expectations. We often refer to this condition as *deference to authority*.[28] This deference occurs when you comply with your boss's request to complete a particular task. If the task is within your job scope and your boss has the right to make this request, then this influence strategy operates without negotiation, threats, persuasion, or other tactics. Silent authority is the most common form of influence in high-power-distance cultures.[29]

Assertiveness

In contrast to silent authority, assertiveness might be called *vocal authority* because it involves actively applying legitimate and coercive power to influence others. Assertiveness includes persistently reminding the target of his or her obligations, frequently checking the target's work, confronting the target, and using threats of sanctions to force compliance. Assertiveness typically applies or threatens to apply punishment if the target does not comply. Explicit or implicit threats range from job loss to losing face by letting down the team. Extreme forms of assertiveness include blackmailing colleagues, such as by threatening to reveal the other person's previously unknown failures unless he or she complies with your request. Referring to the opening story to this chapter, associates claim that Luke Duffy influenced his staff at National Australia Bank largely through assertiveness, including threatening to fire them if they didn't keep quiet and follow his wishes.

Information Control

Luke Duffy also used information control as an influence tactic. Specifically, the rogue National Australia Bank trader hid hundreds of illegal transactions from his boss and other executives, so much so that his team received a sizable bonus when they had actually eaten away a large chunk of the bank's profits! Information control involves explicitly manipulating others' access to information for the purpose of changing their attitudes and/or behavior. With limited access to potentially valuable information, others are at a disadvantage. While the NAB incident is more extreme than most, hiding information isn't unusual in organizations. According to one major survey, almost half of employees believe co-workers keep others in the dark about work issues if it helps their own cause. Employees also influence executive decisions by screening out (filtering) information flowing up the hierarchy. One study found that CEOs influence their board of directors by selectively feeding and withholding information.[30]

Coalition Formation

COALITION: a group that attempts to influence people outside the group by pooling the resources and power of its members

When people lack sufficient power alone to influence others in the organization, they might form a **coalition** of people who support the proposed change. A coalition is influential in three ways.[31] First, it pools the power and resources of many people, so the coalition potentially has more influence than any number of people operating alone. Second, the coalition's mere existence can be a source of power by symbolizing the legitimacy of the issue. In other words, a coalition creates a sense that the issue deserves attention because it has broad support. Third, coalitions tap into the power of the social identity process introduced in Chapter 2. A coalition is essentially an informal group that advocates a new set of norms and behaviors. If the coalition has a broad-based membership (i.e., its members come from various parts of the organization), then other employees are more likely to identify with that group and, consequently, accept the ideas the coalition is proposing.

Upward Appeal

UPWARD APPEAL: a type of influence in which someone with higher authority or expertise is called upon in reality or symbolically to support the influencer's position

Have you ever had a disagreement with a colleague in which one of you eventually says "I'm sure the boss (or teacher) will agree with me on this. Let's find out!" This tactic, called **upward appeal,** ranges from a formal alliance to the perception of informal support from someone with higher authority or expertise. It also occurs when relying on the authority of the firm's policies or values. By reminding others that your request is consistent with the organization's overarching goals, you are implying support from senior executives without formally involving them.

Ingratiation and Impression Management

INGRATIATION: any attempt to increase liking by, or perceived similarity to, some targeted person

Silent authority, assertiveness, information control, coalitions, and upward appeals are somewhat (or very) forceful ways to influence other people. In contrast, a very "soft" influence tactic is **ingratiation**—any attempt to increase liking by, or perceived similarity to, some targeted person.[32] Ingratiation comes in several flavors. For example, employees might flatter their boss in front of others, demonstrate that they have similar attitudes as their boss (e.g., agreeing with the boss's proposal), and ask their boss for advice. Ingratiation is one of the more effective influence tactics at boosting a person's career success (i.e., performance appraisal feedback, salaries, and promotions).[33] However, people who engage in high levels of ingratiation are less (not more) influential and less likely to get promoted.[34] The explanation for the contrasting evidence is that those who engage in too much ingratiation are viewed as insincere and self-serving. The terms *apple-polishing* and *brownnosing* are applied to those who ingratiate to excess or in ways that suggest selfish motives for the ingratiation.

IMPRESSION MANAGEMENT: the practice of actively shaping our public images

Ingratiation is part of a larger influence tactic known as impression management. **Impression management** is the practice of actively shaping our public images.[35] These public images might be crafted as being important, vulnerable, threatening, or pleasant. For the most part, employees routinely engage in pleasant impression management behaviors to satisfy the basic norms of social behavior, such as the way they dress and how they behave toward colleagues and customers. Impression management is a common strategy for people trying to get ahead in the workplace. For instance, job applicants exhibit various forms of impression management in employment interviews.[36] As with ingratiation, employees who use too much impression management tend to be less influential because their behaviors are viewed as insincere. However, that fact hasn't stopped many people from exaggerating their credentials and accomplishments on their résumé, including a Lucent Technologies executive who lied about having a PhD from Stanford University and hid his criminal past involving forgery and embezzlement. Ironically, the executive was Lucent's director of recruiting![37]

Persuasion

Along with ingratiation, **persuasion** is one of the most effective influence strategies for career success. The ability to present facts, logical arguments, and emotional appeals to change another person's attitudes and behavior is not just an acceptable way to influence others; in many societies, it is a noble art and a quality of effective leaders. The effectiveness of persuasion as an influence tactic depends on characteristics of the persuader, message content, communication medium, and the audience being persuaded.[38] People are more persuasive when listeners believe they have expertise and credibility, such as when the persuader does not seem to profit from the persuasion attempt and, in fact, acknowledges one or two arguments against his or her position.

> **PERSUASION:** presenting facts, logical arguments, and emotional appeals to change another person's attitudes and behavior

The message is more important than the messenger when the issue is important to the audience. Messages are more persuasive when they offer more than one point of view so the audience does not feel cornered by the speaker. The message should also be limited to a few strong arguments, which are repeated a few times, but not too frequently. The message should use emotional appeals (such as graphically showing the unfortunate consequences of a bad decision), but only in combination with logical arguments and specific recommendations to overcome the threat. Finally, message content is more persuasive when the audience is warned about opposing arguments. This **inoculation effect** causes listeners to generate counterarguments to the anticipated persuasion attempts, which makes the opponent's subsequent persuasion attempts less effective.[39]

> **INOCULATION EFFECT:** a persuasive communication strategy of warning listeners that others will try to influence them in the future and that they should be wary about the opponent's arguments

Two other considerations when persuading people are the medium of communication and characteristics of the audience. Generally, persuasion works best in face-to-face conversations and through other media-rich communication channels. The personal nature of face-to-face communication increases the persuader's credibility, and the richness of this

Entering the Reality Distortion Field

Wearing his trademark black turtleneck and faded blue jeans, Apple Inc. cofounder and CEO Steve Jobs is famous for stirring up crowds with evangelical fervor as he draws them into his "reality distortion field." A reality distortion field occurs when people are caught in Steve Jobs's visionary headlights. Apple Inc. manager Bud Tribble borrowed the phrase from the TV series *Star Trek* to describe Jobs's overwhelming persuasiveness. "In his presence, reality is malleable," Tribble explained to newly-hired Andy Hertzfeld in 1981. "He [Steve Jobs] can convince anyone of practically anything. It wears off when he's not around, but it makes it hard to have realistic schedules." As one journalist wrote: "Drift too close to Jobs in the grip of one of his manias and you can get sucked in, like a wayward asteroid straying into Jupiter's gravitational zone."[40]

channel provides faster feedback that the influence strategy is working. With respect to audience characteristics, it is more difficult to persuade people who have high self-esteem and intelligence, as well as those whose targeted attitudes are strongly connected to their self-identity.[41]

Exchange

Exchange activities involve the promise of benefits or resources in exchange for the target person's compliance with your request. This tactic also includes reminding the target of past benefits or favors with the expectation that the target will now make up for that debt. The norm of reciprocity is a central and explicit theme in exchange strategies. According to the norm of reciprocity, individuals are expected to help those who have helped them.[42] Negotiation is also an integral part of exchange influence activities. For instance, you might negotiate with your boss for a day off in return for working a less desirable shift at a future date. Networking is another form of exchange as an influence strategy. Active networkers build up "exchange credits" by helping colleagues in the short term for reciprocal benefits in the long term.

Networking as an influence strategy is a deeply ingrained practice in several cultures. The Chinese term *guanxi* refers to special relationships and active interpersonal connectedness. It is based on traditional Confucian values of helping others without expecting future repayment. However, some writers suggest that the original interpretation and practice of guanxi has shifted to include implicit long-term reciprocity, which can slip into cronyism. As a result, some Asian governments are discouraging guanxi-based decisions, preferring more arms-length transactions in business and government decisions.[43]

Consequences and Contingencies of Influence Tactics

Now that the main influence strategies have been described, you are probably asking: Which ones are best? The best way to answer this question is to identify the three ways that people react when others try to influence them: resistance, compliance, or commitment.[44] *Resistance* occurs when people or work units oppose the behavior desired by the influencer and consequently refuse, argue, or delay engaging in the behavior. *Compliance* occurs when people are motivated to implement the influencer's request at a minimal level of effort and for purely instrumental reasons. Without external sources to prompt the desired behavior, it would not occur. *Commitment* is the strongest form of influence, whereby people identify with the influencer's request and are highly motivated to implement it even when extrinsic sources of motivation are no longer present.

Generally, people react more favorably to soft tactics than to hard tactics (see Exhibit 9.3). Soft influence tactics rely on personal power bases (expert and referent power), which tend to build commitment to the influencer's request. In contrast, hard tactics rely on position power (legitimate, reward, and coercion), so they tend to produce compliance or, worse, resistance. Hard tactics also tend to undermine trust, which can hurt future relationships.

Aside from the general preference for soft rather than hard tactics, the most appropriate influence strategy depends on a few contingencies. One obvious contingency is which sources of power are strongest. Those with expertise tend to have more influence using persuasion, whereas those with a strong legitimate power base are usually more successful applying silent authority.[45] A second contingency is whether the person being influenced is higher, lower, or at the same level in the organization. As an example, employees may face adverse career consequences by being too assertive with their boss. Meanwhile, supervisors who engage in ingratiation and impression management tend to lose the respect of their staff.

Finally, the most appropriate influence tactic depends on personal, organizational, and cultural values.[46] People with a strong need for power might feel more comfortable using assertiveness, whereas those who value conformity might feel more comfortable

[Exhibit 9.3] Consequences of Hard and Soft Influence Tactics

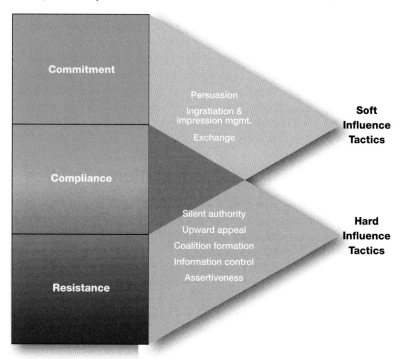

with upward appeals. At an organizational level, firms with a competitive culture might tolerate more use of information control and coalition formation, whereas companies with a learning orientation would likely encourage more influence through persuasion. The preferred influence tactics also vary across societal cultures. Research indicates that ingratiation is much more common among managers in the United States than in Hong Kong, possibly because this tactic disrupts the more distant roles that managers and employees expect in high power distance cultures.

After reading the following section, you should be able to: **learning**objectives**<**

8. *Distinguish influence from organizational politics.*

9. *Describe the organizational conditions and personal characteristics that support organizational politics.*

10. *Identify ways to minimize organizational politics.*

>Influence Tactics and Organizational Politics

You might have noticed that organizational politics has not been mentioned yet, even though some of the practices or examples described over the past few pages are usually considered political tactics. The phrase was carefully avoided because, for the most part, organizational politics is in the eye of the beholder. You might perceive a co-worker's attempt to influence the boss as normal behavior, whereas someone else might perceive the co-worker's tactic as brazen organizational politics.

This perceptual issue explains why OB experts increasingly discuss influence tactics as behaviors and organizational politics as perceptions.[47] The influence tactics described

ORGANIZATIONAL POLITICS: behaviors that others perceive as self-serving tactics for personal gain at the expense of other people and possibly the organization

earlier are perceived as **organizational politics** when observers view the tactics as self-serving behaviors at the expense of others and sometimes contrary to the interests of the entire organization or work unit. Of course, some tactics are so blatantly selfish that almost everyone views them as political. But most influence tactics could be either "political" or beneficial, depending on how they are perceived by others. When employees perceive many incidents of organizational politics, the result is lower job satisfaction, organizational commitment, and organizational citizenship, as well as high levels of work-related stress.[48] And when political tactics really are self-serving, they divert resources away from the organization's effective functioning. In extreme situations, such as in the opening story to this chapter, political activities can result in huge losses and even threaten the company's survival.

Conditions Supporting Organizational Politics

Organizational politics flourishes under the right conditions.[49] One of those conditions is scarce resources. When budgets are slashed, people rely on political tactics to safeguard their resources and maintain the status quo. Office politics also flourishes when resource allocation decisions are ambiguous, complex, or lack formal rules. This occurs because decision makers are given more discretion over resource allocation, so potential recipients of those resources use political tactics to influence the factors that should be considered in the decision. Organizational change encourages political behaviors for this reason. Change creates uncertainty and ambiguity as the company moves from an old set of rules and practices to a new set. During these times, employees apply political strategies to protect their valued resources, position, and self-image.[50]

Personal Characteristics

MACHIAVELLIAN VALUES: the belief that deceit is a natural and acceptable way to influence others

Several personal characteristics affect a person's motivation to engage in self-serving behavior.[51] This includes a strong need for personal as opposed to socialized power. Those with a need for personal power seek power for its own sake and try to acquire more power. Some individuals have strong **Machiavellian values.** Machiavellianism is named after Niccolò Machiavelli, the 16th-century Italian philosopher who wrote *The Prince,* a famous treatise about political behavior. People with high Machiavellian values are comfortable with getting more than they deserve, and they believe that deceit is a natural and acceptable way to achieve this goal. They seldom trust co-workers and tend to use cruder influence tactics, such as bypassing one's boss or being assertive, to get their own way.[52] The opening vignette to this chapter suggests that National Australia Bank's rogue trader displayed Machiavellian characteristics, including rough assertiveness and controlling information.

Minimizing Organizational Politics and its Consequences

The conditions that fuel organizational politics also give us some clues about how to control dysfunctional political activities.[53] One strategy to keep organizational politics in check is to introduce clear rules and regulations that specify the use of scarce resources. Organizational politics can become a problem during times of organizational change, so politics can be minimized through effective organizational change practices. Leaders also need to actively manage group norms to curtail self-serving influence activities. In particular, they can support organizational values that oppose political tactics, such as altruism and customer focus. One of the most important strategies is for leaders to become role models of organizational citizenship rather than symbols of successful organizational politicians.

Along with minimizing organizational politics, companies can limit the adverse effects of political perceptions by giving employees more control over their work and keeping them informed of organizational events. Research has found that employees who are kept informed of what is going on in the organization and who are involved in organizational decisions are less likely to experience stress, job dissatisfaction, and absenteeism as a result of organizational politics.

>Chapter Summary

Power is the capacity to influence others. It exists when one party perceives that he or she is dependent on the other for something of value. However, the dependent person must also have countervailing power—some power over the dominant party—to maintain the relationship.

There are five power bases. Legitimate power is an agreement among organizational members that people in certain roles can request certain behaviors of others. Reward power is derived from the ability to control the allocation of rewards valued by others and to remove negative sanctions. Coercive power is the ability to apply punishment. Expert power is the capacity to influence others by possessing knowledge or skills that they value. People have referent power when others identify with them, like them, or otherwise respect them. Information plays an important role in organizational power. Employees gain power by controlling the flow of information that others need and by being able to cope with uncertainties related to important organizational goals.

Four contingencies determine whether these power bases translate into real power. Individuals and work units are more powerful when they are nonsubstitutable, that is, there is a lack of alternatives. Employees, work units, and organizations reduce substitutability by controlling tasks, knowledge, and labor, and by differentiating themselves from competitors. A second contingency is centrality. People have more power when they have high centrality, that is, the number of people affected is large and people are quickly affected by their actions. Discretion, the third contingency of power, refers to the freedom to exercise judgment. Power increases when people have freedom to use their power. The fourth contingency, visibility, refers to the idea that power increases to the extent that a person's or work unit's competencies are known to others.

Social networking involves cultivating social relationships with others to accomplish one's goals. This activity increases an individual's social capital, which strengthens expert power, referent power, visibility, and possibly centrality. Power has both beneficial and adverse consequences for individuals. On the positive side, empowerment strengthens their well-being and effectiveness. On the negative side, research indicates that when people become more powerful, their perceptual and decision-making skills can suffer.

Influence refers to any behavior that attempts to alter someone's attitudes or behavior. The most widely studied influence tactics are silent authority, assertiveness, information control, coalition formation, upward appeal, ingratiation and impression management, persuasion, and exchange. Soft influence tactics such as friendly persuasion and subtle ingratiation are more acceptable than hard tactics such as upward appeal and assertiveness. However, the most appropriate influence tactic also depends on the influencer's power base; whether the person being influenced is higher, lower, or at the same level in the organization; and personal, organizational, and cultural values regarding influence behavior.

Organizational politics refers to influence tactics that others perceive to be self-serving behaviors at the expense of others and sometimes contrary to the interests of the entire organization or work unit. Organizational politics is more prevalent when scarce resources are allocated using complex and ambiguous decisions and when the organization tolerates or rewards political behavior. Individuals with a high need for personal power and strong Machiavellian values have a higher propensity to use political tactics.

Organizational politics can be minimized by providing clear rules for resource allocation, establishing a free flow of information, using education and involvement during organizational change, supporting team norms and a corporate culture that discourage dysfunctional politics, and having leaders who role model organizational citizenship rather than political savvy.

>key terms

centrality 193	inoculation effect 199	power 190
coalition 198	legitimate power 191	referent power 192
countervailing power 190	Machiavellian values 202	social capital 195
impression management 198	mentoring 195	substitutability 193
influence 196	organizational politics 202	upward appeal 198
ingratiation 198	persuasion 199	

>critical thinking questions

1. What role does countervailing power play in the power relationship? Give an example of your own encounter with countervailing power at school or work.

2. Several years ago, the Major League Baseball Players Association (MLBPA) went on strike in September, just before the World Series started. The players' contract expired at the beginning of the season (May), but they held off the strike until September when they would lose only one-sixth of their salaries. In contrast, a September strike would hurt the owners financially because they earn a larger portion of their revenue during the playoffs. As one player explained: "If we strike next spring, there's nothing stopping [the club owners] from letting us go until next June or July because they don't have that much at stake." Use your knowledge of the sources and contingencies of power to explain why the MLBPA had more power in negotiations by walking out in September rather than March.

3. You have just been hired as a brand manager of toothpaste for a large consumer products company. Your job mainly involves encouraging the advertising and production groups to promote and manufacture your product more effectively. These departments aren't under your direct authority, although company procedures indicate that they must complete certain tasks requested by brand managers. Describe the sources of power you can use to ensure that the advertising and production departments will help you make and sell toothpaste more effectively.

4. How does social networking increase a person's power? What social networking strategies could you initiate now to potentially enhance your future career success?

5. List the eight influence tactics described in this chapter in terms of how they are used by students to influence their university teachers. Which influence tactic is applied most often? Which is applied least often, in your opinion? To what extent is each influence tactic considered legitimate behavior or organizational politics?

6. How do cultural differences affect the following influence factors: (a) silent authority and (b) upward appeal?

7. A few years ago, the CEO of Apple Inc. invited Steve Jobs (who was not associated with the company at the time) to serve as a special adviser and raise morale among Apple employees and customers. While doing this, Jobs spent more time advising the CEO on how to cut costs, redraw the organization chart, and hire new people. Before long, most of the top people at Apple were Jobs's colleagues, who began to systematically evaluate and weed out teams of Apple employees. While publicly supporting Apple's CEO, Jobs privately criticized him and, in a show of nonconfidence, sold 1.5 million shares of Apple stock he had received. This action caught the attention of Apple's board of directors, who soon after decided to replace the CEO with Steve Jobs. The CEO claimed Jobs was a conniving backstabber who used political tactics to get his way. Others suggest that Apple would be out of business today if he hadn't taken over the company. In your opinion, were Steve Jobs's actions examples of organizational politics? Justify your answer.

8. This book frequently emphasizes that successful companies engage in organizational learning. How do political tactics interfere with organizational learning objectives?

>team exercise 9-1

Budget Deliberations

By Sharon Card

Purpose This exercise is designed to help you understand some of the power dynamics and influence tactics that occur across hierarchical levels in organizations.

Materials This activity works best where one small room leads to a larger room, which leads to a larger area.

Instructions

These exercise instructions are based on a class size of about 30 students. The instructor may adjust the size of the first two groups slightly for larger classes. The instructor will organize students as follows: A few (three to four) students are assigned the position of executives. Preferably, they are located in a secluded office or corner of a large classroom. Another six to eight students are assigned positions as middle managers. Ideally, these people will be located in an adjoining room or space, allowing privacy for the executives. The remaining students represent the nonmanagement employees in the organization. They are located in an open area outside the executive and management rooms.

Rules

Members of the executive group are free to enter the space of either the middle management or nonmanagement groups and to communicate whatever they wish, whenever they wish. Members of the middle management group may enter the space of the nonmanagement group whenever they wish, but must request permission to enter the executive group's space. The executive group can refuse the middle management group's request. Members of the nonmanagement group are not allowed to disturb the top group in any way unless specifically invited by members of the executive group. The nonmanagement group does have the right to request permission to communicate with the middle management group. The middle management group can refuse the lower group's request.

Task

Your organization is in the process of preparing a budget. The challenge is to balance needs with the financial resources. Of course, the needs are greater than the resources. The instructor will distribute a budget sheet showing a list of budget requests and their costs. Each group has control over a portion of the budget and must decide how to spend the money over which they have control. Nonmanagement has discretion over a relatively small portion and the executive group has discretion over the greatest portion. The exercise is finished when the organization has negotiated a satisfactory budget, or until the instructor calls time out. The class will then debrief with the following questions and others the instructor might ask.

Discussion Questions

1. What can we learn from this exercise about power in organizational hierarchies?

2. How is this exercise similar to relations in real organizations?

3. How did students in each group feel about the amount of power they held?

4. How did they exercise their power in relations with the other groups?

Find the complete interactive self-assessments at this textbook's Web site at
www.mhhe.com/mcshaneEss2e.

>self-assessment exercise 9-2 [ ]

Guanxi Orientation Scale

Guanxi, which is translated as interpersonal connections, is an important element of doing business in China and some other Asian countries with strong Confucian cultural values. Guanxi is based on traditional Confucian values of helping others without expecting future repayment. This instrument estimates your guanxi orientation; that is, the extent to which you accept and apply guanxi values. This self-assessment is completed alone so that students rate themselves honestly without concerns of social comparison. However, class discussion will focus on the meaning of guanxi and its relevance for organizational power and influence.

>**self-assessment** exercise 9-3

Machiavellianism Scale

Machiavellianism is named after Niccolò Machiavelli, the 16th-century Italian philosopher who wrote *The Prince,* a famous treatise about political behavior. Out of Machiavelli's work emerged this instrument that estimates the degree to which you have a Machiavellian personality. Indicate the extent to which you agree or disagree that each statement in this instrument describes you. Complete each item honestly to get the best estimate of your level of Machiavellianism.

>**self-assessment** exercise 9-4

Perceptions of Politics Scale (POPS)

Organizations have been called *political arenas*—environments where political tactics are common because decisions are ambiguous and resources are scarce. This instrument estimates the degree to which you believe the school where you attend classes has a politicized culture.

This scale consists of several statements that might or might not describe the school where you are attending classes. These statements refer to the administration of the school, not the classroom. Please indicate the extent to which you agree or disagree with each statement.

chapter 10

Conflict Management

>learningobjectives

After reading this chapter, you should be able to:

1. Debate the positive and negative consequences of conflict in the workplace.

2. Distinguish constructive from relationship conflict.

3. Describe three strategies to minimize relationship conflict during constructive conflict episodes.

4. Diagram the conflict process model.

5. Identify six structural sources of conflict in organizations.

6. Outline the five conflict handling styles and discuss the circumstances in which each would be most appropriate.

7. Summarize six structural approaches to managing conflict.

8. Compare and contrast the three types of third-party dispute resolution.

Vigorous debate is part of Intel's culture. The computer chipmaker's leaders believe that arguing out different viewpoints leads to better decisions.

Former Goldman Sachs president John Thornton has had his share of executive debates, but even he was surprised by the animated discussion that permeates Intel, the chipmaker where Thornton is a member of the board. "It can be kind of shocking at first," says Thornton, recalling his first few Intel meetings. "You realize quickly that [Intel managers] practice a form of honesty that borders on brutality." Intel cofounder and former chairman Andy Grove nurtured this culture of conflict—called *constructive confrontation*—many years ago when he noticed that meetings generate better ideas when staff actively debate rather than politely defer to ideas that others put forward. The practice is so important that new Intel employees are taught the fine art of confrontation through supervised debates and role-plays.

Andy Grove emphasizes that conflict is constructive only under specific circumstances. "Constructive confrontation does not mean being loud, unpleasant or rude, and it is not designed to affix blame," warns Grove. "The essence of it is to attack a problem by speaking up in a businesslike way." If you target the other person, then the benefits of constructive debate disintegrate. But some people claim that Intel's constructive confrontation never was very constructive. "I can tell you unequivocally that constructive confrontation was a license for a**holes to be a**holes and express themselves," says former Intel employee Logan Shrine, who coauthored a book with Bob Coleman on Intel's changing culture. "Intel's culture is dysfunctional and anomalous to what's considered acceptable behavior in any other corporation."[1]

///

One of the facts of life is that people hold different points of view. They have unique values hierarchies, develop unique perceptions of reality through learning and reinforcement, and establish different goals and priorities from those of co-workers. At the same time, organizations are living systems that demand dynamic rather than static relationships among employees. In other words, employees at Intel and other companies need to frequently agree on new work arrangements, revise the company's strategic direction, and renegotiate the allocation of scarce resources required to perform their jobs.

Given that people do not have identical viewpoints, this dynamic relationship necessarily leads to conflict. **Conflict** is a process in which one party perceives that its interests are being opposed or negatively affected by another party.[2] It may occur when one party obstructs or plans to obstruct another's goals in some way. For example, Intel employees experience conflict when they believe that one or more colleagues disagree with their proposal, oppose their recommendations, or compete over the budget allocation. But conflict is ultimately based on perceptions, so it also exists whenever one party *believes* that another might obstruct its efforts, whether or not the other party actually intends to do so.

> **CONFLICT:**
> is a process in which one party perceives that its interests are being opposed or negatively affected by another party

This chapter investigates the dynamics of conflict in organizational settings. We begin by considering the age-old question: Is conflict good or bad? Next, we describe the conflict process and examine in detail the main factors that cause or amplify conflict. The five styles of conflict management are then described, followed by a discussion of the structural approaches to conflict management. This chapter closes by looking at the manager's role in third-party conflict management intervention.

>Is Conflict Good or Bad?

For most of the previous century, conflict was widely regarded as undesirable and counter-productive.[3] This is illustrated in Exhibit 10.1a, where the downward line shows that as the level of conflict increases, conflict outcomes get worse. Managers, consultants, and scholars believed that even moderately low levels of disagreement tattered the fabric of workplace relations and sapped energy away from productive activities. Conflict with one's supervisor not only wasted productive time; it violated the hierarchy of command and questioned the efficient assignment of authority (where managers made the decisions and employees followed them).

Consistent with this view, studies report that employees who experience conflict have lower job satisfaction, team cohesion, and information sharing; biased perceptions and decisions; and higher levels of organizational politics, stress, and turnover.[4] Conflict distracts employees from their work and, in some cases, motivates them to withhold valuable knowledge and other resources. People who experience conflict are less motivated to communicate or try to understand the other party, which has the perverse effect of further escalating conflict as each side relies increasingly on distorted perceptions and stereotypes.

By the 1950s and 1960s, a few writers questioned the conflict-is-bad viewpoint, suggesting instead that there is an optimal level of conflict—too little and too much conflict is bad for organizational effectiveness. This upside down U-shaped relationship—shown in Exhibit 10.1b—gained wide acceptance in the 1970s and remains popular today.[5] One benefit of moderate conflict is improved decision making. Conflict energizes people to debate issues and evaluate alternatives more thoroughly. The debate tests the logic of arguments and encourages participants to reexamine their basic assumptions about the problem and its possible solution. Another apparent benefit of moderate conflict, according to some experts, is that it prevents organizations from stagnating and becoming nonresponsive to their external environment. This reflects our earlier observation that conflict occurs in organizations because they are living systems. Moderate levels of conflict are inevitable and necessary in dynamic organizations; conflict episodes occur when employees try to keep the organization responsive to the needs of customers and other stakeholders.[6] A third benefit, which we learned in Chapter 7, is that conflict with people outside the team potentially increases cohesion within the team.

[**Exhibit 10.1**] Past and Current Perspectives of Conflict

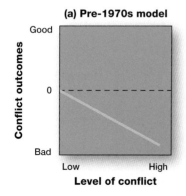

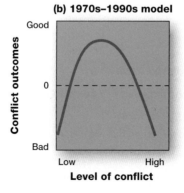

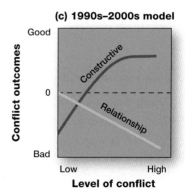

The Emerging View: Constructive and Relationship Conflict

The upside down U-shaped model of conflict was replaced in the 1990s by the perspective that there are actually two types of conflict with opposing consequences (see Exhibit 10.1c).[7] **Constructive conflict** (also known as *task or cognitive conflict*) occurs when people focus their discussion on the issue while maintaining respectfulness for people having other points of view. This conflict is called *constructive* because different viewpoints are encouraged so that ideas and recommendations can be clarified, redesigned, and tested for logical soundness. By keeping the debate focused on the task and logic, participants can re-examine their assumptions and beliefs about the problem and possible solutions without triggering the drive to defend and its associated negative emotions and ego-defense mechanism behaviors. Teams and organizations that have very low levels of constructive conflict are less effective, but there is also likely an upper limit to the level of intensity of constructive conflict.[8] Former Intel employees Logan Shrine and Bob Coleman, described in the opening story to this chapter, were critical of the company's conflict episodes because that conflict may have been more intense than is beneficial.

In contrast to constructive conflict, **relationship conflict** (also known as *socioemotional, affective,* or *destructive conflict*), focuses on people rather than the issues and tasks. The attention is on interpersonal incompatibilities such as personality clashes rather than legitimate differences of opinion regarding tasks or decisions. Employees try to undermine another person's argument by questioning the competency of the person presenting that argument. Attacking a person's credibility or displaying an aggressive response toward that person triggers defense mechanisms and a competitive orientation. The recipients of those verbal attacks become less motivated to communicate and share information, making it more difficult to discover common ground and ultimately resolve the conflict. The parties then rely more on distorted perceptions and stereotypes that, as we noted earlier, tends to further escalate the conflict.

> **CONSTRUCTIVE CONFLICT:**
> (also known as *task or cognitive conflict*) occurs when people focus their discussion on the issue while maintaining respectfulness for people having other points of view

> **RELATIONSHIP CONFLICT:**
> (also known as *socioemotional, affective,* or *destructive conflict*), focuses on people rather than the issues and tasks

Separating Constructive from Relationship Conflict

The idea that there are two types of conflict—constructive and relationship—leads to the logical conclusion that we should encourage constructive conflict for better decision making and minimize relationship conflict in order to avoid dysfunctional emotions and behaviors. This sounds good in theory, but recent evidence suggests that separating these two types of conflict isn't easy. Most of us experience some degree of relationship conflict during or after any constructive debate.[9] In other words, any attempt to engage in constructive conflict, no matter how calmly and rationally, may still sow the seeds of relationship conflict. The stronger the level of debate and the more the issue is tied to the individual's social identity or need fulfillment, the greater the chance that the constructive conflict will evolve into (or mix with) relationship conflict. Fortunately, conflict management experts have identified three strategies that might reduce the level of relationship conflict during constructive conflict episodes.[10]

- *Emotional intelligence.* Relationship conflict is less likely to occur, or is less likely to escalate, when team members have high levels of emotional intelligence. Emotionally intelligent employees are better able to regulate their emotions during debate, which reduces the risk of escalating perceptions of interpersonal hostility. People with high emotional intelligence are also more likely to view a co-worker's emotional reaction as valuable information about that person's needs and expectations, rather than as a personal attack.

- *Cohesive team.* Relationship conflict is suppressed when the conflict occurs within a highly cohesive team. The longer people work together, get to know each other, and develop mutual trust with each other, the more latitude they give to each other to show emotions without being personally offended. Strong cohesion also allows each person to know about and anticipate the behaviors and emotions of their teammates. Another benefit is that cohesion produces a stronger social identity with the group, so team members are motivated to avoid escalating relationship conflict during otherwise emotionally turbulent discussions.

- *Supportive team norms.* Various team norms can hold relationship conflict at bay during constructive debate. When team norms encourage openness, for instance, team members learn to appreciate honest dialogue without personally reacting to any emotional display during the disagreements.[11] Other norms might discourage team members from displaying negative emotions toward co-workers. Team norms also encourage tactics that diffuse relationship conflict when it first appears. For instance, research has found that teams with low relationship conflict use humor to maintain positive group emotions, which offsets negative feelings team members might develop toward some co-workers during debate.

>Conflict Process Model

Now that we have outlined the history and current knowledge about conflict and its outcomes, let's look at the model of the conflict process, shown in Exhibit 10.2.[12] This model begins with the sources of conflict, which we will describe in more detail in the next section. At some point, the sources of conflict lead one or both parties to perceive that conflict exists. They become aware that one party's statements and actions are incompatible with their own goals. These perceptions usually interact with emotions experienced about the conflict.[13] Conflict perceptions and emotions manifest themselves in the decisions and behaviors of one party toward the other. These *conflict episodes* may range from subtle nonverbal behaviors to warlike aggression. Particularly when people experience high levels of conflict emotions, they have difficulty finding the words and expressions that communicate effectively without further irritating the relationship.[14] Conflict is also manifested by the style each side uses to resolve the conflict. Some people tend to avoid the conflict whereas others try to defeat those with opposing views.

Exhibit 10.2 shows arrows looping back from manifest conflict to conflict perceptions and emotions. These arrows illustrate that the conflict process is really a series of episodes

[Exhibit 10.2] Model of the Conflict Process

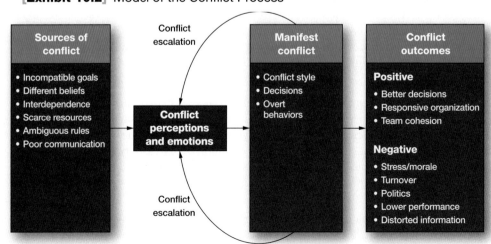

that potentially cycle into conflict escalation.[15] It doesn't take much to start this conflict cycle—just an inappropriate comment, a misunderstanding, or action that lacks diplomacy. These behaviors cause the other party to perceive that conflict exists. Even if the first party did not intend to demonstrate conflict, the second party's response may create that perception.

After reading the next two sections, you should be able to: **learning**objectives<

5. *Identify six structural sources of conflict in organizations.*

6. *Outline the five conflict handling styles and discuss the circumstances in which each would be most appropriate.*

>Structural Sources of Conflict in Organizations

The conflict model starts with the sources of conflict, and it is vital that we understand these sources to effectively diagnose conflict episodes or to identify strategies that will generate more conflict. The six main conditions that cause conflict in organizational settings are incompatible goals, differentiation, interdependence, scarce resources, ambiguous rules, and communication problems.

Incompatible Goals

A common source of conflict is goal incompatibility, which occurs when personal or work goals seem to interfere with another person's or department's goals.[16] This source of conflict is apparent at Microsoft (see accompanying photo story). Each Microsoft division is rewarded for the success of its products, so conflict results when other divisions threaten that success with similar products.

Differentiation

Another source of conflict emerges from unique training, values, beliefs, and experiences. This differentiation tends to produce different perspectives and mental images of ideal goals. Consequently, heterogeneous teams are more likely than homogeneous teams (where people have similar values and backgrounds) to disagree with each other regarding the best decisions and actions.

Differentiation is apparent in mergers where employees bring divergent corporate cultures into the new combined organization. Employees fight over the "right way" to do things because of their unique experiences in the separate

Software Battles

Microsoft Corp. has been highly successful with its operating system, Office software suite, server software, and a host of other products and services. Yet various sources conclude that the company suffers from vicious infighting across product groups. "Pretty much across the board people are saying that Microsoft is dysfunctional," concludes one industry analyst. "They are not cooperating across business groups." For example, MSN delayed releasing search software to compete against Google Desktop because the Windows group, which has a similar search tool for its long-delayed Vista operating system, objected. The MSN group also fought against the Office people over MSN's desire to connect their online calendar with the calendar in Office. The Office group balked because "then MSN could cannibalize Office," says an employee who recently left Microsoft. "Windows and Office would never let MSN have more budget or more control."[17]

companies. A rapidly growing retail clothing chain experienced another variation of differentiation-based conflict when the founder and CEO hired several senior managers from larger organizations to strengthen the experience levels of its senior management group. The new managers soon clashed with executives who had been with the company for some time. "We ended up with an old team and a new team and they weren't on the same wavelength," explains the company owner, who eventually fired most of the new managers.

Many companies are experiencing the rising incidence of cross-generational conflict.[18] Younger and older employees have different needs, different expectations, and somewhat different values, which sometimes produces conflicting preferences and actions. Recent studies conclude that virtual teams have a high incidence of conflict due to differentiation because technology makes it difficult for members of these teams to form common mental models and norms.[19]

Interdependence

Conflict tends to increase with the level of interdependence. Interdependence exists when team members must share materials, information, or expertise in order to perform their jobs.[20] In other words, it represents the collective degree of mutual dependence people have on each other for resources. Higher interdependence increases the risk of conflict because there is a greater chance that each side will disrupt or interfere with the other side's goals.[21]

Other than complete independence, employees tend to have the lowest risk of conflict when working with others in a pooled interdependence relationship. Pooled interdependence occurs where individuals operate independently except for reliance on a common resource or authority (see Chapter 7). The potential for conflict is higher in sequential interdependence work relationships, such as an assembly line. The highest risk of conflict tends to occur in reciprocal interdependence situations. With reciprocal interdependence, employees are highly dependent on each other and, consequently, have a higher probability of interfering with each other's work and personal goals.

Scarce Resources

Resource scarcity generates conflict because each person or unit that requires the same resource necessarily undermines others who also need that resource to fulfill their goals. Consider the lively debates among employees at Intel, described in the opening vignette to this chapter. These conflict episodes occur partly because there aren't enough financial and other resources for everyone to accomplish their goals, so employees need to justify why they should receive the resources. The more resources one project receives, the fewer resources another project will have to accomplish its goals.

Ambiguous Rules

Ambiguous rules—or the complete lack of rules—breed conflict. This occurs because uncertainty increases the risk that one party intends to interfere with the other party's goals. Ambiguity also encourages political tactics and, in some cases, employees enter a free-for-all battle to win decisions in their favor. This explains why conflict is more common during mergers and acquisitions. Employees from both companies have conflicting practices and values, and few rules have developed to minimize the maneuvering for power and resources.[22] When clear rules exist, on the other hand, employees know what to expect from each other and have agreed to abide by those rules.

Communication Problems

Communication plays a critical role in conflict escalation and resolution. As we noted earlier in this chapter, when two parties experience conflict, they become less motivated to communicate with each other. With less communication, the parties rely more on negative stereotypes to understand the other side's behavior and are less likely to empathize with the opponent's situation. In other words, conflict reduces communication, and less communication further escalates the level of relationship conflict.[23] A second influence of communication on conflict is that some people lack the necessary skills to communicate in a diplomatic, nonconfrontational manner. When one party communicates its disagreement arrogantly, opponents are more likely to heighten their perception of the conflict. This may lead the other party to reciprocate with a similar conflict management style.[24]

>Interpersonal Conflict Handling Styles

The six structural conditions described above set the stage for conflict, and these sources lead to conflict perceptions and emotions that, in turn, motivate people to take some sort of action to address the conflict. Dating back to the forward-thinking views of management scholar Mary Parker Follett in the 1920s, organizational behavior experts have identified several conflict handling styles. The number of styles have varied over the years, but most have settled on variations of the five-category model shown in Exhibit 10.3 and described below.[25]

- *Problem solving.* Problem solving tries to find a mutually beneficial solution for both parties. This is known as the **win–win orientation** because people using this style believe that the resources at stake are expandable rather than fixed if the parties work together to find a creative solution. Information sharing is an important feature of this style because both parties collaborate to identify common ground and potential solutions that satisfy everyone involved.

- *Forcing.* Forcing tries to win the conflict at the other's expense. People who use this style typically have a **win–lose orientation**—they believe the parties are drawing from a fixed pie, so the more one party receives, the less the other party will receive. Consequently, this style relies on some of the hard influence tactics described in Chapter 9, particularly assertiveness, to get one's own way.

- *Avoiding.* Avoiding tries to smooth over or avoid conflict situations altogether. It represents a low concern for both self and the other party; in other words, avoiders try to suppress thinking about the conflict. For example, some employees will rearrange their work area or tasks to minimize interaction with certain co-workers.[26]

- *Yielding.* Yielding involves giving in completely to the other side's wishes, or at least cooperating with little or no attention to your own interests. This style involves making unilateral concessions and unconditional promises, as well as offering help with no expectation of reciprocal help.

- *Compromising.* Compromising involves looking for a position in which your losses are offset by equally valued gains. It involves matching the other party's concessions, making conditional promises or threats, and actively searching for a middle ground between the interests of the two parties.

WIN–WIN ORIENTATION: the belief that the parties will find a mutually beneficial solution to their disagreement

WIN–LOSE ORIENTATION: the belief that conflicting parties are drawing from a fixed pie, so the more one party receives, the less the other party will receive

Choosing the Best Conflict Handling Style

Everyone has a preferred conflict handling style. You might have a preference for avoiding or yielding because disagreement makes you feel uncomfortable and is inconsistent with your self-concept as a person who likes to get along with everyone. Or you might

[Exhibit 10.3] Interpersonal Conflict Handling Styles

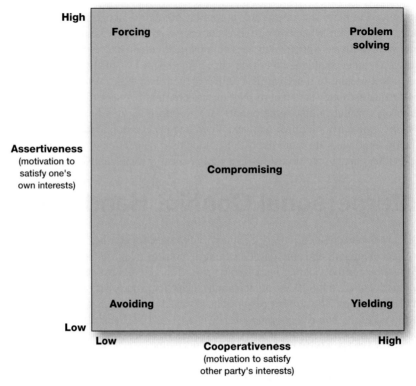

Source: C. K. W. de Dreu, A. Evers, B. Beersma, E. S. Kluwer, and A. Nauta, "A Theory-Based Measure of Conflict Management Strategies in the Workplace," *Journal of Organizational Behavior* 22 (2001), pp. 645–68. For other variations of this model, see T. L. Ruble and K. Thomas, "Support for a Two-Dimensional Model of Conflict Behavior," *Organizational Behavior and Human Performance* 16 (1976), p. 145; R. R. Blake, H. A. Shepard, and J. S. Mouton, *Managing Intergroup Conflict in Industry* (Houston: Gulf Publishing, 1964); and M. A. Rahim, "Toward a Theory of Managing Organizational Conflict," *International Journal of Conflict Management* 13, no. 3 (2002), pp. 206–35.

have a tendency toward compromising and forcing because it reflects your strong need for achievement and to control your environment. In general, people gravitate toward one or two preferred conflict handling styles that match their personality, personal and cultural values, and past experience. For example, studies have found that people in Confucian cultures prefer nonconfrontational conflict handling styles (e.g., avoidance) more than people in the United States and similar Western cultures.[27] Others have reported gender differences, with women having a higher preference for the problem-solving and compromise styles.[28]

However, people do pay attention to circumstances surrounding the conflict and know they should use different conflict handling styles.[29] This is fortunate because the best style does vary with the situation.[30] Exhibit 10.4 summarizes the main contingencies, as well as problems with using each conflict handling style. Problem solving has long been identified as the preferred conflict handling style where possible because dialogue and clever thinking forces people to break out of the limited boundaries of their opposing alternatives to find an integrated solution where both gain value. In addition, recent studies report that problem solving improves long-term relationships, minimizes emotional defensiveness and other indications of relationship conflict, and reduces stress.[31] However, problem solving is the best choice of conflict handling only when there is some potential for mutual gains, which is more likely to occur when the issue is complex, and when the parties have enough trust, openness, and time to share information. If problem solving is used under the wrong conditions, there is an increased risk that the other party will take advantage of the information you have openly shared.

[Exhibit 10.4] Conflict Handling Style Contingencies and Problems

Conflict Handling Style	Preferred Style When . . .	Problems with this Style
Problem solving	• Interests are not perfectly opposing (i.e., not factually win–lose) • Parties have trust, openness, and time to share information • The issues are complex	• Sharing information that the other party might use to their advantage
Avoiding	• Conflict has become too emotionally charged • Cost of trying to resolve the conflict outweighs the benefits	• Doesn't usually resolve the conflict • May increase other party's frustration
Forcing	• You have a deep conviction about your position (e.g., believe other person's behavior is unethical) • Dispute requires a quick solution • The other party would take advantage of more cooperative strategies	• Highest risk of relationship conflict • May damage long-term relations, reducing future problem solving
Yielding	• Other party has substantially more power • Issue is much less important to you than to the other party • The value and logic of your position isn't as clear	• Increases other party's expectations in future conflict episodes
Compromising	• Parties have equal power • Time pressure to resolve the conflict • Parties lack trust/openness for problem solving	• Suboptimal solution where mutual gains are possible

You might think that avoiding is an ineffective conflict management strategy, but it is actually the best approach where conflict has become emotionally charged or where negotiating has a higher cost than the benefits of conflict resolution.[32] At the same time, conflict avoidance is often ineffective because it doesn't resolve the conflict and may increase the other party's frustration. The forcing style of conflict resolution is usually inappropriate because research indicates that it generates relationship conflict more quickly or intensely than other conflict handling styles. However, forcing may be necessary where you know you are correct (e.g., the other party's position is unethical or based on obviously flawed logic), the dispute requires a quick solution, or the other party would take advantage of a more cooperative conflict handling style.

The yielding style may be appropriate when the other party has substantially more power, the issue is not as important to you as to the other party, and you aren't confident that your position has the best value or logical consistency. On the other hand, yielding behaviors may give the other side unrealistically high expectations, thereby motivating them to seek more from you in the future. In the long run, yielding may produce more conflict rather than resolve it. The compromising style may be best when there is little hope for mutual

Healthy Problem Solving at ThedaCare
Soon after being promoted to vice president of hospital administration at ThedaCare, Inc., Kathryn Correia discovered an interdepartmental conflict that dragged down the hospital's efficiency and collegiality. Nurses at the Appleton, Wisconsin, hospital complained that the pharmacy's system for ordering prescriptions was too cumbersome for their hectic schedules and that the pharmacy was inefficient. The pharmacists were equally critical, saying that the nursing group wasn't completing the paperwork required to fill the prescriptions accurately and safely. To resolve this conflict, the hospital held a weeklong rapid improvement event which included nurses, pharmacy staff, employees from other areas, and a facilitator. By thinking creatively in a supportive environment, the team devised a new prescription ordering and distribution system that satisfied both nurses and pharmacy staff. "Instead of pointing fingers, we found collaboration," says Correia. "The most beneficial thing learned from conflict training is taking a proactive approach."[33]

gain through problem solving, both parties have equal power, and both are under time pressure to settle their differences. However, we rarely know for certain that mutual gains are not available, so entering a conflict with the compromise style may cause the parties to overlook better solutions.

>**learning**objectives

After reading the next two sections, you should be able to:

7. *Summarize six structural approaches to managing conflict.*

8. *Compare and contrast the three types of third-party dispute resolution.*

>Structural Approaches to Conflict Management

Conflict management styles refer to how we approach the other party in a conflict situation. But conflict management also involves altering the underlying structural causes of potential conflict. The main structural approaches are emphasizing superordinate goals, reducing differentiation, improving communication and understanding, reducing task interdependence, increasing resources, and clarifying rules and procedures.

Emphasizing Superordinate Goals

SUPERORDINATE GOAL: any goal that both conflicting parties value and whose attainment is beyond the resources and effort of either party alone

One of the oldest recommendations for resolving conflict is to seek out and find common goals.[34] In organizational settings, this typically takes the form of a **superordinate goal,** which is any goal that both conflicting parties value and whose attainment is beyond the resources and effort of either party alone.[35] By increasing commitment to corporatewide goals, employees place less emphasis and therefore feel less conflict with co-workers regarding competing individual or departmental-level goals. They also potentially reduce the problem of differentiation by establishing a common frame of reference. For example, research indicates that the most effective executive teams frame their decisions as superordinate goals that rise above each executive's departmental or divisional goals.[36]

Reducing Differentiation

Another way to minimize dysfunctional conflict is to reduce the differences that produce the conflict in the first place. The more employees think they have common backgrounds or experiences with co-workers, the more motivated they are to coordinate activities and resolve conflict through constructive discussion with those co-workers.[37] One way to increase this commonality is by creating common experiences. The Manila Diamond Hotel in the Philippines accomplishes this by rotating staff across different departments. Multinational peacekeeping forces reduce differentiation among troops from the representative nations by providing opportunities for them to socialize and engage in common activities, including eating together.[38]

Improving Communication and Understanding

A third way to resolve dysfunctional conflict is to give the conflicting parties more opportunities to communicate and understand each other. This recommendation relates back to the contact hypothesis described in Chapter 3. Specifically, the more meaningful interaction we have with someone, the less we rely on stereotypes to understand that person.[39] There are two warnings, however. First, communication and understanding interventions should be applied only *after* differentiation between the two sides has been reduced or where differentiation is already sufficiently low. If perceived differentiation remains high, attempts to manage conflict through dialogue might escalate rather than reduce relationship conflict. The reason is that when forced to interact with people who we believe are quite different and in conflict with us, we tend to select information that reinforces that view.[40]

The second warning is that people in collectivist and high-power-distance cultures are less comfortable with the practice of resolving differences through direct and open communication.[41] As noted earlier, people in Confucian cultures prefer an avoidance conflict management style because it is the most consistent with harmony and face-saving. Direct communication is a high-risk strategy because it easily threatens the need to save face and maintain harmony.

Toyota Drums out Differences

Employees at Toyota Motor Sales U.S.A. are drumming their way to a common bond and cooperation. Over the past three years, more than 3,000 Toyota employees have visited the automaker's training center (University of Toyota) in Torrance, California, to participate in drum circles. Typically in groups of 15 to 50 from one department, employees would begin banging on one of the 150 percussion instruments available in the drum room. Few have played a percussion instrument before, so the first attempt rarely is worth recording. "At first, it sounds pretty terrible, with everyone competing to be the loudest," admits Ron Johnson, Toyota's resident drum guru and a training center manager in Torrance. But most groups soon find a common beat without any guidance or conductor. Johnson recalls his first drum circle experience: "I'll never forget the spirit that came alive inside me. In a

matter of moments, perfect strangers came together in synchronistic rhythm to share a common vision." By the end of the hour-long event, most groups have formed a special bond that apparently increases their cooperation and sense of unity when they return to their jobs.[42]

Reducing Interdependence

Conflict increases with the level of interdependence, so minimizing dysfunctional conflict might involve reducing the level of interdependence between the parties. If cost effective, this might occur by dividing the shared resource so that each party has exclusive use of part of it. Sequentially or reciprocally interdependent jobs might be combined so that they form a pooled interdependence. For example, rather than having one employee serve customers and another operate the cash register, each employee could handle both customer activities alone. Buffers also help to reduce interdependence between people. Buffers include resources, such as adding more inventory between people who perform sequential tasks. Organizations also use human buffers—people who serve as intermediaries between interdependent people or work units who do not get along through direct interaction.

Increasing Resources

An obvious way to reduce conflict due to resource scarcity is to increase the amount of resources available. Corporate decision makers might quickly dismiss this solution because of the costs involved. However, they need to carefully compare these costs with the costs of dysfunctional conflict arising out of resource scarcity.

Clarifying Rules and Procedures

Conflicts that arise from ambiguous rules can be minimized by establishing rules and procedures. Armstrong World Industries, Inc., applied this strategy when consultants and information systems employees clashed while working together on development of a client–server network. Information systems employees at the flooring and building materials company thought they should be in charge, whereas consultants believed they had the senior role. Also, the consultants wanted to work long hours and take Friday off to fly home, whereas Armstrong employees wanted to work regular hours. The company reduced these conflicts by having both parties agree on specific responsibilities and roles. The agreement also assigned two senior executives at both companies to establish rules if future disagreements arose.[43]

>Third-Party Conflict Resolution

THIRD-PARTY CONFLICT RESOLUTION: any attempt by a relatively neutral person to help the parties resolve their differences

Most of this chapter has focused on people directly involved in a conflict, yet many disputes in organizational settings are resolved with the assistance of the manager responsible for the feuding parties, or with some other third party. **Third-party conflict resolution** is any attempt by a relatively neutral person to help the parties resolve their differences. There are generally three types of third-party dispute resolution activities: arbitration, inquisition, and mediation. These activities can be classified by their level of control over the process and control over the decision (see Exhibit 10.5).[44]

- *Arbitration.* Arbitrators have high control over the final decision, but low control over the process. Executives engage in this strategy by following previously agreed rules of due process, listening to arguments from the disputing employees, and making a binding decision. Arbitration is applied as the final stage of grievances by unionized employees, but it is also becoming more common in nonunion conflicts.

- *Inquisition.* Inquisitors control all discussion about the conflict. Like arbitrators, they have high decision control because they choose the form of conflict resolution. However, they also have high process control because they choose which information to

[Exhibit 10.5] Types of Third-Party Intervention

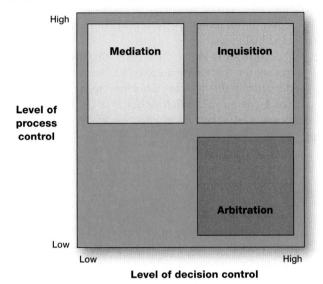

examine and how to examine it, and they generally decide how the conflict resolution process will be handled.

- *Mediation.* Mediators have high control over the intervention process. In fact, their main purpose is to manage the process and context of interaction between the disputing parties. However, the parties make the final decision about how to resolve their differences. Thus, mediators have little or no control over the conflict resolution decision.

Choosing the Best Third-Party Intervention Strategy

Team leaders, executives, and co-workers regularly intervene in disputes between employees and departments. Sometimes they adopt a mediator role; other times they serve as arbitrators. However, research suggests that people in positions of authority (e.g., managers) usually adopt an inquisitional approach whereby they dominate the intervention process as well as making a binding decision.[45] Managers like the inquisition approach because it is consistent with the decision-oriented nature of managerial jobs, gives them control over the conflict process and outcome, and tends to resolve disputes efficiently.

However, the inquisitional approach to third-party conflict resolution is usually the least effective in organizational settings.[46] One problem is that leaders who take an inquisitional role tend to collect limited information about the problem using this approach, so their imposed decision may produce an ineffective solution to the conflict. Also, employees often view inquisitional procedures and outcomes as unfair because they have little control over this approach.

Which third-party intervention is most appropriate in organizations? The answer partly depends on the situation, such as the type of dispute, the relationship between the manager and employees, and cultural values such as power distance.[47] But generally speaking, for everyday disputes between two employees, the mediation approach is usually best because this gives employees more responsibility for resolving their own disputes. The third-party representative merely establishes an appropriate context for conflict resolution. Although not as efficient as other strategies, mediation potentially offers the highest level of employee satisfaction with the conflict process and outcomes.[48]

When employees cannot resolve their differences, arbitration seems to work best because the predetermined rules of evidence and other processes create a higher sense of procedural fairness. Moreover, arbitration is preferred where the organization's goals should take priority over individual goals.

Whether resolving conflict through third-party dispute resolution or direct dialogue, we need to recognize that many solutions come from the sources of conflict that were identified earlier in this chapter. This may seem obvious, but in the heat of conflict, people often focus on each other rather than the underlying causes. Recognizing these conflict sources is the role of effective leadership, which is discussed in the next chapter.

>Chapter Summary

Conflict is the process in which one party perceives that its interests are being opposed or negatively affected by another party. For many years, conflict was viewed as undesirable and counterproductive. There is evidence that conflict can produce undesirable outcomes such as lower job satisfaction, team cohesion, and knowledge sharing, as well as higher organizational politics and turnover. However, experts later formed the opinion that organizations suffer from too little as well as too much conflict. Research reports that moderate conflict can improve decision making, organizational responsiveness to the environment, and team cohesion (when conflict is with sources outside the team).

The current perspective involves distinguishing constructive conflict from relationship conflict. The former focuses on issues and a logical evaluation of ideas, whereas the latter pays attention to interpersonal incompatibilities and flaws. Although the ideal would be to encourage constructive conflict and minimize relationship conflict, relationship conflict tends to emerge in most constructive conflict episodes. However, relationship conflict is less likely to dominate when the parties are emotionally intelligent, have a cohesive team, and have supportive team norms.

The conflict process model begins with the six structural sources of conflict: incompatible goals, differentiation (different values and beliefs), interdependence, scarce resources, ambiguous rules, and communication problems. These sources lead one or more parties to perceive a conflict and to experience conflict emotions. This, in turn, produces manifest conflict, such as behaviors toward the other side. The conflict process often escalates through a series of episodes.

Organizational behavior experts have identified several conflict handling styles: problem solving, avoiding, forcing, yielding, and compromising. People who use problem solving have a win–win orientation. Others, particularly forcing, assume a win–lose orientation. In general, people gravitate toward one or two preferred conflict handling styles that match their personality, personal and cultural values, and past experience. However, the best style depends on various characteristics of the situation.

Structural approaches to conflict management include emphasizing superordinate goals, reducing differentiation, improving communication and understanding, reducing interdependence, increasing resources, and clarifying rules and procedures. These elements can also be altered to stimulate conflict.

Third-party conflict resolution is any attempt by a relatively neutral person to help the parties resolve their differences. The three main forms of third-party dispute resolution are mediation, arbitration, and inquisition. Managers tend to use an inquisition approach, although mediation and arbitration are more appropriate, depending on the situation.

>key terms

>critical thinking questions

1. Distinguish constructive conflict from relationship conflict and explain how to apply the former with minimal levels of the latter.

2. The chief executive officer of Creative Toys, Inc., read about cooperation in Japanese companies and vowed to bring this same philosophy to their company. The goal is to avoid all conflict, so that employees would work cooperatively and be happier at Creative Toys. Discuss the merits and limitations of the CEO's policy.

3. Conflict among managers emerged soon after a French company acquired a Swedish firm. The Swedes perceived the French management as hierarchical and arrogant, whereas the French thought the Swedes were naive, cautious, and lacking an achievement orientation. Describe ways to reduce dysfunctional conflict in this situation.

4. This chapter describes three levels of interdependence that exist in interpersonal and intergroup relationships. Identify examples of these three levels in your work or school activities. How do these three levels affect potential conflict for you?

5. Jane has just been appointed as purchasing manager of Tacoma Technologies Corp. The previous purchasing manager, who recently retired, was known for his winner-take-all approach to suppliers. He continually fought for more discounts and was skeptical about any special deals that suppliers would propose. A few suppliers refused to do business with Tacoma Technologies, but senior management was confident that the former purchasing manager's approach minimized the company's costs. Jane wants to try a more collaborative approach to working with suppliers. Will her approach work? How should she adopt a more collaborative approach in future negotiations with suppliers?

6. You are a special assistant to the commander-in-chief of a peacekeeping mission to a war-torn part of the world. The unit consists of a few thousand peacekeeping troops from the United States, France, India, and four other countries. The troops will work together for approximately one year. What strategies would you recommend to improve mutual understanding and minimize conflict among these troops?

7. The chief operating officer (COO) has noticed that production employees in the company's Mexican manufacturing operations are unhappy with some of the production engineering decisions made by engineers in the company's headquarters in Chicago. At the same time, the engineers complain that production employees aren't applying their engineering specifications correctly and don't understand why those specifications were put in place. The COO believes that the best way to resolve this conflict is to have a frank and open discussion between some of the engineers and employees representing the Mexican production crew. This open dialogue approach worked well recently among managers in the company's Chicago headquarters, so it should work equally well between the engineers and production staff. Based on your knowledge of communication and mutual understanding as a way to resolve conflict, discuss the COO's proposal.

8. Managers tend to use an inquisitional approach to resolving disputes between employees and departments. Describe the inquisitional approach and discuss its appropriateness in organizational settings.

>class exercise 10-1

The Contingencies of Conflict Handling

By Gerard A.Callanan and David F. Perri,
West Chester University of Pennsylvania

Purpose   This exercise is designed to help you understand the contingencies of applying conflict handling styles in organizational settings.

Instructions

- *Step 1:* Participants will read each of the five scenarios presented below and select the most appropriate response from among the five alternatives. Each scenario has a situationally correct response.

- *Step 2 (Optional):* The instructor may ask each student to complete the Dutch Test for Conflict Handling self-assessment in this chapter (Self-Assessment 10-3) or a similar instrument. This instrument will provide an estimate of your preferred conflict handling style.

- *Step 3:* As a class, participants give their feedback on the responses to each of the scenarios, with the instructor guiding discussion on the contextual factors embodied in each scenario. For each scenario, the class should identify the response selected by the majority. In addition, participants will discuss how they decided on the choices they made and the contextual factors they took into account in making their selections.

- *Step 4:* Students will compare their responses to the five scenarios with their results from the conflict handling self-assessment. Discussion will focus on the extent to which each person's preferred conflict handling style influenced their alternatives in this activity, and the implications of this style preference for managing conflict in organizations.

First Scenario

Setting

You are a manager of a division in the accounting department of a large eastern U.S. bank. Nine exempt-level analysts and six nonexempt clerical staff report to you. Recently, one of your analysts, Jane Wilson, has sought the bank's approval for tuition reimbursement for the cost of an evening MBA program specializing in organizational behavior. The bank normally encourages employees to seek advanced degrees on a part-time basis. Indeed, through your encouragement, nearly all of the members of your staff are pursuing additional schoolwork. You consult the bank's policy manual and discover that two approvals are necessary for reimbursement—yours and that of the manager of training and development, Kathy Gordon. Further, the manual states that approval for reimbursement will only be granted if the coursework is "reasonably job related." Based on your review of the matter, you decide to approve Jane's request for reimbursement. However, Kathy Gordon rejects it outright by claiming that coursework

in organizational behavior is not related to an accounting analyst position. She states that the bank will only reimburse the analyst for a degree in either accounting or finance. In your opinion, however, the interpersonal skills and insights to be gained from a degree in organizational behavior are job related and can also benefit the employee in future assignments. The analyst job requires interaction with a variety of individuals at different levels in the organization, and it is important that interpersonal and communication skills be strong.

After further discussion it becomes clear that you and Kathy Gordon have opposite views on the matter. Since both of you are at the same organization level and have equal status, it appears that you are at an impasse. Although the goal of reimbursement is important, you are faced with other pressing demands on your time. In addition, the conflict has diverted the attention of your work group away from its primary responsibilities. Because the school term is about to begin, it is essential that you and Kathy Gordon reach a timely agreement to enable Jane to pursue her coursework.

Action Alternatives for the First Scenario   Please indicate your first (1) and second (2) choices from among the following alternatives by writing the appropriate number in the space provided.

Action Alternative	Ranking (1st & 2nd)
1. You go along with Kathy Gordon's view and advise Jane Wilson to select either accounting or finance as a major for her MBA.	_____
2. You decide to withdraw from the situation completely, and tell Jane to work it out with Kathy Gordon on her own.	_____
3. You decide to take the matter to those in higher management levels and argue forcefully for your point of view. You do everything in your power to ensure that a decision will be made in your favor.	_____
4. You decide to meet Kathy Gordon halfway in order to reach an agreement. You advise Jane to pursue her MBA in accounting or finance, but also recommend she minor in organizational behavior by taking electives in that field.	_____
5. You decide to work more closely with Kathy Gordon by attempting to get a clear as well as flexible policy written that reflects both of your views. Of course, this will require a significant amount of your time.	_____

Second Scenario

Setting

You are the vice president of a relatively large division (80 employees) in a medium-sized consumer products company. Due to the recent turnover of minority staff, your division has fallen behind in meeting the company's goal for Equal Employment Opportunity (EEO) hiring. Because of a scarcity of qualified minority candidates, it appears that you may fall further behind in achieving stated EEO goals.

Although you are aware of the problem, you believe that the low level of minority hiring is due to increased attrition in minority staff as well as the lack of viable replacement candidates. However, the EEO officer believes that your hiring criteria are too stringent, resulting in the rejection of minority candidates with the basic qualifications to do the job. You support the goals and principles of EEO; however, you are concerned that the hiring of less-qualified candidates will weaken the performance of your division. The EEO officer believes that your failure to hire minority employees is damaging to the company in the short term because corporate goals will not be met, and in the long term because it will restrict the pool of minority candidates available for upward mobility. Both of you regard your concerns as important. Further, you recognize that both of you have the company's best interests in mind and that you have a mutual interest in resolving the conflict.

Action Alternatives for the Second Scenario Please indicate your first (1) and second (2) choices from among the following alternatives by writing the appropriate number in the space provided.

Action Alternative	Ranking (1st & 2nd)
1. You conclude that the whole problem is too complex an issue for you to handle right now. You put it on the back burner and decide to reconsider the problem at a later date.	_____
2. You believe that your view outweighs the perspective of the EEO officer. You decide to argue your position more vigorously and hope that your stance will sway the EEO officer to agree with your view.	_____
3. You decide to accept the EEO officer's view. You agree to use less-stringent selection criteria and thereby hire more minority employees.	_____
4. You give in to the EEO officer somewhat by agreeing to relax your standards a little bit. This would allow slightly more minority hiring (but not enough to satisfy the EEO goal) and could cause a small reduction in the overall performance of your division.	_____
5. You try and reach a consensus that addresses each of your concerns. You agree to work harder at hiring more minority applicants and request that the EEO officer agree to help find the most-qualified minority candidates available.	_____

Third Scenario

Setting

You are the manager in charge of the financial reporting section of a large insurance company. It is the responsibility of your group to make periodic written and oral reports to senior management regarding the company's financial performance. The company's senior management has come to rely on your quick and accurate dissemination of financial data as a way to make vital decisions in a timely fashion. This has given you a relatively high degree of organizational influence. You rely on various operating departments to supply you with financial information according to a preestablished reporting schedule.

In two days, you must make your quarterly presentation to the company's board of directors. However, the Claims Department has failed to supply you with several key pieces of information that are critical to your presentation. You check the reporting schedule and realize that you should have had the information two days ago. When you call Bill Jones, the Claims Department manager, he informs you that he cannot possibly have the data to you within the next two days. He states that other pressing work has a higher priority. Although you explain the critical need for this data, he is unwilling to change his position. You believe that your presentation is vital to the company's welfare and explain this to Bill Jones. Although Bill has less status than you, he has been known to take advantage of individuals who are unwilling or unable to push their point of view. With your presentation less than two days away, it is critical that you receive information from the Claims Department within the next 24 hours.

Action Alternatives for the Third Scenario Please indicate your first (1) and second (2) choices from among the following alternatives by writing the appropriate number in the space provided.

Action Alternative	Ranking (1st & 2nd)
1. Accept the explanation from Bill Jones and try to get by without the figures by using your best judgment as to what they would be.	_____
2. Tell Bill Jones that unless you have the data from his department on your desk by tomorrow morning, you will be forced to go over his head to compel him to give you the numbers.	_____
3. Meet Bill Jones halfway by agreeing to receive part of the needed figures and using your own judgment on the others.	_____
4. Try to get your presentation postponed until a later date, if possible.	_____
5. Forget about the short-term need for information and try to achieve a longer-term solution, such as adjusting the reporting schedule to better accommodate your mutual needs.	_____

Fourth Scenario

Setting

You are the production manager of a medium-sized building products company. You control a production line that runs on a three-shift basis. Recently, Ted Smith, the materials handling manager, requested that you accept a different packaging of the raw materials for the production process than what has been customary. He states that new machinery he has installed makes it much easier to provide the material in 100-pound sacks instead of the 50-pound bags that you currently receive. Ted further explains that the provision of the material in the 50-pound bags would put an immense strain on his operation, and he therefore has a critical need for you to accept the change. You know that accepting materials in the new packaging will cause some minor disruption in your production process, but should not cause long-term problems for any of the three shifts. However, you are a little annoyed by the proposed change because Ted did not consult with you before he installed the new equipment. In the past, you and he have been open in your communication. You do not think that this failure to consult you represents a change in your relationship.

Because you work closely with Ted, it is essential that you maintain the harmonious and stable working relationship that you have built over the past few years. In addition, you may need some help from him in the future, since you already know that your operation will have special material

requirements in about two months. You also know that Ted has influence at higher levels of the organization.

Action Alternatives for the Fourth Scenario Please indicate your first (1) and second (2) choices from among the following alternatives by writing the appropriate number in the space provided.

Action Alternative	Ranking (1st & 2nd)
1. Agree to accept the raw material in the different format.	_____
2. Refuse to accept the material in the new format because it would cause a disruption in your operation.	_____
3. Propose a solution where you accept material in the new format during the first shift, but not during the second and third shifts.	_____
4. Tell Ted Smith that you do not wish to deal with the issue at this time, but that you will consider his request and get back to him at a later date.	_____
5. You decide to tell Ted Smith of your concern regarding his failure to consult with you before installing new equipment. You inform him that you wish to find longer-term solutions to the conflict between you.	_____

Fifth Scenario

Setting

You are employed as supervisor of the compensation and benefits section in the human resources department of a medium-sized pharmaceutical company. Your staff of three clerks is responsible for maintaining contacts with the various benefits providers and answering related questions from the company's employees. Your section shares secretarial, word processing, and copier resources with the training and development section of the department. Recently, a disagreement has arisen between you and Beth Hanson, the training and development supervisor, over when the secretarial staff should take their lunches. Beth would like the secretarial staff to take their lunches an hour later to coincide with the time most of her people go to lunch. You know that the secretaries do not want to change their lunch times. Further, the current time is more convenient for your staff.

At this time, you are hard-pressed to deal with the situation. You have an important meeting with the provider of dental insurance in two days. It is critical that you are well prepared for this meeting, and these other tasks are a distraction.

Action Alternatives for the Fifth Scenario   Please indicate your first (1) and second (2) choices from among the following alternatives by writing the appropriate number in the space provided.

Action Alternative	Ranking (1st & 2nd)
1. Take some time over the next day and propose a solution whereby three days a week the secretaries take their lunch at the earlier time and two days at the later time.	_____
2. Tell Beth Hanson you will deal with the matter in a few days, after you have addressed the more-pressing issues.	_____
3. Let Beth Hanson have her way by agreeing to a later lunch hour for the secretarial staff.	_____
4. Flat out tell Beth Hanson that you will not agree to a change in the secretaries' lunchtime.	_____
5. Devote more time to the issue. Attempt to achieve a broad-based consensus with Beth Hanson that meets her needs as well as yours and those of the secretaries.	_____

Source: G. A. Callanan and D. F. Perri, "Teaching Conflict Management Using a Scenario-Based Approach," *Journal of Education for Business* 81 (January/February 2006), pp. 131–39.

>team exercise 10-2

Ugli Orange Role Play

Purpose   This exercise is designed to help you understand the dynamics of interpersonal and intergroup conflict as well as the effectiveness of negotiation strategies under specific conditions.

Materials   The instructor will distribute roles for Dr. Roland, Dr. Jones, and a few observers. Ideally, each negotiation should occur in a private area away from other negotiations.

Instructions

* *Step 1:* The instructor will divide the class into an even number of teams of three people each, with one participant left over for each team formed (e.g., six observers if there are six teams). One-half of the teams will take the role of Dr. Roland and the other half will be Dr. Jones. The instructor will distribute roles after these teams have been formed.

* *Step 2:* Members within each team will be given 10 minutes (or other time limit stated by the instructor) to learn their roles and decide negotiating strategy.

* *Step 3:* After reading their roles and discussing strategy, each Dr. Jones team will be matched with a Dr. Roland team to conduct negotiations. Observers will receive observation forms from the instructor, and two observers will be assigned to watch the paired teams during prenegotiations and subsequent negotiations.

* *Step 4:* As soon as Roland and Jones reach agreement or at the end of the time allotted for the negotiation (whichever comes first), the Roland and Jones teams will report to the instructor for further instruction.

* *Step 5:* At the end of the exercise, the class will congregate to discuss the negotiations. Observers, negotiators, and instructors will then discuss their observations and experiences and the implications for conflict management and negotiation.

Source: This exercise was developed by Robert J. House, Wharton Business School, University of Pennsylvania. A similar incident is also attributed to earlier writing by R. R. Blake and J. S. Mouton.

Find the complete interactive self-assessment at this textbook's Web site at
www.mhhe.com/mcshaneEss2e.

>self-assessment exercise 10-3

The Dutch Test for Conflict Handling

There are many ways to handle a conflict situation, but we tend to prefer one conflict handling style over others. This instrument measures your preference for each of five conflict handling styles. Read each of the statements and select the response that you believe best reflects your position regarding each statement. This exercise is completed alone so students assess themselves honestly without concerns of social comparison. However, class discussion will focus on the different conflict management styles and the situations in which each is most appropriate.

[chapter 11]

Leadership in Organizational Settings

>learningobjectives

After reading this chapter, you should be able to:

1. Define leadership and shared leadership.
2. List seven competencies of effective leaders and discuss the limitations of this leadership perspective.
3. Describe the people-oriented and task-oriented leadership styles.
4. Outline the path-goal theory of leadership.
5. Summarize leadership substitutes theory.
6. Distinguish transformational leadership from transactional and charismatic leadership.
7. Describe the four elements of transformational leadership.
8. Describe the implicit leadership perspective.
9. Discuss similarities and differences in the leadership styles of women and men.

"In essence, leadership is about dreaming the impossible and helping followers achieve the same," says Nandan Nilekani (center in photo), chief executive of Infosys, one of India's largest and most successful information technology companies.

Infosys has grown into one of India's largest and most successful information technology companies, and chief executive Nandan Nilekani wants to maintain that momentum by focusing his attention on leadership development. "Given our pace of growth, transferring the values and beliefs, the DNA of the organization, to the next generations of leaders is one of my most important functions," says Nilekani, who is actively involved in the company's leadership development workshops and mentoring activities.

Building a strong cadre of leaders required Nilekani and his executive team to carefully think about the meaning of effective leadership. "We believe our future leaders need to learn how to set direction, to create a shared vision, encourage execution excellence, embrace inclusive meritocracy," he says. Nilekani particularly emphasizes the importance of values and vision. "In essence, leadership is about dreaming the impossible and helping followers achieve the same. Moreover, the dream has to be built on sound and context-invariant values to sustain the enthusiasm and energy of people over a long time."

Nilekani's definition of leadership bears an uncanny resemblance to the one formed by Pacific Gas & Electric Company (PG&E) CEO Peter Darbee. "A leader needs to first be able to dream great dreams, and establish a vision," he says. Furthermore, great leaders translate that broad vision into more precise objectives, goals, and metrics, all of which are guided by strategy and supported by the organization's culture. Darbee also advises that "the glue that holds this all together is your values. You have to lead from your values."[1]

After reading the next two sections, you should be able to:

1. *Define leadership and shared leadership.*
2. *List seven competencies of effective leaders and discuss the limitations of this leadership perspective.*

learningobjectives<

>The Meaning of Leadership

The world is changing, and so is our concept of leadership. Gone is yesteryear's image of the command-and-control boss. Also gone is the more recent view that leaders are front-and-center charismatic heroes. Instead, as Nandan Nilekani and Peter Darbee stated in the opening vignette, leadership is about values, vision, enabling, and coaching. A few years ago, 54 leadership experts from 38 countries reached a consensus that **leadership** is about influencing, motivating, and enabling others to contribute toward the effectiveness and success of the organizations of which they are members.[2] Leaders apply various forms of influence—from subtle persuasion to direct application of power—to ensure that followers have the motivation and role clarity to achieve specified goals. Leaders also arrange the work environment—such as allocating resources and altering communication patterns—so that employees can achieve corporate objectives more easily.

LEADERSHIP: influencing, motivating, and enabling others to contribute toward the effectiveness and success of the organizations of which they are members

Leadership isn't restricted to the executive suite. Anyone in the organization may be a leader in various ways and at various times.[3] This view is variously known as **shared leadership** or the leaderful organization. Effective self-directed work teams, for example, consist of members who share leadership responsibilities or otherwise allocate this role to a responsible coordinator. W. L. Gore & Associates is a case in point. The company's 6,500 employees are organized around self-directed work teams and, consequently, have few formal leaders. Yet the company has no shortage of leaders. When asked in the company's annual survey "Are you a leader?", more than 50 percent of Gore employees answer "Yes."[4]

SHARED LEADERSHIP: the view that leadership is broadly distributed rather than assigned to one person, such that people within the team and organization lead each other

Leadership has been contemplated since the days of Greek philosophers and it is one of the most popular research topics among organizational behavior scholars. This has resulted in an enormous volume of leadership literature, most of which can be organized into five perspectives: competency, behavioral, contingency, transformational, and implicit.[5] Although some of these perspectives are currently more popular than others, each helps us to more fully understand this complex issue. This chapter explores each of these five perspectives of leadership. In the final section, we also consider cross-cultural and gender issues in organizational leadership.

>Competency Perspective of Leadership

Since the beginning of recorded civilization, people have been interested in the personal characteristics that distinguish great leaders from the rest of us. A major review in the late 1940s concluded that no consistent list of traits could be distilled from the hundreds of studies conducted up to that time. A subsequent review suggested that a few traits are consistently associated with effective leaders, but most are unrelated to effective leadership.[6] These conclusions caused many scholars to give up their search for personal characteristics that distinguish effective leaders.

Leadership researchers and consultants are now returning to the view that leadership requires specific personal characteristics.[7] The recent leadership literature identifies several leadership competencies, most of which can be grouped into the seven categories described below.[8]

- *Emotional intelligence*. Effective leaders have a high level of emotional intelligence.[9] They have the ability to perceive and express emotion, assimilate emotion in thought, understand and reason with emotion, and regulate emotion in themselves and others (see Chapter 4).

- *Integrity*. Integrity refers to the leader's truthfulness and consistency of words and actions. This characteristic is sometimes called *authentic leadership* because the individual acts with sincerity. He or she has a higher moral capacity to judge dilemmas based on sound values and to act accordingly.[10] Several large-scale studies have reported that integrity or honesty is the most important characteristic of effective leaders. Employees and other stakeholders want honest leaders whom they can trust.[11] Unfortunately, recent surveys report that employees don't trust their leaders and don't think they have integrity.[12]

CAREing Leadership Competencies

By all accounts Helene Gayle has the competencies of an effective leader. Recently appointed as president of CARE, the Atlanta-based global aid agency, Gayle brings a wealth of experience from her previous executive positions with the Bill & Melinda Gates Foundation and the Centers for Disease Control (CDC). "Her leadership, commitment, and talents are well demonstrated," says CARE board chairman Lincoln Chen. William Foege, who worked with Gayle when he was head of the CDC, also points to her incredible drive and motivation. "Helene has the capacity to go full-tilt day after day and week after week," he notes. "It's almost as if she doesn't know what fatigue is like." Others have commented on her high degree of integrity. "Helene Gayle may be the most trusted public health leader in the world," says David Satcher, who has served as CDC director and U.S. surgeon general. Still others describe Gayle's high level of emotional intelligence. "Helene has a tremendous natural empathy," says Ashok Alexander, director of the Gates Foundation AIDS program in India.[13]

- *Drive*. Successful leaders have a high need for achievement (see Chapter 5). This drive represents the inner motivation that leaders possess to pursue their goals and encourage others to move forward with theirs. Drive inspires inquisitiveness, an action orientation, and boldness to take the company into uncharted waters.[14]

- *Leadership motivation*. Leaders have a strong need for power because they want to influence others. However, they tend to have a need for *socialized power* because their motivation is constrained by a strong sense of altruism and social responsibility. In other words, effective leaders try to gain power so that they can influence others to accomplish goals that benefit the team or organization.[15]

- *Self-confidence*. Leaders demonstrate confidence in their leadership skills and ability to achieve objectives. Effective leaders are typically extroverted—outgoing, sociable, talkative, and assertive—but they also remain humble.

- *Intelligence*. Leaders have above-average cognitive ability to process enormous amounts of information. Leaders aren't necessarily geniuses; rather, they have superior ability to analyze a variety of complex alternatives and opportunities.

- *Knowledge of the business*. Effective leaders possess tacit and explicit knowledge of the business environment in which they operate.

Although the competency perspective is gaining popularity (again), it has a few limitations.[16] First, it assumes that all effective leaders have the same personal characteristics that are equally important in all situations. This is probably a false assumption; leadership is far too complex to have a universal list of traits that apply to every condition. Some competencies might not be important all the time. Second, alternative combinations of competencies may be equally successful; two people with different sets of competencies might be equally good leaders. Third, the leadership competencies perspective views leadership as something within a person, whereas a few critics point out that leadership is relational. People are effective leaders because of their favorable relationship with followers, so effective leaders cannot be identified without considering the quality of these relationships.[17]

The competency perspective of leadership does not necessarily imply that great leaders are born, not developed. On the contrary, competencies only indicate leadership potential, not leadership performance. People with these characteristics become effective leaders only after they have developed and mastered the necessary leadership behaviors. People with somewhat lower leadership competencies may become very effective leaders because they have leveraged their potential more fully.

After reading the next two sections, you should be able to:

3. *Describe the people-oriented and task-oriented leadership styles.*

4. *Outline the path-goal theory of leadership.*

5. *Summarize leadership substitutes theory.*

learningobjectives<

>Behavioral Perspective of Leadership

In the 1940s and 1950s, leadership experts at several universities launched an intensive research investigation to answer the question: What behaviors make leaders effective? Questionnaires were administered to subordinates, asking them to rate their supervisors on a large number of behaviors. These studies distilled two clusters of leadership behaviors from literally thousands of leadership behavior items.[18]

One cluster represented people-oriented behaviors. This included showing mutual trust and respect for subordinates, demonstrating a genuine concern for their needs, and having a desire to look out for their welfare. Leaders with a strong people-oriented style listen to employee suggestions, do personal favors for employees, support their interests when required, and treat employees as equals. The other cluster represented a task-oriented leadership style and included behaviors that define and structure work roles. Task-oriented leaders assign employees to specific tasks, clarify their work duties and procedures, ensure that they follow company rules, and push them to reach their performance capacity. They establish stretch goals and challenge employees to push beyond those high standards.

Should leaders be task-oriented or people-oriented? This is a difficult question to answer because each style has its advantages and disadvantages. Recent evidence suggests that both styles are positively associated with leader effectiveness, but differences are often apparent only in very high or very low levels of each style. Generally, absenteeism, grievances, turnover, and job dissatisfaction are higher among employees who work with supervisors with very low levels of people-oriented leadership. Job performance is lower among employees who work for supervisors with low levels of task-oriented leadership.[19] Research suggests that university students value task-oriented instructors because they want clear objectives and well-prepared lectures that abide by the unit's objectives.[20]

One problem with the behavioral leadership perspective is that the two categories are broad generalizations that mask specific behaviors within each category. For instance, task-oriented leadership includes planning work activities, clarifying roles, and monitoring operations and performance. Each of these clusters of activities are fairly distinct and likely have different effects on employee well-being and performance. A second concern is that the behavioral approach assumes high levels of both styles are best in all situations. In reality, the best leadership style depends on the situation.[21] On a positive note, the behavioral perspective lays the foundation for two of the main leadership styles—people-oriented and task-oriented—found in many contemporary leadership theories. These contemporary theories adopt a contingency perspective, which is described next.

People-Oriented Leader Takes Britain's Top Spot

What does it take to be voted the best boss in Great Britain? You will likely find the answer by watching Bruce Draper at work. The managing director of Geotechnical Instruments was recently named Britain's best boss. According to personal assistant Hannah Delany, Draper exemplifies the people-oriented leadership style to the company's 85 staff. "Bruce cares about his staff and never takes them for granted," she says. "He appears friendly, approachable and kind and makes sure everyone is content in their job." Fiona Cannon, head of equality and diversity at Lloyds TSB, the financial institution that cosponsored the award, says that people-oriented leadership is vital in organizations today. "Having a good boss can make a huge difference, not only to the success of a business but also to the happiness and well-being of those who work for them." She adds: "Bruce Draper particularly stood out from the crowd."[22]

>Contingency Perspective of Leadership

The contingency perspective of leadership is based on the idea that the most appropriate leadership style depends on the situation. Most, although not all, contingency leadership theories assume that effective leaders must be both insightful and flexible.[23] They must be able to adapt their behaviors and styles to the immediate situation. This isn't easy to do, however. Leaders typically have a preferred style. It takes considerable effort for leaders to learn when and how to alter their styles to match the situation. As we noted earlier, leaders must have high emotional intelligence, so they can diagnose the circumstances and match their behaviors accordingly.

Path-Goal Theory of Leadership

Several contingency theories have been proposed over the years, but **path-goal leadership theory** has withstood scientific critique better than the others. The theory has its roots in the expectancy theory of motivation (see Chapter 5).[24] Early research incorporated expectancy theory into the study of how leader behaviors influence employee perceptions of expectancies (paths) between employee effort and performance (goals). Out of this early work was born path-goal theory as a contingency leadership model.

Path-goal theory states that effective leaders strengthen the performance-to-outcome expectancy and valences of those outcomes by ensuring that employees who perform their jobs well have a higher degree of need fulfillment than employees who perform poorly. Effective leaders strengthen the effort-to-performance expectancy by providing the information, support, and other resources necessary to help employees complete their tasks.[25]

PATH-GOAL LEADERSHIP THEORY: a contingency theory of leadership based on the expectancy theory of motivation that relates several leadership styles to specific employee and situational contingencies

Path-Goal Leadership Styles

Exhibit 11.1 presents the path-goal theory of leadership. This model specifically highlights four leadership styles and several contingency factors leading to three indicators of leader effectiveness. The four leadership styles are:[26]

- *Directive*. These are clarifying behaviors that provide a psychological structure for subordinates. The leader clarifies performance goals, the means to reach those goals,

[Exhibit 11.1] Path-Goal Leadership Theory

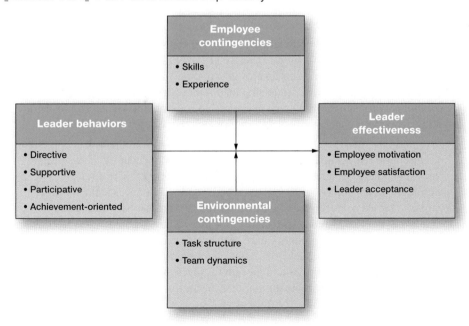

and the standards against which performance will be judged. It also includes judicious use of rewards and disciplinary actions. Directive leadership is the same as task-oriented leadership described earlier and echoes our discussion in Chapter 2 on the importance of clear role perceptions in employee performance.

- *Supportive*. These behaviors provide psychological support for subordinates. The leader is friendly and approachable; makes the work more pleasant; treats employees with equal respect; and shows concern for the status, needs, and well-being of employees. Supportive leadership is the same as people-oriented leadership described earlier and reflects the benefits of social support to help employees cope with stressful situations.

- *Participative*. These behaviors encourage and facilitate subordinate involvement in decisions beyond their normal work activities. The leader consults with employees, asks for their suggestions, and takes these ideas into serious consideration before making a decision. Participative leadership relates to involving employees in decisions.

- *Achievement-oriented*. These behaviors encourage employees to reach their peak performance. The leader sets challenging goals, expects employees to perform at their highest level, continuously seeks improvement in employee performance, and shows a high degree of confidence that employees will assume responsibility and accomplish challenging goals. Achievement-oriented leadership applies goal-setting theory as well as positive expectations in self-fulfilling prophecy.

The path-goal model contends that effective leaders are capable of selecting the most appropriate behavioral style (or styles) for that situation. Leaders might simultaneously use two or more styles. For example, they might be both supportive and participative in a specific situation.

Contingencies of Path-Goal Theory

As a contingency theory, path-goal theory states that each of these four leadership styles will be effective in some situations but not in others. The path-goal leadership model specifies two sets of situational variables that moderate the relationship between a leader's style and effectiveness: (1) employee characteristics and (2) characteristics of the employee's work environment. Several contingencies have already been studied within the path-goal framework, and the model is open for more variables in the future.[27] However, only three contingencies are reviewed here.

- *Skill and experience.* A combination of directive and supportive leadership is best for employees who are (or perceive themselves to be) inexperienced and unskilled.[28] Directive leadership gives subordinates information about how to accomplish the task, whereas supportive leadership helps them cope with the uncertainties of unfamiliar work situations. Directive leadership is detrimental when employees are skilled and experienced because it introduces too much supervisory control.

- *Task structure.* Leaders should adopt the directive style when the task is nonroutine, because this style minimizes role ambiguity that tends to occur in these complex work situations (particularly for inexperienced employees).[29] The directive style is ineffective when employees have routine and simple tasks because the manager's guidance serves no purpose and may be viewed as unnecessarily close control. Employees in highly routine and simple jobs may require supportive leadership to help them cope with the tedious nature of the work and lack of control over the pace of work. Participative leadership is preferred for employees performing nonroutine tasks because the lack of rules and procedures gives them more discretion to achieve challenging goals. The participative style is ineffective for employees in routine tasks because they lack discretion over their work.

- *Team dynamics*. Cohesive teams with performance-oriented norms act as a substitute for most leader interventions. High team cohesiveness substitutes for supportive leadership, whereas performance-oriented team norms substitute for directive and possibly achievement-oriented leadership. Thus, when team cohesiveness is low, leaders should use the supportive style. Leaders should apply a directive style to counteract team norms that oppose the team's formal objectives. For example, the team leader may need to use legitimate power if team members have developed a norm to "take it easy" rather than get a project completed on time.

Path-goal theory has received more research support than other contingency leadership models, but the evidence is far from complete. A few contingencies (i.e., task structure) have limited research support. Other contingencies and leadership styles in the path-goal leadership model haven't received research investigation at all.[30] Another concern is that as path-goal theory expands, the model may become too complex for practical use. Few people would be able to remember all the contingencies and appropriate leadership styles for those contingencies. In spite of these limitations, path-goal theory remains a relatively robust contingency leadership theory.

Leadership Substitutes

Unlike path-goal leadership, which recommends different leadership styles in various situations, the **leadership substitutes** approach identifies conditions that either limit the leader's ability to influence subordinates or make that particular leadership style unnecessary. The literature identifies several conditions that possibly substitute for task-oriented or people-oriented leadership. For example, performance-based reward systems keep employees directed toward organizational goals, so they might replace or reduce the need for task-oriented leadership. Task-oriented leadership is also less important when employees are skilled and experienced. These propositions are similar to path-goal leadership theory, namely that directive leadership is unnecessary—and may be detrimental—when employees are skilled or experienced.[31]

LEADERSHIP SUBSTITUTES: a theory identifying contingencies that either limit the leader's ability to influence subordinates or make that particular leadership style unnecessary

Some research suggests that effective leaders help team members learn to lead themselves through leadership substitutes; in other words, co-workers substitute for leadership in high involvement team structures.[32] Co-workers instruct new employees, thereby providing directive leadership. They also provide social support, which reduces stress among fellow employees. Teams with norms that support organizational goals may substitute for achievement-oriented leadership, because employees encourage (or pressure) co-workers to stretch their performance levels.[33]

Self-leadership—the process of influencing oneself to establish the self-direction and self-motivation needed to perform a task—is another possible leadership substitute.[34] Employees with high self-leadership set their own goals, reinforce their own behavior, maintain positive thought processes, and monitor their own performance, thereby managing both personal motivation and abilities. As employees become more proficient in self-leadership, they presumably require less supervision to keep them focused and energized toward organizational objectives.

The leadership substitutes model has intuitive appeal, but the evidence so far is mixed. Some studies show that a few substitutes do replace the need for task- or people-oriented leadership, but others do not. The difficulties of statistically testing for leadership substitutes may account for some problems, but a few writers contend that the limited support is evidence that leadership plays a critical role regardless of the situation.[35] At this point, we can conclude that a few conditions such as self-directed work teams, self-leadership, and reward systems might reduce the importance of task- or people-oriented leadership, but probably won't completely replace leaders in these roles.

After reading the next section, you should be able to:

6. *Distinguish transformational leadership from transactional and charismatic leadership.*

7. *Describe the four elements of transformational leadership.*

>Transformational Perspective of Leadership

TRANSFOR-MATIONAL LEADERSHIP: a leadership perspective that explains how leaders change teams or organizations by creating, communicating and modeling a vision for the organization or work unit, and inspiring employees to strive for that vision

In the opening vignette to this chapter, Infosys chicf executive Nandan Nilekani stated that effective leaders create a shared vision and encourage excellent execution toward that vision. Leadership, he explains, is essentially "about dreaming the impossible and helping followers achieve the same." Nandan Nilekani is referring to **transformational leadership.** Transformational leaders are agents of change. They create, communicate, and model a shared vision for the team or organization, and inspire followers to strive for that vision.[36]

Transformational versus Transactional Leadership

TRANSACTIONAL LEADERSHIP: leadership that helps organizations achieve their current objectives more efficiently, such as linking job performance to valued rewards and ensuring that employees have the resources needed to get the job done

Transformational leadership differs from **transactional leadership.**[37] Transactional leadership is *managing*—helping organizations achieve their current objectives more efficiently, such as by linking job performance to valued rewards and ensuring that employees have the resources needed to get the job done. The contingency and behavioral theories described earlier adopt the transactional perspective because they focus on leader behaviors that improve employee performance and satisfaction. In contrast, transformational leadership is about *leading*—changing the organization's strategies and culture so that they have a better fit with the surrounding environment.[38] Transformational leaders are change agents who energize and direct employees to a new set of corporate values and behaviors.

Organizations require both transactional and transformational leadership.[39] Transactional leadership improves organizational efficiency, whereas transformational leadership steers companies onto a better course of action. Transformational leadership is particularly important in organizations that require significant alignment with the external environment. Unfortunately, too many leaders get trapped in the daily managerial activities that represent transactional leadership.[40] They lose touch with the transformational aspect of effective leadership. Without transformational leaders, organizations stagnate and eventually become seriously misaligned with their environments.

Transformational versus Charismatic Leadership

One topic that has generated some confusion and controversy is the distinction between transformational and *charismatic leadership*.[41] Many researchers either use the words interchangeably, as if they have the same meaning, or view charismatic leadership as an essential ingredient of transformational leadership. Others take this view further by suggesting that charismatic leadership is the highest degree of transformational leadership.

However, the emerging view, which this book adopts, comes from a third group of experts who contend that charisma is distinct from transformational leadership. These academics point out that charisma is a personal trait or relational quality that provides referent power over followers, whereas transformational leadership is a set of behaviors that people use to lead the change process.[42] Charismatic leaders might be transformational leaders; indeed, their personal power through charisma is a tool to change the behavior of followers. However, some research points out that charismatic or "heroic" leaders easily build allegiance in followers, but do not necessarily change the organization. Other research suggests that charismatic leaders produce dependent followers, whereas transformational leaders have the opposite effect—they support follower empowerment, which tends to reduce dependence on the leader.[43]

The distinction between charismatic and transformational leadership is illustrated in recent leadership dynamics at Procter & Gamble. The American household goods company lost market share and innovativeness under the previous charismatic leader. Yet it has experienced a dramatic turnaround under Alan G. Lafley, who is not known for being charismatic. Instead, Lafley applies the classic elements of transformational leadership that we describe over the next couple of pages.

Elements of Transformational Leadership

There are several descriptions of transformational leadership, but most include the four elements illustrated in Exhibit 11.2. These elements include creating a strategic vision, communicating the vision, modeling the vision, and building commitment toward the vision.

Creating a Strategic Vision

Transformational leaders shape a strategic vision of a realistic and attractive future that bonds employees together and focuses their energy toward a superordinate organizational goal. A shared strategic vision represents the substance of transformational leadership. It reflects a future for the company or work unit that is ultimately accepted and valued by organizational members. Strategic vision creates a "higher purpose" or superordinate goal that energizes and unifies employees.[44] A strategic vision might originate with the leader, but it is just as likely to emerge from employees, clients, suppliers, or other constituents. A shared strategic vision plays an important role in organizational effectiveness.[45] Visions offer the motivational benefits of goal setting, but are compelling future states that bond employees and motivate them to strive for those objectives. Visions are typically described in a way that distinguishes them from the current situation yet makes the goal both appealing and achievable.

Leading without Charisma
Charisma is not a word that comes to mind when seeing Alan George Lafley in action as a leader. Various sources say that the Procter & Gamble (P&G) CEO is distinctly unassuming with "a humble demeanor that belies his status." Lafley is so soft-spoken that colleagues have to bend forward to hear him. One industry observer declared that "if there were 15 people sitting around the conference table, it wouldn't be obvious that he was the CEO." Lafley may lack charisma, but that hasn't stopped him from transforming the household products company where his charismatic predecessor had failed (and was ousted after just 18 months). Lafley's consistent vision as well as symbolic and strategic actions toward a more customer-friendly and innovative organization have provided the direction and clarity that P&G lacked. Importantly, Lafley also walks the talk; for 10 to 15 days each year, he personally interviews and observes customers using P&G products in their homes from Germany to Venezuela. The result: P&G has become the industry's hot spot for innovation, its market share and profitability have experienced sustained growth, and its stock price has soared.[46]

Communicating the Vision

If vision is the substance of transformational leadership, then communicating that vision is the process. Transformational leaders communicate meaning and elevate the importance of the visionary goal to employees. They frame messages around a grand purpose with emotional appeal that captivates employees and other corporate stakeholders. Framing helps transformational leaders establish a common mental model so that the group or organization will act collectively toward the desirable goal.[47] Transformational leaders bring their visions to life through symbols, metaphors, stories, and other vehicles that transcend plain language. Metaphors borrow images of other experiences, thereby creating richer meaning of the vision that has not yet been experienced.

[Exhibit 11.2] Elements of Transformational Leadership

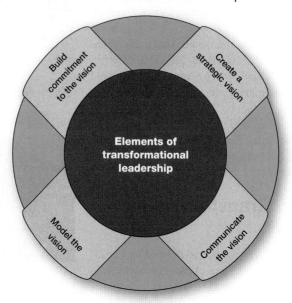

Modeling the Vision

Transformational leaders not only talk about a vision; they enact it. They "walk the talk" by stepping outside the executive suite and doing things that symbolize the vision.[48] They are also reliable and persistent in their actions, thereby legitimizing the vision and providing further evidence that they can be trusted. Leaders walk the talk in both large and small ways. They make effective use of symbolic events, but also ensure that mundane activities such as meeting agendas and office locations are consistent with the vision and its underlying values.

Modeling the vision is important because employees and other stakeholders are executive watchers who look for behaviors that symbolize values and expectations. The greater the consistency between the leader's words and actions, the more employees will believe and follow the leader. Walking the talk also builds employee trust because it is partly determined by the consistency of the person's actions. "As an executive, you're always being watched by employees, and everything you say gets magnified—so you teach a lot by how you conduct yourself," advises Carl Bass, CEO of California software company Autodesk.[49]

Building Commitment toward the Vision

Transforming a vision into reality requires employee commitment. Transformational leaders build this commitment in several ways. Their words, symbols, and stories build a contagious enthusiasm that energizes people to adopt the vision as their own. Leaders demonstrate a can-do attitude by enacting their vision and staying on course. Their persistence and consistency reflect an image of honesty, trust, and integrity. Finally, leaders build commitment by involving employees in the process of shaping the organization's vision.

Evaluating the Transformational Leadership Perspective

Transformational leaders do make a difference. Subordinates are more satisfied and have higher affective organizational commitment under transformational leaders. They also perform their jobs better, engage in more organizational citizenship behaviors, and make better or more creative decisions. One study of bank branches also reported that organizational commitment and financial performance seem to increase where the branch manager completed a transformational leadership training program.[50]

Transformational leadership is currently the most popular leadership perspective, but it faces a number of challenges. One problem is that some writers engage in circular logic by defining transformational leadership in terms of the leader's success.[51] They suggest that leaders are transformational when they successfully bring about change, rather than whether they engage in certain behaviors we call transformational. Another concern is that the transformational leadership model seems to be universal rather than contingency-oriented. Only very recently have writers begun to explore the idea that transformational leadership is more appropriate in some situations than others.[52] For instance, transformational leadership is probably more appropriate when organizations need to adapt than when environmental conditions are stable. Preliminary evidence suggests that the transformational leadership perspective is relevant across cultures. However, there may be specific elements of transformational leadership, such as the way visions are formed and communicated, that are more appropriate in North America than other cultures.

After reading the next two sections, you should be able to:

8. *Describe the implicit leadership perspective.*

9. *Discuss similarities and differences in the leadership styles of women and men.*

learningobjectives<

>Implicit Leadership Perspective

The competency, behavior, contingency, and transformational leadership perspectives make the basic assumption that leaders make a difference. Certainly, there is evidence that senior executives do influence organizational performance. However, leadership is also about followers' perceptions about the characteristics and influence of people they call leaders. This perceptual perspective of leadership is collectively called **implicit leadership theory.**[53]

Implicit leadership theory states that everyone has *leadership prototypes*—preconceived beliefs about the features and behaviors of effective leaders. These prototypes, which develop through socialization within the family and society,[54] shape our expectations and acceptance of people as leaders, which in turn affect their ability to influence us as followers. Equally important, we rely on leadership prototypes to evaluate leaders, particularly where the leader's effectiveness is ambiguous or might not be apparent for a long time. If the leader looks and acts consistently with our prototype, then we are more likely to believe that the leader is effective.[55]

Along with relying on implicit prototypes of effective leaders, followers tend to distort their perception of the influence that leaders have on the environment. This "romance of leadership" effect exists because in most cultures people want to believe that leaders make a difference. There are two basic reasons for this belief.[56] First, leadership is a useful way for us to simplify life events. It is easier to explain organizational successes and failures in terms of the leader's ability than by analyzing a complex array of other forces. Second, there is a strong tendency in the United States and other Western cultures to believe that life events are generated more from people than from uncontrollable natural forces.[57] This illusion of control is satisfied by believing that events result from the rational actions of

IMPLICIT LEADERSHIP THEORY: a theory stating that people evaluate a leader's effectiveness in terms of how well that person fits preconceived beliefs about the features and behaviors of effective leaders (leadership prototypes), and that they tend to inflate the influence of leaders on organizational events

leaders. In other words, employees feel better believing that leaders make a difference, so they actively look for evidence that this is so.

One way that followers support their perceptions that leaders make a difference is through fundamental attribution error (see Chapter 3). Research has found that (at least in Western cultures) leaders are given credit or blame for the company's success or failure because employees do not readily see the external forces that also influence these events. Leaders reinforce this belief by taking credit for organizational successes.[58]

The implicit leadership perspective provides valuable advice to improve leadership acceptance. It highlights the fact that leadership is a perception of followers as much as the actual behaviors and characteristics of people calling themselves leaders. Potential leaders must be sensitive to this fact, understand what followers expect, and act accordingly. Individuals who do not make an effort to fit leadership prototypes will have more difficulty bringing about necessary organizational change.

>Cross-Cultural and Gender Issues in Leadership

Along with the five perspectives of leadership presented throughout this chapter, cultural values and practices affect what leaders do. Culture shapes the leader's values and norms, which influence his or her decisions and actions. These cultural values also shape the expectations that followers have of their leaders. An executive who acts inconsistently with cultural expectations is more likely to be perceived as an ineffective leader. Furthermore, leaders who deviate from those values may experience various forms of influence to get them to conform to the leadership norms and expectations of that society. In other words, implicit leadership theory described in the previous section of this chapter explains differences in leadership practices across cultures.

With respect to gender, studies in field settings have generally found that male and female leaders do not differ in their levels of task-oriented or people-oriented leadership. The main explanation is that real-world jobs require similar behavior from male and female job incumbents.[59] However, women do adopt a participative leadership style more readily than their male counterparts. One possible reason is that, compared to boys, girls are often raised to be more egalitarian and less status oriented, which is consistent with being participative. There is also some evidence that women have somewhat better interpersonal skills than men, and this translates into their relatively greater use of the participative leadership style. A third explanation is that subordinates expect female leaders to be more participative, based on their own sex stereotypes, so female leaders comply with follower expectations to some extent.

Several recent surveys report that women are rated higher than men on the emerging leadership qualities of coaching, teamwork, and empowering employees.[60] Yet, research also suggests that women are evaluated negatively when they try to apply the full range of leadership styles, particularly more directive and autocratic approaches. Thus, ironically, women may be well suited to contemporary leadership roles, yet they often continue to face limitations of leadership through the gender stereotypes and prototypes of leaders held by followers.[61] Overall, both male and female leaders must be sensitive to the fact that followers have expectations about how leaders should act, and negative evaluations may go to leaders who deviate from those expectations.

>Chapter Summary

Leadership is defined as the ability to influence, motivate, and enable others to contribute toward the effectiveness and success of the organizations of which they are members. Leaders use influence to motivate followers, and arrange the work environment so that they do the job more effectively. Leaders exist throughout the organization, not just in the executive suite.

The competency perspective tries to identify the characteristics of effective leaders. Recent writing suggests that leaders have emotional intelligence, integrity, drive, leadership motivation, self-confidence, above-average intelligence, and knowledge of the business. The behavioral perspective of leadership identified two clusters of leader behavior: people-oriented and task-oriented. People-oriented behaviors include showing mutual trust and respect for subordinates, demonstrating a genuine concern for their needs, and having a desire to look out for their welfare. Task-oriented behaviors include assigning employees to specific tasks, clarifying their work duties and procedures, ensuring that they follow company rules, and pushing them to reach their performance capacity.

The contingency perspective of leadership takes the view that effective leaders diagnose the situation and adapt their style to fit that situation. The path-goal model is the prominent contingency theory that identifies four leadership styles—directive, supportive, participative, and achievement-oriented—and several contingencies relating to the characteristics of the employee and of the situation. Leadership substitutes identifies contingencies that either limit the leader's ability to influence subordinates or make that particular leadership style unnecessary.

Transformational leaders create a strategic vision, communicate that vision through framing and use of metaphors, model the vision by "walking the talk" and acting consistently, and build commitment toward the vision. This contrasts with transactional leadership, which involves linking job performance to valued rewards and ensuring that employees have the resources needed to get the job done. The contingency and behavioral perspectives adopt the transactional view of leadership.

According to the implicit leadership perspective, people have leadership prototypes, which they use to evaluate the leader's effectiveness. Furthermore, people want to believe that leaders make a difference, so they engage in fundamental attribution error and other perceptual distortions to support this belief in the leader's impact.

Cultural values also influence the leader's personal values, which in turn influence his or her leadership practices. Women generally do not differ from men in the degree of people-oriented or task-oriented leadership. However, female leaders more often adopt a participative style. Research also suggests that people evaluate female leaders based on gender stereotypes, which may result in higher or lower ratings.

>key terms

implicit leadership theory 241

leadership 231

leadership substitutes 237

path-goal leadership theory 235

shared leadership 231

transactional leadership 238

transformational leadership 238

>critical thinking questions

1. Why is it important for top executives to value and support leadership demonstrated at all levels of the organization?

2. Find two newspaper ads for management or executive positions. What leadership competencies are mentioned in these ads? If you were on the selection panel, what methods would you use to identify these competencies in job applicants?

3. Consider your favorite teacher. What people-oriented and task-oriented leadership behaviors did he or she use effectively? In general, do you think students prefer an instructor who is more people-oriented or task-oriented? Explain your preference.

4. Your employees are skilled and experienced customer service representatives who perform nonroutine tasks, such as solving unique customer problems or special needs with the company's equipment. Use path-goal theory to identify the most appropriate leadership style(s) you should use in this situation. Be sure to fully explain your answer and discuss why other styles are inappropriate.

5. Transformational leadership is currently the most popular perspective of leadership. However, it is far from perfect. Discuss the limitations of transformational leadership.

6. This chapter emphasized that charismatic leadership is not the same as transformational leadership. Still, charisma is often mentioned in the discussions about leadership. In your opinion, how does charisma relate to leadership?

7. Identify a current political leader (e.g., president, governor, mayor) and his or her recent accomplishments. Now, using the implicit leadership perspective, think of ways that these accomplishments of the leader may be over-stated. In other words, explain why they may be due to factors other than the leader.

8. You hear two people debating the merits of women as leaders. One person claims that women make better leaders than do men because women are more sensitive to their employees' needs and involve them in organizational decisions. The other person counters that although these leadership styles may be increasingly important, most women have trouble gaining acceptance as leaders when they face tough situations in which a more autocratic style is required. Discuss the accuracy of the comments made in this discussion.

>team exercise 11-1

Leadership Diagnostic Analysis

Purpose   To help students learn about the different path-goal leadership styles and when to apply each style.

Instructions

- *Step 1:* Students individually write down two incidents in which someone had been an effective manager or leader over them. The leader and situation might be from work, a sports team, a student work group, or any other setting where leadership might emerge. For example, students might describe how their supervisor in a summer job pushed them to reach higher performance goals than they would have done otherwise. Each incident should state the actual behaviors that the leader used, not just general statements (e.g., "My boss sat down with me and we agreed on specific targets and deadlines, then he said several times over the next few weeks that I was capable of reaching those goals."). Each incident only requires two or three sentences.

- *Step 2:* After everyone has written their two incidents, the instructor will form small groups (typically between four or five students). Each team will answer the following questions for each incident presented in that team:

1. Which path-goal theory leadership style(s)—directive, supportive, participative, or achievement-oriented—did the leader apply in this incident?

2. Ask the person who wrote the incident about the conditions that made this leadership style (or these styles, if more than one was used) appropriate in this situation? The team should list these contingency factors clearly and, where possible, connect them to the contingencies described in path-goal theory. (*Note:* The team might identify path-goal leadership contingencies that are not described in the book. These, too, should be noted and discussed.)

- *Step 3:* After the teams have diagnosed the incidents, each team will describe to the entire class the most interesting incidents as well as its diagnosis of that incident. Other teams will critique the diagnosis. Any leadership contingencies not mentioned in the textbook should also be presented and discussed.

Find the complete interactive self-assessment at this textbook's Web site at
www.mhhe.com/mcshaneEss2e.

>self-assessment exercise 11-2

Leadership Dimensions Instrument

This assessment is designed to help you to understand two important dimensions of leadership and to identify which of these dimensions is more prominent in your supervisor, team leader, coach, or other person to whom you are accountable. Read each of the statements in this instrument and select the response that you believe best describes your supervisor. You may substitute "supervisor" with anyone else to whom you are accountable, such as a team leader, CEO, course instructor, or sports coach. After completing this assessment, be prepared to discuss in class the distinctions between these leadership dimensions.

[part 3. case 1] A Mir Kiss?

By Steven L. McShane, The University of Western Australia

A team of psychologists at Moscow's Institute for Biomedical Problems (IBMP) wanted to learn more about the dynamics of long-term isolation in space. This knowledge would be applied to the International Space Station, a joint project of several countries that would send people into space for more than six months. It would eventually include a trip to Mars taking up to three years.

IBMP set up a replica in Moscow of the Mir space station. They then arranged for three international researchers from Japan, Canada, and Austria to spend 110 days isolated in a chamber the size of a train car. This chamber joined a smaller chamber where four Russian cosmonauts had already completed half of their 240 days of isolation. This was the first time an international crew was involved in the studies. None of the participants spoke English as their first language, yet they communicated throughout their stay in English at varying levels of proficiency.

Judith Lapierre, a French-Canadian, was the only female in the experiment. Along with a PhD in public health and social medicine, Lapierre studied space sociology at the International Space University in France and conducted isolation research in the Antarctic. This was her fourth trip to Russia, where she had learned the language. The mission was supposed to have a second female participant from the Japanese space program, but she was not selected by IBMP.

The Japanese and Austrian participants viewed the participation of a woman as a favorable factor, says Lapierre. For example, to make the surroundings more comfortable, they rearranged the furniture, hung posters on the wall, and put a tablecloth on the kitchen table. "We adapted our environment, whereas the Russians just viewed it as something to be endured," she explains. "We decorated for Christmas, because I'm the kind of person who likes to host people."

New Year's Eve Turmoil

Ironically, it was at one of those social events, the New Year's Eve party, that events took a turn for the worse. After drinking vodka (allowed by the Russian space agency), two of the Russian cosmonauts got into a fistfight that left blood splattered on the chamber walls. At one point, a colleague hid the knives in the station's kitchen because of fears that the two Russians were about to stab each other. The two cosmonauts, who

generally did not get along, had to be restrained by other men. Soon after that brawl, the Russian commander grabbed Lapierre, dragged her out of view of the television monitoring cameras, and kissed her aggressively—twice. Lapierre fought him off, but the message didn't register. He tried to kiss her again the next morning.

The next day, the international crew complained to IBMP about the behavior of the Russian cosmonauts. The Russian institute apparently took no action against any of the aggressors. Instead, the institute's psychologists replied that the incidents were part of the experiment. They wanted crew members to solve their personal problems with mature discussion, without asking for outside help. "You have to understand that Mir is an autonomous object, far away from anything," Vadim Gushin, the IBMP psychologist in charge of the project, explained after the experiment had ended in March: "If the crew can't solve problems among themselves, they can't work together."

Following IBMP's response, the international crew wrote a scathing letter to the Russian institute and the space agencies involved in the experiment. "We had never expected such events to take place in a highly controlled scientific experiment where individuals go through a multistep selection process," they wrote. "If we had known . . . we would not have joined it as subjects." The letter also complained about IBMP's response to their concerns.

Informed of the New Year's Eve incident, the Japanese space program convened an emergency meeting on January 2nd to address the incidents. Soon after, the Japanese team member quit, apparently shocked by IBMP's inaction. He was replaced with a Russian researcher on the international team. Ten days after the fight—a little over a month after the international team began the mission—the doors between the Russian and international crew's chambers were barred at the request of the international research team. Lapierre later emphasized that this action was taken because of concerns about violence, not the incident involving her.

A Stolen Kiss or Sexual Harassment

By the end of the experiment in March, news of the fistfight between the cosmonauts and the commander's attempts to kiss Lapierre had reached the public. Russian scientists attempted to play down the kissing incident by saying that it was one fleeting kiss, a clash of cultures, and a female participant who was too emotional.

"In the West, some kinds of kissing are regarded as sexual harassment. In our culture it's nothing," said Russian scientist Vadim Gushin in one interview. In another interview, he explained: "The problem of sexual harassment is given a lot of attention in North America but less in Europe. In Russia it is even less of an issue, not because we are more or less moral than the rest of the world; we just have different priorities."

Judith Lapierre says the kissing incident was tolerable compared to this reaction from the Russian scientists who conducted the experiment. "They don't get it at all," she complains. "They don't think anything is

wrong. I'm more frustrated than ever. The worst thing is that they don't realize it was wrong."

Norbert Kraft, the Austrian scientist on the international team, also disagreed with the Russian interpretation of events. "They're trying to protect themselves," he says. "They're trying to put the fault on others. But this is not a cultural issue. If a woman doesn't want to be kissed, it is not acceptable."

Sources: G. Sinclair Jr., "If You Scream in Space, Does Anyone Hear?" *Winnipeg Free Press,* May 5, 2000, p. A4; S. Martin, "Reining in the Space Cowboys," *Globe & Mail,* April 19, 2000, p. R1; M. Gray, "A Space Dream Sours," *Maclean's,* April 17, 2000, p. 26; E. Niiler, "In Search of the Perfect Astronaut," *Boston Globe,* April 4, 2000, p. E4; J. Tracy, "110-Day Isolation Ends in Sullen . . . Isolation," *Moscow Times,* March 30, 2000, p. 1; M. Warren, "A Mir Kiss?" *Daily Telegraph (London),* March 30, 2000, p. 22; G. York, "Canadian's Harassment Complaint Scorned," *Globe & Mail,* March 25, 2000, p. A2; and S. Nolen, "Lust in Space," *Globe & Mail,* March 24, 2000, p. A3.

[part 3. case 2] Bridging the Two Worlds— The Organizational Dilemma

By William Todorovic, Indiana-Purdue University, Fort Wayne

I had been hired by Aluminum Elements Corp. (AEC), and it was my first day of work. I was 26 years old, and I was now the manager of AEC's customer service group, which looked after customers, logistics, and some of the raw material purchasing. My superior, George, was the vice president of the company. AEC manufactured most of its products from aluminum, a majority of which were destined for the construction industry.

As I walked around the shop floor, the employees appeared to be concentrating on their jobs, barely noticing me. Management held daily meetings, in which various production issues were discussed. No one from the shop floor was invited to the meeting, unless there was a specific problem. Later I also learned that management had separate washrooms, separate lunchrooms, as well as other perks that floor employees did not have. Most of the floor employees felt that management, although polite on the surface, did not really feel they had anything to learn from the floor employees.

John, who worked on the aluminum slitter, a crucial operation required before any other operations could commence, had a number of unpleasant encounters with George. As a result, George usually sent written memos to the floor in order to avoid a direct confrontation with John. Because the directions in the memos were complex, these memos were often more than two pages in length.

One morning, as I was walking around, I noticed that John was very upset. Feeling that perhaps there was something I could do, I approached John and asked him if I could help. He indicated that everything was just fine. From the looks of the situation, and John's body language, I felt that he was willing to talk, but John knew that this was not the way things were done at AEC. Tony, who worked at the machine next to John's, then cursed and said that the office guys only cared about schedules, not about the people down on the floor. I just looked at him, and then said that I only began working here last week, and thought that I could address some of their issues. Tony gave me a strange look, shook his head, and went back to his machine. I could hear him still swearing as I left. Later I realized that most of the office staff was also offended by Tony's language.

On the way back to my office, Lesley, a recently hired engineer from Russia, approached me and pointed out that the employees were not accustomed to management talking to them. Management only issued orders and made demands. As we discussed the different perceptions between office and floor staff, we were interrupted by a very loud lunch bell, which startled me. I was happy to join Lesley for lunch, but she asked me why I was not eating in the office lunch room. I replied that if I was going to understand how AEC worked, I had to get to know all the people better. In addition,

I realized that this was not how things were done, and wondered about the nature of this apparent division between the management and the floor. In the lunchroom, the other workers were amazed to see me there, commenting that I was just new and had not learned the ropes yet.

After lunch, when I asked George, my supervisor, about his recent confrontation with John, George was surprised that John got upset, and exclaimed, "I just wanted John to know that he did a great job, and as a result, we will be able to ship on time one large order to the West Coast. If fact, I thought I was complimenting him."

Earlier, Lesley had indicated that certain behavior was expected from management, and therefore from me. I reasoned that I do not think that this behavior works, and besides it is not what I believe or how I care to behave. For the next couple of months, I simply walked around the floor and took every opportunity to talk to the shop floor employees. Often, when the employees related specific information about their workplaces, I felt that it went over my head. Frequently, I had to write down the information and revisit it later. I made a point of listening to them, identifying where they were coming from, and trying to understand them. I needed to keep my mind open to new ideas. Because the shop employees expected me to make requests and demands, I made a point of not doing any of that. Soon enough, the employees became friendly, and started to accept me as one of their own, or at least as a different type of a management person.

During my third month of work, the employees showed me how to improve the scheduling of jobs, especially those on the aluminum slitter. In fact, the greatest contribution was made by John who demonstrated better ways to combine the most common slitting sizes, and reduce waste by retaining some of the "common-sized" material for new orders. Seeing the opportunity, I programmed a spreadsheet to calculate and track inventory. This, in addition to better planning and forecasting, allowed us to reduce our new order turnarounds from four to five weeks to in by 10 a.m. out by 5 p.m. on the same day.

By the time I was employed for four months, I realized that members from other departments came to me and asked me to relay messages to the shop employees. When I asked why they were delegating this task to me, they stated that I spoke the same language as the shop employees. Increasingly, I became the messenger for the office to floor shop communication.

One morning, George called me into his office and complimented me on the levels of customer service and the improvements that have been achieved. As we talked, I mentioned that we could not have done it without John's help. "He really knows his stuff, and he is good," I said. I suggested that we consider him for some type of a promotion. Also, I hoped that this would be a positive gesture that would improve the communication between the office and shop floor.

George turned and pulled a flyer out of his desk; "Here is a management skills seminar. Do you think we should send John to it?"

"That is a great idea," I exclaimed, "Perhaps it would be good if he were to receive the news from you directly, George." George agreed, and after discussing some other issues, we parted company.

That afternoon, John came into my office, upset and ready to quit. "After all my effort and work, you guys are sending me for training seminars. So, am I not good enough for you?"

[part 3. case 3] Command Performance

By Edward C. Tomlinson, John Carroll University

Coalition forces, including a large number of U.S. military troops, are currently deployed in Iraq in an effort to help secure the country from terrorists and insurgents. A key element of this current strategy involves coalition forces training and developing officers and soldiers in the Iraqi Security Forces (ISF) in order to help this nation's newly reconstituted military develop the capacity to take care of security needs themselves. As this development process unfolds, heavy emphasis is placed on finding and cultivating strong and effective Iraqi military leaders. According to Lt. Gen. David Petraeus, "In an Iraqi unit, the leader is really of paramount importance. There is really a premium on finding, investing in and strengthening good leaders." This real-life challenge offers an opportunity to consider the different leadership styles and the differences these styles may exert on their respective troops.

Capt. Jamie Farrelly commands a U.S. Marine unit that has been assigned to train an ISF unit headed by Col. Yassir. Farrelly places considerable emphasis on maintaining a well-disciplined, highly-trained unit. It is his belief that this approach is essential for both success on the battlefield and the ultimate safe return of his Marines to their families after their tour ends. During his experience in Iraq, however, he has discovered that he is facing a novel leadership challenge: how to use his leadership skills to encourage the further leadership development of his Iraqi counterpart. This problem seems to be exacerbated by the different leadership styles between Farrelly and Yassir that are evident in several incidents during their time together.

For example, Farrelly's unit was training the ISF unit on conducting a vehicle checkpoint one night, when a vehicle approached. The nervous ISF troops suddenly opened fire, with carelessly aimed bullets passing dangerously by the Marines' heads. Infuriated, Capt. Farrelly chastised the Iraqi unit commander, Col. Yassir: ". . . It's your fault. Just like everything here is your fault, because you don't hold anyone accountable. You don't discipline your troops. You don't maintain basic standards."

For his part, Col. Yassir (a former Iraqi Special Forces officer at the time of the U.S. invasion) dismissed Capt. Farrelly's criticism of the checkpoint incident. He asserted that his troops should not be expected to perform at the Marines' level. Commenting on his differences with Capt. Farrelly, he says, "Capt. Farrelly and his Marines are very experienced fighters and concentrate on the technical military point of view. Iraqis focus on building the personal relationships." He continues, "With my troops, I try to treat them like a friend, not a commander. That way, when you ask them to make sacrifices, they will do it because they like you." Nonetheless, when Col. Yassir was reluctant to deliver bad news on an upcoming deployment to Fallujah, he told his men it would only last for 15 days. When it lasted longer than this, about 70 of them attempted to desert.

Fed up with this development, Capt. Farrelly told the crowd of would-be deserters that anyone who left would be sent to a detention facility. He then ordered those wanting to leave to turn their shirts inside out. "I wanted to separate the problem soldiers; make them look different and get inside their head." Forty of the would-be deserters then decided they would stay and continue fighting. The remaining 30 relented after Capt. Farrelly made them stand outside in the cold for several hours without jackets to cover their inverted shirts.

In another incident, Capt. Farrelly heard that some of Col. Yassir's soldiers had crossed into another sector during a patrol without authorization. This is very dangerous because it could lead to friendly-fire accidents. When Capt. Farrelly investigated, he discovered that one of Col. Yassir's platoon leaders had ordered his men to find heaters. It turns out that ISF soldiers from this platoon had stolen heaters, along with DVDs and cigarettes, from houses in the neighborhoods. When Capt. Farrelly informed Col. Yassir of this and demanded that the platoon leader be fired, Col. Yassir declined saying, "I shamed him. I told him what he had done was very bad." Capt. Farrelly vented his frustration: "That platoon leader willfully endangered the lives of his soldiers so he could be a little warmer and he is still here. There are no consequences for anything in this battalion."

Capt. Farrelly's challenge at this point is how he might more effectively lead Col. Yassir and the ISF unit he is training. This challenge is further complicated as ISF units are ultimately controlled by Iraqis: U.S. forces can make suggestions, but Iraqis have the final say on staffing and other operational matters.

Source: Based on Greg Jaffe, "Change of Command," *The Wall Street Journal,* February 4, 2005, pp. A1, A6.

[part 3. case 4] Outstanding Faculty Award Committee

By David J. Cherrington, Brigham Young University

Several years ago I served on the Outstanding Faculty Award committee for the College of Business. This award is the most significant honor that our college bestows on a faculty member and it represents a great personal honor for the recipient and an important ceremony for our college. The award is presented at a formal banquet for the entire faculty and their spouses at the end of the school year.

At the first meeting, our committee discussed the nomination process and decided to use our traditional practice of inviting nominations from both the faculty and students. During the next month, we received six completed files with supporting documentation. Three of the nominations came from department chairs, two from faculty who recommended their colleagues, and one from a group of 16 graduate students.

At the second meeting, we discussed the six applicants and discovered that we didn't know them as well as we should. Finally, we decided that we each needed to read the applications on our own and rank them. We did not identify any ranking criteria; I think we assumed that we shared a common definition of *outstanding.*

Our lack of a common definition became very evident at the third meeting, at which we expected to make a final decision. The discussion was polite, but there was very little agreement. We disagreed about whether this was an award for teaching, or research, or service to the college, or scholarly textbook writing, or consulting, or service to society, or some combination of these. After three hours we were no closer to a decision than when we started. Finally, we decided to identify five criteria and independently rate each candidate on them using a five-point scale.

When we reconvened the next day, our discussion was much more focused as we tried to achieve a consensus regarding how we judged each candidate on each criteria. After a lengthy discussion, we finally completed the task and summed the ratings. The top two scores were 21 and 20 and the lowest score was 12. I assumed the person with the highest total would receive the award and was surprised to see the debate continue over the relevance of our five criteria. We tested different weights for the criteria and found that the top two candidates remained at the top, but not always in the same order. But, more importantly, Dr. H was always on the bottom.

After we had met for almost two hours, the associate dean dropped a real bomb. Turning to one committee member, he said, "Dolan, I sure would like to see Dr. H in your department receive this honor. He retires next year and this would be a great honor for him and no one has received this honor in your department recently."

Dolan agreed, "Yes, this is Dr. H's last year with us and it would be a great way for him to go out. I'm sure he would feel very honored by this award."

I sat there stunned at the suggestion while Dolan retold how Dr. H had been active in public service, his only real strength on our criteria. I was even more stunned when another committee member said, "Well, I so move" and Dolan seconded it.

The associate dean, who was conducting the meeting, said, "Well, if the rest of you think this is a good idea, all in favor say aye." A few members said aye and he quickly proceeded to explain what we needed to do to advertise the winner and arrange the ceremony without calling for nays.

During my conversations with other committee members over the next two weeks, I learned that everyone was as shocked as I was at the outcome of our committee, even two who said aye. I thought we made a terrible decision and I was embarrassed to be a member of the committee. I felt we were appropriately punished when Dr. H gave a 45-minute acceptance speech that started poorly and got worse.

[part 3. case 5] Tomahawk Industries

By David J. Cherrington, Brigham Young University

Tomahawk Industries manufactures motorboats primarily used for waterskiing. During the summer months, a third production line is normally created to help meet the heavy summer demand. This third line is usually created by assigning the experienced workers to all three lines and hiring college students who are home for summer vacation to complete the crews. In the past, however, experienced workers resented having to break up their teams to form a third line. They also resented having to work with a bunch of college kids and complained that they were slow and arrogant.

The foreman, Dan Jensen, decided to try a different strategy this summer and have all the college students work on the new line. He asked Mark Allen to supervise the new crew because Mark claimed that he knew

everything about boats and could perform every job "with my eyes closed." Mark was happy to accept the new job and participated in selecting his own crew. Mark's crew was called "the Greek Team" because all the college students were members of a fraternity or sorority.

Mark spent many hours in training to get his group running at full production. The college students learned quickly, and by the end of June their production rate was up to standard, with an error rate that was only slightly above normal. To simplify the learning process, Dan Jensen assigned the Greek Team long production runs that generally consisted of 30 to 40 identical units. Thus, the training period was shortened and errors were reduced. Shorter production runs were assigned to the experienced teams.

By the middle of July, a substantial rivalry had been created between the Greek Team and the older workers. At first, the rivalry was good-natured. But after a few weeks, the older workers became resentful of the remarks made by the college students. The Greek Team often met its production schedules with time to spare at the end of the day for goofing around. It wasn't uncommon for someone from the Greek Team to go to another line pretending to look for materials just to make demeaning comments. The experienced workers resented having to perform all the shorter production runs and began to retaliate with sabotage. They would sneak over during breaks and hide tools, dent materials, install something crooked, and in other small ways do something that would slow production for the Greek Team.

Dan felt good about his decision to form a separate crew of college students, but when he heard reports of sabotage and rivalry, he became very concerned. Because of complaints from the experienced workers, Dan equalized the production so that all of the crews had similar production runs. The rivalry, however, did

not stop. The Greek Team continued to finish early and flaunt their performance in front of the other crews.

One day the Greek Team suspected that one of their assemblies was going to be sabotaged during the lunch break by one of the experienced crews. By skillful deception, they were able to substitute an assembly from the other experienced line for theirs. By the end of the lunch period, the Greek Team was laughing wildly because of their deception, while one experienced crew was very angry with the other one.

Dan Jensen decided that the situation had to be changed and announced that the job assignments between the different crews would be shuffled. The employees were told that when they appeared for work the next morning, the names of the workers assigned to each crew would be posted on the bulletin board. The announcement was not greeted with much enthusiasm, and Mark Allen decided to stay late to try to talk Dan out of his idea. Mark didn't believe the rivalry was serious enough for this type of action, and he suspected that many of the college students would quit if their team was broken up.

[part 3. case 6] Treetop Forest Products

By Steven L. McShane, The University of Western Australia and David Lebeter, Vancouver, Canada*

Treetop Forest Products Inc. is a sawmill operation in Oregon, which is owned by a major forest products company, but operates independently of headquarters. It was built 30 years ago, and completely updated with new machinery five years ago. Treetop receives raw logs from the area for cutting and planing into building-grade lumber, mostly 2-by-4 and 2-by-6 pieces of standard lengths. Higher-grade logs leave Treetop's sawmill department in finished form and are sent directly to the packaging department. The remaining 40 percent of sawmill output are cuts from lower-grade logs, requiring further work by the planing department.

Treetop has one general manager, 16 supervisors and support staff, and 180 unionized employees. The unionized employees are paid an hourly rate specified in the collective agreement, whereas management and support staff are paid a monthly salary. The mill is divided into six operating departments: boom, sawmill, planer, packaging, shipping, and maintenance. The sawmill, boom, and packaging departments operate a morning shift starting at 6 a.m. and an afternoon shift starting at 2 p.m. Employees in these departments rotate shifts every two weeks. The planer and shipping departments operate

only morning shifts. Maintenance employees work the night shift (starting at 10 p.m.).

Each department, except for packaging, has a supervisor on every work shift. The planer supervisor is responsible for the packaging department on the morning shift, and the sawmill supervisor is responsible for the packaging department on the afternoon shift. However, the packaging operation is housed in a separate building from the other departments, so supervisors seldom visit the packaging department. This is particularly true for the afternoon shift, because the sawmill supervisor is the farthest distance from the packaging building.

Packaging Quality

Ninety percent of Treetop's product is sold on the international market through Westboard Co., a large marketing agency. Westboard represents all forest products mills owned by Treetop's parent company as well as several other clients in the region. The market for building-grade lumber is very price competitive, because there are numerous mills selling a relatively undifferentiated product. However, some differentiation does occur in product packaging and presentation. Buyers will look closely at the packaging when deciding whether to buy from Treetop or another mill.

To encourage its clients to package their products better, Westboard sponsors a monthly package quality award. The marketing agency samples and rates its clients' packages daily, and the sawmill with the highest score at the end of the month is awarded a plaque. Package quality is a combination of how the lumber is piled (e.g., defects turned in), where the bands and dunnage are placed, how neatly the stencil and seal are applied, the stencil's accuracy, and how neatly and tightly the plastic wrap is attached.

Treetop Forest Products won Westboard's packaging quality award several times over the past five years, and received high ratings in the months that it didn't win. However, the mill's ratings have started to decline over the past year or two, and several clients have complained about the appearance of the finished product. A few large customers switched to competitors' lumber, saying that the decision was based on the substandard appearance of Treetop's packaging when it arrived in their lumberyard.

Bottleneck in Packaging

The planing and sawmilling departments have significantly increased productivity over the past couple of years. The sawmill operation recently set a new productivity record on a single day. The planer operation has increased productivity to the point where last year it reduced operations to just one (rather than two) shifts per day. These productivity improvements are due to better operator training, fewer machine breakdowns, and better selection of raw logs. (Sawmill cuts from high-quality logs usually do not require planing work.)

Productivity levels in the boom, shipping, and maintenance departments have remained constant. However, the packaging department has recorded decreasing productivity over the past couple of years, with the result that a large backlog of finished product is typically stockpiled outside the packaging building. The morning shift of the packaging department is unable to keep up with the combined production of the sawmill and planer departments, so the unpackaged output is left for the afternoon shift. Unfortunately, the afternoon shift packages even less product than the morning shift, so the backlog continues to build. The backlog adds to Treetop's inventory costs and increases the risk of damaged stock.

Treetop has added Saturday overtime shifts as well as extra hours before and after the regular shifts for the packaging department employees to process this backlog. Last month, the packaging department employed 10 percent of the workforce but accounted for 85 percent of the overtime. This is frustrating to Treetop's management, because time and motion studies recently confirmed that the packaging department is capable of processing all of the daily sawmill and planer production without overtime. Moreover, with employees earning one and a half or two times their regular pay on overtime, Treetop's cost competitiveness suffers.

Employees and supervisors at Treetop are aware that people in the packaging department tend to extend lunch by 10 minutes and coffee breaks by 5 minutes. They also typically leave work a few minutes before the end of shift. This abuse has worsened recently, particularly on the afternoon shift. Employees who are temporarily assigned to the packaging department also seem to participate in this time loss pattern after a few days. Although they are punctual and productive in other departments, these temporary employees soon adopt the packaging crew's informal schedule when assigned to that department.

>part IV:

Organizational Processes

[chapter 12]

Organizational Structure

Electronic games company BioWare designed an organizational structure that balances various needs for teamwork and information sharing.

>learningobjectives

After reading this chapter, you should be able to:

1. Describe three types of coordination in organizational structures.

2. Justify the optimal span of control in a given situation.

3. Discuss the advantages and disadvantages of centralization and formalization.

4. Distinguish organic from mechanistic organizational structures.

5. Identify and evaluate four pure types of departmentalization.

6. Describe three variations of divisional structure and explain which one should be adopted in a particular situation.

7. Describe the features of team-based organizational structures.

8. Diagram the matrix structure and discuss its advantages and disadvantages.

9. Identify four characteristics of external environments and discuss the preferred organizational structure for each environment.

10. Summarize the influence of organizational size, technology, and strategy on organizational structure.

Physicians Ray Muzyka and Greg Zeschuk didn't think much about organizational structure when they (along with a third partner who later returned to medical practice) launched electronic games company BioWare in the mid-1990s. By default, they relied on a simple team structure in which a handful of talented people worked together to develop the company's first game, Shattered Steel. But when they launched a second project, Baldur's Gate, Muzyka and Zeschuk faced a question that all leaders need to ask themselves when their companies grow: What organizational structure would best support this company for the future?

BioWare's cofounders recognized that one option would be to simply have two (and eventually several) teams working independently. However, they were also concerned that a multiteam structure would duplicate resources, and might undermine resource sharing among people with the same expertise across teams. Alternatively, the game developer could create departments around the various specializations, including art, programming, audio, quality assurance, and design. This would allow employees with similar technical expertise to share information and create new ideas within their specialization. However, employees would not have the same level of teamwork or commitment to the final product as they would in a team-based project structure.[1]

What organizational structure will work best for BioWare? We'll find out in this chapter. **Organizational structure** refers to the division of labor as well as the patterns of coordination, communication, workflow, and formal power that direct organizational activities. The chapter begins by introducing the two fundamental processes in organizational structure: division of labor and coordination. This is followed by a detailed investigation of the four main elements of organizational structure: span of control, centralization, formalization, and departmentalization. The latter part of this chapter examines the contingencies of organizational design, including organizational size, technology, external environment, and strategy.

> **ORGANIZATIONAL STRUCTURE:** the division of labor as well as the patterns of coordination, communication, workflow, and formal power that direct organizational activities

Throughout this chapter, we hope to show that an organization's structure is much more than an organizational chart diagramming which employees report to which managers. Organizational structure includes reporting relationships, but it also relates to job design, information flow, work standards and rules, reliance on teams, and power relationships. Organizational structure is also an important artifact of corporate culture and is often a critical tool for organizational change.[2] For example, when Charles Schwab Co. recently experienced financial trouble, founder Charles Schwab held a two-day marathon session in which the company's top executives were asked to redraw the organization chart in a way that would make the company simpler, more decentralized, and refocused on the customer. Every executive in the room, including those whose jobs would be erased from the new structure, were asked for their input.[3] The point we want to emphasize here is that organizational structure reconfigures power, communication patterns, and possibly the company's culture in the long term. As such, altering the organization's structure is an important component of the CEO's toolkit for organizational change.[4]

After reading the next two sections, you should be able to:

learningobjectives<

1. *Describe three types of coordination in organizational structures.*
2. *Justify the optimal span of control in a given situation.*
3. *Discuss the advantages and disadvantages of centralization and formalization.*
4. *Distinguish organic from mechanistic organizational structures.*

>Division of Labor and Coordination

All organizational structures include two fundamental requirements: the division of labor into distinct tasks and the coordination of that labor so that employees are able to accomplish common goals.[5] Organizations are groups of people who work interdependently toward some purpose. To efficiently accomplish their goals, these groups typically divide the work into manageable chunks, particularly when there are many different tasks to perform. They also introduce various coordinating mechanisms to ensure that everyone is working effectively toward the same objectives.

Division of Labor

Division of labor refers to the subdivision of work into separate jobs assigned to different people. Subdivided work leads to job specialization, because each job now includes a narrow subset of the tasks necessary to complete the product or service. To produce its first electronic game, BioWare's cofounders divided the work among a dozen or more employees. Some people were responsible for programming; others completed the artwork; still others developed the game's sound effects, and so forth. Today's computer games are so sophisticated that a project may require several dozen people with highly specialized expertise. As companies get larger, this horizontal division of labor is accompanied by vertical division of labor, where some people are assigned the task of managing employees.

Why do companies divide the work required to build a computer game into several jobs? As we learned earlier in this book, job specialization increases work efficiency.[6] Job incumbents can master their tasks quickly because work cycles are very short. Less time is wasted changing from one task to another. Training costs are reduced because employees require fewer physical and mental skills to accomplish the assigned work. Finally, job specialization makes it easier to match people with specific aptitudes or skills to the jobs for which they are best suited. Although one person might be able to design a computer game alone, it would take much longer than a game designed by a team of specialists. Also, an individual who produces superb animation might deliver only mediocre computer coding, whereas a highly skilled team of people would have higher quality across all areas of work.

Coordinating Work Activities

As soon as people divide work among themselves, coordinating mechanisms are needed to ensure that everyone works in concert. Coordination is so closely connected to division of labor that the degree of specialization is limited by the feasibility of coordinating that work. Coordination tends to become more expensive and difficult as jobs become more specialized, so companies specialize jobs only to the point where it isn't too costly or challenging to coordinate people in those specialized jobs.[7]

Every organization—from the two-person corner convenience store to the largest corporate entity—uses one or more of the following coordinating mechanisms:[8] informal communication, formal hierarchy, and standardization. These forms of coordination align the work of staff within the same department as well as across work units. Increasingly, they are also recognized as a critical feature of joint ventures, humanitarian aid programs, and other multiorganizational structures.[9]

Coordination through Informal Communication

Informal communication is a coordinating mechanism in all organizations. This includes sharing information on mutual tasks as well as forming common mental models so that employees synchronize work activities using the same mental road map.[10] Informal communication is vital in nonroutine and ambiguous situations because employees can exchange a large volume of information through face-to-face communication and other media-rich channels.

Coordination through informal communication is easiest in small firms such as when BioWare was a start-up firm, although information technologies have further leveraged this coordinating mechanism in large organizations.[11] Companies employing thousands of people also support informal communication by keeping each production site small. Global auto-parts manufacturer Magna International is well known for keeping its plants to a maximum size of around 200 employees, because employees have difficulty remembering each other's names in plants that are any larger. Toyota, Fuji Xerox, and many other companies encourage informal communication as a coordinating mechanism during product development through concurrent engineering, in which specialists from design through to production are organized into a temporary cross-functional team, sometimes moving team members into one large room.[12]

Coordination through Formal Hierarchy

Informal communication is the most flexible form of coordination, but it can be time-consuming. Consequently, as organizations grow, they develop a second coordinating mechanism: formal hierarchy.[13] Hierarchy assigns legitimate power to individuals, who then use this power to direct work processes and allocate resources. In other words, work is coordinated through direct supervision. Any organization with a formal structure coordinates work to some extent through the formal hierarchy. For instance, project leaders at BioWare are responsible for ensuring that employees on their computer game project remain on schedule and that their respective tasks are compatible with tasks completed by other team members.

The formal hierarchy also coordinates work among executives through the division of organizational activities. If the organization is divided into geographic areas, the structure gives those regional group leaders legitimate power over executives responsible for production, customer service, and other activities in those areas. If the organization is divided into product groups, then the heads of those groups have the right to coordinate work across regions. The formal hierarchy has traditionally been applauded as the optimal coordinating mechanism for large organizations. As we'll find out later in this chapter, however, formal hierarchy is not as agile as other forms of coordination.

Coordination through Standardization

Standardization, the third means of coordination, involves creating routine patterns of behavior or output. This coordinating mechanism takes three distinct forms:

- *Standardized processes.* Quality and consistency of a product or service can often be improved by standardizing work activities through job descriptions and procedures.[14] This coordinating mechanism is feasible when the work is routine (such as mass production) or simple (such as making pizzas), but is less effective in nonroutine and complex work such as product design.

- *Standardized outputs.* This form of standardization involves ensuring that individuals and work units have clearly defined goals and output measures (e.g., customer satisfaction, production efficiency). For instance, to coordinate the work of salespeople, companies assign sales targets rather than specific behaviors.

- *Standardized skills.* When work activities are too complex to standardize through processes or goals, companies often coordinate work effort by extensively training employees or hiring people who have learned precise role behaviors from educational programs. This form of coordination is used in hospital operating rooms. Surgeons, nurses, and other operating room professionals coordinate their work more through training than goals or company rules.

Division of labor and coordination of work represent the two fundamental ingredients of all organizations. But how work is divided, which coordinating mechanisms are emphasized, who makes decisions, and other issues are related to the four elements of organizational structure.

>Elements of Organizational Structure

Every company is configured in terms of four basic elements of organizational structure. This section introduces three of them: span of control, centralization, and formalization. The fourth element—departmentalization—is presented in the next section.

Span of Control

Span of control refers to the number of people directly reporting to the next level in the hierarchy. A narrow span of control exists when very few people report directly to a manager, whereas a wide span exists when a manager has many direct reports. A century ago, French engineer and management scholar Henri Fayol strongly recommended a relatively narrow span of control, typically no more than 20 employees per supervisor and 6 supervisors per manager. Fayol championed formal hierarchy as the primary coordinating mechanism, so he believed that supervisors should closely monitor and coach employees. His views were similar to those of Napoleon and other military leaders, who declared that somewhere between three and ten subordinates is the optimal span of control. These prescriptions were based on the belief that managers simply cannot monitor and control any more subordinates closely enough.[15]

Today, we know better. The best performing manufacturing plants currently have an average of 38 production employees per supervisor.[16] What's the secret here? Did Fayol, Napoleon, and others miscalculate the optimal span of control? The answer is that those sympathetic to hierarchical control believed that employees should perform the physical tasks, whereas supervisors and other management personnel should make the decisions and monitor employees to make sure they performed their tasks. In contrast, the best-performing manufacturing operations today rely on self-directed teams, so direct supervision (formal hierarchy) is supplemented with other coordinating mechanisms. Self-directed teams coordinate mainly informal communication and specialized knowledge, so formal hierarchy plays a minor role. Similarly, hospital medical professionals coordinate their work mainly through standardized skills, so the chief physician and head of nursing typically have many direct reports.

A second factor influencing the best span of control is whether employees perform routine tasks. A wider span of control is possible when employees perform routine jobs, because there is less need for direction or advice from supervisors. A narrow span of control is necessary when employees perform novel or complex tasks, because these employees tend to require more supervisory decisions and coaching. A third influence on span of control is the degree of interdependence among employees within the department or team.[17] Generally, a narrow span of control is necessary where employees perform highly interdependent work with others. More supervision is required for highly interdependent jobs because employees tend to experience more conflict with each other, which requires more of a manager's time to resolve. Also, employees are less clear on their personal work performance in highly interdependent tasks, so supervisors spend more time providing coaching and feedback.

Tall and Flat Structures

Span of control is interconnected with organizational size (number of employees) and the number of layers in the organizational hierarchy. Consider two companies with the same number of employees. If company A has a wider span of control (more direct reports per manager) than company B, then company A must have fewer layers of management (i.e., a flatter structure) than does company B. The reason for this relationship is that a company with a wider span of control necessarily has more employees per supervisor, more supervisors for each middle manager, and so on. This larger number of direct reports, compared to a company with a narrower span of control, is only possible by removing layers of management.

Also notice that as companies employ more people, they must widen the span of control, build a taller hierarchy, or both. Most companies end up building taller structures because they rely on direct supervision to some extent as a coordinating mechanism. Unfortunately, increasing the size of the hierarchy creates problems. First, tall structures have higher overhead costs because most layers of hierarchy consist of managers rather than employees who actually make the product or supply the service. Second, senior managers in tall structures often receive lower-quality and less-timely information from the external environment because information from front-line employees is transmitted slowly or not at all up the hierarchy. Also, the more layers of management through which information must pass, the higher the probability that managers will filter out information that does not put them in a positive light. Finally, tall hierarchies tend to undermine employee empowerment and engagement because they focus power around managers rather than employees.[18]

These problems have prompted leaders to "delayer"—remove one or more levels in the organizational hierarchy.[19] Soon after Mark Hurd was hired as CEO of Hewlett-Packard, he stripped the high-technology company's 11 layers of hierarchy down to 8 layers. He argued that this action reduced costs and would make HP more nimble. BASF's European Seal Sands plant went even further when it was dramatically restructured around self-direct teams. "Seven levels of management have been cut basically to two," says a BASF executive.[20] Although many companies enjoy reduced costs and more-empowered employees when they reduce layers of hierarchy, some organizational experts warn that cutting out too much middle management may cause long-term problems. They point out that these managers serve a valuable function by controlling work activities and managing corporate growth. Furthermore, companies will always need managers to make quick decisions and represent a source of appeal over conflicts.[21] The conclusion here is that flatter structures offer several benefits, but cutting out too much management can offset these benefits.

Centralization and Decentralization

Centralization and decentralization represents a second element of organizational design. **Centralization** means that formal decision-making authority is held by a small group of people, typically those at the top of the organizational hierarchy. Most organizations begin with centralized structures, as the founder makes most of the decisions and tries to direct the business toward his or her vision. But as organizations grow, they diversify and their environments become more complex. Senior executives aren't able to process all the decisions that significantly influence the business. Consequently, larger organizations tend to *decentralize,* that is, they disperse decision authority and power throughout the organization.

The optimal level of centralization or decentralization depends on several contingencies that we will examine later in this chapter. However, we also need to keep in mind that different degrees of decentralization can occur simultaneously in different parts of the organization.[22] Nestlé, the Swiss-based food company, has decentralized marketing decisions to remain responsive to local markets, but has centralized production, logistics, and supply chain management activities to improve cost efficiencies and avoid having too much complexity across the organization.

Formalization

Formalization is the degree to which organizations standardize behavior through rules, procedures, formal training, and related mechanisms.[23] In other words, companies become more formalized as they increasingly coordinate work through standardization. McDonald's

CENTRALIZATION: the degree to which formal decision authority is held by a small group of people, typically those at the top of the organizational hierarchy

FORMALIZATION: the degree to which organizations standardize behavior through rules, procedures, formal training, and related mechanisms

7-Eleven's Centralized-Decentralized Structure

7-Eleven has adopted what it calls a "centrally-decentralized" structure. It leverages buying power and efficiencies by centralizing decisions about information technology and supplier purchasing. At the same time, the convenience store chain decentralizes local inventory decisions to store managers so they can adapt quickly to changing circumstances at the local level. Along with ongoing product training and guidance from regional consultants, store managers have the best information about their customers and can respond quickly to local market needs. "We could never predict a busload of football players on a Friday night, but the store manager can," explains a 7-Eleven executive.[24]

restaurants and most other successful fast-food chains typically have a high degree of formalization because they rely on standardization of work processes as a coordinating mechanism. Employees have precisely defined roles, right down to how much mustard should be dispensed, how many pickles should be applied, and how long each hamburger should be cooked. Companies tend to become formalized as they get older and larger. External influences, such as government safety legislation and strict accounting rules, also encourage formalization.

Formalization may increase efficiency and compliance, but it can also create problems. Rules and procedures reduce organizational flexibility, so employees follow prescribed behaviors even when the situation clearly calls for a customized response. High levels of formalization tend to undermine organizational learning and creativity. Some work rules become so convoluted that organizational efficiency would decline if they were actually followed as prescribed. Formalization is also a source of job dissatisfaction and work stress.[25]

Mechanistic versus Organic Structures

MECHANISTIC STRUCTURE: an organizational structure with a narrow span of control and a high degree of formalization and centralization

We discussed span of control, centralization, and formalization together because they cluster around two broader organizational forms: mechanistic and organic structures.[26] A **mechanistic structure** is characterized by a narrow span of control and high degree of formalization and centralization. Mechanistic structures have many rules and procedures, limited decision making at lower levels, tall hierarchies of people in specialized roles, and vertical rather than horizontal communication flows. Tasks are rigidly defined, and are altered only when sanctioned by higher authorities. Companies with an **organic structure** have the opposite characteristics. They operate with a wide span of control, decentralized decision making, and little formalization. Tasks are fluid, adjusting to new situations and organizational needs.

ORGANIC STRUCTURE: an organizational structure with a wide span of control, little formalization and decentralized decision making

As a general rule, mechanistic structures operate better in stable environments because they rely on efficiency and routine behaviors, whereas organic structures work better in rapidly changing (i.e., dynamic) environments because they are more flexible and responsive to these changes. Organic structures are also more compatible with organizational learning, high-performance workplaces, and quality management because they emphasize information sharing and an empowered workforce rather than hierarchy and status.[27] However, the advantages of organic structures rather than mechanistic structures in dynamic environments occur only when employees have developed well-established roles and expertise.[28] Without these conditions, employees are unable to coordinate effectively with each other, resulting in errors and gross inefficiencies. Start-up companies often face this problem, known as the *liability of newness*. Newness makes start-up firms more organic, but their employees often lack industry experience and their teams have not developed sufficiently for peak performance. As a result, the organic structures of new companies cannot compensate for the poorer coordination and significantly lower efficiencies caused by this lack of structure from past experience and team mental models.

After reading the next section, you should be able to:

5. *Identify and evaluate the four pure types of departmentalization.*

6. *Describe three variations of divisional structure and explain which one should be adopted in a particular situation.*

7. *Describe the features of team-based organizational structures.*

8. *Diagram the matrix structure and discuss its advantages and disadvantages.*

learningobjectives<

>Forms of Departmentalization

Span of control, centralization, and formalization are important elements of organizational structure, but most people think about organizational charts when the discussion of organizational structure arises. The organizational chart represents the fourth element in the structuring of organizations, called departmentalization. Departmentalization specifies how employees and their activities are grouped together. It is a fundamental strategy for coordinating organizational activities because it influences organizational behavior in the following ways.[29]

- Departmentalization establishes the chain of command; that is, the system of common supervision among positions and units within the organization. It frames the membership of formal work teams and typically determines which positions and units must share resources. Thus, departmentalization establishes interdependencies among employees and subunits.

- Departmentalization focuses people around common mental models or ways of thinking, such as serving clients, developing products, or supporting a particular skill set. This focus is typically anchored around the common budgets and measures of performance assigned to employees within each departmental unit.

- Departmentalization encourages coordination through informal communication among people and subunits. With common supervision and resources, members within each configuration typically work near each other, so they can use frequent and informal interaction to get the work done.

There are almost as many organizational charts as there are businesses, but the four most common pure types of departmentalization are functional, divisional, team-based, and matrix.

Functional Structure

FUNCTIONAL STRUCTURE: a type of departmentalization that organizes employees around specific knowledge or other resources

A **functional structure** organizes employees around specific knowledge or other resources. The opening vignette to this chapter described how the cofounders of BioWare contemplated the functional structure for the electronic games company. Specifically, they considered the possibility of creating departments around the various specializations, including art, programming, audio, quality assurance, and design. The functional structure creates specialized pools of talent that typically serve everyone in the organization. This provides more economies of scale than if functional specialists are spread over different parts of the organization. It increases employee identity with that specialization or profession. Direct supervision is easier in functional structures because managers oversee people with common issues and expertise.[30]

The functional structure also has limitations.[31] Grouping employees around their skills tends to focus attention on those skills and related professional needs rather than on the company's product/service or client needs. Unless people are transferred from one function to the next, they might not develop a broader understanding of the business. Compared with other structures, the functional structure usually produces higher dysfunctional conflict and poorer coordination in serving clients or developing products. These problems occur because employees need to work with co-workers in other departments to complete organizational tasks, yet they have different subgoals and mental models of ideal work. Together, these problems require substantial formal controls and coordination when people are organized around functions.

Divisional Structure

DIVISIONAL STRUCTURE: a type of departmentalization that groups employees around geographic areas, outputs (products/services), or clients

The **divisional structure** (sometimes called the *multidivisional* or *M-form* structure) groups employees around geographic areas, outputs (products/services), or clients. Exhibit 12.1 illustrates these three variations of divisional structure. The *geographic structure* organizes employees around distinct regions of the country or globe. Exhibit 12.1(a) illustrates a geographic divisionalized structure recently adopted by Hanson PLC, one of the world's largest building materials companies. The *product/service structure* organizes work around distinct outputs. Exhibit 12.1(b) illustrates this type of structure at Philips. The Dutch electronics company divides its workforce mainly into five product divisions, ranging from consumer electronics to medical systems. The *client structure* represents the third form of divisional structure, in which employees are organized around specific customer groups. Exhibit 12.1(c) illustrates the customer-focused structure similar to one adopted by the U.S. Internal Revenue Service.[32]

Which form of divisionalization should large organizations adopt? The answer depends mainly on the primary source of environmental diversity or uncertainty.[33] Suppose an organization has one type of product sold to people across the country. If customer needs vary across regions, or if state governments impose different regulations on the product, then a geographic structure would be best to be more vigilant of this diversity. On the other hand, if the company sells several types of products across the country and customer preferences and government regulations are similar everywhere, then a product structure would likely work best.

[Exhibit 12.1] Three Types of Divisional Structure

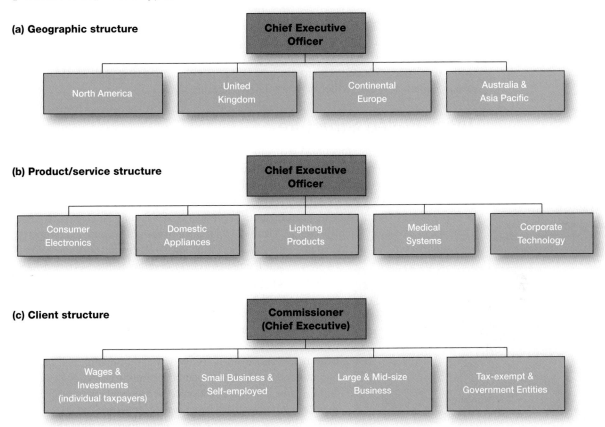

(a) **Geographic structure**

Chief Executive Officer

- North America
- United Kingdom
- Continental Europe
- Australia & Asia Pacific

(b) **Product/service structure**

Chief Executive Officer

- Consumer Electronics
- Domestic Appliances
- Lighting Products
- Medical Systems
- Corporate Technology

(c) **Client structure**

Commissioner (Chief Executive)

- Wages & Investments (individual taxpayers)
- Small Business & Self-employed
- Large & Mid-size Business
- Tax-exempt & Government Entities

Coca-Cola, Nestlé, and many other food and beverage companies are organized mainly around geographic regions because consumer tastes and preferred marketing strategies vary considerably around the world. Even though McDonald's makes the same Big Mac around the planet, it has more fish products in Hong Kong and more vegetarian products in India in line with traditional diets in those countries. Philips, on the other hand, is organized around products because consumer preferences around the world are similar within each group. Hospitals from Geneva, Switzerland, to Santiago, Chile, purchase similar medical equipment from Philips, whereas manufacturing and marketing of these products are quite different from Philips' consumer electronics business.

Many divisionalized companies are moving away from geographical structures.[34] One reason is that clients can purchase online and communicate with businesses from almost anywhere in the world, so local representation is less critical. Reduced geographic variation is another reason for the shift away from geographic structures; freer trade has reduced government intervention for many products, and consumer preferences for many products and services are becoming more similar (converging) around the world. The third reason is that large companies increasingly have global business customers who demand one global point of purchase, not one in every country or region.

Evaluating the Divisionalized Structure

The divisional form is a building block structure; it accommodates growth relatively easily and focuses employee attention on products or customers rather than tasks. Different products, services, or clients can be accommodated by sprouting new divisions. These advantages are offset by a number of limitations. First, the divisionalized structure tends to duplicate resources, such as production equipment and engineering or information technology expertise. Also, unless the division is quite large, resources are not used as efficiently as in functional structures where resources are pooled across the entire organization. The divisionalized structure also creates silos of knowledge. Expertise is spread across several autonomous business units, which reduces the ability and perhaps motivation of these people to share their knowledge with counterparts in other divisions. In contrast, a functional structure groups experts together, which supports knowledge sharing.

Team-Based Structure

TEAM-BASED STRUCTURE: a type of departmentalization built around self-directed teams that complete an entire piece of work

As an alternative to the functional structure, BioWare's cofounders considered a structure based entirely around teams. As was mentioned in the opening vignette to this chapter, this structure would have BioWare employees organized around several projects, each with its own autonomous team. A **team-based structure** is built around self-directed teams that complete an entire piece of work, such as manufacturing a product or developing an electronic game. This type of structure is highly organic. There is a wide span of control because teams operate with minimal supervision. In extreme situations, there is no formal leader, just someone selected by other team members to help coordinate the work and liaise with top management. Team structures are highly decentralized because almost all day-to-day decisions are made by team members rather than someone further up the organizational hierarchy. Finally, many team-based structures have low formalization because teams are given relatively few rules about how to organize their work. Instead, executives assign quality and quantity output targets and often productivity improvement goals to each team. Teams are then encouraged to use available resources and their own initiative to achieve those objectives.

Team-based structures are usually found within the manufacturing operations of larger divisionalized structures. For example, auto-parts giant TRW Automotive has a team-based structure in many of its 200 plants, but these plants are linked together within the company's divisionalized structure. However, a small number of firms apply the team-based structure from top to bottom. Perhaps the most famous example of this is W. L. Gore & Associates, where almost all associates work on teams and no one is the boss.

W. L. Gore's Structural Fabric: Extreme Teams
W. L. Gore & Associates Inc. has an extreme team-based organizational structure that eliminates the traditional hierarchy. Most employees (or "associates" as they are known) at the Newark, Delaware-based manufacturer of fabrics (Gore-Tex), electronics, industrial, and medical products work at four dozen self-sufficient manufacturing and sales offices around the world. Associates make day-to-day decisions within their expertise without approval from anyone higher up. Bigger issues, such as hiring and compensating staff, are decided by teams. Each facility is deliberately limited to about 200 people so they can coordinate more effectively through informal communication. Within those units, new projects are started through individual initiative and support from others.[35]

Evaluating the Team-Based Structure

The team-based organization represents an increasingly popular structure because it is usually more responsive and flexible.[36] It tends to reduce costs because teams have less reliance on formal hierarchy (direct supervision). A cross-functional team structure improves communication and cooperation across traditional boundaries. With greater autonomy, this structure also allows quicker and more informed decision making.[37]

Against these benefits, the team-based structure can be costly to maintain due to the need for ongoing interpersonal skills training. Teamwork potentially takes more time to coordinate than formal hierarchy during the early stages of team development. Employees may experience more stress due to increased ambiguity in their roles. Team leaders also experience more stress due to increased conflict, loss of functional power, and unclear career progression ladders. Also, team structures suffer from duplication of resources and potential competition (and lack of resource sharing) across teams.[38]

Matrix Structure

Throughout this chapter we have referred back to the dilemma that Ray Muzyka and Greg Zeschuk faced regarding the best choice of an organizational structure for BioWare. The company could adopt a functional structure, but this might not generate an optimal level of teamwork or commitment to the final product. Alternatively, BioWare's employees could be organized into a team-based structure. But having several teams would duplicate resources, and possibly undermine resource sharing among people with the same expertise across teams.

After carefully weighing the various organizational structure options, Muzyka and Zeschuk adopted a **matrix structure** to gain the benefits of both a functional structure and a project-based (team) structure. BioWare's matrix structure, which is similar to the diagram in Exhibit 12.2, is organized around both functions (art, audio, programming, etc.) and team-based game development projects. Employees are assigned to a cross-functional team responsible for a specific game project, yet they also belong to a permanent functional unit from which they are redistributed when their work is completed on a particular project.[39] Muzyka and Zeschuk say the matrix structure encourages employees to think in terms of the final product, yet keeps them organized around their expertise to encourage knowledge sharing. "The matrix structure also supports our overall company culture where BioWare is the team, and everyone is always willing to help each other whether they are on the same project or not," they add. BioWare's matrix structure has proven to be a good choice, particularly as the company has now grown to more than 300 employees working on more than a half-dozen game projects.

BioWare's structure, in which project teams overlap with functional departments, is just one form of matrix structure. Another variation, which is common in large global firms, is

> **MATRIX STRUCTURE:** a type of departmentalization that overlays two organizational forms in order to leverage the benefits of both

[Exhibit 12.2] Project-Based Matrix Structure (similar to BioWare's structure)

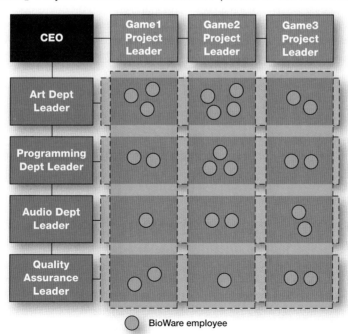

BioWare employee

to have geography on one axis and products/services or client groups on the other. Procter & Gamble recently moved toward this type of global matrix structure with country managers (called *market development organizations*) on one axis and *global business units* representing global brands on the other axis. Previously, P&G had a geographic divisional structure, which gave too much power to country managers and not enough power or priority to globalizing its major brands (e.g., Pantene, Tide, Pringles). P&G's leaders believe that the new matrix structure will balance this power, thereby supporting its philosophy of thinking globally and acting locally.[40]

Evaluating the Matrix Structure

The matrix structure usually optimizes the use of resources and expertise, making it ideal for project-based organizations with fluctuating workloads. When properly managed, it improves communication efficiency, project flexibility, and innovation compared to purely functional or divisional designs. It focuses employees on serving clients or creating products, yet keeps expertise organized around their specialization so knowledge sharing improves and resources are used more efficiently. The matrix structure is also a logical choice when, as in the case of Procter & Gamble, two different dimensions (regions and products) are equally important. Structures determine executive power and what is important; the matrix structure works when two different dimensions deserve equal attention.

In spite of these advantages, the matrix structure has several well-known problems.[41] One concern is that it increases goal conflict and ambiguity. Employees working at the matrix level have two bosses and, consequently, two sets of priorities that aren't always aligned with each other. Project leaders might squabble over specific employees who are assigned to other projects. They may also disagree with employee decisions, but the employee's functional leader has more say than the project leader as to the individual's technical competence. Aware of these concerns, BioWare holds several synchronization meetings each year involving all department directors (art, design, audio, etc.), producers (i.e., game project leaders), and the human resources manager. These meetings sort out differences and ensure that staff members are properly assigned to each game project.

Another challenge is that the existence of two bosses can dilute accountability. In a functional or divisionalized structure, one manager is responsible for everything, even the most unexpected issues. But in a matrix structure, the unusual problems don't get resolved because neither manager takes ownership of them.[42] The result of conflict and ambiguity in matrix structures is that some employees experience more stress, and some managers are less satisfied with their work arrangements.

>**learning**objectives

After reading the next section, you should be able to:

9. *Identify four characteristics of external environments and discuss the preferred organizational structure for each environment.*

10. *Summarize the influences of organizational size, technology, and strategy on organizational structure.*

>Contingencies of Organizational Design

Most organizational behavior theories and concepts have contingencies—ideas that work well in one situation might not work as well in another situation. This contingency approach is certainly relevant when choosing the most appropriate organizational structure.[43] In this section, we introduce four contingencies of organizational design: external environment, size, technology, and strategy. Before doing so, however, we need to warn you that this discussion is necessarily simplified because of an unresolved debate among organizational structure experts.[44] The debate centers around the question of whether specific contingencies can be associated with specific elements of structure (centralization, formalization, etc.), or whether we need to examine *configurations* of contingencies with broad typologies of organizational structure (such as organic versus mechanistic). Some writers further suggest that more than two different structural typologies might work equally well in a particular situational configuration. With these caveats in mind, let's examine the four main contingencies of organizational structure.

External Environment

The best structure for an organization depends on its external environment. The external environment includes anything outside the organization, including most stakeholders (e.g., clients, suppliers, government), resources (e.g., raw materials, human resources, information, finances), and competitors. Four characteristics of external environments influence the type of organizational structure best suited to a particular situation: dynamism, complexity, diversity, and hostility.[45]

Dynamic vs. Stable Environments

Dynamic environments have a high rate of change, leading to novel situations and a lack of identifiable patterns. Organic structures are better suited to this type of environment so that the organization can adapt more quickly to changes, but only if employees are experienced and coordinate well in teamwork.[46] In contrast, stable environments are characterized by regular cycles of activity and steady changes in supply and demand for inputs and outputs. Events are more predictable, enabling the firm to apply rules and procedures. Mechanistic structures are more efficient when the environment is predictable, so they tend to work better than organic structures.

Complex versus Simple Environments

Complex environments have many elements whereas simple environments have few things to monitor. As an example, a major university library operates in a more complex environment than a small town public library. The university library's clients require several types of services—book borrowing, online full-text databases, research centers, course reserve collections, and so on. A small town public library has fewer of these demands placed on it. The more complex the environment, the more decentralized the organization should become. Decentralization is a logical response to complexity because decisions are pushed down to people and subunits with the necessary information to make informed choices.

Diverse versus Integrated Environments

Organizations located in diverse environments have a greater variety of products or services, clients, and regions. In contrast, an integrated environment has only one client, product, and geographic area. The more diversified the environment, the more the firm needs to use a divisionalized form aligned with that diversity. If it sells a single product around the world, a geographic divisionalized structure would align best with the firm's geographic diversity, for example.

Hostile versus Munificent Environments

Firms located in a hostile environment face resource scarcity and more competition in the marketplace. Hostile environments are typically dynamic ones because they reduce the predictability of access to resources and demand for outputs. Organic structures tend to be best in hostile environments. However, when the environment is extremely hostile—such as a severe shortage of supplies or lower market share—organizations tend to temporarily

The Nitro-daptive Ad Agency
How do you design an advertising agency that satisfies client demands for both a global footprint and local expertise? For Nitro Group, the answer is a structure that is mainly decentralized but is adaptive enough to bring in the company's top guns when needed. The upstart ad agency, which was founded in Shanghai in 2002, decentralizes decision making to account staff at its local satellite offices, so that clients have the benefit of creative people who know the local market. Yet, to solve tough advertising challenges, Nitro will parachute in a creative swat team from one of its three global hubs—Shanghai, New York, and London. This structure seems to work. Nitro has landed large regional accounts from Volvo, Mars, and other global companies, and is quickly gaining a reputation for innovation.[47]

centralize so that decisions can be made more quickly and executives feel more comfortable being in control.[48] Ironically, centralization may result in lower-quality decisions during organizational crises, because top management has less information, particularly when the environment is complex.

Organizational Size

Larger organizations should have different structures from smaller organizations.[49] As the number of employees increases, job specialization increases due to a greater division of labor. This greater division of labor requires more elaborate coordinating mechanisms. Thus, larger firms make greater use of standardization (particularly work processes and outcomes) to coordinate work activities. These coordinating mechanisms create an administrative hierarchy and greater formalization. Historically, larger organizations make less use of informal communication as a coordinating mechanism. However, emerging information technologies and increased emphasis on empowerment have caused informal communication to regain its importance in large firms.[50]

Larger organizations also tend to be more decentralized. Executives have neither sufficient time nor expertise to process all the decisions that significantly influence the business as it grows. Therefore, decision-making authority is pushed down to lower levels, where incumbents are able to cope with the narrower range of issues under their control.

Technology

Technology is another factor to consider when designing the best organizational structure for the situation.[51] Technology refers to the mechanisms or processes by which an organization turns out its product or service. One technological contingency is its *variability*—the number of exceptions to standard procedure that tend to occur. In work processes with low variability, jobs are routine and follow standard operating procedures. Another contingency is *analyzability*—the predictability or difficulty of the required work. The less analyzable the work, the more it requires experts with sufficient discretion to address the work challenges. An organic rather than a mechanistic structure should be introduced where employees perform tasks with high variety and low analyzability, such as in a research setting. The reason is that employees face unique situations with little opportunity for repetition. In contrast, a mechanistic structure is preferred where the technology has low variability and high analyzability, such as an assembly line. The work is routine and highly predictable, an ideal situation for a mechanistic structure to operate efficiently.

Organizational Strategy

Organizational strategy refers to the way the organization positions itself in its setting in relation to its stakeholders, given the organization's resources, capabilities, and mission.[52] In other words, strategy represents the decisions and actions applied to achieve the organization's goals. Although size, technology, and environment influence the optimal organizational structure, these contingencies do not necessarily determine structure. Instead, corporate leaders formulate and implement strategies that shape both the characteristics of these contingencies as well as the organization's resulting structure.

This concept is summed up with the simple phrase: structure follows strategy.[53] Organizational leaders decide how large to grow and which technologies to use. They take steps to define and manipulate their environments, rather than let the organization's fate be entirely determined by external influences. Furthermore, organizational structures don't evolve as a natural response to these contingencies. Instead, they result from organizational decisions. Thus, organizational strategy influences both the contingencies of structure and the structure itself. If a company's strategy is to compete through innovation, then a more organic structure would be preferred because it is easier for employees to share knowledge and be creative. If a company chooses a low-cost strategy, then a mechanistic structure is preferred because it maximizes production and service efficiency.[54] Overall, it is now apparent that organizational structure is influenced by size, technology, and environment, but the organization's strategy may reshape these elements and loosen their connection to organizational structure.

>Chapter Summary

Organizational structure refers to the division of labor as well as the patterns of coordination, communication, workflow, and formal power that direct organizational activities. All organizational structures divide labor into distinct tasks and coordinate that labor to accomplish common goals. The primary means of coordination are informal communication, formal hierarchy, and standardization.

The four basic elements of organizational structure include span of control, centralization, formalization, and departmentalization. The optimal span of control, which refers to the number of people directly reporting to the next level in the hierarchy, depends on the presence of coordinating mechanisms other than formal hierarchy, as well as whether employees perform routine tasks and the degree of interdependence among employees within the department.

Centralization occurs when formal decision authority is held by a small group of people, typically senior executives. Many companies decentralize as they become larger and more complex, but some sections of the company may remain centralized while other sections decentralize. Formalization is the degree to which organizations standardize behavior through rules, procedures, formal training, and related mechanisms. Companies become more formalized as they get older and larger. Formalization tends to reduce organizational flexibility, organizational learning, creativity, and job satisfaction.

Span of control, centralization, and formalization cluster into mechanistic and organic structures. Mechanistic structures are characterized by a narrow span of control and high degree of formalization and centralization. Companies with an organic structure have the opposite characteristics.

Departmentalization specifies how employees and their activities are grouped together. It establishes the chain of command, focuses people around common mental models, and encourages coordination through informal communication among people and subunits. A functional structure organizes employees around specific knowledge or other resources. This fosters greater specialization and improves direct supervision, but weakens the focus on serving clients or developing products.

A divisional structure groups employees around geographic areas, clients, or outputs. This structure accommodates growth and focuses employee attention on products or customers rather than tasks. However, this structure duplicates resources and creates silos of knowledge. Team-based structures are very flat with low formalization that organize self-directed teams around work processes rather than functional specialties. The matrix structure combines two structures to leverage the benefits of both types of structure. However, this approach requires more coordination than functional or pure divisional structures, may dilute accountability, and increases conflict.

The best organizational structure depends on the firm's external environment, size, technology, and strategy. The optimal structure depends on whether the environment is dynamic or stable, complex or simple, diverse or integrated, and hostile or munificent. As organizations increase in size, they become more decentralized and more formalized. The work unit's technology—including variety of work and analyzability of problems— influences whether to adopt an organic or mechanistic structure. These contingencies influence but do not necessarily determine structure. Instead, corporate leaders formulate and implement strategies that shape both the characteristics of these contingencies as well as the organization's resulting structure.

>key terms

centralization 259	matrix structure 265	organizational structure 255
divisional structure 262	mechanistic structure 260	span of control 258
formalization 259	organic structure 261	team-based structure 264
functional structure 262	organizational strategy 269	

>critical thinking questions

1. Boutique advertising agency Nitro has an organic, team-based structure. What coordinating mechanism likely dominates in this type of organizational structure? Describe the extent and form in which the other two forms of coordination might be apparent at Nitro.

2. Think about the business school or other organizational unit whose classes you are currently attending. What is the dominant coordinating mechanism used to guide or control the instructor? Why is this coordinating mechanism used the most here?

3. Administrative theorists concluded many decades ago that the most effective organizations have a narrow span of control. Yet, today's top-performing manufacturing firms have a wide span of control. Why is this possible?

Under what circumstances, if any, should manufacturing firms have a narrow span of control?

4. If one could identify trends in organizational structure, one of them would be decentralization. Why is decentralization becoming more common in contemporary organizations? What should companies consider when determining the degree of decentralization?

5. Diversified Technologies LLC (DTL) makes four types of products, each type to be sold to different types of clients. For example, one product is sold exclusively to automobile repair shops, whereas another is used mainly in hospitals. Customer expectations and needs are surprisingly similar throughout the world. However, the company has separate marketing, product design, and manufacturing facilities in Asia, North America, Europe, and South America because, until recently, each jurisdiction had unique regulations governing the production and

sales of these products. However, several governments have begun the process of deregulating the products that DTL designs and manufactures, and trade agreements have opened several markets to foreign-made products. Which form of departmentalization might be best for DTL if deregulation and trade agreements occur?

6. Why are many organizations moving away from the geographic divisional structures?

7. From an employee perspective, what are the advantages and disadvantages of working in a matrix structure?

8. Suppose that you have been hired as a consultant to diagnose the environmental characteristics of your college or university. How would you describe the school's external environment? Is the school's existing structure appropriate for this environment?

>team exercise 12-1

The Club Ed Exercise

By Cheryl Harvey and Kim Morouney, Wilfred Laurier University

Purpose   This exercise is designed to help you understand the issues to consider when designing organizations at various stages of growth.

Materials   Each student team should have enough overhead transparencies or flip chart sheets to display several organizational charts.

Instructions
Each team discusses the scenario presented. The first scenario is presented below. The instructor will facilitate discussion and notify teams when to begin the next step. The exercise and debriefing require approximately 90 minutes, although fewer scenarios can reduce the time somewhat.

- *Step 1*: Students are placed in teams (typically four or five people).

- *Step 2:* After reading Scenario 1 presented below, each team will design an organizational chart (departmentalization) that is most appropriate for this situation. Students should be able to describe the type of structure drawn and explain why it is appropriate. The structure should be drawn on an overhead transparency or flip chart for others

to see later during class discussion. The instructor will set a fixed time (e.g., 15 minutes) to complete this task.

Scenario 1. Determined never to shovel snow again, you are establishing a new resort business on a small Caribbean island. The resort is under construction and is scheduled to open one year from now. You decide it is time to draw up an organizational chart for this new venture, called Club Ed.

- *Step 3*: At the end of the time allowed, the instructor will present scenario 2 and each team will be asked to draw another organizational chart to suit that situation. Again, students should be able to describe the type of structure drawn and explain why it is appropriate.

- *Step 4*: At the end of the time allowed, the instructor will present scenario 3 and each team will be asked to draw another organizational chart to suit that situation.

- *Step 5*: Depending on the time available, the instructor might present a fourth scenario. The class will gather to present their designs for each scenario. During each presentation, teams should describe the type of structure drawn and explain why it is appropriate.

Source: Adapted from C. Harvey and K. Morouney, *Journal of Management Education* 22 (June 1998), pp. 425–29. Used with permission of the authors.

Find the complete interactive self-assessment at this textbook's Web site at
www.mhhe.com/mcshaneEss2e.

>self-assessment exercise 12-2

Identifying Your Preferred Organizational Structure

Personal values influence how comfortable you are working in different organizational structures. You might prefer an organization with clearly defined rules or no rules at all. You might prefer a firm where almost any employee can make important decisions, or where important decisions are screened by senior executives. This self-assessment is designed to help you understand how an organization's structure influences the personal needs and values of people working in that structure. Read each statement and indicate the extent to which you would like to work in an organization with that characteristic. This self-assessment is completed alone so students will complete this self-assessment honestly without concerns of social comparison. However, class discussion will focus on the elements of organizational structure and their relationship to personal needs and values.

chapter 13

Organizational Culture

Dell's culture of killer competition and efficiency is now becoming a liability to the computer-maker's future.

>learningobjectives

After reading this chapter, you should be able to:

1. Describe the elements of organizational culture.
2. Discuss the importance of organizational subcultures.
3. List four categories of artifacts through which corporate culture is deciphered.
4. Identify three functions of organizational culture.
5. Discuss the conditions under which organizational cultural strength improves organizational performance.
6. Identify the four strategies to change or strengthen an organization's culture.
7. Apply attraction-selection-attrition theory to explain how organizational culture strengthens.
8. Describe the stages of organizational socialization.
9. Compare and contrast four strategies for merging organizational cultures.

Propelled by a culture of cost efficiency and competitiveness, Dell, Inc., was the unstoppable leader in the computer industry for more than a decade. Experts praised its low-cost, responsive manufacturing and direct marketing sales model. Founder Michael Dell championed short-term objectives, while Kevin Rollins (until recently Dell CEO) was the architect of efficiency-oriented processes and measures. Dell culture emphasized winning, meaning that it focused on beating the competition and staying on top. "There are some organizations where people think they're a hero if they invent a new thing," Rollins said a few years ago. "Being a hero at Dell means saving money."

Although still an efficient manufacturer of low-cost computers, Dell's spectacular success has stalled while HP, Apple, and other competitors are moving ahead. The reason? Dell's strong "winning" culture blinded leaders to anything other than building low-cost computers at a time when the market shifted toward a preference for style and innovation. "Dell's culture is not inspirational or aspirational," suggests one industry expert. "[Its] culture only wants to talk about execution." A few staff warned of the need for change, but those who dared to criticize Dell's cultural values and assumptions were quickly silenced. "A lot of red flags got waved—but only once," recalls a former Dell manager.

When Dell's financial and market numbers reflected the cultural misalignment, Michael Dell replaced Kevin Rollins as CEO and advised staff of major changes to come. Other senior executives have also left the company. "The company was too focused on the short term," Dell admits. He apparently also repeatedly emphasizes to staff that the Dell model "is not a religion." Dell is convinced that he can turn the company around, but others say that changing Dell's culture will be a mammoth task. "It's not an easy transition," warns a technology analyst. "You've got to change your mind-set and your culture."[1]

//

Dell's current challenges reflect the perils of ignoring organizational culture. **Organizational culture** consists of the values and assumptions shared within an organization.[2] It defines what is important and unimportant in the company and, consequently, directs everyone in the organization toward the "right way" of doing things. You might think of it as the organization's DNA—invisible to the naked eye, yet a powerful template that shapes what happens in the workplace.[3]

> **ORGANIZATIONAL CULTURE:**
> the values and assumptions shared within an organization

This chapter begins by identifying the elements of organizational culture, then describing how culture is deciphered through artifacts. This is followed by a discussion of the relationship between organizational culture and performance, including the effects of cultural strength, fit, and adaptability. Then we examine ways to change or strengthen organizational culture. The final section of this chapter turns our attention to the challenges and solutions to merging organizational cultures.

After reading the next two sections, you should be able to:

learningobjectives<

1. Describe the elements of organizational culture.
2. Discuss the importance of organizational subcultures.
3. List four categories of artifacts through which corporate culture is deciphered.

>Elements of Organizational Culture

Exhibit 13.1 illustrates how the shared values and assumptions of an organization's culture relate to each other and are associated with artifacts, which are discussed later in this chapter. *Values,* which were described in Chapter 1, are stable, evaluative beliefs that guide our preferences for outcomes or courses of action in a variety of situations.[4] They are conscious perceptions about what is good or bad, right or wrong. Values exist as a component of

[Exhibit 13.1] Organizational Culture Assumptions, Values, and Artifacts

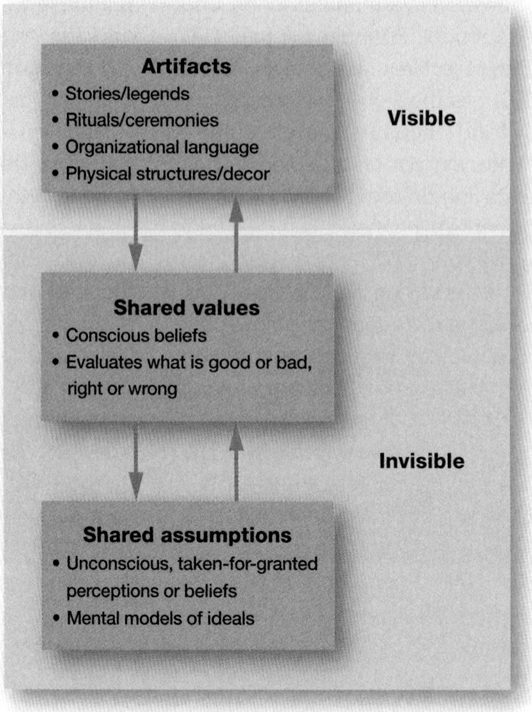

Artifacts
- Stories/legends
- Rituals/ceremonies
- Organizational language
- Physical structures/decor

Visible

Shared values
- Conscious beliefs
- Evaluates what is good or bad, right or wrong

Invisible

Shared assumptions
- Unconscious, taken-for-granted perceptions or beliefs
- Mental models of ideals

Source: Based on information in E. H. Schein, *Organizational Culture and Leadership: A Dynamic View* (San Francisco: Jossey-Bass, 1985).

organizational culture in the form of *shared values,* which are values that people within the organization or work unit have in common and place near the top of their hierarchy of values.[5] Organizational culture also consists of *shared assumptions*—a deeper element that some experts believe is really the essence of corporate culture. Shared assumptions are unconscious taken-for-granted perceptions or beliefs that have worked so well in the past that they are considered the correct way to think and act toward problems and opportunities. Shared assumptions are so deeply ingrained that you probably wouldn't discover them by surveying employees. Only by observing these employees, analyzing their decisions, and debriefing them on their actions would these assumptions rise to the surface.

Content of Organizational Culture

Organizations differ in their cultural content; that is, the relative ordering of values. Dell's culture places efficiency and competitiveness far above innovation and aesthetics, whereas the culture at Apple Inc. gives innovation and style equal or higher priority to cost efficiency. Many experts have tried to classify corporate culture into a few easy-to-remember groups. One of the most popular and respected models identifies seven corporate cultures (see Exhibit 13.2). Another model identifies eight organizational cultures arranged around a circle, indicating that some cultures are opposite to each other. A rules-oriented culture is opposite to an innovation culture, an internally-focused culture is opposed to an externally-focused culture, a controlling culture is opposite to a flexible culture, and a goal-oriented culture is opposite to a supportive culture.[6]

These organizational culture models and surveys are popular with corporate leaders faced with the messy business of diagnosing their company's culture and identifying what kind of culture they want to develop. However, models that organize cultures into seven or eight

[Exhibit 13.2] Organizational Culture Profile Dimensions and Characteristics

Organizational Culture Dimension	Characteristics of the Dimension
Innovation	Experimenting, opportunity seeking, risk taking, few rules, low cautiousness
Stability	Predictability, security, rule-oriented
Respect for people	Fairness, tolerance
Outcome orientation	Action-oriented, high expectations, results-oriented
Attention to detail	Precise, analytic
Team orientation	Collaboration, people-oriented
Aggressiveness	Competitive, low emphasis on social responsibility

Source: Based on information in C. A. O'Reilly III, J. Chatman, and D. F. Caldwell, "People and Organizational Culture: A Profile Comparison Approach to Assessing Person-Organization Fit," *Academy of Management Journal* 34, no. 3 (1991), pp. 487–518.

simple categories mask the reality that there are dozens of individual values, so there are likely as many organizational values. Furthermore, organizational culture consists of assumptions that are too deeply ingrained to be measured through surveys. Overall, organizational culture surveys cannot replace a much more complete analysis of an organization's culture.

Organizational Subcultures

When discussing organizational culture, we are actually referring to the *dominant culture,* that is, the themes shared most widely by the organization's members. However, organizations are also comprised of *subcultures* located throughout its various divisions, geographic regions, and occupational groups.[7] Some subcultures enhance the dominant culture by espousing parallel values and assumptions; other subcultures emphasize somewhat different but not competing values; still others are called *countercultures* because they directly oppose the organization's dominant values.

Subcultures, particularly countercultures, potentially create conflict and dissension among employees, but they also serve two important functions.[8] First, they maintain the organization's standards of performance and ethical behavior. Employees who hold counter-cultural values are an important source of surveillance and critique over the dominant order. They encourage constructive conflict and more creative thinking about how the organization should interact with its environment. Subcultures prevent employees from blindly following one set of values and thereby help the organization to abide by society's ethical values.

The second function of subcultures is that they are the spawning grounds for emerging values that keep the firm aligned with the needs of customers, suppliers, society, and other stakeholders. Companies eventually need to replace their dominant values with ones that are more appropriate for the changing environment. If subcultures are suppressed, the organization may take longer to discover and adopt values aligned with the emerging environment.

>Deciphering Organizational Culture through Artifacts

We can't directly see an organization's cultural assumptions and values. Instead, as Exhibit 13.1 illustrated earlier, we decipher organizational culture indirectly through artifacts. **Artifacts** are the observable symbols and signs of an organization's culture, such as the way visitors are greeted, the organization's physical layout, and how employees are

ARTIFACTS: the observable symbols and signs of an organization's culture

Mayo Clinic's Cultural Expedition

The Mayo Clinic has a well-established culture at its original clinic in Rochester, Minnesota, but maintaining that culture in its expanding operations in Florida and Arizona has been challenging. "We were struggling with growing pains. We didn't want to lose the culture and we were looking at how to keep the heritage alive," explains Matt McElrath, Mayo Clinic human resources director in Arizona. The Mayo Clinic retained anthropologist Linda Catlin to decipher Mayo's culture and identify ways to reinforce it at the two newer sites. Catlin shadowed employees and posed as a patient to observe what happens in waiting rooms. "She did countless interviews, joined physicians on patient visits and even spent time in the operating room," says McElrath. At the end of her six-week cultural expedition, Catlin submitted a report outlining Mayo's culture and how its satellite operations varied from that culture. The Mayo Clinic adopted all of Catlin's 11 recommendations, such as requiring all new physicians at the three sites to attend an orientation in Rochester where they learn about Mayo's history and values.[11]

rewarded.[9] Artifacts are important because they reinforce and potentially support changes to an organization's culture. They are also valuable as evidence about a company's culture. To accurately understand the company's dominant values and assumptions, we need to observe workplace behavior, listen to everyday conversations among staff and with customers, study written documents and e-mails, and interview staff about corporate stories.[10] In other words, we need to sample information from a range of organizational artifacts. In this section, we review the four broad categories of artifacts: organizational stories and legends, rituals and ceremonies, organizational language, and physical structures and symbols.

Organizational Stories and Legends

Stories permeate strong organizational cultures. Some tales recount heroic deeds, such as Michael Dell's determination to build his computer company, beginning from a dorm room at The University of Texas; others ridicule past events that deviated from the firm's core values. These stories and legends serve as powerful social prescriptions of the way things should (or should not) be done. They provide human realism to corporate expectations, individual performance standards, and the criteria for getting fired. These stories also create emotions in listeners, which tends to improve their memory of the lesson within the story. Stories have the greatest effect at communicating corporate culture when they describe real people, are assumed to be true, and known by employees throughout the organization. Stories are also prescriptive—they advise people what to do or not to do.[12]

RITUALS:
the programmed routines of daily organizational life that dramatize the organization's culture

Rituals and Ceremonies

Rituals are the programmed routines of daily organizational life that dramatize the organization's culture. They include how visitors are greeted, how often senior executives visit subordinates, how people communicate with each other, how much time employees take for lunch, and so on. **Ceremonies** are more formal artifacts than rituals. Ceremonies are planned activities conducted specifically for the benefit of an audience. This would include publicly rewarding (or punishing) employees, or celebrating the launch of a new product or newly won contract.

CEREMONIES:
planned displays of organizational culture, conducted specifically for the benefit of an audience

Organizational Language

The language of the workplace speaks volumes about the company's culture. How employees address co-workers, describe customers, express anger, and greet stakeholders are all verbal symbols of cultural values. Employees at The Container Store compliment each other about "being Gumby," meaning that they are being as flexible as the once-popular green toy to help customer or another employee.[13] When Charles Schwab & Co. acquired U.S. Trust, executives at U.S. Trust winced when they heard Schwab executives use the word *customers;* U.S. Trust staff have *clients,* a term that reflects more of a long-term and deep relationship.[14] Language also highlights values held by organizational subcultures. For instance, consultants working at Whirlpool kept hearing employees talk about the appliance company's "PowerPoint culture." This phrase, which names Microsoft's presentation software, is a critique of Whirlpool's hierarchical culture in which communication is one-way (from executives to employees.).[15]

Physical Structures and Symbols

Winston Churchill once said: "We shape our buildings; thereafter, they shape us."[16] The former British Prime Minister was reminding us that buildings both reflect and influence an organization's culture. The size, shape, location, and age of buildings might suggest the company's emphasis on teamwork, environmental friendliness, flexibility, or any other set of values. Even if the building doesn't make much of a statement, there is a treasure trove of physical artifacts inside. Desks, chairs, office space, and wall hangings (or lack of them) are just a few of the items that might convey cultural meaning.[17] Stroll through Wal-Mart's headquarters in Bentonville, Arkansas, and you will find a workplace that almost screams out frugality and efficiency. The world's largest retailer has a Spartan waiting room for suppliers, rather like government-office waiting areas. Visitors pay for their own soft drinks and coffee. In each of the building's inexpensive cubicles, employees sit at inexpensive desks finding ways to squeeze more efficiencies and lower costs out of suppliers as well as their own work processes.[18] Each of these artifacts alone might not say much, but put enough of them together and the company's cultural values become easier to decipher.

After reading the next section, you should be able to:

4. *Identify three functions of organizational culture.*

5. *Discuss the conditions under which organizational cultural strength improves organizational performance.*

learningobjectives<

>Is Organizational Culture Important?

Does corporate culture affect corporate performance? Many writers of popular management books think so.[19] However, the research evidence is somewhat more complicated. Specifically, companies with strong cultures tend to be more successful, but only under a particular set of conditions.[20] A *strong* organizational culture exists when most employees across all subunits hold the dominant values. The company's values are also institutionalized through well-established artifacts, thereby making it difficult for those values to change. Furthermore, strong cultures tend to be long lasting, sometimes traced back to the beliefs and values established by the company's founder. In contrast, companies have weak cultures when the dominant values are short-lived and held mainly by a few people at the top of the organization. A strong corporate culture potentially increases the company's success by serving three important functions:

1. *Control system.* Organizational culture is a deeply embedded form of social control that influences employee decisions and behavior.[21] Culture is pervasive and operates unconsciously. You might think of it as an automatic pilot, directing employees in ways that are consistent with organizational expectations.

2. *Social glue*. Organizational culture is the social glue that bonds people together and makes them feel part of the organizational experience.[22] Employees are motivated to internalize the organization's dominant culture because it fulfils their need for social identity. This social glue is increasingly important as a way to attract new staff and retain top performers.

3. *Sense-making*. Organizational culture assists the sense-making process.[23] It helps employees understand what goes on and why things happen in the company. Corporate culture also makes it easier for them to understand what is expected of them and to interact with other employees who know the culture and believe in it.

Contingencies of Organizational Culture and Performance

The best evidence is that only a modestly positive relationship exists between culture strength and success. One reason is that a strong culture increases organizational performance only when the cultural content is appropriate for the organization's environment. Consider the situation that Dell currently faces. As was described in the opening vignette to this chapter, Dell's culture gives the highest priority to cost efficiency and competitiveness, yet these values and assumptions are no longer ideal for the marketplace. Low-cost computers are still popular, but consumers increasingly demand computers that are innovative and look "cool." Dell has a strong culture, but apparently no longer the right culture for the situation.

The second reason is that very strong cultures lock decision makers into mental models that blind them to new opportunities and unique problems. In strong cultures, decision makers overlook or incorrectly define subtle misalignments between the organization's activities and the changing environment. Dell faced this problem. Although Kevin Rollins and Michael Dell realized that the company's culture put too much emphasis on financial performance (staff even had stock tickers on their computer screens) and tolerated people who didn't collaborate, their solution (called "The Soul of Dell") supplemented, but never questioned, the company's core values and assumptions. "It's not that we didn't have a culture with the qualities that drive business success," explained one Dell executive a few years ago. "We just aspired to do better."[24]

A third reason for the weak link between strong organizational culture and firm performance is that very strong cultures tend to suppress dissenting subcultural values. At Dell, for instance, anyone who questioned the company's almost sacred values and assumptions were quickly silenced. The challenge for organizational leaders is to maintain a strong culture, but one that allows subcultural diversity. Subcultures encourage constructive conflict, which improves creative thinking and offers some level of ethical vigilance over the dominant culture. In the long run, the subculture's nascent values could become important dominant values as the environment changes. Strong cultures suppress subcultures, thereby undermining these benefits.

ADAPTIVE CULTURE: an organizational culture in which employees focus on the changing needs of customers and other stakeholders, and support initiatives to keep pace with those changes

Adaptive Cultures

One last contingency to mention in this discussion on organizational culture and performance is that organizations are more likely to succeed when they have an adaptive culture.[25] An **adaptive culture** exists when employees focus on the changing needs of customers and other stakeholders, and support initiatives to keep pace with these changes. Adaptive cultures have an external focus, and employees assume responsibility for the organization's performance. As a result, they are proactive and quick. Employees seek out opportunities, rather than wait for them to arrive.

Organizational Culture and Business Ethics

An organization's culture influences more than just the bottom line; it can also affect the ethical conduct of its employees. This makes sense because good behavior is driven by ethical values, and ethical values can become embedded into an organization's dominant culture. A few years ago, Michael Dell and former CEO Kevin Rollins saw this connection between culture and ethics when they launched the "Soul of Dell." Concerned about employee obsession with the company's stock price, the executives tried to shift the company's winning culture into one that emphasizes "winning with integrity."[26] For example, one of the revised company values referred to "behaving ethically in every interaction and in every aspect of how we conduct business." Unfortunately, the Soul of Dell initiative probably didn't change the company's culture. The company recently admitted that some Dell executives had manipulated the company books to reach performance targets that would give them a larger bonus.[27]

After reading the next three sections, you should be able to: **learning**objectives<

6. Identify the four strategies to change or strengthen an organization's culture.

7. Apply attraction-selection-attrition theory to explain how organizational culture strengthens.

8. Describe the stages of organizational socialization.

9. Compare and contrast four strategies for merging organizational cultures.

>Changing and Strengthening Organizational Culture

Is it possible to change an organization's culture? Yes, but it isn't easy, it rarely occurs quickly, and oftentimes the culture ends up changing (or replacing) corporate leaders. At the same time, under the right conditions, organizational culture can be a powerful influence on the company's success. So, how do some people successfully change and strengthen organizational culture? Over the next few pages, we will highlight four strategies that have had some success. This list, outlined in Exhibit 13.3, is not exhaustive, but each activity seems to work well under the right circumstances.

Actions of Founders and Leaders

An organization's culture begins with its founders and leaders.[28] You can see this at Dell, Inc., where founder Michael Dell established a competitive and cost-focused culture. Founders are often visionaries who provide a powerful role model for others to follow. Experts suggest that the company's culture sometimes reflects the founder's personality, and that this cultural imprint often remains with the organization for decades. In fact, some observers say that Dell's culture is so much a part of Michael Dell's personal orientation to life that he might not be the best person to try to change Dell's culture. Founders establish an organization's culture, but they and subsequent CEOs are sometimes able to reshape that culture if they apply transformational leadership and organizational change practices. For instance, through his symbolic and substantive actions as a leader, Procter & Gamble chief

[Exhibit 13.3] Strategies to Change and Strengthen Organizational Culture

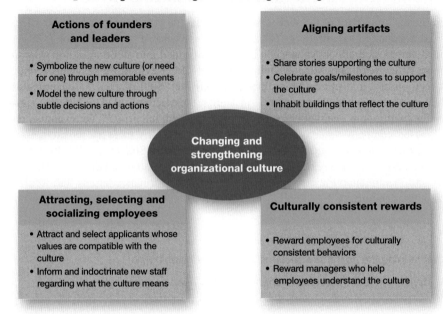

executive A. G. Lafley has transformed the consumer goods company's culture into one that is much more customer focused.

Aligning Artifacts

Artifacts represent more than just the visible indicators of a company's culture. They are also mechanisms that keep the culture in place. By altering artifacts—or creating new ones—leaders can potentially adjust the organization's culture. A dramatic example is moving the company or business unit into new offices that reflect a different culture. National Australia Bank's (NAB) culture is a case in point. By moving into a low-rise campus-like building in Melbourne's docklands area, NAB executives hope to replace the company's hierarchical, bureaucratic culture with one that is more open, egalitarian, and creative. NAB realized that building artifacts can change corporate culture when they observed this happen at MLC, a financial services firm that NAB had acquired a few years earlier. "There's no doubt that MLC has moved its culture over the last few years to a more open and transparent style which is a good example for the rest of the group to follow," admits a NAB executive.[29]

Corporate cultures are also altered and strengthened through the artifacts of stories and behaviors. According to Max De Pree, former CEO of furniture manufacturer Herman Miller Inc., every organization needs "tribal storytellers" to keep the organization's history and culture alive.[30] Leaders play a role by creating memorable events that symbolize the cultural values they want to develop or maintain. At Wall Street investment firm Goldman Sachs, this leadership function is so important that they are called *culture carriers*. Goldman's senior executives live and breathe the company's culture so much that they can effectively transmit and reinforce that culture.[31] Companies also strengthen culture in new operations by transferring current employees who abide by the culture.

Introducing Culturally Consistent Rewards

Reward systems are artifacts that often have a powerful effect on strengthening or reshaping an organization's culture.[32] When Robert Nardelli was hired to transform Home Depot's freewheeling culture, he introduced precise measures of corporate performance and drilled managers with weekly performance objectives around those metrics. A two-hour weekly conference call became a ritual in which Home Depot's top executives were held accountable for the previous week's goals. These actions reinforced a more disciplined (and centralized), performance-oriented culture.[33]

Attracting, Selecting, and Socializing Employees

Organizational culture is strengthened by attracting and hiring people who already embrace the cultural values, then socializing them to more clearly understand the company's culture. This process, along with weeding out people who don't fit the culture, is explained by **attraction-selection-attrition (ASA) theory.**[34] ASA theory states that organizations have a natural tendency to attract, select, and retain people with values and personality characteristics that are consistent with the organization's character, resulting in a more homogeneous organization and a stronger culture.

> **ATTRACTION-SELECTION-ATTRITION (ASA) THEORY:** states that organizations have a natural tendency to attract, select, and retain people with values and personality characteristics that are consistent with the organization's character, resulting in a more homogeneous organization and a stronger culture

- *Attraction.* Job applicants engage in self-selection by avoiding employment in companies whose values seem incompatible with their own values.[35] Companies often encourage this self-selection by actively describing their culture, but applicants will look for evidence of the company's culture even when it is not advertised. Applicants also inspect organizational artifacts when visiting the company.
- *Selection.* How well a job applicant fits in with the company's culture is typically a factor in deciding which job applicants to hire. Companies with strong cultures often put applicants through several interviews and other selection tests, in part to better gauge the applicant's values and their congruence with the company's values.[36]
- *Attrition.* People are motivated to seek out environments that are sufficiently congruent with their personal values, and to leave environments with a poor fit. This occurs because person-organization values congruence supports their social identity and minimizes internal role conflict. Consequently, employees are more likely to quit or be fired if values incongruence is sufficiently high.[37]

>Organizational Socialization

Companies maintain strong cultures through the process of **organizational socialization**—the process by which individuals learn the values, expected behaviors, and social knowledge necessary to assume their roles in the organization.[38] By communicating the company's dominant values, job candidates and new hires are more likely to internalize these values quickly and deeply. "The cultural aspects of our training programs are at least as important as the technical aspects," says an executive at JetBlue, the New York-based discount airline. "The People Department will find the right people and we will inculcate the culture into them and nurture that culture until we release them out into the operation."[39] When employees are effectively socialized into the organization, they tend to perform better and have higher job satisfaction.[40]

> **ORGANIZATIONAL SOCIALIZATION:** the process by which individuals learn the values, expected behaviors, and social knowledge necessary to assume their roles in the organization

Organizational socialization is a process of both learning and adjustment. It is a learning process because newcomers try to make sense of the company's physical workplace, social dynamics, and strategic/cultural environment. Organizational socialization is a process of adjustment because individuals need to adapt to their new work environment. They develop new work roles that reconfigure their social identity, adopt new team norms, and practice new behaviors.

[Exhibit 13.4] Stages of Organizational Socialization

Preemployment socialization (outsider)	Encounter (newcomer)	Role management (insider)	Socialization outcomes
• Learn about the organization and job • Form employment relationship expectations	• Test expectations against perceived realities	• Strengthen work relationships • Practice new role behaviors • Resolve work-nonwork conflicts	• Higher motivation • Higher loyalty • Higher satisfaction • Lower stress • Lower turnover

Socialization is most intense when people move across organizational boundaries, such as when they first join a company or get transferred to an international assignment. Exhibit 13.4 shows the three stages of socialization, which represent the individual's transition from outsider, to newcomer, and then to insider.[41] The preemployment socialization stage encompasses all of the learning and adjustment that occurs prior to the first day of work in a new position. In fact, a large part of the socialization adjustment process occurs prior to the first day of work.[42] As outsiders, however, people rely on indirect and often distorted information about what it is like to work in the organization. Job applicants might distort their résumés, while employers hide their blemishes by presenting overly positive images of organizational life.

The first day on the job typically marks the beginning of the encounter stage of organizational socialization. This is the stage in which newcomers test their prior expectations with the perceived realities. Many companies fail the test, resulting in **reality shock**—the stress that results when employees perceive discrepancies between their preemployment expectations and on-the-job reality.[43] Role management, the third stage of organizational socialization, actually begins during preemployment socialization, but is most active as employees make the transition from newcomers to insiders. They strengthen relationships with co-workers and supervisors, practice new role behaviors, and adopt attitudes and values consistent with their new position and organization. Role

REALITY SHOCK the stress that results when employees perceive discrepancies between their preemployment expectations and on-the-job reality

Whole Foods Spreads Its Culture Like Yoghurt

How do companies maintain their corporate culture when expanding operations? At Whole Foods Market, the solution is yoghurt. "One of our secrets is what I refer to as our 'yoghurt culture,'" explains Whole Foods cofounder John Mackey. This strategy involves transferring employees who carry Whole Foods' unique culture to new stores so recently hired employees learn and embrace that culture more quickly. "For example, in our Columbus Circle store in New York, about 25 percent of the team members transferred from existing stores," Mackey recalls. "They were the starting culture for the fermentation that turned Columbus Circle into a true Whole Foods store." Some employees even took lesser titles just to help Columbus Circle adopt Whole Foods' cultural values. For example, the store's two associate store team leaders previously operated their own stores in Georgetown, Maryland, and Albuquerque, New Mexico, before coming to New York.[44]

management also involves resolving the conflicts between work and nonwork activities, including resolving discrepancies between employees' existing values and those emphasized by the organizational culture.

>Merging Organizational Cultures

4C, Corporate Culture Clash & Chemistry, is a company with an unusual name and mandate. The Dutch consulting firm helps clients to determine whether their culture is aligned (chemistry) or incompatible (clash) with a potential acquisition or merger partner. The firm also analyzes the company's culture with its strategy. There should be plenty of demand for 4C's expertise. According to various studies, the majority of corporate mergers and acquisitions fail, mostly because corporate leaders are so focused on the financial or marketing logistics of a merger that they don't conduct due-diligence audits on their respective corporate cultures.[45]

The marriage of AOL with Time Warner is one of the most spectacular recent examples. In theory, the world's largest merger offered huge opportunities for converging AOL's dominance in Internet services with Time Warner's deep knowledge and assets in traditional media. Instead, the two corporate cultures mixed like oil and water. AOL's culture valued youthful, high-flying, quick deal-making people who were rewarded with stock options. Time Warner, on the other hand, had a button-down, hierarchical, and systematic culture. Executives were older and the reward was a decent retirement package (affectionately known as the "golden rubber band" because people who left earlier in their career usually returned for the retirement benefit).[46]

Organizational leaders can minimize these cultural collisions and fulfill their duty of due diligence by conducting a **bicultural audit,** which diagnoses cultural relations between the companies and determines the extent to which cultural clashes will likely occur.[47] The bicultural audit process begins by identifying cultural differences between the merging companies. Next, the bicultural audit data are analyzed to determine which differences between the two firms will result in conflict and which cultural values provide common ground on which to build a cultural foundation in the merged organization. The final stage involves identifying strategies and preparing action plans to bridge the two organizations' cultures.

> **BICULTURAL AUDIT:** a process of diagnosing cultural relations between the companies and determining the extent to which cultural clashes will likely occur

Strategies to Merge Different Organizational Cultures

In some cases, the bicultural audit results in a decision to end merger talks because the two cultures are too different to merge effectively. However, even with substantially different cultures, two companies may form a workable union if they apply the appropriate merger strategy. The four main strategies for merging different corporate cultures are assimilation, deculturation, integration, and separation (see Exhibit 13.5).[48]

Assimilation

Assimilation occurs when employees at the acquired company willingly embrace the cultural values of the acquiring organization. Typically, this strategy works best when the acquired company has a weak dysfunctional culture, whereas the acquiring company's culture is strong and aligned with the external environment. Culture clash is rare with assimilation because the acquired firm's culture is weak and employees are looking for better cultural alternatives. Research in Motion (RIM), the company that makes BlackBerry wireless devices, applies the assimilation strategy by deliberately acquiring only small start-up firms. "Small companies . . . don't have cultural issues," says RIM co-CEO Jim Balsillie, adding that they are typically absorbed into RIM's culture with little fuss or attention.[49]

[Exhibit 13.5] Strategies for Merging Different Organizational Cultures

Merger Strategy	Description	Works Best When:
Assimilation	Acquired company embraces acquiring firm's culture.	Acquired firm has a weak culture.
Deculturation	Acquiring firm imposes its culture on unwilling acquired firm.	Rarely works—may be necessary only when acquired firm's culture doesn't work but employees don't realize it.
Integration	Combining the two or more cultures into a new composite culture.	Existing cultures can be improved.
Separation	Merging companies remain distinct entities with minimal exchange of culture or organizational practices.	Firms operate successfully in different businesses requiring different cultures.

Source: Based on ideas in A. R. Malekazedeh and A. Nahavandi, "Making Mergers Work by Managing Cultures," *Journal of Business Strategy,* May/June 1990, pp. 55–57; K. W. Smith, "A Brand-New Culture for the Merged Firm," *Mergers and Acquisitions,* 35 (June 2000), pp. 45–50.

Deculturation

Assimilation is rare. Employees usually resist organizational change, particularly when they are asked to throw away personal and cultural values. Under these conditions, some acquiring companies apply a *deculturation* strategy by imposing their culture and business practices on the acquired organization. The acquiring firm strips away artifacts and reward systems that support the old culture. People who cannot adopt the acquiring company's culture are often terminated. Deculturation may be necessary when the acquired firm's culture doesn't work but employees aren't convinced of this. However, this strategy is difficult to apply effectively because the acquired firm's employees resist the cultural intrusions from the buying firm, thereby delaying or undermining the merger process.

Integration

A third strategy is to combine the two or more cultures into a new composite culture that preserves the best features of the previous cultures. Integration is slow and potentially risky, because there are many forces preserving the existing cultures. Still, this strategy should be considered when the companies have relatively weak cultures, or when their cultures include several overlapping values. Integration also works best when people realize that their existing cultures are ineffective and are, therefore, motivated to adopt a new set of dominant values.

Separation

A separation strategy occurs where the merging companies agree to remain distinct entities with minimal exchange of culture or organizational practices. This strategy is most appropriate when the two merging companies are in unrelated industries or operate in different countries, because the most appropriate cultural values tend to differ by industry and national culture. Unfortunately, executives in the acquiring firm have difficulty keeping their hands off the acquired firm. It's not surprising, therefore, that only 15 percent of acquisitions leave the purchased organization as a stand-alone unit.[50]

A Marriage of Cultural Separation

Cisco Systems, the California-based Internet equipment maker, has acquired approximately 90 companies over the past two decades, most of them small, privately held start-up firms with technical expertise in high-growth niches compatible with Cisco's own products. For most acquisitions, Cisco assimilates the smaller firm into its own culture. Linksys, the home wireless network company founded by Janie and Victor Tsao, was an exception. Linksys employs 400 people and was just a few years younger than Cisco. Furthermore, unlike Cisco, Linksys had developed a low-cost business with mass-market retail channels. To avoid disrupting its success, Cisco made sure that Linksys kept its own culture. Cisco executives were so concerned about this that a "filtering team" was formed to prevent Cisco's culture or its leaders from taking over the smaller enterprise. So far, the strategy has worked. Linksys continues to thrive in a competitive low-cost market even though wholly owned by Cisco, which focuses on the high-end network business.[51]

>Chapter Summary

Organizational culture refers to the values and assumptions shared within an organization. Shared assumptions are unconscious taken-for-granted perceptions or beliefs that have worked so well in the past that they are considered the correct way to think and act toward problems and opportunities. Values are stable, evaluative beliefs that guide our preferences for outcomes or courses of action in a variety of situations.

Organizations differ in their cultural content; that is, the relative ordering of values. There are several classifications of organizational culture, but they tend to oversimplify the wide variety of cultures, and completely ignore the underlying assumptions of culture. Organizations have subcultures as well as the dominant culture. Subcultures maintain the organization's standards of performance and ethical behavior. They are also the source of emerging values that replace aging core values.

Artifacts are the observable symbols and signs of an organization's culture. Four broad categories of artifacts include organizational stories and legends, rituals and ceremonies, organizational language, and physical structures and symbols. Understanding an organization's culture requires assessment of many artifacts because they are subtle and often ambiguous.

Organizational culture has three main functions. It is a deeply embedded form of social control. It is also the social glue that bonds people together and makes them feel part of the organizational experience. Third, corporate culture helps employees make sense of the workplace.

Companies with strong cultures generally perform better than those with weak cultures, but only when the cultural content is appropriate for the organization's environment. Also, the culture should not be so strong that it drives out dissenting values, from which may form emerging values for the future. Organizations should have adaptive cultures so that employees focus on the need for change and support initiatives and leadership that keeps pace with these changes.

Organizational culture is very difficult to change, but it has been done and is sometimes necessary for the company's continued survival. Four strategies to change and strengthen an organization's culture are the actions of founders and leaders; aligning artifacts with the desired culture; introducing culturally consistent rewards; and attracting, selecting, and socializing employees.

Attraction-selection-attrition (ASA) theory states that organizations have a natural tendency to attract, select, and retain people with values and personality characteristics that are consistent with the organization's character, resulting in a more homogeneous organization and a stronger culture. Organizational socialization is the process by which individuals learn the values, expected behaviors, and social knowledge necessary to assume their roles in the organization. It is a process of both learning about the work context and adjusting to new work roles, team norms, and behaviors. Employees typically pass through three socialization stages: preemployment, encounter, and role management.

Mergers should include a bicultural audit to diagnose the compatibility of the organizational cultures. The four main strategies for merging different corporate cultures are integration, deculturation, assimilation, and separation.

>key terms

adaptive culture 280

artifacts 277

attraction-selection-attrition (ASA) theory 283

bicultural audit 285

ceremonies 278

organizational culture 275

organizational socialization 283

reality shock 284

rituals 278

>critical thinking questions

1. Superb Consultants have submitted a proposal to analyze the cultural values of your organization. The proposal states that Superb has developed a revolutionary new survey to tap the company's true culture. The survey takes just 10 minutes to complete and the consultants say results can be based on a small sample of employees. Discuss the merits and limitations of this proposal.

2. Some people suggest that the most effective organizations have the strongest cultures. What do we mean by the "strength" of organizational culture, and what possible problems are there with a strong organizational culture?

3. The CEO of a manufacturing firm wants everyone to support the organization's dominant culture of lean efficiency and hard work. The CEO has introduced a new reward system to reinforce this culture and personally interviews all professional and managerial applicants to ensure that they bring similar values to the organization. Some employees who criticized these values had their careers sidelined until they left. Two mid-level managers were fired for supporting contrary values, such as work-life balance. Based on your knowledge of organizational subcultures, what potential problems is the CEO creating?

4. Identify at least two artifacts you have observed in your department or faculty from each of the four broad categories: (a) organizational stories and legends, (b) rituals and ceremonies, (c) organizational language, and (d) physical structures and symbols.

5. "Organizations are more likely to succeed when they have an adaptive culture." What can an organization do to foster an adaptive culture?

6. Suppose you are asked by senior officers of a city government to identify ways to reinforce a new culture of teamwork and collaboration. The senior executive group clearly supports these values, but it wants everyone in the organization to embrace them. Identify four types of activities that would strengthen these cultural values.

7. Socialization is most intense when people pass through organizational boundaries. One example is your entry into the college or university that you are now attending. What learning and adjustment occurred as you moved from outsider to newcomer to insider as a student here.

8. Acme Corp. is planning to acquire Beta Corp., which operates in a different industry. Acme's culture is entrepreneurial and fast-paced, whereas Beta employees value slow, deliberate decision making by consensus. Which merger strategy would you recommend to minimize culture shock when Acme acquires Beta? Explain your answer.

>web exercise 13-1

Diagnosing Corporate Culture Proclamations

Purpose To understand the importance and context in which corporate culture is identified and discussed in organizations.

Instructions

This exercise is a take-home activity, although it can be completed in classes with computers and Internet connections. The instructor will divide the class into small teams (typically four to five people per team). Each team is assigned a specific industry—such as energy, biotechnology, or computer hardware.

The team's task is to search Web sites of several companies in the selected industry for company statements about their corporate culture. Use the company Web site search engine (if it exists) to find documents with key phrases such as "corporate culture" or "company values."

In the next class, or at the end of the time allotted in the current class, students will report on their observations by answering the following three discussion questions:

Discussion Questions

1. What values seem to dominate the corporate culture of the companies you searched? Are these values similar or diverse across companies in the industry?

2. What was the broader content of the Web pages where these companies described or mentioned its corporate culture?

3. Do companies in this industry refer to their corporate culture on the Web sites more or less than companies in other industries searched by the team in this class?

Find the complete interactive self-assessment at this textbook's Web site at
www.mhhe.com/mcshaneEss2e.

>self-assessment exercise 13-2

Corporate Culture Preference Scale

This self-assessment is designed to help you to identify a corporate culture that fits most closely with your personal values and assumptions. The scale does not attempt to measure your preference for every corporate culture, just a few of the more common varieties. Read each pair of the statements, and select the statement that describes the organization you would prefer to work in. Keep in mind that none of these corporate cultures is inherently good or bad. The focus here is on how well you fit within each of them. This self-assessment is completed alone so students assess themselves honestly without concerns of social comparison. However, class discussion will focus on the importance of matching job applicants to the organization's dominant values.

chapter 14

Organizational Change

The 9/11 attacks gave the FBI a new mandate, and the monumental challenge of transforming itself from a reactive law enforcement agency into a proactive domestic intelligence agency.

>learningobjectives

After reading this chapter, you should be able to:

1. Describe the elements of Lewin's force field analysis model.

2. Outline six reasons why people resist organizational change.

3. Discuss six strategies to minimize resistance to change.

4. Outline the conditions for effectively diffusing change from a pilot project.

5. Describe the action research approach to organizational change.

6. Outline the Four-D model of appreciative inquiry and explain how this approach differs from action research.

7. Explain how parallel learning structures assist the change process.

8. Discuss four ethical issues in organizational change.

For the past century, the Federal Bureau of Investigation's (FBI's) structure, work processes, budgets, information systems, reward systems, leadership, and culture were designed for its primary mission—solving crimes and catching criminals. Observers say the FBI is bureaucratic, rigid, and distinctly behind the times in computer technology (most of its records are still paper-based). It is also a highly decentralized organization, with field agents operating without much orchestration from headquarters.

These organizational characteristics work reasonably well for investigating crimes *after* they have been committed. But the FBI's mandate has changed in response to the 9/11 attacks on the World Trade Center. Now, the bureau must become more of a domestic intelligence agency, proactively collecting information and preventing acts of terrorism *before* they occur. This new mandate requires massive change. "It's almost a total transformation of what the bureau does and how it does it. It's staggering," says former U.S. attorney general Dick Thornburgh, who has been asked by Congress to assist FBI director Robert Mueller in the transformation process. Mueller also acknowledges the challenges of changing the FBI. "I've come to find that one of the most difficult things one has to do is to bring an entity through the development of a change of business practices," he says.[1]

Change is difficult enough in small firms. At the Federal Bureau of Investigation and other large organizations, it requires monumental effort and persistence. Organizational change is also very messy. As we will describe throughout this chapter, FBI leaders have introduced numerous strategies to help employees shift their mind-set and behavior toward the agency's new mission. Some of these actions have proven successful; others have not. This chapter examines ways to bring about meaningful change in organizations. We begin by introducing Lewin's model of change and its component parts. This includes sources of resistance to change, ways to minimize this resistance, and stabilizing desired behaviors. Next, this chapter examines three approaches to organizational change—action research, appreciative inquiry, and parallel learning structures. The last section of this chapter considers both cross-cultural and ethical issues in organizational change.

After reading the next two sections, you should be able to:

1. *Describe the elements of Lewin's force field analysis model.*
2. *Outline six reasons why people resist organizational change.*
3. *Discuss six strategies to minimize resistance to change.*
4. *Outline the conditions for effectively diffusing change from a pilot project.*

learningobjectives<

>Lewin's Force Field Analysis Model

Social psychologist Kurt Lewin developed the force field analysis model to help us understand how the change process works (see Exhibit 14.1).[2] Although developed more than 50 years ago, Lewin's **force field analysis** model remains one of the most widely respected ways of viewing this process.[3]

One side of the force field model represents the *driving forces* that push organizations toward a new state of affairs. These might include new competitors or technologies, evolving workforce expectations, or a host of other environmental changes. Corporate leaders also produce driving forces even when external forces for change aren't apparent. For instance, some experts call for "divine discontent" as a key feature of successful organizations, meaning that leaders continually urge employees to strive for higher standards or new innovations even when the company outshines the competition.

FORCE FIELD ANALYSIS: Kurt Lewin's model of system-wide change that helps change agents diagnose the forces that drive and restrain proposed organizational change

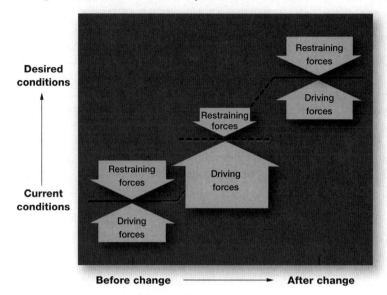

[Exhibit 14.1] Lewin's Force Field Analysis Model

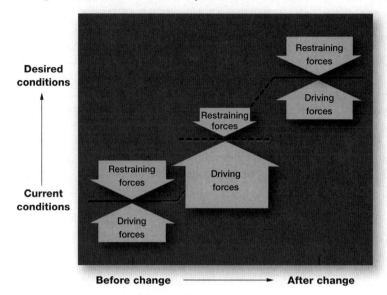

Before change ⟶ After change

UNFREEZING: the first part of the change process whereby the change agent produces disequilibrium between the driving and restraining forces

REFREEZING: the latter part of the change process in which systems and conditions are introduced that reinforce and maintain the desired behaviors

The other side of Lewin's model represents the *restraining forces* that maintain the status quo. These restraining forces are commonly called *resistance to change* because they appear as employee behaviors that block the change process. Stability occurs when the driving and restraining forces are roughly in equilibrium; that is, they are of approximately equal strength in opposite directions.

Lewin's force field model emphasizes that effective change occurs by **unfreezing** the current situation, moving to a desired condition, and then **refreezing** the system so that it remains in this desired state. Unfreezing involves producing disequilibrium between the driving and restraining forces. As we will describe later, this may occur by increasing the driving forces, reducing the restraining forces, or having a combination of both. Refreezing occurs when the organization's systems and structures are aligned with the desired behaviors. They must support and reinforce the new role patterns and prevent the organization from slipping back into the old way of doing things. Over the next few pages, we use Lewin's model to understand why change is blocked and how the process can evolve more smoothly.

Restraining Forces

Economist John Kenneth Galbraith once quipped that when faced with the prospect of changing the status quo or proving why change isn't needed, most people get busy on the proof. The FBI is a classic example of this natural tendency of people to resist change. The bureau's new mandate to develop domestic intelligence capabilities didn't begin after the 9/11 attacks on the World Trade Center; they were issued after the same buildings were attacked eight years earlier. A U.S. presidential commission recently found that the FBI had changed little, which may have contributed to its failure to prevent the 9/11 attacks. The report even stated that the FBI (as well as the CIA) "seem to be working harder and harder just to maintain a status quo that is increasingly irrelevant to the new challenges." John Miller, the FBI's assistant director of the office of public affairs, acknowledges that the FBI faces numerous restraining forces. "The FBI has no corner on the market of people being resistant to change," he says. "We don't recruit people from Planet Perfect; we recruit human beings."[4]

Employee resistance takes many forms, including passive noncompliance, complaints, absenteeism, turnover, and collective action (e.g., strikes, walkouts). This resistance is a symptom of deeper problems in the change process, so leaders need to investigate and remove the causes of resistance.[5] In some situations, employees may be worried about the *consequences* of change, such as how the new conditions will take away their power and status. In other situations, employees show resistance because of concerns about the *process* of change itself, such as the effort required to break old habits and learn new skills. Here are the six main reasons why people resist change:[6]

- *Direct costs*. People tend to block actions that result in higher direct costs or lower benefits than the existing situation. Some FBI managers likely resisted the bureau's new intelligence mandate because it would necessarily remove some of their resources, personal status, and career opportunities.

- *Saving face*. Some people resist change as a political strategy to "prove" that the decision is wrong or that the person encouraging change is incompetent. This not-invented-here syndrome is widespread, according to change experts. Says one consultant: "Unless they're scared enough to listen, they'll never forgive you for being right and for knowing something they don't."[7]

- *Fear of the unknown*. People resist change out of worry that they cannot adjust to the new work requirements. This fear of the unknown increases the *risk* of personal loss. For example, one company owner wanted sales staff to telephone rather than personally visit prospective customers. With no experience in telephone sales, they complained about the changes. Some even avoided the training program that taught them how to make telephone sales.[8]

- *Breaking routines*. The organizational learning perspective introduced in Chapter 1 emphasizes the need to bring in new knowledge, but it also recognizes the need to *unlearn*. This means that employees need to abandon habits and routines that are no longer appropriate. Unfortunately, people like to stay within comfort zones, and typically resist initiatives that force them out of those comfort zones and require investing time and energy learning new role patterns.

- *Incongruent organizational systems*. Rewards, information systems, patterns of authority, career paths, selection criteria, and other systems and structures are both friends and foes of organizational change. When properly aligned, they reinforce desired behaviors. Unfortunately, the FBI and many other organizations fail to realign these systems to reinforce the change initiative. The result is that even enthusiastic employees lose momentum after failing to overcome the structural confines of the past.

- *Incongruent team dynamics*. Teams develop and enforce conformity to a set of norms that guide behavior. However, conformity to existing team norms may discourage employees from accepting organizational change. Team norms that conflict with the desired changes need to be altered.

>Unfreezing, Changing, and Refreezing

According to Lewin's force field analysis model, effective change occurs by unfreezing the current situation, moving to a desired condition, and then refreezing the system so that it remains in this desired state. Unfreezing occurs when the driving forces are stronger than the restraining forces. This happens by making the driving forces stronger, weakening or removing the restraining forces, or a combination of both.

With respect to the first option, driving forces must increase enough to motivate change. Change rarely occurs by increasing driving forces alone, however, because the restraining forces often adjust to counterbalance the driving forces. It is rather like the coils of a mattress. The harder corporate leaders push for change, the stronger the restraining forces push back. This antagonism threatens the change effort by producing tension and conflict within the organization. The preferred option is to both increase the driving forces and reduce or remove the restraining forces. Increasing the driving forces creates an urgency for change, whereas reducing the restraining forces minimizes resistance to change.

Creating an Urgency for Change

New competitors, changing consumer trends, impending government regulations, and other environmental changes represent the driving forces that energize people to face the risks that change creates. In many organizations, however, corporate leaders buffer employees from the external environment to such an extent that these driving forces are hardly felt below the top-executive level. The result is that employees don't understand why they need to change, and leaders are surprised when their change initiatives do not have much effect. Thus, the change process must begin by ensuring employees have an urgency to change, and this typically occurs by informing them about competitors, changing consumer trends, impending government regulations, and other driving forces.[9]

Some companies fuel the urgency to change by putting employees in direct contact with customers. Dissatisfied customers represent a compelling driving force for change because of the adverse consequences for the organization's survival and success. Customers also provide a human element that further energizes employees to change current behavior patterns.[10]

Urging Change without External Forces

Exposing employees to external forces can strengthen the urgency for change, but leaders often need to begin the change process before problems come knocking at the company's door. "You want to create a burning platform for change even when there isn't a need for one," says Steve Bennett, CEO of financial software company Intuit.[11] Creating an urgency for change when the organization is riding high requires a lot of persuasive influence that helps employees visualize future competitive threats and environmental shifts.

For instance, Apple's iPod dominates the digital music market, but Steve Jobs wants the company to be its own toughest competitor. Just when sales of the iPod Mini were soaring, Jobs challenged a gathering of Apple's top 100 executives and engineers to develop a better product to replace it. "Playing it safe is the most dangerous thing we can do," Jobs warned. Nine months later, the company launched the iPod Nano, which replaced the still-popular iPod Mini before competitors could offer a better alternative.[12]

Shell Europe's Bus Ride of Change

Executives at Shell Europe applied customer-driven change when they discovered that middle managers seemed blissfully unaware that Shell wasn't achieving either its financial goals or customer needs. So, to create an urgency for change, the European managers were loaded onto buses and taken out to talk with customers and employees who work with customers every day. "We called these 'bus rides.' The idea was to encourage people to think back from the customer's perspective rather than from the head office," explains Shell Europe's vice president of retailing. "The bus rides were difficult for a lot of people who, in their work history, had hardly ever had to talk to a customer and find out what was good and not so good about Shell from the customer's standpoint."[13]

Reducing the Restraining Forces

Effective change requires more than making employees aware of the driving forces. It also involves reducing or removing the restraining forces. Exhibit 14.2 summarizes six ways to overcome employee resistance. Communication, learning, employee involvement, and stress management try to reduce the restraining forces and, if feasible, should be attempted first.[14] However, negotiation and coercion are necessary for people who will clearly lose something from the change and when the speed of change is critical.

Communication

One of FBI Director Robert Mueller's first strategies to change the bureau has been to communicate in every way possible and to as many audiences as possible that the FBI must change, why it must change, and what the new bureau will look like. "The word is out. Terrorism is the No. 1 priority, and intelligence is what the bureau is about," says former assistant attorney general Paul R. Corts, who has worked closely with the FBI during the change process. "You've got to say it, say it, and say it again." Communication is the highest priority and first strategy required for any organizational change.[15] Leaders rely on communication to create an urgency to change. In addition, communication can potentially

[Exhibit 14.2] Strategies to Minimize Resistance to Change

Strategy	Example	When Used	Problems
Communication	Customer complaint letters shown to employees.	When employees don't feel an urgency for change or don't know how the change will affect them.	Time-consuming and potentially costly.
Learning	Employees learn how to work in teams as company adopts a team-based structure.	When employees need to break old routines and adopt new role patterns.	Time-consuming and potentially costly.
Employee involvement	Company forms task force to recommend new customer service practices.	When the change effort needs more employee commitment, some employees need to save face, and/or employee ideas would improve decisions about the change strategy.	Very time-consuming; might also lead to conflict and poor decisions if employees' interests are incompatible with organizational needs.
Stress management	Employees attend sessions to discuss their worries about the change.	When communication, training, and involvement do not sufficiently ease employee worries.	Time-consuming and potentially expensive; some methods may not reduce stress for all employees.
Negotiation	Employees agree to replace strict job categories with multiskilling in return for increased job security.	When employees will clearly lose something of value from the change and would not otherwise support the new conditions; also necessary when the company must change quickly.	May be expensive, particularly if other employees want to negotiate their support; also tends to produce compliance but not commitment to the change.
Coercion	Company president tells managers to "get on board" the change or leave.	When other strategies are ineffective and the company needs to change quickly.	Can lead to more subtle forms of resistance, as well as long-term antagonism with the change agent.

Sources: Adapted from J. P. Kotter and L. A. Schlesinger, "Choosing Strategies for Change," *Harvard Business Review* 57 (1979), pp. 106–14; P. R. Lawrence, "How to Deal With Resistance to Change," *Harvard Business Review* (May–June 1954), pp. 49–57.

reduce fear of the unknown. The more corporate leaders communicate their images of the future, the more easily employees can visualize their own role in that future. This effort may also begin the process of adjusting team norms to be more consistent with the new reality.

Learning

Learning is an important process in most change initiatives because employees require new knowledge and skills to fit the organization's evolving requirements. The FBI leadership has invested heavily in training to help employees change the bureau into a more intelligence-focused organization. For example, the number of hours of training in counterterrorism and counterintelligence has nearly doubled. Hundreds of FBI executives have also been sent to weeklong courses to learn how to coach employees during the change process. Coaching and other forms of learning are time-consuming, but they help employees break routines by learning new role patterns.

Employee Involvement

Unless the change must occur quickly or employee interests are highly incompatible with the organization's needs, employee involvement is almost an essential part of the change process. Rather than viewing themselves as agents of someone else's decision, employees feel personally responsible for the success of the change effort.[16] Involvement also minimizes problems of saving face and fear of the unknown. Furthermore, the complexity of today's work environment demands that more people provide ideas regarding the best direction of the change effort.

FUTURE SEARCH: system-wide group sessions, usually lasting a few days, in which participants identify trends and identify ways to adapt to those changes

Supporting the change process through employee involvement is also possible in large organizations. **Future search** conferences (and a similar process called *open space*) "put the entire system in the room," meaning that they try to involve as many employees and other stakeholders as possible associated with the organizational system. These multiday events ask participants to identify trends or issues and establish strategic solutions for those conditions. One problem with future search and similar large-group change events is that a few people tend to dominate the process. Another concern is that these events generate high expectations about an ideal future state that are difficult to satisfy in practice. Employees become even more cynical and resistant to change if they do not see meaningful decisions and actions resulting from these meetings.[17] The State of Washington Department of Corrections recently held a future search event that tried to minimize these problems. The event involved a representation of 75 employees and managers who reached a consensus on the department's future direction. Department executives were then assigned specific recommendations to ensure that the conference results were put into place.[18]

Stress Management

Organizational change is a stressful experience for many people because it threatens self-esteem and creates uncertainty about the future. Communication, learning, and employee involvement can reduce some of these stressors. However, research indicates that companies also need to introduce stress management practices to help employees cope with the changes.[19] In particular, stress management minimizes resistance by removing some of the direct costs and fear of the unknown of the change process. Stress also saps energy, so minimizing stress potentially increases employee motivation to support the change process.

Negotiation

As long as people resist change, organizational change strategies will require some influence tactics. Negotiation is a form of influence that involves the promise of benefits or resources in exchange for the target person's compliance with the influencer's request. This strategy potentially activates those who would otherwise lose out from the change. However, it merely gains compliance rather than commitment to the change effort, so it might not be effective in the long term.

Coercion

If all else fails, leaders rely on coercion to change organizations. Coercion can include persistently reminding people of their obligations, frequently monitoring behavior to ensure compliance, confronting people who do not change, and using threats of sanctions to force compliance. Replacing people who will not support the change is an extreme step, but it is fairly common in senior management ranks. Replacing staff is a radical form of organizational unlearning because replacing executives removes knowledge of the organization's past routines. This potentially opens up opportunities for new practices to take hold.[20] At the same time, coercion is a risky strategy because survivors (employees who are not fired) may have less trust in corporate leaders and engage in more political tactics to protect their own job security.

Refreezing the Desired Conditions

Unfreezing and changing behavior patterns won't result in lasting change. People are creatures of habit, so they easily slip back into past patterns. Therefore, leaders need to refreeze the new behaviors by realigning organizational systems and team dynamics with the desired changes.[21] This refreezing is already underway at the FBI. New career paths are being established for intelligence officers rather than only for criminal investigation agents. The compensation system has been redesigned to reward staff who succeed in intelligence work rather than just criminal investigations. And in spite of scrapping a $170 million "virtual file" project a few years ago, the FBI is slowly developing information systems so agents can share knowledge quickly with each other and with other agencies (which is contrary to the bureau's culture of "close holds" on investigation files).

Change Agents and Strategic Visions

Kurt Lewin's force field analysis model is a useful template to explain the dynamics of organizational change. But it overlooks the fact that successful change requires a change agent who communicates an appealing vision of the desired future state.[22] A **change agent** is anyone who possesses enough knowledge and power to guide and facilitate the change effort. Change agents come in different forms, and more than one person is often required

> **CHANGE AGENT:** anyone who possesses enough knowledge and power to guide and facilitate the change effort

Change the School by Changing the Principal

A few years ago, test results at Sun Valley Middle School were so low that the San Fernando Valley, California, school was put on a U.S. federal government watch list for closer scrutiny. The Los Angeles Unified School District tried to help the principal and staff to improve, but to no avail. When a state audit reported that the school suffered from poor management, unsanitary conditions, and uneven classroom instruction, the school district applied a more radical change strategy: it replaced Sun Valley's principal and four assistant principals with new leaders. Sun Valley's new principal, Jeff Davis (shown with students in this photo), brought a more proactive vision for change. For example, he introduced extra English language instruction, reorganized class locations, and launched team teaching to foster a more collegial atmosphere among staff. Sun Valley still has a long way to go, but student test scores in math and English have tripled over the past three years. "That school is absolutely headed in the right direction," says Sue Shannon, superintendent of schools in the eastern San Fernando Valley.[23]

to serve these different roles.[24] Transformational leaders are the primary agents of change because they form a vision of the desired future state, communicate that vision in ways that are meaningful to others, behave in ways that are consistent with the vision, and build commitment to the vision.[25] A strategic vision is particularly important in the change process because it provides a sense of direction and establishes the critical success factors against which the real changes are evaluated. It also minimizes employee fear of the unknown and provides a better understanding about what behaviors employees must learn for the future state.

>**learning**objectives

After reading the next two sections, you should be able to:

5. *Describe the action research approach to organizational change.*

6. *Outline the Four-D model of appreciative inquiry and explain how this approach differs from action research.*

7. *Explain how parallel learning structures assist the change process.*

8. *Discuss three ethical issues in organizational change.*

>Three Approaches to Organizational Change

So far, this chapter has examined the dynamics of change that occur every day in organizations. However, organizational change agents and consultants also apply various approaches to organizational change. This section introduces three of the leading approaches to organizational change: action research, appreciative inquiry, and parallel learning structures.

Action Research Approach

ACTION RESEARCH: a problem-focused change process that combines action orientation (changing attitudes and behavior) and research orientation (testing theory through data collection and analysis)

Along with introducing the force field model, Kurt Lewin recommended an **action research** approach to the change process. Action research takes the view that meaningful change is a combination of action orientation (changing attitudes and behavior) and research orientation (testing theory).[26] On the one hand, the change process needs to be action-oriented because the ultimate goal is to bring about change. An action orientation involves diagnosing current problems and applying interventions that resolve those problems. On the other hand, the change process is a research study because change agents apply a conceptual framework (such as team dynamics or organizational culture) to a real situation. As with any good research, the change process involves collecting data to diagnose problems more effectively and to systematically evaluate how well the theory works in practice.[27]

Action research is also a highly participative process because change requires both the knowledge and commitment of those affected by the change. Indeed, employees are essentially co-researchers as well as participants in the intervention. Overall, action research is a data-based, problem-oriented process that diagnoses the need for change, introduces the intervention, and then evaluates and stabilizes the desired changes.[28]

1. *Form client–consultant relationship.* Action research usually assumes that the change agent originates outside the system (such as a consultant), so the process begins by forming the client–consultant relationship. Consultants need to determine the client's readiness for change, including whether people are motivated to participate in the process, are open to meaningful change, and possess the abilities to complete the process.

2. *Diagnose the need for change.* Action research is a problem-oriented activity that carefully diagnoses the problem through systematic analysis of the situation. Organizational diagnosis identifies the appropriate direction for the change effort by gathering and analyzing data about an ongoing system, such as through interviews and surveys of employees and other stakeholders. Organizational diagnosis also includes employee involvement in agreeing on the appropriate change method, the schedule for these actions, and the expected standards of successful change.

3. *Introduce intervention.* This stage in the action research model applies one or more actions to correct the problem. It may include any of the prescriptions mentioned in this textbook, such as building more effective teams, managing conflict, building a better organizational structure, or changing the corporate culture. An important issue is how quickly the changes should occur.[29] Some experts recommend *incremental change* in which the organization fine-tunes the system and takes small steps toward a desired state. Others claim that *quantum change* is often required, in which the system is overhauled decisively and quickly. Quantum change is usually traumatic to employees and offers little opportunity for correction. But incremental change is also risky when the organization is seriously misaligned with its environment, thereby threatening its survival.

4. *Evaluate and stabilize change.* Action research recommends evaluating the effectiveness of the intervention against the standards established in the diagnostic stage. Unfortunately, even when these standards are clearly stated, the effectiveness of an intervention might not be apparent for several years, or might be difficult to separate from other factors. If the activity has the desired effect, then the change agent and participants need to stabilize the new conditions. This refers to the refreezing process that was described earlier. Rewards, information systems, team norms, and other conditions are redesigned so that they support the new values and behaviors.

The action research approach has dominated organizational change thinking ever since it was introduced in the 1940s. However, some experts complain that the problem-oriented nature of action research—in which something is wrong that must be fixed—focuses on the negative dynamics of the group or system rather than its positive opportunities and potential. This concern with action research has led to the development of a more positive approach to organizational change, called *appreciative inquiry.*[30]

Appreciative Inquiry Approach

Appreciative inquiry tries to break out of the problem-solving mentality of traditional change management practices by reframing relationships around the positive and the possible. It searches for organizational (or team) strengths and capabilities, then adapts or applies that knowledge for further success and well-being. Appreciative inquiry is therefore deeply grounded in the emerging philosophy of *positive organizational behavior* (a variation of *positive psychology*), which focuses on building positive qualities and traits within individuals or institutions as opposed to focusing on just trying to fix what might be wrong with them.[31]

Appreciative inquiry typically directs its inquiry toward successful events and successful organizations or work units. This external focus becomes a form of behavioral modeling, but it also increases open dialogue by redirecting the group's attention away from its own problems. Appreciative inquiry is especially useful when participants are aware of their "problems" or already suffer from enough negativity in their relationships. The positive orientation of appreciative inquiry enables groups to overcome these negative tensions and build a more hopeful perspective of their future by focusing on what is possible.[32]

APPRECIATIVE INQUIRY: an organizational change strategy that directs the group's attention away from its own problems and focuses participants on the group's potential and positive elements

Canadian Tire's Appreciative Journey

After effectively battling the American juggernauts Wal-Mart and Home Depot over the past decade, Canadian Tire's executive team wanted to hear from employees and storeowners about what makes the Canadian hardware and auto parts retailer so successful, then rebuild its core values around those positive experiences. Appreciative inquiry played an important role in this re-visioning process. Internal consultants conducted detailed interviews with 377 staff members across the organization, asking each to describe occasions where they felt Canadian Tire was working at its best and what they value most about the company. Some people described the excitement of holiday season where products are flying out the door. Others recalled the teamwork of employees volunteering to work late to clean up a store after a major delivery. These appreciative incidents were organized around six team values (owners, driven, accountable, etc.), which the executive team discussed and affirmed. Canadian Tire then held a one-day conference in which middle and senior management developed a common understanding of these values. Next, store managers discussed the six team values with their staff and participated in an appreciative exercise in which employees visualized a good news story about Canadian Tire's success.[33]

The Four-D model of appreciative inquiry (named after its four stages) shown in Exhibit 14.3 begins with *discovery*—identifying the positive elements of the observed events or organization.[34] This might involve documenting positive customer experiences elsewhere in the organization. Or it might include interviewing members of another organization to discover its fundamental strengths. As participants discuss their findings, they shift into the *dreaming* stage by envisioning what might be possible in an ideal organization. By directing their attention to a theoretically ideal organization or situation, participants feel safer revealing their hopes and aspirations than if they were discussing their own organization or predicament.

As participants make their private thoughts public to the group, the process shifts into the third stage, called *designing*. Designing involves the process of dialogue, in which participants listen with selfless receptivity to each other's models and assumptions and eventually form a collective model for thinking within the team. In effect, they create a common image of what should be. As this model takes shape, group members shift the focus back to their own situation. In the final stage of appreciative inquiry, called *delivering,* participants

[Exhibit 13.3] The Four-D Model of Appreciative Inquiry

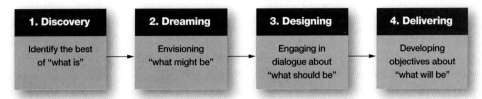

Source: Based on F. J. Barrett and D. L. Cooperrider, "Generative Metaphor Intervention: A New Approach for Working with Systems Divided by Conflict and Caught in Defensive Perception," *Journal of Applied Behavioral Science*, 26 (1990), p. 229; D. Whitney and C. Schau, "Appreciative Inquiry: An Innovative Process for Organization Change," *Employment Relations Today* 25 (Spring 1998), pp. 11–21; J. M. Watkins and B. J. Mohr, *Appreciative Inquiry: Change at the Speed of Imagination* (San Francisco: Jossey-Bass, 2001), pp. 25, 42–45.

establish specific objectives and direction for their own organization based on their model of what will be.

Appreciative inquiry was developed 20 years ago, but it only gained popularity within the past few years, partly due to success stories at Castrol Marine, the U.S. Environmental Protection Agency, AVON Mexico, American Express, Green Mountain Coffee Roasters, and Hunter Douglas, among others.[35] At the same time, this approach has not always been successful and experts warn that it is not always the best approach to changing teams or organizations. Specifically, it requires participants to have a mind-set where they are willing to let go of the problem-oriented approach, and where leaders are willing to accept appreciative inquiry's less-structured process.[36] Another concern is that research has not yet examined the contingencies of this approach.[37] Specifically, we don't yet know under what conditions appreciate inquiry is the best approach to organizational change, and under what conditions it is less effective. Overall, appreciative inquiry has much to offer the organizational change process, but we are just beginning to understand its potential and limitations.

Parallel Learning Structure Approach

Parallel learning structures are highly participative arrangements, composed of people from most levels of the organization who follow the action research model to produce meaningful organizational change. They are social structures developed alongside the formal hierarchy with the purpose of increasing the organization's learning.[38] Ideally, participants in parallel learning structures are sufficiently free from the constraints of the larger organization so they can more effectively solve organizational issues.

Royal Dutch/Shell relied on a parallel learning structure to introduce a more customer-focused organization.[39] Rather than try to change the entire organization at once, executives held week-long "retail boot camps" with six country teams of frontline people (e.g., gas station managers, truck drivers, marketing professionals). Participants learned about competitive trends in their regions and were taught powerful marketing tools to identify new opportunities. The teams then returned home to study their market and develop proposals for improvement. Four months later, boot camp teams returned for a second workshop where each proposal was critiqued by Royal/Dutch Shell executives. Each team had 60 days to put its ideas into action, then return for a third workshop to analyze what worked and what didn't. This parallel learning process did much more than introduce new marketing ideas. It created enthusiasm in participants that spread contagiously to their co-workers, including managers above them, when they returned to their home countries.

PARALLEL LEARNING STRUCTURE: highly participative arrangements, composed of people from most levels of the organization who follow the action research model to produce meaningful organizational change

>Cross-Cultural and Ethical Issues in Organizational Change

One significant concern with some organizational change interventions is that they originate in the United States and other Western countries and may conflict with cultural values in some other countries.[40] A few experts point out that this Western perspective of change is linear, such as in Lewin's force field model shown earlier. It also assumes that the change process is punctuated by tension and overt conflict. But these assumptions are incompatible with cultures that view change as a natural cyclical process with harmony and equilibrium as the objectives.[41] This dilemma suggests that we need to develop a more contingency-oriented perspective with respect to the cultural values of participants.

Some organizational change practices also face ethical issues.[42] One ethical concern is threats to the privacy rights of individuals. The action research model is built on the idea of collecting information from organizational members, yet this requires employees to provide personal information and reveal emotions that they may not want to divulge.[43] A second ethical concern is that some change activities potentially increase management's power by inducing compliance and conformity in organizational members. For instance, action research is a systemwide activity that requires employee participation rather than allowing individuals to get involved voluntarily. A third concern is that some organizational change interventions undermine the individual's self-esteem. The unfreezing process requires participants to disconfirm their existing beliefs, sometimes including their own competence at certain tasks or interpersonal relations.

Organizational change is almost always more difficult than it initially seems. Yet, the dilemma is that most organizations operate in hyperfast environments that demand continuous and rapid adaptation. Organizations survive and gain competitive advantage by mastering the complex dynamics of moving people through the continuous process of change as quickly as the external environment is changing.

>Organizational Behavior: The Journey Continues

Nearly 100 years ago, American industrialist Andrew Carnegie said, "Take away my people, but leave my factories, and soon grass will grow on the factory floors. Take away my factories, but leave my people, and soon we will have a new and better factory." Carnegie's statement reflects the message woven throughout this textbook that organizations are not buildings, machinery, or financial assets. Rather, they are the people in them. Organizations are human entities—full of life, sometimes fragile, always exciting.

>Chapter Summary

Lewin's force field analysis model states that all systems have driving and restraining forces. Change occurs through the process of unfreezing, changing, and refreezing. Unfreezing produces disequilibrium between the driving and restraining forces. Refreezing realigns the organization's systems and structures with the desired behaviors.

Restraining forces are manifested as employee resistance to change. The main reasons why people resist change are direct costs, saving face, fear of the unknown, breaking routines, incongruent organizational systems, and incongruent team dynamics. Resistance to change may be minimized by keeping employees informed about what to expect from the change effort (communicating); teaching employees valuable skills for the desired future (learning); involving them in the change process; helping employees cope with the stress of change; negotiating trade-offs with those who will clearly lose from the change effort; and using coercion (sparingly and as a last resort).

Organizational change also requires driving forces. This means that employees need to have an urgency for change by becoming aware of the environmental conditions that demand change in the organization. The change process also requires refreezing the new behaviors by realigning organizational systems and team dynamics with the desired changes. Every successful change also requires change agents with a clear, well-articulated vision of the desired future state.

Action research is a highly participative, open-systems approach to change management that combines an action orientation (changing attitudes and behavior) with a research orientation (testing theory). It is a data-based, problem-oriented process that diagnoses the need for change, introduces the intervention, and then evaluates and stabilizes the desired changes.

Appreciative inquiry embraces the positive organizational behavior philosophy by focusing participants on the positive and possible. It tries to break out of the problem-solving mentality that dominates organizational change through the action research model. The four stages of appreciative inquiry include discovery, dreaming, designing, and delivering. A third approach, called parallel learning structures, relies on social structures developed alongside the formal hierarchy with the purpose of increasing the organization's learning. They are highly participative arrangements, composed of people from most levels of the organization who follow the action research model to produce meaningful organizational change.

One significant concern is that organizational change theories developed with a Western cultural orientation potentially conflict with cultural values in some other countries. Also, organizational change practices can raise one or more ethical concerns, including increasing management's power over employees, threatening individual privacy rights, undermining individual self-esteem, and making clients dependent on the change consultant.

>key terms

action research 298

appreciative inquiry 299

change agent 297

force field analysis 291

future search 296

parallel learning structure 301

refreezing 292

unfreezing 292

>critical thinking questions

1. Chances are that the school you are attending is currently undergoing some sort of change to adapt more closely with its environment. Discuss the external forces that are driving these changes. What internal drivers for change also exist?

2. Use Lewin's force field analysis to describe the dynamics of organizational change at the Federal Bureau of Investigation (opening vignette to this chapter).

3. Employee resistance is a *symptom,* not a *problem,* in the change process. What are some of the real problems that may underlie employee resistance?

4. Senior management of a large multinational corporation is planning to restructure the organization. Currently, the organization is decentralized around geographical areas so that the executive responsible for each area has considerable autonomy over manufacturing and sales. The new structure will transfer power to the executives responsible for different product groups; the executives responsible for each geographic area will no longer be responsible for manufacturing in their area but will retain control over sales activities. Describe two types of resistance senior management might encounter from this organizational change.

5. Discuss the role of reward systems in organizational change. Specifically, identify where reward systems relate to Lewin's force field model and where they undermine the organizational change process.

6. Web Circuits is a Malaysian-based custom manufacturer for high-technology companies. Senior management wants to introduce lean management practices to reduce production costs and remain competitive. A consultant has recommended that the company start with a pilot project in one department and, when successful, diffuse these practices to other areas of the organization. Discuss the advantages of this recommendation and identify three ways (other than the pilot project's success) to make diffusion of the change effort more successful.

7. Suppose that you are vice president of branch services at the Bank of East Lansing. You notice that several branches have consistently low customer service ratings even though there are no apparent differences in resources or staff characteristics. Describe an appreciative inquiry process in one of these branches that might help to overcome these problems.

8. This chapter suggests that some organizational change activities face ethical concerns. Yet, several consultants actively use these processes because they believe they benefit the organization and do less damage to employees than it seems on the surface. For example, some activities try to open up the employee's hidden area (such as the Johari Window described in Chapter 3) so that there is better mutual understanding with co-workers. Discuss this argument and identify where you think organizational change interventions should limit this process.

>**team** exercise 14-1

Strategic Change Incidents

Purpose   This exercise is designed to help you to identify strategies to facilitate organizational change in various situations.

Instructions

* *Step 1:* The instructor will place students into teams, and each team will be assigned one of the scenarios presented below.

* *Step 2:* Each team will diagnose its assigned scenario to determine the most appropriate set of change management practices. Where appropriate, these practices should (*a*) create an urgency to change, (*b*) minimize resistance to change, and (*c*) refreeze the situation to support the change initiative. Each of these scenarios is based on real events.

* *Step 3:* Each team will present and defend its change management strategy. Class discussion regarding the appropriateness and feasibility of each strategy will occur after all teams assigned the same scenario have presented. The instructor will then describe what the organizations actually did in these situations.

Scenario 1: Greener Telco

The board of directors at a large telephone company wants its executives to make the organization more environmentally friendly by encouraging employees to reduce waste in the workplace. Government and other stakeholders have high expectations for the company to take this action and be publicly successful. Consequently, the managing director wants to significantly reduce the use of paper, refuse, and other waste throughout the company's many widespread offices. Unfortunately, a survey indicates that employees do not value environmental objectives and do not know how to "reduce, reuse, recycle." As the executive responsible for this change, you have been asked to develop a strategy that might bring about meaningful behavioral change toward these environmental goals. What would you do?

Scenario 2: Go Forward Airline

A major airline had experienced a decade of rough turbulence, including two bouts of bankruptcy protection, 10 chief executives, and morale so low that employees had ripped off company logos from their uniforms out of embarrassment. Service was terrible and the airplanes rarely arrived or left the terminal on time. This was costing the airline significant amounts of money in passenger layovers. Managers were paralyzed by anxiety, and many had been with the firm so long that they didn't know how to set strategic goals that worked. One-fifth of all flights were losing money, and the company overall was near financial collapse (just three months to defaulting on payroll obligations). The newly hired CEO and you must get employees to quickly improve operational efficiency and customer service. What actions would you take to bring about these changes in time?

Find the complete interactive self-assessments at this textbook's Web site at
www.mhhe.com/mcshaneEss2e.

>self-assessment exercise 14-2

Tolerance of Change Scale

Some people are naturally less comfortable than other people with the complexity and uncertainty of change. This self-assessment provides an estimate of how tolerant you are of change. Read each of the statements and select the response that best fits your personal belief. This self-assessment is completed alone so students rate themselves honestly without concerns of social comparison. However, class discussion will focus on the meaning of the concept measured by this scale and its implications for managing change in organizational settings.

[part 4 case 1] FTCA—Regional and Headquarters Relations

By Swee C. Goh, University of Ottawa*

The FTCA is a government agency that provides services to the public but also serves an enforcement role. It employs over 20,000 people, who are located at headquarters and in a large number of regional offices across the country. Most staff members are involved with direct counter-type services for both individuals and businesses. This includes collections, inquiries, payments, and audits. The agency also has large centers in various parts of the country to process forms and payments submitted by individuals and businesses.

FTCA is a typical federal government agency; many employees are unionized and have experienced numerous changes over the years. Because of the increasing complexity of regulations and the need to be more cost effective in the delivery of services, FTCA has evolved into an organization that uses technology to a great extent. The agency's leaders increasingly emphasize the need for easier and faster service and turnaround in dealing with clients. They also expect staff to depend more on electronic means of communication for interaction with the public.

As the population has grown over the years, the regional offices of this government organization have expanded. Each regional office is headed by an assistant director (AD) who has a budget and an increasing number of staff for the various functional activities related to the region, such as a manager for information systems. Every region also has offices located in the major cities. The managers of these city center offices report directly to the regional AD. The regional ADs report directly to the director who is the overall head of the agency.

FTCA has a strong emphasis on centralized control, particularly in the functional units. This emphasis occurs because of legal requirements as well as the fact that the agency has extensive direct interaction with the public. For example, one functional unit at headquarters (HQ) is responsible for collections and enforcement. If a regional manager has the same functional activity, FTCA executives believe that that person should be accountable to the HQ functional AD. However, as mentioned earlier, the regional manager also reports directly to the regional AD and the budget for the agency comes from the regional budget allocations and not from the HQ functional group.

This arrangement produces a dual reporting relationship for regional functional managers. Regional managers complain that this situation is very awkward. Who is the real boss under the circumstances: the regional AD or the functional HQ AD for these managers? Also, who should be responsible for evaluating the work performance of these dual-reporting regional managers? And if a regional manager makes a serious error, which of the two supervisors of that manager is ultimately accountable?

The potential for confusion about responsibility and accountability has made the roles and reporting relationships of the senior managers very vague. This has also increased the occurrences of conflict between regional managers and HQ managers.

To address this growing problem, a consultant was brought in to do an independent evaluation of the current organization structure of FTCA. The consultant asked for an organization chart of FTCA, which is shown on page 307. The consultant became aware of the concerns described above by conducting interviews with various staff members throughout the agency. Other information such as budgets and financial allocations, some earlier organizational studies, the mandate of the agency, and so forth, were also provided to the consultant.

The discussions with staff members were very interesting. Some viewed this issue as a people problem and not a structural one. That is, if regional and HQ managers learned how to cooperate and work with each other, this would not be an issue at all: They should take a shared responsibility approach and try to work together. But the view of the HQ functional groups was very different. They argued that FTCA is a functional organization, so these functional unit leaders should have authority and power over regional managers performing the same function. In effect, these regional managers should report to the functional unit ADs or at least be accountable to HQ policies and objectives.

To compound the problem, the regional managers saw this problem completely differently. They argued that the functional HQ managers should have a policy development function. On an annual basis they should develop broad objectives and targets in consultation

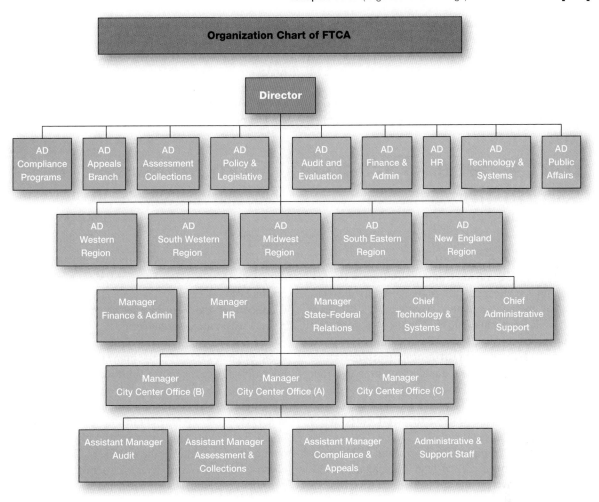

with regional managers. Once approved, it should be the responsibility of the regional managers to carry them out in light of the environment and constraints they face. The functional unit's ADs opposed the regional managers' position, pointing out that if the regional managers do not achieve their objectives, the functional ADs would suffer the consequences.

After hearing these views, the consultant formed the opinion that this was an intractable and complex problem that could be related to both people and structure. The consultant also noted that the regional budgets were huge, sometimes larger than the budgets for functional groups at HQ. Regional ADs also met infrequently—only once a month—with the director and functional ADs at HQ. Most of the time the regions seemed to operate fairly autonomously, whereas the director seemed to have ongoing involvement with the functional ADs.

An HQ staff member observed that over time the regional offices seemed to be getting bigger and had become fairly autonomous with functional staff mirroring the staff functions at HQ. The implication was that the regional staff would soon view the functional units at headquarters as a distant group that only sets policy for the regions to interpret or ignore as they pleased.

A functional AD with several years of seniority at FTCA warned that the functional units must have some control audit and other functional activities in the region. The AD explained that without clear roles, reporting relationships, and accountabilities between the regions and HQ, FTCA could not be able to provide citizens with transparent and fair treatment to the services under their mandate.

The regional ADs, however, saw their responsibilities as facilitating horizontal coordination within the region to ensure that actions and decisions were consistent and reflected the legislative responsibility of the agency.

After a month of study and discussions with staff at FTCA, the consultant realized that this was not going to be an easy problem to resolve. There were also rumblings as the project progressed that some regional ADs did not like the idea of restructuring FTCA to deal with these issues. They seemed to have considerable clout and power in the organization as a group and would resist any change to the status quo.

As the consultant sat down to deliberate a solution to the problem at hand and to write the report, a number of critical questions became apparent: Was FTCA a purely functional organization? Could the accountability issues be resolved through an acceptable organizational process and people training without the need for restructuring? What about power, politics, and conflict in this situation? Finally, will resistance to change become a problem as well?

[part 4 case 2] Woodland Community Center Corporation

By Joseph C. Santora, Essex County College and TST, Inc.*

Fred Chambers, the recently appointed executive director of the Woodland Community Center Corporation (WCCC), leaned back in his overstuffed executive chair and contemplated his new job. At 60 years old, he felt young and fit. His career as a nonprofit executive director had spanned more than 25 years at five very diverse nonprofit organizations. Once he believed his job was done at an organization, he moved on to accept the challenges a new executive position brought with it. Most of all, Chambers resisted complacency, and he wanted to at all costs avoid getting stale in the saddle.

After retiring about four years ago, Chambers heard the trumpet's call to lead once again, so he sought short-term or interim leadership positions in nonprofit organizations. He seemed to enjoy the challenges of the unique organizational niche he had carved out for himself. His last three interim executive director appointments lasted six months, two years, and one year respectively and served both him and the hiring boards of directors well. By hiring Chambers on an interim basis, boards of directors, many of which lacked the foresight to prepare an executive succession plan, were able to conduct a more thorough executive search for a permanent replacement rather than to hastily appoint someone who did not fit the organization.

Once appointed, Chambers was given *carte blanche* by the board to make the necessary internal organizational changes, and despite some initial rocky starts, things worked out well for him and for the nonprofits he led. Chambers got an opportunity to travel to different locations throughout the country, met some interesting people, received a lucrative compensation package, and enjoyed a fixed-term contract agreement; on the other hand, the boards got the opportunity to hire an outsider, someone with diversified senior administrative experiences, to develop and implement a strategy for organizational change. The overall assessment of Chambers as a gun-for-hire by his various board employers was quite respectable.

But unlike past situations Chambers felt uneasy about this new executive appointment. This time, against his wife's advice, he took a full-time permanent executive director position as a replacement for Alain Yates, the articulate, charismatic, long-term executive director at the WCCC. From time to time, the community center board had heard some internal rumblings about the organizational culture at the agency, but it failed to act because Yates held considerable power over the board as a result of his longevity in office and the constant turnover of board members. Chambers's appointment as executive director signaled the community center board's earnest desire to change the organizational culture at the agency. As Chambers conducted his fact-finding mission, he uncovered what the board in general seemed to know about the organizational culture: that Yates encouraged policies of "double standards" which demotivated some long-term and very industrious agency employees. Perhaps, Chambers should have heeded his wife's warning about taking a full-time position. After assessing his situation, he now thought: "Be careful what you wish for; you just might get it."

Gail Katz, a social worker, founded the Woodland Community Center Corporation (WCCC) in 1926 to deliver a variety of social and human services to the indigent population of Woodland, an east coast seaport city. Over time, the organization has had a series of

*© Joseph C. Santora. The names and some managerial actions in this case have been altered to preserve the integrity and anonymity of the organization. This case is intended to be used as a basis for class discussion rather than to illustrate either effective or ineffective handling of a management situation.

executive directors. Alain Yates had been the longest reigning executive director and has led the WCCC for the past 25 years. Yates assumed the leadership of the agency after a tumultuous internal struggle almost caused the agency to cease operations. He gained support for the position from several powerful administrative and staff members in the agency. This internal groundswell forced the board of directors to appoint Yates as the executive director of the agency. Once the board approved his three-year contract as executive director, Yates immediately began repaying the political IOUs he owed these in-group members for their support. He simultaneously initiated a number of bold steps to clean up the agency, and through some legerdemain, the local media turned Yates into a Messiah or savior figure. Yet, some agency employees began to say quietly that Yates was no Messiah at all; rather, they felt that Yates was just an ordinary leader who now began to display a new attitude toward employees. One employee who was especially critical of Yates's leadership stated: "Yates *believes* his own newspaper clippings."

Alain Yates, more so than any previous Woodland Community Center Corporation (WCCC) executive director, shaped the organizational culture of the agency. For him, seniority was sacrosanct, and neither creativity nor hard work replaced it. Many employees enjoyed a very secure work environment, and few, if any, employees were fired for a poor work ethic. The key to employee survival and its attendant rewards was loyalty, not competency. Furthermore, loyalty was the sole way to advance in the agency or to receive a pay increase for employees in the 100-plus employee agency. However, not all employees felt comfortable with Yates's leadership style. For example, some employees were upset with Yates's decision to give certain employees reserved parking spaces, while they had to walk a considerable distance to the agency, a policy that irked them particularly during inclement weather. In addition, other employees became vexed after Yates denied their request to attend a local off-site management seminar, because he often quipped: "We really don't have enough money in the budget" or "Do you really need to attend this seminar. Nothing in management has changed that much." One employee was so outraged when she discovered that Yates had, the very same day, approved a request for an in-group employee to attend a high-priced out-of-state conference that she announced to some colleagues: "I'll do my job, but nothing more as long as Yates is here."

This two-tiered structure created a further wedge between the agencies haves and have-nots. The outcome of Yates's actions resulted in a small, but noticeable, agency fissure that led to a growing rift between employees who sought to excel and those who just got by on their loyalty. One long-time employee opined: "I simply do not believe in just getting by, but . . . ."

Despite this, many employees decided not to leave the agency, because, as a result of Yates's external political contacts and connections with philanthropic funding agencies, employee salaries were superior to those in similar sector organizations. Moreover, members of the out-group—those employees not part of the agency in-group elite whom Yates constantly rewarded—decided to remain at the agency because as one employee succinctly put it, "we are committed to working for the betterment of the agency and its clients, and we will stay despite his preferential treatment of 'pet' employees." But over time, as employees retired or slowly trickled out of the agency because they just could no longer tolerate what one employee called "employment injustices," they were replaced by a class of new employees who were connected to agency in-group members or financial contributors to the agency—both, regardless of how they arrived at the agency, had one characteristic in common: they swore undying loyalty to Yates. The agency was becoming more incestuous and a breeding ground for a groupthink mentality. At this month's staff meeting, Yates informed the staff about some serious agency problems. However, no one dare mention that these problems and their negative organizational impact were a result of several major strategic leadership blunders that Yates made. One astute observer sitting in the last row of the cavernous room where staff meetings were held whispered in a muffled voice: "I guess I am the only one who noticed that the emperor has no clothes."

Yates also informed managers and staff that he was retiring as the executive director of the agency. But prior to announcing his retirement plans after his 25th year in office, Yates had recommended a successor from among his most trusted managers to the board of directors to continue his legacy in perpetuity. His hand-picked successor would continue his policies. Agency managers and employees prepared several lavish retirement celebrations for Yates—they held a formal retirement dinner, hosted several large parties, and even etched Yates's name in gold leaf on the glass entrance doors to the agency.

Despite all the hoopla and festive mood, the board of directors dealt Yates a major blow when it announced that Fred Chambers would succeed him. Board members had been quietly working behind the scene waiting for the right opportunity to create an environment for changing the organizational culture. Board members believed that their charge to Chambers would do this. They had already exerted strong pressure on him to reduce costs, to begin downsizing the nonessential politically connected staff, and to restore a new sense of professionalism to the agency. Chambers knew that he was a good leader, knew he had the confidence of the board, and most importantly, knew he had to change the organizational culture that had existed in the agency for the last quarter of a century. He thought to himself "My legacy won't be etched on any glass doors." But first he had to begin the process of changing the organizational culture that was so deeply embedded in the WCCC.

>**additional**cases

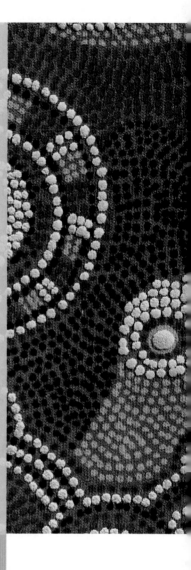

[case.1] Arctic Mining Consultants

By Steven L. McShane, The University of Western Australia, and Tim Neale

Tom Parker enjoyed working outdoors. At various times in the past, he worked as a ranch hand, high steel rigger, headstone installer, prospector, and geological field technician. Now 43, Parker is a geological field technician and field coordinator with Arctic Mining Consultants. He has specialized knowledge and experience in all nontechnical aspects of mineral exploration, including claim staking, line cutting and grid installation, soil sampling, prospecting, and trenching. He is responsible for hiring, training, and supervising field assistants for all of Arctic Mining Consultants' programs. Field assistants are paid a fairly low daily wage (no matter how long they work, which may be up to 12 hours or more) and are provided meals and accommodations. Many of the programs are operated by a project manager who reports to Parker.

Parker sometimes acts as a project manager, as he did on a job that involved staking 15 claims near Eagle Lake, Alaska. He selected John Talbot, Greg Boyce, and Brian Millar, all of whom had previously worked with Parker, as the field assistants. To stake a claim, the project team marks a line with flagging tape and blazes along the perimeter of the claim, cutting a claim post every 500 yards (called a *length*). The 15 claims would require almost 60 miles of line in total. Parker had budgeted seven days (plus mobilization and de-mobilization) to complete the job. This meant that each of the four stakers (Parker, Talbot, Boyce, and Millar) would have to complete a little over seven lengths each day. The following is a chronology of the project.

Day 1

The Arctic Mining Consultants crew assembled in the morning and drove to Eagle Lake, from where they were flown by helicopter to the claim site. On arrival, they set up tents at the edge of the area to be staked, and agreed on a schedule for cooking duties. After supper, they pulled out the maps and discussed the job—how long it would take, the order in which the areas were to be staked, possible helicopter landing spots, and areas that might be more difficult to stake.

Parker pointed out that with only a week to complete the job, everyone would have to average seven and a half lengths per day. "I know that is a lot," he said, "but you've all staked claims before and I'm confident that each of you is capable of it. And it's only for a week. If we get the job done on time, there's a $300 bonus for each man." Two hours later, Parker and his crew members had developed what seemed to be a workable plan.

Day 2

Millar completed six lengths, Boyce six lengths, Talbot eight, and Parker eight. Parker was not pleased with Millar's or Boyce's production. However, he didn't make an issue of it, thinking that they would develop their rhythm quickly.

Day 3

Millar completed five and a half lengths, Boyce four, and Talbot seven. Parker, who was nearly twice as old as the other three, completed eight lengths. He also had enough time remaining to walk over and check the quality of stakes that Millar and Boyce had completed, then walk back to his own area for helicopter pickup back to the tent site.

That night Parker exploded with anger. "I thought I told you that I wanted seven and a half lengths a day!" he shouted at Boyce and Millar. Boyce said that he was slowed down by unusually thick underbrush in his assigned area. Millar said that he had done his best and would try to pick up the pace. Parker did not mention that he had inspected their work. He explained that as far as he was concerned, the field assistants were supposed to finish their assigned area for the day, no matter what.

Talbot, who was sharing a tent with Parker, talked to him later. "I think that you're being a bit hard on them, you know. I know that it has been more by luck than anything else that I've been able to do my quota. Yesterday I only had five lengths done after the first seven hours and there was only an hour before I was supposed to be picked up. Then I hit a patch of really open bush, and was able to do three lengths in 70 minutes. Why don't I take Millar's area tomorrow and he can have mine? Maybe that will help."

"Conditions are the same in all of the areas," replied Parker, rejecting Talbot's suggestion. "Millar just has to try harder."

Day 4

Millar did seven lengths and Boyce completed six and a half. When they reported their production that evening, Parker grunted uncommunicatively. Parker and Talbot did eight lengths each.

Day 5

Millar completed six lengths, Boyce six, Talbot seven and a half, and Parker eight. Once again Parker blew up, but he concentrated his diatribe on Millar. "Why don't you do what you say you are going to do? You know that you have to do seven and a half lengths a day. We went over that when we first got here, so why don't you do it? If you aren't willing to do the job then you never should have taken it in the first place!"

Millar replied by saying that he was doing his best, that he hadn't even stopped for lunch, and that he didn't know how he could possibly do any better. Parker launched into him again: "You have got to work harder! If you put enough effort into it, you will get the area done!"

Later Millar commented to Boyce, "I hate getting dumped on all the time! I'd quit if it didn't mean that I'd have to walk 50 miles to the highway. And besides, I need the bonus money. Why doesn't he pick on you? You don't get any more done than me; in fact, you usually get less. Maybe if you did a bit more he wouldn't be so bothered about me."

"I only work as hard as I have to," Boyce replied.

Day 6

Millar raced through breakfast, was the first one to be dropped off by the helicopter, and arranged to be the last one picked up. That evening the production figures were Millar eight and a quarter lengths, Boyce seven, and Talbot and Parker eight each. Parker remained silent when the field assistants reported their performance for the day.

Day 7

Millar was again the first out and last in. That night, he collapsed in an exhausted heap at the table, too tired to eat. After a few moments, he announced in an abject tone, "Six lengths. I worked like a dog all day and I only got a lousy six lengths!" Boyce completed five lengths, Talbot seven, and Parker seven and a quarter.

Parker was furious. "That means we have to do a total of 34 lengths tomorrow if we are to finish this job on time!" With his eyes directed at Millar, he added: "Why is it that you never finish the job? Don't you realize that you are part of a team, and that you are letting the rest of the team down? I've been checking your lines and you're doing too much blazing and wasting too much time making picture-perfect claim posts! If you worked smarter, you'd get a lot more done!"

Day 8

Parker cooked breakfast in the dark. The helicopter dropoffs began as soon as morning light appeared on the horizon. Parker instructed each assistant to complete eight lengths and, if they finished early, to help the others. Parker said that he would finish the other 10 lengths. Helicopter pickups were arranged for one hour before dark.

By noon, after working as hard as he could, Millar had only completed three lengths. "Why bother," he thought to himself, "I'll never be able to do another five lengths before the helicopter comes, and I'll catch the same amount of abuse from Parker for doing six lengths as for seven and a half." So he sat down and had lunch and a rest. "Boyce won't finish his eight lengths either, so even if I did finish mine, I still wouldn't get the bonus. At least I'll get one more day's pay this way."

That night, Parker was livid when Millar reported that he had completed five and a half lengths. Parker had done ten and a quarter lengths, and Talbot had completed eight. Boyce proudly announced that he finished seven and a half lengths, but sheepishly added that Talbot had helped him with some of it. All that remained were the two and a half lengths that Millar had not completed.

The job was finished the next morning and the crew demobilized. Millar has never worked for Arctic Mining Consultants again, despite being offered work several times by Parker. Boyce sometimes does staking for Arctic, and Talbot works full-time with the company.

[case.2] Big Screen's Big Failure

By Fiona McQuarrie, University College of the Fraser Valley

Bill Brosnan stared at the financial statements in front of him and shook his head. The losses from *Conquistadors,* the movie that was supposed to establish Big Screen Studios as a major Hollywood power, were worse than anyone had predicted. In fact, the losses were so huge that Brosnan's predecessor, Buck Knox, had been fired as a result of this colossal failure. Brosnan had wanted to be the head of a big movie production company for as long as he could remember, and was thrilled to have been chosen by the board of directors to be the new president. But he had never expected that the first task in his dream job would be to deal with the fallout from one of the most unsuccessful movies ever.

The driving force behind *Conquistadors* was its director, Mark Frazier. Frazier had made several profitable movies for other studios and had a reputation as being a maverick with a vision. He was a director with clearly formulated ideas of what his movies should look like, and he also had no hesitations about being forceful with producers, studios, actors, and technical staff to ensure that his idea came to life as he had envisioned it. For several years, while Frazier had been busy on other projects, he had also been working on a script about two Spanish aristocrats in the 16th century who set out for America to find riches and gold, and encountered many amazing adventures on their travels. Frazier was something of an amateur historian, which led to his interest in the real-life stories of the Spanish conquistadors and bringing those stories to life for a 21st century audience. But he also felt that creating an epic tale like this would establish him as a serious writer and filmmaker in the eyes of Hollywood, some of whose major powers had dismissed his past work as unimaginative or clichéd.

At the time Big Screen Studios approached Frazier to see if he would be interested in working for them, the company was going through something of a rough spot. Through several years of hard work and mostly successful productions, Buck Knox, the president of Big Screen, had established Big Screen as a studio that produced cost-efficient and profitable films. The studio also had a good reputation for being supportive of the creative side of filmmaking; actors, writers, directors, and producers generally felt that Big Screen trusted them enough to give them autonomy in making decisions appropriate for their productions. (Other studios had reputations for keeping an overly tight rein on production budgets and for dictating choices based on cost rather than artistic considerations.) However, in the last two years Big Screen had invested in several major productions—a musical, a horror film, and the sequel to a wildly successful film adaptation of a comic book—that for various reasons had all performed well below expectations. Knox had also heard through the grapevine that several of the studio's board members were prepared to join together to force him out of the presidency if Big Screen did not come up with a hit soon.

Knox knew that Frazier was being wooed by several other studios for his next project, and decided to contact Frazier to see if he was interested in directing any of the productions Big Screen was considering in the next year or so. After hearing Knox's descriptions of the upcoming productions, Frazier said, "What I'd really be interested in doing is directing this script I've been writing." He described the plot of *Conquistadors* to Knox, and Knox was enchanted by the possibilities— two strong male lead characters, a beautiful woman the men encountered in South America whose affections they fought over, battles, sea journeys, and challenging journeys over mountains and through jungles. However, Knox could also see that this movie might be extremely expensive to produce. He expressed this concern to Frazier, and Frazier replied, "Yes, but it will be an investment that will pay off. I know this movie will work. And I've mentioned it to two other studios and they are interested in it. I would prefer to make it with Big Screen, but if I have to, I will go somewhere else to get it made. That is how strongly I believe in it. However, any studio I work with has to trust me. I won't make the film without adequate financial commitment from the studio. I want final approval over casting, and I won't make the film if I don't get final cut." (*Final cut* means the director, not the studio, edits the version of the movie that is released to theaters, and that the studio cannot release a version of the movie that the director does not approve.)

Knox told Frazier that he would get back to him later that week, and asked Frazier not to commit to any other project until then. He spent several days mulling over the possibilities. Like Frazier, he believed that *Conquistadors* could be a huge success. It certainly sounded like it had more potential than anything else Big Screen had in development. However, Knox was still concerned about the potential cost, and the amount of control over the project that Frazier was demanding. Frazier's reputation as a maverick meant that he likely would not compromise on his demands. Knox was also concerned about his own vulnerability if the movie failed. But on the other hand, Big Screen needed a big hit, and it needed one soon. Big Screen would look very bad if it turned down *Conquistadors* and the movie became a gigantic hit for some other studio. Frazier had a respectable track record of producing money makers, so even if he might be difficult to work with, the end product usually was successful. At the end of the week, Knox phoned Frazier and told him that Big Screen was willing to produce *Conquistadors*. Frazier thanked Knox, and added, "This film is going to redeem me, and it's going to redeem Big Screen as well."

Preproduction on the film started almost immediately after Frazier and the studio negotiated a budget of $50 million. This was slightly higher than Knox had anticipated, but he believed this was not an excessive amount to permit Frazier to realize the grand vision he had described. Knox further reassured himself by assigning John Connor, one of his trusted vice presidents, to act as the studio's liaison with Frazier and to be executive producer on the film. Connor was a veteran of many years in the movie production industry and was experienced in working with directors and budgets. Knox trusted Connor to be able to make Frazier contain the costs of the production within the agreed-upon limits.

The first major problem the film encountered involved casting. The studio gave Frazier final approval over casting as he had requested. Frazier's first signing was Cole Rogan, a famous action star, to be one of the male leads. The studio did not object to this choice; in fact, Knox and Connor felt that Rogan was an asset because he had a reputation as a star that could "open" a film (in other words, audiences would come to a movie just because he was in it). However, Frazier then decided to cast Frank Monaco as the other male lead. Monaco had made only a few films to date, and those were fluffy romantic comedies. Frazier said that Monaco would bring important qualities of vulnerability and innocence to the role, which would be a strong contrast to Rogan's rugged machismo. However, Connor told Knox, he saw two major problems with Monaco's casting: Monaco had never proven himself in an epic adventure role, and he was an accomplished enough actor that he would make the rather wooden Rogan look bad. Knox told Connor to suggest to Frazier that Rogan's role be recast. Unfortunately, it turned out that Frazier had signed Rogan to a "pay or play" deal, meaning that if the studio released Rogan from the project, the studio would have to pay him a considerable sum of money. Knox was somewhat bothered that Frazier had made this deal with Rogan without consulting either him or Connor, but he told Connor to instruct Frazier to release Rogan and recast the role, and the studio would just accept the payment to Rogan as part of the production costs. Although Frazier complained, he did as the studio asked and chose as a replacement Marty Jones, an actor who had had some success in films but mostly in supporting roles. However, Jones was thrilled to be cast in a major role, and Connor felt that he would be capable of convincingly playing the part.

A few weeks after casting was completed, Connor called Knox and asked to see him immediately. "Buck," he told him once he arrived at Knox's office, "we have a really big problem." Connor said that Frazier was insisting the majority of the production be filmed in the jungles of South America, where most of the action took place, rather than on a studio soundstage or in a more accessible location that resembled the South American locale. Not only that, but Frazier was also insisting that he needed to bring along most of the crew that had worked on his previous films, rather than staffing the production locally. "Why does he want that? That's going to cost a hell of a lot," Knox said. "I know," Connor said, "but he says it's the only way that the film is going to work. He says it just won't be the same if the actors are in a studio or in some swamp in the southern U.S. According to him, the actors and the crew need to be in the real location to truly understand what the conquistadors went through, and audiences won't believe it's a real South American jungle if the film isn't made in one."

Knox told Connor that Frazier had to provide an amended budget to reflect the increased costs before he would approve the location filming. Connor took the request to Frazier, who complained that the studio was weakening on its promise to support the film adequately, and added that he might be tempted to take the film to another studio if he was not allowed to film on location in South America. After a few weeks, he produced an amended budget of $75 million. Knox was horrified that the budget for *Conquistadors* had nearly doubled by half in a few weeks. He told Connor that he would only accept the amended budget under two conditions: one, that Connor would go on the location shoot to ensure that costs stayed within the amended budget; and two, that if the costs exceeded Frazier's estimates, he would have to pay any excess himself. Frazier again complained that the studio was attempting to compromise his vision, but grudgingly accepted the modified terms.

Frazier, Connor, and the cast and crew then headed off to the South American jungles for a scheduled two-month shoot. Immediately it became apparent that there was more trouble. Connor, who reported daily to Knox, told him after two weeks had passed that Frazier was shooting scenes several times over—not because the actors or the crew were making mistakes, or because there was something wrong with the scene, but because the output just didn't meet his artistic standards. This attention to detail meant that the filming schedule was nearly a week behind after only the first week's work. Also, because the filming locations were so remote, the cast and crew were spending nearly four hours of a scheduled seven-hour work day traveling to and from location, leaving only three hours in which they could work at regular pay rates. Work beyond those hours meant they had to be paid overtime, and as Frazier's demanding vision required shooting 10 or 12 hours each day, the production was incurring huge overtime costs. As if that wasn't bad enough, the "rushes" (the finished film produced each day) showed that Monaco and Jones didn't have any chemistry as a pair, and Gia Norman, the European actress Frazier had cast as the love interest, had such a heavy accent that most of her lines couldn't be understood.

Knox told Connor that he was coming to the location right away to meet with Frazier. After several days of very arduous travel, Knox, Connor, and Frazier met in the canvas tent that served as the director's "office" in the middle of the jungle. Knox didn't waste any time with pleasantries. "Mark," he told Frazier, "there is no way you can bring this film in for the budget you have promised or within the deadline you agreed to. John has told me how this production is being managed, and it's just not acceptable. I've done some calculations, and at the rate you are going, this picture is going to cost $85 million and have a running time of four and a half hours. Big Screen is not prepared to support that. We need a film that's a commercially viable length, and we need it at a reasonable cost."

"It needs to be as long as it is," replied Frazier, "because the story has to be told. And if it has to cost this much, it has to cost this much. Otherwise it will look like crap and no one will buy a ticket to see it."

"Mark," replied Knox, "we are prepared to put $5 million more into this picture, and that is it. You have the choice of proceeding under those terms, and keeping John fully appraised of the costs so that he can help you stay within the budget. If you don't agree to that, you can leave the production, and we will hire another director and sue you for breach of contract."

Frazier looked as though he was ready to walk into the jungle and head back to California that very minute, but the thought of losing his dream project was too much for him. He muttered, "OK, I'll finish it."

Knox returned to California, nursing several nasty mosquito bites, and Connor stayed in the jungle and reported to him regularly. Unfortunately, it didn't seem like Frazier was paying much attention to the studio's demands. Connor estimated that the shoot would run three months rather than two, and that the total cost of the shoot would be $70 million. This only left $10 million of the budget for postproduction, distribution, and marketing, which was almost nothing for an epic adventure. To add to Knox's problems, he got a phone call from Richard Garrison, the chairman of Big Screen's board of directors. Garrison had heard gossip about what was going on with *Conquistadors* in the jungles of South America, and wanted to know what Knox was going to do to curb Frazier's excesses. Knox told Garrison that Frazier was operating under clearly understood requirements, and that Connor was on the set to monitor the costs. Unfortunately, Knox thought, Connor was doing a good job of reporting, but he didn't seem to be doing much to correct the problems he was observing.

Frazier eventually came back to California after three and a half months of shooting, and started editing the several hundred hours of film he had produced. Knox requested that Frazier permit Connor or himself to participate in the editing, but Frazier retorted that permitting that would infringe on his right to final cut, and refused to allow anyone associated with the studio to be in the editing room. Knox scheduled a release date for the film in six months' time, and asked the studio's publicity department to start working on an ad campaign for the film, but not much could be done on either of these tasks without at least a rough cut of the finished product.

Three weeks into the editing, Connor called Knox. "I heard from Mark today," he said. "He wants to do some reshoots." "Is that a problem?" Knox asked. "No," said Connor, "most of it is interior stuff that we can do here. But he wants to add a prologue. He says that the story doesn't make sense without more development of how the two lead characters sailed from Spain to South America. He wants to hire a ship."

"He wants to WHAT?" exclaimed Knox.

"He wants to hire a sailing ship, like the conquistadors traveled on. There's a couple of tall ships that would do, but the one he wants is in dry dock in Mexico, and would cost at least a million to make seaworthy and sail up to southern California. And that's on top of the cost of bringing the actors and crew back for a minimum of a week. I suggested to him that we try some special effects or a computerized animation for the scenes of the ship on the ocean, and shoot the shipboard scenes in the studio, but he says that won't be the same and it needs to be authentic."

At this point, Knox was ready to drive over to the editing studios and take care of Frazier himself. Instead, he called Garrison and explained the situation. "I won't commit any more money to this without the board's approval. But we've already invested $80 million into this, so is a few more million that much of a deal if it gets the damn thing finished and gets Frazier out of our hair? If we tell him no, we'll have to basically start all over again, or just dump the whole thing and kiss $80 million goodbye." At the other end of the line, Garrison sighed, and said, "Do whatever you have to do to get it done."

Knox told Connor to authorize the reshoots, with a schedule of two months and the expectation that Frazier would have a rough cut of the film ready for the studio executives to view in three months. However, because of the time Frazier had already spent in editing, Knox had to change the release date, which meant changing the publicity campaign as well—and releasing the film at the same time that one of Big Screen's major competitors was releasing another epic adventure that was considered a sure-fire hit. However, Knox felt he had no choice. If he didn't enforce some deadline, Frazier might sit in the editing room and tinker with his dream forever.

Connor supervised the reshoots, and reported that they went as well as could be expected. The major problem was that Gia Norman had had plastic surgery on her nose after the first shoot was completed, and looked considerably different than she had in the jungles of South America. However, creative lighting, makeup and costuming managed to minimize the change in her appearance. By all accounts, the (very expensive) sailing ship looked spectacular in the rushes, and Frazier was satisfied that his vision had been sufficiently dramatized.

Amazingly, Frazier delivered the rough cut of the film at the agreed-upon time. Knox, Connor, Garrison, and the rest of the studio's executives crowded into the screening room to view the realization of Frazier's dream. Five and a half hours later, they were in shock. No one could deny that the movie looked fantastic, and that it was an epic on a grand scale, but there was no way the studio could release a five and a half hour long film commercially, plus Frazier had agreed to produce a movie that was at most two and a half hours long. Knox was at his wits' end. He cornered Garrison in the

hallway outside the screening room. "Will you talk to Mark? He won't listen to me, he won't listen to John. But we can't release this. It won't work." Garrison agreed, and contacted Frazier the next day. He reported back to Knox that Frazier, amazingly, had agreed to cut the film to two hours and fifteen minutes. Knox, heartened by this news, proceeded with the previously set release date, which by now was a month away, and got the publicity campaign going.

Two days before the scheduled release date, Frazier provided an advance copy of his shortened version of *Conquistadors* for a studio screening. Knox had asked him to provide a copy sooner, but Frazier said that he could not produce anything that quickly. As a consequence, the version of the film that the studio executives were seeing for the first time was the version that had already had thousands of copies duplicated for distribution to movie theatres all across North America. In fact, those copies were on their way by courier to the theatres as the screening started.

At the end of the screening, the studio executives were stunned. Yes, the movie was shorter, but now it made no sense. Characters appeared and disappeared randomly, the plot was impossible to follow, and the dialogue did not make sense at several key points in the small parts of plot that were discernible. The film was a disaster. Several of the executives present voiced the suspicion that Frazier had deliberately edited the movie this way to get revenge on the studio for not "respecting" his vision and forcing him to reduce the film's length. Others suggested that Frazier was simply a lunatic who never should have been given so much autonomy in the first place.

Knox, Garrison, and Connor held a hastily called meeting the next morning. What could the studio do? Recall the film and force Frazier to produce a more coherent shorter version? Recall the film and release the five-and-a-half hour version? Or let the shorter version be released as scheduled and hope that it wouldn't be too badly received? Knox argued that the film should be recalled and Frazier should be forced to produce the product he agreed to produce. Connor said that he thought Frazier had been doing his best to do what the studio wanted, based on what Connor saw on the set, and that making Frazier cut the movie so short compromised the vision that Frazier wanted to achieve. He said the studio should release the long version and present it as a "special cinematic event." Garrison, as chairman of the board, listened to both sides, and after figuring out the costs of recalling and/or reediting the film—not to mention the less tangible costs of further worsening the film's reputation—said, "Gentlemen, we really don't have any choice. *Conquistadors* will be released tomorrow."

Knox immediately cancelled the critics' screenings of *Conquistadors* scheduled for that afternoon, so that bad reviews would not appear on the day of the film's release. Despite that preemptive step and an extensive advertising campaign, *Conquistadors* was a complete and utter flop. On a total outlay of $90 million, the studio recouped less than $9 million. The reviews of the film were terrible, and audiences stayed away in droves. The only place *Conquistadors* was even close to successful was in some parts of Europe, where film critics called the edited version an example of American studios' crass obsession with making money by compromising the work of a genius. The studio attempted to capitalize on this note of hope by releasing the five-and-a-half hour version of *Conquistadors* for screening at some overseas film festivals and cinema appreciation societies, but the revenues from these screenings were so small that they made no difference to the overall financial results.

Three months after *Conquistadors* was released, Garrison called Knox in and told him he was fired. Garrison told Knox the board appreciated what a difficult production *Conquistadors* had been to manage, but that the costs of the production had been unchecked to a degree that the board no longer had confidence in Knox's ability to operate Big Screen Studios efficiently. Connor was offered a very generous early retirement package, and accepted it. The board then hired Bill Brosnan, a vice president at another studio, as Knox's replacement.

After reviewing *Conquistadors'* financial records and the notes that Knox had kept throughout the production, Brosnan was determined that a disaster like this would not undermine his career as it had Knox's. But what could he do to ensure this would not happen?

[case.3] Nirvana Art Gallery

By Christine Ho, University of Adelaide

It was an irony not lost on many of the employees of Nirvana Art Gallery. This gallery was far from being a place of harmony and joy. In fact, some of the employees preferred to refer to management using the acronym NAG in a derogatory manner.

Nirvana was regarded as one of the leading museums of art in Australia. The collection of Australian art was one of the oldest and best known in the country. This museum also housed an enviable Aboriginal collection and an international collection of considerable breadth and depth.

Rod was the assistant curator for the Curatorial unit. Despite his job title, his time was divided between the Curatorial and Research units because there was not enough work in the former to keep him occupied from week to week. It was agreed between the managers of the two units that he work Monday's through Wednesday's at Curatorial and then the remaining days at Research. While Rod would have preferred to work solely for Curatorial because that was where his interests lay, he was in no position to argue with either manager. He hoped that when he finished his PhD in art history he would be employed full-time in Curatorial where he could fully utilize his specialized knowledge and meet his aspiration to be a curator.

Rod did not particularly enjoy coming to work on Thursday's. The research he was asked to do was OK. It was not that stimulating, but he convinced himself that it was useful to understand the functions of the different units in the gallery, and not restrict himself to purely curatorial issues. The Research unit was quite small and the staff were very serious. Because they were located within close proximity to each other, initially, he tried to be friendly to them while they worked.

When he kept getting frowns and annoyed looks from his colleagues, it became obvious that they did not like being disrupted. Further, they assumed he did not have enough work to do, so they kept giving him more tasks. Andrew, one of the researchers, found himself falling behind and having to ask for permission to stay late to finish his work. Because the gallery housed expensive art works, security was tight. All staff was expected to leave by 5 PM and not return until the following morning after 8 AM. Management was very strict about granting this special permission because security had to be notified so that alarm systems could be adjusted and monitored accordingly. Because the research manager, Nelly, often stayed late she did not mind granting Rod permission as well.

On Friday morning, Rod met with Nelly to give her the report he had written on business plans.

"Thanks Rod, it looks good," said Nelly, as she flipped through the document. "You're still working on that draft document on the current spending and budget allocation for this year, aren't you? Andrew can help you with this."

Rod hesitated. "Oh, I think I have all the necessary information, and I'm sure Andrew is busy anyway. If I stay late tonight, I might be able to give it to you before I leave work."

"What's wrong?" asked Nelly.

"It's nothing. I just always get the impression that I'm disturbing everyone in Research. They seem really busy all the time and don't seem to have time for anything else. I'm more of a sociable and friendly person, and like to talk with others while I work."

Nelly gave him a look, which Rod did not know how to decipher. I hope she does not think I am complaining about my job or my colleagues, Rod thought to himself as he walked out of her office. He liked the fact that no one was breathing down his neck all the time. And the last thing he needed was to create animosity between himself and the rest of Research. It was bad enough that they always would go out for lunch together and never invited him. But at least they could say hi whenever he was there.

The following Thursday, when Nelly came into the Research area to talk to one of the researchers, she came by his desk to say that she had read both his reports that he finished last week, thanked him for his hard work, and asked how his work was going. He appreciated the attention. Over the following weeks when he was in Research, she would come by and talk to him. This sometimes included complimenting him on his appearance. How his shirt color emphasized his eyes, or that his new stylish haircut made him look more handsome. At least someone was talking to me, thought Rod. Although he did not think her comments were appropriate, he accepted them graciously with a smile, but made sure he kept his comments professional. He also tried to minimize how often he had to stay late at work so as not to give the wrong impression. But usually that was not possible given his workload.

It was not long before the other researchers noticed the attention she gave him. He started noticing the surreptitious looks and frowns he received whenever she spoke to him. Rod thought he was being paranoid. A couple of times when he had walked into the Research area, some of the researchers were talking in low voices, but they would stop when they noticed him.

Rod wondered what was going on. It was not like he was not pulling his own weight around here. He got the projects done on time even though he only worked two days in Research, and Nelly had told him numerous times that he was doing a good job. Rod put his thoughts aside and focused on his day's tasks. He went home that weekend pleased for once he did not have to work late.

He arrived to work on Monday in good spirits. He had studied all weekend and nearly completed his final draft of his PhD thesis. He always enjoyed working in the Curatorial unit. He found his work preparing upcoming exhibitions interesting. Further, he quite liked the Curatorial team. His manager, Sarah, was approachable and despite being the most junior member, his colleagues regularly asked for his input during the weekly Monday meetings. The team was friendly and he found he had a lot in common with many of them. Sometimes he would be invited to lunch when he was there on one of his Curatorial days. Working in Curatorial also meant that he was not in Research. He would not have to put up with Nelly's comments, which were beginning to really make him feel uncomfortable, and he did not have to put up with the whispers or silent stares he got from his Research colleagues. Rod was looking forward to working on a catalogue for an Aboriginal exhibition the gallery was to host next month when Nelly walked in.

"Rod, you're looking sexy today. Andrew is away sick. Can you come and work in Research today?" she asked.

"Um, I can't Nelly. I'm supposed to work in Curatorial today and it's really busy at the moment. We've got this exhibition coming up and we're behind. Claire is on maternity leave and two others in Curatorial are sick as well with that flu that's going around at the moment. Sorry, but I can't."

Nelly frowned and left without a backwards glance. I'll be at Research soon enough on Thursday anyway, thought Rod.

Later that day, Rod received an e-mail from Nelly.

Rod,

There has been a change in your work arrangement to start this week. The Assistant Director and I have decided that instead of working in Curatorial 3 days and Research 2 days, you will now work in Curatorial only 2 days, and then on Wednesday switch over to Research for the rest of the week.

Nelly.

Rod began to feel panicky. The whole point of this job was to gain curatorial experience, which was why he had changed his PhD status to part-time. He went to see Sarah to see if she could get his work days changed back. Unfortunately, Sarah only confirmed the arrangement.

"There's nothing I can do about this, Rod. I wish I could, but Nelly helped me get this job. You're a valuable member of Curatorial and we both know everyone on the team is flat out with the others away sick or on leave. Nelly has more authority than me and is good friends with the assistant director."

When Rod arrived in Research on Wednesday, Nelly told him that the desk arrangements were to be changed around. His desk was now visible from her office at all times. Other things began to change in Research as well. Nelly rarely spoke to him except to pass on job assignments. And because he was there an extra day each week, he was able to complete his tasks without having to stay after hours. Rod was pleased about that. However, as the weeks passed, there were not even enough tasks to keep him occupied and he would be told to "find something to do." He felt like he was wasting his time, especially since Curatorial continued to be short staffed and Research was now brimming with staff and limited work. Rod hated that sometimes he had to pretend to be busy.

To make matters worse, when he would arrive at work Nelly had started to remark, "So *now* you've decided to turn up to work," or "getting our beauty sleep, were we?" His fellow researchers began to chime in with similar snide remarks, like "while you've been having your latte, we've been at work since 8 AM."

It was getting unbearable in Research for Rod. Even though his colleagues were talking to him now, he much preferred it when they were not.

Rod was unhappy. He was at lunch with some of the Curatorial staff and told them about the e-mail.

"You'll just have to do the time with Research, and hope that you get back on the good side of Nelly. She may eventually change things back so that you can work more in Curatorial. She's a NAG who likes to use her power over others. It's happened before."

[case.4] The Regency Grand Hotel

By Elizabeth Ho, Prada Singapore

The Regency Grand Hotel is a five-star hotel in Bangkok, Thailand. The hotel was established 15 years ago by a local consortium of investors and has been operated by a Thai general manager throughout this time. The hotel is one of Bangkok's most prestigious hotels and its 700 employees enjoy the prestige of being associated with the hotel. The hotel provides good welfare benefits, above market-rate salary, and job security. In addition, a good year-end bonus amounting to four months' salary was awarded to employees regardless of the hotel's overall performance during the year.

Recently, the Regency was sold to a large American hotel chain that was very keen to expand its operations into Thailand. When the acquisition was announced, the general manager decided to take early retirement when the hotel changed ownership. The American hotel chain kept all of the Regency employees, although a few were transferred to other positions. John Becker, an American with 10 years of management experience with the hotel chain, was appointed as the new general manager of the Regency Grand Hotel. Becker was selected as the new general manager because of his previous successes in integrating newly acquired hotels in the United States. In most of the previous acquisitions, Becker took over operations with poor profitability and low morale.

Becker is a strong believer in empowerment. He expects employees to go beyond guidelines/standards to consider guest needs on a case-by-case basis. That is, employees must be guest-oriented at all times so as to provide excellent customer service. From his U.S. experience, Becker has found that empowerment increases employee motivation, performance, and job satisfaction, all of which contribute to the hotel's profitability and customer service ratings. Soon after becoming general manager at the Regency Grand, Becker introduced the practice of empowerment so as to replicate the successes that he had achieved back home.

The Regency Grand Hotel has been very profitable since it opened 15 years ago. The employees have always worked according to management's instructions. Their responsibility was to ensure that the instructions from their managers were carried out diligently and conscientiously. Innovation and creativity were discouraged under the previous management. Indeed, employees were punished for their mistakes and discouraged from trying out ideas that had not been approved by management. As a result, employees were afraid to be innovative and to take risks.

Becker met with Regency's managers and department heads to explain that empowerment would be introduced in the hotel. He told them that employees must be empowered with decision-making authority so that they can use their initiative, creativity, and judgment to satisfy guest needs or handle problems effectively and efficiently. However, he stressed that the more complex issues and decisions were to be referred to superiors, who were to coach and assist rather than provide direct orders. Furthermore, Becker stressed that mistakes were allowed but he could not tolerate it if the same mistakes were made more than twice. He advised his managers and department heads not to discuss with him minor issues/problems and not to consult with him about minor decisions. Nevertheless, he told them that they are to discuss important/major issues and decisions with him. He concluded the meeting by asking for feedback. Several managers and department heads told him that they liked the idea and would support it, while others simply nodded their heads. Becker was pleased with the response, and was eager to have his plan implemented.

In the past, the Regency had emphasized administrative control, resulting in many bureaucratic procedures throughout the organization. For example, the front-counter employees needed to seek approval from their manager before they could upgrade guests to another category of room. The front-counter manager would then have to write and submit a report to the general manager justifying the upgrade. Soon after his meeting with managers, Becker reduced the number of bureaucratic rules at the Regency and allocated more decision-making authority to front-line employees. This action upset those who previously had decision-making power over these issues. As a result, several of these employees left the hotel.

Becker also began spending a large portion of his time observing and interacting with the employees at the front desk, lobby, restaurants, and various departments. This direct interaction with Becker helped many employees to understand what he wanted and expected of them. However, the employees had much difficulty trying to distinguish between a major and minor issue/decision. More often than not, supervisors would reverse employee decisions by stating that they were major issues requiring management approval. Employees who displayed initiative and made good decisions in satisfying the needs of the guests rarely received any positive feedback from their supervisors. Eventually, most of these employees lost confidence in making

decisions, and reverted back to relying on their superiors for decision making.

Not long after the implementation of the practice of empowerment, Becker realized that his subordinates were consulting him more frequently than before. Most of them came to him with minor issues and consulted with him about minor decisions. He had to spend most of his time attending to his subordinates. Soon he began to feel highly frustrated and exhausted, and very often would tell his secretary that "unless the hotel is on fire, don't let anyone disturb me."

Becker thought that the practice of empowerment would benefit the overall performance of the hotel. However, contrary to his expectation, the business and overall performance of the hotel began to deteriorate. There had been an increasing number of guest complaints. In the past, the hotel had minimal guest complaints. Now there has been a significant number of formal written complaints every month. Many other guests voiced their dissatisfaction verbally to hotel employees. The number of mistakes made by employees had been on the increase. Becker was very upset when he realized that two of the local newspapers and an overseas newspaper had published negative feedback about the hotel in terms of service standards. He was most distressed when an international travel magazine had voted the hotel as "one of Asia's nightmare hotels."

The stress levels of the employees were continuously mounting since the introduction of the practice of empowerment. Absenteeism due to illness was increasing at an alarming rate. In addition, the employee turnover rate had reached an all-time high. The good working relationships that were established under the old management had been severely strained. The employees were no longer united and supportive of each other. They were quick to "point fingers" at or to "back stab" one another when mistakes were made and when problems occurred.

>**video**summaries

>**video**summaries

Celebrity CEO Charisma

Does the cult of CEO charisma really make a difference to company profits? This NBC program takes a brief look at chief executives who acted like superheroes but failed to deliver, as well as a few low-key executives who really made a difference. Harvard Business School professor Rakesh Khurana, author of *Searching for a Corporate Savior,* a book warning that charismatic leaders are not necessarily effective leaders contributes to the program.

Discussion Questions
1. Why do company boards tend to hire charismatic CEOs?
2. What can corporate boards do to minimize the charisma effect when filling chief executive officer and other senior executive positions?

Good Business Deeds

You might not expect to see British American Tobacco, McDonald's, and Microsoft at a meeting on corporate social responsibility, but in their own way these firms are taking steps to become better employers and citizens in the community. This video program describes how these and other firms are embracing values and corporate social responsibility. It particularly highlights a few firms that serve as role models in this regard. One of these is Greyston Bakery, a multimillion dollar gourmet operation that takes people who need help and turns them into contributing members of the organization and society. Another is Eileen Fisher Company, which promotes good labor practices both at home and overseas, and helps customers meet their needs. In each case, the company's values are aligned more closely with employee values than at your typical organization.

Discussion Questions
1. Employees at Greyston Bakery, Eileen Fisher Company, Feed the Children, Green@Work, and other organizations described in this video program seem to have a strong congruence of their personal values with the organization's values. What are the apparent benefits of this values congruence?
2. Discuss the implications of corporate social responsibility in terms of employer branding. What companies come to mind whose employer brand is "doing good" for the community?

JetBlue Airways

JetBlue Airways is one of America's great aviation success stories. In just a few short years after its startup, the New York-based discount airline has become both profitable and highly popular among customers. Founder David Neeleman

claims that the notion of a "JetBlue experience" emerged from customer feedback about their travels on JetBlue. This unique experience is based on the company's customer-focused culture and the many decisions focused on giving customers the best possible encounters.

Discussion Questions
1. Identify the activities or conditions that have developed and maintained JetBlue's customer service culture.
2. How has JetBlue's culture and explicit values influenced its decision making?

Johnson & Johnson: (a) Creating a Global Learning Organization: The Credo; (b) Management Fundamentals Training at Johnson & Johnson

Johnson & Johnson (J&J) is a family-oriented health care and personal products company with about 330 operating units and more than 150,000 employees around the world. The company is well known for "The Credo," a set of values statements introduced in 1938 to help J&J's executives and employees make better decisions. The Credo helps J&J staff to continuously be aware of and serve the needs of its core stakeholders. It also serves as the glue that holds the company's geographically and industrially diverse operating units together. This program introduces Johnson & Johnson's credo and shows how the company instills those values in its managers.

Discussion Questions
1. Why does Johnson & Johnson place so much importance on "The Credo"?
2. How does Johnson & Johnson ensure that managers understand and apply The Credo in their daily decisions and actions?

Pike Place Fish Market

Several years ago, Pike Place Fish Market in Seattle had unhappy employees and was in financial trouble. Rather than close shop, owner John Yokoyama sought help from consultant Jim Bergquist to improve his leadership and energize the workforce. Rather than rule as a tyrant, Yokoyama learned how to actively involve employees in the business. Soon, staff felt more empowered and gained more enjoyment from their work. They also began to actively have fun at work, including setting goals as a game, throwing fish to each other as sport, and pretending they are "world famous." Today, thanks to these and other strategies described in this video case, Pike Place *is* world famous. The little shop has become a tourist attraction and customers from California to New York call in orders.

Discussion Questions

1. Based on the model of emotions and attitudes in Chapter 4, explain how the changes at Pike Place Fish Market improved job satisfaction and reduced turnover. How did these attitude changes affect customer satisfaction?

2. Goal setting is discussed as an important activity at Pike Place. Evaluate the effectiveness of this goal setting process in the context of the characteristics of effective goals described in this textbook.

3. How is coaching applied at Pike Place, and how does this coaching influence employee performance?

Southwest CEO: Get to Know Gary Kelly

Southwest Airlines remains one of the most successful airlines in the United States. Its secret to success? Treat customers as kings and queens, and treat employees even better. This video program shows how Southwest Airlines CEO Gary Kelly keeps in touch with day-to-day activities at the airline. It also describes some of the challenges that Kelly and his executive team have ahead of them.

Discussion Questions

1. Discuss the transactional and transformational leadership of Gary Kelly.

2. How does Gary Kelly's leadership reinforce Southwest Airlines' organizational culture?

Workplace Bias

Wal-Mart is known for its low prices, but many former and current female employees claim the company also has discriminatory low pay and promotional opportunities for women. This video program presents the views of several women who have joined in one of the largest class action sex discrimination lawsuits in history. They claim that qualified women at Wal-Mart receive fewer promotions than their male counterparts. Others say they were fired for launching a sexual harassment complaint. The program describes statistics showing that male district managers earn significantly more than their female counterparts.

Discussion Questions

1. Use your knowledge of social identity theory, stereotyping, and prejudice to explain how sex discrimination might exist at Wal-Mart and in other large retail organizations. Be sure to note any evidence described in this program to support your explanation.

2. If you were a senior manager at Wal-Mart and believed that some of these complaints are due to stereotyping and other biases among middle managers, what interventions would you recommend to correct these biases?

>glossary

A

ability The natural aptitudes and learned capabilities required to successfully complete a task.

achievement-nurturing orientation A cross-cultural value describing the degree to which people in a culture emphasize competitive versus cooperative relations with other people.

action research A problem-focused change process that combines action orientation (changing attitudes and behavior) and research orientation (testing theory through data collection and analysis).

adaptive culture An organizational culture in which employees focus on the changing needs of customers and other stakeholders, and support initiatives to keep pace with those changes.

appreciative inquiry An organizational change strategy that directs the group's attention away from its own problems and focuses participants on the group's potential and positive elements.

artifacts The observable symbols and signs of an organization's culture.

attitudes The cluster of beliefs, assessed feelings, and behavioral intentions toward a person, object, or event.

attraction-selection-attrition (ASA) theory States that organizations have a natural tendency to attract, select, and retain people with values and personality characteristics that are consistent with the organization's character, resulting in a more homogeneous organization and a stronger culture.

attribution process The perceptual process of deciding whether an observed behavior or event is caused largely by internal or external factors.

B

behavior modification A theory that explains learning in terms of the antecedents and consequences of behavior.

bicultural audit A process of diagnosing cultural relations between the companies and determining the extent to which cultural clashes will likely occur.

bounded rationality Processing limited and imperfect information and satisficing rather than maximizing when choosing between alternatives.

brainstorming A freewheeling, face-to-face meeting where team members aren't allowed to criticize, but are encouraged to speak freely, generate as many ideas as possible, and build on the ideas of others.

Brooks's law Also called the "mythical man-month," this principle says that adding more people to a late software project only makes it later.

C

categorical thinking Organizing people and objects into preconceived categories that are stored in our long-term memory.

centrality A contingency of power referring to the degree and nature of interdependence between the power holder and others.

centralization The degree to which formal decision authority is held by a small group of people, typically those at the top of the organizational hierarchy.

ceremonies Planned displays of organizational culture, conducted specifically for the benefit of an audience.

change agent Anyone who possesses enough knowledge and power to guide and facilitate the change effort.

coalition A group that attempts to influence people outside the group by pooling the resources and power of its members.

cognitive dissonance Occurs when we perceive an inconsistency between our beliefs, feelings, and behavior.

collectivism A cross-cultural value describing the degree to which people in a culture emphasize duty to groups to which people belong, and to group harmony.

communication The process by which information is transmitted and *understood* between two or more people.

competencies Skills, knowledge, aptitudes, and other personal characteristics that lead to superior performance.

conflict Is a process in which one party perceives that its interests are being opposed or negatively affected by another party.

conscientiousness A personality dimension describing people who are careful, dependable, and self-disciplined.

constructive conflict (Also known as *task or cognitive conflict.*) Occurs when people focus their discussion on the issue while maintaining respectfulness for people having other points of view.

continuance commitment An employee's calculative attachment to the organization, whereby an employee is motivated to stay only because leaving would be costly.

corporate social responsibility (CSR) Organizational activities intended to benefit society and the environment beyond the firm's immediate financial interests or legal obligations.

counterproductive work behaviors, (CWs) Voluntary behaviors that have the potential to directly or indirectly harm the organization.

countervailing power The capacity of a person, team or organization to keep a more powerful person or group in the exchange relationship.

creativity The development of original ideas that make a socially recognized contribution.

D

decision making A conscious process of making choices among alternatives with the intention of moving toward some desired state of affairs.

deep-level diversity Differences in the psychological characteristics of employees, including personalities, beliefs, values, and attitudes.

distributive justice Perceived fairness in the outcomes we receive relative to our contributions and the outcomes and contributions of others.

divergent thinking Reframing the problem in a unique way and generating different approaches to the issue.

divisional structure A type of departmentalization that groups employees around geographic areas, outputs (products/services), or clients.

drives Neural states that energize individuals to correct deficiencies or maintain an internal equilibrium.

E

electronic brainstorming A recent form of brainstorming that relies on networked computers to submit and share creative ideas.

emotional dissonance The conflict between required and true emotions.

emotional intelligence (EI) The ability to monitor our own and others' feelings and emotions, to discriminate between them and to use this information to guide our thinking and actions.

emotional labor The effort, planning, and control needed to express organizationally desired emotions during interpersonal transactions.

emotions Physiological, behavioral, and psychological episodes experienced toward an object, person, or event that create a state of readiness.

empathy A person's understanding of and sensitivity to the feelings, thoughts, and situation of others.

employee involvement The degree to which employees influence how their work is organized and carried out.

empowerment A psychological concept in which people experience more self-determination, meaning, competence and impact regarding their role in the organization.

equity theory A theory that explains how people develop perceptions of fairness in the distribution and exchange of resources.

ERG theory A needs hierarchy theory consisting of three fundamental needs—existence, relatedness, and growth.

escalation of commitment The tendency to repeat an apparently bad decision or allocate more resources to a failing course of action.

ethical sensitivity A personal characteristic that enables people to recognize the presence and determine the relative importance of an ethical issue.

ethics The study of moral principles or values that determine whether actions are right or wrong and outcomes are good or bad.

evaluation apprehension Occurs when individuals are reluctant to mention ideas that seem silly because they believe (often correctly) that other team members are silently evaluating them.

exit-voice-loyalty-neglect (EVLN) model The four ways, as indicated in the name, that employees respond to job dissatisfaction.

expectancy theory A motivation theory based on the idea that work effort is directed toward behaviors that people believe will lead to desired outcomes.

extroversion A personality dimension describing people who are outgoing, talkative, sociable, and assertive.

F

false-consensus effect A perceptual error in which we overestimate the extent to which others have beliefs and characteristics similar to our own.

five-factor model (FFM) The five abstract dimensions representing most personality traits: conscientiousness, emotional stability, openness to experience, agreeableness and extroversion.

force field analysis Kurt Lewin's model of system-wide change that helps change agents diagnose the forces that drive and restrain proposed organizational change.

formalization The degree to which organizations standardize behavior through rules, procedures, formal training, and related mechanisms.

four-drive theory A motivation theory based on the innate drives to acquire, bond, learn, and defend that incorporates both emotions and rationality.

functional structure A type of departmentalization that organizes employees around specific knowledge or other resources.

fundamental attribution error The tendency to see the person rather than the situation as the main cause of that person's behavior.

future search —system-wide group sessions, usually lasting a few days, in which participants identify trends and identify ways to adapt to those changes.

G

general adaptation syndrome A model of the stress experience, consisting of three stages: alarm reaction, resistance and exhaustion.

globalization Economic, social, and cultural connectivity with people in other parts of the world.

goal setting The process of motivating employees and clarifying their role perceptions by establishing performance objectives.

grapevine An unstructured and informal network founded on social relationships rather than organizational charts or job descriptions.

groupthink The tendency of highly cohesive groups to value consensus at the price of decision quality.

H

halo effect A perceptual error whereby our general impression of a person, usually based on one prominent characteristic, colors our perception of other characteristics of that person.

high-performance work practices (HPWP) A perspective that effective organizations incorporate several workplace practices that leverage the potential of human capital.

I

implicit favorite A preferred alternative that the decision maker uses repeatedly as a comparison.

implicit leadership theory A theory stating that people evaluate a leader's effectiveness in terms of how well that person fits preconceived beliefs about the features and behaviors of effective leaders (leadership prototypes), and that they tend to inflate the influence of leaders on organizational events.

impression management The practice of actively shaping our public images.

individualism A cross-cultural value describing the degree to which people in a culture emphasize independence and personal uniqueness.

influence Any behavior that attempts to alter someone's attitudes or behavior.

information overload Occurs when the volume of information received exceeds the person's capacity to get through it.

ingratiation Any attempt to increase liking by, or perceived similarity to, some targeted person.

inoculation effect A persuasive communication strategy of warning listeners that others will try to influence them in the future and that they should be wary about the opponent's arguments.

intellectual capital Company's stock of knowledge, including human capital, structural capital and relationship capital.

intuition The ability to know when a problem or opportunity exists and to select the best course of action without conscious reasoning.

J

job characteristics model A job design model that relates the motivational properties of jobs to specific personal and organizational consequences of those properties.

job design The process of assigning tasks to a job, including the interdependency of those tasks with other jobs.

job enrichment Occurs when employees are given more responsibility for scheduling, coordinating and planning their own work.

job satisfaction Person's evaluation of his or her job and work context.

job specialization The result of division of labor in which each job includes a subset of the tasks required to complete the product or service.

Johari Window A model of mutual understanding that encourages disclosure and feedback to increase our own open area and reduce the blind, hidden, and unknown areas.

L

leadership Influencing, motivating, and enabling others to contribute toward the effectiveness and success of the organizations of which they are members.

leadership substitutes A theory identifying contingencies that either limit the leader's ability to influence subordinates or make that particular leadership style unnecessary.

learning A relatively permanent change in behavior (or behavior tendency) that occurs as a result of a person's interaction with the environment.

learning orientation The extent to which an organization or individual supports knowledge management, particularly opportunities to acquire knowledge through experience and experimentation.

legitimate power An agreement among organizational members that people in certain roles can request certain behaviors of others.

locus of control A person's general belief about the amount of control he or she has over personal life events.

M

Machiavellian values The belief that deceit is a natural and acceptable way to influence others.

management by walking around (MBWA) A communication practice in which executives get out of their offices and learn from others in the organization through face-to-face dialogue.

Maslow's needs hierarchy theory A motivation theory of needs arranged in a hierarchy, whereby people are motivated to fulfill a higher need as a lower one becomes gratified.

matrix structure A type of departmentalization that overlays two organizational forms in order to leverage the benefits of both.

mechanistic structure An organizational structure with a narrow span of control and a high degree of formalization and centralization.

media richness The medium's data-carrying capacity, that is, the volume and variety of information that can be transmitted during a specific time.

mental models Visual or relational images in our mind representing the external world.

mentoring A relationship in which a more senior member of the organization provides coaching and other career development support to a junior member—also increases power through visibility.

moral intensity The degree to which an issue demands the application of ethical principles.

motivation The forces within a person that affect his or her direction, intensity, and persistence of voluntary behavior.

N

needs Goal-directed forces that people experience.

neuroticism A personality dimension describing people with high levels of anxiety, hostility, depression, and self-consciousness.

nominal group technique A variation of traditional brainstorming that tries to combine the benefits of team decision making without the problems mentioned earlier.

norms The informal rules and shared expectations that groups establish to regulate the behavior of their members.

O

open systems A perspective that organizations take their sustenance from the environment and, in turn, affect that environment through their output.

organic structure An organizational structure with a wide span of control, little formalization and decentralized decision making.

organizational (affective) commitment The employee's emotional attachment to, identification with, and involvement in a particular organization.

organizational behavior (OB) The study of what people think, feel, and do in and around organizations.

organizational citizenship behaviors (OCBs) Various forms of cooperation and helpfulness to others that support the organization's social and psychological context.

organizational culture The values and assumptions shared within an organization.

organizational effectiveness A broad concept represented by several perspectives, including the organization's fit with the external environment, internal subsystems configuration for high-performance, emphasis on organizational learning, and ability to satisfy the needs of key stakeholders.

organizational efficiency The ratio of inputs to outcomes in the organization's transformation process.

organizational learning A perspective that organizational effectiveness depends on the organization's capacity to acquire, share, use, and store valuable knowledge.

organizational politics Behaviors that others perceive as self-serving tactics for personal gain at the expense of other people and possibly the organization.

organizational socialization The process by which individuals learn the values, expected behaviors, and social knowledge necessary to assume their roles in the organization.

organizational strategy The way the organization positions itself in its setting in relation to its stakeholders, given the organization's resources, capabilities, and mission.

organizational structure The division of labor as well as the patterns of coordination, communication, workflow, and formal power that direct organizational activities.

organizations Groups of people who work interdependently toward some purpose.

P

parallel learning structure —highly participative arrangements, composed of people from most levels of the organization who follow the action research model to produce meaningful organizational change.

path-goal leadership theory A contingency theory of leadership based on the expectancy theory of motivation that relates several leadership styles to specific employee and situational contingencies.

perception The process of receiving information about and making sense of the world around us.

personality The relatively enduring pattern of thoughts, emotions, and behaviors that characterize a person, along with the psychological processes behind those characteristics.

persuasion Presenting facts, logical arguments, and emotional appeals to change another person's attitudes and behavior.

positive organizational behavior A perspective of organizational behavior that focuses on building positive qualities and traits within individuals or institutions as opposed to focusing on what is wrong with them.

power The capacity of a person, team, or organization to influence others.

power distance A cross-cultural value describing the degree to which people in a culture accept unequal distribution of power in a society.

primacy effect A perceptual error in which we quickly form an opinion of people based on the first information we receive about them.

procedural justice Perceived fairness of the procedures used to decide the distribution of resources.

process losses Resources (including time and energy) expended toward team development and maintenance rather than the task.

production blocking A time constraint in team decision making due to the procedural requirement that only one person may speak at a time.

prospect theory An effect in which losing a particular amount is more disliked than gaining the same amount.

psychological harassment Repeated and hostile or unwanted conduct, verbal comments, actions or gestures that affect an employee's dignity or psychological or physical integrity and that result in a harmful work environment for the employee.

R

rational choice paradigm A deeply held perspective of decision making that that people should—and typically do—make decisions based on pure logic and rationality.

reality shock The stress that results when employees perceive discrepancies between their preemployment expectations and on-the-job reality.

recency effect A perceptual error in which the most recent information dominates our perception of others.

referent power The capacity to influence others based on an identification with and respect for the power-holder.

refreezing —the latter part of the change process in which systems and conditions are introduced that reinforce and maintain the desired behaviors.

relationship conflict (Also known as *socioemotional, affective,* or *destructive conflict.*) Focuses on people rather than the issues and tasks.

resilience The capability of individuals to cope successfully in the face of significant change, adversity, or risk.

rituals The programmed routines of daily organizational life that dramatize the organization's culture.

role A set of behaviors that people are expected to perform because they hold certain positions in a team and organization.

S

satisficing Selecting a solution that is satisfactory or "good enough," rather than optimal or "the best."

scenario planning A systematic process of thinking about alternative futures and what the organization should do to anticipate and react to those environments.

scientific management Systematically partitioning work into its smallest elements and standardizing tasks to achieve maximum efficiency.

selective attention The process of attending to some information received by our senses and ignoring other information.

self-concept An individual's self-beliefs and self-evaluations.

self-directed teams (SDTs) Cross-functional work groups organized around work processes, that complete an entire piece of work requiring several interdependent tasks, and that have substantial autonomy over the execution of those tasks.

self-efficacy A person's belief that he or she has the ability, motivation, correct role perceptions, and favorable situation to complete a task successfully.

self-fulfilling prophecy Occurs when our expectations about another person cause that person to act in a way that is consistent with those expectations.

self-reinforcement Occurs whenever an employee has control over a reinforcer but doesn't "take" it until completing a self-set goal.

self-serving bias The tendency to attribute our favorable outcomes to internal factors and our failures to external factors.

sexual harassment Unwelcome conduct of a sexual nature that detrimentally affects the work environment or leads to adverse job-related consequences for its victims.

shared leadership The view that leadership is broadly distributed rather than assigned to one person, such that people within the team and organization lead each other.

skill variety The extent to which employees must use different skills and talents to perform tasks within their job.

social capital The knowledge and other resources available to people or social units (teams, organizations) due to a durable network that connects them to others.

social identity theory A theory that explains self-concept in terms of the person's unique characteristics (personal identity) and membership in various social groups (social identity).

social learning theory A theory stating that much learning occurs by observing others and then modeling the behaviors that lead to favorable outcomes and avoiding behaviors that lead to punishing consequences.

social loafing Occurs when people exert less effort (and usually perform at a lower level) when working in groups than when working alone.

span of control The number of people directly reporting to the next level in the organizational hierarchy.

stakeholders Individuals, organizations, or other entities who affect, or are affected by, the organization's objectives and actions.

stereotyping The process of assigning traits to people based on their membership in a social category.

stress An adaptive response to a situation that is perceived as challenging or threatening to the person's well-being.

stressors Any environmental conditions that place a physical or emotional demand on the person.

substitutability A contingency of power referring to the availability of alternatives.

superordinate goal Any goal that both conflicting parties value and whose attainment is beyond the resources and effort of either party alone.

surface-level diversity The observable demographic or physiological differences in people, such as their race, ethnicity, gender, age, and physical disabilities.

T

tacit knowledge Knowledge embedded in our actions and ways of thinking, and transmitted only through observation and experience.

task identity The degree to which a job requires completion of a whole or an identifiable piece of work.

task interdependence The extent that team members must share materials, information, or expertise in order to perform their jobs.

task significance The degree to which the job has a substantial impact on the organization and/or larger society.

team-based structure A type of departmentalization built around self-directed teams that complete an entire piece of work.

team cohesion The degree of attraction people feel toward the team and their motivation to remain members.

teams Groups of two or more people who interact and influence each other, are mutually accountable for achieving common goals associated with organizational objectives, and perceive themselves as a social entity within an organization.

third-party conflict resolution Any attempt by a relatively neutral person to help the parties resolve their differences.

transactional leadership Leadership that helps organizations achieve their current objectives more efficiently, such as linking job performance to valued rewards and ensuring that employees have the resources needed to get the job done.

transformational leadership A leadership perspective that explains how leaders change teams or organizations by creating, communicating and modeling a vision for the organization or work unit, and inspiring employees to strive for that vision.

trust A psychological state comprising the intention to accept vulnerability based on positive expectations of the intent or behavior of another person.

trust Positive expectations one person has toward another person in situations involving risk.

U

uncertainty avoidance A cross-cultural value describing the degree to which people in a culture tolerate ambiguity (low uncertainty avoidance) or feel threatened by ambiguity and uncertainty (high uncertainty avoidance).

unfreezing —the first part of the change process whereby the change agent produces disequilibrium between the driving and restraining forces.

upward appeal A type of influence in which someone with higher authority or expertise is called upon in reality or symbolically to support the influencer's position.

V

values Relatively stable, evaluative beliefs that guide a person's preferences for outcomes or courses of action in a variety of situations.

virtual teams Teams whose members operate across space, time, and organizational boundaries and are linked through information technologies to achieve organizational tasks.

virtual work Work performed away from the traditional physical workplace using information technology.

W

wikis Collaborative Web spaces in which anyone in a group can write, edit, or remove material from the Web site.

win–lose orientation The belief that conflicting parties are drawing from a fixed pie, so the more one party receives, the less the other party will receive.

win–win orientation The belief that the parties will find a mutually beneficial solution to their disagreement.

workaholic A person who is highly involved in work, feels compelled to work and has a low enjoyment of work.

work/life balance The degree to which a person minimizes conflict between work and nonwork demands.

>**end**notes

chapter 1

1. G. Whipp, "Swimming against the Tide," *Daily News of Los Angeles,* May 30, 2003, p. U6; "The Pixar Principle," *The Age (Melbourne, AU),* May 28, 2006; D. F. Locke, J. Ressner, and R. Corliss, "When Woody Met Mickey," *Time,* February 6, 2006, p. 46; W. C. Taylor and P. LaBarre, "How Pixar Adds a New School of Thought to Disney," *New York Times,* January 29, 2006; N. Wingfield and M. Marr, "A Techie's Task," *The Wall Street Journal,* January 30, 2006, p. B7; and R. Grover, "How Bob Iger Unchained Disney," *BusinessWeek,* February 5, 2007, p. 74.

2. M. Warner, "Organizational Behavior Revisited," *Human Relations* 47 (October 1994), pp. 1151–66; R. Westwood and S. Clegg, "The Discourse of Organization Studies: Dissensus, Politics, and Paradigms," in *Debating Organization: Point-Counterpoint in Organization Studies,* ed. R. Westwood and S. Clegg (Malden, MA: Blackwood, 2003), pp. 1–42. Some of the historical bases of OB mentioned in this paragraph are described in J. A. Conger, "Max Weber's Conceptualization of Charismatic Authority: Its Influence on Organizational Research," *The Leadership Quarterly* 4, no. 3–4 (1993), pp. 277–88; R. Kanigel, *The One Best Way: Frederick Winslow Taylor and the Enigma of Efficiency* (New York: Viking, 1997); J. H. Smith, "The Enduring Legacy of Elton Mayo," *Human Relations* 51, no. 3 (1998), pp. 221–49; T. Takala, "Plato on Leadership," *Journal of Business Ethics* 17 (May 1998), pp. 785–98; and J. A. Fernandez, "The Gentleman's Code of Confucius: Leadership by Values," *Organizational Dynamics* 33, no. 1 (February 2004), pp. 21–31.

3. D. Katz and R. L. Kahn, *The Social Psychology of Organizations* (New York: Wiley, 1966), Chap. 2; and R. N. Stern and S. R. Barley, "Organizations as Social Systems: Organization Theory's Neglected Mandate," *Administrative Science Quarterly* 41 (1996), pp. 146–62.

4. B. Schlender, "The Three Faces of Steve," *Fortune,* November 9, 1998, pp. 96–101.

5. S. L. Rynes et al., "Behavioral Coursework in Business Education: Growing Evidence of a Legitimacy Crisis," *Academy of Management Learning & Education* 2, no. 3 (2003), pp. 269–83; R. P. Singh and A. G. Schick, "Organizational Behavior: Where Does It Fit in Today's Management Curriculum?" *Journal of Education for Business* 82, no. 6 (July 2007), p. 349.

6. P. R. Lawrence and N. Nohria, *Driven: How Human Nature Shapes Our Choices* (San Francisco: Jossey-Bass, 2002), Chap. 6.

7. P. R. Lawrence "Historical Development of Organizational Behavior," in *Handbook of Organizational Behavior,* ed. L. W. Lorsch (Englewood Cliffs, NJ: Prentice-Hall, 1987), pp. 1–9; and S. A. Mohrman, C. B. Gibson, and A. M. Mohrman Jr., "Doing Research That Is Useful to Practice: A Model and Empirical Exploration," *Academy of Management Journal* 44 (April 2001), pp. 357–75. For a contrary view, see A. P. Brief and J. M. Dukerich, "Theory in Organizational Behavior: Can It Be Useful?" *Research in Organizational Behavior* 13 (1991), pp. 327–52.

8. M. S. Myers, *Every Employee a Manager* (New York: McGraw Hill, 1970).

9. D. Yankelovich, "Got to Give to Get," *Mother Jones* 22 (July 1997), pp. 60–63; D. MacDonald, "Good Managers Key to Buffett's Acquisitions," *Montreal Gazette,* November 16, 2001. The two studies on OB and financial performance are B. N. Pfau and I. T. Kay, *The Human Capital Edge* (New York: McGraw-Hill, 2002); and I. S. Fulmer, B. Gerhart, and K. S. Scott, "Are the 100 Best Better? An Empirical Investigation of the Relationship between Being a 'Great Place to Work' and Firm Performance," *Personnel Psychology* 56, no. 4 (Winter 2003), pp. 965–93.

10. Mohrman, Gibson, and Mohrman Jr., "Doing Research That Is Useful to Practice: A Model and Empirical Exploration"; and J. P. Walsh et al., "On the Relationship between Research and Practice: Debate and Reflections," *Journal of Management Inquiry* 16, no. 2 (June 2007), pp. 128–54. Similarly, in 1961, Harvard business professor Fritz Roethlisberger proposed that the field of OB is concerned with human behavior "from the points of view of both (a) its determination . . . and (b) its improvement." See P. B. Vaill, "F. J. Roethlisberger and the Elusive Phenomena of Organizational Behavior," *Journal of Management Education* 31, no. 3 (June 2007), pp. 321–38.

11. R. H. Hall, "Effectiveness Theory and Organizational Effectiveness," *Journal of Applied Behavioral Science* 16, no. 4 (Oct. 1980), pp. 536–45; and K. Cameron, "Organizational Effectiveness: Its Demise and Re-Emergence through Positive Organizational Scholarship," in *Great Minds in Management,* ed. K. G. Smith and M. A. Hitt (New York: Oxford University Press, 2005), pp. 304–30.

12. J. L. Price, "The Study of Organizational Effectiveness," *The Sociological Quarterly* 13 (1972), pp. 3–15.

13. S. C. Selden and J. E. Sowa, "Testing a Multi-Dimensional Model of Organizational Performance: Prospects and Problems," *Journal of Public Administration Research and Theory* 14, no. 3 (July 2004), pp. 395–416.

14. F. E. Kast and J. E. Rosenzweig, "General Systems Theory: Applications for Organization and Management," *Academy of Management Journal* (1972), pp. 447–65; P. M. Senge, *The Fifth Discipline: The Art and Practice of the Learning Organization* (New York: Doubleday Currency, 1990); A. De Geus, *The Living Company* (Boston: Harvard Business School Press, 1997); and R. T. Pascale, M. Millemann, and L. Gioja, *Surfing on the Edge of Chaos* (London: Texere, 2000).

15. V. P. Rindova and S. Kotha, "Continuous 'Morphing': Competing through Dynamic Capabilities, Form, and Function," *Academy of Management Journal* 44 (2001), pp. 1263–80; and J. McCann, "Organizational Effectiveness: Changing Concepts

for Changing Environments," *Human Resource Planning* 27, no. 1 (2004), pp. 42–50.

16. J. Arlidge, "McJobs That All the Family Can Share," *Daily Telegraph (London),* January 26, 2006, p. 1.

17. C. Ostroff and N. Schmitt, "Configurations of Organizational Effectiveness and Efficiency," *Academy of Management Journal* 36, no. 6 (1993), p. 1345.

18. P. S. Adler et al., "Performance Improvement Capability: Keys to Accelerating Performance Improvement in Hospitals," *California Management Review* 45, no. 2 (2003), pp. 12–33; and J. Jamrog, M. Vickers, and D. Bear, "Building and Sustaining a Culture That Supports Innovation," *Human Resource Planning* 29, no. 3 (2006), pp. 9–19. Klaus Kleinfeld's quotation is from "Siemens CEO Klaus Kleinfeld: 'Nobody's Perfect, but a Team Can Be'," *Knowledge@Wharton,* April 19, 2006.

19. G. Huber, "Organizational Learning: The Contributing Processes and Literature," *Organizational Science* 2 (1991), pp. 88–115; D. A. Garvin, *Learning in Action: A Guide to Putting the Learning Organization to Work* (Boston: Harvard Business School Press, 2000); and H. Shipton, "Cohesion or Confusion? Towards a Typology for Organizational Learning Research," *International Journal of Management Reviews* 8, no. 4 (2006), pp. 233–52.

20. W. C. Bogner and P. Bansal, "Knowledge Management as the Basis of Sustained High Performance," *Journal of Management Studies* 44, no. 1 (2007), pp. 165–88; and D. Jiménez-Jiménez and J. G. Cegarra-Navarro, "The Performance Effect of Organizational Learning and Market Orientation," *Industrial Marketing Management* 36, no. 6 (2007), pp. 694–708.

21. M. Liedtke, "Google vs. Yahoo: Heavyweights Attack from Different Angles," *Associated Press Newswires,* December 18, 2004; R. Basch, "Doing Well by Doing Good," *Searcher Magazine,* January 2005, pp. 18–28; and A. Ignatius and L. A. Locke, "In Search of the Real Google," *Time,* February 20, 2006, pp. 36.

22. T. A. Stewart, *Intellectual Capital: The New Wealth of Organizations* (New York: Currency/Doubleday, 1997); H. Saint-Onge and D. Wallace, *Leveraging Communities of Practice for Strategic Advantage* (Boston: Butterworth-Heinemann, 2003), pp. 9–10; J. A. Johannessen, B. Olsen, and J. Olaisen, "Intellectual Capital as a Holistic Management Philosophy: A Theoretical Perspective," *International Journal of Information Management* 25, no. 2 (2005), pp. 151–71.

23. M. E. McGill and J. W. Slocum Jr., "Unlearn the Organization," *Organizational Dynamics* 22, no. 2 (1993), pp. 67–79; and A. E. Akgün, G. S. Lynn, and J. C. Byrne, "Antecedents and Consequences of Unlearning in New Product Development Teams," *Journal of Product Innovation Management* 23 (2006), pp. 73–88.

24. J. Pfeffer, *The Human Equation: Building Profits by Putting People First* (Boston: Harvard University Press, 1998); E. Appelbaum et al., *Manufacturing Advantage: Why High-Performance Work Systems Pay Off* (Ithaca, NY: Cornell University Press, 2000); G. S. Benson, S. M. Young, and E. E. Lawler III, "High-Involvement Work Practices and Analysts' Forecasts of Corporate Earnings," *Human Resource Management* 45, no. 4 (2006), pp. 519–37; and L. Sels et al.,

"Unravelling the HRM-Performance Link: Value-Creating and Cost-Increasing Effects of Small Business HRM," *Journal of Management Studies* 43, no. 2 (2006), pp. 319–42.

25. M. A. Huselid, "The Impact of Human Resource Management Practices on Turnover, Productivity, and Corporate Financial Performance," *Academy of Management Journal* 38, no. 3 (1995), pp. 635–72; B. E. Becker and M. A. Huselid, "Strategic Human Resources Management: Where Do We Go from Here?" *Journal of Management* 32, no. 6 (December 2006), pp. 898–925; and J. Combs et al., "How Much Do High-Performance Work Practices Matter? A Meta-Analysis of Their Effects on Organizational Performance," *Personnel Psychology* 59, no. 3 (2006), pp. 501–28.

26. J. Barney, "Firm Resources and Sustained Competitive Advantage," *Journal of Management* 17, no. 1 (1991), pp. 99–120.

27. V. L. Parker, "Org Charts Turn around with Teams," *News & Observer (Raleigh, NC),* July 21, 2005, p. D1; and N. Byrnes and M. Arndt, "The Art of Motivation," *BusinessWeek,* May 1, 2006, p. 56.

28. E. E. Lawler III, S. A. Mohrman, and G. E. Ledford Jr., *Strategies for High Performnce Organizations* (San Francisco: Jossey-Bass, 1998); S. H. Wagner, C. P. Parker, and D. Neil, "Employees That Think and Act Like Owners: Effects of Ownership Beliefs and Behaviors on Organizational Effectiveness," *Personnel Psychology* 56, no. 4 (Winter 2003), pp. 847–71; P. J. Gollan, "High Involvement Management and Human Resource Sustainability: The Challenges and Opportunities," *Asia Pacific Journal of Human Resources* 43, no. 1 (April 2005), pp. 18–33; Y. Liu et al., "The Value of Human Resource Management for Organizational Performance," *Business Horizons* 50 (2007), pp. 503–11; and P. Tharenou, A. M. Saks, and C. Moore, "A Review and Critique of Research on Training and Organizational-Level Outcomes," *Human Resource Management Review* 17, no. 3 (2007), pp. 251–73.

29. S. Fleetwood and A. Hesketh, "HRM-Performance Research: Under-Theorized and Lacking Explanatory Power," *International Journal of Human Resource Management* 17, no. 12 (December 2006), pp. 1977–93.

30. J. Godard, "High Performance and the Transformation of Work? The Implications of Alternative Work Practices for the Experience and Outcomes of Work," *Industrial and Labor Relations Review* 54, no. 4 (July 2001), pp. 776–805; G. Murray et al., eds., *Work and Employment Relations in the High-Performance Workplace* (London: Continuum, 2002); and B. Harley, "Hope or Hype? High Performance Work Systems," in *Participation and Democracy at Work: Essays in Honour of Harvie Ramsay,* ed. B. Harley, J. Hyman, and P. Thompson (Houndsmills, UK: Palgrave Macmillan, 2005), pp. 38–54.

31. A. L. Friedman and S. Miles, *Stakeholders: Theory and Practice* (New York: Oxford University Press, 2006); M. L. Barnett, "Stakeholder Influence Capacity and the Variability of Financial Returns to Corporate Social Responsibility," *Academy of Management Review* 32, no. 3 (2007), pp. 794–816; and R. E. Freeman, J. S. Harrison, and A. C. Wicks, *Managing for Stakeholders: Survival, Reputation, and Success* (New Haven, CT: Yale University Press, 2007).

32. C. Eden and F. Ackerman, *Making Strategy: The Journey of Strategic Management* (London: Sage, 1998).

33. Three of the many recent sources on Wal-Mart's stakeholder dilemmas and failings are T. A. Hemphill, "Rejuvenating Wal-Mart's Reputation," *Business Horizons* 48, no. 1 (2005), pp. 11–21; A. Bianco, *The Bully of Bentonville: How the High Cost of Wal-Mart's Everyday Low Prices Is Hurting America* (New York: Random House, 2006); and C. Fishman, *The Wal-Mart Effect* (New York: Penguin, 2006).

34. G. R. Salancik and J. Pfeffer, *The External Control of Organizations: A Resource Dependence Perspective* (New York: Harper Row, 1978); T. Casciaro and M. J. Piskorski, "Power Imbalance, Mutual Dependence, and Constraint Absorption: A Closer Look at Dependence Theory," *Administrative Science Quarterly* 50 (2005), pp. 167–99; and N. Roome and F. Wijen, "Stakeholder Power and Organizational Learning in Corporate Environmental Management," *Organization Studies* 27, no. 2 (2005), pp. 235–63.

35. R. E. Freeman, A. C. Wicks, and B. Parmar, "Stakeholder Theory and 'the Corporate Objective Revisited'," *Organization Science* 15, no. 3 (May–June 2004), pp. 364–69; D. Balser and J. McClusky, "Managing Stakeholder Relationships and Nonprofit Organization Effectiveness," *Nonprofit Management & Leadership* 15, no. 3 (Spring 2005), pp. 295–315; and Friedman and Miles, *Stakeholders: Theory and Practice,* Chap. 3.

36. B. M. Meglino and E. C. Ravlin, "Individual Values in Organizations: Concepts, Controversies, and Research," *Journal of Management* 24, no. 3 (1998), pp. 351–89; B. R. Agle and C. B. Caldwell, "Understanding Research on Values in Business," *Business and Society* 38, no. 3 (September 1999), pp. 326–87; A. Bardi and S. H. Schwartz, "Values and Behavior: Strength and Structure of Relations," *Personality and Social Psychology Bulletin* 29, no. 10 (October 2003), pp. 1207–20; and S. Hitlin and J. A. Pilavin, "Values: Reviving a Dormant Concept," *Annual Review of Sociology* 30 (2004), pp. 359–93.

37. "Lockheed Martin Is Top Choice as Ideal Employer for Engineering Students," PRNewswire News release, (Bethesda, MD: May 15, 2006).

38. M. van Marrewijk, "Concepts and Definitions of CSR and Corporate Sustainability: Between Agency and Communion," *Journal of Business Ethics* 44 (May 2003), pp. 95–105; and Barnett, "Stakeholder Influence Capacity and the Variability of Financial Returns to Corporate Social Responsibility."

39. L. S. Paine, *Value Shift* (New York: McGraw-Hill, 2003); and A. Mackey, T. B. Mackey, and J. B. Barney, "Corporate Social Responsibility and Firm Performance: Investor Preferences and Corporate Strategies," *Academy of Management Review* 32, no. 3 (2007), pp. 817–35.

40. S. Zadek, *The Civil Corporation: The New Economy of Corporate Citizenship* (London: Earthscan, 2001); and S. Hart and M. Milstein, "Creating Sustainable Value," *Academy of Management Executive* 17, no. 2 (2003), pp. 56–69.

41. "Believe It," *BC Business,* July 2004, p. 130; "Multi-Year Study Finds 21% Increase in Americans Who Say Corporate Support of Social Issues Is Important in Building Trust," *Business Wire,* December 9, 2004; and J. Milne, "Do the Right Thing," *MIS UK,* December 1, 2005, p. 20.

42. R. Martin, "The Virtue Matrix: Calculating the Return on Corporate Responsibility," *Harvard Business Review* 80 (March 2002), pp. 68–85.

43. J. P. Campbell, "The Definition and Measurement of Performance in the New Age," in *The Changing Nature of Performance: Implications for Staffing, Motivation, and Development,* ed. D. R. Ilgen and E. D. Pulakos (San Francisco: Jossey-Bass, 1999), pp. 399–429; and R. D. Hackett, "Understanding and Predicting Work Performance in the Canadian Military," *Canadian Journal of Behavioural Science* 34, no. 2 (2002), pp. 131–40.

44. D. W. Organ, "Organizational Citizenship Behavior: It's Construct Clean-up Time," *Human Performance* 10 (1997), pp. 85–97; S. J. Motowidlo, "Some Basic Issues Related to Contextual Performance and Organizational Citizenship Behavior in Human Resource Management," *Human Resource Management Review* 10, no. 1 (2000), pp. 115–26; and J. A. LePine, A. Erez, and D. E. Johnson, "The Nature and Dimensionality of Organizational Citizenship Behavior: A Critical Review and Meta-Analysis," *Journal of Applied Psychology* 87 (February 2002), pp. 52–65.

45. K. Lee and N. J. Allen, "Organizational Citizenship Behavior and Workplace Deviance: The Role of Affect and Cognitions," *Journal of Applied Psychology* 87, no. 1 (2002), pp. 131–42.

46. M. Rotundo and P. Sackett, "The Relative Importance of Task, Citizenship, and Counterproductive Performance to Global Ratings of Job Performance: A Policy-Capturing Approach," *Journal of Applied Psychology* 87 (February 2002), pp. 66–80; and P. D. Dunlop and K. Lee, "Workplace Deviance, Organizational Citizenship Behaviour, and Business Unit Performance: The Bad Apples Do Spoil the Whole Barrel," *Journal of Organizational Behavior* 25 (2004), pp. 67–80.

47. B. Carey, "Truckload's New Recruiting Routes," *Traffic World,* August 22, 2005; and D. Simanoff, "Hotels Plagued by Staff Vacancies," *Tampa Tribune,* January 30, 2006, p. 1.

48. Watson Wyatt, "U.S. Workers Cite Hypocrisy and Favoritism—Rather Than Financial Misdeeds—as Biggest Ethical Lapses at Work," Watson Wyatt News release, (Washington, DC: January 12, 2005); and Watson Wyatt, *WorkCanada 2004/2005—Pursuing Productive Engagement,* (Toronto: Watson Wyatt, January 2005).

49. T. R. Mitchell, B. C. Holtom, and T. W. Lee, "How to Keep Your Best Employees: Developing an Effective Retention Policy," *Academy of Management Executive* 15 (November 2001), pp. 96–108; K. Morrell, J. Loan-Clarke, and A. Wilkinson, "The Role of Shocks in Employee Turnover," *British Journal of Management* 15 (2004), pp. 335–49; and B. C. Holtom, T. R. Mitchell, and T. W. Lee, "Increasing Human and Social Capital by Applying Job Embeddedness Theory," *Organizational Dynamics* 35, no. 4 (2006), pp. 316–31.

50. D. A. Harrison and J. J. Martocchio, "Time for Absenteeism: A 20-Year Review of Origins, Offshoots, and Outcomes," *Journal of Management* 24 (Spring 1998), pp. 305–50; C. M.

Mason and M. A. Griffin, "Group Absenteeism and Positive Affective Tone: A Longitudinal Study," *Journal of Organizational Behavior* 24, no. 6 (2003), pp. 667–87; and A. Vaananen et al., "Job Characteristics, Physical and Psychological Symptoms, and Social Support as Antecedents of Sickness Absence among Men and Women in the Private Industrial Sector," *Social Science & Medicine* 57, no. 5 (2003), pp. 807–24.

51. "'Huge Responsibility' on Globalco to Perform," *New Zealand Herald,* June 18, 2001; "A Major Player on the World Milk Stage," *Weekly Times (Sydney),* September 8, 2004, p. 91; K. Newman, "Greener Pastures," *MIS New Zealand,* September 2004, p. 18; and D. Blayney et al., *U.S. Dairy at a Global Crossroads,* (Washington, DC: United States Department of Agriculture. Economic Research Service, November 2006).

52. S. Fischer, "Globalization and Its Challenges," *American Economic Review* (May 2003), pp. 1–29. For discussion of the diverse meanings of *globalization,* see M. F. Guillén, "Is Globalization Civilizing, Destructive or Feeble? A Critique of Five Key Debates in the Social Science Literature," *Annual Review of Sociology* 27 (2001), pp. 235–60.

53. The ongoing debate regarding the advantages and disadvantages of globalization are discussed in Guillén, "Is Globalization Civilizing, Destructive or Feeble?"; D. Doane, "Can Globalization Be Fixed?" *Business Strategy Review* 13, no. 2 (2002), pp. 51–58; J. Bhagwati, *In Defense of Globalization* (New York: Oxford University Press, 2004); and M. Wolf, *Why Globalization Works* (New Haven, CT: Yale University Press, 2004).

54. K. Ohmae, *The Next Global Stage* (Philadelphia: Wharton School Publishing, 2005).

55. R. House, M. Javidan, and P. Dorfman, "Project Globe: An Introduction," *Applied Psychology: An International Journal* 50 (2001), pp. 489–505; M. A. Von Glinow, E. A. Drost, and M. B. Teagarden, "Converging on IHRM Best Practices: Lessons Learned from a Globally Distributed Consortium on Theory and Practice," *Human Resource Management* 41, no. 1 (April 2002), pp. 123–40; and M. M. Javidan et al., "In the Eye of the Beholder: Cross-Cultural Lessons in Leadership from Project Globe," *Academy of Management Perspectives* 20, no. 1 (February 2006), pp. 67–90.

56. Verizon, *Making Connections: Verizon Corporate Responsibility Report 2004,* (New York: Verizon, December 2004); P. Goffney, "Champions of Diversity: The Path to Corporate Enlightenment," *Essence,* May 2005, 149–57.

57. M. F. Riche, "America's Diversity and Growth: Signposts for the 21st Century," *Population Bulletin* (June 2000), pp. 3–43; and U.S. Census Bureau, *Statistical Abstract of the United States: 2004–2005,* (Washington, DC: U.S. Census Bureau, May 2005).

58. D. A. Harrison et al., "Time, Teams, and Task Performance: Changing Effects of Surface- and Deep-Level Diversity on Group Functioning," *Academy of Management Journal* 45, no. 5 (2002), pp. 1029–46.

59. R. Zemke, C. Raines, and B. Filipczak, *Generations at Work: Managing the Clash of Veterans, Boomers, Xers, and Nexters in Your Workplace* (New York: Amacom, 2000); M. R. Muetzel, *They're Not Aloof, Just Generation X* (Shreveport, LA: Steel Bay, 2003); S. H. Applebaum, M. Serena, and B. T.

Shapiro, "Generation X and the Boomers: Organizational Myths and Literary Realities," *Management Research News* 27, no. 11/12 (2004), pp. 1–28; and N. Howe and W. Strauss, "The Next 20 Years: How Customer and Workforce Attitudes Will Evolve," *Harvard Business Review* (July–August 2007), pp. 41–52.

60. O. C. Richard, "Racial Diversity, Business Strategy, and Firm Performance: A Resource-Based View," *Academy of Management Journal* 43 (2000), pp. 164–77; D. D. Frink et al., "Gender Demography and Organization Performance: A Two-Study Investigation with Convergence," *Group & Organization Management* 28 (March 2003), pp. 127–47; and T. Kochan et al., "The Effects of Diversity on Business Performance: Report of the Diversity Research Network," *Human Resource Management* 42 (2003), pp. 3–21.

61. C. Hymowitz, "The New Diversity," *The Wall Street Journal,* November 14, 2005, p. R1.

62. R. J. Ely and D. A. Thomas, "Cultural Diversity at Work: The Effects of Diversity Perspectives on Work Group Processes and Outcomes," *Administrative Science Quarterly* 46 (June 2001), pp. 229–73; T. Kochan et al., "The Effects of Diversity on Business Performance: Report of the Diversity Research Network," *Human Resource Management* 42, no. 1 (2003), pp. 3–21; D. van Knippenberg and S. A. Haslam, "Realizing the Diversity Dividend: Exploring the Subtle Interplay between Identity, Ideology and Reality," in *Social Identity at Work: Developing Theory for Organizational Practice,* ed. S. A. Haslam et al. (New York: Taylor and Francis, 2003), pp. 61–80; D. van Knippenberg, C. K. W. De Dreu, and A. C. Homan, "Work Group Diversity and Group Performance: An Integrative Model and Research Agenda," *Journal of Applied Psychology* 89, no. 6 (2004), pp. 1008–22; and E. Molleman, "Diversity in Demographic Characteristics, Abilities and Personality Traits: Do Faultlines Affect Team Functioning?" *Group Decision and Negotiation* 14, no. 3 (2005), pp. 173–93.

63. W. G. Bennis and R. J. Thomas, *Geeks and Geezers* (Boston: Harvard Business School Press, 2002), pp. 74–79; and E. D. Y. Greenblatt, "Work/Life Balance: Wisdom or Whining," *Organizational Dynamics* 31, no. 2 (2002), pp. 177–93.

64. Australian Telework Advisory Committee (ATAC), *Telework— International Developments (Paper III),* (Canberra: Commonwealth of Australia, March 2005); and M. Conlin, "The Easiest Commute of All," *BusinessWeek,* December 12, 2005, p. 78.

65. J. Zemke, "The World Is Their Cubicle," *Metromode,* March 8, 2007.

66. "AT&T Telecommute Survey Indicates Productivity Is Up," AT&T News release, (New York: August 6, 2002); L. Duxbury and C. Higgins, "Telecommute: A Primer for the Millennium Introduction," in *The New World of Work: Challenges and Opportunities,* ed. C. L. Cooper and R. J. Burke (Oxford: Blackwell, 2002), pp. 157–99; V. Illegems and A. Verbeke, "Telework: What Does It Mean for Management?" *Long Range Planning* 37 (2004), pp. 319–34; and S. Raghuram and B. Wiesenfeld, "Work-Nonwork Conflict and Job Stress among Virtual Workers," *Human Resource Management* 43, no. 2/3 (Summer/Fall 2004), pp. 259–77.

67. D. E. Bailey and N. B. Kurland, "A Review of Telework Research: Findings, New Directions, and Lessons for the Study of Modern Work," *Journal of Organizational Behavior* 23 (2002), pp. 383–400; D. W. McCloskey and M. Igbaria, "Does 'Out of Sight' Mean 'Out of Mind'? An Empirical Investigation of the Career Advancement Prospects of Telecommuters," *Information Resources Management Journal* 16 (April–June 2003), pp. 19–34; and Sensis, *Sensis® Insights Report: Teleworking,* (Melbourne: Sensis, June 2005).

68. M. N. Zald, "More Fragmentation? Unfinished Business in Linking the Social Sciences and the Humanities," *Administrative Science Quarterly* 41 (1996), pp. 251–61. Concerns about the "trade deficit" in OB are raised in C. Heath and S. B. Sitkin, "Big-B Versus Big-O: What Is Organizational About Organizational Behavior?" *Journal of Organizational Behavior* 22 (2001), pp. 43–58.

69. J. Pfeffer and R. I. Sutton, *Hard Facts, Dangerous Half-Truths, and Total Nonsense* (Boston: Harvard Business School Press, 2006); and D. M. Rousseau and S. McCarthy, "Educating Managers from an Evidence-Based Perspective," *Academy of Management Learning & Education* 6, no. 1 (2007), pp. 84–101.

70. C. M. Christensen and M. E. Raynor, "Why Hard-Nosed Executives Should Care About Management Theory," *Harvard Business Review* (September 2003), pp. 66–74. For excellent critique of the "one best way" approach in early management scholarship, see P. F. Drucker, "Management's New Paradigms," *Forbes* (October 5, 1998), pp. 152–77.

71. H. L. Tosi and J. W. Slocum Jr., "Contingency Theory: Some Suggested Directions," *Journal of Management* 10 (1984), pp. 9–26.

72. D. M. Rousseau and R. J. House, "Meso Organizational Behavior: Avoiding Three Fundamental Biases," in *Trends in Organizational Behavior,* ed. C. L. Cooper and D. M. Rousseau (Chichester, UK: John Wiley & Sons, 1994), pp. 13–30.

chapter 2

1. S. Lath, "Johnson & Johnson: Living by Its Credo," *Business Today (India)*, November 5, 2006, pp. 126–29; R. Alsop, "How Boss's Deeds Buff a Firm's Reputation," *The Wall Street Journal*, January 21, 2007, p. B1; F. Catteeuw, E. Flynn, and J. Vonderhorst, "Employee Engagement: Boosting Productivity in Turbulent Times," *Organization Development Journal* 25, no. 2 (Summer 2007), pp. 151–57; C. J. Corace, "Engagement—Enrolling the Quiet Majority," *Organization Development Journal* 25, no. 2 (Summer 2007), pp. 171–75; and F. van de Ven, "Fulfilling the Promise of Career Development: Getting to the 'Heart' of the Matter," *Organization Development Journal* 25, no. 3 (Fall 2007), pp. 45–51.

2. L. L. Thurstone, "Ability, Motivation, and Speed," *Psychometrika* 2, no. 4 (1937), pp. 249–54; N. R. F. Maier, *Psychology in Industry*, 2nd ed. (Boston: Houghton Mifflin Company, 1955); V. H. Vroom, *Work and Motivation* (New York: John Wiley & Sons, 1964); and J. P. Campbell et al., *Managerial Behavior, Performance, and Effectiveness* (New York: McGraw-Hill, 1970).

3. E. E. Lawler and L. W. Porter, "Antecedent Attitudes of Effective Managerial Performance," *Organizational Behavior and Human Performance* 2 (1967), pp. 122–42; and M. A. Griffin, A. Neal, and S. K. Parker, "A New Model of Work Role Performance: Positive Behavior in Uncertain and Interdependent Contexts," *Academy of Management Journal* 50, no. 2 (April 2007), pp. 327–47.

4. Senior officers in the Singapore Armed Forces introduced the acronym "MARS." Chris Perryer at the University of Western Australia has pointed out that the full model should be called the "MARS BAR" because the outcomes might be labeled "behavior and results"! Only a few literature reviews have included all four factors. These include J. P. Campbell and R. D. Pritchard, "Motivation Theory in Industrial and Organizational Psychology," in *Handbook of Industrial and Organizational Psychology*, ed. M. D. Dunnette (Chicago: Rand McNally, 1976), pp. 62–130; T. R. Mitchell, "Motivation: New Directions for Theory, Research, and Practice," *The Academy of Management Review* 7, no. 1 (January 1982), pp. 80–88; G. A. J. Churchill et al., "The Determinants of Salesperson Performance: A Meta-Analysis," *Journal of Marketing Research (JMR)* 22, no. 2 (1985), pp. 103–18; and R. E. Plank and D. A. Reid, "The Mediating Role of Sales Behaviors: An Alternative Perspective of Sales Performance and Effectiveness," *Journal of Personal Selling & Sales Management* 14, no. 3 (Summer 1994), pp. 43–56.

5. C. C. Pinder, *Work Motivation in Organizational Behavior* (Upper Saddle River, NJ: Prentice-Hall, 1998); and G. P. Latham and C. C. Pinder, "Work Motivation Theory and Research at the Dawn of the Twenty-First Century," *Annual Review of Psychology* 56 (2005), pp. 485–516.

6. P. Tharenou, A. M. Saks, and C. Moore, "A Review and Critique of Research on Training and Organizational-Level Outcomes," *Human Resource Management Review* 17, no. 3 (2007), pp. 251–73.

7. "New Euro 16m Centre to Train 1,000 Toyota Staff a Year," *Just-Auto*, March 24, 2006; and Y. Kageyama, "Toyota Workers Learn Knack of Auto Production in New Global Push," *Associated Press Newswires*, April 17, 2006.

8. K. F. Kane, "Special Issue: Situational Constraints and Work Performance," *Human Resource Management Review* 3 (Summer 1993), pp. 83–175; S. B. Bacharach and P. Bamberger, "Beyond Situational Constraints: Job Resources, Inadequacy, and Individual Performance at Work," *Human Resource Management Review* 5, no. 2 (1995), pp. 79–102; and G. Johns, "Commentary: In Praise of Context," *Journal of Organizational Behavior* 22 (2001), pp. 31–42.

9. W. Immen, "Prospective Hires Put to the Test," *Globe & Mail*, January 26, 2005, p. C1.

10. Personality researchers agree on one point about the definition of personality: it is difficult to pin down. A definition necessarily captures one perspective of the topic more than others, and the concept of personality is itself very broad. The definition presented here is based on C. S. Carver and M. F. Scheier, *Perspectives on Personality*, 6th ed. (Boston: Allyn & Bacon, 2007); and D. C. Funder, *The Personality Puzzle*, 4th ed. (New York: W. W. Norton & Company, 2007).

11. D. P. McAdams and J. L. Pals, "A New Big Five: Fundamental Principles for an Integrative Science of Personality," *American Psychologist* 61, no. 3 (2006), pp. 204–17.

12. B. Reynolds and K. Karraker, "A Big Five Model of Disposition and Situation Interaction: Why a 'Helpful' Person May Not Always Behave Helpfully," *New Ideas in Psychology* 21 (April 2003), pp. 1–13; and W. Mischel, "Toward an Integrative Science of the Person," *Annual Review of Psychology* 55 (2004), pp. 1–22.

13. B. W. Roberts and A. Caspi, "Personality Development and the Person-Situation Debate: It's Déjà Vu All over Again," *Psychological Inquiry* 12, no. 2 (2001), pp. 104–9.

14. K. L. Jang, W. J. Livesley, and P. A. Vernon, "Heritability of the Big Five Personality Dimensions and Their Facets: A Twin Study," *Journal of Personality* 64, no. 3 (1996), pp. 577–91; N. L. Segal, *Entwined Lives: Twins and What They Tell Us About Human Behavior* (New York: Plume, 2000); T. Bouchard and J. Loehlin, "Genes, Evolution, and Personality," *Behavior Genetics* 31, no. 3 (May 2001), pp. 243–73; G. Lensvelt-Mulders and J. Hettema, "Analysis of Genetic Influences on the Consistency and Variability of the Big Five across Different Stressful Situations," *European Journal of Personality* 15, no. 5 (2001), pp. 355–71; and P. Borkenau et al., "Genetic and Environmental Influences on Person X Situation Profiles," *Journal of Personality* 74, no. 5 (2006), pp. 1451–80.

15. Segal, *Entwined Lives*, 116–18. For critiques of the genetics perspective of personality, see J. Joseph, "Separated Twins and the Genetics of Personality Differences: A Critique," *American Journal of Psychology* 114, no. 1 (Spring 2001), pp. 1–30; and P. Ehrlich and M. W. Feldman, "Genes, Environments & Behaviors," *Daedalus* 136, no. 2 (Spring 2007), pp. 5–12.

16. B. W. Roberts and W. F. DelVecchio, "The Rank-Order Consistency of Personality Traits from Childhood to Old Age: A Quantitative Review of Longitudinal Studies," *Psychological Bulletin* 126, no. 1 (2000), pp. 3–25; and A. Terracciano, P. T. Costa, and R. R. McCrae, "Personality Plasticity after Age 30," *Personality and Social Psychology Bulletin* 32, no. 8 (Aug. 2006), pp. 999–1009.

17. M. Jurado and M. Rosselli, "The Elusive Nature of Executive Functions: A Review of Our Current Understanding," *Neuropsychology Review* 17, no. 3 (2007), pp. 213–33.

18. B. W. Roberts and E. M. Pomerantz, "On Traits, Situations, and Their Integration: A Developmental Perspective," *Personality & Social Psychology Review* 8, no. 4 (2004), pp. 402–16; and W. Fleeson, "Situation-Based Contingencies Underlying Trait-Content Manifestation in Behavior," *Journal of Personality* 75, no. 4 (2007), pp. 825–62.

19. J. M. Digman, "Personality Structure: Emergence of the Five-Factor Model," *Annual Review of Psychology* 41 (1990), pp. 417–40; O. P. John and S. Srivastava, "The Big Five Trait Taxonomy: History, Measurement, and Theoretical Perspectives," in *Handbook of Personality: Theory and Research*, ed. L. A. Pervin and O. P. John, 2nd ed. (New York: Guilford Press, 1999), pp. 102–38; and A. Caspi, B. W. Roberts, and R. L. Shiner, "Personality Development: Stability and Change," *Annual Review of Psychology* 56, no. 1 (2005), pp. 453–84.

20. J. Hogan and B. Holland, "Using Theory to Evaluate Personality and Job-Performance Relations: A Socioanalytic Perspective," *Journal of Applied Psychology* 88, no. 1 (2003), pp. 100–12; and D. S. Ones, C. Viswesvaran, and S. Dilchert, "Personality at Work: Raising Awareness and Correcting Misconceptions," *Human Performance* 18, no. 4 (2005), pp. 389–404.

21. M. R. Barrick and M. K. Mount, "Yes, Personality Matters: Moving on to More Important Matters," *Human Performance* 18, no. 4 (2005), pp. 359–72.

22. M. R. Barrick, M. K. Mount, and T. A. Judge, "Personality and Performance at the Beginning of the New Millennium: What Do We Know and Where Do We Go Next?" *International Journal of Selection and Assessment* 9, no. 1&2 (2001), pp. 9–30; T. A. Judge and R. Ilies, "Relationship of Personality to Performance Motivation: A Meta-Analytic Review," *Journal of Applied Psychology* 87, no. 4 (2002), pp. 797–807; A. Witt, L. A. Burke, and M. R. Barrick, "The Interactive Effects of Conscientiousness and Agreeableness on Job Performance," *Journal of Applied Psychology* 87 (February 2002), pp. 164–69; and J. Moutafi, A. Furnham, and J. Crump, "Is Managerial Level Related to Personality?" *British Journal of Management* 18, no. 3 (2007), pp. 272–80.

23. K. M. DeNeve and H. Cooper, "The Happy Personality: A Meta-Analysis of 137 Personality Traits and Subjective Well-Being," *Psychological Bulletin* 124 (September 1998), pp. 197–229; R. Ilies, M. W. Gerhardt, and H. Le, "Individual Differences in Leadership Emergence: Integrating Meta-Analytic Findings and Behavioral Genetics Estimates," *International Journal of Selection and Assessment* 12, no. 3 (September 2004), pp. 207–19; and B. Kozak, J. Strelau, and J. N. V. Miles, "Genetic Determinants of Individual Differences in Coping Styles," *Anxiety, Stress & Coping* 18, no. 1 (March 2005), pp. 1–15.

24. J. D. Campbell, S. Assanand, and A. Di Paula, "The Structure of the Self-Concept and Its Relation to Psychological Adjustment," *Journal of Personality* 71, no. 1 (2003), pp. 115–40; and M. J. Constantino et al., "The Direct and Stress-Buffering Effects of Self-Organization on Psychological Adjustment: The Direct and Stress-Buffering Effects of Self-Organization on Psychological Adjustment," *Journal of Social & Clinical Psychology* 25, no. 3 (2006), pp. 333–60.

25. C. Sedikides and A. P. Gregg, "Portraits of the Self," in *The Sage Handbook of Social Psychology*, ed. M. A. Hogg and J. Cooper (London: Sage Publications, 2003), pp. 110–38; and M. R. Leary, "Motivational and Emotional Aspects of the Self," *Annual Review of Psychology* 58, no. 1 (2007), pp. 317–44.

26. D. A. Moore, "Not So above Average after All: When People Believe They Are Worse Than Average and Its Implications for Theories of Bias in Social Comparison," *Organizational Behavior and Human Decision Processes* 102, no. 1 (2007), pp. 42–58.

27. N. J. Hiller and D. C. Hambrick, "Conceptualizing Executive Hubris: The Role of (Hyper-)Core Self-Evaluations in Strategic Decision-Making," *Strategic Management Journal* 26, no.

4 (2005), pp. 297–319; U. Malmendier and G. Tate, "CEO Overconfidence and Corporate Investment," *The Journal of Finance* 60, no. 6 (2005), pp. 2661–2700; and J. A. Doukas and D. Petmezas, "Acquisitions, Overconfident Managers and Self-Attribution Bias," *European Financial Management* 13, no. 3 (2007), pp. 531–77.

28. W. B. Swann Jr, "To Be Adored or to Be Known? The Interplay of Self-Enhancement and Self-Verification," in *Foundations of Social Behavior*, ed. R. M. Sorrentino and E. T. Higgins (New York: Guilford, 1990), pp. 408–48; and W. B. Swann Jr, P. J. Rentfrow, and J. S. Guinn, "Self-Verification: The Search for Coherence," in *Handbook of Self and Identity*, ed. M. R. Leary and J. Tagney (New York: Guilford, 2002), pp. 367–83.

29. Leary, "Motivational and Emotional Aspects of the Self."

30. T. A. Judge and J. E. Bono, "Relationship of Core Self-Evaluations Traits—Self-Esteem, Generalized Self-Efficacy, Locus of Control, and Emotional Stability—with Job Satisfaction and Job Performance: A Meta-Analysis," *Journal of Applied Psychology* 86, no. 1 (2001), pp. 80–92; and T. A. Judge and C. Hurst, "Capitalizing on One's Advantages: Role of Core Self-Evaluations," *Journal of Applied Psychology* 92, no. 5 (2007), pp. 1212–27.

31. W. B. Swann Jr, C. Chang-Schneider, and K. L. McClarty, "Do People's Self-Views Matter?: Self-Concept and Self-Esteem in Everyday Life," *American Psychologist* 62, no. 2 (2007), pp. 84–94.

32. M. T. Bitti, "Rewards of Hard Work," *National Post*, October 17, 2007, p. WK2.

33. A. Bandura, *Self-Efficacy: The Exercise of Control* (New York: W. H. Freeman, 1997).

34. G. Chen, S. M. Gully, and D. Eden, "Validation of a New General Self-Efficacy Scale," *Organizational Research Methods* 4, no. 1 (January 2001), pp. 62–83.

35. P. E. Spector, "Behavior in Organizations as a Function of Employee's Locus of Control," *Psychological Bulletin* 91 (1982), pp. 482–97; K. Hattrup, M. S. O'Connell, and J. R. Labrador, "Incremental Validity of Locus of Control after Controlling for Cognitive Ability and Conscientiousness," *Journal of Business and Psychology* 19, no. 4 (2005), pp. 461–81; and T. W. H. Ng, K. L. Sorensen, and L. T. Eby, "Locus of Control at Work: A Meta-Analysis," *Journal of Organizational Behavior* 27 (2006), pp. 1057–87.

36. H. Tajfel, *Social Identity and Intergroup Relations* (Cambridge: Cambridge University Press, 1982); B. E. Ashforth and F. Mael, "Social Identity Theory and the Organization," *Academy of Management Review* 14 (1989), pp. 20–39; M. A. Hogg and D. J. Terry, "Social Identity and Self-Categorization Processes in Organizational Contexts," *Academy of Management Review* 25 (January 2000), pp. 121–40; and S. A. Haslam, R. A. Eggins, and K. J. Reynolds, "The Aspire Model: Actualizing Social and Personal Identity Resources to Enhance Organizational Outcomes," *Journal of Occupational and Organizational Psychology* 76 (2003), pp. 83–113.

37. Sedikides and Gregg, "Portraits of the Self." The history of the social self in human beings is described in M. R. Leary and N.

R. Buttermore, "The Evolution of the Human Self: Tracing the Natural History of Self-Awareness," *Journal for the Theory of Social Behaviour* 33, no. 4 (2003), pp. 365–404.

38. M. R. Edwards, "Organizational Identification: A Conceptual and Operational Review," *International Journal of Management Reviews* 7, no. 4 (2005), pp. 207–30; D. A. Whetten, "Albert and Whetten Revisited: Strengthening the Concept of Organizational Identity," *Journal of Management Inquiry* 15, no. 3 (Sept. 2006), pp. 219–34.

39. B. M. Meglino and E. C. Ravlin, "Individual Values in Organizations: Concepts, Controversies, and Research," *Journal of Management* 24, no. 3 (1998), pp. 351–89; B. R. Agle and C. B. Caldwell, "Understanding Research on Values in Business," *Business and Society* 38, no. 3 (September 1999), pp. 326–87; and S. Hitlin and J. A. Pilavin, "Values: Reviving a Dormant Concept," *Annual Review of Sociology* 30 (2004), pp. 359–93.

40. D. Lubinski, D. B. Schmidt, and C. P. Benbow, "A 20-Year Stability Analysis of the Study of Values for Intellectually Gifted Individuals from Adolescence to Adulthood," *Journal of Applied Psychology* 81 (1996), pp. 443–51.

41. B. Kabanoff and J. Daly, "Espoused Values in Organisations," *Australian Journal of Management* 27, no. Special Issue (2002), pp. 89–104.

42. S. H. Schwartz, "Universals in the Content and Structure of Values: Theoretical Advances and Empirical Tests in 20 Countries," *Advances in Experimental Social Psychology* 25 (1992), pp. 1–65; S. H. Schwartz, "Are There Universal Aspects in the Structure and Contents of Human Values?" *Journal of Social Issues* 50 (1994), pp. 19–45; M. Schwartz, "The Nature of the Relationship between Corporate Codes of Ethics and Behaviour," *Journal of Business Ethics* 32, no. 3 (2001), p. 247; D. Spini, "Measurement Equivalence of 10 Value Types from the Schwartz Value Survey across 21 Countries," *Journal of Cross-Cultural Psychology* 34, no. 1 (January 2003), pp. 3–23; and S. H. Schwartz and K. Boehnke, "Evaluating the Structure of Human Values with Confirmatory Factor Analysis," *Journal of Research in Personality* 38, no. 3 (2004), pp. 230–55.

43. G. R. Maio and J. M. Olson, "Values as Truisms: Evidence and Implications," *Journal of Personality and Social Psychology* 74, no. 2 (1998), pp. 294–311; G. R. Maio et al., "Addressing Discrepancies between Values and Behavior: The Motivating Effect of Reasons," *Journal of Experimental Social Psychology* 37, no. 2 (2001), pp. 104–17; B. Verplanken and R. W. Holland, "Motivated Decision Making: Effects of Activation and Self-Centrality of Values on Choices and Behavior," *Journal of Personality and Social Psychology* 82, no. 3 (2002), pp. 434–47; A. Bardi and S. H. Schwartz, "Values and Behavior: Strength and Structure of Relations," *Personality and Social Psychology Bulletin* 29, no. 10 (October 2003), pp. 1207–20; and M. M. Bernard and G. R. Maio, "Effects of Introspection About Reasons for Values: Extending Research on Values-as-Truisms," *Social Cognition* 21, no. 1 (2003), pp. 1–25.

44. A. L. Kristof, "Person-Organization Fit: An Integrative Review of Its Conceptualizations, Measurement, and Implications," *Personnel Psychology* 49, no. 1 (Spring 1996),

pp. 1–49; M. L. Verquer, T. A. Beehr, and S. H. Wagner, "A Meta-Analysis of Relations between Person-Organization Fit and Work Attitudes," *Journal of Vocational Behavior* 63 (2003), pp. 473–89; J. W. Westerman and L. A. Cyr, "An Integrative Analysis of Person-Organization Fit Theories," *International Journal of Selection and Assessment* 12, no. 3 (September 2004), pp. 252–61; and D. Bouckenooghe et al., "The Prediction of Stress by Values and Value Conflict," *Journal of Psychology* 139, no. 4 (2005), pp. 369–82.

45. T. A. Joiner, "The Influence of National Culture and Organizational Culture Alignment on Job Stress and Performance: Evidence from Greece," *Journal of Managerial Psychology* 16 (2001), pp. 229–42; Z. Aycan, R. N. Kanungo, and J. B. P. Sinha, "Organizational Culture and Human Resource Management Practices: The Model of Culture Fit," *Journal Of Cross-Cultural Psychology* 30 (July 1999), pp. 501–26.

46. D. Oyserman, H. M. Coon, and M. Kemmelmeier, "Rethinking Individualism and Collectivism: Evaluation of Theoretical Assumptions and Meta-Analyses," *Psychological Bulletin* 128 (2002), pp. 3–72; C. P. Earley and C. B. Gibson, "Taking Stock in Our Progress on Individualism-Collectivism: 100 Years of Solidarity and Community," *Journal of Management* 24 (May 1998), pp. 265–304; and F. S. Niles, "Individualism-Collectivism Revisited," *Cross-Cultural Research* 32 (November 1998), pp. 315–41.

47. Oyserman, Coon, and Kemmelmeier, "Rethinking Individualism and Collectivism: Evaluation of Theoretical Assumptions and Meta-Analyses." Also see F. Li and L. Aksoy, "Dimensionality of Individualism–Collectivism and Measurement Equivalence of Triandis and Gelfand's Scale," *Journal of Business and Psychology* 21, no. 3 (2007), pp. 313–29. The relationship between individualism and collectivism is still being debated, but most experts now agree that individualism and collectivism have serious problems with conceptualization and measurement.

48. G. Hofstede, *Culture's Consequences: Comparing Values, Behaviors, Institutions, and Organizations across Nations*, 2nd ed. (Thousand Oaks, CA: Sage, 2001).

49. G. Hofstede, *Cultures and Organizations: Software of the Mind* (New York: McGraw-Hill, 1991). Hofstede used the terms *masculinity* and *femininity* for achievement and nurturing orientation, respectively. We have adopted the latter to minimize the sexist perspective of these concepts.

50. J. S. Osland et al., "Beyond Sophisticated Stereotyping: Cultural Sensemaking in Context," *Academy of Management Executive* 14 (February 2000), pp. 65–79; S. S. Sarwono and R. W. Armstrong, "Microcultural Differences and Perceived Ethical Problems: An International Business Perspective," *Journal of Business Ethics* 30 (March 2001), pp. 41–56; M. Voronov and J. A. Singer, "The Myth of Individualism-Collectivism: A Critical Review," *Journal of Social Psychology* 142 (August 2002), pp. 461–80; and N. Jacob, "Cross-Cultural Investigations: Emerging Concepts," *Journal of Organizational Change Management* 18, no. 5 (2005), pp. 514–28.

51. C. Savoye, "Workers Say Honesty Is Best Company Policy," *Christian Science Monitor*, June 15, 2000; J. M. Kouzes and B. Z. Posner, *The Leadership Challenge*, 3rd ed. (San Francisco: Jossey-Bass, 2002); and J. Schettler, "Leadership in Corporate America," *Training & Development*, September 2002, pp. 66–73.

52. P. L. Schumann, "A Moral Principles Framework for Human Resource Management Ethics," *Human Resource Management Review* 11 (Spring–Summer 2001), pp. 93–111; J. Boss, *Analyzing Moral Issues*, 3rd ed. (New York: McGraw-Hill, 2005), Chap. 1; and M. G. Velasquez, *Business Ethics: Concepts and Cases*, 6th ed. (Upper Saddle River, NJ: Prentice-Hall, 2006), Chap. 2.

53. T. J. Jones, "Ethical Decision Making by Individuals in Organizations: An Issue Contingent Model," *Academy of Management Review* 16 (1991), pp. 366–95; B. H. Frey, "The Impact of Moral Intensity on Decision Making in a Business Context," *Journal of Business Ethics* 26 (August 2000), pp. 181–95; and D. R. May and K. P. Pauli, "The Role of Moral Intensity in Ethical Decision Making," *Business and Society* 41 (March 2002), pp. 84–117.

54. J. R. Sparks and S. D. Hunt, "Marketing Researcher Ethical Sensitivity: Conceptualization, Measurement, and Exploratory Investigation," *Journal of Marketing* 62 (April 1998), pp. 92–109.

55. K. F. Alam, "Business Ethics in New Zealand Organizations: Views from the Middle and Lower Level Managers," *Journal of Business Ethics* 22 (November 1999), pp. 145–53; K. Blotnicky, "Is Business in Moral Decay?" *Chronicle-Herald (Halifax)*, June 11, 2000; and B. Stoneman and K. K. Holliday, "Pressure Cooker," *Banking Strategies*, January–February 2001, p. 13.

56. S. Greengard, "Golden Values," *Workforce Management*, March 2005, pp. 52–53.

57. B. Farrell, D. M. Cobbin, and H. M. Farrell, "Codes of Ethics: Their Evolution, Development and Other Controversies," *Journal of Management Development* 21, no. 2 (2002), pp. 152–63; and G. Wood and M. Rimmer, "Codes of Ethics: What Are They Really and What Should They Be?" *International Journal of Value-Based Management* 16, no. 2 (2003), p. 181.

58. P. J. Gnazzo and G. R. Wratney, "Are You Serious About Ethics?" *Across the Board* 40 (July/August 2003), p. 46ff; T. F. Lindeman, "A Matter of Choice," *Pittsburgh Post-Gazette*, March 30, 2004; B. Schultz, "Ethics under Investigation," *Network World*, April 26, 2004; and K. Tyler, "Do the Right Thing," *HRMagazine* 50, no. 2 (February 2005), pp. 99–103.

59. E. Aronson, "Integrating Leadership Styles and Ethical Perspectives," *Canadian Journal of Administrative Sciences* 18 (December 2001), pp. 266–76; and D. R. May et al., "Developing the Moral Component of Authentic Leadership," *Organizational Dynamics* 32 (2003), pp. 247–60. The Vodafone director quotation is from R. Van Lee, L. Fabish, and N. McGaw, "The Value of Corporate Values," *Strategy+Business* (Summer 2005), pp. 1–13.

chapter 3

1. J. Lynch and M. Dagostino, "Man in Motion," *People*, August 26, 2002, p. 89; N. Hooper, "Call Me Irresistible," *Australian Financial Review*, December 5, 2003, p. 38; D. Knight, "Hands-on CEO Gets IPL Back on Track," *Indianapolis Star*, November 21, 2004; K. Capell, "Ikea; How the Swedish Retailer Became a Global Cult Brand," *BusinessWeek*, November 14, 2005, p. 96; W. Frey, "Rubbish Boy Doing Well as Junk Man," *Metro-Vancouver*, April 25, 2005, p. 11; and L. Morrell, "Taking the Floor," *Retail Week*, November 18, 2005.

2. The effect of the target in selective attention is known as *bottom-up selection*; the effect of the perceiver's psychodynamics on this process is known as *top-down selection*. C. E. Connor, H. E. Egeth, and S. Yantis, "Visual Attention: Bottom-Up Versus Top-Down," *Current Biology* 14, no. 19 (2004), pp. R850–52; and E. I. Knudsen, "Fundamental Components of Attention," *Annual Review of Neuroscience* 30, no. 1 (2007), pp. 57–78.

3. A. Mack et al., "Perceptual Organization and Attention," *Cognitive Psychology* 24, no. 4 (1992), pp. 475–501; A. R. Damasio, *Descartes' Error: Emotion, Reason, and the Human Brain* (New York: Putnam Sons, 1994); C. Frith, "A Framework for Studying the Neural Basis of Attention," *Neuropsychologia* 39, no. 12 (2001), pp. 1367–71; N. Lavie, "Distracted and Confused? Selective Attention under Load," *Trends in Cognitive Sciences* 9, no. 2 (2005), pp. 75–82; D. Westin, *The Political Brain: The Role of Emotion in Deciding the Fate of the Nation* (Cambridge, MA: PublicAffairs, 2007).

4. E. Byron, "To Master the Art of Solving Crimes, Cops Study Vermeer," *The Wall Street Journal*, July 27, 2005, p. A1; D. J. Hall, "The Justice System Isn't Always Just," *Capital Times & Wisconsin State Journal*, November 27, 2005, p. D1.

5. C. N. Macrae and G. V. Bodenhausen, "Social Cognition: Thinking Categorically about Others," *Annual Review of Psychology* 51 (2000), pp. 93–120. For literature on the automaticity of the perceptual organization and interpretation process, see J. A. Bargh, "The Cognitive Monster: The Case against the Controllability of Automatic Stereotype Effects," in *Dual Process Theories in Social Psychology*, ed. S. Chaiken and Y. Trope (New York: Guilford, 1999), pp. 361–82; J. A. Bargh and M. J. Ferguson, "Beyond Behaviorism: On the Automaticity of Higher Mental Processes," *Psychological Bulletin* 126, no. 6 (2000), pp. 925–45; and M. Gladwell, *Blink: The Power of Thinking without Thinking* (New York: Little, Brown, 2005).

6. E. M. Altmann and B. D. Burns, "Streak Biases in Decision Making: Data and a Memory Model," *Cognitive Systems Research* 6, no. 1 (2005), pp. 5–16. For discussion of cognitive closure and perception, see A. W. Kruglanski and D. M. Webster, "Motivated Closing of the Mind: 'Seizing' And 'Freezing,'" *Psychological Review* 103, no. 2 (1996), pp. 263–83.

7. N. Ambady and R. Rosenthal, "Half a Minute: Predicting Teacher Evaluations from Thin Slices of Nonverbal Behavior and Physical Attractiveness," *Journal of Personality and Social Psychology* 64, no. 3 (March 1993), pp. 431–41. For other research on thin slices, see N. Ambady and R. Rosenthal, "Thin Slices of Expressive Behavior as Predictors of Interpersonal Consequences: A Meta-Analysis," *Psychological Bulletin* 111, no. 2 (1992), pp. 256–74; and N. Ambady et al., "Surgeons' Tone of Voice: A Clue to Malpractice History," *Surgery* 132, no. 1 (July 2002), pp. 5–9.

8. P. M. Senge, *The Fifth Discipline: The Art and Practice of the Learning Organization* (New York: Doubleday Currency, 1990), Chap. 10; P. N. Johnson-Laird, "Mental Models and Deduction," *Trends in Cognitive Sciences* 5, no. 10 (2001), pp. 434–42; A. B. Markman and D. Gentner, "Thinking," *Annual Review of Psychology* 52 (2001), pp. 223–47; and T. J. Chermack, "Mental Models in Decision Making and Implications for Human Resource Development," *Advances in Developing Human Resources* 5, no. 4 (2003), pp. 408–22.

9. M. A. Hogg et al., "The Social Identity Perspective: Intergroup Relations, Self-Conception, and Small Groups," *Small Group Research* 35, no. 3 (June 2004), pp. 246–76; and J. Jetten, R. Spears, and T. Postmes, "Intergroup Distinctiveness and Differentiation: A Meta-Analytic Integration," *Journal of Personality and Social Psychology* 86, no. 6 (2004), pp. 862–79.

10. J. W. Jackson and E. R. Smith, "Conceptualizing Social Identity: A New Framework and Evidence for the Impact of Different Dimensions," *Personality & Social Psychology Bulletin* 25 (January 1999), pp. 120–35.

11. L. Falkenberg, "Improving the Accuracy of Stereotypes within the Workplace," *Journal of Management* 16 (1990), pp. 107–18; S. T. Fiske, "Stereotyping, Prejudice, and Discrimination," in *Handbook of Social Psychology*, ed. D. T. Gilbert, S. T. Fiske, and G. Lindzey, 4th ed. (New York: McGraw-Hill, 1998), pp. 357–411; and Macrae and Bodenhausen, "Social Cognition: Thinking Categorically about Others."

12. C. N. Macrae, A. B. Milne, and G. V. Bodenhausen, "Stereotypes as Energy-Saving Devices: A Peek inside the Cognitive Toolbox," *Journal of Personality and Social Psychology* 66 (1994), pp. 37–47; J. W. Sherman et al., "Stereotype Efficiency Reconsidered: Encoding Flexibility under Cognitive Load," *Journal of Personality and Social Psychology* 75 (1998), pp. 589–606; and Macrae and Bodenhausen, "Social Cognition: Thinking Categorically about Others."

13. L. Sinclair and Z. Kunda, "Motivated Stereotyping of Women: She's Fine if She Praised Me but Incompetent if She Criticized Me," *Personality and Social Psychology Bulletin* 26 (November 2000), pp. 1329–42; and J. C. Turner and S. A. Haslam, "Social Identity, Organizations, and Leadership," in *Groups at Work: Theory and Research*, ed. M. E. Turner (Mahwah, NJ: Lawrence Erlbaum Associates, 2001), pp. 25–65.

14. A. L. Friedman and S. R. Lyne, "The Beancounter Stereotype: Towards a General Model of Stereotype Generation," *Critical Perspectives on Accounting* 12, no. 4 (2001), pp. 423–51.

15. "Employers Face New Danger: Accidental Age Bias," *Omaha World-Herald*, October 10, 2005, p. D1; and "Tiptoeing through the Employment Minefield of Race, Sex, and Religion? Here's Another One," *North West Business Insider (Manchester, UK)*, February 2006.

16. J. A. Bargh and T. L. Chartrand, "The Unbearable Automaticity of Being," *American Psychologist* 54, no. 7 (July 1999), pp. 462–79; S. T. Fiske, "What We Know Now about Bias and Intergroup Conflict, the Problem of the Century," *Current Directions in Psychological Science* 11, no. 4 (August 2002), pp. 123–28. For recent evidence that shows that intensive training can minimize stereotype activation, see K. Kawakami et al., "Just Say No (to Stereotyping) Effects of Training in the Negation of Stereotypic Associations on Stereotype Activation," *Journal of Personality and Social Psychology* 78, no. 5 (2000), pp. 871–88; and E. A. Plant, B. M. Peruche, and D. A. Butz, "Eliminating Automatic Racial Bias: Making Race Non-Diagnostic for Responses to Criminal Suspects," *Journal of Experimental Social Psychology* 41, no. 2 (2005), pp. 141–56.

17. H. H. Kelley, *Attribution in Social Interaction* (Morristown, NJ: General Learning Press, 1971).

18. J. M. Feldman, "Beyond Attribution Theory: Cognitive Processes in Performance Appraisal," *Journal of Applied Psychology* 66 (1981), pp. 127–48.

19. J. M. Crant and T. S. Bateman, "Assignment of Credit and Blame for Performance Outcomes," *Academy of Management Journal* 36 (1993), pp. 7–27; B. Weiner, "Intrapersonal and Interpersonal Theories of Motivation from an Attributional Perspective," *Educational Psychology Review* 12 (2000), pp. 1–14; and N. Bacon and P. Blyton, "Worker Responses to Teamworking: Exploring Employee Attributions of Managerial Motives," *International Journal of Human Resource Management* 16, no. 2 (February 2005), pp. 238–55.

20. Fundamental attribution error is part of a larger phenomenon known as *correspondence bias.* See D. T. Gilbert and P. S. Malone, "The Correspondence Bias," *Psychological Bulletin* 117, no. 1 (1995), pp. 21–38.

21. I. Choi, R. E. Nisbett, and A. Norenzayan, "Causal Attribution across Cultures: Variation and Universality," *Psychological Bulletin* 125, no. 1 (1999), pp. 47–63; D. S. Krull et al., "The Fundamental Fundamental Attribution Error: Correspondence Bias in Individualist and Collectivist Cultures," *Personality and Social Psychology Bulletin* 25, no. 10 (October 1999), pp. 1208–19; R. E. Nisbett, *The Geography of Thought: How Asians and Westerners Think Differently—and Why* (New York: Free Press, 2003), Chap. 5.

22. F. Lee and L. Z. Tiedens, "Who's Being Served? 'Self-Serving' Attributions in Social Hierarchies," *Organizational Behavior and Human Decision Processes* 84, no. 2 (2001), pp. 254–87; E. W. K. Tsang, "Self-Serving Attributions in Corporate Annual Reports: A Replicated Study," *Journal of Management Studies* 39, no. 1 (January 2002), pp. 51–65; and N. J. Roese and J. M. Olson, "Better, Stronger, Faster: Self-Serving Judgment, Affect Regulation, and the Optimal Vigilance Hypothesis," *Perspectives on Psychological Science* 2, no. 2 (2007), pp. 124–41.

23. Similar models are presented in D. Eden, "Self-Fulfilling Prophecy as a Management Tool: Harnessing Pygmalion," *Academy of Management Review* 9 (1984), pp. 64–73; R. H. G. Field and D. A. Van Seters, "Management by Expectations (MBE): The Power of Positive Prophecy," *Journal of General Management* 14 (Winter 1988), pp. 19–33; and D. O. Trouilloud et al., "The Influence of Teacher Expectations on Student Achievement in Physical Education Classes: Pygmalion Revisited," *European Journal of Social Psychology* 32 (2002), pp. 591–607.

24. D. Eden, "Interpersonal Expectations in Organizations," in *Interpersonal Expectations: Theory, Research, and Applications* (Cambridge, UK: Cambridge University Press, 1993), 154–78.

25. D. Eden, "Pygmalion Goes to Boot Camp: Expectancy, Leadership, and Trainee Performance," *Journal of Applied Psychology* 67 (1982), pp. 194–99; and R. P. Brown and E. C. Pinel, "Stigma on My Mind: Individual Differences in the Experience of Stereotype Threat," *Journal of Experimental Social Psychology* 39, no. 6 (2003), pp. 626–33.

26. A. R. Remo, "Nurture the Good to Create an Asset," *Philippine Daily Inquirer*, December 6, 2004.

27. S. Madon, L. Jussim, and J. Eccles, "In Search of the Powerful Self-Fulfilling Prophecy," *Journal of Personality and Social Psychology* 72, no. 4 (April 1997), pp. 791–809; A. E. Smith, L. Jussim, and J. Eccles, "Do Self-Fulfilling Prophecies Accumulate, Dissipate, or Remain Stable over Time?" *Journal of Personality and Social Psychology* 77, no. 3 (1999), pp. 548–65; and S. Madon et al., "Self-Fulfilling Prophecies: The Synergistic Accumulative Effect of Parents' Beliefs on Children's Drinking Behavior," *Psychological Science* 15, no. 12 (2005), pp. 837–45.

28. W. H. Cooper, "Ubiquitous Halo," *Psychological Bulletin* 90 (1981), pp. 218–44; K. R. Murphy, R. A. Jako, and R. L. Anhalt, "Nature and Consequences of Halo Error: A Critical Analysis," *Journal of Applied Psychology* 78 (1993), pp. 218–25; and T. H. Feeley, "Comment on Halo Effects in Rating and Evaluation Research," *Human Communication Research* 28, no. 4 (October 2002), pp. 578–86.

29. C. L. Kleinke, *First Impressions: The Psychology of Encountering Others* (Englewood Cliffs, N.J.: Prentice-Hall, 1975); E. A. Lind, L. Kray, and L. Thompson, "Primacy Effects in Justice Judgments: Testing Predictions from Fairness Heuristic Theory," *Organizational Behavior and Human Decision Processes* 85 (July 2001), pp. 189–210; and O. Ybarra, "When First Impressions Don't Last: The Role of Isolation and Adaptation Processes in the Revision of Evaluative Impressions," *Social Cognition* 19 (October 2001), pp. 491–520.

30. D. D. Steiner and J. S. Rain, "Immediate and Delayed Primacy and Recency Effects in Performance Evaluation," *Journal of Applied Psychology* 74 (1989), pp. 136–42; K. T. Trotman, "Order Effects and Recency: Where Do We Go from Here?" *Accounting & Finance* 40 (2000), pp. 169–82; and W. Green, "Impact of the Timing of an Inherited Explanation on Auditors' Analytical Procedures Judgements," *Accounting and Finance* 44 (2004), pp. 369–92.

31. R. W. Clement and J. Krueger, "The Primacy of Self-Referent Information in Perceptions of Social Consensus," *British Journal of Social Psychology* 39 (2000), pp. 279–99; R. L. Gross and S. E. Brodt, "How Assumptions of Consensus Undermine Decision Making," *Sloan Management Review* (January 2001), pp. 86–94; and J. Oliver et al., "Projection of Own on

Others' Job Characteristics: Evidence for the False Consensus Effect in Job Characteristics Information," *International Journal of Selection and Assessment* 13, no. 1 (2005), pp. 63–74.

32. M. Bendick, M. L. Egan, and S. M. Lofhjelm, "Workforce Diversity Training: From Anti-Discrimination Compliance to Organizational Development HR," *Human Resource Planning* 24 (2001), pp. 10–25; L. Roberson, C. T. Kulik, and M. B. Pepper, "Using Needs Assessment to Resolve Controversies in Diversity Training Design," *Group & Organization Management* 28, no. 1 (March 2003), pp. 148–74; and D. E. Hogan and M. Mallott, "Changing Racial Prejudice through Diversity Education," *Journal of College Student Development* 46, no. 2 (March/April 2005), pp. 115–25.

33. P. Babcock, "Detecting Hidden Bias," *HRMagazine*, February 2006, p. 50.

34. D. Eden et al., "Implanting Pygmalion Leadership Style through Workshop Training: Seven Field Experiments," *Leadership Quarterly* 11 (2000), pp. 171–210; and S. S. White and E. A. Locke, "Problems with the Pygmalion Effect and Some Proposed Solutions," *Leadership Quarterly* 11 (Autumn 2000), pp. 389–415.

35. T. W. Costello and S. S. Zalkind, *Psychology in Administration: A Research Orientation* (Englewood Cliffs, NJ: Prentice-Hall, 1963), pp. 45–46; and J. M. Kouzes and B. Z. Posner, *The Leadership Challenge*, 3rd ed. (San Francisco: Jossey-Bass, 2002), Chap. 3.

36. J. Luft, *Group Processes* (Palo Alto, CA: Mayfield Publishing, 1984). For a variation of this model, see J. Hall, "Communication Revisited," *California Management Review* 15 (Spring 1973), pp. 56–67.

37. L. C. Miller and D. A. Kenny, "Reciprocity of Self-Disclosure at the Individual and Dyadic Levels: A Social Relations Analysis," *Journal of Personality and Social Psychology* 50 (1986), pp. 713–19.

38. T. F. Pettigrew, "Intergroup Contact Theory," *Annual Review of Psychology* 49 (1998), pp. 65–85; S. Brickson, "The Impact of Identity Orientation on Individual and Organizational Outcomes in Demographically Diverse Settings," *Academy of Management Review* 25 (January 2000), pp. 82–101; and J. Dixon and K. Durrheim, "Contact and the Ecology of Racial Division: Some Varieties of Informal Segregation," *British Journal of Social Psychology* 42 (March 2003), pp. 1–23.

39. W. G. Stephen and K. A. Finlay, "The Role of Empathy in Improving Intergroup Relations," *Journal of Social Issues* 55 (Winter 1999), pp. 729–43; S. K. Parker and C. M. Axtell, "Seeing Another Viewpoint: Antecedents and Outcomes of Employee Perspective Taking," *Academy of Management Journal* 44 (December 2001), pp. 1085–100; and G. J. Vreeke and I. L. van der Mark, "Empathy, an Integrative Model," *New Ideas in Psychology* 21, no. 3 (2003), pp. 177–207.

40. I. Nonaka and H. Takeuchi, *The Knowledge-Creating Company* (New York: Oxford University Press, 1995); P. Duguid, "'The Art of Knowing': Social and Tacit Dimensions of Knowledge and the Limits of the Community of Practice," *The Information Society* 21 (2005), pp. 109–18.

41. B. F. Skinner, *About Behaviorism* (New York: Alfred A. Knopf, 1974); J. Komaki, T. Coombs, and S. Schepman, "Motivational Implications of Reinforcement Theory," in *Motivation and Leadership at Work*, ed. R. M. Steers, L. W. Porter, and G. A. Bigley (New York: McGraw-Hill, 1996), pp. 34–52; and R. G. Miltenberger, *Behavior Modification: Principles and Procedures* (Pacific Grove, CA: Brooks/Cole, 1997).

42. T. K. Connellan, *How to Improve Human Performance* (New York: Harper & Row, 1978), pp. 48–57; and F. Luthans and R. Kreitner, *Organizational Behavior Modification and Beyond* (Glenview, IL: Scott, Foresman, 1985), pp. 85–88.

43. Miltenberger, *Behavior Modification,* Chaps. 4–6.

44. Punishment can also include removing a pleasant consequence, such as when employees must switch from business to economy class flying when their sales fall below the threshold for top tier sales "stars."

45. L. K. Trevino, "The Social Effects of Punishment in Organizations: A Justice Perspective," *Academy of Management Review* 17 (1992), pp. 647–76; and L. E. Atwater et al., "Recipient and Observer Reactions to Discipline: Are Managers Experiencing Wishful Thinking?" *Journal of Organizational Behavior* 22, no. 3 (May 2001), pp. 249–70.

46. G. P. Latham and V. L. Huber, "Schedules of Reinforcement: Lessons from the Past and Issues for the Future," *Journal of Organizational Behavior Management* 13 (1992), pp. 125–49; and B. A. Williams, "Challenges to Timing-Based Theories of Operant Behavior," *Behavioural Processes* 62 (April 2003), pp. 115–23.

47. S. Overman, "Many Offer Basic Wellness Initiatives, Few Track Results," *Employee Benefit News*, April 15, 2006; and H. Wecsler, "Sick Day Incentive Plan Favored by NLR Board," *Arkansas Democrat Gazette*, February 17, 2006, p. 14.

48. Bargh and Ferguson, "Beyond Behaviorism." Some writers argue that behaviorists long ago accepted the relevance of cognitive processes in behavior modification. See I. Kirsch et al., "The Role of Cognition in Classical and Operant Conditioning," *Journal of Clinical Psychology* 60, no. 4 (April 2004), pp. 369–92.

49. M. Colias, "Obese Police," *Crain's Chicago Business*, February 26, 2007, p. 1.

50. A. Bandura, *Social Foundations of Thought and Action: A Social Cognitive Theory* (Englewood Cliffs, NJ: Prentice-Hall, 1986).

51. A. Pescuric and W. C. Byham, "The New Look of Behavior Modeling," *Training & Development* 50 (July 1996), pp. 24–30.

52. M. E. Schnake, "Vicarious Punishment in a Work Setting," *Journal of Applied Psychology* 71 (1986), pp. 343–45; Trevino, "The Social Effects of Punishment in Organizations." ; and J. B. DeConinck, "The Effect of Punishment on Sales Managers' Outcome Expectancies and Responses to Unethical Sales Force Behavior," *American Business Review* 21, no. 2 (June 2003), pp. 135–40.

53. A. Bandura, "Self-Reinforcement: Theoretical and Methodological Considerations," *Behaviorism* 4 (1976), pp. 135–55;

C. A. Frayne and J. M. Geringer, "Self-Management Training for Improving Job Performance: A Field Experiment Involving Salespeople," *Journal of Applied Psychology* 85, no. 3 (June 2000), pp. 361–72; and J. B. Vancouver and D. V. Day, "Industrial and Organisation Research on Self-Regulation: From Constructs to Applications," *Applied Psychology* 54, no. 2 (April 2005), pp. 155–85.

54. D. A. Kolb, *Experiential Learning* (Englewood Cliffs, NJ: Prentice-Hall, 1984); S. Gherardi, D. Nicolini, and F. Odella, "Toward a Social Understanding of How People Learn in Organizations," *Management Learning* 29 (September 1998), pp. 273–97; and D. A. Kolb, R. E. Boyatzis, and C. Mainemelis, "Experiential Learning Theory: Previous Research and New Directions," in *Perspectives on Thinking, Learning, and Cognitive Styles*, ed. R. J. Sternberg and L. F. Zhang (Mahwah, NJ: Lawrence Erlbaum, 2001), 227–48.

55. W. E. Baker and J. M. Sinkula, "The Synergistic Effect of Market Orientation and Learning Orientation on Organizational Performance," *Academy of Marketing Science Journal* 27, no. 4 (Fall 1999), pp. 411–29; and Z. Emden, A. Yaprak, and S. T. Cavusgil, "Learning from Experience in International Alliances: Antecedents and Firm Performance Implications," *Journal of Business Research* 58, no. 7 (2005), pp. 883–92.

56. H. Shipton, "Cohesion or Confusion? Towards a Typology for Organizational Learning Research," *International Journal of Management Reviews* 8, no. 4 (2006), pp. 233–52; and D. Jiménez-Jiménez and J. G. Cegarra-Navarro, "The Performance Effect of Organizational Learning and Market Orientation," *Industrial Marketing Management* 36, no. 6 (2007), pp. 694–708.

57. R. Garud and A. Kumaraswamy, "Vicious and Virtuous Circles in the Management of Knowledge: The Case of Infosys Technologies," *MIS Quarterly* 29, no. 1 (March 2005), pp. 9–33.

chapter 4

1. T. Knauss, "Small Local Company Is a Happy Place to Work," *Post Standard/Herald-Journal (Syracuse, NY),* March 21, 2006, p. A1; M. Rubado, "Great Job," *Post Standard/Herald-Journal (Syracuse, NY),* July 31, 2006, p. D8; C. Hannagan, "Workers at Cxtec Have Something to Cheer About," *Post-Standard (Syracuse, NY),* August 5, 2007; and K. Tyler, "Leveraging Long Tenure," *HRMagazine,* May 2007, pp. 54–60.

2. The centrality of emotions in marketing, economics, and sociology is discussed in G. Loewenstein, "Emotions in Economic Theory and Economic Behavior," *American Economic Review* 90, no. 2 (May 2000), pp. 426–32; D. S. Massey, "A Brief History of Human Society: The Origin and Role of Emotion in Social Life," *American Sociological Review* 67 (February 2002), pp. 1–29; and J. O'Shaughnessy and N. J. OShaughnessy, *The Marketing Power of Emotion* (New York: Oxford University Press, 2003).

3. The definition presented here is constructed from the following sources: N. M. Ashkanasy, W. J. Zerbe, and C. E. J. Hartel, "Introduction: Managing Emotions in a Changing Workplace," in *Managing Emotions in the Workplace,* ed. N. M. Ashkanasy, W. J. Zerbe, and C. E. J. Hartel (Armonk, NY: M. E. Sharpe,

2002), pp. 3–18; and H. M. Weiss, "Conceptual and Empirical Foundations for the Study of Affect at Work," in *Emotions in the Workplace,* ed. R. G. Lord, R. J. Klimoski, and R. Kanfer (San Francisco: Jossey-Bass, 2002), pp. 20–63. However, the meaning of emotions is still being debated. See, for example, M. Cabanac, "What Is Emotion?" *Behavioural Processes* 60 (2002), pp. 69–83.

4. R. Kanfer and R. J. Klimoski, "Affect and Work: Looking Back to the Future," in *Emotions in the Workplace,* ed. R. G. Lord, R. J. Klimoski, and R. Kanfer (San Francisco: Jossey-Bass, 2002), pp. 473–90; and J. A. Russell, "Core Affect and the Psychological Construction of Emotion," *Psychological Review* 110, no. 1 (2003), pp. 145–72.

5. R. B. Zajonc, "Emotions," in *Handbook of Social Psychology,* ed. D. T. Gilbert, S. T. Fiske, and L. Gardner (New York: Oxford University Press, 1998), pp. 591–634.

6. N. A. Remington, L. R. Fabrigar, and P. S. Visser, "Reexamining the Circumplex Model of Affect," *Journal of Personality and Social Psychology* 79, no. 2 (2000), pp. 286–300; R. J. Larson, E. Diener, and R. E. Lucas, "Emotion: Models, Measures, and Differences," in *Emotions in the Workplace,* ed. R. G. Lord, R. J. Klimoski, and R. Kanfer (San Francisco: Jossey-Bass, 2002), pp. 64–113; and L. F. Barrett et al., "The Experience of Emotion," *Annual Review of Psychology* 58, no. 1 (2007), pp. 373–403.

7. A. H. Eagly and S. Chaiken, *The Psychology of Attitudes* (Orlando, FL: Harcourt Brace Jovanovich, 1993); A. P. Brief, *Attitudes in and around Organizations* (Thousand Oaks, CA: Sage, 1998). There is an amazing lack of consensus on the definition of attitudes. This book adopts the three-component model, whereas some experts define attitude as only the "feelings" component, with "beliefs" as a predictor and "intentions" as an outcome. Some writers specifically define attitudes as an "evaluation" of an attitude object, whereas others distinguish attitudes from evaluations of an attitude object. For some of these definitional variations, see I. Ajzen, "Nature and Operation of Attitudes," *Annual Review of Psychology* 52 (2001), pp. 27–58; D. Albarracín et al., "Attitudes: Introduction and Scope," in *The Handbook of Attitudes,* ed. D. Albarracín, B. T. Johnson, and M. P. Zanna (Mahwah, NJ: Lawrence Erlbaum Associates, 2005), pp. 3–20; and W. A. Cunningham and P. D. Zelazo, "Attitudes and Evaluations: A Social Cognitive Neuroscience Perspective," *TRENDS in Cognitive Sciences* 11, no. 3 (2007), pp. 97–104.

8. C. D. Fisher, "Mood and Emotions While Working: Missing Pieces of Job Satisfaction?" *Journal of Organizational Behavior* 21 (2000), pp. 185–202; Cunningham and Zelazo, "Attitudes and Evaluations"; and M. D. Lieberman, "Social Cognitive Neuroscience: A Review of Core Processes," *Annual Review of Psychology* 58, no. 1 (2007), pp. 259–89.

9. S. Orbell, "Intention-Behavior Relations: A Self-Regulation Perspective," in *Contemporary Perspectives on the Psychology of Attitudes,* ed. G. Haddock and G. R. Maio (East Sussex, UK: Psychology Press, 2004), pp. 145–68.

10. H. M. Weiss and R. Cropanzano, "Affective Events Theory: A Theoretical Discussion of the Structure, Causes, and

Consequences of Affective Experiences at Work," *Research in Organizational Behavior* 18 (1996), pp. 1–74; and J. Wegge et al., "A Test of Basic Assumptions of Affective Events Theory (AET) in Call Centre Work," *British Journal of Management* 17 (2006), pp. 237–54.

11. J. A. Bargh and M. J. Ferguson, "Beyond Behaviorism: On the Automaticity of Higher Mental Processes," *Psychological Bulletin* 126, no. 6 (2000), pp. 925–45; R. H. Fazio, "On the Automatic Activation of Associated Evaluations: An Overview," *Cognition and Emotion* 15, no. 2 (2001), pp. 115–41; and M. Gladwell, *Blink: The Power of Thinking without Thinking* (New York: Little, Brown, 2005).

12. A. R. Damasio, *Descartes' Error: Emotion, Reason, and the Human Brain* (New York: Putnam Sons, 1994); A. Damasio, *The Feeling of What Happens* (New York: Harcourt Brace and Co., 1999); P. Ekman, "Basic Emotions," in *Handbook of Cognition and Emotion,* ed. T. Dalgleish and M. Power (San Francisco: Jossey-Bass, 1999), pp. 45–60; J. E. LeDoux, "Emotion Circuits in the Brain," *Annual Review of Neuroscience* 23 (2000), pp. 155–84; and R. J. Dolan, "Emotion, Cognition, and Behavior," *Science* 298, no. 5596 (November 8, 2002), pp. 1191–94.

13. N. Schwarz, "Emotion, Cognition, and Decision Making," *Cognition and Emotion* 14, no. 4 (2000), pp. 433–40; and M. T. Pham, "The Logic of Feeling," *Journal of Consumer Psychology* 14, no. 4 (2004), pp. 360–69.

14. G. R. Maio, V. M. Esses, and D. W. Bell, "Examining Conflict between Components of Attitudes: Ambivalence and Inconsistency Are Distinct Constructs," *Canadian Journal of Behavioural Science* 32, no. 2 (2000), pp. 71–83.

15. P. C. Nutt, *Why Decisions Fail* (San Francisco, CA: Berrett-Koehler, 2002); S. Finkelstein, *Why Smart Executives Fail* (New York: Viking, 2003); and P. C. Nutt, "Search During Decision Making," *European Journal of Operational Research* 160 (2005), pp. 851–76.

16. Weiss and Cropanzano, "Affective Events Theory."

17. L. Festinger, *A Theory of Cognitive Dissonance* (Evanston, IL: Row, Peterson, 1957); G. R. Salancik, "Commitment and the Control of Organizational Behavior and Belief," in *New Directions in Organizational Behavior,* ed. B. M. Staw and G. R. Salancik (Chicago: St. Clair, 1977), pp. 1–54; and A. D. Galinsky, J. Stone, and J. Cooper, "The Reinstatement of Dissonance and Psychological Discomfort Following Failed Affirmation," *European Journal of Social Psychology* 30, no. 1 (2000), pp. 123–47.

18. B. E. Ashforth and R. H. Humphrey, "Emotional Labor in Service Roles: The Influence of Identity," *Academy of Management Review* 18 (1993), pp. 88–115. For a recent review of the emotional labor concept, see T. M. Glomb and M. J. Tews, "Emotional Labor: A Conceptualization and Scale Development," *Journal of Vocational Behavior* 64, no. 1 (2004), pp. 1–23.

19. J. A. Morris and D. C. Feldman, "The Dimensions, Antecedents, and Consequences of Emotional Labor," *Academy of Management Review* 21 (1996), pp. 986–1010; and D. Zapf, "Emotion Work and Psychological Well-Being: A Review of the Literature and Some Conceptual Considerations," *Human Resource Management Review* 12 (2002), pp. 237–68.

20. E. Forman, "'Diversity Concerns Grow as Companies Head Overseas,' Consultant Says," *Sun–Sentinel (Fort Lauderdale, FL),* June 26, 1995. Cultural differences in emotional expression are discussed in F. Trompenaars, "Resolving International Conflict: Culture and Business Strategy," *Business Strategy Review* 7, no. 3 (Autumn 1996), pp. 51–68; F. Trompenaars and C. Hampden-Turner, *Riding the Waves of Culture,* 2nd ed. (New York: McGraw-Hill, 1998), Chap. 6; and A. E. Raz and A. Rafaeli, "Emotion Management in Cross-Cultural Perspective: 'Smile Training' in Japanese and North American Service Organizations," *Research on Emotion in Organizations* 3 (2007), pp. 199–220.

21. R. Hallowell, D. Bowen, and C. I. Knoop, "Four Seasons Goes to Paris," *Academy of Management Executive* 16, no. 4 (November 2002), pp. 7–24.

22. This relates to the automaticity of emotion, which is summarized in P. Winkielman and K. C. Berridge, "Unconscious Emotion," *Current Directions in Psychological Science* 13, no. 3 (2004), pp. 120–23; and K. N. Ochsner and J. J. Gross, "The Cognitive Control of Emotions," *TRENDS in Cognitive Sciences* 9, no. 5 (May 2005), pp. 242–49.

23. W. J. Zerbe, "Emotional Dissonance and Employee Well-Being," in *Managing Emotions in the Workplace.* ed. N. M. Ashkanasy, W. J. Zerbe, and C. E. J. Hartel (Armonk, NY: M. E. Sharpe, 2002), pp. 189–214; and R. Cropanzano, H. M. Weiss, and S. M. Elias, "The Impact of Display Rules and Emotional Labor on Psychological Well-Being at Work," *Research in Occupational Stress and Well Being* 3 (2003), pp. 45–89.

24. J. Verdon, "They Can Hardly Contain Themselves," *The Record (Bergen, NJ),* April 21, 2007, p. A15.

25. C. M. Brotheridge and A. A. Grandey, "Emotional Labor and Burnout: Comparing Two Perspectives of 'People Work,'" *Journal of Vocational Behavior* 60 (2002), pp. 17–39; Zapf, "Emotion Work and Psychological Well-Being"; and J. M. Diefendorff, M. H. Croyle, and R. H. Gosserand, "The Dimensionality and Antecedents of Emotional Labor Strategies," *Journal of Vocational Behavior* 66, no. 2 (2005), pp. 339–57.

26. C. Fox, "Shifting Gears," *Australian Financial Review,* August 13, 2004, p. 28; and J. Thomson, "True Team Spirit," *Business Review Weekly,* March 18, 2004, p. 92.

27. J. D. Mayer, P. Salovey, and D. R. Caruso, "Models of Emotional Intelligence," in *Handbook of Human Intelligence,* ed. R. J. Sternberg, 2nd ed. (New York: Cambridge University Press, 2000), pp. 396–420. This definition is also recognized in C. Cherniss, "Emotional Intelligence and Organizational Effectiveness," in *The Emotionally Intelligent Workplace,* ed. C. Cherniss and D. Goleman (San Francisco: Jossey-Bass, 2001), pp. 3–12; and M. Zeidner, G. Matthews, and R. D. Roberts, "Emotional Intelligence in the Workplace: A Critical Review," *Applied Psychology: An International Review* 53, no. 3 (2004), pp. 371–99.

28. These four dimensions of emotional intelligence are discussed in detail in D. Goleman, R. Boyatzis, and A. McKee, *Primal Leadership* (Boston: Harvard Business School Press, 2002),

Chap. 3. Slight variations of this model are presented in R. Boyatzis, D. Goleman, and K. S. Rhee, "Clustering Competence in Emotional Intelligence," in *The Handbook of Emotional Intelligence,* ed. R. Bar-On and J. D. A. Parker (San Francisco: Jossey-Bass, 2000), pp. 343–62; and D. Goleman, "An EI-Based Theory of Performance," in *The Emotionally Intelligent Workplace,* ed. C. Cherniss and D. Goleman (San Francisco: Jossey-Bass, 2001), pp. 27–44.

29. Which model best represents EI and its abilities is debated in several sources, including several chapters in K. R. Murphy, ed., *A Critique of Emotional Intelligence: What Are the Problems and How Can They Be Fixed?* (Mahwah, NJ: Lawrence Erlbaum Associates, 2006).

30. H. A. Elfenbein and N. Ambady, "Predicting Workplace Outcomes from the Ability to Eavesdrop on Feelings," *Journal of Applied Psychology* 87, no. 5 (2002), pp. 963–71.

31. The hierarchical nature of the four EI dimensions is discussed by Goleman, but is more explicit in the Salovey and Mayer model. See D. R. Caruso and P. Salovey, *The Emotionally Intelligent Manager* (San Francisco: Jossey-Bass, 2004).

32. P. N. Lopes et al., "Emotional Intelligence and Social Interaction," *Personality and Social Psychology Bulletin* 30, no. 8 (August 2004), pp. 1018–34; C. S. Daus and N. M. Ashkanasy, "The Case for the Ability-Based Model of Emotional Intelligence in Organizational Behavior," *Journal of Organizational Behavior* 26 (2005), pp. 453–66; J. E. Barbuto Jr and M. E. Burbach, "The Emotional Intelligence of Transformational Leaders: A Field Study of Elected Officials," *Journal of Social Psychology* 146, no. 1 (2006), pp. 51–64; M. A. Brackett et al., "Relating Emotional Abilities to Social Functioning: A Comparison of Self-Report and Performance Measures of Emotional Intelligence," *Journal of Personality and Social Psychology* 91, no. 4 (2006), pp. 780–95; and D. L. Reis et al., "Emotional Intelligence Predicts Individual Differences in Social Exchange Reasoning," *NeuroImage* 35, no. 3 (2007), pp. 1385–91.

33. Some studies have reported situations where EI has a limited effect on indivsual performance. For example, see A. L. Day and S. A. Carroll, "Using an Ability-Based Measure of Emotional Intelligence to Predict Individual Performance, Group Performance, and Group Citizenship Behaviours," *Personality and Individual Differences* 36 (2004), pp. 1443–58; Z. Ivcevic, M. A. Brackett, and J. D. Mayer, "Emotional Intelligence and Emotional Creativity," *Journal of Personality* 75, no. 2 (2007), pp. 199–236; and J. C. Rode et al., "Emotional Intelligence and Individual Performance: Evidence of Direct and Moderated Effects," *Journal of Organizational Behavior* 28, no. 4 (2007), pp. 399–421.

34. Lopes et al., "Emotional Intelligence and Social Interaction,"; and C. S. Wong et al., "The Feasibility of Training and Development of EI: An Exploratory Study in Singapore, Hong Kong and Taiwan," *Intelligence* 35, no. 2 (2007), pp. 141–50.

35. Goleman, Boyatzis, and McKee, *Primal Leadership*; S. C. Clark, R. Callister, and R. Wallace, "Undergraduate Management Skills Courses and Students' Emotional Intelligence," *Journal of Management Education* 27, no. 1 (February 2003), pp. 3–23; and H. A. Elfenbein, "Learning in

Emotion Judgments: Training and the Cross-Cultural Understanding of Facial Expressions," *Journal of Nonverbal Behavior* 30, no. 1 (2006), pp. 21–36.

36. D. A. Harrison, D. A. Newman, and P. L. Roth, "How Important Are Job Attitudes? Meta-Analytic Comparisons of Integrative Behavioral Outcomes and Time Sequences," *Academy of Management Journal* 49, no. 2 (2006), pp. 305–25.

37. E. A. Locke, "The Nature and Causes of Job Satisfaction," in *Handbook of Industrial and Organizational Psychology,* ed. M. Dunnette (Chicago: Rand McNally, 1976), 1297–1350; and H. M. Weiss, "Deconstructing Job Satisfaction: Separating Evaluations, Beliefs and Affective Experiences," *Human Resource Management Review,* no. 12 (2002), pp. 173–94. Some definitions still include emotion as an element of job satisfaction, whereas the definition presented in this book views emotion as a cause of job satisfaction. Also, this definition views job satisfaction as a *collection of attitudes,* not several *facets* of job satisfaction.

38. T. W. Smith, *Job Satisfaction in America: Trends and Socio-Demographic Correlates,* (Chicago: National Opinion Research Center/University of Chicago, August 2007).

39. Ipsos-Reid, "Ipsos-Reid Global Poll Finds Major Differences in Employee Satisfaction around the World," News release, (Toronto: January 8, 2001); International Survey Research, *Employee Satisfaction in the World's 10 Largest Economies: Globalization or Diversity?* (Chicago: International Survey Research, 2002); Watson Wyatt Worldwide, "Asia-Pacific Workers Satisfied with Jobs Despite Some Misgivings with Management and Pay," Watson Wyatt news release, (Singapore: November 16, 2004).

40. K. Macklem, "Vancity Confidential," *Maclean's,* October 11–18, 2004, p. 22; Watson Wyatt Worldwide, "Malaysian Workers More Satisfied with Their Jobs Than Their Companies' Leadership and Supervision Practices," Watson Wyatt Worldwide news release, (Kuala Lumpur: November 30, 2004); K. and Keis, "HR Needs Happy Staff to Show Its Success," *Canadian HR Reporter,* February 14, 2005, p. 14.

41. M. J. Withey and W. H. Cooper, "Predicting Exit, Voice, Loyalty, and Neglect," *Administrative Science Quarterly,* no. 34 (1989), pp. 521–39; W. H. Turnley and D. C. Feldman, "The Impact of Psychological Contract Violations on Exit, Voice, Loyalty, and Neglect," *Human Relations,* no. 52 (July 1999), pp. 895–922. Subdimensions of silence and voice also exist. See L. van Dyne, S. Ang, and I. C. Botero, "Conceptualizing Employee Silence and Employee Voice as Multidimensional Constructs" *Journal of Management Studies* 40, no. 6 (September 2003), pp. 1359–92.

42. T. R. Mitchell, B. C. Holtom, and T. W. Lee, "How to Keep Your Best Employees: Developing an Effective Retention Policy," *Academy of Management Executive* 15 (November 2001), pp. 96–108; and C. P. Maertz and M. A. Campion, "Profiles of Quitting: Integrating Process and Content Turnover Theory," *Academy of Management Journal* 47, no. 4 (2004), pp. 566–82.

43. A. A. Luchak, "What Kind of Voice Do Loyal Employees Use?" *British Journal of Industrial Relations* 41 (March 2003), pp. 115–34.

44. J. D. Hibbard, N. Kumar, and L. W. Stern, "Examining the Impact of Destructive Acts in Marketing Channel Relationships," *Journal of Marketing Research* 38 (February 2001), pp. 45–61; and J. Zhou and J. M. George, "When Job Dissatisfaction Leads to Creativity: Encouraging the Expression of Voice," *Academy of Management Journal* 44 (August 2001), pp. 682–96.

45. M. J. Withey and I. R. Gellatly, "Situational and Dispositional Determinants of Exit, Voice, Loyalty and Neglect," *Proceedings of the Administrative Sciences Association of Canada, Organizational Behaviour Division* (June 1998); D. C. Thomas and K. Au, "The Effect of Cultural Differences on Behavioral Responses to Low Job Satisfaction," *Journal of International Business Studies* 33, no. 2 (2002), pp. 309–26; S. F. Premeaux and A. G. Bedeian, "Breaking the Silence: The Moderating Effects of Self-Monitoring in Predicting Speaking up in the Workplace," *Journal of Management Studies* 40, no. 6 (2003), pp. 1537–62.

46. T. A. Judge et al., "The Job Satisfaction–Job Performance Relationship: A Qualitative and Quantitative Review," *Psychological Bulletin* 127 (2001), pp. 376–407; and L. Saari and T. A. Judge, "Employee Attitudes and Job Satisfaction," *Human Resource Management* 43, no. 4 (Winter 2004), pp. 395–407. Other studies report stronger correlations with job performance when both the beliefs and feelings components of job satisfaction are consistent with each other, and when measuring overall job attitude (satisfaction and commitment combined). See D. J. Schleicher, J. D. Watt, and G. J. Greguras, "Reexamining the Job Satisfaction-Performance Relationship: The Complexity of Attitudes," *Journal of Applied Psychology* 89, no. 1 (2004), pp. 165–77; and Harrison, Newman, and Roth, "How Important Are Job Attitudes?"

47. "The Greatest Briton in Management and Leadership," *Personnel Today* (February 18, 2003), p. 20.

48. J. I. Heskett, W. E. Sasser, and L. A. Schlesinger, *The Service Profit Chain* (New York: Free Press, 1997); D. J. Koys, "The Effects of Employee Satisfaction, Organizational Citizenship Behavior, and Turnover on Organizational Effectiveness: A Unit-Level, Longitudinal Study," *Personnel Psychology* 54 (April 2001), pp. 101–14; W. C. Tsai and Y. M. Huang, "Mechanisms Linking Employee Affective Delivery and Customer Behavioral Intentions," *Journal of Applied Psychology* 87, no. 5 (2002), pp. 1001–8; T. DeCotiis et al., "How Outback Steakhouse Created a Great Place to Work, Have Fun, and Make Money," *Journal of Organizational Excellence* 23, no. 4 (Autumn 2004), pp. 23–33; and G. A. Gelade and S. Young, "Test of a Service Profit Chain Model in the Retail Banking Sector," *Journal of Occupational & Organizational Psychology* 78 (2005), pp. 1–22.

49. P. Guenzi and O. Pelloni, "The Impact of Interpersonal Relationships on Customer Satisfaction and Loyalty to the Service Provider," *International Journal Of Service Industry Management* 15, no. 3–4 (2004), pp. 365–84; and S. J. Bell, S. Auh, and K. Smalley, "Customer Relationship Dynamics: Service Quality and Customer Loyalty in the Context of Varying Levels of Customer Expertise and Switching Costs," *Journal*

of the Academy of Marketing Science* 33, no. 2 (Spring 2005), pp. 169–83.

50. F. Bilovsky, "Wegmans Is Named America's No. 1 Employer," *Democrat & Chronicle (Rochester, NY)*, January 11, 2005; M. Boyle, "The Wegmans Way," *Fortune*, January 24, 2005, p. 62; B. Niedt, "Wegmans Reaches No. 1 on List of Workplaces," *Post Standard (Syracuse, NY)*, January 11, 2005, p. A1; and M. Sommer and J. F. Bonfatti, "Wegmans Employees Feel Challenged, Valued," *Buffalo News (Buffalo, NY)*, January 16, 2005, p. B7.

51. R. T. Mowday, L. W. Porter, and R. M. Steers, *Employee Organization Linkages: The Psychology of Commitment, Absenteeism, and Turnover* (New York: Academic Press, 1982).

52. J. P. Meyer, "Organizational Commitment," *International Review of Industrial and Organizational Psychology* 12 (1997), pp. 175–228. Along with affective and continuance commitment, Meyer identifies *normative commitment,* which refers to employee feelings of obligation to remain with the organization. This commitment has been excluded so that students focus on the two most common perspectives of commitment.

53. R. D. Hackett, P. Bycio, and P. A. Hausdorf, "Further Assessments of Meyer and Allen's (1991) Three-Component Model of Organizational Commitment," *Journal of Applied Psychology* 79 (1994), pp. 15–23.

54. J. P. Meyer et al., "Affective, Continuance, and Normative Commitment to the Organization: A Meta-Analysis of Antecedents, Correlates, and Consequences," *Journal of Vocational Behavior* 61 (2002), pp. 20–52; and M. Riketta, "Attitudinal Organizational Commitment and Job Performance: A Meta-Analysis," *Journal of Organizational Behavior* 23 (2002), pp. 257–66.

55. J. P. Meyer et al., "Organizational Commitment and Job Performance: It's the Nature of the Commitment That Counts," *Journal of Applied Psychology* 74 (1989), pp. 152–56; A. A. Luchak and I. R. Gellatly, "What Kind of Commitment Does a Final-Earnings Pension Plan Elicit?" *Relations Industrielles* 56 (Spring 2001), pp. 394–417; Z. X. Chen and A. M. Francesco, "The Relationship between the Three Components of Commitment and Employee Performance in China," *Journal of Vocational Behavior* 62, no. 3 (2003), pp. 490–510; and D. M. Powell and J. P. Meyer, "Side-Bet Theory and the Three-Component Model of Organizational Commitment," *Journal of Vocational Behavior* 65, no. 1 (2004), pp. 157–77.

56. E. W. Morrison and S. L. Robinson, "When Employees Feel Betrayed: A Model of How Psychological Contract Violation Develops," *Academy of Management Review* 22 (1997), pp. 226–56; and J. E. Finegan, "The Impact of Person and Organizational Values on Organizational Commitment," *Journal of Occupational and Organizational Psychology* 73 (June 2000), pp. 149–69.

57. D. M. Cable and T. A. Judge, "Person-Organization Fit, Job Choice Decisions, and Organizational Entry," *Organizational Behavior and Human Decision Processes* 67, no. 3 (1996), pp. 294–311; T. J. Kalliath, A. C. Bluedorn, and M. J. Strube, "A Test of Value Congruence Effects," *Journal of Organizational Behavior* 20, no. 7 (1999), pp. 1175–98; and J. W. Westerman

and L. A. Cyr, "An Integrative Analysis of Person-Organization Fit Theories," *International Journal of Selection and Assessment* 12, no. 3 (September 2004), pp. 252–61.

58. D. M. Rousseau et al., "Not So Different after All: A Cross-Disicipline View of Trust," *Academy of Management Review* 23 (1998), pp. 393–404.

59. S. Ashford, C. Lee, and P. Bobko, "Content, Causes, and Consequences of Job Insecurity: A Theory-Based Measure and Substantive Test," *Academy of Management Journal* 32 (1989), pp. 803–29; and C. Hendry and R. Jenkins, "Psychological Contracts and New Deals," *Human Resource Management Journal* 7 (1997), pp. 38–44.

60. T. S. Heffner and J. R. Rentsch, "Organizational Commitment and Social Interaction: A Multiple Constituencies Approach," *Journal of Vocational Behavior* 59 (2001), pp. 471–90.

61. N. Davidson, "Vancouver Developer Looks to Make Video Games without Burning out Staff," *Canadian Press,* February 21, 2006. Some quotations are from Propaganda's Web site: www.propagandagames.go.com

62. J. C. Quick et al., *Preventive Stress Management in Organizations* (Washington, DC: American Psychological Association, 1997), pp. 3–4; and R. S. DeFrank and J. M. Ivancevich, "Stress on the Job: An Executive Update," *Academy of Management Executive* 12 (August 1998), pp. 55–66.

63. Quick et al., *Preventive Stress Management in Organizations* pp. 5–6; and B. L. Simmons and D. L. Nelson, "Eustress at Work: The Relationship between Hope and Health in Hospital Nurses," *Health Care Management Review* 26, no. 4 (October 2001), p. 7ff.

64. H. Selye, *Stress without Distress* (Philadelphia: J. B. Lippincott, 1974).

65. S. E. Taylor, R. L. Repetti, and T. Seeman, "Health Psychology: What Is an Unhealthy Environment and How Does It Get under the Skin?" *Annual Review of Psychology* 48 (1997), pp. 411–47.

66. D. Ganster, M. Fox, and D. Dwyer, "Explaining Employees' Health Care Costs: A Prospective Examination of Stressful Job Demands, Personal Control, and Physiological Reactivity," *Journal of Applied Psychology* 86 (May 2001), pp. 954–64; M. Kivimaki et al., "Work Stress and Risk of Cardiovascular Mortality: Prospective Cohort Study of Industrial Employees," *British Medical Journal* 325 (October 19, 2002), pp. 857–60; and A. Rosengren et al., "Association of Psychosocial Risk Factors with Risk of Acute Myocardial Infarction in 11,119 Cases and 13,648 Controls from 52 Countries (the Interheart Study) Case-Control Study," *The Lancet* 364, no. 9438 (September 11, 2004), pp. 953–62.

67. R. C. Kessler, "The Effects of Stressful Life Events on Depression," *Annual Review of Psychology* 48 (1997), pp. 191–14; L. Greenburg and J. Barling, "Predicting Employee Aggression against Coworkers, Subordinates and Supervisors: The Roles of Person Behaviors and Perceived Workplace Factors," *Journal of Organizational Behavior* 20 (1999), pp. 897–913; M. Jamal and V. V. Baba, "Job Stress and Burnout among Canadian Managers and Nurses: An Empirical Examination," *Canadian Journal of Public Health* 91, no. 6

(November–December 2000), pp. 454–58; L. Tourigny, V. V. Baba, and T. R. Lituchy, "Job Burnout among Airline Employees in Japan: A Study of the Buffering Effects of Absence and Supervisory Support," *International Journal of Cross Cultural Management* 5, no. 1 (April 2005), pp. 67–85; and M. S. Hershcovis et al., "Predicting Workplace Aggression: A Meta-Analysis," *Journal of Applied Psychology* 92, no. 1 (2007), pp. 228–38.

68. K. Danna and R. W. Griffin, "Health and Well-Being in the Workplace: A Review and Synthesis of the Literature," *Journal of Management* (Spring 1999), pp. 357–84.

69. This is a slight variation of the definition in the Quebec anti-harassment legislation. See www.cnt.gouv.qc.ca. For related definitions and discussion of workplace incivility, see H. Cowiea et al., "Measuring Workplace Bullying," *Aggression and Violent Behavior* 7 (2002), pp. 33–51; and C. M. Pearson and C. L. Porath, "On the Nature, Consequences and Remedies of Workplace Incivility: No Time for 'Nice'? Think Again," *Academy of Management Executive* 19, no. 1 (February 2005), pp. 7–18.

70. Pearson and Porath, "On the Nature, Consequences and Remedies of Workplace Incivility"; and J. Przybys, "How Rude!," *Las Vegas Review-Journal,* April 25, 2006, p. 1E.

71. "HR Bullied Just as Much as Anyone Else," *Personnel Today*, November 2005, p. 3; and S. Toomey, "Bullying Alive and Kicking," *The Australian,* July 16, 2005, p. 9.

72. Past predictions of future work hours are described in B. K. Hunnicutt, *Kellogg's Six-Hour Day* (Philadelphia: Temple University Press, 1996).

73. Hunnicutt, *Kellogg's Six-Hour Day*; E. Galinsky et al., *Overwork in America: When the Way We Work Becomes Too Much,* (New York: Families and Work Institute, March 2005); and R. G. Netemeyer, J. G. Maxham III, and C. Pullig, "Conflicts in the Work-Family Interface: Links to Job Stress, Customer Service Employee Performance, and Customer Purchase Intent," *Journal of Marketing* 69 (April 2005), pp. 130–45.

74. R. Drago, D. Black, and M. Wooden, *The Persistence of Long Work Hours,* Melbourne Institute Working Paper Series (Melbourne: Melbourne Institute of Applied Economic and Social Research, University of Melbourne, August 2005).

75. C. B. Meek, "The Dark Side of Japanese Management in the 1990s: Karoshi and Ijime in the Japanese Workplace," *Journal of Managerial Psychology* 19, no. 3 (2004), pp. 312–31; J. Shi, "Beijing's High Flyers Dying to Get Ahead," *South China Morning Post (Hong Kong)*, October 8, 2005, p. 8; and N. You, "Mantra: Work for Life, Rather Than Live to Work," *China Daily,* March 26, 2005.

76. L. Wahyudi S, "'Traffic Congestion Makes Me Crazy," *Jakarta Post,* March 18, 2003. The effect of traffic congestion on stress is reported in G. W. Evans, R. E. Wener, and D. Phillips, "The Morning Rush Hour: Predictability and Commuter Stress," *Environment and Behavior* 34 (July 2002), pp. 521–30.

77. F. Kittell et al., "Job Conditions and Fibrinogen in 14,226 Belgian Workers: The Belstress Study," *European Heart Journal* 23 (2002), pp. 1841–48; and S. K. Parker, "Longitudinal Effects of Lean Production on Employee Outcomes and the

Mediating Role of Work Characteristics," *Journal of Applied Psychology* 88, no. 4 (2003), pp. 620–34.

78. S. J. Havlovic and J. P. Keenen, "Coping with Work Stress: The Influence of Individual Differences; Handbook on Job Stress [Special Issue]," *Journal of Social Behavior and Personality* 6 (1991), pp. 199–212.

79. S. S. Luthar, D. Cicchetti, and B. Becker, "The Construct of Resilience: A Critical Evaluation and Guidelines for Future Work," *Child Development* 71, no. 3 (May–June 2000), pp. 543–62; F. Luthans, "The Need for and Meaning of Positive Organizational Behavior," *Journal of Organizational Behavior* 23 (2002), pp. 695–706; and G. A. Bonanno, "Loss, Trauma, and Human Resilience: Have We Underestimated the Human Capacity to Thrive after Extremely Aversive Events?" *American Psychologist* 59, no. 1 (2004), pp. 20–28.

80. M. Beasley, T. Thompson, and J. Davidson, "Resilience in Response to Life Stress: The Effects of Coping Style and Cognitive Hardiness," *Personality and Individual Differences* 34, no. 1 (2003), pp. 77–95; M. M. Tugade, B. L. Fredrickson, and L. Feldman Barrett, "Psychological Resilience and Positive Emotional Granularity: Examining the Benefits of Positive Emotions on Coping and Health," *Journal of Personality* 72, no. 6 (2004), pp. 1161–90; I. Tsaousis and I. Nikolaou, "Exploring the Relationship of Emotional Intelligence with Physical and Psychological Health Functioning," *Stress and Health* 21, no. 2 (2005), pp. 77–86; and L. Campbell-Sills, S. L. Cohan, and M. B. Stein, "Relationship of Resilience to Personality, Coping, and Psychiatric Symptoms in Young Adults," *Behaviour Research and Therapy* 44, no. 4 (April 2006), pp. 585–99.

81. J. T. Spence, A. S., and Robbins, "Workaholism: Definition, Measurement and Preliminary Results," *Journal of Personality Assessment* 58 (1992), pp. 160–78; R. J. Burke, "Workaholism in Organizations: Psychological and Physical Well-Being Consequences," *Stress Medicine* 16, no. 1 (2000), pp. 11–16; I. Harpaz and R. Snir, "Workaholism: Its Definition and Nature," *Human Relations* 56 (2003), pp. 291–319; and R. J. Burke, A. M. Richardson, and M. Martinussen, "Workaholism among Norwegian Senior Managers: New Research Directions," *International Journal of Management* 21, no. 4 (December 2004), pp. 415–26.

82. R. J. Burke and G. MacDermid, "Are Workaholics Job Satisfied and Successful in Their Careers?" *Career Development International* 4 (1999), pp. 277–82; and R. J. Burke and S. Matthiesen, "Short Communication: Workaholism among Norwegian Journalists: Antecedents and Consequences," *Stress and Health* 20, no. 5 (2004), pp. 301–8.

83. L. T. Eby et al., "Work and Family Research in IO/OB: Content Analysis and Review of the Literature (1980–2002)," *Journal of Vocational Behavior* 66, no. 1 (2005), pp. 124–97.

84. Y. Iwasaki et al., "A Short-Term Longitudinal Analysis of Leisure Coping Used by Police and Emergency Response Service Workers," *Journal of Leisure Research* 34 (July 2002), pp. 311–39.

85. M. Waung, "The Effects of Self-Regulatory Coping Orientation on Newcomer Adjustment and Job Survival," *Personnel Psychology* 48 (1995), pp. 633–50; and A. M. Saks and B. E. Ashforth, "Proactive Socialization and Behavioral Self-Management," *Journal of Vocational Behavior* 48 (1996), pp. 301–23.

86. The effectiveness of these programs are reported in numerous studies, including V. A. Barnes, F. A. Treiber, and M. H. Johnson, "Impact of Transcendental Meditation on Ambulatory Blood Pressure in African-American Adolescents," *American Journal of Hypertension* 17, no. 4 (2004), pp. 366–69; and W. M. Ensel and N. Lin, "Physical Fitness and the Stress Process," *Journal of Community Psychology* 32, no. 1 (January 2004), pp. 81–101.

87. S. E. Taylor et al., "Biobehavioral Responses to Stress in Females: Tend-and-Befriend, Not Fight-or-Flight," *Psychological Review* 107, no. 3 (July 2000), pp. 411–29; and R. Eisler and D. S. Levine, "Nurture, Nature, and Caring: We Are Not Prisoners of Our Genes," *Brain and Mind* 3 (2002), pp. 9–52.

chapter 5

1. D. Creelman, "Interview: Bob Catell & Kenny Moore," HR.com, February 2005; W. L. Lee, "Net Value: That Loving Feeling," The Edge Financial Daily (Malaysia), April 25, 2005; N. Mwaura, "Honour Staff for Good Work," Daily Nation (Nairobi, Kenya), September 27, 2005; and E. White, "Praise from Peers Goes a Long Way," The Wall Street Journal, December 19, 2005, p. B3.

2. C. C. Pinder, Work Motivation in Organizational Behavior (Upper Saddle River, NJ: Prentice-Hall, 1998); and R. M. Steers, R. T. Mowday, and D. L. Shapiro, "The Future of Work Motivation Theory," Academy of Management Review 29 (2004), pp. 379-87.

3. "Towers Perrin Study Finds, Despite Layoffs and Slow Economy, a New, More Complex Power Game Is Emerging between Employers and Employees," Business Wire news release, New York), August 30, 2001; and C. Lachnit, "The Young and the Dispirited," Workforce 81 (August 2002), p. 18.

4. The confusing array of definitions about drives and needs has been the subject of criticism for a half century. See, for example, R. S. Peters, "Motives and Motivation," Philosophy 31 (1956), pp. 117-30; H. Cantril, "Sentio, Ergo Sum: 'Motivation' Reconsidered," Journal of Psychology 65, no. 1 (January 1967), pp. 91-107; and G. R. Salancik and J. Pfeffer, "An Examination of Need-Satisfaction Models of Job Attitudes," Administrative Science Quarterly 22, no. 3 (September 1977), pp. 427-56.

5. A. Blasi, "Emotions and Moral Motivation," Journal for the Theory of Social Behaviour 29, no. 1 (1999), pp. 1-19; D. W. Pfaff, Drive: Neurobiological and Molecular Mechanisms of Sexual Motivation (Cambridge, MA: MIT Press, 1999); T. V. Sewards and M. A. Sewards, "Fear and Power-Dominance Drive Motivation: Neural Representations and Pathways Mediating Sensory and Mnemonic Inputs, and Outputs to Premotor Structures," Neuroscience and Biobehavioral Reviews 26 (2002), pp. 553-79; and K. C. Berridge, "Motivation Concepts in Behavioral Neuroscience," Physiology & Behavior 81, no. 2 (2004), pp. 179-209. We distinguish drives from

emotions, but future research may find that the two concepts are not so different as is stated here.

6. K. Passyn and M. Sujan, "Self-Accountability Emotions and Fear Appeals: Motivating Behavior," Journal of Consumer Research 32, no. 4 (2006), pp. 583-89; and S. G. Barsade and D. E. Gibson, "Why Does Affect Matter in Organizations? " Academy of Management Perspectives 21, no. 2 (February 2007), pp. 36-59.

7. G. Loewenstein, "The Psychology of Curiosity: A Review and Reinterpretation," Psychological Bulletin 116, no. 1 (1994), pp. 75-98; R. E. Baumeister and M. R. Leary, "The Need to Belong: Desire for Interpersonal Attachments as a Fundamental Human Motivation," Psychological Bulletin 117 (1995), pp. 497-529; and A. E. Kelley, "Neurochemical Networks Encoding Emotion and Motivation: An Evolutionary Perspective," in Who Needs Emotions? The Brain Meets the Robot, ed. J.-M. Fellous and M. A. Arbib (New York: Oxford University Press, 2005), pp. 29-78.

8. S. Hitlin, "Values as the Core of Personal Identity: Drawing Links between Two Theories of Self," Social Psychology Quarterly 66, no. 2 (2003), pp. 118-37; D. D. Knoch and E. E. Fehr, "Resisting the Power of Temptations. The Right Prefrontal Cortex and Self-Control," Annals of the New York Academy of Sciences 1104, no. 1 (2007), p. 123; and B. Monin, D. A. Pizarro, and J. S. Beer, "Deciding Versus Reacting: Conceptions of Moral Judgment and the Reason-Affect Debate," Review of General Psychology 11, no. 2 (2007), 99-111.

9. N. M. Ashkanasy, W. J. Zerbe, and C. E. J. Hr****tel, "A Bounded Emotionality Perspective on the Individual in the Organization," in Emotions in Organizational Behavior, ed. C. E. J. Hr****tel, W. J. Zerbe, and N. M. Ashkanasy (Mahwah, N. J.: Lawrence Erlbaum Associates, 2005), pp. 113-17.

10. A. H. Maslow, "A Theory of Human Motivation," Psychological Review 50 (1943), pp. 370-96; and A. H. Maslow, Motivation and Personality (New York: Harper & Row, 1954).

11. D. T. Hall and K. E. Nougaim, "An Examination of Maslow's Need Hierarchy in an Organizational Setting," Organizational Behavior and Human Performance 3, no. 1 (1968), p. 12; M. A. Wahba and L. G. Bridwell, "Maslow Reconsidered: A Review of Research on the Need Hierarchy Theory," Organizational Behavior and Human Performance 15 (1976), pp. 212-40; andE. L. Betz, "Two Tests of Maslow's Theory of Need Fulfillment," Journal of Vocational Behavior 24, no. 2 (1984), pp. 204-20; P. A. Corning, "Biological Adaptation in Human Societies: A 'Basic Needs' Approach," Journal of Bioeconomics 2, no. 1 (2000), pp. 41-86.

12. A. H. Maslow, "A Preface to Motivation Theory," Psychsomatic Medicine 5 (1943), pp. 85-92.

13. A. H. Maslow, Maslow on Management (New York: John Wiley & Sons, 1998).

14. F. F. Luthans, "Positive Organizational Behavior: Developing and Managing Psychological Strengths," The Academy of Management Executive 16, no. 1 (2002), pp. 57-72; S. L. Gable and J. Haidt, "What (and Why) Is Positive Psychology?," Review of General Psychology 9, no. 2 (2005), pp. 103-10; and M. E. P. Seligman et al., "Positive Psychology Progress: Empirical Validation of Interventions," American Psychologist 60, no. 5 (2005), pp. 410-21.

15. C. P. Alderfer, Existence, Relatedness, and Growth (New York: Free Press, 1972).

16. J. Rauschenberger, N. Schmitt, and J. E. Hunter, "A Test of the Need Hierarchy Concept by a Markov Model of Change in Need Strength," Administrative Science Quarterly 25, no. 4 (December 1980), pp. 654-70; and J. P. Wanous and A. A. Zwany, "A Cross-Sectional Test of Need Hierarchy Theory," Organizational Behavior and Human Performance 18 (1977), pp. 78-97.

17. B. A. Agle and C. B. Caldwell, "Understanding Research on Values in Business," Business and Society 38 (September 1999), pp. 326-87; B. Verplanken and R. W. Holland, "Motivated Decision Making: Effects of Activation and Self-Centrality of Values on Choices and Behavior," Journal of Personality and Social Psychology 82, no. 3 (2002), pp. 434-47; and S. Hitlin and J. A. Pilavin, "Values: Reviving a Dormant Concept," Annual Review of Sociology 30 (2004), pp. 359-93.

18. D. C. McClelland, The Achieving Society (New York: Van Nostrand Reinhold, 1961); D. C. McClelland and D. H. Burnham, "Power Is the Great Motivator," Harvard Business Review 73 (January-February 1995), pp. 126-39; D. Vredenburgh and Y. Brender, "The Hierarchical Abuse of Power in Work Organizations," Journal of Business Ethics 17 (September 1998), pp. 1337-47; and S. Shane, E. A. Locke, and C. J. Collins, "Entrepreneurial Motivation," Human Resource Management Review 13, no. 2 (2003), pp. 257-79.

19. D. Miron and D. C. McClelland, "The Impact of Achievement Motivation Training on Small Business," California Management Review 21 (1979), pp. 13-28.

20. P. R. Lawrence and N. Nohria, Driven: How Human Nature Shapes Our Choices (San Francisco: Jossey-Bass, 2002).

21. L. Gaertner et al., "The 'I,' The 'We,' And The 'When': A Meta-Analysis of Motivational Primacy in Self-Definition," Journal of Personality and Social Psychology 83, no. 3 (2002), pp. 574-91; and M. R. Leary, "Motivational and Emotional Aspects of the Self," Annual Review of Psychology 58, no. 1 (2007), 317-44.

22. Baumeister and Leary, "The Need to Belong."

23. J. Litman, "Curiosity and the Pleasures of Learning: Wanting and Liking New Information," Cognition and Emotion 19, no. 6 (2005), pp. 793-14; and T. G. Reio Jr et al., "The Measurement and Conceptualization of Curiosity," Journal of Genetic Psychology 167, no. 2 (2006), pp. 117-35.

24. A. R. Damasio, Descartes' Error: Emotion, Reason, and the Human Brain (New York: Putnam Sons, 1994); J. E. LeDoux, "Emotion Circuits in the Brain," Annual Review of Neuroscience 23 (2000), pp. 155-84; and P. Winkielman and K. C. Berridge, "Unconscious Emotion," Current Directions in Psychological Science 13, no. 3 (2004), pp. 120-23.

25. Lawrence and Nohria, Driven: How Human Nature Shapes Our Choices, pp. 145-47.

26. Lawrence and Nohria, Driven: How Human Nature Shapes Our Choices, Chap. 11.

27. P. Dvorak, "Out of Tune," The Wall Street Journal, June 29, 2005, p. A1.

28. Expectancy theory of motivation in work settings originated in V. H. Vroom, Work and Motivation (New York: Wiley, 1964). The version of expectancy theory presented here was developed by Edward Lawler. Lawler's model provides a clearer presentation of the model's three components. P-to-O expectancy is similar to "instrumentality" in Vroom's original expectancy theory model. The difference is that instrumentality is a correlation whereas P-to-O expectancy is a probability. See J. P. Campbell et al., Managerial Behavior, Performance, and Effectiveness (New York: McGraw-Hill, 1970); E. E. Lawler III, Motivation in Work Organizations (Monterey, CA: Brooks-Cole, 1973); and D. A. Nadler and E. E. Lawler, "Motivation: A Diagnostic Approach," in Perspectives on Behavior in Organizations, ed. J. R. Hackman, E. E. Lawler III, and L. W. Porter, second ed. (New York: McGraw-Hill, 1983), pp. 67-78.

29. M. Zeelenberg et al., "Emotional Reactions to the Outcomes of Decisions: The Role of Counterfactual Thought in the Experience of Regret and Disappointment," Organizational Behavior and Human Decision Processes 75, no. 2 (1998), pp. 117-41; B. A. Mellers, "Choice and the Relative Pleasure of Consequences," Psychological Bulletin 126, no. 6 (November 2000), pp. 910-24; and R. P. Bagozzi, U. M. Dholakia, and S. Basuroy, "How Effortful Decisions Get Enacted: The Motivating Role of Decision Processes, Desires, and Anticipated Emotions," Journal of Behavioral Decision Making 16, no. 4 (October 2003), pp. 273-95.

30. Nadler and Lawler, "Motivation: A Diagnostic Approach."

31. T. Matsui and I. Terai, "A Cross-Cultural Study of the Validity of the Expectancy Theory of Motivation," Journal of Applied Psychology 60 (1979), pp. 263-65; and D. H. B. Welsh, F. Luthans, and S. M. Sommer, "Managing Russian Factory Workers: The Impact of U.S.-Based Behavioral and Participative Techniques," Academy of Management Journal 36 (1993), pp. 58-79.

32. This limitation was recently acknowledged by Victor Vroom, who had introduced expectancy theory in his 1964 book. See G. P. Latham, Work Motivation: History, Theory, Research, and Practice (Thousand Oaks, CA: Sage, 2007), pp. 47-48.

33. G. P. Latham, "Goal Setting: A Five-Step Approach to Behavior Change," Organizational Dynamics 32, no. 3 (2003), pp. 309-18; and E. A. Locke and G. P. Latham, A Theory of Goal Setting and Task Performance (Englewood Cliffs, N.J: Prentice Hall, 1990). Some practitioners rely on the acronym "SMART" goals, referring to goals that are specific, measurable, acceptable, relevant, and timely. However, this list overlaps key elements (e.g., specific goals are measurable and timely) and overlooks the key elements of challenging and feedback-related.

34. A. Li and A. B. Butler, "The Effects of Participation in Goal Setting and Goal Rationales on Goal Commitment: An Exploration of Justice Mediators," Journal of Business and Psychology 19, no. 1 (Fall 2004), pp. 37-51.

35. Locke and Latham, A Theory of Goal Setting and Task Performance, Chap. 6 and 7; and J. Wegge, "Participation in Group Goal Setting: Some Novel Findings and a Comprehensive Model as a New Ending to an Old Story," Applied Psychology: An International Review 49 (2000), pp. 498-516.

36. M. London, E. M. Mone, and J. C. Scott, "Performance Management and Assessment: Methods for Improved Rater Accuracy and Employee Goal Setting," Human Resource Management 43, no. 4 (Winter 2004), pp. 319-36; and G. P. Latham and C. C. Pinder, "Work Motivation Theory and Research at the Dawn of the Twenty-First Century," Annual Review of Psychology 56 (2005), pp. 485-516.

37. E. White, "For Relevance, Firms Revamp Worker Reviews," The Wall Street Journal, July 17, 2006, p. B1.

38. S. P. Brown, S. Ganesan, and G. Challagalla, "Self-Efficacy as a Moderator of Information-Seeking Effectiveness," Journal of Applied Psychology 86, no. 5 (2001), pp. 1043-51; P. A. Heslin and G. P. Latham, "The Effect of Upward Feedback on Managerial Behaviour," Applied Psychology: An International Review 53, no. 1 (2004), pp. 23-37; D. Van-Dijk and A. N. Kluger, "Feedback Sign Effect on Motivation: Is It Moderated by Regulatory Focus?," Applied Psychology: An International Review 53, no. 1 (2004), pp. 113-35; and J. E. Bono and A. E. Colbert, "Understanding Responses to Multi-Source Feedback: The Role of Core Self-Evaluations," Personnel Psychology 58, no. 1 (Spring 2005), pp. 171-03.

39. A. Dragoon, "Sleepless in Manhattan," CIO, April 2005, p. 1; and S. E. Ante, "Giving the Boss the Big Picture," Business-Week, February 13, 2006, p. 48.

40. J. B. Miner, "The Rated Importance, Scientific Validity, and Practical Usefulness of Organizational Behavior Theories: A Quantitative Review," Academy of Management Learning and Education 2, no. 3 (2003), pp. 250-68. Also see C. C. Pinder, Work Motivation in Organizational Behavior (Upper Saddle River, NJ: Prentice-Hall, 1997), p. 384.

41. P. M. Wright, "Goal Setting and Monetary Incentives: Motivational Tools That Can Work Too Well," Compensation and Benefits Review 26 (May-June 1994), pp. 41-49; and E. A. Locke and G. P. Latham, "Building a Practically Useful Theory of Goal Setting and Task Motivation: A 35-Year Odyssey," American Psychologist 57, no. 9 (2002), pp. 705-17.

42. Latham, Work Motivation, p. 188.

43. J. Greenberg and E. A. Lind, "The Pursuit of Organizational Justice: From Conceptualization to Implication to Application," in Industrial and Organizational Psychology: Linking Theory with Practice, ed. C. L. Cooper and E. A. Locke (London: Blackwell, 2000), pp. 72-108; R. Cropanzano and M. Schminke, "Using Social Justice to Build Effective Work Groups," in Groups at Work: Theory and Research, ed. M. E. Turner (Mahwah, N.J.: Lawrence Erlbaum Associates, 2001), pp. 143-71; and D. T. Miller, "Disrespect and the Experience of Injustice," Annual Review of Psychology 52 (2001), pp. 527-53.

44. J. S. Adams, "Toward an Understanding of Inequity," Journal of Abnormal and Social Psychology 67 (1963), pp. 422-36; R. T. Mowday, "Equity Theory Predictions of Behavior in Organizations," in Motivation and Work Behavior, ed. L. W. Porter and R. M. Steers, 5th ed. (New York: McGraw-Hill, 1991),

pp. 111-31; R. G. Cropanzano and J. Greenberg, "Progress in Organizational Justice: Tunneling through the Maze," in International Review of Industrial and Organizational Psychology, ed. C. L. Cooper and I. T. Robertson (New York: Wiley, 1997), pp. 317-72; and L. A. Powell, "Justice Judgments as Complex Psychocultural Constructions: An Equity-Based Heuristic for Mapping Two- and Three-Dimensional Fairness Representations in Perceptual Space," Journal of Cross-Cultural Psychology 36, no. 1 (January 2005), pp. 48-73.

45. C. T. Kulik and M. L. Ambrose, "Personal and Situational Determinants of Referent Choice," Academy of Management Review 17 (1992), pp. 212-37; and G. Blau, "Testing the Effect of Level and Importance of Pay Referents on Pay Level Satisfaction," Human Relations 47 (1994), pp. 1251-68.

46. T. P. Summers and A. S. DeNisi, "In Search of Adams' Other: Reexamination of Referents Used in the Evaluation of Pay," Human Relations 43 (1990), pp. 497-511.

47. Y. Cohen-Charash and P. E. Spector, "The Role of Justice in Organizations: A Meta-Analysis," Organizational Behavior and Human Decision Processes 86 (November 2001), pp. 278-321.

48. M. Ezzamel and R. Watson, "Pay Comparability across and within UK Boards: An Empirical Analysis of the Cash Pay Awards to CEOs and Other Board Members," Journal of Management Studies 39, no. 2 (March 2002), pp. 207-32; and J. Fizel, A. C. Krautman, and L. Hadley, "Equity and Arbitration in Major League Baseball," Managerial and Decision Economics 23, no. 7 (October-November 2002), pp. 427-35.

49. Greenberg and Lind, "The Pursuit of Organizational Justice: From Conceptualization to Implication to Application." For recent studies of voice and injustice, see K. Roberts and K. S. Markel, "Claiming in the Name of Fairness: Organizational Justice and the Decision to File for Workplace Injury Compensation," Journal of Occupational Health Psychology 6 (October 2001), pp. 332-47; and J. B. Olson-Buchanan and W. R. Boswell, "The Role of Employee Loyalty and Formality in Voicing Discontent," Journal of Applied Psychology 87, no. 6 (2002), pp. 1167-74.

50. J. R. Edwards, J. A. Scully, and M. D. Brtek, "The Nature and Outcomes of Work: A Replication and Extension of Interdisciplinary Work-Design Research," Journal of Applied Psychology 85, no. 6 (2000), pp. 860-68; F. P. Morgeson and M. A. Campion, "Minimizing Tradeoffs When Redesigning Work: Evidence from a Longitudinal Quasi-Experiment," Personnel Psychology 55, no. 3 (Autumn 2002), pp. 589-612.

51. P. Siekman, "This Is Not a BMW Plant," Fortune, April 18, 2005, p. 208.

52. M. Valverde, G. Ryan, and M. Gorjup, "An Examination of the Quality of Jobs in the Call Center Industry," International Advances in Economic Research 13, no. 2 (2007), pp. 146-56.

53. H. Fayol, General and Industrial Management, trans. C. Storrs (London: Pitman, 1949); E. E. Lawler III, Motivation in Work Organizations (Monterey, CA: Brooks/Cole, 1973), Chap. 7; and M. A. Campion, "Ability Requirement Implications of Job Design: An Interdisciplinary Perspective," Personnel Psychology 42 (1989), pp. 1-24.

54. F. W. Taylor, The Principles of Scientific Management (New York: Harper & Row, 1911); and R. Kanigel, The One Best Way: Frederick Winslow Taylor and the Enigma of Efficiency (New York: Viking, 1997).

55. C. R. Walker and R. H. Guest, The Man on the Assembly Line (Cambridge, MA: Harvard University Press, 1952); W. F. Dowling, "Job Redesign on the Assembly Line: Farewell to Blue-Collar Blues?" Organizational Dynamics (Autumn 1973), pp. 51-67; and E. E. Lawler III, High-Involvement Management (San Francisco: Jossey-Bass, 1986).

56. J. R. Hackman and G. Oldham, Work Redesign (Reading, MA: Addison-Wesley, 1980).

57. J. E. Champoux, "A Multivariate Test of the Job Characteristics Theory of Work Motivation," Journal of Organizational Behavior 12, no. 5 (September 1991), pp. 431-46; and R. B. Tiegs, L. E. Tetrick, and Y. Fried, "Growth Need Strength and Context Satisfactions as Moderators of the Relations of the Job Characteristics Model," Journal of Management 18, no. 3 (September 1992), pp. 575-93.

58. M. A. Campion and C. L. McClelland, "Follow-up and Extension of the Interdisciplinary Costs and Benefits of Enlarged Jobs," Journal of Applied Psychology 78 (1993), pp. 339-51; and N. G. Dodd and D. C. Ganster, "The Interactive Effects of Variety, Autonomy, and Feedback on Attitudes and Performance," Journal of Organizational Behavior 17 (1996), pp. 329-47.

59. J. R. Hackman et al., "A New Strategy for Job Enrichment," California Management Review 17, no. 4 (1975), pp. 57-71; and R. W. Griffin, Task Design: An Integrative Approach (Glenview, IL: Scott Foresman, 1982).

60. P. E. Spector and S. M. Jex, "Relations of Job Characteristics from Multiple Data Sources with Employee Affect, Absence, Turnover Intentions, and Health," Journal of Applied Psychology 76 (1991), pp. 46-53; P. Osterman, "How Common Is Workplace Transformation and Who Adopts It?" Industrial and Labor Relations Review 47 (1994), pp. 173-88; and R. Saavedra and S. K. Kwun, "Affective States in Job Characteristics Theory," Journal of Organizational Behavior 21 (2000), pp. 131-46.

61. Hackman and Oldham, Work Redesign, pp. 137-38.

62. K. Tyler, "The Boss Makes the Weather," HRMagazine, May 2004, pp. 93-96.

63. The varied history of the empowerment concept is wonderfully detailed in J. M. Bartunek and G. M. Spreitzer, "The Interdisciplinary Career of a Popular Construct Used in Management: Empowerment in the Late 20th Century," Journal of Management Inquiry 15, no. 3 (Sept. 2006), pp. 255-73.

64. This definition is based mostly on G. M. Spreitzer and R. E. Quinn, A Company of Leaders: Five Disciplines for Unleashing the Power in Your Workforce (San Francisco: Jossey-Bass, 2001). However, most elements of this definition appear in other discussions of empowerment. See, for example, R. Forrester, "Empowerment: Rejuvenating a Potent Idea," Academy of Management Executive 14 (August 2000), pp. 67-80; W. A. Randolph, "Re-Thinking Empowerment: Why Is It So Hard to Achieve? " Organizational Dynamics 29 (November 2000),

pp. 94-107; and S. T. Menon, "Employee Empowerment: An Integrative Psychological Approach," *Applied Psychology: An International Review* 50 (2001), pp. 153–80.

65. The positive relationship between these structural empowerment conditions and psychological empowerment is reported in H. K. S. Laschinger et al., "A Longitudinal Analysis of the Impact of Workplace Empowerment on Work Satisfaction," *Journal of Organizational Behavior* 25, no. 4 (June 2004), pp. 527–45.

66. C. S. Koberg et al., "Antecedents and Outcomes of Empower-ment," *Group and Organization Management* 24 (1999), pp. 71–91; and Y. Melhem, "The Antecedents of Customer-Contact Employees' Empowerment," *Employee Relations* 26, no. 1/2 (2004), pp. 72–93.

67. B. J. Niehoff et al., "The Influence of Empowerment and Job Enrichment on Employee Loyalty in a Downsizing Environ-ment," *Group and Organization Management* 26 (March 2001), pp. 93–113; J. Yoon, "The Role of Structure and Motivation for Workplace Empowerment: The Case of Korean Employees," *Social Psychology Quarterly* 64 (June 2001), pp. 195–206; and T. D. Wall, J. L. Cordery, and C. W. Clegg, "Empowerment, Performance, and Operational Uncertainty: A Theoretical Integration," *Applied Psychology: An International Review* 51 (2002), pp. 146–69.

68. G. M. Spreitzer, "Social Structural Characteristics of Psycho-logical Empowerment," *Academy of Management Journal* 39 (April 1996), pp. 483–504.

69. D. Furlonger, "Best Company to Work For," *Financial Mail (South Africa)*, September 30, 2005, p. 20; A. Hogg, "John Gomersall: CEO, PPC," (South Africa, October 26, 2005), http://www.moneyweb.co.za/specials/corp_gov/509689.htm, (accessed January 4, 2006); and Pretoria Portland Cement, "PPC Wins Best Company to Work for 2005," Meropa Com-munications news release, (Sandton, South Africa, September 29, 2005). Information was also collected from the 2003, 2004, and 2005 annual reports of Pretoria Portland Cement.

70. J.C. Chebat and P. Kollias, "The Impact of Empowerment on Customer Contact Employees' Role in Service Organizations," *Journal of Service Research* 3 (August 2000), pp. 66–81; and H. K. S. Laschinger, J. Finegan, and J. Shamian, "The Impact of Workplace Empowerment, Organizational Trust on Staff Nurses' Work Satisfaction and Organizational Commitment," *Health Care Management Review* 26 (Summer 2001), pp. 7–23.

chapter 6

1. P. Withers, "Few Rules Rule," *B.C. Business,* January 2002, p. 24; G. Huston, I. Wilkinson, and D. Kellogg, "Dare to Be Great," *B.C. Business,* May 2004, pp. 28–29; P. Withers and L. Kloet, "The Best Companies to Work for in B.C.," *B.C. Busi-ness,* December 2004, pp. 37–53; M. Andrews, "How to Make Robot Bees, and Other Sound Secrets," *National Post,* March 5, 2005, p. TO32; and P. Wilson, "Radical Entertainment to Hire Staff, Expand Studio," *Vancouver Sun,* May 6, 2005, p. C3.

2. F. A. Shull Jr., A. L. Delbecq, and L. L. Cummings, *Organiza-tional Decision Making* (New York: McGraw-Hill, 1970), p. 31.

3. R. E. Nisbett, *The Geography of Thought: How Asians and Westerners Think Differently—and Why* (New York: Free Press, 2003); D. Baltzly, "Stoicism," (Stanford Encyclopedia of Philosophy, 2004), http://plato.stanford.edu/entries/stoicism/, (accessed March 8, 2005); R. Hanna, "Kant's Theory of Judgment," (Stanford Encyclopedia of Philosophy, 2004), http://plato.stanford.edu/entries/kant-judgment/, (accessed March 12, 2005).

4. This model is adapted from several sources, including H. A. Simon, *The New Science of Management Decision* (New York: Harper & Row, 1960); H. Mintzberg, D. Raisinghani, and A. Théorét, "The Structure of 'Unstructured' Decision Processes," *Administrative Science Quarterly* 21 (1976), pp. 246–75; and W. C. Wedley and R. H. G. Field, "A Predecision Support System," *Academy of Management Review* 9 (1984), pp. 696–703.

5. P. F. Drucker, *The Practice of Management* (New York: Harper & Brothers, 1954), pp. 353–57; and B. M. Bass, *Organizational Decision Making* (Homewood, IL: Irwin, 1983), Chap. 3.

6. L. R. Beach and T. R. Mitchell, "A Contingency Model for the Selection of Decision Strategies," *Academy of Management Review* 3 (1978), pp. 439–49; I. L. Janis, *Crucial Decisions* (New York: The Free Press, 1989), pp. 35–37; and W. Zhongtuo, "Meta-Decision Making: Concepts and Paradigm," *Systematic Practice and Action Research* 13, no. 1 (February 2000), pp. 111–15.

7. J. G. March and H. A. Simon, *Organizations* (New York: John Wiley & Sons, 1958).

8. N. Schwarz, "Social Judgment and Attitudes: Warmer, More Social, and Less Conscious," *European Journal of Social Psychology* 30 (2000), pp. 149–76; N. M. Ashkanasy and C. E. J. Hartel, "Managing Emotions in Decision-Making," in *Managing Emotions in the Workplace,* ed. N. M. Ashkanasy, W. J. Zerbe, and C. E. J. Hartel (Armonk, NY: M. E. Sharpe, 2002); and S. Maitlis and H. Ozcelik, "Toxic Decision Processes: A Study of Emotion and Organizational Decision Making," *Organization Science* 15, no. 4 (July–August 2004), pp. 375–93.

9. A. Howard, "Opinion," *Computing,* July 8, 1999, p. 18.

10. A. R. Damasio, *Descartes' Error: Emotion, Reason, and the Human Brain* (New York: Putnam Sons, 1994); P. Winkielman and K. C. Berridge, "Unconscious Emotion," *Current Direc-tions in Psychological Science* 13, no. 3 (2004), pp. 120–23; A. Bechara and A. R. Damasio, "The Somatic Marker Hypoth-esis: A Neural Theory of Economic Decision," *Games and Economic Behavior* 52, no. 2 (2005), pp. 336–72.

11. T. K. Das and B. S. Teng, "Cognitive Biases and Strategic Decision Processes: An Integrative Perspective," *Journal Of Management Studies* 36, no. 6 (November 1999), pp. 757–78; P. Bijttebier, H. Vertommen, and G. V. Steene, "Assessment of Cognitive Coping Styles: A Closer Look at Situation-Response Inventories," *Clinical Psychology Review* 21, no. 1 (2001), pp. 85–104; and P. C. Nutt, "Expanding the Search for Alternatives During Strategic Decision-Making," *Academy of Management Executive* 18, no. 4 (November 2004), pp. 13–28.

12. J. Brandtstadter, A. Voss, and K. Rothermund, "Perception of Danger Signals: The Role of Control," *Experimental Psychology* 51, no. 1 (2004), pp. 24–32; and M. Hock and H. W. Krohne, "Coping with Threat and Memory for Ambiguous Information: Testing the Repressive Discontinuity Hypothesis," *Emotion* 4, no. 1 (2004), pp. 65–86.

13. P. C. Nutt, *Why Decisions Fail* (San Francisco, CA: Berrett-Koehler, 2002); and S. Finkelstein, *Why Smart Executives Fail* (New York: Viking, 2003).

14. E. Witte, "Field Research on Complex Decision-Making Processes—the Phase Theorum," *International Studies of Management and Organization* (1972), pp. 156–82; and J. A. Bargh and T. L. Chartrand, "The Unbearable Automaticity of Being," *American Psychologist* 54, no. 7 (July 1999), pp. 462–79.

15. S. Jefferson, "NASA Let Arrogance on Board," *Palm Beach Post,* August 30, 2003; R. J. Smith, "NASA Culture, Columbia Probers Still Miles Apart," *Washington Post,* August 22, 2003, p. A3; Columbia Accident Investigation Board, *Report, Volume 1,* (Washington, DC: Government Printing Office, August 2003); "NASA Managers Differed Over Shuttle Strike," *Reuters,* July 22, 2003; and C. Gibson, "Columbia: The Final Mission," *NineMSN (Australia),* July 13, 2003.

16. R. Rothenberg, "Ram Charan: The Thought Leader Interview," *strategy + business* (Fall 2004).

17. H. A. Simon, *Administrative Behavior,* 2nd ed. (New York: The Free Press, 1957); and H. A. Simon, "Rational Decision Making in Business Organizations," *American Economic Review* 69, no. 4 (September 1979), pp. 493–513.

18. Simon, *Administrative Behavior,* pp. 25, 80–84.

19. P. O. Soelberg, "Unprogrammed Decision Making," *Industrial Management Review* 8 (1967), pp. 19–29; and J. E. Russo, V. H. Medvec, and M. G. Meloy, "The Distortion of Information During Decisions," *Organizational Behavior & Human Decision Processes* 66 (1996), pp. 102–10.

20. A. L. Brownstein, "Biased Predecision Processing," *Psychological Bulletin* 129, no. 4 (2003), pp. 545–68.

21. H. A. Simon, "Rational Choice and the Structure of Environments," *Psychological Review* 63 (1956), pp. 129–38; and H. Schwartz, "Herbert Simon and Behavioral Economics," *Journal of Socio-Economics* 31 (2002), pp. 181–89.

22. P. C. Nutt, "Search During Decision Making," *European Journal of Operational Research* 160 (2005), pp. 851–76.

23. J. P. Forgas and J. M. George, "Affective Influences on Judgments and Behavior in Organizations: An Information Processing Perspective," *Organizational Behavior and Human Decision Processes* 86 (September 2001), pp. 3–34; G. Loewenstein and J. S. Lerner, "The Role of Affect in Decision Making," in *Handbook of Affective Sciences,* ed. R. J. Davidson, K. R. Scherer, and H. H. Goldsmith (New York: Oxford University Press, 2003), pp. 619–42; J. S. Lerner, D. A. Small, and G. Loewenstein, "Heart Strings and Purse Strings: Carryover Effects of Emotions on Economic Decisions," *Psychological Science* 15, no. 5 (2004), pp. 337–41; and J. P. Forgas, "Affective Influences on Interpersonal Behavior: Towards Understanding the Role of Affect in Everyday Interactions," in *Affect in Social Thinking and Behavior,* ed. J. P. Forgas (Philadelphia, PA: Psychology Press, 2006).

24. M. T. Pham, "The Logic of Feeling," *Journal of Consumer Psychology* 14 (September 2004), pp. 360–69; and N. Schwarz, "Metacognitive Experiences in Consumer Judgment and Decision Making," *Journal of Consumer Psychology* 14 (September 2004), pp. 332–49.

25. L. Sjöberg, "Intuitive vs. Analytical Decision Making: Which Is Preferred?," *Scandinavian Journal of Management* 19 (2003), pp. 17–29.

26. W. H. Agor, "The Logic of Intuition," *Organizational Dynamics* (Winter 1986), pp. 5–18; H. A. Simon, "Making Management Decisions: The Role of Intuition and Emotion," *Academy of Management Executive* (February 1987), pp. 57–64; and O. Behling and N. L. Eckel, "Making Sense out of Intuition," *Academy of Management Executive* 5 (February 1991), pp. 46–54.

27. M. D. Lieberman, "Intuition: A Social Cognitive Neuroscience Approach," *Psychological Bulletin* 126 (2000), pp. 109–37; G. Klein, *Intuition at Work* (New York: Currency/Doubleday, 2003); and E. Dane and M. G. Pratt, "Intuition: It's Boundaries and Role in Organizational Decision-Making" in *Academy of Management Best Papers Proceedings,* New Orleans, 2004, pp. A1–A6.

28. Y. Ganzach, A. H. Kluger, and N. Klayman, "Making Decisions from an Interview: Expert Measurement and Mechanical Combination," *Personnel Psychology* 53 (Spring 2000), pp. 1–20; and A. M. Hayashi, "When to Trust Your Gut," *Harvard Business Review* 79 (February 2001), pp. 59–65. Evidence of high failure rates from quick decisions is reported in Nutt, *Why Decisions Fail;* and Nutt, "Search During Decision Making."

29. P. Goodwin and G. Wright, "Enhancing Strategy Evaluation in Scenario Planning: A Role for Decision Analysis," *Journal of Management Studies* 38 (January 2001), pp. 1–16; and R. Bradfield et al., "The Origins and Evolution of Scenario Techniques in Long Range Business Planning," *Futures* 37, no. 8 (2005), pp. 795–812.

30. J. Pfeffer and R. I. Sutton, "Knowing 'What' to Do Is Not Enough: Turning Knowledge into Action," *California Management Review* 42, no. 1 (Fall 1999), pp. 83–108; and R. Charan, C. Burke, and L. Bossidy, *Execution: The Discipline of Getting Things Done* (New York: Crown Business, 2002). The survey of managerial competencies is reported in D. Nilsen, B. Kowske, and A. Kshanika, "Managing Globally," *HRMagazine,* August 2005, pp. 111–15.

31. G. Whyte, "Escalating Commitment to a Course of Action: A Reinterpretation," *Academy of Management Review* 11 (1986), pp. 311–21; and J. Brockner, "The Escalation of Commitment to a Failing Course of Action: Toward Theoretical Progress," *Academy of Management Review* 17, no. 1 (January 1992), pp. 39–61.

32. D. Collins, "Senior Officials Tried to Stop Spending," *Irish Examiner,* October 5, 2005; M. Sheehan, "Throwing Good Money after Bad," *Sunday Independent (Dublin),* October 9, 2005; "Computer System Was Budgeted at Eur9m . . . Its Cost

Eur170m . . . Now Health Chiefs Want a New One," *Irish Mirror,* July 7, 2007, p. 16; and E. Kennedy, "Health Boss Refuses to Ditch Ill-Fated PPARS System," *Irish Independent,* February 5, 2007.

33. F. D. Schoorman and P. J. Holahan, "Psychological Antecedents of Escalation Behavior: Effects of Choice, Responsibility, and Decision Consequences," *Journal of Applied Psychology* 81 (1996), pp. 786–93.

34. G. Whyte, "Escalating Commitment in Individual and Group Decision Making: A Prospect Theory Approach," *Organizational Behavior and Human Decision Processes* 54 (1993), pp. 430–55; and D. J. Sharp and S. B. Salter, "Project Escalation and Sunk Costs: A Test of the International Generalizability of Agency and Prospect Theories," *Journal of International Business Studies* 28, no. 1 (1997), pp. 101–21.

35. J. D. Bragger et al., "When Success Breeds Failure: History, Hysteresis, and Delayed Exit Decisions," *Journal of Applied Psychology* 88, no. 1 (2003), pp. 6–14. A second logical reason for escalation, called the *martingale strategy,* is described in J. A. Aloysius, "Rational Escalation of Costs by Playing a Sequence of Unfavorable Gambles: The Martingale," *Journal of Economic Behavior & Organization* 51 (2003), pp. 111–29.

36. I. Simonson and B. M. Staw, "De-Escalation Strategies: A Comparison of Techniques for Reducing Commitment to Losing Courses of Action," *Journal of Applied Psychology* 77 (1992), pp. 419–26; W. Boulding, R. Morgan, and R. Staelin, "Pulling the Plug to Stop the New Product Drain," *Journal of Marketing Research,* no. 34 (1997), pp. 164–76; B. M. Staw, K. W. Koput, and S. G. Barsade, "Escalation at the Credit Window: A Longitudinal Study of Bank Executives' Recognition and Write-Off of Problem Loans," *Journal of Applied Psychology,* no. 82 (1997), pp. 130–42; and M. Keil and D. Robey, "Turning around Troubled Software Projects: An Exploratory Study of the Deescalation of Commitment to Failing Courses of Action," *Journal of Management Information Systems* 15 (Spring 1999), pp. 63–87.

37. M. Fenton-O'Creevy, "Employee Involvement and the Middle Manager: Saboteur or Scapegoat?" *Human Resource Management Journal,* no. 11 (2001), pp. 24–40. Also see V. H. Vroom and A. G. Jago, *The New Leadership: Managing Participation in Organizations* (Englewood Cliffs, NJ: Prentice Hill, 1988).

38. K. T. Dirks, L. L. Cummings, and J. L. Pierce, "Psychological Ownership in Organizations: Conditions under Which Individuals Promote and Resist Change," *Research in Organizational Change and Development,* no. 9 (1996), pp. 1–23; A. Kleingeld, H. Van Tuijl, and J. A. Algera, "Participation in the Design of Performance Management Systems: A Quasi-Experimental Field Study," *Journal of Organizational Behavior* 25, no. 7 (2004), pp. 831–51; A. G. Robinson and D. M. Schroeder, *Ideas Are Free* (San Francisco: Berrett-Koehler, 2004); and A. Cox, S. Zagelmeyer, and M. Marchington, "Embedding Employee Involvement and Participation at Work," *Human Resource Management Journal* 16, no. 3 (2006), pp. 250–67.

39. J. Giles, "Wisdom of the Crowd," *Nature* 438, no. 7066 (November 17, 2005), p. 281; and J. Surowiecki, *The Wisdom of Crowds* (New York: Anchor, 2005).

40. S. W. Crispin, "Workers' Paradise," *Far Eastern Economic Review,* April 17, 2003, pp. 40–41; and "Thai Carbon Black: Worker-Driven Focus Key to Firm's Success," *The Nation (Thailand),* June 3, 2004.

41. G. P. Latham, D. C. Winters, and E. A. Locke, "Cognitive and Motivational Effects of Participation: A Mediator Study," *Journal of Organizational Behavior,* no. 15 (1994), pp. 49–63; and J. A. Wagner III et al., "Cognitive and Motivational Frameworks in U.S. Research on Participation: A Meta-Analysis of Primary Effects," *Journal of Organizational Behavior,* no. 18 (1997), pp. 49–65.

42. J. Zhou and C. E. Shalley, "Research on Employee Creativity: A Critical Review and Directions for Future Research," *Research in Personnel and Human Resources Management* 22 (2003), pp. 165–217; and M. A. Runco, "Creativity," *Annual Review of Psychology* 55 (2004), pp. 657–87.

43. B. Kabanoff and J. R. Rossiter, "Recent Developments in Applied Creativity," *International Review of Industrial and Organizational Psychology* no. 9 (1994), pp. 283–324.

44. R. S. Nickerson, "Enhancing Creativity," in *Handbook of Creativity,* ed. R. J. Sternberg (New York: Cambridge University Press, 1999), pp. 392–430.

45. For a thorough discussion of insight, see R. J. Sternberg and J. E. Davidson, *The Nature of Insight* (Cambridge, MA: MIT Press, 1995).

46. R. J. Sternberg and L. A. O'Hara, "Creativity and Intelligence," in *Handbook of Creativity,* ed. R. J. Sternberg (New York: Cambridge University Press, 1999), pp. 251–72; and S. Taggar, "Individual Creativity and Group Ability to Utilize Individual Creative Resources: A Multilevel Model," *Academy of Management Journal* 45 (April 2002), pp. 315–30.

47. G. J. Feist, "The Influence of Personality on Artistic and Scientific Creativity," in *Handbook of Creativity,* ed. R. J. Sternberg (New York: Cambridge University Press, 1999), pp. 273–96; and R. I. Sutton, *Weird Ideas That Work* (New York: Free Press, 2002), pp. 8–9, Chap. 10.

48. R. W. Weisberg, "Creativity and Knowledge: A Challenge to Theories," in *Handbook of Creativity,* ed. R. J. Sternberg (New York: Cambridge University Press, 1999), pp. 226–50.

49. Sutton, *Weird Ideas That Work,* pp. 121, 153–54; and C. Andriopoulos, "Six Paradoxes in Managing Creativity: An Embracing Act," *Long Range Planning* 36 (2003), pp. 375–88.

50. D. K. Simonton, "Creativity: Cognitive, Personal, Developmental, and Social Aspects," *American Psychologist* 55 (January 2000), pp. 151–58.

51. M. D. Mumford, "Managing Creative People: Strategies and Tactics for Innovation," *Human Resource Management Review* 10 (Autumn 2000), pp. 313–51; T. M. Amabile et al., "Leader Behaviors and the Work Environment for Creativity: Perceived Leader Support," The *Leadership Quarterly* 15, no. 1 (2004), pp. 5–32; and C. E. Shalley, J. Zhou, and G. R. Oldham, "The Effects of Personal and Contextual Characteristics on Creativity: Where Should We Go from Here?" *Journal of Management* 30, no. 6 (2004), pp. 933–58.

52. R. Westwood and D. R. Low, "The Multicultural Muse: Culture, Creativity and Innovation," *International Journal of Cross Cultural Management* 3, no. 2 (2003), pp. 235–59.

53. T. M. Amabile, "Motivating Creativity in Organizations: On Doing What You Love and Loving What You Do," *California Management Review* 40 (Fall 1997), pp. 39–58; and A. Cummings and G. R. Oldham, "Enhancing Creativity: Managing Work Contexts for the High Potential Employee," *California Management Review,* no. 40 (Fall 1997), pp. 22–38.

54. T. M. Amabile, "Changes in the Work Environment for Creativity During Downsizing," *Academy of Management Journal* 42 (December 1999), pp. 630–40; J. M. Howell and K. Boies, "Champions of Technological Innovation: The Influence of Contextual Knowledge, Role Orientation, Idea Generation, and Idea Promotion on Champion Emergence," *The Leadership Quarterly* 15, no. 1 (2004), pp. 123–43; and M. Baer and G. R. Oldham, "The Curvilinear Relation between Experienced Creative Time Pressure and Creativity: Moderating Effects of Openness to Experience and Support for Creativity," *Journal of Applied Psychology* 91, no. 4 (2006), pp. 963–70.

55. A. Hiam, "Obstacles to Creativity—and How You Can Remove Them," *Futurist* 32 (October 1998), pp. 30–34.

56. M. A. West, *Developing Creativity in Organizations* (Leicester, UK: BPS Books, 1997), pp. 33–35.

57. S. Hemsley, "Seeking the Source of Innovation," *Media Week,* August 16, 2005, p. 22; and S. Planting, "When You Need to Get Serious, Get Playful," *Financial Mail (South Africa),* February 4, 2005, p. 14.

58. A. Hargadon and R. I. Sutton, "Building an Innovation Factory," *Harvard Business Review* 78 (May–June 2000), pp. 157–66; and T. Kelley, *The Art of Innovation* (New York: Currency Doubleday, 2001), pp. 158–62.

59. K. S. Brown, "The Apple of Jonathan Ive's Eye," *Investor's Business Daily,* September 19, 2003.

chapter 7

1. C. Fishman, "The Anarchist's Cookbook," *Fast Company,* July 2004, p. 70; A. Kimball-Stanley, "Bucking the Trend in Benefits," *Providence Journal (Rhode Island),* May 14, 2006, p. H01; and K. Zimbalist, "Green Giant," Time, April 24, 2006, p. 24.

2. V. L. Parker, "Org Charts Turn around with Teams," *News & Observer (Raleigh, N.C.),* July 21, 2005, p. D1; J. Springer, "Eyes on the Prize," *Supermarket News,* August 1, 2005, p. 12; and D. Hechler, "Teamwork Is Job One at Ford," *Fulton County Daily Report (Atlanta),* May 16, 2006, p. 16.

3. M. E. Shaw, *Group Dynamics,* 3rd ed. (New York: McGraw-Hill, 1981), p. 8; S. A. Mohrman, S. G. Cohen, and A. M. Mohrman Jr., *Designing Team-Based Organizations: New Forms for Knowledge Work* (San Francisco: Jossey-Bass, 1995), pp. 39–40; and E. Sundstrom, "The Challenges of Supporting Work Team Effectiveness," in *Supporting Work Team Effectiveness,* ed. E. Sundstrom and Associates (San Francisco, CA: Jossey-Bass, 1999), pp. 6–9.

4. R. A. Guzzo and M. W. Dickson, "Teams in Organizations: Recent Research on Performance and Effectiveness," *Annual Review of Psychology* 47 (1996), pp. 307–38; D. A. Nadler, "From Ritual to Real Work: The Board as a Team," *Directors and Boards* 22 (Summer 1998), pp. 28–31; and L. R. Offerman and R. K. Spiros, "The Science and Practice of Team Development: Improving the Link," *Academy of Management Journal* 44 (April 2001), pp. 376–92.

5. B. D. Pierce and R. White, "The Evolution of Social Structure: Why Biology Matters," *Academy of Management Review* 24 (October 1999), pp. 843–53; P. R. Lawrence and N. Nohria, *Driven: How Human Nature Shapes Our Choices* (San Francisco: Jossey-Bass, 2002); and J. R. Spoor and J. R. Kelly, "The Evolutionary Significance of Affect in Groups: Communication and Group Bonding," *Group Processes & Intergroup Relations* 7, no. 4 (2004), pp. 398–412.

6. M. A. Hogg et al., "The Social Identity Perspective: Intergroup Relations, Self-Conception, and Small Groups," *Small Group Research* 35, no. 3 (June 2004), pp. 246–76; N. Michinov, E. Michinov, and M. C. Toczek-Capelle, "Social Identity, Group Processes, and Performance in Synchronous Computer-Mediated Communication," *Group Dynamics: Theory, Research, and Practice* 8, no. 1 (2004), pp. 27–39; and M. Van Vugt and C. M. Hart, "Social Identity as Social Glue: The Origins of Group Loyalty," *Journal of Personality and Social Psychology* 86, no. 4 (2004), pp. 585–98.

7. S. Schacter, *The Psychology of Affiliation* (Stanford, CA: Stanford University Press, 1959), pp. 12–19; R. Eisler and D. S. Levine, "Nurture, Nature, and Caring: We Are Not Prisoners of Our Genes," *Brain and Mind* 3 (2002), pp. 9–52; and A. C. DeVries, E. R. Glasper, and C. E. Detillion, "Social Modulation of Stress Responses," *Physiology & Behavior* 79, no. 3 (August 2003), pp. 399–407.

8. M. Moldaschl and W. Weber, "The 'Three Waves' of Industrial Group Work: Historical Reflections on Current Research on Group Work," *Human Relations* 51 (March 1998), pp. 347–88. The survey quotation is found in J. N. Choi, "External Activities and Team Effectiveness: Review and Theoretical Development," *Small Group Research* 33 (April 2002), pp. 181–208. Several popular books in the 1980s encouraged team work, based on the Japanese economic miracle. These books included W. Ouchi, *Theory Z: How American Management Can Meet the Japanese Challenge* (Reading, MA: Addison-Wesley, 1981); and R. T. Pascale and A. G. Athos, *Art of Japanese Management* (New York: Simon and Schuster, 1982).

9. C. R. Emery and L. D. Fredenhall, "The Effect of Teams on Firm Profitability and Customer Satisfaction," *Journal of Service Research* 4 (February 2002), pp. 217–29; and G. S. Van der Vegt and O. Janssen, "Joint Impact of Interdependence and Group Diversity on Innovation," *Journal of Management* 29 (2003), pp. 729–51.

10. R. E. Baumeister and M. R. Leary, "The Need to Belong: Desire for Interpersonal Attachments as a Fundamental Human Motivation," *Psychological Bulletin* 117 (1995), pp. 497–529; S. Chen, H. C. Boucher, and M. P. Tapias, "The Relational Self Revealed: Integrative Conceptualization and Implications for Interpersonal Life," *Psychological Bulletin* 132, no. 2 (2006), pp. 151–79; J. M. Feinberg and J. R. Aiello, "Social Facilitation: A Test of Competing Theories," *Journal of Applied Social Psychology* 36, no. 5 (2006), pp. 1087–1109; A. M. Grant, "Relational Job Design and the Motivation to Make a Prosocial Difiference," *Academy of Management Review* 32, no. 2

(2007), pp. 393–417; and N. L. Kerr et al., "Psychological Mechanisms Underlying the Kohler Motivation Gain," *Personality & Social Psychology Bulletin* 33, no. 6 (2007), pp. 828–41.

11. E. A. Locke et al, "The Importance of the Individual in an Age of Groupism," in *Groups at Work: Theory and Research,* ed. M. E. Turner (Mahwah, NJ: Lawrence Erbaum Associates, 2001), pp. 501–28; N. J. Allen and T. D. Hecht, "The 'Romance of Teams': Toward an Understanding of Its Psychological Underpinnings and Implications," *Journal of Occupational and Organizational Psychology* 77 (2004), pp. 439–61.

12. I. D. Steiner, *Group Process and Productivity* (New York: Academic Press, 1972); and N. L. Kerr and S. R. Tindale, "Group Performance and Decision Making," *Annual Review of Psychology* 55 (2004), pp. 623–55.

13. D. Dunphy and B. Bryant, "Teams: Panaceas or Prescriptions for Improved Performance?" *Human Relations* 49 (1996), pp. 677–99. For discussion of Brooks's law, see F. P. Brooks, ed., *The Mythical Man-Month: Essays on Software Engineering,* 2nd ed. (Reading, MA: Addison-Wesley, 1995).

14. S. J. Karau and K. D. Williams, "Social Loafing: A Meta-Analytic Review and Theoretical Integration," *Journal of Personality and Social Psychology* 65 (1993), pp. 681–706; R. C. Liden et al., "Social Loafing: A Field Investigation," *Journal of Management* 30 (2004), pp. 285–304; L. L. Chidambaram, "Is Out of Sight, Out of Mind? An Empirical Study of Social Loafing in Technology-Supported Groups," *Information Systems Research* 16, no. 2 (2005), pp. 149–68; and U. C. Klehe and N. Anderson, "The Moderating Influence of Personality and Culture on Social Loafing in Typical Versus Maximum Performance Situations," *International Journal of Selection and Assessment* 15, no. 2 (2007), pp. 250–62.

15. M. Erez and A. Somech, "Is Group Productivity Loss the Rule or the Exception? Effects of Culture and Group-Based Motivation," *Academy of Management Journal* 39 (1996), pp. 1513–1537; and Kerr and Tindale, "Group Performance and Decision Making."

16. M. A. West, C. S. Borrill, and K. L. Unsworth, "Team Effectiveness in Organizations," *International Review of Industrial and Organizational Psychology* 13 (1998), pp. 1–48; R. Forrester and A. B. Drexler, "A Model for Team-Based Organization Performance," *Academy of Management Executive* 13 (August 1999), pp. 36–49; J. E. McGrath, H. Arrow, and J. L. Berdahl, "The Study of Groups: Past, Present, and Future," *Personality & Social Psychology Review* 4, no. 1 (2000), pp. 95–105; and M. A. Marks, J. E. Mathieu, and S. J. Zaccaro, "A Temporally Based Framework and Taxonomy of Team Processes," *Academy of Management Review* 26, no. 3 (July 2001), pp. 356–76.

17. G. P. Shea and R. A. Guzzo, "Group Effectiveness: What Really Matters?," *Sloan Management Review* 27 (1987), pp. 33–46; J. R. Hackman et al., "Team Effectiveness in Theory and in Practice," in *Industrial and Organizational Psychology: Linking Theory with Practice,* ed. C. L. Cooper and E. A. Locke (Oxford, UK: Blackwell, 2000), pp. 109–29.

18. J. S. DeMatteo, L. T. Eby, and E. Sundstrom, "Team-Based Rewards: Current Empirical Evidence and Directions for Future Research," *Research in Organizational Behavior* 20 (1998), pp. 141–83; E. E. Lawler III, *Rewarding Excellence: Pay Strategies for the New Economy* (San Francisco: Jossey-Bass, 2000), pp. 207–14; amd G. Hertel, S. Geister, and U. Konradt, "Managing Virtual Teams: A Review of Current Empirical Research," *Human Resource Management Review* 15 (2005), pp. 69–95.

19. These and other environmental conditions for effective teams are discussed in R. Wageman, "Case Study: Critical Success Factors for Creating Superb Self-Managing Teams at Xerox," *Compensation and Benefits Review* 29 (September–October 1997), pp. 31–41; Sundstrom, "The Challenges of Supporting Work Team Effectiveness"; Choi, "External Activities and Team Effectiveness: Review and Theoretical Development"; T. L. Doolen, M. E. Hacker, and E. M. Van Aken, "The Impact of Organizational Context on Work Team Effectiveness: A Study of Production Team," *IEEE Transactions on Engineering Management* 50, no. 3 (August 2003), pp. 285–96; and S. D. Dionne et al., "Transformational Leadership and Team Performance," *Journal Of Organizational Change Management* 17, no. 2 (2004), pp. 177–93.

20. L. Adams, "Medrad Works and Wins as a Team," *Quality Magazine,* October 2004, p. 42; and "Lean Manufacturing Increases Productivity, Decreases Cycle Time," *Industrial Equipment News,* October 2005.

21. M. A. Campion, E. M. Papper, and G. J. Medsker, "Relations between Work Team Characteristics and Effectiveness: A Replication and Extension," *Personnel Psychology* 49 (1996), pp. 429–52; and D. C. Man and S. S. K. Lam, "The Effects of Job Complexity and Autonomy on Cohesiveness in Collectivistic and Individualistic Work Groups: A Cross-Cultural Analysis," *Journal of Organizational Behavior* 24 (2003), pp. 979–1001.

22. G. S. Van der Vegt, J. M. Emans, and E. Van de Vliert, "Patterns of Interdependence in Work Teams: A Two-Level Investigation of the Relations with Job and Team Satisfaction," *Personnel Psychology* 54 (Spring 2001), pp. 51–69; R. Wageman, "The Meaning of Interdependence," in *Groups at Work: Theory and Research,* ed. M. E. Turner (Mahwah, NJ: Lawrence Erlbaum Associates, 2001), pp. 197–217; S. M. Gully et al., "A Meta-Analysis of Team-Efficacy, Potency, and Performance: Interdependence and Level of Analysis as Moderators of Observed Relationships," *Journal of Applied Psychology* 87, no. 5 (October 2002), pp. 819–32; and M. R. Barrick et al., "The Moderating Role of Top Management Team Interdependence: Implications for Real Teams and Working Groups," *Academy of Management Journal* 50, no. 3 (2007), pp. 544–57.

23. Fishman, "The Anarchist's Cookbook."

24. F. P. Morgeson, M. H. Reider, and M. A. Campion, "Selecting Individuals in Team Settings: The Importance of Social Skills, Personality Characteristics, and Teamwork Knowledge," *Personnel Psychology* 58, no. 3 (2005), pp. 583–611; and V. Rousseau, C. Aubé, and A. Savoie, "Teamwork Behaviors: A Review and an Integration of Frameworks," *Small Group Research* 37, no. 5 (2006), pp. 540–70. For a detailed examination of the characteristics of effective team members, see M. L. Loughry, M. W. Ohland, and D. D. Moore, "Development of a Theory-Based Assessment of Team Member Effectiveness,"

Educational and Psychological Measurement 67, no. 3 (June 2007), pp. 505–24.

25. C. O. L. H. Porter et al., "Backing up Behaviors in Teams: The Role of Personality and Legitimacy of Need," *Journal of Applied Psychology* 88, no. 3 (2003), pp. 391–403; and C. E. Hårtel and D. Panipucci, "How 'Bad Apples' Spoil the Bunch: Faultlines, Emotional Levers, and Exclusion in the Workplace," *Research on Emotion in Organizations* 3 (2007), pp. 287–310.

26. S. Ganesan, "Reality-Style Recruitment," *Malaysia Star,* October 9, 2005; Z. Nazeer, "You're Hired!" *The New Paper (Singapore),* October 31, 2005; and J. Ng, "Shell Uses 'The Apprentice' Contest to Recruit Staff," *Straits Times (Singapore),* October 3, 2005.

27. D. van Knippenberg, C. K. W. De Dreu, and A. C. Homan, "Work Group Diversity and Group Performance: An Integrative Model and Research Agenda," *Journal of Applied Psychology* 89, no. 6 (2004), pp. 1008–1022; D. C. Lau and J. K. Murnighan, "Interactions within Groups and Subgroups: The Effects of Demographic Faultlines," *Academy of Management Journal* 48, no. 4 (August 2005), pp. 645–59; and R. Rico et al., "The Effects of Diversity Faultlines and Team Task Autonomy on Decision Quality and Social Integration," *Journal of Management* 33, no. 1 (Feb. 2007), pp. 111–32.

28. The NTSB and NASA studies are summarized in J. R. Hackman, "New Rules for Team Building," *Optimize* (July 2002), pp. 50–62.

29. B. W. Tuckman and M. A. C. Jensen, "Stages of Small-Group Development Revisited," *Group and Organization Studies* 2 (1977), pp. 419–42; and B. W. Tuckman, "Developmental Sequence in Small Groups," *Group Facilitation* (Spring 2001), pp. 66–81.

30. D. L. Miller, "The Stages of Group Development: A Retrospective Study of Dynamic Team Processes," *Canadian Journal of Administrative Sciences* 20, no. 2 (2003), pp. 121–34.

31. G. R. Bushe and G. H. Coetzer, "Group Development and Team Effectiveness: Using Cognitive Representations to Measure Group Development and Predict Task Performance and Group Viability," *Journal of Applied Behavioral Science* 43, no. 2 (June 2007), pp. 184–212.

32. J. E. Mathieu and G. F. Goodwin, "The Influence of Shared Mental Models on Team Process and Performance," *Journal of Applied Psychology* 85 (April 2000), pp. 273–84; J. Langan-Fox and J. Anglim, "Mental Models, Team Mental Models, and Performance: Process, Development, and Future Directions," *Human Factors and Ergonomics in Manufacturing* 14, no. 4 (2004), pp. 331–52; B. C. Lim and K. J. Klein, "Team Mental Models and Team Performance: A Field Study of the Effects of Team Mental Model Similarity and Accuracy," *Journal of Organizational Behavior* 27 (2006), pp. 403–18; and R. Rico, M. Sánchez-Manzanares, and C. Gibson, "Team Implicit Coordination Processes: A Team Knowledge-Based Approach," *Academy of Management Review* in press (2008).

33. A. P. Hare, "Types of Roles in Small Groups: A Bit of History and a Current Perspective," *Small Group Research* 25 (1994), pp. 443–48; and A. Aritzeta, S. Swailes, and B. Senior,

"Belbin's Team Role Model: Development, Validity and Applications for Team Building," *Journal of Management Studies* 44, no. 1 (January 2007), pp. 96–118.

34. S. H. N. Leung, J. W. K. Chan, and W. B. Lee, "The Dynamic Team Role Behavior: The Approaches of Investigation," *Team Performance Management* 9 (2003), pp. 84–90; and G. L. Stewart, I. S. Fulmer, and M. R. Barrick, "An Exploration of Member Roles as a Multilevel Linking Mechanism for Individual Traits and Team Outcomes," *Personnel Psychology* 58, no. 2 (2005), pp. 343–65.

35. D. C. Feldman, "The Development and Enforcement of Group Norms," *Academy of Management Review* 9 (1984), pp. 47–53; E. Fehr and U. Fischbacher, "Social Norms and Human Cooperation," *Trends in Cognitive Sciences* 8, no. 4 (2004), pp. 185–90.

36. N. Ellemers and F. Rink, "Identity in Work Groups: The Beneficial and Detrimental Consequences of Multiple Identities and Group Norms for Collaboration and Group Performance," *Advances in Group Processes* 22 (2005), pp. 1–41.

37. J. J. Dose and R. J. Klimoski, "The Diversity of Diversity: Work Values Effects on Formative Team Processes," *Human Resource Management Review* 9, no. 1 (Spring 1999), pp. 83–108.

38. S. Taggar and R. Ellis, "The Role of Leaders in Shaping Formal Team Norms," *Leadership Quarterly* 18, no. 2 (2007), pp. 105–20.

39. D. J. Beal et al., "Cohesion and Performance in Groups: A Meta-Analytic Clarification of Construct Relations," *Journal of Applied Psychology* 88, no. 6 (2003), pp. 989–1004; and S. W. J. Kozlowski and D. R. Ilgen, "Enhancing the Effectiveness of Work Groups and Teams," *Psychological Science in the Public Interest* 7, no. 3 (2006), pp. 77–124.

40. K. A. Jehn, G. B. Northcraft, and M. A. Neale, "Why Differences Make a Difference: A Field Study of Diversity, Conflict, and Performance in Workgroups," *Administrative Science Quarterly* 44, no. 4 (1999), pp. 741–63; and van Knippenberg, De Dreu, and Homan, "Work Group Diversity and Group Performance: An Integrative Model and Research Agenda." For evidence that diversity/similarity does not always influence cohesion, see S. S. Webber and L. M. Donahue, "Impact of Highly and Less Job-Related Diversity on Work Group Cohesion and Performance: A Meta-Analysis," *Journal of Management* 27, no. 2 (2001), pp. 141–62.

41. E. Aronson and J. Mills, "The Effects of Severity of Initiation on Liking for a Group," *Journal of Abnormal and Social Psychology* 59 (1959), pp. 177–81; and J. E. Hautaluoma and R. S. Enge, "Early Socialization into a Work Group: Severity of Initiations Revisited," *Journal of Social Behavior & Personality* 6 (1991), pp. 725–48.

42. B. Mullen and C. Copper, "The Relation between Group Cohesiveness and Performance: An Integration," *Psychological Bulletin* 115 (1994), pp. 210–27.

43. M. Rempel and R. J. Fisher, "Perceived Threat, Cohesion, and Group Problem Solving in Intergroup Conflict," *International Journal of Conflict Management* 8 (1997), pp. 216–34; and M. E. Turner and T. Horvitz, "The Dilemma of Threat: Group Effectiveness and Ineffectiveness under Adversity," in *Groups*

at Work: Theory and Research, ed. M. E. Turner (Mahwah, NJ: Lawrence Erlbaum Associates, 2001), pp. 445–70.

44. W. Piper et al., "Cohesion as a Basic Bond in Groups," *Human Relations* 36 (1983), pp. 93–108; and C. A. O'Reilly, D. E. Caldwell, and W. P. Barnett, "Work Group Demography, Social Integration, and Turnover," *Administrative Science Quarterly* 34 (1989), pp. 21–37.

45. Mullen and Copper, "The Relation between Group Cohesiveness and Performance"; A. V. Carron et al., "Cohesion and Performance in Sport: A Meta-Analysis," *Journal of Sport and Exercise Psychology* 24 (2002), pp. 168–88; and Beal et al., "Cohesion and Performance in Groups."

46. C. Langfred, "Is Group Cohesiveness a Double-Edged Sword? An Investigation of the Effects of Cohesiveness on Performance," *Small Group Research* 29 (1998), pp. 124–43; and K. L. Gammage, A. V. Carron, and P. A. Estabrooks, "Team Cohesion and Individual Productivity: The Influence of the Norm for Productivity and the Identifiablity of Individual Effort," *Small Group Research* 32 (February 2001), pp. 3–18.

47. S. L. Robinson, "Trust and Breach of the Psychological Contract," *Administrative Science Quarterly* 41 (1996), pp. 574–99; D. M. Rousseau et al., "Not So Different after All: A Cross-Discipline View of Trust," *Academy of Management Review* 23 (1998), pp. 393–404; and D. L. Duarte and N. T. Snyder, *Mastering Virtual Teams: Strategies, Tools, and Techniques That Succeed,* 2nd ed. (San Francisco, CA: Jossey-Bass, 2000), pp. 139–55.

48. D. J. McAllister, "Affect- and Cognition-Based Trust as Foundations for Interpersonal Cooperation in Organizations," *Academy of Management Journal* 38, no. 1 (February 1995), pp. 24–59; and M. Williams, "In Whom We Trust: Group Membership as an Affective Context for Trust Development," *Academy of Management Review* 26, no. 3 (July 2001), pp. 377–96.

49. O. E. Williamson, "Calculativeness, Trust, and Economic Organization," *Journal of Law and Economics* 36, no. 1 (1993), pp. 453–86.

50. E. M. Whitener et al., "Managers as Initiators of Trust: An Exchange Relationship Framework for Understanding Managerial Trustworthy Behavior," *Academy of Management Review* 23 (July 1998), pp. 513–30; J. M. Kouzes and B. Z. Posner, *The Leadership Challenge,* 3rd ed. (San Francisco: Jossey-Bass, 2002), Chap. 2; and T. Simons, "Behavioral Integrity: The Perceived Alignment between Managers' Words and Deeds as a Research Focus," *Organization Science* 13, no. 1 (January–February 2002), pp. 18–35.

51. S. L. Jarvenpaa and D. E. Leidner, "Communication and Trust in Global Virtual Teams," *Organization Science* 10 (1999), pp. 791–815; and M. M. Pillutla, D. Malhotra, and J. Keith Murnighan, "Attributions of Trust and the Calculus of Reciprocity," *Journal of Experimental Social Psychology* 39, no. 5 (2003), pp. 448–55.

52. K. T. Dirks and D. L. Ferrin, "The Role of Trust in Organizations," *Organization Science* 12, no. 4 (July–August 2004), pp. 450–67.

53. S. A. Mohrman, S. G. Cohen, and A. M. Mohrman, Jr., *Designing Team-Based Organizations: New Forms for Knowledge Work* (San Francisco: Jossey-Bass, 1995); D. E. Yeatts and C. Hyten, *High-Performing Self-Managed Work Teams: A Comparison of Theory and Practice* (Thousand Oaks, CA: Sage, 1998); E. E. Lawler, *Organizing for High Performance* (San Francisco: Jossey-Bass, 2001); and R. J. Torraco, "Work Design Theory: A Review and Critique with Implications for Human Resource Development," *Human Resource Development Quarterly* 16, no. 1 (Spring 2005), pp. 85–109.

54. J. Mackey, "Open Book Company," *Newsweek,* November 28, 2005, p. 42.

55. J. Smith, "Building Cars, Building Teams," *Plant Engineering,* December 2005, pp. 41–50.

56. M. Connelly, "Chrysler Wants to Put Team Assembly in All Plants," *Automotive News,* May 30, 2005, p. 53; J. Leute, "Union, Management Work in Lockstep at Belvidere, Ill., Plant," *Janesville Gazette (Janesville, WI),* July 18, 2005; Smith, "Building Cars, Building Teams"; and M. Connelly, "Chrysler Boosts Belvidere Flexibility," *Automotive News,* February 13, 2006, p. 44.

57. P. Panchak, "Production Workers Can Be Your Competitive Edge," *Industry Week,* October 2004, p. 11; and S. K. Muthusamy, J. V. Wheeler, and B. L. Simmons, "Self-Managing Work Teams: Enhancing Organizational Innovativeness," *Organization Development Journal* 23, no. 3 (Fall 2005), pp. 53–66.

58. C. R. Emery and L. D. Fredendall, "The Effect of Teams on Firm Profitability and Customer Satisfaction," *Journal of Service Research* 4 (February 2002), pp. 217–29; A. Krause and H. Dunckel, "Work Design and Customer Satisfaction: Effects of the Implementation of Semi-Autonomous Group Work on Customer Satisfaction Considering Employee Satisfaction and Group Performance (Translated Abstract)," *Zeitschrift fur Arbeits-und Organisationspsychologie* 47, no. 4 (2003), pp. 182–93; and H. van Mierlo et al., "Self-Managing Teamwork and Psychological Well-Being: Review of a Multilevel Research Domain," *Group & Organization Management* 30, no. 2 (April 2005), pp. 211–35.

59. M. Moldaschl and W. G. Weber, "The 'Three Waves' of Industrial Group Work: Historical Reflections on Current Research on Group Work," *Human Relations* 51 (March 1998), pp. 259–87; and W. Niepce and E. Molleman, "Work Design Issues in Lean Production from Sociotechnical System Perspective: Neo-Taylorism or the Next Step in Sociotechnical Design?" *Human Relations* 51, no. 3 (March 1998), pp. 259–87.

60. E. Ulich and W. G. Weber, "Dimensions, Criteria, and Evaluation of Work Group Autonomy," in *Handbook of Work Group Psychology,* ed. M. A. West (Chichester, UK: John Wiley and Sons, 1996), 247–82.

61. K. P. Carson and G. L. Stewart, "Job Analysis and the Sociotechnical Approach to Quality: A Critical Examination," *Journal of Quality Management* 1 (1996), pp. 49–65; and C. C. Manz and G. L. Stewart, "Attaining Flexible Stability by Integrating Total Quality Management and Socio-Technical Systems Theory," *Organization Science* 8 (1997), pp. 59–70.

62. J. Gordon, "Do Your Virtual Teams Deliver Only Virtual Performance?" *Training,* June 2005, 20–24.

63. J. Lipnack and J. Stamps, *Virtual Teams: People Working across Boundaries with Technology* (New York: John Wiley and Sons, 2001); B. S. Bell and W. J. Kozlowski, "A Typology of Virtual Teams: Implications for Effective Leadership," *Group & Organization Management* 27 (March 2002), pp. 14–49; and Hertel, Geister, and Konradt, "Managing Virtual Teams: A Review of Current Empirical Research."

64. G. Gilder, *Telecosm: How Infinite Bandwidth Will Revolutionize Our World* (New York: Free Press, 2001); and L. L. Martins, L. L. Gilson, and M. T. Maynard, "Virtual Teams: What Do We Know and Where Do We Go Form Here?" *Journal of Management* 30, no. 6 (2004), pp. 805–35. The Novartis quotation is from S. Murray, "Pros and Cons of Technology: The Corporate Agenda: Managing Virtual Teams," *Financial Times (London),* May 27, 2002, p. 6.

65. Martins, Gilson, and Maynard, "Virtual Teams"; and G. Hertel, U. Konradt, and K. Voss, "Competencies for Virtual Teamwork: Development and Validation of a Web-Based Selection Tool for Members of Distributed Teams," *European Journal of Work and Organizational Psychology* 15, no. 4 (2006), pp. 477–04.

66. G. Buckler, "Staking One for the Team," *Computing Canada,* October 22, 2004, p. 16.

67. V. H. Vroom and A. G. Jago, *The New Leadership* (Englewood Cliffs, NJ: Prentice-Hall, 1988), pp. 28–29.

68. M. Diehl and W. Stroebe, "Productivity Loss in Idea-Generating Groups: Tracking Down the Blocking Effects," *Journal of Personality and Social Psychology* 61 (1991), pp. 392–403; R. B. Gallupe et al., "Blocking Electronic Brainstorms," *Journal of Applied Psychology* 79 (1994), pp. 77–86; B. A. Nijstad, W. Stroebe, and H. F. M. Lodewijkx, "Production Blocking and Idea Generation: Does Blocking Interfere with Cognitive Processes?" *Journal of Experimental Social Psychology* 39, no. 6 (November 2003), pp. 531–48; and B. A. Nijstad and W. Stroebe, "How the Group Affects the Mind: A Cognitive Model of Idea Generation in Groups," *Personality & Social Psychology Review* 10, no. 3 (2006), pp. 186–213.

69. B. E. Irmer, P. Bordia, and D. Abusah, "Evaluation Apprehension and Perceived Benefits in Interpersonal and Database Knowledge Sharing," *Academy of Management Proceedings* (2002), pp. B1–B6.

70. I. L. Janis, *Groupthink: Psychological Studies of Policy Decisions and Fiascoes,* 2nd ed. (Boston: Houghton Mifflin, 1982); and J. K. Esser, "Alive and Well after 25 Years: A Review of Groupthink Research," *Organizational Behavior and Human Decision Processes* 73, no. 2–3 (1998), pp. 116–41.

71. J. N. Choi and M. U. Kim, "The Organizational Application of Groupthink and Its Limitations in Organizations," *Journal of Applied Psychology* 84, no. 2 (April 1999), pp. 297–06; W. W. Park, "A Comprehensive Empirical Investigation of the Relationships among Variables of the Groupthink Model," *Journal of Organizational Behavior* 21, no. 8 (December 2000), pp. 873–87; and D. D. Henningsen et al., "Examining the Symptoms of Groupthink and Retrospective Sensemaking," *Small Group Research* 37, no. 1 (Feb. 2006), pp. 36–64.

72. D. Miller, *The Icarus Paradox: How Exceptional Companies Bring About Their Own Downfall* (New York: HarperBusiness, 1990); S. Finkelstein, *Why Smart Executives Fail* (New York: Viking, 2003); K. Tasa and G. Whyte, "Collective Efficacy and Vigilant Problem Solving in Group Decision Making: A Non-Linear Model," *Organizational Behavior and Human Decision Processes* 96, no. 2 (March 2005), pp. 119–29.

73. H. Collingwood, "Best-Kept Secrets of the World's Best Companies: Outside-in R&D," *Business 2.0,* April 2006, p. 82.

74. K. M. Eisenhardt, J. L. Kahwajy, and L. J. Bourgeois III, "Conflict and Strategic Choice: How Top Management Teams Disagree," *California Management Review* 39 (1997), pp. 42–62; R. Sutton, *Weird Ideas That Work* (New York: Free Press, 2002); and C. J. Nemeth et al., "The Liberating Role of Conflict in Group Creativity: A Study in Two Countries," *European Journal of Social Psychology* 34, no. 4 (2004), pp. 365–74. For discussion on how all conflict is potentially detrimental to teams, see C. K. W. De Dreu and L. R. Weingart, "Task Versus Relationship Conflict, Team Performance, and Team Member Satisfaction: A Meta-Analysis," *Journal of Applied Psychology* 88 (August 2003), pp. 587–604; and P. Hinds and D. E. Bailey, "Out of Sight, Out of Sync: Understanding Conflict in Distributed Teams," *Organization Science* 14, no. 6 (2003), pp. 615–32.

75. K. Darce, "Ground Control: NASA Attempts a Cultural Shift," *Seattle Times,* April 24, 2005, p. A3; and R. Shelton, "NASA Attempts to Change Mindset in Wake of Columbia Tragedy," *Macon Telegraph (Macon, GA),* July 7, 2005.

76. B. Mullen, C. Johnson, and E. Salas, "Productivity Loss in Brainstorming Groups: A Meta-Analytic Integration," *Basic and Applied Psychology* 12 (1991), pp. 2–23. The original description of brainstorming appeared in A. F. Osborn, *Applied Imagination* (New York: Scribner, 1957).

77. R. I. Sutton and A. Hargadon, "Brainstorming Groups in Context: Effectiveness in a Product Design Firm," *Administrative Science Quarterly* 41 (1996), pp. 685–718; T. Kelley, *The Art of Innovation* (New York: Currency Doubleday, 2001); V. R. Brown and P. B. Paulus, "Making Group Brainstorming More Effective: Recommendations from an Associative Memory Perspective," *Current Directions in Psychological Science* 11, no. 6 (2002), pp. 208–12; and K. Leggett Dugosh and P. B. Paulus, "Cognitive and Social Comparison Processes in Brainstorming," *Journal of Experimental Social Psychology* 41, no. 3 (2005), pp. 313–20.

78. R. B. Gallupe, L. M. Bastianutti, and W. H. Cooper, "Unblocking Brainstorms," *Journal of Applied Psychology* 76 (1991), pp. 137–42; W. H. Cooper et al., "Some Liberating Effects of Anonymous Electronic Brainstorming," *Small Group Research* 29, no. 2 (April 1998), pp. 147–78; A. R. Dennis, B. H. Wixom, and R. J. Vandenberg, "Understanding Fit and Appropriation Effects in Group Support Systems Via Meta-Analysis," *MIS Quarterly* 25, no. 2 (June 2001), pp. 167–93; and D. M. DeRosa, C. L. Smith, and D. A. Hantula, "The Medium Matters: Mining the Long-Promised Merit of

Group Interaction in Creative Idea Generation Tasks in a Meta-Analysis of the Electronic Group Brainstorming Literature," *Computers in Human Behavior* 23, no. 3 (2007), pp. 1549–1581.

79. A. L. Delbecq, A. H. Van de Ven, and D. H. Gustafson, *Group Techniques for Program Planning: A Guide to Nominal Group and Delphi Processes* (Middleton, WI: Green Briar Press, 1986).

80. S. Frankel, "NGT + MDS: An Adaptation of the Nominal Group Technique for Ill-Structured Problems," *Journal of Applied Behavioral Science* 23 (1987), pp. 543–51; and H. Barki and A. Pinsonneault, "Small Group Brainstorming and Idea Quality: Is Electronic Brainstorming the Most Effective Approach?" *Small Group Research* 32, no. 2 (April 2001), pp. 158–205.

chapter 8

1. J. Bennett and M. Beith, "Alternate Universe," *Newsweek,* July 30, 2007; and S. Hatch, "Virtual Worlds, Real Meetings," *Corporate Meetings & Incentives,* February 2007, pp. 12–17.

2. C. Barnard, *The Functions of the Executive* (Cambridge, MA: Harvard University Press, 1938).

3. M. T. Hansen, M. L. Mors, and B. Løvås, "Knowledge Sharing in Organizations: Multiple Networks, Multiple Phases," *Academy of Management Journal* 48, no. 5 (2005), pp. 776–93; R. Du, S. Ai, and Y. Ren, "Relationship between Knowledge Sharing and Performance: A Survey in Xu'an, China," *Expert Systems with Applications* 32 (2007), pp. 38–46; and S. R. Murray and J. Peyrefitte, "Knowledge Type and Communication Media Choice in the Knowledge Transfer Process," *Journal of Managerial Issues* 19, no. 1 (Spring 2007), pp. 111–33.

4. N. Ellemers, R. Spears, and B. Doosje, "Self and Social Identity," *Annual Review of Psychology* 53 (2002), pp. 161–86; S. A. Haslam and S. Reicher, "Stressing the Group: Social Identity and the Unfolding Dynamics of Responses to Stress," *Journal of Applied Psychology* 91, no. 5 (2006), pp. 1037–1052; and M. T. Gailliot and R. F. Baumeister, "Self-Esteem, Belongingness, and Worldview Validation: Does Belongingness Exert a Unique Influence Upon Self-Esteem?" *Journal of Research in Personality* 41, no. 2 (2007), pp. 327–45.

5. S. Cohen, "The Pittsburgh Common Cold Studies: Psychosocial Predictors of Susceptibility to Respiratory Infectious Illness," *International Journal of Behavioral Medicine* 12, no. 3 (2005), pp. 123–31; and B. N. Uchino, "Social Support and Health: A Review of Physiological Processes Potentially Underlying Links to Disease Outcomes," *Journal of Behavioral Medicine* 29, no. 4 (2006), pp. 377–87.

6. D. Kirkpatrick, "It's Not a Game," *Fortune,* February 5, 2007, pp. 34–38.

7. C. E. Shannon and W. Weaver, *The Mathematical Theory of Communication* (Urbana, IL: University of Illinois Press, 1949); and R. M. Krauss and S. R. Fussell, "Social Psychological Models of Interpersonal Communication," in *Social Psychology: Handbook of Basic Principles,* ed. E. T. Higgins and A. Kruglanski (New York: Guilford Press, 1996), pp. 655–701.

8. J. R. Carlson and R. W. Zmud, "Channel Expansion Theory and the Experiential Nature of Media Richness Perceptions," *Academy of Management Journal* 42 (April 1999), pp. 153–70.

9. P. Shachaf and N. Hara, "Behavioral Complexity Theory of Media Selection: A Proposed Theory for Global Virtual Teams," *Journal of Information Science* 33 (2007), pp. 63–75.

10. N. B. Ducheneaut and L. A. Watts, "In Search of Coherence: A Review of E-Mail Research," *Human-Computer Interaction* 20, no. 1–2 (2005), pp. 11–48.

11. W. Lucas, "Effects of E-Mail on the Organization," *European Management Journal* 16, no. 1 (February 1998), pp. 18–30; D. A. Owens, M. A. Neale, and R. I. Sutton, "Technologies of Status Management Status Dynamics in E-Mail Communications," *Research on Managing Groups and Teams* 3 (2000), pp. 205–30; and N. B. Ducheneaut, "Ceci N'est Pas Un Objet? Talking About Objects in E-Mail," *Human-Computer Interaction* 18, no. 1–2 (2003), pp. 85–110.

12. N. B. Ducheneaut, "The Social Impacts of Electronic Mail in Organizations: A Case Study of Electronic Power Games Using Communication Genres," *Information, Communication, & Society* 5, no. 2 (2002), pp. 153–88; and N. Panteli, "Richness, Power Cues and Email Text," *Information & Management* 40, no. 2 (2002), pp. 75–86.

13. N. Epley and J. Kruger, "When What You Type Isn't What They Read: The Perseverance of Stereotypes and Expectancies over E-Mail," *Journal of Experimental Social Psychology* 41, no. 4 (2005), pp. 414–22.

14. J. B. Walther, "Language and Communication Technology: Introduction to the Special Issue," *Journal of Language and Social Psychology* 23, no. 4 (December 2004), pp. 384–96; J. B. Walther, T. Loh, and L. Granka, "Let Me Count the Ways: The Interchange of Verbal and Nonverbal Cues in Computer-Mediated and Face-to-Face Affinity," *Journal of Language and Social Psychology* 24, no. 1 (March 2005), pp. 36–65; and K. Byron, "Carrying Too Heavy a Load? The Communication and Miscommunication of Emotion by Email," *Academy of Management Review* 33, no. 1 (2008).

15. G. Hertel, S. Geister, and U. Konradt, "Managing Virtual Teams: A Review of Current Empirical Research," *Human Resource Management Review* 15 (2005), pp. 69–95; H. Lee, "Behavioral Strategies for Dealing with Flaming in an Online Forum," *The Sociological Quarterly* 46, no. 2 (2005), pp. 385–403.

16. D. D. Dawley and W. P. Anthony, "User Perceptions of E-Mail at Work," *Journal of Business and Technical Communication* 17, no. 2 (April 2003), pp. 170–200; "Email Brings Costs and Fatigue," *Western News (University of Western Ontario) (London, Ontario),* July 9, 2004; G. F. Thomas and C. L. King, "Reconceptualizing E-Mail Overload," *Journal of Business and Technical Communication* 20, no. 3 (July 2006), pp. 252–87; and S. Carr, "Email Overload Menace Growing," *Silicon.com,* July 12, 2007.

17. S. Williams, "Apologies and Rows by Email Are a New Sin for Hi-Tech Cowards," *Western Mail (Cardiff, Wales),* April 1, 2006, p. 11.

18. W. M. Bulkeley, "Playing Well with Others: How IBM's Employees Have Taken Social Networking to an Unusual Level," *The Wall Street Journal,* June 18, 2007, p. R10; and M. Rauch, "Virtual Reality," *Sales & Marketing Management* 159, no. 1 (January 2007), pp. 18–23.

19. A. F. Cameron and J. Webster, "Unintended Consequences of Emerging Communication Technologies: Instant Messaging in the Workplace," *Computers in Human Behavior* 21, no. 1 (2005), pp. 85–103.

20. L. Z. Tiedens and A. R. Fragale, "Power Moves: Complementarity in Dominant and Submissive Nonverbal Behavior," *Journal of Personality and Social Psychology* 84, no. 3 (2003), pp. 558–68.

21. P. Ekman and E. Rosenberg, *What the Face Reveals: Basic and Applied Studies of Spontaneous Expression Using the Facial Action Coding System* (Oxford, England: Oxford University Press, 1997); P. Winkielman and K. C. Berridge, "Unconscious Emotion," *Current Directions in Psychological Science* 13, no. 3 (2004), pp. 120–23.

22. L. K. Trevi o, J. Webster, and E. W. Stein, "Making Connections: Complementary Influences on Communication Media Choices, Attitudes, and Use," *Organization Science* 11, no. 2 (2000), pp. 163–82; B. Barry and I. S. Fulmer, "The Medium Is the Message: The Adaptive Use of Communication Media in Dyadic Influence," *Academy of Management Review* 29, no. 2 (2004), pp. 272–92; J. W. Turner et al., "Exploring the Dominant Media: How Does Media Use Reflect Organizational Norms and Affect Performance?" *Journal of Business Communication* 43, no. 3 (July 2006), pp. 220–50; and M. B. Watson-Manheim and F. Bélanger, "Communication Media Repertoires: Dealing with the Multiplicity of Media Choices," *MIS Quarterly* 31, no. 2 (2007), pp. 267–93.

23. R. C. King, "Media Appropriateness: Effects of Experience on Communication Media Choice," *Decision Sciences* 28, no. 4 (1997), pp. 877–910.

24. K. Griffiths, "KPMG Sacks 670 Employees by E-Mail," *The Independent (London),* November 5, 2002, p. 19; and "Shop Worker Sacked by Text Message," The Post *(Claremont/Nedlands, Western Australia),* July 28, 2007, pp. 1, 78.

25. R. L. Daft and R. H. Lengel, "Information Richness: A New Approach to Managerial Behavior and Organization Design," *Research in Organizational Behavior* 6 (1984), pp. 191–233; and R. H. Lengel and R. L. Daft, "The Selection of Communication Media as an Executive Skill," *Academy of Management Executive* 2 (1988), pp. 225–32.

26. R. E. Rice, "Task Analyzability, Use of New Media, and Effectiveness: A Multi-Site Exploration of Media Richness," *Organization Science* 3 (1992), pp. 475–500.

27. J. W. Turner and N. L. Reinsch Jr, "The Business Communicator as Presence Allocator," *Journal of Business Communication* 44, no. 1 (2007), pp. 36–58; and J. Reinsch, N. Lamar, J. W. Turner, and C. H. Tinsley, "Multicommunicating: A Practice Whose Time Has Come?" *Academy of Management Review* (in press).

28. Carlson and Zmud, "Channel Expansion Theory and the Experiential Nature of Media Richness Perceptions"; and N. Kock, "Media Richness or Media Naturalness? The Evolution of Our Biological Communication Apparatus and Its Influence on Our Behavior toward E-Communication Tools," *IEEE Transactions on Professional Communication* 48, no. 2 (June 2005), pp. 117–30.

29. D. Muller, T. Atzeni, and F. Butera, "Coaction and Upward Social Comparison Reduce the Illusory Conjunction Effect: Support for Distraction-Conflict Theory," *Journal of Experimental Social Psychology* 40, no. 5 (2004), pp. 659–65; and L. P. Robert and A. R. Dennis, "Paradox of Richness: A Cognitive Model of Media Choice," *IEEE Transactions on Professional Communication* 48, no. 1 (2005), pp. 10–21.

30. J. Kruger et al., "Egocentrism over E-Mail: Can We Communicate as Well as We Think?" *Journal of Personality and Social Psychology* 89, no. 6 (2005), pp. 925–36.

31. D. Goleman, R. Boyatzis, and A. McKee, *Primal Leaders* (Boston: Harvard Business School Press, 2002), pp. 92–95.

32. D. Woodruff, "Crossing Culture Divide Early Clears Merger Paths," *Asian Wall Street Journal,* May 28, 2001, p. 9.

33. R. M. Krauss, "The Psychology of Verbal Communication," in *International Encyclopedia of the Social and Behavioral Sciences,* ed. N. Smelser and P. Baltes (London: Elsevier, 2002), pp. 16161–16165.

34. L. L. Putnam, N. Phillips, and P. Chapman, "Metaphors of Communication and Organization," in *Handbook of Organization Studies,* ed. S. R. Clegg, C. Hardy, and W. R. Nord (London: Sage, 1996), 373–408; G. Morgan, *Images of Organization,* 2nd ed. (Thousand Oaks, CA: Sage, 1997); and M. Rubini and H. Sigall, "Taking the Edge Off of Disagreement: Linguistic Abstractness and Self-Presentation to a Heterogeneous Audience," *European Journal of Social Psychology* 32 (2002), pp. 343–51.

35. T. Koski, "Reflections on Information Glut and Other Issues in Knowledge Productivity," *Futures* 33 (August 2001), pp. 483–95.

36. A. G. Schick, L. A. Gordon, and S. Haka, "Information Overload: A Temporal Approach," *Accounting, Organizations & Society* 15 (1990), pp. 199–220; and A. Edmunds and A. Morris, "The Problem of Information Overload in Business Organisations: A Review of the Literature," *International Journal of Information Management* 20 (2000), pp. 17–28.

37. D. C. Thomas and K. Inkson, *Cultural Intelligence: People Skills for Global Business* (San Francisco: Berrett-Koehler, 2004), Chap. 6; and D. Welch, L. Welch, and R. Piekkari, "Speaking in Tongues," *International Studies of Management & Organization* 35, no. 1 (Spring 2005), pp. 10–27.

38. S. Ohtaki, T. Ohtaki, and M. D. Fetters, "Doctor-Patient Communication: A Comparison of the USA and Japan," *Family Practice* 20 (June 2003), pp. 276–82; and M. Fujio, "Silence During Intercultural Communication: A Case Study," *Corporate Communications* 9, no. 4 (2004), pp. 331–39.

39. D. C. Barnlund, *Communication Styles of Japanese and Americans: Images and Realities* (Belmont, CA: Wadsworth, 1988); H. Yamada, *American and Japanese Business Discourse: A*

Comparison of Interaction Styles (Norwood, NJ: Ablex, 1992), Chap. 2; and H. Yamada, *Different Games, Different Rules* (New York: Oxford University Press, 1997), pp. 76–79.

40. P. Harris and R. Moran, *Managing Cultural Differences* (Houston: Gulf, 1987); H. Blagg, "A Just Measure of Shame?" *British Journal of Criminology* 37 (Autumn 1997), pp. 481–501; and R. E. Axtell, *Gestures: The Do's and Taboos of Body Language around the World,* Revised ed. (New York: Wiley, 1998).

41. M. Griffin, "The Office, Australian Style," *Sunday Age,* June 22, 2003, p. 6.

42. D. Tannen, *You Just Don't Understand: Men and Women in Conversation* (New York: Ballentine Books, 1990); D. Tannen, *Talking from 9 to 5* (New York: Avon, 1994); M. Crawford, *Talking Difference: On Gender and Language* (Thousand Oaks, CA: Sage, 1995), pp. 41–44; and L. L. Namy, L. C. Nygaard, and D. Sauerteig, "Gender Differences in Vocal Accommodation: The Role of Perception," *Journal of Language and Social Psychology* 21, no. 4 (December 2002), pp. 422–32.

43. A. Mulac et al., "'Uh-Huh. What's That All About?' Differing Interpretations of Conversational Backchannels and Questions as Sources of Miscommunication across Gender Boundaries," *Communication Research* 25 (December 1998), pp. 641–68; N. M. Sussman and D. H. Tyson, "Sex and Power: Gender Differences in Computer-Mediated Interactions," *Computers in Human Behavior* 16 (2000), pp. 381–94; D. R. Caruso and P. Salovey, *The Emotionally Intelligent Manager* (San Francisco: Jossey-Bass, 2004), p. 23; and D. Fallows, *How Women and Men Use the Internet,* (Washington, DC: Pew Internet and American Life Project, December 28, 2005).

44. The three components of listening discussed here are based on several recent studies in the field of marketing, including S. B. Castleberry, C. D. Shepherd, and R. Ridnour, "Effective Interpersonal Listening in the Personal Selling Environment: Conceptualization, Measurement, and Nomological Validity," *Journal of Marketing Theory and Practice* 7 (Winter 1999), pp. 30–38; L. B. Comer and T. Drollinger, "Active Empathetic Listening and Selling Success: A Conceptual Framework," *Journal of Personal Selling & Sales Management* 19 (Winter 1999), pp. 15–29; and K. de Ruyter and M. G. M. Wetzels, "The Impact of Perceived Listening Behavior in Voice-to-Voice Service Encounters," *Journal of Service Research* 2 (February 2000), pp. 276–84.

45. A. Leaman and B. Bordass, "Productivity in Buildings: The Killer Variables," *Building Research & Information* 27, no. 1 (1999), pp. 4–19; T. J. Allen, "Architecture and Communication among Product Development Engineers," *California Management Review* 49, no. 2 (Winter 2007), pp. 23–41; and F. Becker, "Organizational Ecology and Knowledge Networks," *California Management Review* 49, no. 2 (Winter 2007), pp. 42–61.

46. S. P. Means, "Playing at Pixar," *Salt Lake Tribune (Utah),* May 30, 2003, p. D1; and G. Whipp, "Swimming against the Tide," *Daily News of Los Angeles,* May 30, 2003, p. U6.

47. M. Gardner, "Democratic Principles Make Businesses More Transparent," *Christian Science Monitor,* March 19, 2007, p. 13.

48. G. Evans and D. Johnson, "Stress and Open-Office Noise," *Journal of Applied Psychology* 85 (2000), pp. 779–83; and F. Russo, "My Kingdom for a Door," *Time Magazine,* October 23, 2000, p. B1.

49. C. Wagner and A. Majchrzak, "Enabling Customer-Centricity Using Wikis and the Wiki Way," *Journal of Management Information Systems* 23, no. 3 (2006), pp. 17–43; R. B. Ferguson, "Build a Web 2.0 Platform and Employees Will Use It," *eWeek,* June 20, 2007; and C. Karena, "Working the Wiki Way," *Sydney Morning Herald,* March 6, 2007.

50. The original term is "management by *wandering* around," but this has been replaced with "walking" over the years. See W. Ouchi, *Theory Z* (New York: Avon Books, 1981), pp. 176–77; and T. Peters and R. Waterman, *In Search of Excellence* (New York: Harper and Row, 1982), p. 122.

51. R. Rodwell, "Regular Staff Meetings Help Build Morale," *South China Morning Post (Hong Kong),* August 27, 2005, p. 4.

52. R. Rousos, "Trust in Leaders Lacking at Utility," *The Ledger (Lakeland, FL),* July 29, 2003, p. B1; and B. Whitworth and B. Riccomini, "Management Communication: Unlocking Higher Employee Performance," *Communication World,* March–April 2005, pp. 18–21.

53. K. Davis, "Management Communication and the Grapevine," *Harvard Business Review* 31 (September–October 1953), pp. 43–49; and W. L. Davis and J. R. O'Connor, "Serial Transmission of Information: A Study of the Grapevine," *Journal of Applied Communication Research* 5 (1977), pp. 61–72.

54. H. Mintzberg, *The Structuring of Organizations* (Englewood Cliffs, NJ: Prentice-Hall, 1979), pp. 46–53; and D. Krackhardt and J. R. Hanson, "Informal Networks: The Company Behind the Chart," *Harvard Business Review* 71 (July–August 1993), pp. 104–11.

55. C. J. Walker and C. A. Beckerle, "The Effect of State Anxiety on Rumor Transmission," *Journal of Social Behaviour & Personality* 2 (August 1987), pp. 353–60; R. L. Rosnow, "Inside Rumor: A Personal Journey," *American Psychologist* 46 (May 1991), pp. 484–96; and M. Noon and R. Delbridge, "News from Behind My Hand: Gossip in Organizations," *Organization Studies* 14 (1993), pp. 23–36.

56. N. Nicholson, "Evolutionary Psychology: Toward a New View of Human Nature and Organizational Society," *Human Relations* 50 (September 1997), pp. 1053–1078.

chapter 9

1. R. Gluyas, "Fear and Loathing in NAB's Forex Fiasco," *The Australian,* August 6, 2005, p. 35; E. Johnston, "'Anything Goes,' Ex-Trader Says," *Australian Financial Review,* August 2, 2005, p. 3; E. Johnston, "Expletives and Stench in Hothouse of NAB Dealers," *Australian Financial Review,* August 6, 2005, p. 3; M. Moncrief and D. Miletic, "The End Is Nigh for NAB's Rogue Traders," *Sydney Morning Herald,* July 3, 2006, p. 19.

2. J. R. P. French and B. Raven, "The Bases of Social Power," in *Studies in Social Power,* ed. D. Cartwright (Ann Arbor, MI: University of Michigan Press, 1959), pp. 150–167; and A. D. Galinsky et al., "Power and Perspectives Not Taken," *Psychological Science* 17, no. 12 (2006), pp. 1068–74. Also see H. Mintzberg, *Power in and around Organizations* (Englewood Cliffs, NJ: Prentice-Hall, 1983), Chap. 1; and J. Pfeffer, *Managing with Power* (Boston: Harvard Business University Press, 1992), pp. 17, 30.

3. R. A. Dahl, "The Concept of Power," *Behavioral Science* 2 (1957), pp. 201–18; R. M. Emerson, "Power-Dependence Relations," *American Sociological Review* 27 (1962), pp. 31–41; and A. M. Pettigrew, *The Politics of Organizational Decision-Making* (London: Tavistock, 1973).

4. R. Gulati and M. Sytch, "Dependence Asymmetry and Joint Dependence in Interorganizational Relationships: Effects of Embeddedness on a Manufacturer's Performance in Procurement Relationships," *Administrative Science Quarterly* 52, no. 1 (2007), pp. 32–69.

5. French and Raven, "The Bases of Social Power"; P. Podsakoff and C. Schreisheim, "Field Studies of French and Raven's Bases of Power: Critique, Analysis, and Suggestions for Future Research," *Psychological Bulletin* 97 (1985), pp. 387–411; and P. P. Carson and K. D. Carson, "Social Power Bases: A Meta-Analytic Examination of Interrelationships and Outcomes," *Journal of Applied Social Psychology* 23 (1993), pp. 1150–69.

6. C. Barnard, *The Function of the Executive* (Cambridge, MA: Harvard University Press, 1938); and C. Hardy and S. R. Clegg, "Some Dare Call It Power," in *Handbook of Organization Studies,* ed. S. R. Clegg, C. Hardy, and W. R. Nord (London: Sage, 1996), pp. 622–41.

7. A. I. Shahin and P. L. Wright, "Leadership in the Context of Culture: An Egyptian Perspective," *Leadership & Organization Development Journal* 25, no. 5/6 (2004), pp. 499–511; and Y. J. Huo et al., "Leadership and the Management of Conflicts in Diverse Groups: Why Acknowledging Versus Neglecting Subgroup Identity Matters," *European Journal of Social Psychology* 35, no. 2 (2005), pp. 237–54.

8. L. S. Sya, "Flying to Greater Heights," *New Sunday Times (Kuala Lumpur),* July 31, 2005, p. 14.

9. J. M. Peiro and J. L. Melia, "Formal and Informal Interpersonal Power in Organisations: Testing a Bifactorial Model of Power in Role-Sets," *Applied Psychology* 52, no. 1 (2003), pp. 14–35.

10. P. F. Drucker, "The New Workforce," *The Economist,* November 3, 2001, pp. 8–12.

11. K. Miyahara, "Charisma: From Weber to Contemporary Sociology," *Sociological Inquiry* 53, no. 4 (Fall 1983), pp. 368–88; J. D. Kudisch and M. L. Poteet, "Expert Power, Referent Power, and Charisma: Toward the Resolution of a Theoretical Debate," *Journal of Business & Psychology* 10 (Winter 1995), pp. 177–95; and D. Ladkin, "The Enchantment of the Charismatic Leader: Charisma Reconsidered as Aesthetic Encounter," Leadership 2, no. 2 (May 2006), pp. 165–79.

12. G. Yukl and C. M. Falbe, "Importance of Different Power Sources in Downward and Lateral Relations," *Journal of Applied Psychology* 76 (1991), pp. 416–23; and B. H. Raven, "Kurt Lewin Address: Influence, Power, Religion, and the Mechanisms of Social Control," *Journal of Social Issues* 55 (Spring 1999), pp. 161–86.

13. P. L. Dawes, D. Y. Lee, and G. R. Dowling, "Information Control and Influence in Emergent Buying Centers," *Journal of Marketing* 62, no. 3 (July 1998), pp. 55–68; D. Willer, "Power-at-a-Distance," *Social Forces* 81, no. 4 (2003), pp. 1295–1334; and D. J. Brass et al., "Taking Stock of Networks and Organizations: A Multilevel Perspective," *Academy of Management Journal* 47, no. 6 (December 2004), pp. 795–817.

14. C. R. Hinings et al., "Structural Conditions of Intraorganizational Power," *Administrative Science Quarterly* 19 (1974), pp. 22–44. Also see C. S. Saunders, "The Strategic Contingency Theory of Power: Multiple Perspectives," *The Journal of Management Studies* 27 (1990), pp. 1–21.

15. S. Elliott, "Hunting for the Next Cool in Advertising," *The New York Times,* December 1, 2003, p. C19; S. Delaney, "Predicting the Birth of the Cool," *The Independent (London),* September 5, 2005, p. 15; and A. McMains, "Trend-Spotting Division Adds to Lowe's Evolution," *Adweek,* April 11, 2005, p. 11.

16. D. J. Hickson et al., "A Strategic Contingencies' Theory of Intraorganizational Power," *Administrative Science Quarterly* 16 (1971), pp. 216–27; Hinings et al., "Structural Conditions of Intraorganizational Power"; and R. M. Kanter, "Power Failure in Management Circuits," *Harvard Business Review* (July–August 1979), pp. 65–75.

17. Hickson et al., "A Strategic Contingencies' Theory of Intraorganizational Power"; J. D. Hackman, "Power and Centrality in the Allocation of Resources in Colleges and Universities," *Administrative Science Quarterly* 30 (1985), pp. 61–77; and D. J. Brass and M. E. Burkhardt, "Potential Power and Power Use: An Investigation of Structure and Behavior," *Academy of Management Journal* 36 (1993), pp. 441–70.

18. S. D. Harrington and B. Ivry, "For Commuters, a Day to Adapt," *The Record (Bergen, NJ),* December 21, 2005, p. A1; and S. McCarthy, "Transit Strike Cripples New York," *Globe & Mail (Toronto),* December 21, 2005, p. A17.

19. Kanter, "Power Failure in Management Circuits"; B. E. Ashforth, "The Experience of Powerlessness in Organizations," *Organizational Behavior and Human Decision Processes* 43 (1989), pp. 207–42; and L. Holden, "European Managers: HRM and an Evolving Role," *European Business Review* 12 (2000), pp. 251–60.

20. D. Hambrick, C. and E. Abrahamson, "Assessing Managerial Discretion across Industries: A Multimethod Approach," *Academy of Management Journal* 38, no. 5 (1995), pp. 1427–41; and M. A. Carpenter and B. R. Golden, "Perceived Managerial Discretion: A Study of Cause and Effect," *Strategic Management Journal* 18, no. 3 (1997), pp. 187–206.

21. R. Madell, "Ground Floor," *Pharmaceutical Executive (Women in Pharma Supplement),* June 2000, pp. 24–31.

22. B. R. Ragins and J. L. Cotton, "Mentor Functions and Outcomes: A Comparison of Men and Women in Formal and Informal Mentoring Relationships," *Journal of Applied Psychology* 84, no. 4 (1999), pp. 529–50; T. D. Allen et al., "Career Benefits Associated with Mentoring for Protégés: A Meta-Analysis," *Journal of Applied Psychology* 89, no. 1 (2004), pp. 127–36; and S. Tonidandel, D. R. Avery, and M. G. Phillips, "Maximizing Returns on Mentoring: Factors Affecting Subsequent Protègè Performance," *Journal of Organizational Behavior* 28, no. 1 (2007), pp. 89–110.

23. D. Krackhardt and J. R. Hanson, "Informal Networks: The Company Behind the Chart," *Harvard Business Review* 71 (July–August 1993), pp. 104–111; and P. S. Adler and S. W. Kwon, "Social Capital: Prospects for a New Concept," *Academy of Management Review* 27, no. 1 (2002), pp. 17–40.

24. A. Mehra, M. Kilduff, and D. J. Brass, "The Social Networks of High and Low Self-Monitors: Implications for Workplace Performance," *Administrative Science Quarterly* 46 (March 2001), pp. 121–46.

25. D. Keltner, D. H. Gruenfeld, and C. Anderson, "Power, Approach, and Inhibition," *Psychological Review* 110, no. 2 (2003), pp. 265–84; B. Simpson and C. Borch, "Does Power Affect Perception in Social Networks? Two Arguments and an Experimental Test," *Social Psychology Quarterly* 68, no. 3 (2005), pp. 278–87; and Galinsky et al., "Power and Perspectives Not Taken."

26. K. Atuahene-Gima and H. Li, "Marketing's Influence Tactics in New Product Development: A Study of High Technology Firms in China," *Journal of Product Innovation Management* 17 (2000), pp. 451–70; and A. Somech and A. Drach-Zahavy, "Relative Power and Influence Strategy: The Effects of Agent/Target Organizational Power on Superiors' Choices of Influence Strategies," *Journal of Organizational Behavior* 23 (2002), pp. 167–79.

27. D. Kipnis, S. M. Schmidt, and I. Wilkinson, "Intraorganizational Influence Tactics: Explorations in Getting One's Way," *Journal of Applied Psychology* 65 (1980), pp. 440–52; A. Rao and K. Hashimoto, "Universal and Culturally Specific Aspects of Managerial Influence: A Study of Japanese Managers," *Leadership Quarterly* 8 (1997), pp. 295–312; and L. A. McFarland, A. M. Ryan, and S. D. Kriska, "Field Study Investigation of Applicant Use of Influence Tactics in a Selection Interview," *Journal of Psychology* 136 (July 2002), pp. 383–98.

28. R. B. Cialdini and N. J. Goldstein, "Social Influence: Compliance and Conformity," *Annual Review of Psychology* 55 (2004), pp. 591–621.

29. Rao and Hashimoto, "Universal and Culturally Specific Aspects of Managerial Influence." Silent authority as an influence tactic in non-Western cultures is also discussed in S. F. Pasa, "Leadership Influence in a High Power Distance and Collectivist Culture," *Leadership & Organization Development Journal* 21 (2000), pp. 414–26.

30. "Be Part of the Team If You Want to Catch the Eye," *Birmingham Post (UK)*, August 31, 2000, p. 14; and S. Maitlis, "Taking It from the Top: How CEOs Influence (and Fail to Influence) Their Boards," *Organization Studies* 25, no. 8 (2004), pp. 1275–311.

31. A. T. Cobb, "Toward the Study of Organizational Coalitions: Participant Concerns and Activities in a Simulated Organizational Setting," *Human Relations* 44 (1991), pp. 1057–79; E. A. Mannix, "Organizations as Resource Dilemmas: The Effects of Power Balance on Coalition Formation in Small Groups," *Organizational Behavior and Human Decision Processes* 55 (1993), pp. 1–22; and D. J. Terry, M. A. Hogg, and K. M. White, "The Theory of Planned Behavior: Self-Identity, Social Identity and Group Norms," *British Journal of Social Psychology* 38 (September 1999), pp. 225–44.

32. D. Strutton and L. E. Pelton, "Effects of Ingratiation on Lateral Relationship Quality within Sales Team Settings," *Journal of Business Research* 43 (1998), pp. 1–12; and R. Vonk, "Self-Serving Interpretations of Flattery: Why Ingratiation Works," *Journal of Personality and Social Psychology* 82 (2002), pp. 515–26.

33. C. A. Higgins, T. A. Judge, and G. R. Ferris, "Influence Tactics and Work Outcomes: A Meta-Analysis," *Journal of Organizational Behavior* 24 (2003), pp. 90–106.

34. D. Strutton, L. E. Pelton, and J. F. Tanner, "Shall We Gather in the Garden: The Effect of Ingratiatory Behaviors on Buyer Trust in Salespeople," *Industrial Marketing Management* 25 (1996), pp. 151–62; and J. O'Neil, "An Investigation of the Sources of Influence of Corporate Public Relations Practitioners," *Public Relations Review* 29 (June 2003), pp. 159–69.

35. M. C. Bolino and W. H. Tunley, "More Than One Way to Make an Impression: Exploring Profiles of Impression Management," *Journal of Management* 29 (2003), pp. 141–60.

36. A. P. J. Ellis et al., "The Use of Impression Management Tactics in Structured Interviews: A Function of Question Type?" *Journal of Applied Psychology* 87 (December 2002), pp. 1200–8; C. A. Higgins and T. A. Judge, "The Effect of Applicant Influence Tactics on Recruiter Perceptions of Fit and Hiring Recommendations: A Field Study," *Journal of Applied Psychology* 89, no. 4 (2004), pp. 622–32; and H. H. Peeters and F. F. Lievens, "Verbal and Nonverbal Impression Management Tactics in Behavior Description and Situational Interviews," *International Journal of Selection and Assessment* 14, no. 3 (September 2006), pp. 206–22.

37. S. L. McShane, "Applicant Misrepresentations in Résumés and Interviews in Canada," *Labor Law Journal* (January 1994), pp. 15–24; S. Romero and M. Richtel, "Second Chance," *The New York Times,* March 5, 2001, p. C1; and P. Sabatini, "Fibs on Résumés Commonplace," *Pittsburgh Post–Gazette,* February 24, 2006.

38. A. P. Brief, *Attitudes in and around Organizations* (Thousand Oaks, CA: Sage, 1998), pp. 69–84; and D. J. O'Keefe, *Persuasion: Theory and Research* (Thousand Oaks, CA: Sage Publications, 2002).

39. S. Gilmor, "Ahead of the Curve," *Infoworld,* January 13, 2003, p. 58; and M. Hiltzik, "Apple CEO's Visions Don't Guarantee Sustained Gains," *Los Angeles Times,* April 14, 2003, p. C1. The origin of "reality distortion field" is described at www.folklore.org.

40. These and other features of message content in persuasion are detailed in R. Petty and J. Cacioppo, *Attitudes and*

Persuasion: Classic and Contemporary Approaches (Dubuque, IA: W. C. Brown, 1981); M. Pfau, E. A. Szabo, and J. Anderson, "The Role and Impact of Affect in the Process of Resistance to Persuasion," *Human Communication Research* 27 (April 2001), pp. 216–52; O'Keefe, *Persuasion: Theory and Research,* Chap. 9; R. Buck et al., "Emotion and Reason in Persuasion: Applying the Ari Model and the Casc Scale," *Journal of Business Research* 57, no. 6 (2004), pp. 647–56; and W. D. Crano and R. Prislin, "Attitudes and Persuasion," *Annual Review of Psychology* 57 (2006), pp. 345–74.

41. N. Rhodes and W. Wood, "Self-Esteem and Intelligence Affect Influenceability: The Mediating Role of Message Reception," *Psychological Bulletin* 111, no. 1 (1992), pp. 156–71.

42. A. W. Gouldner, "The Norm of Reciprocity: A Preliminary Statement," *American Sociological Review* 25 (1960), pp. 161–78.

43. Y. Fan, "Questioning Guanxi: Definition, Classification, and Implications," *International Business Review* 11 (2002), pp. 543–61; D. Tan and R. S. Snell, "The Third Eye: Exploring Guanxi and Relational Morality in the Workplace," *Journal of Business Ethics* 41 (December 2002), pp. 361–84; and W. R. Vanhonacker, "When Good Guanxi Turns Bad," *Harvard Business Review* 82, no. 4 (April 2004), pp. 18–19.

44. C. M. Falbe and G. Yukl, "Consequences for Managers of Using Single Influence Tactics and Combinations of Tactics," *Academy of Management Journal* 35 (1992), pp. 638–52.

45. R. C. Ringer and R. W. Boss, "Hospital Professionals' Use of Upward Influence Tactics," *Journal of Managerial Issues* 12 (2000), pp. 92–108.

46. G. Blickle, "Do Work Values Predict the Use of Intraorganizational Influence Strategies?" *Journal Of Applied Social Psychology* 30, no. 1 (January 2000), pp. 196–205; P. P. Fu et al., "The Impact of Societal Cultural Values and Individual Social Beliefs on the Perceived Effectiveness of Managerial Influence Strategies: A Meso Approach," *Journal of International Business Studies* 35, no. 4 (July 2004), pp. 284–305.

47. This definition of organizational politics has become the dominant perspective over the past 15 years. See G. R. Ferris and K. M. Kacmar, "Perceptions of Organizational Politics," *Journal of Management* 18 (1992), pp. 93–116; R. Cropanzano et al., "The Relationship of Organizational Politics and Support to Work Behaviors, Attitudes, and Stress," *Journal of Organizational Behavior* 18 (1997), pp. 159–80; and E. Vigoda and A. Cohen, "Influence Tactics and Perceptions of Organizational Politics: A Longitudinal Study," *Journal of Business Research* 55 (2002), pp. 311–24. However, organizational politics was previously viewed as influence tactics outside the formal role that could be either selfish or altruistic. This older definition is less common today, possibly because it is incongruent with popular views of politics and because it overlaps too much with the concept of influence. For the older perspective of organizational politics, see J. Pfeffer, *Power in Organizations* (Boston: Pitman, 1981); and Mintzberg, *Power in and around Organizations.*

48. K. M. Kacmar and R. A. Baron, "Organizational Politics: The State of the Field, Links to Related Processes, and an Agenda for Future Research," in *Research in Personnel and Human Resources Management,* ed. G. R. Ferris (Greenwich, CT: JAI Press, 1999), 1–39; L. A. Witt, T. F. Hilton, and W. A. Hochwarter, "Addressing Politics in Matrix Teams," *Group & Organization Management* 26 (June 2001), pp. 230–47; and E. Vigoda, "Stress-Related Aftermaths to Workplace Politics: The Relationships among Politics, Job Distress, and Aggressive Behavior in Organizations," *Journal of Organizational Behavior* 23 (2002), pp. 571–91.

49. C. Hardy, *Strategies for Retrenchment and Turnaround: The Politics of Survival* (Berlin: Walter de Gruyter, 1990), Chap. 14; and M. C. Andrews and K. M. Kacmar, "Discriminating among Organizational Politics, Justice, and Support," *Journal of Organizational Behavior* 22 (2001), pp. 347–66.

50. S. Blazejewski and W. Dorow, "Managing Organizational Politics for Radical Change: The Case of Beiersdorf-Lechia S. A., Poznan," *Journal of World Business* 38 (August 2003), pp. 204–23.

51. L. W. Porter, R. W. Allen, and H. L. Angle, "The Politics of Upward Influence in Organizations," *Research in Organizational Behavior* 3 (1981), pp. 120–22; and R. J. House, "Power and Personality in Complex Organizations," *Research in Organizational Behavior* 10 (1988), pp. 305–57.

52. R. Christie and F. Geis, *Studies in Machiavellianism* (New York: Academic Press, 1970); S. M. Farmer et al., "Putting Upward Influence Strategies in Context," *Journal of Organizational Behavior* 18 (1997), pp. 17–42; and K. S. Sauleya and A. G. Bedeian, "Equity Sensitivity: Construction of a Measure and Examination of Its Psychometric Properties," *Journal of Management* 26 (September 2000), pp. 885–910.

53. G. R. Ferris et al., "Perceptions of Organizational Politics: Prediction, Stress-Related Implications, and Outcomes," *Human Relations* 49 (1996), pp. 233–63.

chapter 10

1. A. Grove, "How to Make Confrontation Work for You," in *The Book of Management Wisdom*, ed. P. Krass (New York: John Wiley & Sons, 2000), 83–89; B. Schlender, "Inside Andy Grove's Latest Crusade," *Fortune*, August 23, 2004, p. 68; and J. Detar, "Andy Grove, Intel's Inside Man," *Investor's Business Daily*, July 24, 2007.

2. D. Tjosvold, *Working Together to Get Things Done* (Lexington, MA: Lexington, 1986), 114–15; J. A. Wall and R. R. Callister, "Conflict and Its Management," *Journal of Management* 21 (1995), pp. 515–58; M. A. Rahim, "Toward a Theory of Managing Organizational Conflict," *International Journal of Conflict Management* 13, no. 3 (2002), pp. 206–35; and D. Tjosvold, "Defining Conflict and Making Choices About Its Management," *International Journal of Conflict Management* 17, no. 2 (2006), pp. 87–95.

3. For example, see L. Urwick, *The Elements of Administration*, 2nd ed. (London: Pitman, 1947); C. Argyris, "The Individual and Organization: Some Problems of Mutual Adjustment," *Administrative Science Quarterly* 2, no. 1 (1957), pp. 1–24; K. E. Boulding, "Organization and Conflict," *Conflict Resolution* 1, no. 2 (June 1957), pp. 122–34; and R. R. Blake, H. A.

Shepard, and J. S. Mouton, *Managing Intergroup Conflict in Industry* (Houston: Gulf Publishing, 1964).

4. C. K. W. de Dreu and L. R. Weingart, "A Contingency Theory of Task Conflict and Performance in Groups and Organizational Teams," in *International Handbook of Organizational Teamwork and Cooperative Working*, ed. M. A. West, D. Tjosvold, and K. G. Smith (Chicester, UK: John Wiley & Sons, 2003), 151–66; and K. A. Jehn and C. Bendersky, "Intragroup Conflict in Organizations: A Contingency Perspective on the Conflict-Outcome Relationship," *Research In Organizational Behavior* 25 (2003), pp. 187–242.

5. Rahim, "Toward a Theory of Managing Organizational Conflict"; and M. Duarte and G. Davies, "Testing the Conflict-Performance Assumption in Business-to-Business Relationships," *Industrial Marketing Management* 32 (2003), pp. 91–99. For early writing on the optimal level of conflict, see L. A. Coser, *The Functions of Social Conflict* (New York: Free Press, 1956); J. A. Litterer, "Conflict in Organization: A Re-Examination," *Academy of Management Journal* 9 (1966), pp. 178–86; H. Assael, "Constructive Role of Interorganizational Conflict," *Administrative Science Quarterly* 14, no. 4 (1969), pp. 573–82.

6. K. M. Eisenhardt, J. L. Kahwajy, and L. J. Bourgeois III, "How Management Teams Can Have a Good Fight," *Harvard Business Review* (July–August 1997), pp. 77–85; K. M. Eisenhardt, J. L. Kahwajy, and L. J. Bourgeois III, "Conflict and Strategic Choice: How Top Management Teams Disagree," *California Management Review* 39 (Winter 1997), pp. 42–62; T. Greitemeyer et al., "Information Sampling and Group Decision Making: The Effects of an Advocacy Decision Procedure and Task Experience," *Journal of Experimental Psychology-Applied* 12, no. 1 (Mar 2006), pp. 31–42; and U. Klocke, "How to Improve Decision Making in Small Groups: Effects of Dissent and Training Interventions," *Small Group Research* 38, no. 3 (June 2007), pp. 437–68.

7. H. Guetzkow and J. Gyr, "An Analysis of Conflict in Decision-Making Groups," *Human Relations* 7, no. 3 (Aug. 1954), pp. 367–82; and L. H. Pelled, K. M. Eisenhardt, and K. R. Xin, "Exploring the Black Box: An Analysis of Work Group Diversity, Conflict, and Performance," *Administrative Science Quarterly* 44 (March 1999), pp. 1–28; Jehn and Bendersky, "Intragroup Conflict in Organizations." The notion of two types of conflict dates back to the 1950s (see first reference above), but became the dominant perspective in the 1990s. We have avoided using the cognitive and affective conflict labels because each type of conflict includes both cognitive and emotional elements.

8. C. K. W. de Dreu, "When Too Little or Too Much Hurts: Evidence for a Curvilinear Relationship between Task Conflict and Innovation in Teams," *Journal of Management* 32, no. 1 (Feb. 2006), pp. 83–107.

9. C. K. W. de Dreu and L. R. Weingart, "Task Versus Relationship Conflict, Team Performance, and Team Member Satisfaction: A Meta-Analysis," *Journal of Applied Psychology* 88 (August 2003), pp. 587–604; and A. C. Mooney, P. J. Holahan, and A. C. Amason, "Don't Take It Personally: Exploring Cognitive Conflict as a Mediator of Affective Conflict," *Journal of Management Studies* 44, no. 5 (2007), pp. 733–58.

10. J. Yang and K. W. Mossholder, "Decoupling Task and Relationship Conflict: The Role of Intergroup Emotional Processing," *Journal of Organizational Behavior* 25 (2004), pp. 589–605.

11. A. C. Amason and H. J. Sapienza, "The Effects of Top Management Team Size and Interaction Norms on Cognitive and Affective Conflict," *Journal of Management* 23, no. 4 (1997), pp. 495–516.

12. L. Pondy, "Organizational Conflict: Concepts and Models," *Administrative Science Quarterly* 2 (1967), pp. 296–320; and K. W. Thomas, "Conflict and Negotiation Processes in Organizations," in *Handbook of Industrial and Organizational Psychology*, ed. M. D. Dunnette and L. M. Hough, 2nd ed. (Palo Alto, CA: Consulting Psychologists Press, 1992), 651–718.

13. H. Barki and J. Hartwick, "Conceptualizing the Construct of Interpersonal Conflict," *International Journal of Conflict Management* 15, no. 3 (2004), pp. 216–44.

14. M. A. Von Glinow, D. L. Shapiro, and J. M. Brett, "Can We Talk, and Should We? Managing Emotional Conflict in Multicultural Teams," *Academy of Management Review* 29, no. 4 (2004), pp. 578–92.

15. G. E. Martin and T. J. Bergman, "The Dynamics of Behavioral Response to Conflict in the Workplace," *Journal of Occupational & Organizational Psychology* 69 (December 1996), pp. 377–87; and J. M. Brett, D. L. Shapiro, and A. L. Lytle, "Breaking the Bonds of Reciprocity in Negotiations," *Academy of Management Journal* 41 (August 1998), pp. 410–24.

16. R. E. Walton and J. M. Dutton, "The Management of Conflict: A Model and Review," *Administrative Science Quarterly* 14 (1969), pp. 73–84; and S. M. Schmidt and T. A. Kochan, "Conflict: Toward Conceptual Clarity," *Administrative Science Quarterly* 17, no. 3 (Sept. 1972), pp. 359–70.

17. B. Dudley, "Bring Back the Dazzle," *Seattle Times*, September 23, 2005; J. Greene, "Troubling Exits at Microsoft," *BusinessWeek*, September 26, 2005, p. 98; A. Linn, "Microsoft Reorganizes to Compete Better with Google, Yahoo," *Associated Press Newswires*, September 21, 2005; V. Murphy, "Microsoft's Midlife Crisis," *Forbes*, October 3, 2005, p. 88; L. Vaas, "Microsoft Expands Bureaucracy, Crowns MSN King," *eWeek*, September 20, 2005; and J. L. Yang, "Microsoft's New Brain," *Fortune*, May 1, 2006, p. 56.

18. R. Zemke and B. Filipczak, *Generations at Work: Managing the Clash of Veterans, Boomers, Xers, and Nexters in Your Workplace* (New York: Amacom, 1999); and P. Harris, "Boomers vs. Echo Boomer: The Work War," *T+D* (May 2005), pp. 44–49.

19. P. Hinds and D. E. Bailey, "Out of Sight, Out of Sync: Understanding Conflict in Distributed Teams," *Organization Science* 14, no. 6 (2003), pp. 615–32; and P. Hinds and M. Mortensen, "Understanding Conflict in Geographically Distributed Teams: The Moderating Effects of Shared Identity, Shared Context, and Spontaneous Communication," *Organization Science* 16, no. 3 (May–June 2005), pp. 290–307.

20. R. Wageman and G. Baker, "Incentives and Cooperation: The Joint Effects of Task and Reward Interdependence on Group Performance," *Journal of Organizational Behavior* 18, no. 2 (1997), pp. 139–58; and G. S. van der Vegt, B. J. M. Emans, and E. van der Vliert, "Patterns of Interdependence in Work Teams: A Two-Level Investigation of the Relations with Job and Team Satisfaction," *Personnel Psychology* 54, no. 1 (2001), pp. 51–69.

21. P. C. Earley and G. B. Northcraft, "Goal Setting, Resource Interdependence, and Conflict Management," in *Managing Conflict: An Interdisciplinary Approach*, ed. M. A. Rahim (New York: Praeger, 1989), pp. 161–70; and K. Jelin, "A Multimethod Examination of the Benefits and Detriments of Intragroup Conflict," *Administrative Science Quarterly* 40 (1995), pp. 245–82.

22. A. Risberg, "Employee Experiences of Acquisition Processes," *Journal of World Business* 36 (March 2001), pp. 58–84.

23. M. Hewstone, M. Rubin, and H. Willis, "Intergroup Bias," *Annual Review of Psychology* 53 (2002), pp. 575–604; and J. Jetten, R. Spears, and T. Postmes, "Intergroup Distinctiveness and Differentiation: A Meta-Analytic Integration," *Journal of Personality and Social Psychology* 86, no. 6 (2004), pp. 862–79.

24. Jehn and Bendersky, "Intragroup Conflict in Organizations."

25. M. P. Follett, "Constructive Conflict," in *Dynamic Administration: The Collected Papers of Mary Parker Follett*, ed. H. C. Metcalf and L. Urwick (New York: Harper and Brothers, 1942), pp. 30–37; Blake, Shepard, and Mouton, *Managing Intergroup Conflict in Industry*; T. Ruble and K. Thomas, "Support for a Two-Dimensional Model of Conflict Behavior," *Organizaiotnal Behavior and Human Performance* 16 (1976), pp. 143–55; C. K. W. de Dreu et al., "A Theory-Based Measure of Conflict Management Strategies in the Workplace," *Journal of Organizational Behavior* 22 (2001), pp. 645–68; and Rahim, "Toward a Theory of Managing Organizational Conflict."

26. Jelin, "A Multimethod Examination of the Benefits and Detriments of Intragroup Conflict."

27. D. A. Cai and E. L. Fink, "Conflict Style Differences between Individualists and Collectivists," *Communication Monographs* 69 (March 2002), pp. 67–87; C. H. Tinsley and E. Weldon, "Responses to a Normative Conflict among American and Chinese Managers," *International Journal of Conflict Management* 3, no. 2 (2003), pp. 183–94; and F. P. Brew and D. R. Cairns, "Styles of Managing Interpersonal Workplace Conflict in Relation to Status and Face Concern: A Study with Anglos and Chinese," *International Journal of Conflict Management* 15, no. 1 (2004), pp. 27–57.

28. N. Brewer, P. Mitchell, and N. Weber, "Gender Role, Organizational Status, and Conflict Management Styles," *International Journal of Conflict Management* 13 (2002), pp. 78–95; and N. B. Florea et al., "Negotiating from Mars to Venus: Gender in Simulated International Negotiations," *Simulation & Gaming* 34 (June 2003), pp. 226–48.

29. G. A. Callanan, C. D. Benzing, and D. F. Perri, "Choice of Conflict-Handling Strategy: A Matter of Context," *Journal of Psychology* 140, no. 3 (2006), pp. 269–88.

30. D. W. Johnson et al., "Effects of Cooperative, Competitive, and Individualistic Goal Structures on Achievement: A Meta-Analysis," *Psychological Bulletin* 89 (1981), pp. 47–62; and Rahim, "Toward a Theory of Managing Organizational Conflict."

31. R. A. Friedman et al., "What Goes around Comes Around: The Impact of Personal Conflict Style on Work Conflict and Stress," *International Journal of Conflict Management* 11, no. 1 (2000), pp. 32–55; X. M. Song, J. Xile, and B. Dyer, "Antecedents and Consequences of Marketing Managers' Conflict-Handling Behaviors," *Journal of Marketing* 64 (January 2000), pp. 50–66; M. Song, B. Dyer, and R. J. Thieme, "Conflict Management and Innovation Performance: An Integrated Contingency Perspective," *Academy of Marketing Science* 34, no. 3 (2006), pp. 341–56; and L. A. DeChurch, K. L. Hamilton, and C. Haas, "Effects of Conflict Management Strategies on Perceptions of Intragroup Conflict," *Group Dynamics* 11, no. 1 (2007), pp. 66–78.

32. C. K. W. de Dreu and A. E. M. Van Vianen, "Managing Relationship Conflict and the Effectiveness of Organizational Teams," *Journal of Organizational Behavior* 22 (2001), pp. 309–28; and R. J. Lewicki et al., *Negotiation*, 4th ed. (New York: McGraw-Hill/Irwin, 2003), pp. 35–36.

33. Based on information in J. L. Dreachslin and D. Kiddy, "From Conflict to Consensus: Managing Competing Interest in Your Organization," *Healthcare Executive*, November/December 2006, 8–14.

34. K. Lewin, *Resolving Social Conflicts* (New York: Harper, 1948).

35. J. D. Hunger and L. W. Stern, "An Assessment of the Functionality of the Superordinate Goal in Reducing Conflict," *Academy of Management Journal* 19, no. 4 (1976), pp. 591–605; and M. Sherif, "Superordinate Goals in the Reduction of Intergroup Conflict," *The American Journal of Sociology* 63, no. 4 (1958), pp. 349–56.

36. M. Sherif, "Superordinate Goals in the Reduction of Intergroup Conflict"; Eisenhardt, Kahwajy, and Bourgeois III, "How Management Teams Can Have a Good Fight"; and Song, Xile, and Dyer, "Antecedents and Consequences of Marketing Managers' Conflict-Handling Behaviors."

37. H. C. Triandis, "The Future of Workforce Diversity in International Organisations: A Commentary," *Applied Psychology: An International Journal* 52, no. 3 (2003), pp. 486–95.

38. E. Elron, B. Shamir, and E. Bem-Ari, "Why Don't They Fight Each Other? Cultural Diversity and Operational Unity in Multinational Forces," *Armed Forces & Society* 26 (October 1999), pp. 73–97; and "Teamwork Polishes This Diamond," *Philippine Daily Inquirer*, October 4, 2000, p. 10.

39. K. R. Lewis, "(Drum) Beatings Build Corporate Spirit," *Star Tribune (Minneapolis, MN)*, June 3, 2003, p. 3E; "Oh What a Feeling! " *Music Trades*, May 2004, pp. 94–95; and D. Cole, "Joining the Tom-Tom Club," *U.S. News & World Report*, March 22, 2004, p. D12.

40. T. F. Pettigrew, "Intergroup Contact Theory," *Annual Review of Psychology* 49 (1998), pp. 65–85; S. Brickson, "The Impact of Identity Orientation on Individual and Organizational Outcomes

in Demographically Diverse Settings," *Academy of Management Review* 25 (January 2000), pp. 82–101; and J. Dixon and K. Durrheim, "Contact and the Ecology of Racial Division: Some Varieties of Informal Segregation," *British Journal of Social Psychology* 42 (March 2003), pp. 1–23.

41. Triandis, "The Future of Workforce Diversity in International Organisations."

42. Von Glinow, Shapiro, and Brett, "Can We Talk, and Should We? "

43. E. Horwitt, "Knowledge, Knowledge, Who's Got the Knowledge," *Computerworld,* April 8, 1996, pp. 80, 81, 84.

44. L. L. Putnam, "Beyond Third-Party Role: Disputes and Managerial Intervention," *Employee Responsibilities and Rights Journal* 7 (1994), pp. 23–36; and A. R. Elangovan, "The Manager as the Third Party: Deciding How to Intervene in Employee Disputes," in *Negotiation: Readings, Exercises, and Cases,* ed. R. J. Lewicki, J. A. Litterer, and D. Saunders, 3rd ed. (New York: McGraw-Hill, 1999), pp. 458–69. For a somewhat different taxonomy of managerial conflict intervention, see P. G. Irving and J. P. Meyer, "A Multidimensional Scaling Analysis of Managerial Third-Party Conflict Intervention Strategies," *Canadian Journal of Behavioural Science* 29, no. 1 (January 1997), pp. 7–18.

45. B. H. Sheppard, "Managers as Inquisitors: Lessons from the Law," in *Bargaining inside Organizations*, ed. M. H. Bazerman and R. J. Lewicki (Beverly Hills, CA: Sage, 1983); and N. H. Kim, D. W. Sohn, and J. A. Wall, "Korean Leaders' (and Subordinates') Conflict Management," *International Journal of Conflict Management* 10, no. 2 (April 1999), pp. 130–53.

46. R. Karambayya and J. M. Brett, "Managers Handling Disputes: Third Party Roles and Perceptions of Fairness," *Academy of Management Journal* 32 (1989), pp. 687–704; and R. Cropanzano et al., "Disputant Reactions to Managerial Conflict Resolution Tactics," *Group & Organization Management* 24 (June 1999), pp. 124–53.

47. A. R. Elangovan, "Managerial Intervention in Organizational Disputes: Testing a Prescriptive Model of Strategy Selection," *International Journal of Conflict Management* 4 (1998), pp. 301–35; and P. S. Nugent, "Managing Conflict: Third-Party Interventions for Managers," *Academy of Management Executive* 16, no. 1 (February 2002), pp. 139–54.

48. J. P. Meyer, J. M. Gemmell, and P. G. Irving, "Evaluating the Management of Interpersonal Conflict in Organizations: A Factor-Analytic Study of Outcome Criteria," *Canadian Journal of Administrative Sciences* 14 (1997), pp. 1–13; and M. Hyde et al., "Workplace Conflict Resolution and the Health of Employees in the Swedish and Finnish Units of an Industrial Company," *Social Science & Medicine* 63, no. 8 (2006), pp. 2218–27.

chapter 11

1. N. Nilekani, "How Do I Develop Next Generation Leaders," *Economic Times (India),* November 25, 2005; and R. Stavros, "The Ultimate CEOs," *Public Utilities Fortnightly,* June 1, 2006, p. 40.

2. R. House, M. Javidan, and P. Dorfman, "Project Globe: An Introduction," *Applied Psychology: An International Review* 50 (2001), pp. 489–505; and R. House et al., "Understanding Cultures and Implicit Leadership Theories across the Globe: An Introduction to Project Globe," *Journal of World Business* 37 (2002), pp. 3–10.

3. R. G. Isaac, W. J. Zerbe, and D. C. Pitt, "Leadership and Motivation: The Effective Application of Expectancy Theory," *Journal of Managerial Issues* 13 (Summer 2001), pp. 212–26; C. L. Pearce and J. A. Conger, eds., *Shared Leadership: Reframing the Hows and Whys of Leadership* (Thousand Oaks, CA: Sage, 2003); and J. S. Nielson, *The Myth of Leadership* (Palo Alto, CA: Davies-Black, 2004).

4. J. Raelin, "Preparing for Leaderful Practice," *T&D,* March 2004, p. 64.

5. Many of these perspectives are summarized in R. N. Kanungo, "Leadership in Organizations: Looking Ahead to the 21st Century," *Canadian Psychology* 39 (Spring 1998), pp. 71–82; and G. A. Yukl, *Leadership in Organizations,* 6th ed. (Upper Saddle River, NJ: Pearson Education, 2006).

6. R. M. Stogdill, *Handbook of Leadership* (New York: The Free Press, 1974), Chap. 5.

7. "Care Board Names Dr. Helene Gayle as New President/CEO," CARE news release, (Atlanta: December 2, 2005); M. Bixler, "Chief's Global View to Influence Goals," *Atlanta Journal-Constitution,* April 12, 2006, p. F1; and P. Bock, "In Every Way, Helene Gayle Cares in All Capital Letters," *Washington Post,* January 1, 2006, p. D01.

8. J. Intagliata, D. Ulrich, and N. Smallwood, "Leveraging Leadership Competencies to Produce Leadership Brand: Creating Distinctiveness by Focusing on Strategy and Results," *Human Resources Planning* 23, no. 4 (2000), pp. 12–23; J. A. Conger and D. A. Ready, "Rethinking Leadership Competencies," *Leader to Leader* (Spring 2004), pp. 41–47; and S. J. Zaccaro, C. Kemp, and P. Bader, "Leader Traits and Attributes," in *The Nature of Leadership,* ed. J. Antonakis, A. T. Cianciolo, and R. J. Sternberg (Thousand Oaks, CA: Sage, 2004), pp. 101–24.

9. This list is based on S. A. Kirkpatrick and E. A. Locke, "Leadership: Do Traits Matter?" *Academy of Management Executive* 5 (May 1991), pp. 48–60; R. M. Aditya, R. J. House, and S. Kerr, "Theory and Practice of Leadership: Into the New Millennium," in *Industrial and Organizational Psychology: Linking Theory with Practice,* ed. C. L. Cooper and E. A. Locke (Oxford, UK: Blackwell, 2000), pp. 130–165; D. Goleman, R. Boyatzis, and A. McKee, *Primal Leaders* (Boston: Harvard Business School Press, 2002); T. A. Judge et al., "Personality and Leadership: A Qualitative and Quantitative Review," *Journal Of Applied Psychology* 87, no. 4 (August 2002), pp. 765–80; T. A. Judge, A. E. Colbert, and R. Ilies, "Intelligence and Leadership: A Quantitative Review and Test of Theoretical Propositions," *Journal Of Applied Psychology* 89, no. 3 (June 2004), pp. 542–52; and Zaccaro, Kemp, and Bader, "Leader Traits and Attributes."

10. J. George, "Emotions and Leadership: The Role of Emotional Intelligence," *Human Relations* 53 (August 2000), pp. 1027–55; Goleman, Boyatzis, and McKee, *Primal Leaders;* R. G. Lord and R. J. Hall, "Identity, Deep Structure and the Development of Leadership Skill," *Leadership Quarterly* 16, no. 4 (August 2005), pp. 591–615; and C. Skinner and P. Spurgeon, "Valuing

Empathy and Emotional Intelligence in Health Leadership: A Study of Empathy, Leadership Behaviour and Outcome Effectiveness," *Health Services Management Research* 18, no. 1 (February 2005), pp. 1–12.

11. W. L. Gardner et al., "'Can You See the Real Me?' a Self-Based Model of Authentic Leader and Follower Development," *Leadership Quarterly* 16 (2005), pp. 343–72; and M. E. Palanski and F. J. Yammarino, "Integrity and Leadership: Clearing the Conceptual Confusion," *European Management Journal* 25, no. 3 (2007), pp. 171–84.

12. The large-scale studies are reported in C. Savoye, "Workers Say Honesty Is Best Company Policy," *Christian Science Monitor,* June 15, 2000, p. 3; J. M. Kouzes and B. Z. Posner, *The Leadership Challenge,* 3rd ed. (San Francisco: Jossey-Bass, 2002), Chap. 2; and J. Schettler, "Leadership in Corporate America," *Training & Development,* September 2002, pp. 66–73.

13. Watson Wyatt Worldwide, "Asia-Pacific Workers Satisfied with Jobs Despite Some Misgivings with Management and Pay," Watson Wyatt Worldwide news release, (Singapore: November 16, 2004); J. Cremer, "Asian Workers Give Low Marks to Leaders," *South China Morning Post (Hong Kong),* July 30, 2005, p. 8; D. Jones, "Optimism Puts Rose-Colored Tint in Glasses of Top Execs," *USA Today,* December 16, 2005, p. B1; and E. Pondel, "Friends & Bosses?" *Seattle Post-Intelligencer,* April 10, 2006, p. C1.

14. R. Charan, C. Burke, and L. Bossidy, *Execution: The Discipline of Getting Things Done* (New York: Crown Business, 2002); and D. Nilsen, B. Kowske, and A. Kshanika, "Managing Globally," *HRMagazine,* August 2005, pp. 111–15.

15. R. J. House and R. N. Aditya, "The Social Scientific Study of Leadership: Quo Vadis?" *Journal of Management* 23 (1997), pp. 409–73.

16. R. Jacobs, "Using Human Resource Functions to Enhance Emotional Intelligence," in *The Emotionally Intelligent Workplace,* ed. C. Cherniss and D. Goleman (San Francisco: Jossey-Bass, 2001), pp. 161–63; and Conger and Ready, "Rethinking Leadership Competencies."

17. R. G. Lord and D. J. Brown, *Leadership Processes and Self-Identity: A Follower-Centered Approach to Leadership* (Mahwah, NJ: Lawrence Erlbaum Associates, 2004); and R. Bolden and J. Gosling, "Leadership Competencies: Time to Change the Tune?" *Leadership* 2, no. 2 (May 2006), pp. 147–63.

18. P. G. Northouse, *Leadership: Theory and Practice,* 3rd ed. (Thousand Oaks, CA: Sage, 2004), Chap. 4; and Yukl, *Leadership in Organizations,* Chap. 3.

19. A. K. Korman, "Consideration, Initiating Structure, and Organizational Criteria—A Review," *Personnel Psychology* 19 (1966), pp. 349–62; E. A. Fleishman, "Twenty Years of Consideration and Structure," in *Current Developments in the Study of Leadership,* ed. E. A. Fleishman and J. C. Hunt (Carbondale, IL: Southern Illinois University Press, 1973), pp. 1–40; T. A. Judge, R. F. Piccolo, and R. Ilies, "The Forgotten Ones? The Validity of Consideration and Initiating Structure in Leadership Research," *Journal of Applied Psychology* 89, no. 1 (2004), pp. 36–51; and Yukl, *Leadership in Organizations,* pp. 62–75.

20. V. V. Baba, "Serendipity in Leadership: Initiating Structure and Consideration in the Classroom," *Human Relations* 42 (1989), pp. 509–25.

21. "Why Geotechnical Instruments Boss Draper Is One in a Million," *Birmingham Post (United Kingdom),* June 2, 2006, p. 26; and N. Whitten, "Best Boss Sets Examples to Staff," *Evening Chronicle (Newcastle, U.K.),* June 15, 2006, p. 24.

22. S. Kerr et al., "Towards a Contingency Theory of Leadership Based Upon the Consideration and Initiating Structure Literature," *Organizational Behavior and Human Performance* 12 (1974), pp. 62–82; and L. L. Larson, J. G. Hunt, and R. N. Osbom, "The Great Hi–Hi Leader Behavior Myth: A Lesson from Occam's Razor," *Academy of Management Journal* 19 (1976), pp. 628–41.

23. R. Tannenbaum and W. H. Schmidt, "How to Choose a Leadership Pattern," *Harvard Business Review,* May–June 1973, pp. 162–80.

24. For a thorough study of how expectancy theory of motivation relates to leadership, see R. G. Isaac, W. J. Zerbe, and D. C. Pitt, "Leadership and Motivation: The Effective Application of Expectancy Theory," *Journal of Managerial Issues* 13 (Summer 2001), pp. 212–26.

25. R. J. House, "A Path-Goal Theory of Leader Effectiveness," *Administrative Science Quarterly* 16 (1971), pp. 321–38; M. G. Evans, "Extensions of a Path-Goal Theory of Motivation," *Journal of Applied Psychology* 59 (1974), pp. 172–78; R. J. House and T. R. Mitchell, "Path-Goal Theory of Leadership," *Journal of Contemporary Business* (Autumn 1974), pp. 81–97; and M. G. Evans, "Path-Goal Theory of Leadership," in *Leadership,* ed. L. L. Neider and C. A. Schriesheim (Greenwich, CT: Information Age Publishing, 2002), pp. 115–38.

26. R. J. House, "Path-Goal Theory of Leadership: Lessons, Legacy, and a Reformulated Theory," *Leadership Quarterly* 7 (1996), pp. 323–52.

27. J. Indvik, "Path-Goal Theory of Leadership: A Meta-Analysis," *Academy of Management Proceedings* (1986), pp. 189–92; and J. C. Wofford and L. Z. Liska, "Path-Goal Theories of Leadership: A Meta-Analysis," *Journal of Management* 19 (1993), pp. 857–76.

28. J. D. Houghton and S. K. Yoho, "Toward a Contingency Model of Leadership and Psychological Empowerment: When Should Self-Leadership Be Encouraged?" *Journal of Leadership & Organizational Studies* 11, no. 4 (2005), pp. 65–83.

29. R. T. Keller, "A Test of the Path-Goal Theory of Leadership with Need for Clarity as a Moderator in Research and Development Organizations," *Journal of Applied Psychology* 74 (1989), pp. 208–12.

30. C. A. Schriesheim and L. L. Neider, "Path-Goal Leadership Theory: The Long and Winding Road," *Leadership Quarterly* 7 (1996), pp. 317–21.

31. This observation has also been made by C. A. Schriesheim, "Substitutes-for-Leadership Theory: Development and Basic Concepts," *Leadership Quarterly* 8 (1997), pp. 103–8.

32. D. F. Elloy and A. Randolph, "The Effect of Superleader Behavior on Autonomous Work Groups in a Government Operated Railway Service," *Public Personnel Management* 26

(Summer 1997), pp. 257–72; and C. C. Manz and H. Sims Jr., *The New SuperLeadership: Leading Others to Lead Themselves* (San Francisco: Berrett-Koehler, 2001).

33. M. L. Loughry, "Coworkers Are Watching: Performance Implications of Peer Monitoring," *Academy of Management Proceedings* (2002), pp. O1–O6.

34. C. C. Manz and C. Neck, *Mastering Self-Leadership,* 3rd ed. (Upper Saddle River, NJ: Prentice-Hall, 2004).

35. P. M. Podsakoff and S. B. MacKenzie, "Kerr and Jermier's Substitutes for Leadership Model: Background, Empirical Assessment, and Suggestions for Future Research," *Leadership Quarterly* 8 (1997), pp. 117–32; S. D. Dionne et al., "Neutralizing Substitutes for Leadership Theory: Leadership Effects and Common-Source Bias," *Journal Of Applied Psychology* 87, no. 3 (June 2002), pp. 454–64; J. R. Villa et al., "Problems with Detecting Moderators in Leadership Research Using Moderated Multiple Regression," *Leadership Quarterly* 14, no. 1 (February 2003), pp. 3–23; and S. D. Dionne et al., "Substitutes for Leadership, or Not," *The Leadership Quarterly* 16, no. 1 (2005), pp. 169–93.

36. J. M. Burns, *Leadership* (New York: Harper & Row, 1978); B. M. Bass, *Transformational Leadership: Industrial, Military, and Educational Impact* (Hillsdale, NJ: Erlbaum, 1998); S. B. Proctor-Thomson and K. W. Parry, "What the Best Leaders Look Like," in *Leadership in the Antipodes: Findings, Implications and a Leader Profile,* ed. K. W. Parry (Wellington, N. Z.: Institute of Policy Studies and Centre for the Study of Leadership, 2001), pp. 166–91; and B. J. Avolio and F. J. Yammarino, eds., *Transformational and Charismatic Leadership: The Road Ahead* (Greenwich, CT: JAI Press, 2002).

37. V. L. Goodwin, J. C. Wofford, and J. L. Whittington, "A Theoretical and Empirical Extension to the Transformational Leadership Construct," *Journal of Organizational Behavior* 22 (November 2001), pp. 759–74.

38. A. Zaleznik, "Managers and Leaders: Are They Different?" *Harvard Business Review* 55, no. 5 (1977), pp. 67–78; and W. Bennis and B. Nanus, *Leaders: The Strategies for Taking Charge* (New York: Harper & Row, 1985). For a recent discussion regarding managing versus leading, see G. Yukl and R. Lepsinger, "Why Integrating the Leading and Managing Roles Is Essential for Organizational Effectiveness," *Organizational Dynamics* 34, no. 4 (2005), pp. 361–75.

39. Both transformational and transactional leadership improve work unit performance. See B. M. Bass et al., "Predicting Unit Performance by Assessing Transformational and Transactional Leadership," *Journal of Applied Psychology* 88 (April 2003), pp. 207–18. This point is also argued in Yukl and Lepsinger, "Why Integrating the Leading and Managing Roles Is Essential for Organizational Effectiveness."

40. For discussion on the tendency to slide from transformational to transactional leadership, see W. Bennis, *An Invented Life: Reflections on Leadership and Change* (Reading, MA: Addison-Wesley, 1993).

41. R. J. House, "A 1976 Theory of Charismatic Leadership," in *Leadership: The Cutting Edge,* ed. J. G. Hunt and L. L. Larson (Carbondale, IL: Southern Illinois University Press, 1977),

189–207; and J. A. Conger, "Charismatic and Transformational Leadership in Organizations: An Insider's Perspective on These Developing Streams of Research," *Leadership Quarterly* 10 (Summer 1999), pp. 145–79.

42. J. E. Barbuto, "Taking the Charisma out of Transformational Leadership," *Journal of Social Behavior & Personality* 12 (September 1997), pp. 689–97; Y. A. Nur, "Charisma and Managerial Leadership: The Gift That Never Was," *Business Horizons* 41 (July 1998), pp. 19–26; and M. D. Mumford and J. R. Van Doorn, "The Leadership of Pragmatism—Reconsidering Franklin in the Age of Charisma," *Leadership Quarterly* 12, no. 3 (Fall 2001), pp. 279–309.

43. R. E. De Vries, R. A. Roe, and T. C. B. Taillieu, "On Charisma and Need for Leadership," *European Journal of Work and Organizational Psychology* 8 (1999), pp. 109–33; and R. Khurana, *Searching for a Corporate Savior: The Irrational Quest for Charismatic CEOs* (Princeton, NJ: Princeton University Press, 2002).

44. K. Brooker and J. Schlosser, "The Un-CEO," *Fortune,* September 16, 2002, pp. 88–93; B. Nussbaum, "The Power of Design," *BusinessWeek,* May 17, 2004, p. 86; N. Buckley, "The Calm Reinventor," *Financial Times (London),* January 29, 2005, p. 11; S. Ellison, "Women's Touch Guides P&G Chief's Firm Hand in Company Turnaround," *The Wall Street Journal Europe,* June 1, 2005, p. A1; S. Hill Jr., "P&G's Turnaround Proves Listening to Customer Pays," *Manufacturing Business Technology,* July 2005, p. 64; and J. Tylee, "Procter's Creative Gamble," *Campaign,* March 18, 2005, pp. 24–26.

45. Bennis and Nanus, *Leaders,* pp. 27–33, 89; I. M. Levin, "Vision Revisited," *Journal of Applied Behavioral Science* 36 (March 2000), pp. 91–107; R. E. Quinn, *Building the Bridge as You Walk on It: A Guide for Leading Change* (San Francisco: Jossey-Bass, 2004), Chap. 11; and J. M. Strange and M. D. Mumford, "The Origins of Vision: Effects of Reflection, Models, and Analysis," *Leadership Quarterly* 16, no. 1 (2005), pp. 121–48.

46. J. R. Baum, E. A. Locke, and S. A. Kirkpatrick, "A Longitudinal Study of the Relation of Vision and Vision Communication to Venture Growth in Entrepreneurial Firms," *Journal of Applied Psychology* 83 (1998), pp. 43–54; and S. L. Hoe and S. L. McShane, "Leadership Antecedents of Informal Knowledge Acquisition and Dissemination," *International Journal of Organisational Behaviour* 5 (2002), pp. 282–91.

47. J. A. Conger, "Inspiring Others: The Language of Leadership," *Academy of Management Executive* 5 (February 1991), pp. 31–45; G. T. Fairhurst and R. A. Sarr, *The Art of Framing: Managing the Language of Leadership* (San Francisco, CA: Jossey-Bass, 1996); and A. E. Rafferty and M. A. Griffin, "Dimensions of Transformational Leadership: Conceptual and Empirical Extensions," *Leadership Quarterly* 15, no. 3 (2004), pp. 329–54.

48. D. E. Berlew, "Leadership and Organizational Excitement," *California Management Review* 17, no. 2 (Winter 1974), pp. 21–30; Bennis and Nanus, *Leaders,* pp. 43–55; and T. Simons, "Behavioral Integrity: The Perceived Alignment between Managers' Words and Deeds as a Research Focus,"

Organization Science 13, no. 1 (January–February 2002), pp. 18–35.

49. C. Hymowitz, "Today's Bosses Find Mentoring Isn't Worth the Time and Risks," *The Wall Street Journal,* March 13, 2006, p. B1.

50. J. Barling, T. Weber, and E. K. Kelloway, "Effects of Transformational Leadership Training on Attitudinal and Financial Outcomes: A Field Experiment," *Journal of Applied Psychology* 81 (1996), pp. 827–32.

51. A. Bryman, "Leadership in Organizations," in *Handbook of Organization Studies,* ed. S. R. Clegg, C. Hardy, and W. R. Nord (Thousand Oaks, CA: Sage, 1996), pp. 276–92.

52. B. S. Pawar and K. K. Eastman, "The Nature and Implications of Contextual Influences on Transformational Leadership: A Conceptual Examination," *Academy of Management Review* 22 (1997), pp. 80–109; and C. P. Egri and S. Herman, "Leadership in the North American Environmental Sector: Values, Leadership Styles, and Contexts of Environmental Leaders and Their Organizations," *Academy of Management Journal* 43, no. 4 (2000), pp. 571–604.

53. J. R. Meindl, "On Leadership: An Alternative to the Conventional Wisdom," *Research in Organizational Behavior* 12 (1990), pp. 159–203; L. R. Offermann, J. J. K. Kennedy, and P. W. Wirtz, "Implicit Leadership Theories: Content, Structure, and Generalizability," *Leadership Quarterly* 5, no. 1 (1994), pp. 43–58; R. J. Hall and R. G. Lord, "Multi-Level Information Processing Explanations of Followers' Leadership Perceptions," *Leadership Quarterly* 6 (1995), pp. 265–87; and O. Epitropaki and R. Martin, "Implicit Leadership Theories in Applied Settings: Factor Structure, Generalizability, and Stability over Time," *Journal of Applied Psychology* 89, no. 2 (2004), pp. 293–310.

54. R. G. Lord et al., "Contextual Constraints on Prototype Generation and Their Multilevel Consequences for Leadership Perceptions," *Leadership Quarterly* 12, no. 3 (2001), pp. 311–38; T. Keller, "Parental Images as a Guide to Leadership Sensemaking: An Attachment Perspective on Implicit Leadership Theories," *Leadership Quarterly* 14 (2003), pp. 141–60; and K. A. Scott and D. J. Brown, "Female First, Leader Second? Gender Bias in the Encoding of Leadership Behavior," *Organizational Behavior and Human Decision Processes* 101 (2006), pp. 230–42.

55. S. F. Cronshaw and R. G. Lord, "Effects of Categorization, Attribution, and Encoding Processes on Leadership Perceptions," *Journal of Applied Psychology* 72 (1987), pp. 97–106; and J. L. Nye and D. R. Forsyth, "The Effects of Prototype-Based Biases on Leadership Appraisals: A Test of Leadership Categorization Theory," *Small Group Research* 22 (1991), pp. 360–79.

56. Meindl, "On Leadership: An Alternative to the Conventional Wisdom"; J. Felfe and L.-E. Petersen, "Romance of Leadership and Management Decision Making," *European Journal of Work and Organizational Psychology* 16, no. 1 (2007), pp. 1–24; and B. Schyns, J. R. Meindl, and M. A. Croon, "The Romance of Leadership Scale: Cross-Cultural Testing and Refinement," *Leadership* 3, no. 1 (February 2007), pp. 29–46.

57. J. Pfeffer, "The Ambiguity of Leadership," *Academy of Management Review* 2 (1977), pp. 102–12.

58. R. Weber et al., "The Illusion of Leadership: Misattribution of Cause in Coordination Games," *Organization Science* 12, no. 5 (2001), pp. 582–98; N. Ensari and S. E. Murphy, "Cross-Cultural Variations in Leadership Perceptions and Attribution of Charisma to the Leader," *Organizational Behavior and Human Decision Processes* 92 (2003), pp. 52–66; and M. L. A. Hayward, V. P. Rindova, and T. G. Pollock, "Believing One's Own Press: The Causes and Consequences of CEO Celebrity," *Strategic Management Journal* 25, no. 7 (July 2004), pp. 637–53.

59. G. N. Powell, "One More Time: Do Female and Male Managers Differ?" *Academy of Management Executive* 4 (1990), pp. 68–75; and M. L. van Engen and T. M. Willemsen, "Sex and Leadership Styles: A Meta-Analysis of Research Published in the 1990s," *Psychological Reports* 94, no. 1 (February 2004), pp. 3–18.

60. R. Sharpe, "As Leaders, Women Rule," *BusinessWeek,* November 20, 2000, p. 74; M. Sappenfield, "Women, It Seems, Are Better Bosses," *Christian Science Monitor,* January 16, 2001; A. H. Eagly and L. L. Carli, "The Female Leadership Advantage: An Evaluation of the Evidence," *The Leadership Quarterly* 14, no. 6 (December 2003), pp. 807–34; and A. H. Eagly, M. C. Johannesen-Schmidt, and M. L. van Engen, "Transformational, Transactional, and Laissez-Faire Leadership Styles: A Meta-Analysis Comparing Women and Men," *Psychological Bulletin* 129 (July 2003), pp. 569–91.

61. A. H. Eagly, S. J. Karau, and M. G. Makhijani, "Gender and the Effectiveness of Leaders: A Meta-Analysis," *Psychological Bulletin* 117 (1995), pp. 125–45; J. G. Oakley, "Gender-Based Barriers to Senior Management Positions: Understanding the Scarcity of Female CEOs," *Journal of Business Ethics* 27 (2000), pp. 821–34; N. Z. Stelter, "Gender Differences in Leadership: Current Social Issues and Future Organizational Implications," *Journal of Leadership Studies* 8 (2002), pp. 88–99; M. E. Heilman et al., "Penalties for Success: Reactions to Women Who Succeed at Male Gender-Typed Tasks," *Journal of Applied Psychology* 89, no. 3 (2004), pp. 416–27; and A. H. Eagly, "Achieving Relational Authenticity in Leadership: Does Gender Matter?" *The Leadership Quarterly* 16, no. 3 (June 2005), pp. 459–74.

chapter 12

1. R. Muzyka and G. Zeschuk, "Managing Multiple Projects," *Game Developer,* March 2003, pp. 34–42; M. Saltzman, "The Ex-Doctors Are In," *National Post,* March 24, 2004, p. AL4; R. McConnell, "For Edmonton's BioWare, Today's the Big Day," *Edmonton Journal,* April 14, 2005, p. C1; and D. Gladstone and S. Molloy, "Doctors & Dragons," *Computer Gaming World,* December 2006.

2. S. Ranson, R. Hinings, and R. Greenwood, "The Structuring of Organizational Structure," *Administrative Science Quarterly* 25 (1980), pp. 1–14; and K. Walsh, "Interpreting the Impact of Culture on Structure," *Journal of Applied Behavioral Science* 40, no. 3 (Sept. 2004), pp. 302–22.

3. B. Morris, "Charles Schwab's Big Challenge," *Fortune,* May 30, 2005, pp. 60–69.

4. J. E. Johanson, "Intraorganizational Influence," *Management Communication Quarterly* 13 (February 2000), pp. 393–435.

5. H. Mintzberg, *The Structuring of Organizations* (Englewood Cliffs, NJ: Prentice-Hall, 1979), pp. 2–3.

6. E. E. Lawler III, *Motivation in Work Organizations* (Monterey, CA: Brooks/Cole, 1973); and M. A. Campion, "Ability Requirement Implications of Job Design: An Interdisciplinary Perspective," *Personnel Psychology* 42 (1989), pp. 1–24.

7. G. S. Becker and K. M. Murphy, "The Division-of-Labor, Coordination Costs and Knowledge," *Quarterly Journal of Economics* 107, no. 4 (Nov 1992), pp. 1137–60; and L. Borghans and B. Weel, "The Division of Labour, Worker Organisation, and Technological Change," *The Economic Journal* 116, no. 509 (2006), pp. F45–F72.

8. Mintzberg, *The Structuring of Organizations,* Chap. 1; D. A. Nadler and M. L. Tushman, *Competing by Design: The Power of Organizational Architecture* (New York: Oxford University Press, 1997), Chap. 6; and J. R. Galbraith, *Designing Organizations: An Executive Guide to Strategy, Structure, and Process* (San Francisco: Jossey-Bass, 2002), Chap. 4.

9. J. Stephenson, Jr., "Making Humanitarian Relief Networks More Effective: Operational Coordination, Trust and Sense Making," *Disasters* 29, no. 4 (2005), pp. 337–50.

10. A. Willem, M. Buelens, and H. Scarbrough, "The Role of Inter-Unit Coordination Mechanisms in Knowledge Sharing: A Case Study of a British MNC," *Journal of Information Science* 32, no. 6 (2006), pp. 539–61; and R. R. Gulati, "Silo Busting," *Harvard Business Review* 85, no. 5 (2007), pp. 98–108.

11. Borghans and Weel, "The Division of Labour, Worker Organisation, and Technological Change."

12. K. Umemoto, A. Endo, and M. Machado, "From Sashimi to Zen-In: The Evolution of Concurrent Engineering at Fuji Xerox," *Journal of Knowledge Management* 8, no. 4 (2004), pp. 89–99; M. Hoque, M. Akter, and Y. Monden, "Concurrent Engineering: A Compromise Approach to Develop a Feasible and Customer-Pleasing Product," *International Journal of Production Research* 43, no. 8 (2005), pp. 1607–24.

13. A. H. Van De Ven, A. L. Delbecq, and R. J. Kocnig Jr., "Determinants of Coordination Modes within Organizations," *American Sociological Review* 41, no. 2 (1976), pp. 322–38.

14. Y. M. Hsieh and A. Tien-Hsieh, "Enhancement of Service Quality with Job Standardisation," *Service Industries Journal* 21 (July 2001), pp. 147–66.

15. H. Fayol, *General and Industrial Management,* trans. C. Storrs (London: Pitman, 1949); D. D. Van Fleet and A. G. Bedeian, "A History of the Span of Management," *Academy of Management Review* 2 (1977), pp. 356–72; and D. A. Wren, A. G. Bedeian, and J. D. Breeze, "The Foundations of Henri Fayol's Administrative Theory," *Management Decision* 40, no. 9 (2002), pp. 906–18.

16. D. Drickhamer, "Lessons from the Leading Edge," *Industry Week,* February 21, 2000, pp. 23–26.

17. J. H. Gittell, "Supervisory Span, Relational Coordination and Flight Departure Performance: A Reassessment of Postbureaucracy Theory," *Organization Science* 12, no. 4 (July–August 2001), pp. 468–83.

18. T. D. Wall, J. L. Cordery, and C. W. Clegg, "Empowerment, Performance, and Operational Uncertainty: A Theoretical Integration," *Applied Psychology: An International Review* 51 (2002), pp. 146–69.

19. J. Morris, J. Hassard, and L. McCann, "New Organizational Forms, Human Resource Management and Structural Convergence? A Study of Japanese Organizations," *Organization Studies* 27, no. 10 (2006), pp. 1485–511.

20. "BASF Culling Saves (GBP) 4m," *Personnel Today,* February 19, 2002, p. 3; and A. Lashinsky, "The Hurt Way," *Fortune,* April 17, 2006, p. 92.

21. Q. N. Huy, "In Praise of Middle Managers," *Harvard Business Review* 79 (September 2001), pp. 72–79; and H. J. Leavitt, *Top Down: Why Hierarchies Are Here to Stay and How to Manage Them More Effectively* (Cambridge, MA: Harvard Business School Press, 2005).

22. J. G. Kelley, "Slurpees and Sausages: 7-Eleven Holds School," *Richmond (VA) Times-Dispatch,* March 12. 2004, p. C1; and S. Marling, "The 24-Hour Supply Chain," *InformationWeek,* January 26, 2004, p. 43.

23. H. A. Richardson et al., "Does Decentralization Make a Difference for the Organization? An Examination of the Boundary Conditions Circumscribing Decentralized Decision-Making and Organizational Financial Performance," *Journal of Management* 28, no. 2 (2002), pp. 217–44; and G. Masada, "To Centralize or Decentralize?" *Optimize,* May 2005, pp. 58–61. Nestlé's centralized-decentralized structure is discussed in S. Wetlaufer, "The Business Case against Revolution: An Interview with Nestlé's Peter Brabeck," *Harvard Business Review* 79, no. 2 (February 2001), pp. 112–19; and T. Demos, "Going Global," *Fortune,* March 6, 2006, p. 48.

24. Mintzberg, *The Structuring of Organizations,* Chap. 5.

25. W. Dessein and T. Santos, "Adaptive Organizations," *Journal of Political Economy* 114, no. 5 (2006), pp. 956–95; A. A. M. Nasurdin et al., "Organizational Structure and Organizational Climate as Potential Predictors of Job Stress: Evidence from Malaysia," *International Journal of Commerce and Management* 16, no. 2 (2006), pp. 116–29; and C. J. Chen and J. W. Huang, "How Organizational Climate and Structure Affect Knowledge Management—the Social Interaction Perspective," *International Journal of Information Management* 27, no. 2 (2007), pp. 104–18.

26. T. Burns and G. Stalker, *The Management of Innovation* (London: Tavistock, 1961).

27. J. Tata, S. Prasad, and R. Thom, "The Influence of Organizational Structure on the Effectiveness of TQM Programs," *Journal of Managerial Issues* 11, no. 4 (Winter 1999), pp. 440–53; and A. Lam, "Tacit Knowledge, Organizational Learning and Societal Institutions: An Integrated Framework," *Organization Studies* 21 (May 2000), pp. 487–513.

28. W. D. Sine, H. Mitsuhashi, and D. A. Kirsch, "Revisiting Burns and Stalker: Formal Structure and New Venture Performance in Emerging Economic Sectors," *Academy of Management Journal* 49, no. 1 (2006), pp. 121–32.

29. Mintzberg, *The Structuring of Organizations,* p. 106.

30. Galbraith, *Designing Organizations,* pp. 23–25.

31. E. E. Lawler III, *Rewarding Excellence: Pay Strategies for the New Economy* (San Francisco: Jossey-Bass, 2000), pp. 31–34.

32. These structures were identified from corporate Web sites and annual reports. These companies include a mixture of other structures, so the charts shown are adapted for learning purposes.

33. M. Goold and A. Campbell, "Do You Have a Well-Designed Organization," *Harvard Business Review* 80 (March 2002), pp. 117–24.

34. J. R. Galbraith, "Structuring Global Organizations," in *Tomorrow's Organization,* ed. S. A. Mohrman et al. (San Francisco: Jossey-Bass, 1998), pp. 103–29; C. Homburg, J. P. Workman Jr., and O. Jensen, "Fundamental Changes in Marketing Organization: The Movement toward a Corganizational Structure," *Academy of Marketing Science Journal* 28 (Fall 2000), pp. 459–78; T. H. Davenport, J. G. Harris, and A. K. Kohli, "How Do They Know Their Customers So Well?" *Sloan Management Review* 42 (Winter 2001), pp. 63–73; and J. R. Galbraith, "Organizing to Deliver Solutions," *Organizational Dynamics* 31 (2002), pp. 194–207.

35. "The Firm That Lets Staff Breathe," *Sunday Times (London)*, March 24, 2002; M. Weinreb, "Power to the People," *Sales & Marketing Management,* April 2003, pp. 30–35; A. Deutschman, "The Fabric of Creativity," *Fast Company,* December 2004, p. 54; M. L. Diamond, "Change in Management for Medical Device Company," *Asbury Park Press (Asbury Park, NJ),* February 6, 2006; and P. J. Kiger, "Power to the Individual," *Workforce Management,* February 27, 2006, pp. 1–7.

36. J. R. Galbraith, E. E. Lawler III, and Associates, *Organizing for the Future: The New Logic for Managing Complex Organizations* (San Francisco, CA: Jossey-Bass, 1993); and R. Bettis and M. Hitt, "The New Competitive Landscape," *Strategic Management Journal* 16 (1995), pp. 7–19.

37. P. C. Ensign, "Interdependence, Coordination, and Structure in Complex Organizations: Implications for Organization Design," *Mid-Atlantic Journal of Business* 34 (March 1998), pp. 5–22.

38. R. Cross, "Looking before You Leap: Assessing the Jump to Teams in Knowledge-Based Work," *Business Horizons* (September 2000), pp. 29–36; M. Fenton-O'Creevy, "Employee Involvement and the Middle Manager: Saboteur or Scapegoat?," *Human Resource Management Journal* 11 (2001), pp. 24–40; G. Garda, K. Lindstrom, and M. Dallnera, "Towards a Learning Organization: The Introduction of a Client-Centered Team-Based Organization in Administrative Surveying Work," *Applied Ergonomics* 34 (2003), pp. 97–105; and C. Douglas and W. L. Gardner, "Transition to Self-Directed Work Teams: Implications of Transition Time and Self-Monitoring for Managers' Use of Influence Tactics," *Journal of Organizational Behavior* 25 (2004), pp. 47–65.

39. R. C. Ford and W. A. Randolph, "Cross-Functional Structures: A Review and Integration of Matrix Organization and Project Management," *Journal of Management* 18 (1992), pp. 267–94.

40. N. Buckley, "P&G Shakes up Its Global Units," *Financial Times (London),* May 19, 2004; and "Merely Splitting Hairs," *Marketing Week,* February 17, 2005, p. 26. Procter & Gamble's structure is actually more complex than we have described here. Its "four pillars" also include global business services and corporate functions. See P&G Corporate Info, Corporate Structure, Four Pillars at www.pg.com/jobs/corporate_ structure/four_pillars.jhtml.

41. G. Calabrese, "Communication and Co-Operation in Product Development: A Case Study of a European Car Producer," *R & D Management* 27 (July 1997), pp. 239–52; and T. Sy and L. S. D'Annunzio, "Challenges and Strategies of Matrix Organizations: Top-Level and Mid-Level Managers' Perspectives," *Human Resource Planning* 28, no. 1 (2005), pp. 39–48.

42. Nadler and Tushman, *Competing by Design,* Chap. 6; and M. Goold and A. Campbell, "Structured Networks: Towards the Well-Designed Matrix," *Long Range Planning* 36, no. 5 (October 2003), pp. 427–39.

43. L. Donaldson, *The Contingency Theory of Organizations* (Thousand Oaks, CA: Sage, 2001); J. Birkenshaw, R. Nobel, and J. Ridderstråle, "Knowledge as a Contingency Variable: Do the Characteristics of Knowledge Predict Organizational Structure?" *Organization Science* 13, no. 3 (May–June 2002), pp. 274–89.

44. A. D. Meyer, A. S. Tsui, and C. R. Hinings, "Configurational Approaches to Organizational Analysis," *Academy of Management Journal* 36, no. 6 (December 1993), pp. 1175–95; and K. K. Sinha and A. H. Van De Ven, "Designing Work within and between Organizations," *Organization Science* 16, no. 4 (July–August 2005), pp. 389–408.

45. P. R. Lawrence and J. W. Lorsch, *Organization and Environment* (Homewood, IL: Irwin, 1967); Mintzberg, *The Structuring of Organizations,* Chap. 15.

46. Burns and Stalker, *The Management of Innovation;* and Lawrence and Lorsch, *Organization and Environment.*

47. R. Gardner, "Charismatic Clarke Brings His Client Service Approach to UK," *Campaign*, October 8, 2004, p. 18; N. O'Leary, "Chris Clarke Is Coming for Your Business," *Adweek,* April 9, 2007, pp. 8, 39; and S. Russell, "Global Ambitions," *B&T,* June 8, 2007, p. 17.

48. Mintzberg, *The Structuring of Organizations,* p. 282.

49. D. S. Pugh and C. R. Hinings, *Organizational Structure: Extensions and Replications* (Farnborough, England: Lexington Books, 1976); and Mintzberg, *The Structuring of Organizations,* Chap. 13.

50. Galbraith, *Designing Organizations,* pp. 52–55; G. Hertel, S. Geister, and U. Konradt, "Managing Virtual Teams: A Review of Current Empirical Research," *Human Resource Management Review* 15 (2005), pp. 69–95.

51. C. Perrow, "A Framework for the Comparative Analysis of Organizations," *American Sociological Review* 32 (1967), pp. 194–208; D. Gerwin, "The Comparative Analysis of Structure and Technology: A Critical Appraisal," *Academy of Management Review* 4, no. 1 (1979), pp. 41–51; and C. C. Miller et al., "Understanding Technology-Structure Relationships: Theory Development and Meta-Analytic Theory Testing," *Academy of Management Journal* 34, no. 2 (1991), pp. 370–99.

52. R. H. Kilmann, *Beyond the Quick Fix* (San Francisco: Jossey-Bass, 1984), p. 38.

53. A. D. Chandler, *Strategy and Structure* (Cambridge, MA: MIT Press, 1962).

54. D. Miller, "Configurations of Strategy and Structure," *Strategic Management Journal* 7 (1986), pp. 233–49.

chapter 13

1. L. M. Fisher, "How Dell Got Soul," *strategy+business* 2004, pp. 1–14; N. Byrnes, P. Burrows, and L. Lee, "Dark Days at Dell," *BusinessWeek*, September 4, 2006, p. 26; M. Kessler, "Dell Reverses, Steps into Wal-Mart," *USA Today*, May 25, 2007, p. B1; S. Lohr, "Can Michael Dell Refocus His Namesake?" *New York Times*, September 9, 2007, p. 1; and D. Zehr, "Dell Challenge: New Ideas and Less Red Tape," *Austin American-Statesman (TX)*, February 4, 2007, p. A1.

2. A. Williams, P. Dobson, and M. Walters, *Changing Culture: New Organizational Approaches* (London: Institute of Personnel Management, 1989); and E. H. Schein, "What Is Culture?" in *Reframing Organizational Culture*, ed. P. J. Frost et al. (Newbury Park, CA: Sage, 1991), pp. 243–53.

3. Williams, Dobson, and Walters, *Changing Culture: New Organizational Approaches*; Schein, "What Is Culture?"

4. B. M. Meglino and E. C. Ravlin, "Individual Values in Organizations: Concepts, Controversies, and Research," *Journal of Management* 24, no. 3 (1998), pp. 351–89; B. R. Agle and C. B. Caldwell, "Understanding Research on Values in Business," *Business and Society* 38, no. 3 (September 1999), pp. 326–87; and S. Hitlin and J. A. Pilavin, "Values: Reviving a Dormant Concept," *Annual Review of Sociology* 30 (2004), pp. 359–93.

5. N. M. Ashkanasy, "The Case for Culture," in *Debating Organization*, ed. R. Westwood and S. Clegg (Malden, MA: Blackwell, 2003), pp. 300–10.

6. C. A. O'Reilly III, J. Chatman, and D. F. Caldwell, "People and Organizational Culture: A Profile Comparison Approach to Assessing Person-Organization Fit," *Academy of Management Journal* 34 (1991), pp. 487–516; and J. J. van Muijen, "Organizational Culture," in *A Handbook of Work and Organizational Psychology: Organizational Psychology,* ed. P. J. D. Drenth, H. Thierry, and C. J. de Wolff, 2nd ed. (East Sussex, UK: Psychology Press, 1998), pp. 113–32. For recent reviews of organizational culture survey instruments, see T. Scott et al., "The Quantitative Measurement of Organizational Culture in Health Care: A Review of the Available Instruments," *Health Services Research* 38, no. 3 (2003), pp. 923–45; D. E. Leidner and T. Kayworth, "A Review of Culture in Information Systems Research: Toward a Theory of Information Technology Culture Conflict," *MIS Quarterly* 30, no. 2 (2006), pp. 357–99; and S. Scott-Findlay and C. A. Estabrooks, "Mapping the Organizational Culture Research in Nursing: A Literature Review," *Journal of Advanced Nursing* 56, no. 5 (2006), pp. 498–513.

7. J. Martin and C. Siehl, "Organizational Culture and Counterculture: An Uneasy Symbiosis," *Organizational Dynamics* (Autumn 1983), pp. 52–64; G. Hofstede, "Identifying Organizational Subcultures: An Empirical Approach," *Journal of Management Studies* 35, no. 1 (1990), pp. 1–12; and E. Ogbonna and L. C. Harris, "Organisational Culture in the Age of the Internet: An Exploratory Study," *New Technology, Work and Employment* 21, no. 2 (2006), pp. 162–75.

8. A. Sinclair, "Approaches to Organizational Culture and Ethics," *Journal of Business Ethics* 12 (1993); and A. Boisnier and J. Chatman, "The Role of Subcultures in Agile Organizations," in *Leading and Managing People in Dynamic Organizations*, ed. R. Petersen and E. Mannix (Mahwah, NJ: Lawrence Erlbaum Associates, 2003), pp. 87–112.

9. J. S. Ott, *The Organizational Culture Perspective* (Pacific Grove, CA: Brooks/Cole, 1989), Chap. 2; J. S. Pederson and J. S. Sorensen, *Organizational Cultures in Theory and Practice* (Aldershot, England: Gower, 1989), pp. 27–29; and M. O. Jones, *Studying Organizational Symbolism: What, How, Why?* (Thousand Oaks, CA: Sage, 1996).

10. E. H. Schein, "Organizational Culture," *American Psychologist* (February 1990), pp. 109-19; A. Furnham and B. Gunter, "Corporate Culture: Definition, Diagnosis, and Change," *International Review of Industrial and Organizational Psychology* 8 (1993), pp. 233–61; and E. H. Schein, *The Corporate Culture Survival Guide* (San Francisco: Jossey-Bass, 1999), Chap. 4.

11. M. Doehrman, "Anthropologists—Deep in the Corporate Bush," *Daily Record (Kansas City, MO)*, July 19, 2005, p. 1.

12. A. L. Wilkins, "Organizational Stories as Symbols Which Control the Organization," in *Organizational Symbolism*, ed. L. R. Pondy et al. (Greenwich, CT: JAI Press, 1984), pp. 81–92; R. Zemke, "Storytelling: Back to a Basic," *Training* 27 (March 1990), pp. 44–50; J. C. Meyer, "Tell Me a Story: Eliciting Organizational Values from Narratives," *Communication Quarterly* 43 (1995), pp. 210–24; and W. Swap et al., "Using Mentoring and Storytelling to Transfer Knowledge in the Workplace," *Journal of Management Information Systems* 18 (Summer 2001), pp. 95–114.

13. D. Roth, "My Job at the Container Store," *Fortune*, January 10, 2000, pp. 74–78.

14. R. Frank and S. Craig, "White-Shoe Shuffle," *The Wall Street Journal*, September 15, 2004, p. A1.

15. R. E. Quinn and N. T. Snyder, "Advance Change Theory: Culture Change at Whirlpool Corporation," in *The Leader's Change Handbook,* ed. J. A. Conger, G. M. Spreitzer, and E. E. Lawler III (San Francisco: Jossey-Bass, 1999), pp. 162–93.

16. Churchill apparently made this statement on October 28, 1943, in the British House of Commons, when London, damaged by bombings in World War II, was about to be rebuilt.

17. K. D. Elsbach and B. A. Bechky, "It's More Than a Desk: Working Smarter through Leveraged Office Design," *California Management Review* 49, no. 2 (Winter 2007), pp. 80–101.

18. A. D'Innocenzio, "Wal-Mart's Town Becomes New Address for Corporate America," *Associated Press,* September 19, 2003; and J. Useem, "One Nation under Wal-Mart," *Fortune*, March 3, 2003, pp. 65–78.

19. J. C. Collins and J. I. Porras, *Built to Last: Successful Habits of Visionary Companies* (London: Century, 1994); T. E. Deal and A. A. Kennedy, *The New Corporate Cultures* (Cambridge, MA: Perseus Books, 1999); J. M. Kouzes and B. Z. Posner, *The Leadership Challenge*, 3rd ed. (San Francisco: Jossey-Bass, 2002); R. Barrett, *Building a Values-Driven Organization: A Whole System Approach to Cultural Transformation* (Burlington, MA: Butterworth-Heinemann, 2006).

20. C. Siehl and J. Martin, "Organizational Culture: A Key to Financial Performance? " in *Organizational Climate and Culture,* ed. B. Schneider (San Francisco, CA: Jossey-Bass, 1990), pp. 241–81; G. G. Gordon and N. DiTomasco, "Predicting Corporate Performance from Organizational Culture," *Journal of Management Studies* 29 (1992), pp. 783–98; J. P. Kotter and J. L. Heskett, *Corporate Culture and Performance* (New York: Free Press, 1992); C. P. M. Wilderom, U. Glunk, and R. Maslowski, "Organizational Culture as a Predictor of Organizational Performance," in *Handbook of Organizational Culture and Climate*, ed. N. M. Ashkanasy, C. P. M. Wilderom, and M. F. Peterson (Thousand Oaks, CA: Sage, 2000), pp. 193–210; A. Carmeli and A. Tishler, "The Relationships between Intangible Organizational Elements and Organizational Performance," *Strategic Management Journal* 25 (2004), pp. 1257–78; and S. Teerikangas and P. Very, "The Culture-Performance Relationship in M&A: From Yes/No to How," *British Journal of Management* 17, no. s1 (2006), pp. S31–S48.

21. C. A. O'Reilly and J. A. Chatman, "Culture as Social Control: Corporations, Cults, and Commitment," *Research in Organizational Behavior* 18 (1996), pp. 157–200; J. C. Helms Mills and A. J. Mills, "Rules, Sensemaking, Formative Contexts, and Discourse in the Gendering of Organizational Culture," in *International Handbook of Organizational Climate and Culture*, eds. N. Ashkanasy, C. Wilderom, and M. Peterson (Thousand Oaks, CA: Sage, 2000), pp. 55–70; and J. A. Chatman and S. E. Cha, "Leading by Leveraging Culture," *California Management Review* 45 (Summer 2003), pp. 20–34.

22. B. Ashforth and F. Mael, "Social Identity Theory and the Organization," *Academy of Management Review* 14 (1989), pp. 20–39.

23. M. R. Louis, "Surprise and Sensemaking: What Newcomers Experience in Entering Unfamiliar Organizational Settings," *Administrative Science Quarterly* 25 (1980), pp. 226–51; and S. G. Harris, "Organizational Culture and Individual Sensemaking: A Schema-Based Perspective," *Organization Science* 5 (1994), pp. 309–21.

24. Fisher, "How Dell Got Soul," p. 6.

25. Kotter and Heskett, *Corporate Culture and Performance* ; and J. P. Kotter, "Cultures and Coalitions," *Executive Excellence* 15 (March 1998), pp. 14–15.

26. A. Maitland and K. Rollins, "The Two-in-a-Box World of Dell," *Financial Times (London)*, March 20, 2003, p. 14.

27. D. Ho, "Michael Dell Says He Had No Role in Accounting Scandal," *Cox News Service,* September 6, 2007.

28. E. H. Schein, "The Role of the Founder in Creating Organizational Culture," *Organizational Dynamics* 12, no. 1 (Summer 1983), pp. 13–28; R. House, M. Javidan, and P. Dorfman, "Project Globe: An Introduction," *Applied Psychology: An International Review* 50 (2001), pp. 489–505; and R. House et al., "Understanding Cultures and Implicit Leadership Theories across the Globe: An Introduction to Project Globe," *Journal of World Business* 37 (2002), pp. 3–10.

29. J. Hewett, "Office Politics," *Australian Financial Review*, September 27, 2003, p. 29.

30. M. De Pree, *Leadership Is an Art* (East Lansing, MI: Michigan State University Press, 1987).

31. B. McLean, "Inside the Money Machine," *Fortune*, September 6, 2004, p. 84.

32. J. Kerr and J. W. Slocum Jr., "Managing Corporate Culture through Reward Systems," *Academy of Management Executive* 1 (May 1987), pp. 99–107; K. R. Thompson and F. Luthans, "Organizational Culture: A Behavioral Perspective," in *Organizational Climate and Culture*, ed. B. Schneider (San Francisco: Jossey-Bass, 1990), pp. 319–44.

33. R. Charan, "Home Depot's Blueprint for Culture Change," *Harvard Business Review* (April 2006), pp. 61–70; and B. Grow, D. Brady, and M. Arndt, "Renovating Home Depot," *BusinessWeek,* March 6, 2006, pp. 50–57.

34. B. Schneider, "The People Make the Place," *Personnel Psychology* 40, no. 3 (1987), pp. 437–53; B. Schneider et al., "Personality and Organizations: A Test of the Homogeneity of Personality Hypothesis," *Journal of Applied Psychology* 83, no. 3 (June 1998), pp. 462–70; and T. R. Giberson, C. J. Resick, and M. W. Dickson, "Embedding Leader Characteristics: An Examination of Homogeneity of Personality and Values in Organizations," *Journal of Applied Psychology* 90, no. 5 (2005), pp. 1002–10.

35. T. A. Judge and D. M. Cable, "Applicant Personality, Organizational Culture, and Organization Attraction," *Personnel Psychology* 50, no. 2 (1997), pp. 359–94; D. Chapman, S. et al., "Applicant Attraction to Organizations and Job Choice: A Meta-Analytic Review of the Correlates of Recruiting Outcomes," *Journal of Applied Psychology* 90, no. 5 (2005), pp. 928–44; A. L. Kristof-Brown, R. D. Zimmerman, and E. C. Johnson, "Consequences of Individuals' Fit at Work: A Meta-Analysis of Person-Job, Person-Organization, Person-Group, and Person-Supervisor Fit," *Personnel Psychology* 58, no. 2 (2005), pp. 281–342; and C. Hu, H.-C. Su, and C.-I. B. Chen, "The Effect of Person-Organization Fit Feedback Via Recruitment Web Sites on Applicant Attraction," *Computers in Human Behavior* 23, no. 5 (2007), pp. 2509–23.

36. A. Kristof-Brown, "Perceived Applicant Fit: Distinguishing between Recruiters' Perceptions of Person-Job and Person-Organization Fit," *Personnel Psychology* 53, no. 3 (Autumn 2000), pp. 643–71; and A. E. M. Van Vianen, "Person-Organization Fit: The Match between Newcomers' and Recruiters' Preferences for Organizational Cultures," *Personnel Psychology* 53 (Spring 2000), pp. 113–49.

37. D. M. Cable and J. R. Edwards, "Complementary and Supplementary Fit: A Theoretical and Empirical Integration," *Journal of Applied Psychology* 89, no. 5 (2004), pp. 822–34.

38. J. Van Maanen, "Breaking In: Socialization to Work," in *Handbook of Work, Organization, and Society*, ed. R. Dubin (Chicago: Rand McNally, 1976).

39. S. Huettel, "Soaring Ahead," *St. Petersburg Times (FL)*, October 24, 2005, p. 1D; and E. P. Lima, "Winning Cultures," *Air Transport World*, February 1, 2006, p. 54.

40. C. L. Adkins, "Previous Work Experience and Organizational Socialization: A Longitudinal Examination," *Academy of*

Management Journal 38 (1995), pp. 839–62; J. D. Kammeyer-Mueller and C. R. Wanberg, "Unwrapping the Organizational Entry Process: Disentangling Multiple Antecedents and Their Pathways to Adjustment," *Journal of Applied Psychology* 88, no. 5 (2003), pp. 779–94.

41. L. W. Porter, E. E. Lawler III, and J. R. Hackman, *Behavior in Organizations* (New York: McGraw-Hill, 1975), pp. 163–67; Van Maanen, "Breaking In: Socialization to Work" ; and D. C. Feldman, "The Multiple Socialization of Organization Members," *Academy of Management Review* 6 (1981), pp. 309–18.

42. B. E. Ashforth and A. M. Saks, "Socialization Tactics: Longitudinal Effects on Newcomer Adjustment," *Academy of Management Journal* 39 (1996), pp. 149–78; Kammeyer-Mueller and Wanberg, "Unwrapping the Organizational Entry Process."

43. Louis, "Surprise and Sensemaking: What Newcomers Experience in Entering Unfamiliar Organizational Settings."

44. C. Fishman, "The Anarchist's Cookbook," *Fast Company*, July 2004, p. 70; and "World's Finest Food Retailers: Whole Foods, Not Holy Food," *The Grocer*, November 12, 2005, p. 32.

45. M. L. Marks, "Adding Cultural Fit to Your Diligence Checklist," *Mergers & Acquisitions* 34, no. 3 (November–Dececember 1999), pp. 14–20; Schein, *The Corporate Culture Survival Guide,* Chap. 8; M. L. Marks, "Mixed Signals," *Across the Board* (May 2000), pp. 21–26; and J. P. Daly, R. W. Pouder, and B. Kabanoff, "The Effects of Initial Differences in Firms' Espoused Values on Their Postmerger Performance," *Journal of Applied Behavioral Science* 40, no. 3 (September 2004), pp. 323–43.

46. A. Klein, "A Merger Taken AO-Ill," *Washington Post*, October 21. 2002, p. E1; and A. Klein, *Stealing Time: Steve Case, Jerry Levin, and the Collapse of AOL Time Warner* (New York: Simon & Shuster, 2003).

47. S. Greengard, "Due Diligence: The Devil in the Details," *Workforce* (October 1999), p. 68; and Marks, "Adding Cultural Fit to Your Diligence Checklist."

48. A. R. Malekazedeh and A. Nahavandi, "Making Mergers Work by Managing Cultures," *Journal of Business Strategy* (May–June 1990), pp. 55–57; and K. W. Smith, "A Brand-New Culture for the Merged Firm," *Mergers and Acquisitions* 35 (June 2000), pp. 45–50.

49. T. Hamilton, "RIM on a Roll," *Toronto Star*, February 22, 2004, p. C01.

50. Hewitt Associates, "Mergers and Acquisitions May Be Driven by Business Strategy—but Often Stumble over People and Culture Issues," PR Newswire news release, (Lincolnshire, IL: August 3, 1998).

51. I. Mount, "Be Fast Be Frugal Be Right," *Inc* 26, no. 1 (January 2004), pp. 64–70; and S. Anthony and C. Christensen, "Mind over Merger," *Optimize* (February 2005), pp. 22–27.

chapter 14

1. C. Ragavan and C. S. Hook, "Fixing the FBI," *U.S. News & World Report,* March 28, 2005, pp. 18–24, 26, 29–30; The Commission on the Intelligence Capabilities of the United States Regarding Weapons of Mass Destruction, *Report to the President of the United States,* (Washington, DC: March 31, 2005); and J. J. Brazil, "Mission: Impossible?" *Fast Company,* April 2007, pp. 92–97, 108–9.

2. K. Lewin, *Field Theory in Social Science* (New York: Harper & Row, 1951).

3. Recent affirmation of Lewin's force field model is found in D. Coghlan and T. Brannick, "Kurt Lewin: The 'Practical Theorist' for the 21st Century," *Irish Journal of Management* 24, no. 2 (2003), pp. 31–37; and B. Burnes, "Kurt Lewin and the Planned Approach to Change: A Re-Appraisal," *Journal of Management Studies* 41, no. 6 (Sept. 2004), pp. 977–1002.

4. D. Eggen, "FBI Fails to Transform Itself, Panel Says," *Washington Post,* June 7, 2005, p. A04; The Commission on the Intelligence Capabilities of the United States Regarding Weapons of Mass Destruction, *Report to the President of the United States,* p. 4; and Brazil, "Mission: Impossible?"

5. E. B. Dent and S. G. Goldberg, "Challenging 'Resistance to Change'," *Journal of Applied Behavioral Science* 35 (March 1999), pp. 25–41; and D. B. Fedor, S. Caldwell, and D. M. Herold, "The Effects of Organizational Changes on Employee Commitment: A Multilevel Investigation," *Personnel Psychology* 59, no. 1 (2006), pp. 1–29.

6. D. A. Nadler, "The Effective Management of Organizational Change," in *Handbook of Organizational Behavior,* ed. J. W. Lorsch (Englewood Cliffs, NJ: Prentice-Hall, 1987), pp. 358–69; R. Maurer, *Beyond the Wall of Resistance: Unconventional Strategies to Build Support for Change* (Austin, TX: Bard Books, 1996); P. Strebel, "Why Do Employees Resist Change?" *Harvard Business Review* (May–June 1996), pp. 86–92; and D. A. Nadler, *Champions of Change* (San Francisco, CA: Jossey-Bass, 1998).

7. V. Newman, "The Psychology of Managing for Innovation," *KM Review* 9, no. 6 (2007), pp. 10–15.

8. "Making Change Work for You—Not against You," *Agency Sales Magazine* 28 (June 1998), pp. 24–27.

9. T. G. Cummings, "The Role and Limits of Change Leadership," in *The Leader's Change Handbook,* ed. J. A. Conger, G. M. Spreitzer, and E. E. Lawler III (San Francisco: Jossey-Bass, 1999), pp. 301–20; and J. P. Kotter and D. S. Cohen, *The Heart of Change* (Boston: Harvard Business School Press, 2002), pp. 15–36.

10. L. D. Goodstein and H. R. Butz, "Customer Value: The Linchpin of Organizational Change," *Organizational Dynamics* 27 (June 1998), pp. 21–35.

11. I. J. Bozon and P. N. Child, "Refining Shell's Position in Europe," *McKinsey Quarterly,* no. 2 (2003), pp. 42–51.

12. D. Darlin, "Growing Tomorrow," *Business 2.0,* May 2005, p. 126.

13. L. Grossman and S. Song, "Stevie's Little Wonder," *Time,* September 19, 2005, p. 63; and S. Levy, "Honey, I Shrunk the iPod. A Lot," *Newsweek,* September 19, 2005, p. 58.

14. J. P. Kotter and L. A. Schlesinger, "Choosing Strategies for Change," *Harvard Business Review* (March–April 1979), pp. 106–14.

15. B. Nanus and S. M. Dobbs, *Leaders Who Make a Difference* (San Francisco: Jossey-Bass, 1999); and Kotter and Cohen, *The Heart of Change,* pp. 83–98.

16. K. T. Dirks, L. L. Cummings, and J. L. Pierce, "Psychological Ownership in Organizations: Conditions under Which Individuals Promote and Resist Change," *Research in Organizational Change and Development* 9 (1996), pp. 1–23; and A. Cox, S. Zagelmeyer, and M. Marchington, "Embedding Employee Involvement and Participation at Work," *Human Resource Management Journal* 16, no. 3 (2006), pp. 250–67.

17. For criticism of a recent search conference for lacking innovative or realistic ideas, see A. Oels, "Investigating the Emotional Roller-Coaster Ride: A Case Study-Based Assessment of the Future Search Conference Design," *Systems Research and Behavioral Science* 19 (July–August 2002), pp. 347–55; and M. F. D. Polanyi, "Communicative Action in Practice: Future Search and the Pursuit of an Open, Critical and Non-Coercive Large-Group Process," *Systems Research and Behavioral Science* 19 (July 2002), pp. 357–66.

18. B. B. Bunker and B. T. Alban, *Large Group Interventions: Engaging the Whole System for Rapid Change* (San Francisco, CA: Jossey-Bass, 1996); D. Shaw et al., "Problem Structuring Methods for Large Group Interventions," *Journal of the Operational Research Society* 55, no. 5 (May 2004), pp. 453–63; and S. Janoff and M. Weisbord, "Future Search as 'Real-Time' Action Research," *Futures* 38, no. 6 (2006), pp. 716–22. The State of Washington future search conference is described in T. Shapley, "Trying to Fix What Everyone Else Has Broken," *Seattle Post-Intelligencer,* November 16, 2005, p. B8.

19. M. McHugh, "The Stress Factor: Another Item for the Change Management Agenda?" *Journal of Organizational Change Management* 10 (1997), pp. 345–62; and D. Buchanan, T. Claydon, and M. Doyle, "Organisation Development and Change: The Legacy of the Nineties," *Human Resource Management Journal* 9 (1999), pp. 20–37.

20. D. Nicolini and M. B. Meznar, "The Social Construction of Organizational Learning: Conceptual and Practical Issues in the Field," *Human Relations* 48 (1995), pp. 727–46.

21. R. H. Miles, "Leading Corporate Transformation: Are You up to the Task?" in *The Leader's Change Handbook,* ed. J. A. Conger, G. M. Spreitzer, and E. E. Lawler III (San Francisco: Jossey-Bass, 1999), pp. 221–67; E. E. Lawler III, "Pay Can Be a Change Agent," *Compensation & Benefits Management* 16 (Summer 2000), pp. 23–26; and Kotter and Cohen, *The Heart of Change,* pp. 161–77.

22. R. E. Quinn, *Building the Bridge as You Walk on It: A Guide for Leading Change* (San Francisco: Jossey-Bass, 2004), Chap. 11.

23. R. Caldwell, "Models of Change Agency: A Fourfold Classification," *British Journal of Management* 14 (June 2003), pp. 131–42.

24. J. P. Kotter, "Leading Change: Why Transformation Efforts Fail," *Harvard Business Review* (March–April 1995), pp. 59–67; and J. P. Kotter, "Leading Change: The Eight Steps to Transformation," in *The Leader's Change Handbook,* ed. J. A. Conger, G. M. Spreitzer, and E. E. Lawler III (San Francisco: Jossey-Bass, 1999), pp. 221–67.

25. D. Helfand, "School Is Down but Looking Up," *Los Angeles Times,* October 14, 2004, p. B1; "Mrs. Bush Remarks on Helping America's Youth in Sun Valley, California," White House news release, (Sun Valley, CA: April 27, 2005), http://www.whitehouse.gov/news/releases/2005/04/20050427-5.html.

26. P. Reason and H. Bradbury, *Handbook of Action Research* (London: Sage, 2001); Coghlan and Brannick, "Kurt Lewin: The 'Practical Theorist' for the 21st Century"; and C. Huxham and S. Vangen, "Researching Organizational Practice through Action Research: Case Studies and Design Choices," *Organizational Research Methods* 6 (July 2003), pp. 383–403.

27. V. J. Marsick and M. A. Gephart, "Action Research: Building the Capacity for Learning and Change," *Human Resource Planning* 26 (2003), pp. 14–18

28. L. Dickens and K. Watkins, "Action Research: Rethinking Lewin," *Management Learning* 30 (June 1999), pp. 127–40; and J. Heron and P. Reason, "The Practice of Co-Operative Inquiry: Research 'with' Rather Than 'on' People," in *Handbook of Action Research,* ed. P. Reason and H. Bradbury (Thousand Oaks, CA: Sage, 2001), pp. 179–88.

29. D. A. Nadler, "Organizational Frame Bending: Types of Change in the Complex Organization," in *Corporate Transformation: Revitalizing Organizations for a Competitive World,* ed. R. H. Kilmann, T. J. Covin, and Associates (San Francisco: Jossey-Bass, 1988), pp. 66–83; and K. E. Weick and R. E. Quinn, "Organizational Change and Development," *Annual Review of Psychology* (1999), pp. 361–86.

30. T. M. Egan and C. M. Lancaster, "Comparing Appreciative Inquiry to Action Research: OD Practitioner Perspectives," *Organization Development Journal* 23, no. 2 (Summer 2005), pp. 29–49.

31. F. F. Luthans, "Positive Organizational Behavior: Developing and Managing Psychological Strengths," *The Academy of Management Executive* 16, no. 1 (2002), pp. 57–72; N. Turner, J. Barling, and A. Zacharatos, "Positive Psychology at Work," in *Handbook of Positive Psychology,* ed. C. R. Snyder and S. Lopez (Oxford, UK: Oxford University Press, 2002), pp. 715–30; K. Cameron, J. E. Dutton, and R. E. Quinn, eds., *Positive Organizational Scholarship: Foundation of a New Discipline* (San Francisco: Berrett Koehler Publishers, 2003); J. I. Krueger and D. C. Funder, "Towards a Balanced Social Psychology: Causes, Consequences, and Cures for the Problem-Seeking Approach to Social Behavior and Cognition," *Behavioral and Brain Sciences* 27, no. 3 (June 2004), pp. 313–27; S. L. Gable and J. Haidt, "What (and Why) Is Positive Psychology?" *Review of General Psychology* 9, no. 2 (2005), pp. 103–10; and M. E. P. Seligman et al., "Positive Psychology Progress: Empirical Validation of Interventions," *American Psychologist* 60, no. 5 (2005), pp. 410–21.

32. D. Whitney and D. L. Cooperrider, "The Appreciative Inquiry Summit: Overview and Applications," *Employment Relations Today* 25 (Summer 1998), pp. 17–28; and J. M. Watkins and B. J. Mohr, *Appreciative Inquiry: Change at the Speed of Imagination* (San Francisco: Jossey-Bass, 2001).

[378] endnotes

33. Canadian Tire, *Team Values Development Process (Powerpoint File),* (Toronto: Canadian Tire, September 24, 2001); and Canadian Tire, *Leadership Guide* (Toronto: Canadian Tire, 2002).

34. F. J. Barrett and D. L. Cooperrider, "Generative Metaphor Intervention: A New Approach for Working with Systems Divided by Conflict and Caught in Defensive Perception," *Journal of Applied Behavioral Science* 26 (1990), pp. 219–39; Whitney and Cooperrider, "The Appreciative Inquiry Summit: Overview and Applications"; Watkins and Mohr, *Appreciative Inquiry: Change at the Speed of Imagination,* pp. 15–21.

35. M. Schiller, "Case Study: Avon Mexico," in *Appreciative Inquiry: Change at the Speed of Imagination,* ed. J. M. Watkins and B. J. Mohr (San Francisco: Jossey-Bass, 2001), pp. 123–26; D. Whitney and A. Trosten-Bloom, *The Power of Appreciative Inquiry: A Practical Guide to Positive Change* (San Francisco: Berrett-Koehler Publishers, 2003); P. Babcock, "Seeing a Brighter Future," *HRMagazine* 50, no. 9 (September 2005), p. 48; D. S. Bright, D. L. Cooperrider, and W. B. Galloway, "Appreciative Inquiry in the Office of Research and Development: Improving the Collaborative Capacity of Organization," *Public Performance & Management Review* 29, no. 3 (2006), p. 285; D. Gilmour and A. Radford, "Using OD to Enhance Shareholder Value: Delivering Business Results in BP Castrol Marine," *Organization Development Journal* 25, no. 3 (2007), pp. P97–P102.

36. T. F. Yaeger, P. F. Sorensen, and U. Bengtsson, "Assessment of the State of Appreciative Inquiry: Past, Present, and Future," *Research in Organizational Change and Development* 15 (2004), pp. 297–19; and G. R. Bushe and A. F. Kassam, "When Is Appreciative Inquiry Transformational? A Meta-Case Analysis," *Journal of Applied Behavioral Science* 41, no. 2 (June 2005), pp. 161–81.

37. G. R. Bushe, "Five Theories of Change Embedded in Appreciative Inquiry," in *18th Annual World Congress of Organization Development,* (Dublin, Ireland, July 14–18, 1998).

38. G. R. Bushe and A. B. Shani, *Parallel Learning Structures* (Reading, MA: Addison-Wesley, 1991); and E. M. Van Aken, D. J. Monetta, and S. D. Sink, "Affinity Groups: The Missing Link in Employee Involvement," *Organization Dynamics* 22 (Spring 1994), pp. 38–54.

39. D. J. Knight, "Strategy in Practice: Making It Happen," *Strategy & Leadership* 26 (July–August 1998), pp. 29–33; R. T. Pascale, "Grassroots Leadership—Royal Dutch/Shell," *Fast Company,* no. 14 (April–May 1998), pp. 110–20; R. T. Pascale, "Leading from a Different Place," in *The Leader's Change Handbook,* ed. J. A. Conger, G. M. Spreitzer, and E. E. Lawler III (San Francisco: Jossey-Bass, 1999), pp. 301–20; and R. Pascale, M. Millemann, and L. Gioja, *Surfing on the Edge of Chaos* (London: Texere, 2000).

40. C. M. Lau, "A Culture-Based Perspective of Organization Development Implementation," *Research in Organizational Change and Development* 9 (1996), pp. 49–79.

41. T. C. Head and P. F. Sorenson, "Cultural Values and Organizational Development: A Seven-Country Study," *Leadership and Organization Development Journal* 14 (1993), pp. 3–7; R. J. Marshak, "Lewin Meets Confucius: A Review of the OD Model of Change," *Journal of Applied Behavioral Science* 29 (1993), pp. 395–415; and C. M. Lau and H. Y. Ngo, "Organization Development and Firm Performance: A Comparison of Multinational and Local Firms," *Journal Of International Business Studies* 32, no. 1 (2001), pp. 95–114.

42. M. McKendall, "The Tyranny of Change: Organizational Development Revisited," *Journal of Business Ethics* 12 (February 1993), pp. 93–104; and C. M. D. Deaner, "A Model of Organization Development Ethics," *Public Administration Quarterly* 17 (1994), pp. 435–46.

43. G. A. Walter, "Organization Development and Individual Rights," *Journal of Applied Behavioral Science* 20 (1984), pp. 423–39.

chapter 1

Photo 1.1, © Keizo Mori/UPI/Landov. Photo 1.2,© Will Crockett, Shoot Smarter. Photo 1.3, Lockheed Martin Corporation. Photo 1.4, © Dave Krieger.

chapter 2

Photo 2.1, © India Today Group. Reprinted with permission. Photo 2.2, © AP/Wide World Photos. Photo 2.3, photo by Nathan Denette/ National Post. Photo 2.4, courtesy of Molson Coors.

chapter 3

Photo 3.1, © Bob Finlayson/Newspix. Photo 3.2, © AP/Wide World Photos. Photo 3.3, courtesy of COCOPLANS. Photo 3.4, © IT Stock International/Jupiter Images.

chapter 4

Photo 4.1, courtesy of CXtec. Photo 4.2, courtesy of Four Seasons Hotels and Resorts. Photo 4.3, courtesy of Wegmans. Photo 4.4, © Larry Dale Gordon/Getty Images.

chapter 5

Photo 5.1, Photos Sarova, Panafric Hotel in Nairobi, Kenya. Photo 5.2, © TW Photo/Corbis. P5.3, courtesy of Verizon. Photo 5.4, courtesy of Pretoria Portland Cement Company.

chapter 6

Photo 6.1, © Ron Sangha Photography. Photo 6.2, photo courtesy Scott Andrews/NASA. Photo 6.3, © Irish Times LTD. Photo 6.4, OnAsia Images/ Yvan Cohen.

chapter 7

Photo 7.1, Tom Starkweather/Bloomberg News/Landov. Photo 7.2, Shell Photographic Services, Shell International Ltd. Photo 7.3, © AP/Wide World Photos. Photo 7.4, Johnson Space Center/NASA.

chapter 8

Photo 8.1, courtesy of International Business Machines Corporation. Unauthorized use not permitted. Photo 8.2, photo courtesy of Admiral Insurance. Photo 8.3, © Mark M. Lawrence/Corbis. Photo 8.4, photo courtesy of Kowloon Shangri-La.

chapter 9

Photo 9.1, Craig Abraham/Fairfax Photos. Photo 9.2, Photo courtesy of Lowe Worldwide. Photo 9.3, © AP/Wide World Photos. Photo 9.4, © Adrian Sanchez-Gonzalez/Landov.

chapter 10

Photo 10.1, © Monica Davey/Reuters/Corbis. Photo 10.2, © Peter Yates/The New York Times. Photo 10.3, © ThedaCare. Photo 10.4, Edward Carreon/Newhouse News Service.

chapter 11

Photo 11.1, © India Today Group. Reprinted with permission. Photo 11.2, UPI Photo/Dominic Bracco II /Newscom. Photo 11.3, © Empics. Photo 11.4, © AP/Wide World Photos.

chapter 12

Photo 12.1, © The Edmonton Journal. Photo 12.2, © Tim Boyle/ Getty Images. Photo 12.3, © Bill Cramer. Photo 12.4, Photo courtesy of Nitro Group.

chapter 13

Photo 13.1, © AP/Wide World Photos. Photo 13.2, used with permission, Mayo Foundation for Medical Education and Research. Photo 13.3, © AP/Wide World Photos. Photo 13.4, © Mark Leong/Redux.

chapter 14

Photo 14.1, Stan Honda/AFP/Getty Images. Photo 14.2, Adrian Brown/Bloomberg News/Landov. Photo 14.3, © Brian Vander Brug, 2004, Los Angeles Times. Reprinted with permission. Photo 14.4, Charlottetown Guardian/The Canadian Press/Brian McInnis.

>company index

A

Admiral Insurance, 173
Adolph Coors Co. (Coors), 41
Agilent Technologies, 16
Air Asia, 191
Allied Signal, 122
Amazon.com, 59
American Express, 301
AOL, 285
Apple Inc., 4, 97, 128, 199, 275, 276, 294
Aria, 14
Armstrong World Industries, Inc., 220
Astral Media Inc., 29
AstraZeneca, 83
AT&T, 16
Autodesk, 240
AVON Mexico, 301

B

BASF, 259
Bill & Melinda Gates Foundation, 232
BioWare, 254, 255, 256, 257, 262, 264, 265, 266
Britain's National Health System, 195

C

Canadian Tire, 300
CARE, 232
Castrol Marine, 301
CDC (U.S. Centers for Disease Control), 232
Charles Schwab & Co., 255, 279
Chrysler, 158
CIA (U.S. Central Intelligence Agency), 292
Cisco Systems, 287
Coca-Cola, 263
Cocoplans, 53
The Container Store, 72, 278–279
Continuum, 181
Contract Freighters, 13
Coors (Adolph Coors Co.), 41
Corning Inc., 162
C&S Wholesale Grocers, 145, 147
CXtec Inc., 66, 67, 69

D

Dairy Farmers of America, 14
Dell, Inc., 274, 275, 276, 280, 281
Denver International Airport, 122
Department of Corrections, State of Washington, 296
Disney Co., 3, 5, 79

E

EA (Electronic Arts), 79
EEOC (U.S. Equal Employment Opportunity Commission), 81
Eileen Fisher Company, 324

Electronic Arts (EA), 79
Enron, 41
EPA (U.S. Environmental Protection Agency), 301

F

Fairmont Hotels & Resorts, 33
Families and Work Institute, 81
FBI (U.S. Federal Bureau of Investigation), 290, 291, 292–293, 295–297
Fifth Third Securities, 149
Fonterra, 14
Ford Motor Company, 101, 145, 147
Four Seasons Hotels and Resorts, 71
4C, Corporate Culture Clash & Chemistry, 285
Fuji Xerox, 257

G

GE (General Electric), 145, 147
General Electric (GE), 145, 147
General Motors (GM), 72, 74
Geotechnical Instruments, 234
GlobalCo, 14
GM (General Motors), 72, 74
Goldman Sachs, 209, 282
Google, 7, 213
Green Mountain Coffee Roasters, 301
Greyston Bakery, 324

H

H. J. Heinz Co., 40
Hanson PLC, 262
Harvard Business School, 95
Hay Associates, 123
Herman Miller Inc., 282
Hewitt Associates, 125
Hewlett-Packard (HP), 183, 259, 275
Home Depot, 283, 300
Honeywell, 122
Horton Group, 59
HP (Hewlett-Packard), 183, 259, 275
Hunter Douglas, 301

I

IBM, 39, 159, 160, 168, 169, 170, 173–174, 181–183
IDEO, 128
Indianapolis Power & Light (IPL), 47
Infosys, 230, 231
Intel, 208, 209, 211
Intuit, 294
IPL (Indianapolis Power & Light), 47
IRS (U.S. Internal Revenue Service), 262

J

JetBlue Airways, 47, 283, 324
Johnson & Johnson (J&J), 24, 25, 32, 35, 41, 324

K

Keyhold, Inc., 7
KFC, 91
Kowloon Shangri-La, 182

L

Linksys, 287
Lloyds TSB, 234
Lockheed Martin, 11
Los Angeles Unified School District, 297
Lowe Worldwide, 192
Lucent Technologies, 199

M

Magna International, 257
Manila Diamond Hotel, 219
Mars, 268
Mayo Clinic, 278
McDonald's, 7, 71, 259, 263
Medrad, Inc., 149
Metropolitan Transit Authority, 194
Microsoft Corp., 213, 279
MLC, 282

N

NAB (National Australia Bank), 188, 189, 192, 197–198, 202, 282
NASA, 117, 118, 152–153, 162, 171
National Australia Bank (NAB), 188, 189, 192, 197–198, 202, 282
National Transportation Safety Board (NTSB), 152–153
Nestlé, 259, 263
New York Police Department (NYPD), 48
Nitro Group, 268
Nortel Networks, 16
NTSB (National Transportation Safety Board), 152–153
Nucor, 9
NYPD (New York Police Department), 48

O

OMD, 127
1-800-GOT-JUNK?, 47
Oracle Corporation, 33

P

Pacific Gas & Electric Company (PG&E), 231
Panafric Hotel, 90, 91
PepsiCo, 15
P&G (Procter & Gamble), 239, 266, 281–282
PG&E (Pacific Gas & Electric Company), 231
Philips, 262, 263
Pike Place Fish Market, 324
Pixar Animation Studios, 3, 4, 5, 149, 181

[389]